Probability and the Logic

of Rational Belief

Probability and the Logic
of Rational Belief

By HENRY E. KYBURG, Jr.

Wesleyan University Press
MIDDLETOWN, CONNECTICUT

for Marian

Contents

PART ONE: *Problem*

Introduction

1. The answers to three groups of questions hinge on an adequate definition of probability:

(A) What does it mean to say that something is probable? What do people intend to convey by statements making use of such words as 'probable', 'chances', and 'practically certain'? And how may disagreements about the use of these terms be resolved?

(B) What does it mean to take probability as a guide in life? How can we tell when a hypothesis is 'adequately confirmed by the evidence' or when a prediction has a high probability? How can experience make an inductive conclusion probable, and how can you tell *when* it is probable?

(C) Why *should* I take probability as a guide in life? Why should my expectations conform to the predictions of well-tested scientific hypotheses? Why should I refuse an even-money bet when the chances are against my winning? And in general, what are the criteria and sanctions of rationality?

We would expect answers to these questions to be apparent once an adequate understanding of probability has been achieved. But the definitions of probability that have been proposed in the past do not provide plausible answers. Not only do I find that there are contexts which reveal the inadequacy of each proposal, but also that there are contexts which none of these proposals can be made to fit without strain: specifically, contexts in which general inductive conclusions—such as, 'All men are mortal', 'half the tosses performed with this coin will result in heads'—are asserted to be highly probable. And yet the uniformity of practical opinion concerning probabilities gives some foundation to the hope that a definition offensive only to those with a special philosophical bone to pick can be found.

If there were complete agreement concerning the use of the term 'probability' we might want to overlook the lack of a clear understanding of its meaning. But while the probability assessments of ordinary people often agree, there are also occasions when they don't agree. In a group of people planning to go on a picnic, there is often a wet blanket who maintains, in opposition to the others, that it will very probably rain on the day of the picnic. Such disagreements concerning what is probable also occur in more rarified and scientific circles; there are those who argue that the evidence makes it highly probable that there is a relationship between smoking and cancer, and there are those who argue that it does not. There are those who claim that there is a strong probability in favor of the existence of psychic phenomena, and those who deny it. And there are always those who ignore evidence ("It won't happen to me") and those who jump to conclusions ("Tradesmen always try to cheat you") both of which may be construed as errors in probability assessments. To resolve these conflicting claims we require a clearer conception of probability than that provided by ordinary usage.

Probability statements serve in discourse not only to express opinions (well-grounded or otherwise) about future occurrences, but to guide our decisions and inform our actions in an uncertain world. As Bishop Butler said, "But to us [as opposed to the deity] probability is the very guide of life."[1] It is obvious to many people that you shouldn't take an even money bet unless your chances of winning are about even. It is also obvious—perhaps even more so— that you shouldn't attempt to cross a road unless the odds on your reaching the other side are very much in your favor. We are a long way from being able to say on what rational grounds, if any, even such commonplace maxims as these hold. But it is clear that to take account of one's chances is (or may be) to take probability as a guide in life, as Bishop Butler advised. While most people agree that the worthy Bishop had a point, there is no uniformity of opinion on what his point was. Before we can take his advice, the questions must be asked and answered, "*How* are we to take probability as a guide in life? And how are we to know what *is* probable?"

Another maxim which has the sanction of popular acceptance is that one should take experience as one's guide. But how are we to do this? The fact that something has happened once provides no logical warrant for supposing that it will happen again. If we have observed that A has followed B once, or *n* times, we are still free to suppose, without contradicting ourselves, that A will not follow B the next time B occurs. This thesis was cogently argued by Hume, and is periodically reasserted in the philosophical periodicals. But while we may readily admit that no amount of evidence will in itself logically entail that a given statement about the future will be true, it is nevertheless easy to say that when we have enough evidence this predictive statement becomes overwhelmingly probable. Unless it covers all crows no finite amount of evidence can force us on pain of inconsistency to accept a general statement such as "All crows are black." Yet it is clear that there comes a

1. Joseph Butler, *Analogy*, *Works*, Ed. Gladstone, Oxford, 1896, Vol. I, p. 5.

point in the collection of evidence when no sane person (not to mention a *rational* one) to whom the evidence is available can have really serious doubts about the generalization.

This is directly related to Bishop Butler's maxim: if experience is to be taken as a guide in life, it must be understood as providing probabilities only. To base one's expectations on past experience is to take probability as one's guide in life. This applies almost transparently to inductions based on repetitions in everyday experience: every time I have gone fishing by the first red nun in the harbor, I have caught fish; if I go fishing there today, I will probably also catch fish. But it seems plausible to suppose that it applies with equal force to the most sophisticated and far flung ramifications of modern science. No statement, theory, or law which can logically be refuted by future experience can be more than probable, regardless of its evidential support.

At the same time, it is generally felt that to act in the expectation that these laws, theories, etc., will *fail* to hold in the future as they have held in the past, would be absurd, crazy, asking for trouble. What is the justification, if any, for this feeling? The obvious answer is that although actions of this absurd sort *may* turn out to be successful, the probability is overwhelmingly against it.

There is a close connection between probability and rationality. The virtue of rationality is not cited explicitly so often as is the advisability of taking probability as a guide, but it is nonetheless implied when we say of someone who fails to take account of his chances, "He's crazy." Rationality is an important concept not only in philosophy, but in science, in business, in ordinary life. To be irrational is often to invite disaster. I am speaking only of rationality as it is involved in anticipating the future or as it is embodied in the judicious acceptance of empirical conclusions on the basis of empirical evidence; but even in this limited sense the concept of rationality remains vague. How can it be made clear?

We may suppose, first, that rationality demands consistency: a creature whose beliefs were inconsistent (e.g., one who believed that all men were mortal, and that he, although a man, was immortal) would hardly be called rational. The beliefs of a rational animal must be consistent. This requirement can be expressed formally; we may define consistency for the language that this rational animal uses, and consider his beliefs consistent if there are no direct contradictions among the statements to which he gives his assent.

We may generalize this requirement, and say that if a being is to be called rational, the statements to which he gives assent must not only be *directly* consistent, but must not *entail* any self-contradictory statements. Thus we may not only demand that he withhold his assent from either "P" or "not-P", but we may also demand that he withhold his assent from one or more of the following three statements: "P", "If P then Q", and "not-Q". This is going a bit far already; perhaps not every man is rational in this sense. But rationality is nevertheless a plausible and useful goal, an important value. Only those with a theoretical bone to pick deny the virtue of rationality, and then only during their professional moments. If not everybody who wants to be rational succeeds, that's too bad; rationality is still important and many people strive to approach it. The existence of the ideal of consistency not only gives us a standard by which to measure their approach, but it serves another function: if someone who accepts this ideal can be shown that his beliefs are inconsistent, he will modify his beliefs and come closer to perfect rationality.

But a man's beliefs may be consistent without deserving the honorific epithet 'rational'; a person could with perfect consistency maintain (a) that all men born before 1800 are mortal, and (b) that he himself is immortal. We would, rightly I think, feel that he was being irrational in maintaining this conjunction of beliefs. The requirement of consistency places very little restriction on what a man is free to believe; by making suitable adjustments among his other beliefs, he can, without violating this requirement, believe any statement which is not self-contradictory.

Many of the most important criteria of rationality, then, are tied up with questions of probability and induction; we must be able to answer such questions as: When is it irrational to reject a conclusion that is supported by given evidence? When and how can empirical evidence render a hypothesis so probable that it is irrational not to accept it? More than this, if we can find a satisfactory interpretation of probability, we can answer *all* of the questions which arise with respect to rationality (of the ordinary, nontranscendental variety) by the single answer: it is rational to believe what is highly probable, irrational not to believe it; and it is irrational to believe what is highly improbable, and rational not to believe it. There may, of course, be some things which are, relative to the evidence available, neither probable nor improbable; this definition of rationality would leave us free to accept or reject such things as our fancy, or some other requirement than rationality, dictated.

2.   This book is an attempt to make precise a formal analogue of the intuitive concept of rational belief. Surely we ought to be able to give some grounds for saying, "It is *irrational* of a college graduate, in the twentieth century, to be highly confident that the

earth is flat." There are many statements in which everybody (philosophers and fanatics excepted) agrees that it is rational to have a high degree of belief ("The sun will rise tomorrow."), and there are many statements which everybody agrees that it is irrational to take too seriously ("The moon is made of green cheese."). There are things that ought to be believed, and there are things that ought not to be believed. We are rational when we believe that which is warranted by the evidence; and in particular we are rational when we have a *degree* of belief in a given statement (as indicated, for example, by the odds at which we are willing to bet on its truth) which is precisely that degree justified by the evidence. We are irrational when we refuse to believe what the evidence indicates, or when we have more (or less) confidence in a hypothesis than is justified by the evidence. The theory of probability presented here is designed to provide a practical framework for assessing the rationality of given beliefs on given evidence. My interpretation of probability, like Keynes,[2] demands that the probability of a statement be understood as indicating the degree of belief which a person ought, rationally, to attach to that statement on given evidence. Probability is to be legislative for rational belief.

It is said that the scientific method (and only the scientific method) can lead us to beliefs which are warranted by the evidence, and hence rational. (It is sometimes implied, rather unrealistically, that in this sense scientific method is a recent invention, as though none of the beliefs of those who lived before 1500 were rational.) Scientific method, understood in a sufficiently broad sence, could perhaps provide a rationale for rational belief, were it not for three difficulties: (a) we must be able to tell what is and what is not scientific in practical, down to earth situations; (b) we must be able to show how it is that this method leads to conclusions which are intuitively acceptable and not to conclusions which are absurd; and (c) we must make the criteria of the method precise enough not only to distinguish between more and less acceptable conclusions, but also to arbitrate between conflicting claims as to the degree of credibility of a given hypothesis on given evidence. Instead of attempting to meet these difficulties, and instead of writing in generalities about the virtues of being scientific, I shall provide a formal interpretation of the concept of a rational corpus, or body of knowledge, and of the related concept of probability.

We usually apply the terms 'rational' and 'irrational' to people.[3] I am going to offer a formal interpretation of the terms, such that

---

2. J. M. Keynes, *A Treatise on Probability*, London, 1921, pp. 3, 4.

3. But we also apply these terms to numbers in a way analogous to that in which I shall apply them to expressions.

they apply to a triplet of expressions: a statement, a set of evidence statements, and a fraction. My formal interpretation can be related to the ordinary sense of the terms in the following way. The degree of a person's belief in a given statement may often be measured, e.g., by discovering the least odds at which he would be willing to bet on the truth of the statement. He may defend his belief by reference to certain items of knowledge that constitute the evidence for that statement. The fraction representing his degree of belief, the statement in question, and the evidence statements that he cites as determining his degree of belief, constitute a triplet of expressions which either fulfil or do not fulfil the requirements of the formal calculus. A rational corpus will constitute, so to speak, a model into which the beliefs of a rational man can be translated. A man will be considered rational to the extent that his beliefs, when translated into the formal notation, form a rational corpus.

The term 'consistent', in the same way, has both a psychological and a formal sense. We speak of a person as being consistent or inconsistent, and at the same time we speak of a set of statements as being consistent or inconsistent. We may use formal inconsistency as a criterion of psychological inconsistency: if among the statements that a person is willing to assert we find a formal inconsistency, we say that he is inconsistent in his beliefs.

It may be helpful to pursue this analogy a bit further. Let us consider that limited sense of rationality which is embodied in systems of deductive logic. How, for example, may we use a logical system such as that presented by Quine[4] to evaluate the rationality of a set of beliefs? The answer to this question may give us some indication of what we may hope to find in a theory of probability and a logic of rational belief. First of all, it is obvious that no one is intended by Quine to 'think' in formal deductions. Quine does not even write his textbook in formal deductions; instead, he contents himself with showing that for each of his theorems a formal deduction is possible. Similarly, a person would surely be counted as rational if, for each of his inferences, a formal deduction of the conclusion from the premises were possible. The object of having a formal system is not to have every argument presented in full-blown logical form, but to be certain that it is always *possible* to carry out a valid argument in any degree of detail necessary to convince someone who doubts its validity, but accepts the logical system as a standard of validity. A formal deduction represents only the maximum degree of detail in which every step of the ar-

4. W. V. O. Quine, *Mathematical Logic*, Revised Edition, Cambridge (Mass.), 1951. Both the book and the system of logic embodied in it will be referred to hereafter as ML; the context will make clear which is intended.

gument can be checked mechanically against the formal criteria of a valid deduction.

There are two ways in which the formal system can function in the justification of beliefs. By itself, it can be used as a standard in terms of which to justify such statements as, "6 x 7 = 42". This statement is one that ought to be believed. As many a parent knows, however, it is not always believed, even though it ought to be. People (especially very young ones) sometimes have serious doubts about it. Nevertheless it is (a) rational to believe it, and (b) possible to *show* that it is rational to believe it. I am not, of course, suggesting that when your child comes home from first grade and wants to know why six sevens are forty-two rather than forty-three, you should sit him down in front of Quine's *Mathematical Logic* until he is convinced. What I am suggesting is that the most reluctant skeptic must admit that the statement in question is worthy of rational belief, or maintain that the system of *Mathematical Logic* is a poor standard of rationality (by showing, e.g., that it is inconsistent), or repudiate rationality as such. A psychotic may still insist that six sevens are forty-three, but even a neurotic must admit that six sevens are forty-two, however intolerable he may find it. The system of ML may thus serve as a standard of rational belief where purely logical or mathematical statements are concerned.

The other way in which a deductive system may function is as a standard of validity for arguments leading from empirical premises to an empirical conclusion. Relative to the evidence that my cold frame is an Euclidian rectangle measuring six feet on one side and seven on the other, what degree of belief may I be entitled to have in the conclusion that the area of my cold frame is forty-two square feet? Here the obvious answer is that I may be just as certain of the conclusion as I am of the premise, if the conclusion really *follows from* the premise. (This 'obvious answer' requires justification by reference to a principle of rationality lying outside of the system of ML itself; such a principle will be forthcoming in my logic of rational belief.) A skeptic may demand that I *show* that the conclusion follows from the premise; and here I may turn to ML as a standard of deductive validity—i.e., as giving a formal interpretation of the conventional phrase 'follows from',

In general, the justification of a deductive argument, or the demonstration that two statements contradict each other, is not quite so simple and straightforward as is the demonstration that a purely formal statement is a theorem in ML. There is generally no possibility of simply plugging the statements concerned into the system. This limitation holds for the above example; we would have to introduce primitive terms (or matrices) into the object language of ML which would enable us to express the statements concerned in that language, and we would have to introduce axioms reflecting any logical relationships that may hold among these terms. The translation of statements in ordinary language into the notation of ML may be more or less complete, depending upon how recalcitrant our skeptic is. It is not a purely mechanical process, since the logical properties of many of the terms of ordinary discourse depend upon the sense in which these terms are used; nevertheless it is often possible to agree on a translation for the sake of settling a given question. This is quite sufficient to make ML useful in the analysis of deductive arguments employing empirical premises.

In ordinary discourse arguments are usually presented in a highly abbreviated form. But if two people accept the axioms of ML and accept *modus ponens*[5] as a rule of inference, and can agree on a translation of the premises and conclusion of an argument into a formal notation (the translation does not need to be one they would agree to accept in *every* context), then we *know* that it is possible for them to expand and formalize the argument to any degree necessary to assure agreement about whether or not the conclusion follows from the premises. The formal logical system of ML assures eventual agreement on logical matters among those who accept it as a standard.

We may suppose that in the same way a logic of rational belief will function as a standard such that those who accept it will be able to resolve disagreements concerning the degree of belief in a given statement warranted by given evidence. Just as agreement concerning the validity of an argument counts for little, unless both parties to the argument are willing to accept the premises of the argument, so agreement about degrees of belief in a statement authorized by given evidence will count for little unless this evidence (a) is acceptable to both parties, and (b) is all the evidence available to them bearing on the matter at issue. The second requirement, (b), has no analogue in the deductive situation as it is usually pictured, and, as we shall see in the following chapters, it is the rock on which most theories of probability founder, despite their acceptance of the requirement 'in principle'.

The degrees of confidence a person actually has in a given statement must be measured empirically, e.g., by a series of bets, just as any actual inconsistency among his beliefs must be determined empirically by finding out what it is that he believes. But we

5. *Modus ponens* is the rule of inference that authorizes the assertion of "Q" on the basis of the premises "P" and "If P, then Q."

do not have to examine people to find out what degree of support given evidence gives to a hypothesis, any more than we have to examine people to find out whether or not two statements are inconsistant. Similarly, the degree of confidence a person *ought* to have in a given hypothesis, on a given totality of evidence, just like the amount of inconsistency he *ought* to exhibit, can be determined on purely logical grounds.

The parallel between deductive logic and the logic of rational belief may be further illustrated by a pair of relatively non-controversial examples. If a person believes that there are ten million people in greater New York, and that no person has more than five million hairs on his head, then the logic of consistency bids him refrain from believing that no two New Yorkers have the same number of hairs on their heads. On the evidence that a given die lands with the one-spot up on a sixth of its tosses, and that the next toss is not rigged in any way, a person ought to have a degree of belief equal to about a sixth of certainty that the next toss of that die will land with the one-spot up. It is possible for him to accept and refuse bets in such a way as to indicate that his degree of belief in this occurrence differs from one sixth, just as it is possible for a person to believe that no two people in New York have the same number of hairs on their heads, that there are ten million people in New York, and that no human being has more than five million hairs. But in neither case would we call the person rational.

Within rather wide limits, both logics can be dealt with in syntax. That one well-formed-formula is a consequence of another well-formed-formula in a system of logic can be shown (a) without regard to the factual truth of either formula, and (b) without regard to the interpretation or meaning of any non-logical signs that may appear in either formula, provided that any 'logical' relationships among the primitive terms be expressed axiomatically. In the same way, given a set of statements that qualifies as a rational corpus, we can determine the degree of belief which this rational corpus would compel its holder (if any) to attach to a given statement (a) without reference to the factual truth of any statement in the rational corpus or of the statement in question, and (b) without regard to the interpretation of any of the non-logical signs that occur in any of the statements concerned, subject to the same proviso as before. In examining the logical relationships among a set of statements expressing beliefs, we are concerned only with the set of statements and not with the world at large. We must examine statements, not sticks and stones, if we wish to elucidate the term 'rationality'. As Keynes says, in a similar context, "The validity and reasonable nature of inductive generalization is ... a question of logic and not of

experience, of formal and not of material laws. The actual constitution of the phenomenal universe determines the character of our
evidence, but it cannot determine what conclusions *given* evidence
rationally supports.''[6] The logic of rational belief is that which determines what conclusions given evidence rationally supports.

3.   The three major approaches to the problem of defining probability will be considered in some detail in the next three chapters.
The object of this examination is not to point out new difficulties
with these theories—since the partisans of each have amply criti-
cized the others—but to make clearer the difficulties and complications to which any theory of probability is subject, and to clarify
further the problems raised by the everyday use of the term 'probability'.

We might begin, however, by asking if a rigorous, formal interpretation of probability is possible at all; perhaps it is impossible
to go any further than common sense has already gone in achieving
agreement about probabilities. It may be that we shall have to accept probability as indefinable, as Keynes sugests.[7] And would this
be so bad? Isn't it only in rare cases that people disagree about
what beliefs are rational and what ones are not?

The proposal to treat probability as a primitive, undefinable
logical relation has several drawbacks. In the first place it is not
philosophically satisfying. We would like to be able to *show* that on
such and such evidence, such and such a belief is rational. Even if
everyone's intuitions of probability agreed (which we know they do
not) with respect to what beliefs are warranted by given evidence,
the situation remains rather unsatisfactory as long as we can give
no reason why just these beliefs and no others are rational. In the
second place, disputes about probability would not be amenable to
adjudication by any set procedure and there would be no guarantee
of eventual agreement. In the third place, many philosophical disputes hinge on the question of evidence, and remain unresolved despite the analytical effort expended on them: Is it or is it not rational to believe that when I leave my office my dictionary remains
on my desk? Some idealists say, ''There are no empirical grounds
at all for believing this,'' while some realists say, ''There is a
plethora of empirical evidence in its favor.''

There is one other drawback to the proposal to regard probability as indefinable. Usually one feels that a *rational* belief is one
that can be defended (I would say 'justified demonstratively', were
'demonstrative' not preempted by deductive logic), while a mere
hunch or intuition that admits of no rational defense is considered

6. Keynes, *op. cit.*, p. 221.
7. *Ibid.*, p. 8.

irrational, or, at best, non-rational. This feeling may well be related to that which led to the characterization of $\sqrt{2}$ as an *irrational*
number. If my belief in a given statement is *rational*, I feel that I
should be able to *show* that it is rational, not only by citing the evidence which supports the belief, but by exhibiting the *relation* between the statement believed and the evidence which renders it
probable. I should be able to show how and to what extent the evidence is relevant to and justifies the belief.

If rationality entails defensibility and thus communicability of
beliefs, then to be required to intuit the rationality of a belief is
out of the question. It may be, as Keynes points out, that one also
has to intuit the validity of *modus ponens* in deductive logic; but
the important distinction remains that you can state an explicit
rule authorizing the use of *modus ponens* which can be followed
even by those (if any) who cannot *see* its validity. No such simple
rule suffices to replace the required intuitions in Keynes' system
of probability. His basic probability relations cannot be *rationalized*
in the way the rule, "From 'P' and 'If P then Q' you may infer 'Q',"
rationalizes the intuitively valid principle of *modus ponens*. And it
is precisely such a rationalization that we would like to achieve.

4.   The fact that this rationalization is performed only in a formal
system creates some difficulties and leaves some lacunae. The
major gap, and the one which will strike pragmatists and their rel-
atives as the most debilitating, is that the formal language in which
rationality is defined is treated as *given;* the system therefore
cannot reflect the process of change that takes place in our scientific language. Such changes do take place every time an important
theory is accepted. In this sense the system does not adequately
describe the process of scientific investigation, even on a linguistic level.

While the pragmatic (or sociological?) description of the scientific situation serves an important function, the analysis of the
fixed relations between evidence and conclusion is also important
and worthy of study. While the pragmatic view of the scientific
process gives a more realistic picture of what scientists do—in the
sense that a moving picture is realistic—the formal view which I
am presenting here allows for a more detailed examination of the
justification for their doing what they do. A series of snapshots
makes possible a closer examination of each scene than does a
moving picture. Both snapshots and movies are useful: the one for
presenting an overall picture, the other for studying details. And of
course at different stages of inquiry, we will be interested in studying different snapshots.

Another gap, and one which is more serious from a general

philosophical point of view, is that while I suppose we have a ready-made language to begin with, it is clear that no language can come into existence until we have made and accepted some generalizations about the world. The word 'dog' will not be part of our language, unless we know that dogs are among those kinds of things that the world is full of, i.e., that there are very few, if any, objects which are *almost* dogs. Most general nouns are useful precisely because we know that they refer to a class of objects of which we have experienced only a small part, and because we also know that the members of this class have a large number of properties in common and are definitely distinguishable from members of neighboring classes. This is already inductive generalization. The formal language, on the other hand, springs into being ready-made. We suppose that it is intelligible, but we also suppose, in developing our inductive logic from the beginning (the logical beginning, not the historical beginning), that we know nothing about the world except what can be expressed in reports of our experience. This is a highly artificial situation; but it does not mean that the system cannot reflect the relationships which obtain between evidence and conclusion in less artificial situations.

It may also be considered a lack that I have not provided a *calculus* of probability. Most books on probability are concerned primarily with the mathematical treatment of relations between probability statements. One of the theses that will be defended here, however, is that there *is* no calculus of probability. On the interpretation of probability statements I have to offer, the 'calculus of probability' is merely the reflection, on a syntactical level, of the calculus of class ratios that can be discovered in the object language. This calculus can be established for finite classes on purely logical grounds.

For example, one of the theorems or axioms found among the statements in most books on probability is that the probability of both A and B, given C (where A, B, and C are properties, events, or the like), is equal to the probability of A, given C, multiplied by the probability of B, given A and C. This can be expressed as a theorem in a class-ratio calculus, if A, B, and C, are understood as classes; if the classes are finite, then it will be simply a theorem in logic: the proportion of objects in C which belong to the intersection of A and B is equal to the proportion of objects in C belonging to A, multiplied by the proportion of objects in the intersection of C and A which belong to B.

Calculations like this lie behind many probability statements; but it does not follow either that the class ratio interpretation of probability is the only plausible one, or, what is less often recognized, that this theorem is one which must apply directly to *proba-bility* statements. I shall maintain that such calculations are to be performed on class ratio statements, but not on probability state-ments. Probability will not be interpreted as a class ratio, and I shall argue that we have no need for a special calculus of proba-bility with its own axioms and theorems. Probability will be de-fined by reference to class ratios, among other things, and the cal-culus of class ratios will be mirrored by a pale reflection of itself in certain special cases which can arise in the application of the theory of probability.

It may be asked, "What good is a theory of probability which doesn't provide a calculus?" If the point of developing a theory of probability is to facilitate the calculations that statisticians and scientists make, then a theory without a calculus is like a house without doors: it will lack any connection with the outside world. But I do not believe that this can be the point of developing a theory of probability. It strikes me as almost absurd for a philosopher to presume to audit the arithmetical accounts of statisticians. Statis-ticians have made their calculations without the help of philoso-phers in the past and can probably continue to do so in the future—just as a grocer can know when he has sold a dozen eggs without the help of the logical definition of '12'. On the other hand, the in-terpretation and clarification of the probability statements issued by statisticians and scientists (including the ones they make when they are off guard) is surely a plausible and useful task for the philosopher; even more important, and equally dependent on an ad-equate theory of probability is the analysis of the rational use of general probability statements in determining our expectations. But no calculus is needed to perform either of these functions.

Similarly (but from the other side of the fence), it may be felt as a lack that I shall have almost nothing to say about truth. Since I am concerned with the syntax of rational belief, and since truth is a semantical concept (as opposed, e.g., to theoremhood), I cannot legitimately talk about truth. But I don't have to. It is possible to develop a formal logic without referring to truth, and there is no reason for referring to it in discussing a rational corpus. I will speak instead about statements being included in a rational corpus (in virtue of their probability), but this is obviously completely in-dependent of the truth-value of the statements. That a statement is true is not a sufficient condition for its being included in a rational corpus, because it must also be probable relative to the evidence available. And that a statement is true is not a necessary condi-tion for its being included in a rational corpus, because if the evi-dence is overwhelmingly in favor of the statement, the statement *ought* to be included, even if new evidence turns up later which shows that it is actually false, and ought therefore to be excluded at this later time.

All of this will become clearer in the chapters that follow. I wish merely to emphasize here (a) that I am not presenting a 'new foundation' for the 'calculus of probability', and (b) that this is primarily a syntactical investigation, based on the supposition that there is a syntax of rational belief, just as there is a syntax of logical consistency. I am concerned only with the *logic* of rational belief, not with the 'how to' aspects of scientific research or theory- or concept-formation, nor with an anthropological investigation of scientific practise.

The major difficulty, as those readers will know who, like me, flip through a book before settling down to read it, is that the formal system itself seems rather formidably complicated. Now since the system is intended to elucidate the perfectly ordinary, common-sense, intuitively recognizable relation between evidence and conclusion encountered in every day experience and courts of law, as well as in laboratories, the fact that I become embroiled in relatively unfamiliar symbolism deserves some explanation.

Even though the perception of the relationship between evidence and conclusion is one in which people do not make too many more errors than they do in perceiving deductive relationships, we should hardly expect, after having waited so long for a formalization of this relationship, that it would turn out to be very simple after all. The difficulties that have hindered this formalization still exist; the relationship is exceedingly complicated, as we see when we attempt to make it clear to ourselves discursively in ordinary language. It was only through the medium of protosyntax that I was able to formulate my ideas clearly enough to begin to develop a formal system; the informal characterizations which accompany my formal definitions are largely *post hoc* translations of requirements I saw originally in protosyntactical terms.

There is a marked contrast between my formalization of the inductive relationship and Quine's formalization of the deductive relationship. It is easy for Quine to express, in ordinary language, that relation which must hold between a statement S and the axioms of his *Mathematical Logic* in virtue of which S may be said to be a theorem. It is somewhat more complicated for him to define theoremhood formally in the machinery of protosyntax. He does so only because he is interested in establishing that his system is incomplete and incompletable, which he can do even more impressively in protosyntax than he can in syntax. But the situation with regard to probability is just the reverse of this: it is the protosyntactical definition which is simple, and the discursive characterization which is complicated. The general relation which holds between S and the large class of statements which constitutes the basis of our rational knowledge about the world, in virtue of which S is worthy of a high degree of rational belief, is far more complicated than the relation between "P, and if P then Q" and "Q". This is unfortunate, but not surpirsing. The necessity of turning directly to protosyntax in order to make this relation clear can be seen readily by the reader who is willing to compare my stumbling, lengthy, discursive characterizations of various aspects of this relationship with their crisp protosyntactical expression. I cannot think of any way of making the relationship simpler or clearer, and to depend on ordinary language would accomplish precisely the opposite result.

Although the protosyntactical expression of the inductive relationship is not complicated (in principle), the notation of protosyntax may itself constitute a stumbling block through its unfamiliarity. I have therefore attempted to state every important result in comprehensible prose, so that the reader who is unacquainted with the notation can nevertheless follow the argument and understand the results. To do less would be to restrict unnecessarily the number of people who can read the book, as well as to be discourteous to those who can read protosyntax only with difficulty; to do more, however—to reduce the formal developments to footnotes or to abandon them altogether—would be to lower the text to the level of homily and unsupported assertion. The assertion that the crudest form of induction by simple enumeration can be justified with probability under some circumstances is in one sense homiletic (no ordinary person ever doubted it) and in another sense, highly problematic (no definition of probability has been given heretofore from which this result follows formally and consistently). It is important that the formal definitions be available, and that they have the consequences that they actually have; but if the reader is willing to take my word with regard to what I have proved in the formal development of the metatheorems and definitions, the informal parts of the text may be read independently. I can only hope that the reader will be patient, that he will skip only when he must, and even that he may eventually be inspired to study protosyntax in Quine's *Mathematical Logic*.

Although protosyntax may seem to be an extraordinary complication to add to the already complicated relationship between empirical evidence and empirical conclusion, it is in reality the simplest and most convenient means of expressing this relationship. It is also, once it is familiar, simple in an absolute sense. Even if it were not, however, the importance of the relationship, the need for having a standard against which to evaluate disputed or disputable instances of it, and the need for rationality in a world that is a jungle of claims and counterclaims on behalf of everything from brands of deodorant to brands of politics, make the clarification of the relation of evidence to conclusion worthy of any amount of effort.

5.   One important activity of philosophers is to think rationally and intelligently. Intelligence may be imponderable, but it is the thesis underlying this book that rationality is not, and that what is rational can be communicated and supported by argument. This holds not only for deductive argument, but for inductive argument as well—the form of argument we employ in learning from experience, in anticipating the future, in pursuing scientific knowledge, and so on. It is a not uncommon feeling that philosophy has depended too much on the former (to the embarrassment of the philosopher's premises), and not enough on the latter.

There is another activity of philosophers that has the sanction of tradition: it is the clarification of obscure ideas. This is, as many philosophers have maintained, a worthy task. It is even worthy when this clarification must be accomplished by the introduction of special symbols and technical terminology. Certainly the syntactical criteria of validity in formal logic are simpler than the criteria of validity embodied in the scholastic rules about moods and figures. But whether clarification is the sole function, or even the main function, of philosophy is open to question. I myself think that philosophers have more important tasks than that of analyzing confusing concepts, although I am willing to agree that many of these tasks must follow a preliminary clearing (or analysis) of the ground on which they are to rest.

The analysis of probability and rational belief is to perform the latter function for the sake of the former. While it was once a great service for philosophers to be skeptical, too many people have learned their lesson too well. It is said, for example, that "To know that P" entails "P". If this is so, of course a claim to knowledge must always be empty, or at best open to dispute. But I know, and most ordinary people know, a great number of things, and we *know* that we know them! Perhaps professional philosophers will be happier if I replace 'know' with 'have a high degree of rational belief in'—though Reichenbach and others allow *no* form of rational belief. Since people are not agreed what it is (if anything!) in the relation between evidence and conclusion of an inductive argument which makes belief in the conclusion rational, or which allows us to say that we know the conclusion, we have excellent reasons for analyzing the concept of rational belief.

But the matter does not end here. In one sense, it does not even begin here, since I consider it not only important (as any analytical philosopher would) to know what rationality is, but also to be rational; the logic of rational belief may be simply construed as an elucidation of the prior imperative: Be rational! But the acceptance of rationality as a duty (among others), and the clarification of what it is that this duty consists in, are only the beginnings of an answer to the classical philosophical problems of knowledge. In a very real sense we now know more than people used to know; and what it is that we know and don't know may be made clearer by applying the litmus of the logic of rational belief.

The ramifications, the significance, the uses, the meanings, the implications of what we know or what we ought to know or what we don't know, constitute an almost unlimited field for the most traditional forms of philosophical endeavor. The analysis of rational belief is not a curious exercise in syntax, but an extension of the range of that knowledge of which philosophy is alleged to be the love, and a justification for the replacement of academic exercises in logical analysis by a treatment of live issues by live men. Perhaps it will help to lead philosophy back to the problems of life and meaning, of freedom and security, with which the amateur philosopher is so often concerned. Or have we traded our right to deal with these problems for the privilege of being always right about trivia?

CHAPTER TWO

Frequency Theories

1. In this chapter I shall discuss theories of probability which either directly interpret probability statements as statements about relative frequencies or class ratios, or take probability as an abstract property of certain sequences of events, obeying the laws of the probability calculus and finding its connection with the ordinary world through derived relative frequencies (observed or contemplated) in finite classes. This view of the meaning of probability recommends itself not only by its antiquity (it has been attributed to Aristotle,[1] and received an explicit formulation in 1866[2]), but by its conformity to current feelings about empiricism and verifiability.

Frequency theories, in one form or another, have been particularly popular among statisticians since Venn[3] defined the probability that an A will be a B as the limit of the relative frequency of B's among A's as the number of A's is increased without limit. More recently, von Mises has provided a reformulation of this thesis, which is mathematically and logically more sophisticated than Venn's original statement.[4] In von Mises' formulation, the sequence of A's is referred to as a *collective,* and is subject to the condition that the B's occur *randomly* in the sequence. Randomness is defined objectively without reference to anything anyone does or does not know as 'after-effect-freedom'—*Widerspruchsfreiheit.* Although the original formulation of the randomness-requirement led to difficulties, the requirement has been reformulated by Wald[5] in such a way that it can be shown that sequences exist (in the mathematical sense) in which a given property occurs randomly (in Wald's sense) and in which the limit of the relative frequency of this property

1. By Richard von Mises, *Positivism,* Harvard University Press, Cambridge, 1951, p. 164. Curiously enough, Reichenbach, another frequency theorist, demurs in *Theory of Probability,* University of California Press, Berkeley and Los Angeles, 1949.
2. John Venn, *The Logic of Chance,* London and New York, 1866 and later editions.
3. *op. cit.*
4. Richard von Mises, *Wahrscheinlichkeit, Statistik, und Wahrheit,* Springer, Vienna, 1928. (Translated as *Probability, Statistics, and Truth,* London, 1939.) See also Reichenbach, *Wahrscheinlichkeitslehre,* Leiden, 1935. (Translated as *Theory of Probability,* University of California Press, 1949.)
5. Abraham Wald, "Die Widerspruchfreiheit des Kollektivbegriffs der Wahrscheinlichkeitsrechnung," *Ergebnisse eines mathematische Kolloquium* 8, 1937.

exists. The interpretation of probability is thus completely objective on this theory: a given sequence either is or is not a collective, regardless of what anyone knows or believes; and similarly, the probability that A is a B has a certain value p (if it has any value at all—i.e., if the limit of the relative frequency of B's among the A's exists) regardless of what anyone knows or believes. It may be noted, however, that no finite collection *can* qualify as a collective, and also that even if there are infinite sequences composed of natural events, it may be that none of them are collectives.

There are other interpretations of probability which share this characteristic of objectivity. Russell[6] and Neyman[7] have offered finite frequency interpretations, in which probability is defined as a proportion in a finite class. The probability that a card in an ordinary deck is an ace, for example, is 1/13, since 1/13'th of the cards are aces. In this formulation there are no restrictions regarding randomness, and the difficulties of infinite sequences are avoided.

Yet another variety of objective interpretation has been proposed by R. B. Braithwaite.[8] Here probability is taken as an abstract characteristic of 'selections' from a population. There is again no restriction in regard to randomness. The probability that an A will be a B is interpreted concretely as a class ratio in a model. The model consists of an arbitrary number of bags, each of which contains black and white balls in the same ratio, p. An n-fold sample drawn from the class of A's corresponds to a selection of one ball from each of n bags in the model. If the model with the parameter p gives a valid picture of the relationship between the A's and the B's, we say that the probability that an A will be a B is p.

The most general interpretation along these lines, and the one which is most popular among the members of the influential British-American school of statisticians, is that which takes probability as an entirely abstract property applicable to some sequences or classes of events. The connection between the abstract property of probability (which has certain mathematical characteristics by postulation, so that the conventional calculus of probability can be applied to it, but which is not otherwise defined) and concrete experimental evidence, is provided by some form of decision theory. The concrete meaning of a probability statement is given informally by Cramér as follows: "Whenever we say that the probability of an event E with respect to an experiment ε is equal to P, the

6. Bertrand Russell, *Human Knowledge*, New York, 1948.
7. Jerzy Neyman, *First Course in Probability and Statistics*, New York, 1950.
8. R. B. Braithwaite, *Scientific Explanation*. Cambridge University Press, 1953.

concrete meaning of this assertion will thus simply be the following: In a long series of repetitions of ε, it is practically certain that the frequency of E will be approximately equal to P.''[9] Given a probability statement, we can thus roughly anticipate the result of a long experiment; given the result of an experiment we may decide what probability statement to accept on the basis of a decision technique.

In general, the result of an experiment ε can be expressed numerically as the value of a random variable. For example, in tossing a coin, we might let the random variable representing the result take the value 1 if the result is heads and the value 0 otherwise. A mathematical probability may then be interpreted as the *conceptual counterpart* of the relative frequency with which this random variable takes on certain values, rather than being directly identified with this relative frequency. The conceptual counterpart theory, like the limiting frequency theory of von Mises, takes probability as an empirical (though abstract) and objective relation. If the probability of an event E with respect to an experiment ε is P, it is so independently of anything that anyone knows, believes, or expects. To make a statement about a probability is no less factual and objective than to make a statement about the length of a stick.[10]

2.   Most of those who entertain frequency, or more generally, objectivistic theories of probability admit that the explication they offer is applicable only to certain uses of the term. There is no obvious way to provide a frequency interpretation for the statement, "It is very probable that Caesar crossed the Rubicon," or for the statement, "It is improbable that there is life on Jupiter."

Hans Reichenbach[11] was one of the few frequency theorists who thought that it was possible to give such statements a frequency interpretation. It might be maintained, for example, that statements of the type, "Caesar crossed the Rubicon," supported by evidence similar to the historical evidence we have for this statement, are true with a certain relative frequency. But this involves two difficulties: First, the probability statement will only refer to types of statements or classes of statements (and how do we decide what a type is?) and not to the specific statement with which we are concerned; on the usual frequency interpretation we must construe "It is very probable that Caesar crosses the Rubicon" as an ellipsis

9. Harald Cramér, *Mathematical Methods of Statistics*, Princeton University Press, 1946, p. 149.
10. Similar conceptions have been presented by a number of statisticians, e.g., Feller, Doob, Neyman, and Wald. Writing from a philosophical point of view, Churchman, von Wright, Margenau, and N. R. Campbell have also presented similar theories. For detailed references, see the bibliography.
11. *op. cit.* See also Reichenbach, *Experience and Prediction*, Chicago, 1938.

for, "Most statements of such and such a type are true." Second, in order to get evidence about the relative frequency of truth of this type of statement, we must count the true and false statements of this type. But this merely multiplies our problem, for in order to count the true statements, we must know that they are true; and this seems quite as difficult as knowing whether or not the particular statement that interests us is true. Reichenbach attempted to avoid these difficulties by means of his system of *posits*—i.e., estimates of relative frequency—but few scholars have felt that he was successful.

Most frequency theorists are satisfied to maintain only that their interpretation serves adequately in those probability statements that occur in science and statistics. They would make no attempt to apply their theory to contexts (11) through (14) of Appendix II. With regard to these contexts frequency theorists either adopt a personalistic view,[12] such as will be considered in the next chapter, or a logical view,[13] such as will be considered in Chapter Four, or (more often) they ignore these contexts altogether as not being amenable to formal treatment.[14]

The remaining contexts (1) through (10) all seem to have something to do with frequencies. Contexts (1) through (5) are tailor-made for the frequency interpretation; contexts (6) through (10) raise certain difficulties. First of all, consider statement (1): "The probability of getting a head in a toss of this well-tested coin is 1/2." On the frequency interpretation, this means that if the coin is tossed a large number of times, the relative frequency of heads will be approximately 1/2, or rather, that this outcome is 'practically certain'. This sounds reasonable enough: if I were to toss the coin a large number of times and to discover that the relative frequency of heads was closer to 1/4 than to 1/2, I might consider my original statement to have been in error. Similarly, if the results of my experiment agree roughly with the prediction based on (1), I shall consider (1) to have been, to some degree, confirmed. But the truth or falsity of (1) is quite independent of the results of my experiment; if statement (1) is true, it is so (on this interpretation) regardless of whether I believe it, or of whether I have any evi-

12. E.g., Ramsey, *The Foundations of Mathematics*, New York, 1931.
13. E.g., Carnap, "The Two Concepts of Probability," *Philosophy and Phenomenological Research* 5, 1945, and *The Logical Foundations of Probability*, Chicago, 1951; Nagel, *Principles of the Theory of Probability*, Volume I, no. 6, of the International Encyclopedia of Unified Science, Chicago, 1939; Kemble, "Is the Frequency Theory of Probability Adequate for All Scientific Purposes?" *American Journal of Physics* 10, 1942.
14. E.g., Cramér, *op. cit.*, p. 151; G. H. von Wright, *The Logical Problem of Induction*, Helsinki, 1941; R. von Mises, *Positivism*, p. 166.

dence for it. If it is false, similarly, it is false regardless of what grounds I have for thinking it true.

Now let us suppose that I have been somehow informed of the truth of (1)—perhaps by finding a brazen tablet with (1) engraved on it. Consider statement (5): ''The probability of 10 heads occurring in 10 successive tosses of this coin is $(1/2)^{10}$.'' If statement (1) is true, then, subject to certain conditions, statement (5) will be true. The concrete frequency interpretation of (5) is that if we perform the experiment which consists of 10 tosses of the coin a very large number of times, then the relative frequency of experiments with the property that each of the ten tosses resulted in a head will be approximately $1/2^{10}$. This also seems reasonable; on the frequency theory, we can infer (5) from (1), subject to a few simple requirements. The theory seems to stand up quite well in contexts (1) and (5), and would presumably hold equally well for contexts (2) through (4).

There is only one point on which issue might be taken, and that is the grammatical oddity of offering a statement about a class or a sequence as an explication of a statement which grammatically and intuitively is about a single object: *an* A. We are to replace a statement referring to the probability of *a* member of a certain class having a certain property by a statement referring to the proportion of *all* members of the class which have the property. As I say, this is no more than a grammatical oddity; but it would be nice if we could eliminate it by providing some translation of the indefinite article instead of replacing the reference to *a* member by a reference to *all* members.

Now consider statement (8): ''The probability that the next toss will yield heads is $1/2$.'' There is only one 'next' toss, as indicated by the definite article 'the'. It is a unique experiment, never performed before, and never to be performed again. Since we are dealing here with a finite (one-fold) class, we can be sure that the relative frequency with which heads occur in it will be either 1 or 0. The result of a single experiment will be either heads or tails. No matter what form of frequency interpretation we adopt, we can be sure in advance that if the probability of heads on the next toss exists at all (perhaps most theories would deny that it does), its value is either 0 or 1. We can be sure that in any case it will not be $1/2$.

This does not conform to any conventional use of the term 'probability'. The frequency theorists have attempted to get around this difficulty in two ways: first by treating statement (8) as an elliptical equivalent of statement (1), and second by simply ruling out statement (8) as meaningless, on the grounds that it does not refer to a repeatable experiment, and therefore involves no random variable whose behavior can be described by a probability statement.

The first approach does not seem plausible. When I make a statement about the *next* toss of a coin, I am making a statement about a particular event; I refuse to be told that I am talking directly about a whole class of events. (There may be implicit in my statement some indirect reference to the whole class of events, but this is not what I am talking *about*.) This becomes even plainer if I make a statement about the 17'th toss of the coin, rather than about the next toss. If I knew nothing about this toss, I might say that the probability is 1/2 that it resulted in heads; if I knew that the 17'th toss was one which resulted in heads, it would seem plausible to say that the probability that this toss resulted in heads was 1; and if I knew that 15 out of the first 20 tosses resulted in heads, the most plausible probability would seem to be .75. To interpret (8) as an ellipsis of (1) does violence to common usage, which in speaking of the probability of a definite event takes into account anything that is known about that event. What (8) is an ellipsis of will depend on the circumstances in which it is asserted.

The second approach is the one which is most often adopted.[15] According to this approach, (8) does not involve probability (in the frequency sense) at all. There is no random variable which can take on various values, for the experiment can be performed only once; there is no infinite sequence in which we can look for a limiting frequency. This is a perfectly legitimate solution to the problem; the frequency theorist is perfectly free to say, "Oh well, I'm not talking about *that* sense of probability." But it is a bit startling to find that the frequency explication of probability does not allow us to say, even of a *thoroughly tested* coin, being tossed under *carefully controlled* conditions, that the probability of heads on the next toss is 1/2.

The same analysis must be applied to statement (7): "The probability that the next ten tosses will all yield heads is $1/2^{10}$." Again, on a frequency interpretation, the probability of this event (if it exists at all) must be either 0 or 1, depending on whether or not the event in question occurs. We can discover which value the probability has only by performing the requisite ten tosses. Now consider the statement, "It is practically certain that out of a thousand tosses of this well tested coin, between 450 and 550 will result in heads. This, or rather the corresponding probability statement, follows from (1) in exactly the same way, and subject to exactly the same conditions, as (5) does. But this kind of probability statement cannot be applied to the *next* thousand tosses, any more

15. By von Mises, Cramér, Neyman, and others.

than statement (5) can be applied to the next ten tosses. The next thousand tosses will have this property, or it won't; the probability is 1, or 0, or, if we insist on having a random variable, does not exist. In spite of the fact that statisticians and frequency theorists seem to be willing to pass from a very high probability (frequency) which refers to a class of experiments to a practical certainty which refers to one specific experiment, it must be noted that this transition is perfectly analogous to the transition whose legitimacy they deny when it occurs between (1) and (8) or between (5) and (7).

It might be thought that the number of heads could be taken as a random variable in the next thousand tosses—after all, it can take values from 0 to 1000. But it cannot actually take more than one value; it is not something that can vary, but something that, though temporarily unknown, is definitely constant. Whether or not the outcome of the experiment is causally determined is irrelevant; no matter how whimsical the world, when once the experiment has been performed the proportion of heads *will have been determined,* and it is this proportion which interests us. When we consider all sets of a thousand consecutive tosses, then the proportion which result in heads is a random variable, for then it takes on a specific value in *each* of these sets. But when we are talking about only *one* such set, it can have only one value, and not a sequence of values.

Statement (9) reads, "Given an n-fold random sample of P's, m of which are Q's, the probability is t that between $m/n - d$ and $m/n + d$ of all the P's are Q's." This statement fares even worse than the preceding one. The proportion of P's which are Q's (or more generally, the population parameter) is certainly not a random variable: it has some (presumably unknown) constant value which either does or does not fall within these limits. Nor is it easy to find a probability statement which is related to this statement as (5) is to (7), though some statisticians have looked hard for one.[16]

It should also be clear that statements (6) and (10) are in the same boat as statements (7), (8), and (9). The term 'probability' in these contexts cannot be explicated by the frequency theory. Nevertheless, these statements and others like them are of the utmost importance in every application of statistics. If I am running an insurance agency, I will be interested in statement (4) primarily because I feel that it enables me to assert statement (6) under the appropriate conditions. It is due to the restrictions embodied in the phrase 'appropriate conditions' that I must take statement (6) and not statement (4) as a guide in life. If I am running a gambling casino, my interest in statements (1) and (5) will be due to my

---

16. E.g., by considering a class of inferences drawn on the basis of similar samples. See, for example, Wald, *On the Principles of Statistical Inference,* Notre Dame, 1942.

feeling that they help to justify statements like (7) and (8), and these statements about definite complex events are the ones I shall use in determining the risk I am running and in estimating my profits.

It appears that whenever probability is used as a guide in life, it is used to refer, not to the frequency with which a random variable will take a certain value, but to the likelihood that a certain *constant* will have a certain value. When probability is taken as a guide in life, it is in the face of some concrete situation which will have *one* outcome—whether the concrete situation is a simple one like the toss of a coin, or is a complex one, like a series of 10,000 tosses of a coin, or is somewhat vague, like the results of all the games played at a casino during a given month. The properties of this outcome may or may not be determined in advance by physical laws, but this is beside the point: the properties are determinate after the event, and what we really want to know is what *will have happened*. We take probability as our guide in life by taking into account the probability that the outcome will have a certain property. Since there is only one outcome, and since that outcome has only those properties that it actually has, there are no random variables involved in our *use* of probability statements. In these important contexts the frequency theory no longer applies.[17]

It may be interesting to note some of the attempts to make the frequency interpretation apply to such contexts indirectly. The simplest attempt takes the form of justifying expectations by reference to long run results. It is suggested that you should offer no more than even money on a single toss of a coin, since, if you offer greater odds, then in the long run you would almost certainly lose money. This argument is obviously not cogent. I am contemplating a wager on *one* toss of a coin only—what *would* happen in a very large number of tosses is irrelevant when I am only considering one toss. On the single toss, I am no more likely to lose if I offer 10 to 1 odds than if I offer even money. Furthermore, the frequency argument does not say what *would* happen in a long sequence of tosses—it only tells me what is very likely or practically certain to happen. But this is just the sort of conception that, when it is applied to a single event, the frequency theory is trying to avoid. And even if I offer 10 to 1 odds on each toss of a million tosses of a coin, there is no random variable to which the frequency theory may be applied: I shall either win more than 10/11'ths of the tosses

17. This has been pointed out by Carnap, "Probability as a Guide in Life," *Journal of Philosophy* 44, 1947; Kemble, *op. cit.*; D. C. Williams, "On the Derivation of Probabilities from Frequencies," *Philosophy and Phenomenological Research* 5, 1945; and others.

or I shan't. A further application of the long-run argument would be not only silly, but, possibly, a temptation to get into an infinite regress. As Keynes once said, somewhere, "In the long run, we are all dead."

A better attempt to show how frequency probability can be used as a guide in life makes direct use of mathematical expectation. Mathematical expectation can be defined on the frequency theory in such a way that it can be applied to single events. The mathematical expectation of *every* even-money bet on the toss of a well-tested coin will be 0. This clearly can be applied to a definite (e.g., the next) toss, while probability cannot. Arguments have been presented in favor of employing mathematical expectation as a guide in life, but they must obviously all break down for the reasons indicated above. An argument purporting to establish the advantages of acting in a certain way in a certain situation can only establish the probability or liklihood or practical certainty that the outcome will be advantageous.

It may be said that no argument is required, that it is, by definition, to be considered irrational not to take mathematical expectation as a guide in life. But there remain, nevertheless, some difficulties with this view. In the first place, we can only determine mathematical expectations if we somehow quantify the values involved in the different possible outcomes of a given situation. This is easy enough when we are tossing pennies, and not an insurmountable problem when we are manufacturing telephone receivers; but as a general guide to the good life the maxim that we should maximize our mathematical expectations must be kept in abeyance until the hedonistic calculus is perfected and every rational man has agreed that ethical hedonism is right. In the second place, although the mathematical expectation of each party to a coin-tossing contest is 0, this does not imply that they will come out even; the chances are that one will come out ahead of the other, and that the longer the game has gone on, the greater will be the absolute amount that the winner is ahead. Finally, and this seems to be the most cogent argument against the direct use of mathematical expectation as a guide in life, mathematical expectation as defined on the frequency theory of probability applies to *every* member of a certain class of situations. It applies equally to every bet on the outcome of a coin-toss, past as well as future. According to the letter of the theory, then, and in the absence of any explicit proviso to the contrary, the odds at which I ought to bet on the occurrence of a head on the toss of the coin which just now resulted in tails are even money. If we are to make a suitable proviso explicit, however, we must take into account whatever relevant knowledge we have about the event under consideration; and to do this, we must turn elsewhere than to the theory of mathematical expectation as presented by the frequency theorists. We must be able to say what knowledge is *relevant*, and we must be able to say *how* this knowledge is to be taken into account.[18]

The most common objection to the frequency theory is that it does not lead to a justification of scientific hypotheses.[19] Regardless of whether or not the frequency theory is adequate to other uses of the term 'probable', it is obvious that our scientific knowledge cannot be 'highly probable' in the frequency sense. But frequency theorists and statisticians have been very much concerned with the problem of arriving inductively at sound statistical hypotheses, or, as they would say, sound probability statements. In Chapter Eighteen I shall have more to say about some of the limitations of decision theories and theories of statistical inference. But we might just note a few interesting facts here.

First, the evidence for a statistical hypothesis often leads to the assignment of a number to this hypothesis; the number does not represent a probability (on the frequency theory), but rather a 'confidence coefficient'. Nevertheless, confidence coefficients act very much in the way in which we might expect probability—in the sense in which it is legislative for rational belief—to act. In the second place, the general applicability of decision theory clearly depends on the general applicability of mathematical expectation as a guide in life; but we have already seen that this is questionable. Finally, the omnipresent assumptions about randomness admit of no plausible interpretation on the frequency theory, and on the implausible interpretation which *is* offered, the assumptions are almost always patently false, if not nonsensical.[20]

It has been maintained that it is sufficient for us to know how to *use* probability statements and statistical hypotheses, and that we therefore do not have to worry about justifying statistical inferences in terms of some other theory of probability. But a distinction may be made between knowing how we *do* use statistical hy-

---

18. The problem of formulating suitable provisos in this context is essentially the same as that of choosing a suitable reference class for probabilities on either the logical or the frequency interpretations of probability; and it is a problem on which very little seems to have been done.

19. Nagel (*op. cit.*) and Carnap (*Logical Foundations of Probability*) make this objection to the thesis of Reichenbach that probability has a univocal meaning. C. I. Lewis (*An Analysis of Knowledge and Valuation*, Open Court, 1946) maintains, largely because of this fact, that the frequency theory is altogether wrong.

20. As has been pointed out by a close neighbor of the frequency theorists, G. Spencer Brown, in *Probability and Scientific Inference*, Longmans, Green & Co., New York, 1957.

potheses and knowing how we *ought* to use them; and for the justification of the use we do make of them or for the analysis of how we ought to use them, we must turn, if not to another theory of probability, at least to some general and yet-to-be-presented theory of scientific inference. Even if this should prove feasible, however, I think we require a non-statistical conception of probability in order to state explicitly what we practise intuitively in making sensible statistical hypotheses, in confirming them, and in employing them as guides to the future.

3.   So far I have shown that the frequency interpretation of probability breaks down in all but contexts (1) through (5). There is no way in which probability as it is interpreted according to this theory can be predicated of scientific conclusions or taken as a guide in life. Even in contexts (6) through (10), although they seem at first sight to involve a frequency concept, this interpretation cannot be accepted literally, and no derivative concept which is not defined by reference to knowledge and ignorance will serve. The fact that the frequency definition seems to be perfectly adequate for the first five contexts, if not for the others, has led a number of people to accept a dual interpretation of probability, according to which some probability statements are to be interpreted in one way, others in another way. Nagel accepts this conclusion in his *Principles of the Theory of Probability*,[21] and Carnap has defended it in a number of publications.[22] Other scholars have also come to this way of thinking.[23]

But there are some difficulties even with this liberal attitude. I have just argued that the frequency interpretation cannot be accepted in certain contexts in which it seems that an 'objective' interpretation of probability would be plausible. While it is not unreasonable to suppose that 'probability' may occur in different senses in contexts (1) through (5) and in contexts (10) through (14), it is a little surprising to discover that the sense of probability employed in contexts (6) through (9) is the same as the latter, rather than the same as the former. When I say that the probability of heads on the next toss of this well-tested coin is 1/2, I may be referring not only to the state of my knowledge about this particular toss, but also to the state of my knowledge about the general behavior of this coin. And I will *assert* (1) not when the relative frequency of heads among tosses of this coin is 1/2, but when I *know* that it is 1/2.

21. And also in his later writings, e.g., in "Probability and Non-Demonstrative Inference," *Philosophy and Phenomenological Research* 5, 1945.
22. Any of those mentioned earlier, but particularly, "The Two Concepts of Probability," *Philosophy and Phenomenological Research* 5, 1945.
23. E.g., Leblanc, Hempel, Kemeny. See the bibliography for detailed references.

Obviously there is some connection between frequency and probability in the first five contexts; it seems almost equally obvious that there is a similar connection in the next four; and it does not seem too far fetched to suppose that there may even be *some* connection between frequency and probability in the last group of contexts as well. I shall maintain that a probability statement implicitly *mentions* a frequency statement, but that it does not, as the frequency theorists suppose, constitute a direct *use* of a statement about relative frequencies. This connection will be shown to hold in the first and last groups of contexts as well as in the middle group, where it seems rather obvious. And of course this renders a dual view of probability unnecessary.[24]

---

24. Lewis, *op. cit.*, makes this same point, and presents (informally) a similar thesis concerning probability. But he seems to consider the problem of providing grounds for the choice of a reference class to which to refer probabilities an insoluble one, for he accepts the rather questionable thesis that the same event may have several different probabilities, relative to the same body of knowledge.

CHAPTER THREE

The Personalistic Theory of Probability

1.   The subjective, or personalistic, theory of probability was first explicitly suggested by Ramsey; it is mentioned in his book of essays, *The Foundations of Mathematics*.[1] It has not been considered very important until recently, and Ramsey himself seems to have considered it only a supplement to a relative frequency or class ratio theory.[2] De Finetti[3] was the first statistician to take it seriously, and in 1954 J. L. Savage published a detailed presentation of the foundations of the theory.[4] Recently certain parts of the personalistic theory have been employed to provide a justification for the axioms conventionally laid down for confirmation functions of the type that I shall discuss in the next chapter.[5]

The basic thesis of the theory is that probability statements are statements concerning actual degrees of belief. Some statements are certain, e.g., statements known to be logical or mathematical theorems, while others are believed only to a certain degree, e.g., the statement, "It will rain tomorrow." I neither completely believe nor completely disbelieve this statement; instead, I partially believe it, or, in the language of the personalistic theory, attach a certain degree of probability to it.

According to Ramsey, it is possible to discover the degree of probability I attach to the proposition that it will rain tomorrow by considering a hypothetical sequence of bets. The actual value of the probability, for me, now, is that indicated by the highest odds I would offer in betting on the occurrence of rain tomorrow. If these odds were $5:2$, the probability would be $5/(2+5)$, or $0.7142\ldots$ Due to the diminishing marginal utility of money, this technique is difficult to apply in practise, although as the sums involved become smaller

1. Ramsey, *The Foundations of Mathematics*, p. 166 ff.
2. As do Braithwaite (*Scientific Explanations*), von Wright (*The Logical Problem of Induction*), and others, who generally attach even less importance to it than Ramsey did.
3. De Finetti, *La prévision: ses lois logiques, ses sources subjectives. Annales de l'Institut Henri Poincaré* 7, 1937.
4. L. J. Savage, *The Foundations of Statistics*, New York, 1954.
5. Abner Shimony, "Coherence and the Axioms of Confirmation," *Journal of Symbolic Logic* 20, 1955. John Kemeny, "Fair Bets and Inductive Probabilities," *Journal of Symbolic Logic* 20, 1955. R. Sherman Lehman, "On Confirmation and Rational Betting," *Journal of Symbolic Logic* 20, 1955.

and smaller it becomes more and more plausible. Savage provides an alternative method of measuring degrees of belief, however, which eliminates the difficulties that crop up in trying to apply Ramsey's technique directly.

Savage begins with a set of *states* (of the world); a set of *consequences; acts,* which are functions from states to consequences; and a relation, 'is not preferred to', which holds between acts. In a given context, one of a certain set of states actually obtains, although we may not know which one it is. An act is a function that tells us, for every state, which consequence would result from that act if that state actually obtained. The primitive relation 'is not preferred to' provides a simple ordering among acts: for every two acts, f and g, either f is not preferred to g, or g is not preferred to f, or both.

On this basis it is possible to define preference between acts, given B, where B is a subset of the set of states S. It is then possible to define preference between consequences. The definition of probability then proceeds as follows: Let A and B be subsets of the set S of states. We offer a person a choice between two acts. The first of these acts is that he is to receive a prize f in case A obtains, or a prize f' in case A does not obtain. The second of these acts is that he is to receive a prize f in case B obtains, or a prize f' in case B does not obtain. The prize f is definitely preferred to the prize f' by this person. We now say, "A is not more probable than B" if and only if the first act is not preferred to the second act.[6]

This definition yields an ordering among events (subsets of S) with respect to the relation, 'is not more probable than'. From here to quantitative probabilities is an easy step. A *probability measure* P is defined as a function assigning to every subset B of S a real number $P(B)$ such that:

(1) $P(B) \geq 0$, for every B.

(2) If $B \cap C \equiv 0$, $P(B \cup C) = P(B) + P(C)$.

(3) $P(S) = 1$.

In order to arrive at quantitative probabilities, now, we merely have to assume some postulate to the effect that there exist partitions of S into arbitrarily many equivalent (equiprobable) subsets. (B and C constitute a partition of S if every element of S belongs to either B or C, and if no element of S belongs to both B and C.) If there is an

6. Savage, *op. cit.*, p. 31 ff.

n-fold partition of S into equivalent subsets, for example, the probability of each of these subsets is $1/n$.

2.   It is clear that some probability statements on this theory are empirical. To find out whether A is more probable than B for person Z at time t, we must conduct an inquiry. We must discover whether he would prefer to stake a possible gain on the occurrence of A or on the occurrence of B. This is a problem (and not necessarily a trivial one) in experimental psychology. To find the numerical probability which the person attaches to the occurrence of A, we may take B as a sequence of coin tosses, in which the person is absolutely convinced that the tosses are independent and that the coin is fair, and make comparisons accordingly. If the person would just as soon stake a possible gain on the occurrence of A as on the occurrence of three consecutive heads, the probability of A, for him, at this time, is 0.12500 ... Now if we have such a coin, we can go down the list of possible events or states in the person's world, and discover the precise degree of probability that he attaches to each possibility; and we may do this to any degree of accuracy we please. We can evaluate the probability, for him, now, that the next president will be a republican, to 1000 decimal places. Every probability statement would then be empirical; it would make an assertion about the actual state of the person's beliefs.

To say, then, that the postulates, theorems, etc., of the theory hold good for these probabilities, would be to advance a psychological theory. This theory would have such consequences as this: If a person has a degree of belief equal to p_1 in A, and a degree of belief equal to p_2 in B, and a degree of belief equal to 0 in the conjunction of A and B, then he will have a degree of belief in the alternation of A or B equal to p_1 plus p_2. This psychological theory is clearly false in general, although it may hold approximately, for some people, some of the time, in some areas of belief.

But the subjective theory of probability has never been proposed as a $purely$ empirical theory about the relationships among people's beliefs. Instead of this, the personalistic $calculus$ of probability has been taken as normative for relations between degrees of belief in related propositions. The theory of probability as a whole is partly normative. According to Savage, a person has certain degrees of confidence in certain propositions; should the person discover empirically that the confidence he has in related propositions violates the rules of the calculus, he will modify his beliefs. A distribution of probabilities (degrees of confidence) is called 'consistent' by Savage if no two related probability statements violate the rules of the calculus. (Ramsey also uses the term 'consistent' in this sense.)

Savage offers the following illustration. A person considers the

32 possible outcomes of tossing a coin five times to be equally probable. He also considers it more probable that there will be four or five heads in the five tosses than that the first two tosses will both be heads. These are straight-forward psychological statements about the degrees of belief that the person actually has in the propositions concerned. Now reference to the rules of the calculus shows that if the tosses are regarded by this person as independent, and if each of the 32 possibilities has a probability of 1/32, then the probability of four or five heads out of the five tosses is 6/32, while the probability of two heads on the first two tosses is 8/32. The person has caught himself in an inconsistency, but, "The theory does not tell him how to resolve the inconsistency; there are literally an infinite number of possibilities among which he must choose."[7]

In general, the most plausible choice seems to be to hold fast to the position that all 32 outcomes of the five tosses are equally probable, and to adjust the other beliefs accordingly. Savage attempts to explain this by distinguishing between "those probability statements about which we feel sure" and "those about which we feel unsure." "When our opinions, as reflected in real or envisaged action, are inconsistent, we sacrifice the unsure opinions to the sure ones."[8] (But perhaps it would be in better conformity with Savage's treatment of 'learning from experience' to abandon the opinion that the tosses are independent and that all 32 outcomes are equally probable.) He admits that the distinction between sure and unsure opinions cannot be explained by reference to his theory of probability.[9]

3.   Savage suggests that it is perfectly plausible to suppose that two perfectly rational people, "faced with the same evidence, may have different degrees of confidence in the truth of the same propositions."[10] People do seem to differ in the confidence they have in the same propositions, even when they are presumably faced with the same evidence. But this can occur even in mathematics: Alice was sure that 1 from 365 was 364; Humpty Dumpty preferred to see it done on paper. The interesting point is that there exists a procedure by which (within rather wide limits) a mathematical disagreement can be resolved to the satisfaction of everybody concerned. Savage does not feel that it is possible to formulate such a procedure for probability statements. However, he points out that on his theory, as two people accumulate *new* evidence about a proposition

7. *Ibid.*, p. 68.
8. *Ibid.*, p. 57.
9. But isn't it precisely *this* distinction that probability statements are often intended to express? This shortcoming of the theory, which applies equally to logical theories of probability, will be discussed in the next chapter.
10. Savage, *op. cit.*, p. 3.

they will come closer and closer to agreement about the degree of confidence which is justified. "...in certain contexts, any two opinions, provided that neither is extreme in the technical sense, are almost sure to be brought very close to one another by a sufficiently large body of evidence."[11] An *extreme* opinion is one which assigns a probability of 0 or 1 to a proposition. In this case no evidence is relevant. If your prejudices are deepseated enough, it is unreasonable *not* to disregard the evidence.

It is true that people do not have to agree precisely in their assignments of probability in order to arrive at an agreement concerning some future action. But the fact that they agree even approximately seems to be no more than a fortunate psychological quirk; the theory itself regards *no* distribution of beliefs which is in accord with the rules of the calculus as 'unreasonable'. This includes the 'technically extreme' distributions as well as the more conventional ones. The fundamentalist is being reasonable when he refuses to admit that the evidence in favor of evolution carries any weight. Most people, I think, would balk at calling the extreme positions reasonable; and in spite of the fact that we may wish to allow for some minor differences of opinion about probabilities, we surely do not wish to call *every* non-extreme distribution reasonable merely because it is 'consistent'. If someone maintains that a certain long shot it 'practically certain' to win a given race, but can give me no evidence supporting this hypothesis, I shall decline to call him 'reasonable' however consistent his degrees of belief may be.

The personalistic theory of probability cannot be called upon to settle disputes about probability; in fact, there can be no disputes except about whether or not a given person's assignments of probability are consistent. Savage seems to feel that it is asking too much to expect two people having the same information to agree about the probability of a given proposition. Now it may be that he is right in feeling that it is impossible to lay down a plausible set of rules which will guarantee that they will eventually achieve some measure of agreement, in the same sense in which there is a set of rules which will guarantee that Humpty Dumpty and Alice will eventually agree about the result of subtracting 1 from 365. It may not be possible (although I think it is) to offer any more specific explication of 'reasonableness of belief' than that provided by the personalistic theory. But there is no *a priori* reason why this should be so, and in fact people do seem to use the word 'reasonable' much less lavishly than Savage would allow them to use it.[12]

11. *Ibid.*, p. 58.
12. Shimony, Kemeny, and Lehman are on the side of the angels in this matter; they consider consistency of degrees of belief only a necessary and not a sufficient condition of rationality.

New problems arise when we attempt to apply the personalistic theory of probability to general statements. Braithwaite has pointed this out in connection with Ramsey's theory.[13] How can we interpret, "The probability that the theory T is true is (at least) 0.99?" According to the general scheme of personalistic probability, this should be interpreted as meaning that I would just as soon risk a possible gain on the truth of the theory as on (say) the truth of the hypothesis that the outcome of a hundred tosses of a coin will have a certain character — e.g., exhibit a relative frequency of heads within such and such limits. But the truth of the theory can never be definitively established, and it therefore seems absurd to say that I would prefer to risk a possible gain on the truth of the theory than on any other possible fact at all. If I choose to stake a possible gain on the occurrence of a hundred heads on the next hundred tosses of a coin, at least I stand *some* chance of collecting. On the other hand, even if I am quite sure that the theory is true, I might prefer to stake a possible gain on the falsehood of the theory — or rather, the event of its being falsified during the next two years — than upon (say) the occurrence of a thousand tails in the next thousand tosses of a fair coin. But already I am being inconsistent — since I am expressing a very low degree of belief in the falsity of the theory, and a very low degree of belief in the truth of the theory, in spite of the fact that I am certain that the theory is either true or false.

The most plausible way out seems to be to avoid reference to the 'probability' of statements that cannot be definitively confirmed in some finite time. This, of course, applies with as much force to statistical statements about indefinitely large classes as to universal generalizations and theories, and it renders the use of Bayes' theorem for induction impossible. To use Bayes' theorem, we must assume that some general statistical statement (e.g., the statement that the proportion of A's which are B's falls between p_1 and p_2) has a finite probability. But to say that such a statement has a finite probability (for me) is to say that I would prefer to risk a possible gain on the truth of this general statement than on the truth of some practically testible statement such as "The next one hundred tosses of this coin will all land heads."

Savage does not attempt to get along without Bayes' theorem; he uses it to show that, as the evidence accumulates, two people will come to agreement about the probable state of the world, even though their initial assignments of probability differ, and also to show that with a large amount of evidence at hand, a non-extreme person will be almost certain that the state s obtains when s is in fact the state

13. Braithwaite, *op. cit.*, p. 357 ff.

that obtains. Both these uses of Bayes' theorem depend on the explicit assumption that the *a priori* probability of the actual state is represented by some definite number greater than zero. (As Nicod has shown[14] it is not sufficient to demand that the probability in question be 'greater than 0' — we must demand that it be greater than some definite positive number ϵ.) But this is precisely what seems questionable on the personalistic theory. To suppose that there are only a finite number of statistical hypotheses to be considered could provide us with our *a priori* probabilities, but it is difficult to see how these probabilities can be interpreted as personalistic ones.

We might get around the difficulty of assigning non-zero probabilities to theories and general statements by having an angel perform our psychological tests for us. Since the angel would presumably know which state of the world obtained, the person would be able to collect even if he voted for the theory. But this begins to seem a little far fetched.

The personalistic theory breaks down altogether with regard to contexts (1) through (5), even if we suppose that the angelic hypothesis suffices to save contexts dealing with the probability of general statements and theories. In the first place it is obvious that not even an angel would decide whether or not to pay off on the state of the world corresponding to 'a toss of this coin will result in heads.' The indefinite article here cannot be translated into 'some' or 'there is a' or 'all'. We cannot interpret, "The probability that a toss of this coin will result in heads is $1/2$," as a personalistic probability at all. The holders of the personalistic theory are therefore obliged to reject these contexts as containing an improper use of the word 'probability'. The problem created by these contexts is usually called the problem of 'unknown' probabilities; this is somewhat misleading, for the problem is just as great a one when the 'probability' in question is supposed to be known.

These contexts are among the most important for science, and they have received much attention from the holders of personalistic views. De Finetti has provided an indirect interpretation of these contexts which does make use of personalistic probability. This is accomplished by introducing a 'probability measure' in the abstract mathematical sense. This abstract probability measure, which is merely a species of bounded measure, may or may not correspond to an actual probability. There are, however, certain sequences of events (such as the tossing of a coin) in which this abstract probability measure may be supposed to exist, and in which it may some-

14. Nicod, *Foundations of Geometry and Induction*, New York, 1950.

times be interpreted as a personal probability. These interesting sequences are called *symmetric*, which means that with respect to a certain property P, the personal probability that any b members of the sequence have the property, and any c members lack it, depends solely on the integers b and c.[15]

Savage gives the following example: "If, for example, a statistician were to say, 'I do not know the p of this coin, but I am sure that it is at most one half,' that would mean in personalistic terms, 'I regard the sequence of tosses of this coin as a symmetric sequence, the measure M of which assigns unit measure to the interval $(0, 1/2)$.'"[16] If the statistician were sure that the p of the coin were very close to $1/2$, he would say that the measure M assigns unit measure to a small interval around $1/2$. The first five contexts from Appendix II must therefore be construed as statements about abstract probability measures and symmetric sequences. The first statement will be rendered: "I regard the sequence of tosses of this well-tested coin as a symmetric sequence, the measure M of which assigns unit measure to a small interval about the value $1/2$." Anyone who accepts this statement will assign a personal probability of $1/2$ to the occurrence of heads on a given future toss of the coin, provided he interprets the probability measure M as a personal probability. (He is not obligated to do so, and since personal probability must be represented by a real number rather than by an interval, he has to use his imagination in any case.)

Much of the apparent objectivity of the first five contexts, as well as the word 'probability' itself, seems to disappear in the translation into acceptable personalistic terminology. On the personalistic theory two people may very well reasonably disagree about statements like these, even though they have exactly the same information to go on. In the first place one of them may regard the sequence as symmetric; the other may not. There are quite a number of people who consider the sequence of results of tossing a coin, HTHHTHTTH, more probable than the sequence HHHHHTTTT; for these people the sequence of coin tosses will not be symmetrical. Savage does not discuss the relation of evidence (if any) to the supposed symmetry of a sequence; it appears to be merely another fortunate psychological coincidence that statisticians generally seem to agree that the sequences that concern them are symmetric. In the second place, the assignment of a measure M to the sequence brings up all the problems mentioned earlier in connection with general statements. We may be led to assign very different meas-

15. Savage, *op. cit.*, p. 52.
16. *Ibid.*, p. 53.

ures to the sequence (on a given amount of evidence) depending on the *a priori* probabilities with which we start.

To sum up: The personalistic theory does not provide a direct interpretation for 'probability' as it occurs in the first five contexts; the holders of personalistic views do attempt to deal with these contexts, but their interpretations, in addition to being very indirect, do not seem to be at all true to life. Contexts (9) through (12), which refer to general statements, cannot be handled by the personalistic theory without recourse to what I have called the angelic hypothesis. The remaining statements, which refer to the probability of some definite event, can be handled by the personalistic theory as it stands. But even here the theory has shortcomings. It seems too liberal to be taken as the sole criterion of reasonableness, and too strict when it demands consistency to an arbitrary number of decimal places. It does not provide a framework within which disagreements can be settled: Two people, given the same evidence, are free on this theory to assign any probability whatsoever to the same proposition, provided only that they adjust their other beliefs to avoid inconsistency. Essentially, there *can* be no disagreements about probability between different people. The distinction between sure and unsure opinions, which may have been offered as a means of alleviating the oddity of this situation, is altogether too vague to be of much help.

CHAPTER FOUR

Logical Theories

1. According to this final group of theorists, the theory of probability is a part of logic. Probability is taken to be completely legislative for rational belief; it does not merely dictate 'consistency', as it does on the personalistic interpretation. The goal of such a theory is to lay down rules such that the probability of a given statement, relative to given evidence, is a real number determined on logical grounds alone; consequently the degree of belief which it is *rational* to have in that statement, *on that evidence,* is also determined on logical grounds alone. Probability is a logical concept, according to these theories, and probability statements are logically true, if they are true at all. If they are false, they are logically false—self-contradictory.

The first person to defend this thesis explicitly was J. M. Keynes, in his *Treatise on Probability.* He wrote, "All propositions are true or false, but the knowledge we have of them depends on our circumstances; and while it is often convenient to speak of propositions as certain or probable, this expresses strictly a relationship in which they stand to a *corpus* of knowledge, actual or hypothetical..." "But in the sense important to logic, probability is not subjective ... A Proposition is not probable because we think it so. When once the facts are given which determine our knowledge, what is probable or improbable in these circumstances has been fixed objectively, and is independent of our opinion." The theory of probability "involves purely logical relations between the propositions which embody our direct knowledge and the propositions about which we seek indirect knowledge." [1]

If these relations are 'purely logical' and if probability statements are to be taken as analytic or conventional, then we must accept the fact that experience is irrelevant to the probability of a given statement on given evidence. But this is not so strange as some people (e.g., von Wright[2]) have attempted to make it sound. The probability of the given statement on the given evidence may be fixed and determined, once and for all, by the logical relations involved; yet it is certainly a rule of rational behavior that if experience yields new evidence, this evidence should be included in any

1. J. M. Keynes, *A Treatise on Probability*, New York, 1921, p. 3-4.
2. G. H. von Wright, *The Logical Problem of Induction*, Helsinki, 1941.

future evaluation of the probability of the statement concerned. While the old probability statement is not changed in any way by the acquisition of new evidence, it no longer interests us; what does interest us is the new probability statement which is determined by the statement in question and *all* of the evidence, new as well as old. New evidence does not enable us to 'correct' the old probability statement; it obligates us to consider instead a new probability statement.

This is precisely the kind of concept of probability we need if we are to use probability as a guide in life, if we are to speak of the 'high probability' of scientific inferences, and so on. But the system of probability which Keynes develops in his *Treatise* is vague in a number of respects, and embodies one difficulty in particular which cannot be overlooked. He takes the probability relation as primitive, saying that it does not seem to be possible to define it in terms of the conventional logical primitives. The basic relations of probability, then, must be known intuitively, just as we must recognize intuitively that 'q' follows from 'p' and 'if p then q'. However, we can lay down a purely formal rule to the effect that from 'p' and '$p \supset q$' we can obtain 'q'; Keynes cannot do anything like this with his probability relation; he cannot provide us with formal rules which will eliminate the necessity of intuition. Yet, because of the additional complexity of the probability relation, as opposed to the deductive relation embodied in *modus ponens,* it is imperative that we be able to dispense with intuitions if we are to demand that any two rational animals, faced with the same evidence, ultimately come to agreement on the probability of a given statement.

Keynes admits that there are variations in people's abilities to intuit probability relations: some can detect probability relations that escape others, or can intuit them with greater precision. One of the purposes of the calculus of probability, on Keynes' view, is that it makes it possible to argue from simple probability statements, which most people are capable of intuiting, to more complex ones.[3] An analogy with mathematical thinking gives this, at first sight, some plausibility. It is certainly true that some people are better at 'mathematical intuition' than others; it is possible for some people to see that a certain statement is a theorem, while others cannot. But there remains this important difference: while I may not be able to see that 'A' is a theorem, and you may, it is nevertheless possible, in general, for you to produce a proof of 'A' which even I can follow. But if you claim to see a probability rela-

3. Keynes, *op. cit.*, p. 53.

tion which I cannot see, it is not generally true on Keynes' view that you can produce a proof, or anything analogous to a proof, which will convince me. Even in those special cases in which a complex probability statement is derivable from simpler ones, I will have to intuit *some* probability relations—relations far more complex than those involved in *modus ponens*.

Keynes' development of his theory also makes use of a principle of indifference. It is carefully formulated to avoid certain well-known paradoxes, but it is still rather vague, for it is stated in terms of his indefinable concept of probability. Another difficulty encountered in Keynes' system is that there are alleged to be probability relations which are incomparable in magnitude.[4] Yet if probability is to be completely legislative for rational belief, this should entail that there are incomparable degrees of belief. How are we to understand the assertion that different degrees of the same thing are incomparable?

A number of these difficulties are eliminated in Carnap's logical theory of probability.[5] Carnap's 'degree of confirmation' is a purely logical concept, and is defined relative to specific formalized languages only. No extra-logical reference is required for its definition, and no extraordinary intuitions are required for its application. It functions in the same way in which Keynes' probability concept functions, but it is definable in terms of conventional logical concepts. Since my own view is a logical one, and since Carnap's research is not only the most extensive that has been done in the field, but also includes a very general perspective, I shall consider his results in some detail.[6]

2. Carnap picks no fights with the frequency theorists: he accepts the thesis that the frequency explication of probability is adequate

---

4. *Ibid.,* p. 159: "Many probabilities ... are numerically measurable in the sense that there is *some* other probability with which they are comparable in the manner described above. But they are not numerically measurable ... unless the probability with which they are thus comparable is the relation of certainty." (Italics in the original.)

5. R. Carnap, *The Logical Foundations of Probability*, Chicago, 1951.

6. Other writers who have contributed notably to the logical theory of probability include F. Waismann, "Logische Analyse der Wahrscheinlichkeitsbegriffs," *Erkenntnis* 1, 1930-31; C. G. Hempel, "A purely Syntactical Definition of Confirmation," *Journal of Symbolic Logic* 8, 1943; C. Hempel and P. Oppenheim, "A Definition of 'Degree of Confirmation,'" *Philosophy of Science* 12, 1945; O. Helmer and P. Oppenheim, "A Syntactical Definition of Probability and of Degree of Confirmation," *Journal of Symbolic Logic* 10, 1945; J. Kemeny, "A Logical Measure Function," *Journal of Symbolic Logic* 18, 1953. For a mathematician's refinement of the Keynesian concept, see B. O. Koopman, "The Axioms and Algebra of Intuitive Probability," *Annals of Mathematics* 41, 1940; "Intuitive Probabilities and Sequences," *Annals of Mathematics* 42, 1941. A still different logical theory is presented by Th. Hailperin, "Foundations of Probability in Mathematical Logic," *Philosophy of Science* 4, 1937.

to many uses of the concept in science. However, he also empha-
sizes the importance of another concept of probability—a concept
analogous to that discussed by Keynes. To avoid confusion, Carnap
refers to this concept as that of probability$_1$, while the frequency
concept is referred to as probability$_2$.[7] The explication of proba-
bility$_2$ is provided by the frequency interpretation of probability,
while the explication of probability$_1$ is to be provided by Carnap's
formally defined *degree of confirmation*.

Carnap has so far only examined the concept of degree of confirmation as it might be defined in languages of fairly simple structure. These languages, L, contain signs of the following varieties:
(a) Individual constants; N of them in L_N, an infinite number in L_∞
(b) A finite number of primitive predicates
(c) An infinite number of variables.
(d) The logical constants
The general formation rules for these languages are given, and
then the basic semantical rules of truth. These are essentially the
same for all languages of the group with which Carnap is concerned.

In Carnap's system, the basic concept of both deductive and inductive logic is that of a state description. A *state description* in a
language L states for every individual of L, and for every property
designated by a primitive predicate of L, whether or not this individual has this property.[8] Thus if we have only one primitive predicate and two individual constants, the only state descriptions are:

(1) $P(a) \cdot P(b)$

(2) $P(a) \cdot \overline{P}(b)$

(3) $\overline{P}(a) \cdot P(b)$

(4) $\overline{P}(a) \cdot \overline{P}(b)$

The *range* of a sentence in L is defined as the class of all state
descriptions in which this sentence holds. Thus in the above illustration, the range of 'P(a)' is the class (of state descriptions) whose
members are (1) and (2). The range of 'P(a) · P(b)' is the class
whose only element is (1). The range of 'P(a) v P(b)' is the class
whose members are (1), (2), and (3). The basic concepts of deductive logic can be defined by reference to ranges. For example, we
may say, "A sentence i L-implies a sentence $j =_{Df}$ the range of i
is included in the range of j. Other concepts may be defined similarly. In order for the definitions of deductive concepts to be ade-

7. R. Carnap, "The Two Concepts of Probability," *Philosophy and Phenomenological
Research* 5, 1945.
8. Carnap, *The Logical Foundations of Probability*, p. 71.

quate, we must impose a condition on the language; we must demand
that the primitive predicates be logically independent. In order for
our definitions of inductive concepts to be adequate, we must impose an additional requirement on the language; we must demand
completeness as well as independence. Both of these requirements
will be discussed in the following section.[9]
     The next important concept to be introduced is that of a *struc-
ture description*. While a state description tells us the properties
possessed by each individual in the universe, a structure description only tells us what properties are possessed and by how *many*
individuals in the universe. A structure description may be represented by a disjunction of state descriptions which are *isomorphic*.
Two state descriptions are isomorphic when one can be obtained
from the other by replacing individual constants in the first by the
individual constants in the second, in such a way that different constants are replaced by different constants, and a given constant is
replaced by the same constant throughout. In my example above, (2)
and (3) are isomorphic state descriptions, since if we replace 'a' by
'b' and 'b' by 'a' in (2), we obtain (3). The following three structure
descriptions correspond to the four state descriptions listed above:

(5) $P(a) \cdot P(b)$

(6) $\overline{P}(a) \cdot \overline{P}(b)$

(7) $P(a) \cdot \overline{P}(b) \cdot v \cdot \overline{P}(a) \cdot P(b)$

     The *Q-predicates* are introduced as the strongest predicates in
the language. If the language contains two primitive predicates,
'P_1' and 'P_2', then a given individual may have the properties designated by both of these predicates, the property designated by the
first, but not that designated by the second; the property designated
by the second, but not that designated by the first; or, finally, it
may lack both properties. A Q-predicate, then, completely describes an *individual*. On the basis of the two primitive predicates,
we may define four Q-predicates:

(8) $Q_1(x)$ *for* $P_1(x) \cdot P_2(x)$

(9) $Q_2(x)$ *for* $P_1(x) \cdot \overline{P}_2(x)$

(10) $Q_3(x)$ *for* $\overline{P}_1(x) \cdot P_2(x)$

(11) $Q_4(x)$ *for* $\overline{P}_1(x) \cdot \overline{P}_2(x)$

For a language L^π of the type Carnap is considering, where π is

9. *Ibid.*, p. 72-76.

the (finite) number of primitive one-place predicates (all of the same type) available in the language, the number of Q-predicates is 2^π. Any predicate expression in a language of this kind is equivalent to a disjunction of Q-predicates. In the above example 'P_1' is equivalent to 'Q_1 v Q_2', '$\overline{P}_2$' is equivalent to 'Q_2 v Q_4', and so on.[10]

The *logical width* of a predicate expression is defined as follows: If the predicate expression is logically empty (e.g., '$P_1 \cdot \overline{P}_1$') we assign it the width 0; otherwise it is equivalent to a definite disjunction of Q-predicates, and its width is taken to be the number of Q-predicates in that disjunction. In the above example, the width of 'P_1' is 2, the width of '$P_1 \cdot \overline{P}_2$' is 1, the width of 'P_1 v P_2' is 3, and so on. The *relative width* of a predicate expression is the ratio of the width of the expression to the total number of Q-predicates in the language. It is clear that the width of a predicate expression depends on the number of predicates in the language; in L^π the width of a primitive predicate is $2^{\pi-1}$. The relative width does not depend on the number of primitive predicates; the relative width of a primitive predicate is always $2^{\pi-1}/2^\pi$, or $1/2$.[11]

Before going on to the consideration of various quantitative c-functions (confirmation functions) which might be proposed as explicata for probability₁, Carnap lays down certain conventions to which any such explicatum should conform. The expression '$c(h,e) = p$' is to be read, 'the degree of confirmation of hypothesis h, relative to evidence e, is p.' The conventions are:[12]

(1) (a) if e and e' are L-equivalent, then $c(h,e) = c(h,e')$.

(b) if h and h' are L-equivalent, then $c(h,e) = c(h',e)$.

(c) $c(h \cdot j, e) = c(h,e) \times c(j, e \cdot h)$.

(d) if $e \cdot h \cdot j$ is L-false, then $c(h \text{ v } j, e) = c(h,e) + c(j,e)$.

(2) if e is not L-false, and t is tautological, then $c(t,e) = 1$.

(3) for any state description Z in L_N, $c(Z, t) > 0$.

Carnap then shows that *if* we accept these conventions, then we must, in virtue of (1)c and (1)a, be able to write:

$$c(h,e) = \frac{m(e \cdot h)}{m(e)}$$

where $m(e)$ corresponds to $c(e,t)$, or the *null confirmation*, or

10. *Ibid.*, p. 124-125.
11. *Ibid.*, p. 127.
12. *Ibid.*, p. 285-289.

the *a priori* probability of e.[13] In this way the problem of finding
an adequate c-function is reduced to that of finding an adequate m-
function, or *measure-function*. The problem can be further reduced,
since any statement in L_N can be written as a disjunction of state
descriptions, to that of finding a suitable measure-function for all
state descriptions in L_N. (State descriptions are logically exclusive
in pairs, and we may therefore apply convention (1)d to the appropriate disjunction.)

Carnap then turns to a special class of m- and c-functions, the
regular m- and c-functions. A function m is a *regular measure-
function* if it fulfils the two requirements:[14]

(1) for every state description Z in L_N, $m(Z)$ is a positive real
number.

(2) the sum of the values of m for all the state descriptions in L_N
is 1.

A confirmation function c is *based upon* m if, for any pair of sentences e and h in L_N such that $m(e) \neq 0$, $c(h,e) = m(e \cdot h)/m(e)$.
A function c is a *regular confirmation-function* if it is based on a
regular measure-function.[15] All of the classical theorems in probability, with the exception of those based upon the principle of indifference, hold for all regular c-functions satisfying the conventions of adequacy.

Carnap next considers a special subclass of the regular m- and
c-functions; these are the *symmetrical* measure-functions and the
corresponding confirmation-functions. These functions treat all individuals on a par, so that, for example, 'P(c)' is confirmed by
'P(a) · P(b)' to precisely the same degree as it is confirmed by
'P(d) · P(f)'. A symmetrical measure-function is a regular measure-function such that if the state descriptions Z_i and Z_j are isomorphic, then $m(Z_i) = m(Z_j)$. A symmetrical c-function is, of
course, one which is based on a symmetrical m-function.

Symmetrical confirmation-functions have the following very important characteristic: if the relative frequency of the property P
in a population is r, then, relative to this evidence, any symmetrical c-function will assign the probability₁ r to the hypothesis that
a given member of the population has the property P. This will be
the case regardless of the logical width of the property P, and regardless of which particular symmetrical m- and c-functions are
employed. This type of inference is called the direct inductive inference, and is the only form of probability₁ statement in Carnap's

13. *Ibid.*, p. 295.
14. *Ibid.*, p. 295.
15. *Ibid.*, p. 295.

system which is independent of the logical width of the predicates involved.

Carnap finally proposes, tentatively, a particular measure-function $m*$, and suggests that the confirmation-function $c*$ based on this may serve as an adequate explication of probability$_1$. Since $m*$ is a symmetrical m-function, it has the same value for all isomorphic state descriptions; it also assigns the same value to each structure description in L_N.[16] (Carnap also considers another c-function, $c\dagger$, which is based on a measure-function assigning equal values to each state description.[17]) In effect, $m*$ assigns the same measure to each of the distinct statistical distributions of the individuals among the Q-predicates. For any given state description, Z_i, $m*(Z_i) = 1/Th_i$, where T is the number of structure descriptions in L_N and h_i is the number of state descriptions isomorphic to Z_i, or, what is the same thing, the number of state descriptions belonging to the structure description to which Z_i belongs.

In the simple case of one predicate and two individuals, this leads to the following measures:

$$m*(P(a) \cdot P(b)) = 1/3$$

$$m*(\overline{P}(a) \cdot P(b)) = 1/6$$

$$m*(P(a) \cdot \overline{P}(b)) = 1/6$$

$$m*(\overline{P}(a) \cdot \overline{P}(b)) = 1/3$$

Carnap presents several theorems concerning $c*$, the confirmation-function based on $m*$. Let h be a singular prediction of the form 'M(c)', where 'M' is a predicate of width w_1, and 'c' is an individual not occurring in e. The evidence e states that in a sample of s individuals, s_1 specified individuals had the property M. Then $c*(h, e) = (s_1 + w_1)/(s + k)$, where k is the number of Q-predicates.[18] Carnap also shows that in a language containing an infinite number of individual constants, the $c*$ of any empirical law is 0, regardless of the evidence in favor of it. Similarly, in a language containing a very large number of individual constants, the $c*$ of a universal generalization is very close to 0.[19] Carnap engages in a valiant attempt to make this seem plausible, maintaining that we are really interested in instance confirmations, rather than in laws, and that we wish it to be well-confirmed that in the next

16. *Ibid.*, p. 562 ff.
17. *Ibid.*, p. 564 ff.
18. *Ibid.*, p. 568.
19. *Ibid.*, p. 571.

instance the law will hold, rather than that it will hold always and everywhere.

This does not seem to be quite true to life. I am not only quite sure that the next crow I see will be black; I am quite sure that the next n crows I see will each be black, and even that *all* crows are black. Am I mad? While it may be possible to get along without talking about the probability of a law, it is a little discomforting to discover after all this work on degree of confirmation that we do not end up with any way of saying of a law that it is 'well confirmed.' People do say this of laws, and while we may expect that they are not speaking quite as precisely as we (as logicians) would like them to, we should have some pretty good reasons on hand if we are going to tell them that they are speaking nonsense or falsehoods. Within the framework of Carnap's system, we have excellent reasons for telling them this, of course. But in some other framework we may be able to come closer to everyday usage. There are several more fundamental and important difficulties with his system, however, and it is to these that I shall now turn.

3. The most frustrating thing about Carnap's system, in its present state, is that it can be applied only to very simple languages which cannot possibly be adequate to the needs of any contemporary science. These languages must meet two general requirements: the requirement of completeness and the requirement of independence. I shall discuss independence first, and then turn to completeness.

Logical independence demands (1) that the atomic sentences be logically independent of each other, (2) that the individual constants in L designate different individuals, and (3) that the primitive predicates designate attributes which are logically independent of each other.[20] This is a more serious restriction than it may seem to be at first glance. It means that we cannot employ predicates like 'red' and 'green' if we consider it a logical truth that if an object is red, it is not green. (And note that if it is not logically true its degree of confirmation is 0.) Nor can we employ relational predicates which are irreflexive or transitive, for 'a is not warmer than a' and 'if a is warmer than b, and b is warmer than c, then a is warmer than c' are logical truths, which rule out certain state descriptions as logically impossible. On the other hand, if we decide to treat these truths as empirical, rather than logical, then we will find that the probability of 'no object is warmer than itself' is 0 or very close to it.

But a way of avoiding this requirement has been suggested by

20. *Ibid.*, p. 72-73.

Kemeny.[21] His suggestion is essentially this: that we employ any predicates we wish, set down axioms reflecting the logical relationships among these predicates, and define a regular measure function as one which meets Carnap's requirements, but which assigns zero measure to any 'state description' which describes a logically impossible state. Kemeny's system, based upon his "New Approach to Semantics"[22] has been developed to apply to functional calculi of all finite orders.[23] As Kemeny[24] and Carnap[25] have both pointed out, it is possible to pass from one system to the other by considering the 'meaning postulates' to be part of our evidence. The system, that is to say, is not changed essentially by employing this method of avoiding the independence requirement.[26]

The requirement of completeness constitutes a more serious difficulty in itself, and it leads to considerations which militate against the whole logical-range conception of probability. The requirement of logical completeness demands (1) that any two individuals differ only in a finite number of (independent) respects, and (2) that "a system of pr [predicates] be taken which is sufficiently comprehensive for expressing all the qualitative attributes in the given universe,"[27] to which inductive logic, as formulated for the language, is to be applied.

In the first place, this requirement has a decidely ontological ring to it; it sounds very much like an old-fashioned postulate-of-the-uniformity-of-nature. In the second place, it would surely be advantageous to be free to provide names in our language for new primitive properties, if these new properties should come to light in the application of new experimental techniques. Most theories seem to involve the introduction of new, non-eliminable predicates. There may also be some difficulty in supposing that there are an infinite number of individuals, which differ from each other in only a finite number of respects. We must be concerned only with *sci-*

21. John Kemeny, Review of *The Logical Foundations of Probability*, *Journal of Symbolic Logic* 16, 1951. Also see his "Extension of the Methods of Inductive Logic," *Philosophical Studies* 3, 1952, in which he goes into more detail.
22. John Kemeny, "A New Approach to Semantics, Part I," *Journal of Symbolic Logic* 21, 1956.
23. J. Kemeny, "A Logical Measure Function," *Journal of Symbolic Logic* 18, 1953.
24. *Ibid.*, p. 301.
25. Carnap, "Meaning Postulates," *Philosophical Studies* 3, 1952.
26. Kemeny's system in "A Logical Measure Function" does embody some important changes, due to the fact that he replaces 'state descriptions' in the object language by an analysis of possible models of the system in the meta-language. In some cases this leads to more plausible confirmation values than those provided by Carnap's system. But the degree of confirmation of a law is still 0.
27. Carnap, *The Logical Foundations of Probability*, p. 74-75.

entifically important respects—but how can we decide which these are on logical grounds alone?

Completeness is required, however, in any theory for which degrees of confirmation depend on the logical width of the predicates involved. This may be seen in Carnap's formula for the degree of confirmation of the singular predictive inference, $(s_1 + w_1)/(s + k)$, where s is the number of individuals examined, s_1 is the number of individuals examined, s_1 is the number with the property M, w_1 is the logical width of M, and k is the number of Q-predicates. Suppose that our language has 10 primitive predicates, and that M is defined by a conjunction of two of them. Suppose that we have examined 1000 objects and found 800 of them to have the property M. What is the probability that the next object to be examined will have the property M? The number of Q-predicates is (in Carnap's simple language, for 10 primitive predicates) 1024; the width of M is 256. We therefore have,

$$c^*(h, e) = \frac{s_1 + w_1}{s + k} = \frac{800 + 256}{1000 + 1024} = 0.522 > \frac{1}{2}$$

If we introduce one new primitive predicate, so that our total is 11, the number of Q-predicates becomes 2048, and the width of M becomes 512. The relative width of M (or the *a priori* probability of h) remains the same: $256/1024 = 512/2048$. But we get a new value for $c^*(h, e)$:

$$c^*(h, e) = \frac{800 + 512}{1000 + 2048} = 0.430 < \frac{1}{2}$$

It seems odd that the introduction of a new predicate, logically independent of the predicates occurring in the hypothesis as well as of the predicates occurring in the evidence statement, should materially alter the numerical value of the degree of confirmation of that hypothesis on that evidence.

The larger the number of predicates, relative to the size of our samples, the less pronounced is the effect of adding a new primitive predicate. But the above example shows also that even for a very modest number of primitive predicates, logical width is more important than the composition of a large sample. If we had a thousand primitive predicates, or even a hundred, no humanly attainable samples would have any appreciable effect on the degree of confirmation of the singular predictive inference.

Finally, suppose that the language of science can be formalized in such a way that the requirement of completeness is met. If the practical difficulties involved in this can be overcome at all, we may find that there are several different ways of performing the required formalization, and that they do not all lead to the same number of primitive predicates. The degree of confirmation of a given hypothesis on given evidence will then depend which particular method of formalization we employ. To put the matter as paradoxically as possible, the more articulate and the more finely attuned to reality our language, the lower the degree of confirmation of a given hypothesis on given evidence.

To be sure, Carnap proposes $c*$ only tentatively; there is, in fact, a continuum of possible explicata for probability$_1$ which may be defined in his system. Thus if we find that the number of primitive predicates is such that the above formula for the singular predictive inference seems implausible, we can increase or decrease the force of logical width by using the formula:[28]

$$c\,(h_M, e_M) = \frac{s_M + (w/k)\lambda\,(k)}{s + \lambda\,(k)}$$

where h_M, e_M, s_M, and w correspond to h, e, s_1, and w_1 in the earlier formula. The function λ is simply a function of k, the number of Q-predicates, tailored to make the formula seem plausible. If the world were different, in the sense that we could discriminate more (or less) properties, we would want to use a different confirmation function. Given any particular function λ, there will be a number of primitive predicates which will make the formula for confirmation seem implausible; and the implausibility will be of the same sort that leads Carnap to reject the confirmation function $c\dagger$: if we adopt $c\dagger$, it will be impossible to learn from experience; if we adopt $c*$ in a language which contains a thousand primitive predicates, it will be practically impossible to learn from experience.

This characteristic of Carnap's system has not gone unnoticed. Kemeny has suggested that we simply adopt a universal constant, k, an index of caution, and define the degree of confirmation of the hypothesis that the next object will have the property M, where M is a conjunction of t primitive properties, and s_1 of s examined objects have been found to have the property M, by:[29]

$$c\,(h, e) = \frac{s_1 + k\,(1/2)^t}{s + k}$$

If we let k be 2^P, where P is the number of primitive predicates, we get Carnap's function $c*$. Carnap points out that this is the same

28. Carnap, *The Continuum of Inductive Methods*, Chicago, 1952, p. 30.
29. Kemeny, "A Contribution to Inductive Logic," *Philosophy and Phenomenological Research* 13, 1952-53. Carnap's *Continuum of Inductive Methods* had not yet appeared.

as letting the function $\lambda(2^P)$ be the constant function $\lambda(2^P) = k$.[30] But this does not, of course, eliminate the arbitrary character of confirmation functions. We may still ask, why pick one confirmation function rather than another; or why pick one value of k rather than another.

Carnap suggests that among other factors influencing our selection of a c-function will be its success in predicting.[31] In some worlds one function will work better, in other worlds another will. Burks has boldly asserted that this arbitrariness is ineliminable, and that any calculation of degree of confirmation will reflect not only the evidence available, but our "presuppositions" concerning the world, as embodied in our choice of a confirmation function.[32] All we can say is that ordinarily our presuppositions are such as to lead to a confirmation function similar to c^*. There can be no inductive confirmation of our presuppositions. As Lenz has pointed out,[33] in choosing one c-function rather than another, we will generally employ (presuppose) the ordinary principle of induction: we will suppose that the future adequacy of a c-function is indicated by its past adequacy. This, of course, is a synthetic hypothesis; Carnap's theory of induction cannot lead to a justification of induction free of assumptions about the nature of the world.

All c-functions defined in the way that Carnap has suggested yield values for the confirmation of a hypothesis on null evidence. This seems a little questionable in itself, and it leads to some consequences which do not seem to have been sufficiently considered. Let K be any non-empty class of individuals. Carnap shows that for any Q-predicate, the *a priori* probability of the hypothesis that a given individual in K has the property denoted by this predicate is $1/k$, where k is the number of Q-predicates, and furthermore that the estimate of the relative frequency of this property in K should also be $1/k$.[34] By analogy with the examples given earlier, we may suppose that the degree of confirmation of the hypothesis that the next individual drawn from K have the property, relative to the evidence provided by a reasonably small sample drawn from K, will be very close to $1/k$. If the number of primitive predicates

30. Carnap, "Remarks to Kemeny's Paper," *Philosophy and Phenomenological Research* 13, 1952-53.
31. R. Carnap, *The Continuum of Inductive Methods*, p. 53-55.
32. A. W. Burks, "The Presupposition Theory of Induction," *Philosophy of Science* 20, 1954. Also see his "On the Presuppositions of Induction," *Review of Metaphysics* 8, 1954-55.
33. J. W. Lenz, "Carnap on Defining 'Degree of Confirmation,'" *Philosophy of Science* 23, 1956.
34. Carnap, *Logical Foundations of Probability*, p. 556.

is large (say, fifteen or twenty), then the probability of the predictive hypothesis will be close to $1/k$, even on the basis of a rather large sample (say a thousand-fold sample). In virtue of this fact, and with the help of conventions (1)c and (1)d, we may apply Bernoulli's theorem as a good approximation, and show that $c^*(h',t)$ is very close to 1, where h' states that a proportion lying between $1/k - d$ and $1/k + d$ of the first n individuals we draw from K will have the property designated by the Q-predicate in question. But this is precisely to say that we can be practically certain, *a priori*, that the relative frequency of objects in a given n-fold subclass of K which have the property in question will be close to $1/k$. This certainly does not seem plausible; but it is a consequence, not only of Carnap's suggested explicatum, but of any theory meeting Carnap's criteria of adequacy, provided only that the instance confirmation, relative to a not-too-large amount of evidence, be close to the *a priori* probability.

Carnap would explain this by saying that we are not much concerned with statements like $c^*(h',t)$, since these statements have a very low *reliability*. "The estimate ... on the null evidence, has only a low reliability..."[35] This brings me to the final and (to my mind) most serious difficulty involved in any approach to probability₁ which accepts the conventional conventions for manipulating probabilities. Probability₁ is supposed to be legislative for rational belief, and yet if a confirmation function is adopted as the explication of probability₁, we find that we have to distinguish between more and less reliable probability₁ statements. At the same time, probability₁ statements are all logically true. This seems strange in itself: to talk about the reliability of a logically true statement. It seems even stranger when we consider that we often speak of the reliability of an estimate in just about the same sense as we speak of the probability of a hypothesis.

This distinction between reliability and probability must nevertheless be made if we are to offer a confirmation function as an explication of probability.[36] In any such explication we may find that the probability of a given statement, relative to no evidence at all, may be p, and that the probability of the same statement, relative to a huge amount of highly relevant evidence may also be p. We certainly want to make some sort of distinction between the two situations; and it would certainly be nice if this distinction could be reflected in the legislated degrees of belief. But so long as *a priori*

---

35. *Ibid.*, p. 559.
36. This is very clearly brought out by C. I. Lewis, *An Analysis of Knowledge and Valuation*, Open Court, 1946, p. 292.

probabilities exist, and are identified with real (or rational) numbers, the distinction cannot be represented within the probability measure itself. The fact that the reliability of a probability statement increases as the amount of evidence e increases, and that e is represented in the formal framework of the theory, is interesting, but hardly seems to be a sufficient characterization of reliability. We want something that will indicate the *degree* of reliability and will allow us to measure the weight of different kinds of evidence in this respect. It is this desire that has led Carnap to suggest a concept analogous to 'standard error' as a measure of reliability;[37] but this measure is a conventional one lying outside of the formal framework of the theory, and it does not conveniently lead to distinctions between different types of evidence. One might have a completely different standard of reliability and yet retain the same probability theory.

As long as an external element enters into the application of the logical theory of probability and into the characterization of rational beliefs, it is tempting to go along with the frequency theorists who maintain that it is impossible to systematize completely the considerations involved in the use of (statistical) probability as a guide in life, a determiner of beliefs, etc. The object of a logical theory is to formalize and standardize these considerations; if the logical theory cannot do this without introducing such supplementary notions as 'reliability' and the 'weight of the evidence' (Keynes' term), then we are not much better off than we are with only a frequency theory.

Carnap has provided us with a most comprehensive analysis of the possible confirmation functions which fulfil his basic requirements. As he points out, the class of concepts with which he deals includes every concept which has been proposed as an explicatum for probability₁ by previous investigators, to the extent that this concept has been made precise and has not depended on a self-contradictory principle of indifference.[38] Most of the above mentioned difficulties, if such they be, apply to any definition of probability which meets the conventional criteria. Although these criteria seem simple and straight-forward enough—perhaps even minimal[39]—I shall attempt to present a plausible theory which does not meet them.

In particular, I shall find it convenient to reject altogether the

37. Carnap, *The Logical Foundations of Probability*, p. 549.
38. The concept defined by Helmer and Oppenheim (*op. cit.*, note 5) is an exception; for this concept neither the general nor the special multiplication principles hold.
39. Shimony, Lehman, and Kemeny regard them as minimal; see note 5, Chapter Three, for references.

general multiplication principle (1) c, and the special addition principle (1) d, and the convention demanding an *a priori* probability greater than 0 for any state description (3) will be modified by the fact that probability statements will not be identified with numbers, but will be taken simply as mentioning (among other things) numbers; and instead of mentioning a single number, a probability statement will mention a pair of numbers. Carnap's other conventions, concerning L-equivalent evidence, L-equivalent hypotheses, and the maximum value of a probability, (conventions (1) a, (1) b, and (2)), will be retained in suitably modified form.

PART TWO: *Theory*

CHAPTER FIVE

The Object Language

1. The object language to which my definitions will refer is ML, supplemented by one primitive sign, p, and a set of axioms governing the use of p together with its accented variants. This extensional object language seems admirably suited to be a formalized language of science. It is recommended not only by its elegance and syntactical simplicity, but also by its flexibility with regard to type restrictions. The assignment of a rigid system of types in a scientific language can be problematic. What are we to take as the lowest type? Chairs and tables? Sense data? Sub-atomic events? Point-instants? If a chair is to be a class of sense data and a class of point events, what is to be the type relationship between point events and sense data? Quine's system enables us to ignore these questions, or at least to postpone them. They may come up again through the identification of individuals with their unit classes: "...individuals are distinguished from other classes by the peculiar circumstance of being their own sole members..." But, "From a formal standpoint actually there is no need of assuming that there is any such x at all." [1]

Freedom to add or delete matrices, or to change the logical relationships among them, without having to perform a major reconstruction of our language, is very important in a formal scientific language. The meanings of ordinary words often seem to change as we discover new things about the world; linguistic rules and conventions which are convenient at one time may not be so convenient at another. If relationships between meanings are reflected in the rules of our formal language, it should be possible to change the rules without too much difficulty, and without making any great changes in our body of knowledge. All of this is accomplished easily in the framework of ML.

Quine suggests that, "... languages for any extra-logical purposes can presumably be formed merely by supplementing our primitive logical notation by indefinitely many extra-logical predicates such as 'eur', 'red', etc. Such signs are of the same category as 'ϵ'; each attaches to one or more variables to produce an atomic formula." [2] There are advantages, as Quine points out, in treating

---

1. Quine, *Mathematical Logic* (revised edition), p. 135.
2. *Ibid.*, p. 151.

even proper names as terms defined on the basis of primitive predicates, rather than introducing them into the language directly.

Objections have been raised[3] to this suggestion; but even in ordinary usage a proper name seems generally to be equivalent to some description: "John Jones is the fellow who runs the local grocery." Even 'ostensive definitions' may be supposed to have this form: "Jane Smith is the lady occupying that spatiotemporal location." We may thus be able not only to restrict ourselves to definite descriptions, but to limit our primitive name-matrices to one— 'I-now', or 'place 0-0-0, time 0'. This does not mean, of course, that Quine's dictum—"To be is to be the value of a variable"—is to be taken as solving all ontological problems; we may also take the dictum to mean simply that ontology is not a proper part of logic.

For the sake of syntactical symplicity, I shall suppose that each of the extra-logical predicates consists of the sign 'p' followed by from 1 to n accents. This will give us n extralogical predicates. If we wish to change the language to the extent of adding a new predicate (the most usual sort of change), we merely say that from now on the extra-logical predicates are those expressions which consists of 'p' followed by from 1 to $n + 1$ accents.

Just as it seems plausible to lay down certain axioms of membership (AM) governing the sign 'ϵ', it seems plausible to lay down axioms of the primitive matrices, APM, governing the various signs formed from 'p' and strings of accents. Just as we want to be able to say, "If x is a member of y, and y is included in z, then x is a member of z," we shall want to be able to say, "If x is longer than y, and y is longer than z, then x is longer than z." And of course we want to be able to show that such statements as, "Socrates is longer than," and "The distance from here to New York bears the relation mortal to the distance from here to Boston," are false, without having to exhibit empirical evidence.

This system of expressions is not what Carnap and others would honor with the name 'language'; but even in what Carnap calls a 'calculus' where no reference to meaning is legitimate, it is possible to arrange for statements which would ordinarily be 'true by virtue of the meanings of the terms involved' to be 'theorems' which depend for their provability on the axioms governing the primitive matrices. This is merely to say that many of the semantical rules of a language can be reflected in the formal structure of a corresponding calculus. The axioms of the primitive matrices will thus represent certain statements which are to count as theo-

3. For example, H. Hochberg, "On Pegasizing," *Philosophy and Phenomenological Research* 17, 1957.

rems in the object language. And of course ponentials of these statements will also count as theorems. The *grounds* for supposing these statements to be *true* may be semantical—or may not concern us at all—but this is irrelevant to my present purpose.

When we add a new primitive predicate to the language, we will, in all likelihood, want to add to the axioms governing the primitive matrices. This is simple enough, and in general involves only minor adjustments, if any, to what we know and the grounds on which we know it. Changing the meaning of a term which already exists in the language is more complicated; but at worst we can simply forget about the old term and introduce a new one, defined by reference to one or more new primitive predicates which obey one or more new sets of axioms. In practise, this would mean that whenever a special symbol is to be introduced, all aspects of its logical relations to other symbols must be given. (Many a student of science would be grateful for such consideration.) If the new term is not a primitive predicate, this requirement is satisfied by a formal definition; but, more important, if it is a primitive predicate, the requirement will be satisfied only by a list of all the types of axioms that govern its logical behavior.

So far the object language is logically richer and empirically poorer than any of those considered by Carnap. Logically richer because we may have primitive predicates of any number of places and of any desired relative types; empirically poorer, because we do not demand that the system of predicates be complete: we remain free to add new primitive predicates should the occasion arise. Nor do we have to be concerned about logical independence; we need only suppose that the logical relationships among the primitive predicates are expressed by appropriate axioms.[4] Nevertheless, there is one point of similarity: the number of primitive predicates is assumed to be finite. In order to be sure that this is plausible in a language of science, we must be sure that it is possible to develop 'real-number predicates' within the framework of ML, supplemented by a finite number of primitive predicates and a finite number of kinds of axioms governing them.

Let there be a primitive predicate π such that the following two expressions are metatheorems:

(1) $\ulcorner (\alpha)(\beta)(\pi(\alpha;\beta) \supset \sim\pi(\beta;\alpha))\urcorner$

(2) $\ulcorner (\alpha)(\beta)(\gamma)(\pi(\alpha;\beta) \cdot \pi(\beta;\gamma) \cdot \supset \pi(\alpha;\gamma))\urcorner$

Now let us suppose that it is possible to define a certain function ξ

---

4. R. Carnap, "Meaning Postulates," *Philosophical Studies* 3, 1952, indicates that Carnap would now agree to this procedure.

by functional abstraction from logical material together with the primitive predicates; and let us further suppose that ξ correlates the elements of $\ulcorner \hat{\alpha} \, (\exists \beta)(\pi(\alpha;\beta) \text{ v } \pi(\beta;\alpha)) \urcorner$ with real numbers in such a way that (3) is satisfied:

(3) $\ulcorner (\gamma)(\gamma')(\gamma,\gamma' \, \epsilon \, \hat{\alpha} \, (\exists \beta)(\pi(\alpha;\beta) \text{ v } \pi(\beta;\alpha)) \supset \cdot \, \xi'\gamma \, _r{>} \, \xi'\gamma' \equiv$

$\pi(\gamma;\gamma')) \urcorner$

This is apparently always possible—at least when the class in question is finite—for if worst comes to worst we can always take $\ulcorner \xi' \eta = _r 1 \urcorner$ for some η, and assign arbitrary values to $\ulcorner \xi' \zeta \urcorner$ as each new object ζ turns up, in such a way as to satisfy (3). (This technique seems often to be employed by social scientists.) Given a primitive predicate π and a function ξ satisfying the above requirements, it is of course an easy matter to introduce an infinite array of matrices as follows:

(4) $\ulcorner _\eta \Pi(\alpha) \urcorner$ for $\ulcorner \alpha \, \epsilon \, \hat{\beta}(\xi' \beta = \eta) \urcorner$

These matrices can all be defined for every real number η whether or not they determine classes which have members; we can even define them (and this is important for my purposes) when there are only a finite number of elements between which the relation π holds.

There is one very interesting kind of array of matrices: that which arises when we have some method of *combining* the objects between which the relation holds. Let π' be such a combining function, so that $\ulcorner \pi''(\alpha;\beta) \urcorner$ is the object produced by the addition of α to β. Let (5) be a metatheorem:

(5) $\ulcorner \alpha,\beta \, \epsilon \, \hat{\gamma}(\exists \delta)(\pi(\gamma;\delta) \text{ v } \pi(\delta;\gamma)) \supset \pi''(\alpha;\beta) \, \epsilon \, \hat{\gamma}(\exists \delta)(\pi(\gamma;\delta) \text{ v }$

$\pi(\delta;\gamma)) \urcorner$

We are often, in this situation, able to find a mapping function ξ with the logically provable or empirically discoverable property expressed by equation (6):

(6) $\ulcorner _\eta \Pi(\alpha) \cdot \, _\zeta \Pi(\beta) \cdot \supset _{\eta_r +} \, \zeta \, \Pi(\pi''(\alpha;\beta)) \urcorner$

This is merely a crude suggestion as to how we might be able to arrive at the quantitative matrices required for a scientific language on the basis of a finite number of primitive predicates. It is interesting to note that on this view an abstract quantity such as 'two grams' comes to be the 'class of two-gram objects', just as the abstract number 2 is the class of all pairs. The difference is that the class of all two-gram objects may be empty, while in ML we have a theorem to the effect that the class of pairs is not empty. The real pecularity is that if there are neither two-gram objects nor four-gram objects, then the class of two-gram objects will be the same as the class of four-gram objects; i.e., "two grams = four grams" will be true. But it will certainly not be a theorem; and it is doubtful that we could ever have any empirical reasons for accepting it. In practise we will not be particularly interested in the class of two-gram objects anyway, but rather in the class of $2 \pm .001$ gram objects. And we have excellent inductive reasons for believing that *this* class is not empty.

The importance of being able to employ primitive predicates which are not logically independent should not be underestimated. Theoretical terms, such as 'entropy', 'instantaneous velocity', etc., must somehow be connected with the terms which describe ordinary experience. If they are not to be completely reducible (via formal definitions) to the terms of ordinary experience—which even the most ardent empiricists are beginning to acknowledge—then it seems plausible to suppose that this connection is established by a logical relationship. Carnap's reduction sentences, for example, formulate just such relationships.

The primitive predicates can be related to a set of ordinary words by a sequence of semantical rules; and in fact it is only by reference to such a semantical relationship that we can *justify* the axioms governing the primitive predicates, if we feel that they need to be justified. But the primitive predicates may also be related, for convenience, to a set of predicates like 'eur', 'red', etc., as suggested by Quine, by means of a series of formal definitions. The syntactical advantage of having to be concerned with only one new primitive sign is obvious; and the formal definitions would enable us to use a more suggestive notation in practise.[5]

2.   The most persuasive argument in favor of an empirical interpretation of probability is that there are many contexts in which probability statements are used to express matters of fact. No one would say that the probability of a human birth being the birth of a male was 0.515, unless he knew that in fact 51.5% of human births are the births of males. And conversely, no one would accept the latter statement unless he was willing to accept the former. The two statements are therefore *practically* equivalent, since one will be accepted if and only if the other is accepted. In asserting this

---

5. It must be remembered that we are constructing this language for a very definite purpose—the elucidation of some of the fundamental criteria of scientific knowledge—and that we are not offering it as an 'analysis of ordinary language.' If suffices to be able to say in our object language whatever can be said in ordinary language when it is used for predicting, describing, communicating factual information, etc. For comments on this aspect of formalization, see G. Bergmann, *Philosophy of Science*, The University of Wisconsin Press, 1957; A. J. Ayer, "Individuals," *Mind* n.s. 61, 1952.

type of probability statement, we are implicitly asserting a statement about relative frequencies or class ratios.

This does not require us to accept a frequency statement as an explication of this form of probability statement. To accept this explication would be to accept the thesis that in *using* a probability statement of this type, we are *using* an empirical statement about relative frequencies. But we can also say that in using a probability statement of this type, we are *mentioning,* in a certain context, a statement about relative frequencies. On this latter view, we can (by a judicious selection of context) save the practical equivalence of the two statements mentioned in the preceding paragraph without *identifying* the statistical statement with the probability statement. This is the technique that I shall employ. A probability statement will be construed as a statement in syntax, mentioning, among other things, a statistical statement belonging to the object language. This will explain the fact that we often require empirical statistical knowledge in order to make a probability statement—for we may plausibly demand that the statistical statement mentioned be known. Unknown probabilities, hypothetical probabilities, and so on, may be construed in the same way with the help of hypothetical rational corpora.

It is only in connection with statistical statements in the object language—which are to be kept distinct from probability statements—that the conventional rules of the 'probability calculus' hold simply and automatically. We thus need an efficient way of stating and manipulating such statements as "Half the people in this room are dogs," "3.74% of the alpha particles fired in situation S will miss the target," etc. The remainder of this chapter will be devoted to developing the required class ratio calculus within the framework of ML, and showing that it can be expanded to meet the requirements of classical statistics.[6]

The simplest form of class ratio calculus is one in which the classes concerned are finite, and in which the class ratios are given precisely. The following definitions, D 63 to D 68, are taken directly from ML, pages 266-269.

D 63 $\ulcorner (\zeta/\eta) \urcorner$ *for* $\ulcorner \hat{\alpha}\hat{\beta}(\alpha,\beta \ \epsilon \ \mathrm{Nn} \cdot \eta \ \mathrm{x} \ \alpha = \zeta \ \mathrm{x} \ \beta) \urcorner$

D 64 $\ulcorner (\zeta \underset{s}{>} \eta) \urcorner$ *for* $\ulcorner (\exists \alpha)(\exists \beta)(\exists \gamma)(\exists \delta)(\zeta = \alpha/\beta \cdot \eta = \gamma/\delta \cdot$

$\alpha \ \mathrm{x} \ \delta > \gamma \ \mathrm{x} \ \beta) \urcorner$

D 65   'Ra' *for* '$\hat{\mathrm{x}}(\exists \mathrm{y})(\exists \mathrm{z})(\mathrm{y} \ \epsilon \ \mathrm{Nn} \cdot \mathrm{z} > 0 \cdot \mathrm{x} = \mathrm{y/z})$'

---

6. The readers who plan to skip the formal developments as far as possible would do well to glance at D 70 before going on to page 64 where the narrative is resumed.

D 66 $\ulcorner(\zeta\ _{s}+\eta\ )\urcorner$ for $\ulcorner(\ _{\gamma}\gamma)(\exists\alpha)(\exists\beta)(\exists\alpha')(\exists\beta')(\zeta=\alpha/\beta\cdot\eta=$
$$\alpha'/\beta'\cdot\gamma=((\alpha\times\beta')+$$
$$(\alpha'\times\beta))/(\beta\times\beta'))\urcorner$$

D 67 $\ulcorner(\zeta\ _{s}\times\eta\ )\urcorner$ for $\ulcorner(\ _{\gamma}\gamma)(\exists\alpha)(\exists\beta)(\exists\alpha')(\exists\beta')(\zeta=\alpha/\beta\cdot\eta=$
$$\alpha'/\beta'\cdot\gamma=(\alpha\times\alpha')/(\beta\times\beta'))\urcorner$$

D 68 $\ulcorner(\zeta\ _{s}\div\eta\ )\urcorner$ for $\ulcorner(\ _{\gamma}\beta)(\zeta=\eta\ _{s}\times\beta\ )\urcorner$

It will be convenient to define the difference between two ratios; if x is greater than y, the difference '$y\ _{s}-x$' will not exist, but in a class ratio calculus this causes no particular inconvenience.

D 69 $\ulcorner(\zeta\ _{s}-\eta\ )\urcorner$ for $\ulcorner(\ _{\gamma}\beta)(\zeta=\eta\ _{s}+\beta)\urcorner$

The basic form of statistical statement will be rendered, '$\%(x,y,z\ )$', which is to be read, 'the proportion of the x's which are also y's is z.'

D 70 $\ulcorner\%(\zeta,\eta,\theta\ )\urcorner$ for $\ulcorner(\exists\alpha)(\exists\beta)(\alpha,\beta\ \epsilon\ \mathrm{Nn}\cdot\zeta\ \epsilon\ \alpha\cdot\zeta\cap\eta\ \epsilon\ \beta\cdot$
$$\theta=\beta/\alpha\urcorner$$

Finally, we want to have a convenient notation for mentioning the class consisting of n-fold selections from the class x, in formal notation, x_{n}.

D 71 $\ulcorner\zeta_{\eta}\urcorner$ for $\ulcorner\hat{\alpha}\ (\eta\ \epsilon\ \mathrm{Nn}\cdot\alpha\ \epsilon\ \eta\cdot\alpha\subset\zeta\ )\urcorner$

There follow, without proof, a few metatheorems which suffice to establish the conventional statistical calculus.

*810 $\vdash\ulcorner\eta\ \epsilon\ \mathrm{Fin}\cdot\eta\subset\zeta\cdot\supset\%(\eta,\zeta,_{s}1)\urcorner$

*811 $\vdash\ulcorner\eta\ \epsilon\ \mathrm{Fin}\cdot\eta\subset\bar{\zeta}\cdot\supset\%(\eta,\zeta,_{s}0)\urcorner$

*812 $\vdash\ulcorner\%(\eta,\zeta,\xi)\supset\%(\eta,\bar{\zeta},_{s}1\ _{s}-\ \xi)\urcorner$

*813 $\vdash\ulcorner\eta\cap\zeta=\Lambda:\supset\cdot\%(\theta,\eta,\xi)\cdot\%(\theta,\zeta,\psi)\cdot\supset\%(\theta,\eta\cup\zeta,\xi\ _{s}+\psi)\urcorner$

It is easy to see that these metatheorems do suffice to establish the calculus of probability, with regard to any finite class K, by comparing them with the axioms provided by Kolmogorov in his *Elementary Theory of Probability*.[7] Let K be any finite class; $\hat{x}(x\subset\mathrm{K})$ will correspond to Kolmogorov's $\mathfrak{Z}$.

Kolmogorov		ML
I	$\mathfrak{Z}$ is a field of sets	I* $\hat{x}(x\subset\mathrm{K})$ is a field; i.e.,

$$(y\ )(z\ )(y,z\ \epsilon\ \hat{x}(x\subset\mathrm{K})\supset:$$
$$y\cap z\ \epsilon\ \hat{x}(x\subset\mathrm{K})\cdot$$
$$y\cup z\ \epsilon\ \hat{x}(x\subset\mathrm{K})\cdot$$
$$y\cap\bar{z}\ \epsilon\ \hat{x}(x\subset\mathrm{K}))$$

7. Kolmogoroff, *Foundations of the Theory of Probability*, New York, 1950, p. 95.

III   To each set A in $\mathfrak{F}$ is assigned a non-negative real number P(A).

III*   To each element y of $\hat{x}(x \subset K)$ we assign a number P*(y) such that P*(y) = $_r$z $\cdot \equiv \cdot$ %(K,y,z)

II $\mathfrak{F}$ contains the set E

II*   K ϵ $\hat{x}(x \subset K)$

IV   P(E) = 1

IV*   P*(K) = $_r$1.   (*810)

V   If A and B have no element in common, then P(A $\cup$ B) = P(A) + P(B).

V*   (*813)

The following three metatheorems may also be of some interest.

*814 $\vdash^\lceil (\exists \beta)(\eta \epsilon \beta \cdot \beta \epsilon \text{Nn}) \supset (\exists \theta)(\%(\eta,\zeta,\theta))^\rceil$

*815 $\vdash^\lceil \%(\theta,\eta,\xi) \cdot \%(\theta \cap \eta,\zeta,\psi) \cdot \supset (\theta,\eta \cap \zeta,\xi \,_s\text{x} \, \psi)^\rceil$

*816 $\vdash^\lceil \%(\eta,\zeta,\xi) \cdot \%(\eta,\zeta,\psi) \cdot \supset (\xi = \psi)^\rceil$

There are two things about the above calculus of class ratios which seem at first sight to vitiate its significance. The first is that the classes with which the calculus deals are all supposed to be finite. The usual machinery of statistics makes use of the assumption that the classes with which it deals are infinite—so that, for example, drawing a sample from a population will not affect the composition of the population. But of course we do not have to suppose that the classes with which we are concerned are literally infinite in order to say that drawing a sample will not change the composition of the population, any more than we have to suppose that the number of measurable lengths is the same as the number of real numbers in order to say that the length of a steel bar forming the hypoteneuse of a triangle is the-square-root-of-two feet long. It suffices to suppose that the difference between $\sqrt{2}$ feet and the true length of the bar is trivial; in the same way, it suffices to suppose that the classes with which we are concerned are very large indeed, so that in drawing a sample, no *practical* difference is made in its composition. More important, even in describing what in reality must be a discrete distribution by means of a continuous distribution function, we need only suppose that the class is large enough, relative to the smallest *useful* intervals of that which we are describing, so that we will not be led into any noticeable error.

The question remains, however, of whether or not we are free to suppose that the classes of objects that interest us in our scientific pursuits are all finite. Are we ever compelled to suppose that a definite class is literally infinite? Philosophers—and even some scientists—often talk as if the number of people (past, present, and future), or the number of electrons, were infinite. The reason that this sounds plausible is not far to seek: it would be very difficult to name a natural number to which they belong. We simply don't know how many members they have. But this is merely to say that we don't know how big they are—it is very different from saying that there is no number to which they belong. On the other hand, there may be situations in which we must deal with classes which we do have reason to believe are literally infinite. Even here, however, since these classes must be ordered in some way, if we are to pick out any members at all, we may use the definitions suggested above by restricting our considerations to a finite initial segment of the class—say the first googolplex[8] of members (i.e., $(10)^{10^{100}}$). Or we may introduce a special limit conception to use when the conditions of the problem dictate a specific way of proceeding to a limit.

The other difficulty with the above calculus of class ratios is that it does not give us a convenient way of saying that a certain class ratio has *approximately* such and such a value. The usual approach in statistical texts has been to treat the necessity of assigning approximate values to parameters as a more or less unfortunate accident which there is little or no point in attempting to treat formally; on the other hand, it is supposed that the material about which statistics generalizes is such that infinite classes and continuous distributions and the like are the rule rather than the exception. I shall suppose just the opposite. I shall suppose that the approximateness of parameters is something which is so pervasive and inevitable that it should be taken account of in the formal development of the theory of probability, while the mathematical convenience of infinite classes and continuous distributions is just—a mathematical convenience.

The obvious way of expressing this vagueness (which must be sharply distinguished from the uncertainty expressed by probability statements) is to mention in our statistical statements two numbers rather than one; so that a statistical statement will be interpreted as saying that a certain class ratio lies between such and such limits, rather than that it has such and such a value. This modification is easily introduced; if we wish to say that the proportion of x's which are y's lies between the limits z_1 and z_2, we shall simply arrange to write the ordered pair $(z_1; z_2)$ in the place where we would ordinarily write the single parameter.

---

8. The term 'googolplex' is due to Kasner and Newman, "New Names for Old," reprinted in *The World of Mathematics*, (Newmann, ed.), New York, 1956.

D 72 $\ulcorner \% (\eta, \zeta, (\xi; \psi)) \urcorner$ for $\ulcorner (\exists \alpha)(\exists \beta)(\eta \in \alpha \cdot \eta \cap \zeta \in \beta \cdot$

$$\alpha/\beta \;_s> \xi \text{ v } \alpha/\beta = \xi \cdot$$

$$\psi \;_s> \alpha/\beta \text{ v } \psi = \alpha/\beta) \urcorner$$

The metatheorems stated for D 70 hold as they stand for statistical statements of the form $\ulcorner \% (\eta, \zeta, (\xi; \xi)) \urcorner$. They also have more general counterparts which appear as the next four metatheorems.

*817 $\vdash \ulcorner \eta \cap \zeta = \Lambda \supset : \% (\theta, \eta, (\psi; \psi')) \cdot \% (\theta, \zeta, (\xi; \xi')) \cdot \supset$

$$\% (\theta, \eta \cap \zeta, (\psi \;_s+ \xi; \psi' \;_s+ \xi')) \urcorner$$

*818 $\vdash \ulcorner \% (\theta, \zeta, (\psi; \psi')) \cdot \% (\theta \cap \zeta, \eta, (\xi; \xi')) \cdot \supset$

$$\% (\theta, \zeta \cap \eta, (\psi \;_sx \; \xi; \psi' \;_sx \; \xi')) \urcorner$$

*819 $\vdash \ulcorner \% (\zeta, \eta, (\psi; \psi')) \cdot \% (\zeta, \eta, (\xi; \xi')) \cdot \psi \;_s> \xi \cdot \psi' \;_s> \xi' \cdot \supset$

$$\% (\zeta, \eta, (\psi; \xi')) \urcorner$$

*820 $\vdash \ulcorner \% (\zeta, \eta, (\psi; \xi)) \cdot \supset \% (\zeta, \overline{\eta}, (\;_s1 \;_s- \xi; \;_s1 \;_s- \psi)) \urcorner$

The introduction of approximate parameters into the formal machinery of the statistical calculus has one rather interesting consequence. This is the progressive weakening of our statistical knowledge as we try to treat more objects at the same time. We may know within very narrow limits the proportion of x's which are y's; but when we argue from this proportion, by *818, to the proportion of all n-fold selections from the x's which consist entirely of y's, our knowledge becomes less precise; relatively speaking, the limits are wider in the second case.

One further definition is useful enough to be given a place here; its usefulness will only become apparent in later chapters, but it does pertain to expressions in the object language. Given two classes, x and y, we shall sometimes want to form the class of all pairs such that the first member of the pair belongs to x, and the second member to y. This is the cartesian product of x and y.

D 73 $\ulcorner (\eta \otimes \zeta) \urcorner$ for $\ulcorner \hat{\alpha}\hat{\beta}(\alpha \in \eta \cdot \beta \in \zeta) \urcorner$

4.   To illustrate in greater detail the connection between the class ratio calculus which I have added to (or found in) ML, and the conventional concepts of statistics, I shall suggest a few additional definitions. One of the most important concepts in statistics is that of a *distribution* of a class of objects into a class of classes, e.g., the distribution of a group of people into those who have had no college, those who have had just one year of college, those who have had just two years, and so on. It is clear that to assert that a

distribution in this sense describes a population is merely to assert that a number of ordinary statistical statements together describe the population. Thus we may simply write, "Dist$(x,(y_1,y_2, y_3, \ldots y_n),((z_1;z_1'),(z_2;z_2'), \ldots ,(z_n;z_n')))$" to mean that the proportion of x's which belong to the class y_1 lies between z_1 and z_1', and the proportion of x's which belong to the class y_2 lies between z_2 and z_2', and ... and the proportion of x's which belong to the class y_n lies between z_n and z_n'.

If we take $y_1 \ldots y_n$ as being mutually exclusive and exhausting x, we have the conventional *discrete distribution*. If we select $y_1 \ldots y_n$ in such a way that for every i, y_i is included in $y_i + 1$, and x is included in y_n, then we have the conventional *cumulative distribution*.

Continuous distributions offer many advantages over the discrete variety—the chief of which is that they allow us to use the powerful and efficient tools of analysis. I have already argued that we need be concerned only with finite classes; how then can we employ continuous distributions? Let $y_1 \ldots y_n$ be a finite set of classes defined on the basis of rational (or real) valued abstracts as described earlier; e.g., let y_1 be the class of objects weighing less than 1 gram, y_2 the class of objects weighing at least 1 grams but less than two grams, ... and y_n the class of objects weighing at least $n - 1$ grams. Let Z and Z' be functions of one variable, such that $Z(1) = z_1$, $Z'(1) = z_1'$, $Z(2) = z_2$, and so on. Instead of writing "Dist $(x,(y_1, y_2, \ldots, y_n),((z_1;z_1'),(z_2;z_2'), \ldots, (z_n;z_n')))$" to describe the distribution of the finite class x into the class of classes $y_1 \ldots y_n$, we may more simply write, "Dist $(x, (y_1,y_2, \ldots y_n),(Z;Z'))$". The values that the functions Z and Z' take for non-integral values of the argument are merely irrelevant here; there are any number of pairs of functions which will serve to describe the distribution. But we may be interested also in a somewhat more detailed description— e.g., in the distribution of the x's into classes only a tenth, or a hundredth of a gram in width. And sometimes—for example, when we have grounds for believing that a *normal* distribution function will give us the desired ˙distribution—the fact that Z and Z' work for one-gram intervals will constitute good evidence for the hypothesis that these same functions will work for any size of interval we happen to be interested in, no matter how small, *within reasonable limits*, this size happens to be.

Another assumption which we may make, even though we have all the evidence in the world for its falsity, is that the number of classes y_i for which the distribution holds is infinite. We may assume, in the first place, that Z and Z' will work, not only for intervals of any degree of smallness we have some reason to be interested in, but for intervals of any degree of smallness whatever. In the second place, we may wish to eliminate the limits that have been placed on the distribution. If x is the class of pollywogs, it is a safe enough assumption that we need be concerned only with weights falling between 0 grams and 500 grams. But it may be simpler to suppose that pollywogs may have any weight whatever; our continuous distribution function will then assert that there is some definite proportion of pollywogs which weigh more than 1000 kilograms: a proportion different from $_r0$. The supposition is false, as well as its consequence; it is made solely in the interest of mathematical efficiency, and we are free to make it only because we know better than to take such consequences seriously.[9]

Finally, if we have a great deal of information about the distribution of the x's among the y's, we may find that we can for all practical purposes eliminate the pair of distribution functions Z and Z' in favor of a single function Z*. If, for every value of the argument, the functions Z and Z' have *practically* the same value, we will simply pick a function Z* which gives us approximately this value. This function Z* is the usual *frequency function*, or *probability density function*.

On the basis of all these simplifying assumptions, we can describe a distribution in a very simple way. Letting Y be the class of all weights, or lengths, or whatever we are interested in, we may simply write, "Dist $(x,Y,(Z*;Z*))$" to mean that for any real numbers i and j, the integral of Z* between i and j will give approximately the proportion of x's belonging to the subclass of Y which includes all the weights (or what have you) that fall between i units and j units, provided we do not take i and j absurdly close together, and provided that we do not take an i and j which lie too far outside the normal range in which the x's fall. To make these necessary provisos precise, of course, we require the formal machinery of probability. But it is interesting both that they are often neglected in statistical texts, and that they are rarely neglected in statistical practise.

This puts us well within the realm of mathematical statistics. But we have not had to suppose that the class of x's is literally infinite—all we require is that there be a fairly large number of x's in each of the smallest subclasses of Y in which we are interested; and this requirement can be met when we are only interested in a few broad subclasses of Y, as well as when there are enormous numbers of x's.

9. On not taking our arithmetic too seriously, see Spencer Brown, *Probability and Scientific Inference.*

This completes the outline of the class ratio calculus and some of its useful extensions which I have supposed to be added to Quine's ML. It includes potentially all of the relatively non-controversial parts of the mighty machinery of modern mathematical statistics, as well as much of what has been traditionally subsumed under the theory of probability.

CHAPTER SIX

The Metalanguage

1. To show that a statement is 'probable', as Keynes and Carnap, among others, have pointed out, it is necessary to refer to the *evidence* relative to which this statement has its probability. Two possibilities present themselves: we may mention the evidence by using statements which describe the facts that constitute the evidence, or we may introduce the evidence somewhat more indirectly by mentioning only the latter statements (not the evidential facts themselves), using, for this purpose, statements of the metalanguage. On the former view, probability would seem to be interpreted as a relation between facts or states of affairs: *that* so and so is the case is probable relative to the fact *that* such and such is the case. But this seems to lead to certain difficulties. To discuss the probability of a certain fact for a certain individual, we must include as evidence only the facts that that person knows, or ought to know. But he may claim to know the fact expressed by one statement, and not that expressed by another statement, even though the two facts are precisely the same. "Smith is an anarchist," and "Jones is an anarchist," may express the same fact (when "Smith" and "Jones" are aliases of the same man), but a given person may very well be quite sure that one of these statements is true and that the other is false. And we cannot even insist that he *ought* to believe that the two statements are both true or that the two statements are both false, unless it just happens that he has evidence supporting the hypothesis that Smith and Jones are the same man.

Matters are somewhat simplified if we adopt the second point of view; on this view probability is to be expressed as a relation between statements, not facts, so that it is not odd at all that "Smith is an anarchist" can be evidence in favor of "Smith blew up the town hall," while "Jones is an anarchist" does not constitute evidence in favor of it unless we happen to know (or have grounds for believing) that Smith and Jones are the same person. In order to talk about probability as a relation between statements, we require the resources of a metalanguage. Just as we require a formalized metalanguage in order to define 'logically true' or 'theorem' or 'logically false', we require a formalized metalanguage to define 'randomness' and 'probability'.

Again there are two possibilities: we may adopt a metalanguage

in which the rules concerning the object language are purely syntactical, or we may adopt one which makes use of semantical rules
as well. If we employ syntax, the rules will refer only to the typo-
graphical shapes occurring in statements in the object language; if
we employ semantics, the rules of the metalanguage will refer to
the meanings of the expressions in the object language as well. Semantics allows a somewhat greater variety of rules and definitions
than does syntax, but, as I suggested earlier, it seems possible to
provide syntactical counterparts to many of the more significant
semantical rules by providing suitable postulates in the metalanguage
to govern the non-logical primitive predicates. In Carnap's terminology, the result of doing this is that the object language becomes
a mere calculus, and the metalanguage becomes merely a set of
rules for manipulating the signs in the object language.

We obtain a real *language* only when we provide some interpretation of the signs in the calculus — and this, of course, must be
done by means of semantical rules. (That is, it must be done by
means of semantic rules if it is to be done formally; but I am not
sure that there is a genuine necessity for doing it formally.) Now
usually the formal analogues of such statements as, "No bachelors
are married," are discovered to be logically true only after the
calculus is interpreted; they are true only by virtue of the semantical rules of the language, or in other words, by virtue of the meanings of the terms involved. On my procedure the formal analogues
of these statements are supposed to be *theorems* in the object language. This can be arranged in two ways: first, by seeing to it that
no interpretation is accepted which does not (by way of the syntactical rules governing the use of primitive predicates) lead to this
result, and second, by starting out with an interpretation in mind,
and selecting syntactical rules accordingly. The latter method seems
to be the most plausible, and is probably the one that anyone would
follow if he were seriously going to try to formalize a part of the
language of science. The 'justification' of the syntactical rules governing the primitive predicates may then simply be found in the
conventions of an informal language, rather than in the semantical
rules of a formal system. If we desire to be able to define 'truth',
'logical truth', etc., then of course we do have to give, at some point,
semantic rules; but it is still an open methodological question whether
it is better to work with syntax so far as it is possible, or whether
it is better from the outset to treat logic as a part of semantics.
Since the syntactical treatment seems simpler to me, I shall adopt
the former technique.

The fact that it is not possible to formulate a general definition
of 'truth' in syntax will be of only slight concern to us. We shall be

interested, in the first place, in statements which are 'theorems' in the object language; although the theorems do not exhaust the syntactical truths, we can always arrange for any particular syntactical truth we happen to be interested in to be a theorem. (In so doing, we run some risk of inconsistency.) In the second place, we are interested in statements which are more or less probable — and particularly in the ones which are more probable. But the probability of a statement is quite independent of its truth or falsity; and I shall also maintain that probability, like theoremhood, is syntactically definable.

Insofar as it is sometimes an open question whether a given statement in a natural language is to be construed as an analytic statement, or merely as a well-confirmed generalization, it will be an open question whether a given set of syntactical rules will be representative of the intent of the original language: i.e., whether the calculus really fits the informal 'interpretation' with which we start. The problem arises, however, with regard to semantical rules as well; it can be avoided only by Carnap's somewhat Alexandrian technique of postulating that the primitive predicates are to be logically independent. But the difficulty, however interesting philosophically, does not strike me as a serious one so far as the logic of rational belief is concerned. Any statement with regard to which the difficulty can arise will be one which anybody *ought* to believe, on one ground or another; the question of the 'real' reason for believing it, if it is a meaningful question at all, is irrelevant to the central question of the degree to which certain more or less doubtful statements ought to be believed.

Probability will ultimately be defined relative to a 'rational corpus.' The rational corpus, in the formal development of the theory, will be interpreted as a bare set of statements fulfilling certain requirements. Probability will then be defined formally relative to such sets of statements. The same statement may clearly have different probabilities relative to different sets of statements taken as a rational corpus. It is my contention that this relationship is a 'formal' one. Quine gives the following criterion of formality: "... translatability into a notation containing only names of signs, a connective indicating concatenation, and the notation of logic ..."[1] I hope to show that it is plausible to interpret probability statements as formal in this sense. So far as the present volume is concerned, semantics will play no part. This is not to say that a theory of probability like the one worked out here could not be extended to apply to a semantical system; it is only to say that this is not what I am doing.

1. Quine, *Mathematical Logic*, p. 286.

2. It is possible to formulate the definition of probability not only in syntax, but in the more restricted medium of Quine's protosyntax. Protosyntax employs only joint denial and quantification; syntax itself employs membership as well. Since the last section of Quine's ML seems to be the least read, I shall give here a brief review of his protosyntax.[2]

The primitive matrix of protosyntax refers to an ordered alphabet of the signs which occur in the object language. Quine lists nine signs; we must list ten, in order to include the basic non-logical predicate 'p'. The alphabet is thus:

$$w, x, y, z, ', (,), \epsilon, p$$

The primitive matrix $\ulcorner M \alpha\beta\gamma \urcorner$ allows us to form a name for each of these signs as well as names for expressions made up of finite rows of them, provided we give it the following meaning: '$Mxyz$' is to mean,

(1) if x is a single sign, x alphabetically just succeeds y.

(2) if x is a complex expression, x is the result of writing y followed by z.

(3) if x is not an expression at all (e.g., if it is a fly speck or a set), $x = y$.

The protosyntactical definitions $\Delta 1 - \Delta 8$ serve to introduce the conventional logical notation based on joint denial and universal quantification. Since membership is ruled out of protosyntax, special definitions must be provided for identity and for definite descriptions. These are given as $\Delta 9 - \Delta 14$ below. The greek letters α, β, γ, and δ represent variables, η and ζ represent terms, and ψ and ξ represent formulas — all in protosyntax.

$\Delta 9 \quad \ulcorner (\alpha = \beta) \urcorner \quad$ *for* $\quad \ulcorner (\gamma)(M\gamma\alpha\alpha \equiv M\gamma\beta\beta) \urcorner$

$\Delta 10 \quad \ulcorner M(\exists\alpha)\psi\beta\gamma \urcorner \quad$ *for* $\quad \ulcorner (\exists\delta)(M\delta\beta\gamma \cdot (\alpha)(\alpha = \delta \cdot \equiv \psi)) \urcorner$

$\Delta 11 \quad \ulcorner M\zeta(\exists\alpha)\psi\gamma \urcorner \quad$ *for* $\quad \ulcorner (\exists\delta)(M\zeta\delta\gamma \cdot (\alpha)(\alpha = \delta \cdot \equiv \psi)) \urcorner$

$\Delta 12 \quad \ulcorner M\zeta\eta(\exists\alpha)\psi \urcorner \quad$ *for* $\quad \ulcorner (\exists\delta)(M\zeta\eta\delta \cdot (\alpha)(\alpha = \delta \cdot \equiv \psi)) \urcorner$

$\Delta 13 \quad \ulcorner (\zeta = \eta) \urcorner \quad$ *for* $\quad \cdot \ulcorner (\gamma)(M\gamma\zeta\zeta \equiv M\gamma\eta\eta) \urcorner$

$\Delta 14 \quad \ulcorner (\zeta \neq \eta) \urcorner \quad$ *for* $\quad \ulcorner \sim(\zeta = \eta) \urcorner$

This clears the way for the definitions of the signs constituting the alphabet of the object language, and for the definition of a sign for concatenation, '$\frown$'; $x \frown y$ is to be the name of the complex ex-

---

2. The greater part of the material in this section (which continues to the end of the chapter) has been lifted bodily from the last part of Quine's text. The whole section may be omitted by those who wish to avoid the details of my formal definitions.

pression formed by writing the expression x followed by the expression y. These definitions follow as $\Delta 15 - \Delta 18$.

$\Delta 15$ 'S$_1$' for '$(\imath x)(y)(z) \sim \mathrm{M}xyz$.'

$\Delta 16$ 'S$_2$' for '$(\imath x)\mathrm{M}x\mathrm{S}_1 x$', 'S$_3$' for '$(\imath x)\mathrm{M}x\mathrm{S}_2 x$', etc. to 'S$_{10}$'

$\Delta 17$ $\ulcorner(\zeta \frown \eta)\urcorner$ for $\ulcorner(\imath \alpha)(\mathrm{M}\alpha\zeta\eta \cdot \sim \mathrm{M}\alpha\zeta\alpha)\urcorner$

$\Delta 18$ $\ulcorner(\zeta_1 \frown \zeta_2 \frown \zeta_3)\urcorner$ for $\ulcorner((\zeta_1 \frown \zeta_2) \frown \zeta_3)\urcorner$

   $\ulcorner(\zeta_1 \frown \zeta_2 \frown \zeta_3 \frown \zeta_4)\urcorner for$ $\ulcorner((\zeta_1 \frown \zeta_2 \frown \zeta_3) \frown \zeta_4)\urcorner$ etc.

An expression x begins an expression y, symbolically, $x \mathrel{B} y$, if y consists of x alone or of x followed by something:

$\Delta 19$ $\ulcorner(\zeta \mathrel{B} \eta)\urcorner for$ $\ulcorner(\zeta = \eta \cdot \mathrm{v} \; (\exists\alpha)(\zeta \frown \alpha = \eta))\urcorner$

An expression x ends an expression y, symbolically, $x \mathrel{E} y$, if y consists of x alone, or of x preceded by something:

$\Delta 20$ $\ulcorner(\zeta \mathrel{E} \eta)\urcorner for \ulcorner(\zeta = \eta \cdot \mathrm{v} \; (\exists\alpha)(\alpha \frown \zeta = \eta))\urcorner$

An expression x is part (or all) of an expression y, symbolically, $x \mathrel{P} y$, if there is an initial segment of y which ends in x:

$\Delta 21$ $\ulcorner(\zeta \mathrel{P} \eta)\urcorner for \ulcorner(\exists\alpha)(\alpha \mathrel{B} \eta \cdot \zeta \mathrel{E} \alpha)\urcorner$

An expression x is a string of accents, symbolically, Ac x, if every initial segment of x ends in an accent:

$\Delta 22$ $\ulcorner(\mathrm{Ac} \; \zeta)\urcorner for \ulcorner(\alpha)(\alpha \mathrel{B} \zeta \cdot \supset \cdot \mathrm{S}_5 \mathrel{E} \alpha)\urcorner$

The result of writing the expression x, followed by epsilon, followed by y, and enclosing the whole thing in parentheses, will be called $x \mathrel{e} y$:

$\Delta 23$ $\ulcorner(\zeta \mathrel{e} \eta)\urcorner for \ulcorner(\mathrm{S}_6 \frown \zeta \frown \mathrm{S}_9 \frown \eta \frown \mathrm{S}_7)\urcorner$

The result of writing the expression x, followed by a down-arrow, followed by the expression y, and enclosing the whole thing in parentheses, will be called $x \mathrel{j} y$:

$\Delta 24$ $\ulcorner(\zeta \mathrel{j} \eta)\urcorner for \ulcorner(\mathrm{S}_6 \frown \zeta \frown \mathrm{S}_8 \frown \eta \frown \mathrm{S}_7)\urcorner$

The result of putting an expression x in parentheses and prefixing it to y will be called $x \mathrel{qu} y$:

$\Delta 25$ $\ulcorner(\zeta \mathrel{qu} \eta)\urcorner for \ulcorner(\mathrm{S}_6 \frown \zeta \frown \mathrm{S}_7 \frown \eta)\urcorner$

An expression x is a variable, symbolically, Vbl x, if it is one of the first four signs in the alphabet, or if it is one of these signs followed by a string of accents:

$\Delta 26$ $\ulcorner$ Vbl ζ $\urcorner$ *for* $\ulcorner$ $(\exists\alpha)(\alpha = S_1 \cdot v \cdot \alpha = S_2 \cdot v \cdot \alpha = S_3 \cdot v \cdot \alpha = S_4:$

$\zeta = \alpha \cdot v \ (\exists\beta)(Ac\ \beta \cdot \zeta = \alpha^\frown \beta))$ $\urcorner$

In my version of Quine's system, we must also be able to speak of the primitive non-logical predicates. A definition along the lines of $\Delta 26$ will do admirably. An expression x is a primitive non-logical predicate if it consists of S_{10} followed by one accent, or S_{10} followed by two accents, or ..., or S_{10} followed by n accents. (While we are happy to have an infinite number of variables, we do not want an infinite number of primitive predicates.)

$\Delta 261$ $\ulcorner$ Pr ζ $\urcorner$ *for* $\ulcorner$ $(\zeta = S_{10}^\frown S_5 \cdot v \cdot \zeta = S_{10}^\frown S_5^\frown S_5 \cdot v \cdots)$ $\urcorner$

The definition of a primitive non-logical predicate will clearly depend for its detail on the number of primitive non-logical predicates there are in the object language. This definition will also have to be changed when new primitive non-logical predicates are added to the language.

An expression x is a quantification of an expression y, symbolically, x Q y, if it is formed by prefixing a parenthesized variable to y:

$\Delta 27$ $\ulcorner$ $(\zeta$ Q $\eta)$ $\urcorner$ *for* $\ulcorner$ $(\exists\alpha)(Vbl\ \alpha \cdot \zeta = \alpha$ qu $\eta)$ $\urcorner$

The atomic logical formulas may now be defined by Quine's $\Delta 28$; and the atomic non-logical formulas may be defined by my $\Delta 281$. It will be noticed that according to $\Delta 281$, the atomic non-logical formulas will consist merely of a primitive predicate followed by a variable in parentheses; this does not mean that all of our predicates are simple one-place predicates — the classes defined on the basis of the primitive non-logical formulas will be included (axiomatically) in the class of pairs, triplets, etc., as the case may be. Thus 'longer(x)' will be a perfectly good atomic non-logical formula — except that for 'longer' we will have 'p' followed by a suitable string of accents. It will just happen that '$\hat{x}$ longer$(x) \subset \hat{y}$ $(\exists z)$ $(\exists w)$ $(y = (z; w))$' will be a theorem — in fact an axiom governing the primitive matrix corresponding to "longer".

$\Delta 28$ $\ulcorner$ LFmla$_0\zeta$ $\urcorner$ *for* $\ulcorner$ $(\exists\alpha)(\exists\beta)(Vbl\ \alpha \cdot Vbl\ \beta \cdot \zeta = \alpha$ e $\beta)$ $\urcorner$

$\Delta 281$ $\ulcorner$ PFmla$_0\zeta$ $\urcorner$ *for* $\ulcorner$ $(\exists\alpha)(\exists\beta)(Vbl\ \alpha \cdot Pr\ \beta \cdot \zeta = \beta^\frown S_6^\frown \alpha^\frown S_7)$ $\urcorner$

From here on we shall often have occasion to speak of groups of expressions; but since the concept of membership is not available to protosyntax, we must employ a special technique for this purpose. Quine employs the ingenious device of treating a set of expressions x_1, x_2, x_3, ... x_n as a single complicated expression in which the expressions in which we are interested occur as 'framed ingredients' — flanked on each side by the ungrammatical combination of signs $S_6 \frown S_7$. The set of expressions x_1, x_2, ...x_n will thus be rendered as the single expression: $S_6 \frown S_7 \frown x_1 \; S_6 \frown S_7 \frown x_2 \; S_6 \frown S_7 \frown$ ... $\frown S_6 \frown S_7 \frown x_n \; \frown S_6 \frown S_7$. An expression x is a framed ingredient of an expression y, symbolically x Ing y, if $S_6 \frown S_7 \frown x \frown S_6 \frown S_7$ is part or all of y and $S_6 \frown S_7$ is not part of x:

Δ29 $\lceil (\zeta \text{ Ing } \eta) \rceil$ *for* $\lceil (S_6 \frown S_7 \frown \zeta \frown S_6 \frown S_7 \; P \; \eta \cdot \sim (S_6 \frown S_7 \; P \; \zeta)) \rceil$

One framed ingredient x of z is prior to another framed ingredient y of z, symbolically x Pr_z y, if x is a framed ingredient of an initial segment of z in which y is not a framed ingredient:

Δ30 $\lceil (\zeta \; \text{Pr}_\theta \; \eta) \rceil$ *for* $\lceil (\exists \alpha)(\alpha \; B \; \theta \cdot \zeta \; \text{Ing } \alpha \cdot \eta \; \text{Ing } \theta \cdot \sim (\eta \; \text{Ing } \alpha)) \rceil$

The protosyntactical definition of a formula is now apparent; the following definition differs from Quine's only in that I have replaced the expression describing atomic formulas in general by a pair of expressions describing atomic logical formulas and atomic non-logical formulas.

Δ31 $\lceil$ Fmla $\zeta \rceil$ *for* $\lceil (\exists \alpha)(\zeta \; \text{Ing } \alpha \cdot (\beta)(\beta \; \text{Ing } \alpha \supset \cdot \text{LFmla}_0 \; \beta \; \text{v}$

$$\text{PFmla}_0 \; \beta \; \text{v} \; (\exists \gamma)(\exists \delta)(\gamma \; \text{Pr}_\alpha \; \beta \cdot \delta \; \text{Pr}_\alpha \; \beta :$$

$$\beta = \gamma \; \text{j} \; \delta \cdot \text{v} \cdot \beta \; Q \; \gamma))) \rceil$$

It will be noticed that according to the above definitions, some rather unorthodox expressions will turn out to be formulas — for example, "Two is longer than." Although some philosophers might prefer to consider this a meaningless expression, rather than a false statement, I do not think that the distinction is terribly significant. Any statement which is patently false on logical grounds alone seems absurd; and whether its absurdity is to be rendered as formal meaninglessness or formal falsity (or theoremhood of its denial) strikes me as essentially arbitrary.

Quine goes on to establish further definitions which lead, eventually, to a protosyntactical definition of "Thm x", or the "the expression x is a theorem." He defines the four kinds of axioms of quantification; $\text{AQ}_A \; x$ for x is an axiom of quantification of the first kind (the closure of a tautology), $\text{AQ}_B \; x$ for x is an axiom of quantification of the second kind, $\text{AQ}_C \; x$ and $\text{AQ}_D \; x$ for x is an axiom of quantification of the third and fourth kinds, respectively. In the same way he defines $\text{AM}_A \; x$, $\text{AM}_B \; x$, and $\text{AM}_C \; x$, for x is an axiom of membership of the first, second, and third kinds respectively. There is little point in reproducing his definitions here, not only because the interested reader can find them in the last section of Quine's book, but also because my supplemented version of ML requires additional axioms to govern the logical behavior of the primitive non-logical predicates; and these can be supplied only if we have a particular language in mind. For my purposes it will suffice merely to suppose that a third species of axiom has been defined which includes (by alternation) all of the kinds of axioms which we require for the non-logical primitive predicates. I shall write AP x to mean that the expression x is one or another of these axioms. Thus Quine's general definition of an axiom ($\Delta 76$) will be modified only to the extent of including these new axioms:

$\Delta 76$ $\ulcorner$ Ax ζ $\urcorner$ for $\ulcorner$ $(AQ_A$ ζ v AQ_B ζ v AQ_C ζ v AQ_D ζ v AM_A ζ v

AM_B ζ v AM_C ζ v AP ζ $)$ $\urcorner$

Quine's definition of a theorem remains unchanged:

$\Delta 77$ $\ulcorner$ Thm ζ $\urcorner$ for $\ulcorner$ $(\exists\alpha)(\zeta$ Ing α $\cdot$ $(\beta)(\beta$ Ing α $\supset$ $\cdot$

Ax β v $(\exists\gamma)(\gamma$ Pr_α β $\cdot$ γ cd β Pr_α $\beta)))$ $\urcorner$

There are a number of other definitions presented by Quine in the process of defining theoremhood, which will also be useful to me. Where x is a formula, nx is the denial of x; where x and y are formulas, x al y is the alternation formed from x and y, and x cd y is the conditional whose antecedent is x and whose consequent is y.

$\Delta 47$ $\ulcorner$ n ζ $\urcorner$ for $\ulcorner$ $(\zeta$ j $\zeta)$ $\urcorner$

$\Delta 48$ $\ulcorner$ $(\zeta$ al $\eta)$ $\urcorner$ for $\ulcorner$ n $(\zeta$ j $\eta)$ $\urcorner$

$\Delta 49$ $\ulcorner$ $(\zeta$ cd $\eta)$ $\urcorner$ for $\ulcorner$ $(n\zeta$ al $\eta)$ $\urcorner$

Where x and y are formulas, x cj y is their conjunction, and x b y is their biconditional. Where z is a variable, z qe x is the existential quantification of x with respect to z.

$\Delta 62$ $\ulcorner$ $(\zeta$ cj $\eta)$ $\urcorner$ for $\ulcorner$ $($ nζ j n$\eta)$ $\urcorner$

$\Delta 63$ $\ulcorner$ $(\zeta$ b $\eta)$ $\urcorner$ for $\ulcorner$ $((\zeta$ cd $\eta)$ cj $(\eta$ cd $\zeta)$ $\urcorner$

$\Delta 64$ $\ulcorner$ $(\zeta$ qe $\eta)$ $\urcorner$ for $\ulcorner$ n $(\zeta$ qu n$\eta)$ $\urcorner$

Numbers, ratios, statistical statements, etc., will be very important in the rest of the book; but instead of attempting to set up machinery which will allow us to use explicit protosyntactical definitions in each situation, I shall merely provide informal explanations of the more extended (proper) protosyntactical notation. This will not lead to any difficulty as long as we are careful not to treat something as protosyntactically definable which is not really definable in that sense. But I shall allow myself one further degree of latitude; I shall pretend to define (in this informal way) expressions such as abstracts, which cannot be defined *out of context* in protosyntax. But again this will lead to no difficulty so long as we do not employ these protosyntactical expressions in contexts from which they could not be defined away. In this sense $\Delta 83 - \Delta 86$ and $\Delta 89 - \Delta 94$ are not only informal, but also somewhat fictive.

$\Delta 81$ $\ulcorner(\zeta \, {}_\mathrm{s}\mathrm{gr} \, \eta)\urcorner$ *for*   the expression whose abbreviation under the definitions of the object language consists of the expression ζ followed by '${}_\mathrm{s}{>}$', followed by η, the whole enclosed in parentheses.

$\Delta 82$ $\ulcorner(\zeta \, \mathrm{id} \, \eta)\urcorner$ *for*   the expression whose abbreviation in the object language consists of the expression ζ, followed by '$=$', followed by η, the whole enclosed in parentheses.

$\Delta 83$ $\ulcorner(\zeta \, {}_\mathrm{s}\mathrm{min} \, \eta)\urcorner$ *for*   the expression whose abbreviation in the object language consists of the expression ζ, followed by '${}_\mathrm{s}{-}$', followed by η, the whole enclosed in parentheses.

$\Delta 84$ $\ulcorner(\zeta \, {}_\mathrm{s}\mathrm{pl} \, \eta)\urcorner$ *for*   the expression whose abbreviation in the object language consists of the expression ζ, followed by '${}_\mathrm{s}{+}$', followed by η, the whole enclosed in parentheses.

$\Delta 85$ $\ulcorner(\zeta \, {}_\mathrm{s}\mathrm{tms} \, \eta)\urcorner$ *for*   the expression whose abbreviation in the object language consists of the expression ζ, followed by '${}_\mathrm{s}{\times}$', followed by η, the whole enclosed in parentheses.

$\Delta 86$ $\ulcorner(\zeta \, {}_\mathrm{s}\mathrm{div} \, \eta)\urcorner$ *for*   the expression whose abbreviation in the object language consists of the expression ζ, followed by '${}_\mathrm{s}{\div}$', followed by η, the whole enclosed in parentheses.

$\Delta 87$ $\ulcorner\mathrm{pct} \, (\zeta, \, \eta, \, (\xi; \, \psi))\urcorner$ *for* the expression whose abbreviation in the object language consists of the expression '%', followed by S_6, followed by ζ, followed by a comma, followed by η, followed by a comma, followed by S_8, followed by ξ, followed by a semicolon, followed by ψ, followed by S_7, followed by S_7.

Δ88 $\ulcorner(\zeta \text{ incl } \eta)\urcorner$ *for*   the expression whose abbreviation in the object language consists of the expression ζ, followed by '$\subset$', followed by η, the whole enclosed in parentheses.

Δ89 $\ulcorner(\zeta \text{ int } \eta)\urcorner$ *for*   the expression whose abbreviation in the object language consists of the expression ζ, followed by '$\cap$', followed by η, the whole enclosed in parentheses.

Δ90 $\ulcorner(\zeta \text{ un } \eta)\urcorner$ *for*   the expression whose abbreviation in the object language consists of the expression ζ, followed by '$\cup$', followed by η, the whole enclosed in parentheses.

Δ91 $\ulcorner \text{compl } \zeta \urcorner$ *for*   the expression whose abbreviation is formed in ML by putting the expression ζ under a bar: '$-$'.

Δ92 $\ulcorner \text{unt } \zeta \urcorner$ *for*   the expression whose abbreviation is formed in ML by prefixing the expression 'ι' to the expression ζ.

Δ93 $\ulcorner(\zeta \text{ cp } \eta)\urcorner$ *for*   the expression whose abbreviation in the object language consists of ζ, followed by '$\otimes$', followed by η, the whole enclosed in parentheses.

Δ94 $\ulcorner(\zeta \text{ pr } \eta)\urcorner$ *for*   the expression whose abbreviation in the object language consists of ζ, followed by ';', followed by η, the whole enclosed in parentheses.

On occasion I shall want to refer to the names of particular sets —numbers, ratios, etc. Instead of defining the fraction '1/2' (or '$_s 1$', or '$_s 0$', as the case may be) in each of its acceptable contexts, I shall simply employ the technique of forming the names of these expressions of the object language by writing the expressions themselves in single quotes in suitable protosyntactical contexts. Thus the expression '1/2' in the object language will be named protosyntactically by the expression " '1/2' " in the metalanguage.

There are several more definitions provided by Quine which I shall employ, but they will be used only briefly and I shall explain them informally at the time when I use them. The above definitions are more important, and will be employed often in what follows.

CHAPTER SEVEN

The Rational Corpus

1. So far, I have merely been adding details to Quine's system as it stands—no fundamentally new concepts, either in the object language or in the metalanguage, have been introduced. Now, however, we are ready for the introduction of the concept of a rational corpus. This concept is central to that of rational belief; and it is central to the *use* of a deductive system such as that of ML as well as to the use of the system of probability I shall outline.

One of the interesting and important uses of logic is the justification of beliefs: if I have reason to believe that all men are mortal and that Socrates is a man, then I have *reason* to believe that Socrates is mortal. Furthermore, if I have reason to believe the first two statements, then I am not only privileged to believe the third, but obligated to believe it. ML, of course, says no such thing. Supposing that we have the appropriate primitive predicates, there will be a *theorem* in ML corresponding to, "If all men are mortal and Socrates is a man, then Socrates is mortal." Similarly, there will be a statement in the protosyntax of ML which says that this statement is a theorem. But even the latter statement makes no reference to 'truth' or 'belief' — it still does not either obligate me or entitle me to pass from belief in the antecedent to belief in the consequent.

But surely we wish to be able to take the system of ML as legislative for rational belief; if a person says that he believes that all men are mortal and that he is a man, but persists in maintaining that he is immortal, we wish to feel free to say that he is not being rational; that his beliefs violate the canons of logic; in short, that he ought to have his head examined. Note that this goes beyond the use of ML to settle disputes about consistency and derivability and theoremhood; for these purposes the disputants must agree to use ML. Here we want to say that whether or not the person agrees to speak the language of ML, he is being inconsistent, and he *ought not* to be.

If we restrict ourselves to translations into the supplemented version of ML of statements in ordinary factual discourse, so that instead of talking about beliefs themselves we can talk about the statements which express these beliefs, this legislative function of logic can be expressed protosyntactically. Just as we can define a theorem protosyntactically as a statement which is an axiom or a ponential of ponentials of axioms, etc., we can define a class of statements which *ought to be believed,* given that a certain set of other statements *are* believed: *viz.,* the class of statements such that each statement is one of those which are believed, or a theorem, or a ponential of the original statements or theorems, and so on.

We will want the original statements on which the rational corpus is based to be statements expressing those beliefs which are based on the 'immediate experience' of the individual or group of individuals whose rational corpus we are discussing. For my purposes, however, it does not really matter what these statements are; I shall suppose only that there is a protosyntactically definable expression F whose framed ingredients are simply those statements of matters of fact (whatever kinds of statements these may be) that are known without inference to the bearer of the rational corpus under discussion.[1] It is one of the outstanding virtues of Quine's system in this respect that as it requires no prior assignment of logical types to the primitive predicates, the way is left open for inferences proceeding from the objects about which we have immediate knowledge either to classes of these objects or to 'subobjects' of which these objects are the classes. From a knowledge of chairs we can proceed to inferred knowledge of chair-type point events, or to inferred knowledge of whole classes of chairs. There is no need to suppose that statements employing predicates of the lowest type are the only ones mentioned in F.

Given such an expression F, then, we can see how we might demand that any statement which is derivable from the statements in F (or from the axioms of ML) be an ingredient of a rational corpus based on F. But we would like to demand more; we would also like to demand that any person's rational corpus contain the statement expressing the hypothesis that the sun will rise tomorrow, although this statement is neither an ingredient of F, nor a theorem, nor is the statement in question derivable from the axioms of ML together with the statements in F. We want to demand this because if someone maintains that the sun will not rise tomorrow, we want to be able to say that his belief is *irrational.* Anyone has enough evidence to render it highly probable that the sun will rise tomorrow — and so this statement is something that *ought* to be included in every well-equipped rational corpus. Since the statement is only highly probable, we must, if we are to demand that it appear in a certain rational corpus, elucidate this demand in terms of probability.

1. Or, better, are justifiably self-evident to him.

To sum up: there are a number of things which we shall want to be embodied in a logic of rational belief. Given a set of primitive beliefs concerning the data of experience (whatever *that* may be) we want to be able to show that any statement derivable from the axioms of ML alone, or from the axioms of ML together with statements expressing these primitive beliefs, ought to be believed; and we want to be able to show that any statement which is highly probable relative to what is already believed ought also to be believed.[2]

2. Before embarking on the formal development of the logic of rational belief, there are a few remarks which perhaps had best be made here to avoid misunderstanding. I am *not* talking about the psychological aspects of belief, nor about beliefs in general. I am talking solely about belief in matters of fact (such as the belief that the sun rose this morning, or that it will rise tomorrow, or the belief that all men are mortal). I am furthermore proposing to formalize my study of these beliefs by ignoring the facts themselves, concentrating instead on the statements of ML by which these facts might be expressed. It is an open question anyway, I think, whether it is facts or statements which may best be said to be believed. I incline toward the latter view, although most philosophers seem to incline toward the former.[3]

In this simplified and formalized sense of belief, we might be able to take a partial inventory of someone's rational corpus, provided he understood the supplemented language of ML, by presenting him with a list of statements in that language and asking him to check off the ones that he believes. A refinement of this is to adopt Savage's technique (discussed earlier) and by making the person choose between certain alternative courses of action to determine the degree of belief he assigns to the various statements in the list.

Needless to say, it would be impossible to take a complete inventory of someone's beliefs — it would be impossible to present someone with all the statements that can be formulated in ML, much less all the statements in my supplemented version of ML, for the purpose of discovering which ones he believes. In addition, a com-

2. For further discussion of the desirability of having a formal analogue of the concept of a rational corpus, see my article, "The Justification of Deduction," *Review of Metaphysics* 12, 1958.

3. The issue between Alonzo Church ("On Carnap's Statements of Assertion and Belief") and Rudolf Carnap ("On Belief Sentences: Reply to Alonzo Church") concerning the possibility of dispensing with propositions in favor of sentences is largely irrelevant here; we are not proposing to analyze all belief contexts in terms of statements, but only those relevant to the formalization of a language capable of being used to express scientific knowledge. The papers referred to may be found in M. McDonald (editor), *Philosophy and Analysis*, New York, 1954.

pletely rational person would include in his rational corpus all the theorems of ML; but of course no actual person knows all the theorems of ML. We thus know from the outset that no person is completely rational and that it is impossible to discover precisely the extent of the person's rationality. Nevertheless our logic of rational belief will be sufficiently useful if only we can take any statement of ML which a person believes to a certain degree, and by examining *some* of the other statements he believes, or ought to believe, — ultimately by examining merely the finite set of statements appearing in F — to determine the rationality of this belief. In other words, our logic of rational belief will perform its function if we can determine in any particular instance (or even in most instances) whether a person is being rational or not.

The fact that no person is completely rational is irrelevant; I am not formulating a psychological hypothesis, but establishing an ideal; and it is an ideal that is closely approached in limited areas of belief by many people — e.g., a physicist may be expected to be fairly rational about the statements of physics. Similarly, the fact that it may be psychologically difficult to believe (in some sense) more than one or a few things at a time is irrelevant; it is not belief in this sense with which I am concerned, but belief in the sense of potential assent.

A person's rational corpus will be changing constantly in time as he experiences new things, learns new facts, and so on. In the following formal treatment I shall ignore this phenomenon by taking a rational corpus to be a snapshot, as it were, of this constantly changing body of beliefs. The basic form of change is simply an increase in the number of basic statements in F;[4] the investigation of the grounds on which statements come to be ingredients of the expression F is not strictly a logical inquiry, but an epistemological one. It is not this process of change that interests me here, but the constant and (I shall maintain) purely formal relationships that hold between a given set of basic statements and other statements for which these original statements constitute evidence.

Many of the things which a person may be held responsible for believing, if he is to be rational, are things for which the evidence is second hand. The evidence I have for quantum theory, say, is not experimental at all, but only the fact that certain individuals (who have taken account of the experimental evidence) have written certain sentences. This is nevertheless relatively good evidence, since I have other evidence (mostly also second hand) which supports the

---

4. But the language itself will also change, through changes in the meanings of terms, as well as through the introduction of new (usually theoretical) terms.

hypothesis that these people are honest, conscientious, etc., scientific workers. A theory of rational belief must take into account the rationality of believing statements on the basis of second hand evidence; among the statements in F will be statements about sounds, printed pages, etc.

Although I have been talking only about a person's rational corpus, there is nothing to prevent our considering the rational corpus of a whole scientific discipline. A rational corpus, on my formal interpretation, is merely a set of statements which stand in certain relationships to the given set of basic statements appearing in F. In an individual, we suppose this set of basic statements to express his own experience (including his experience of the reports of other people's experience); if we want to consider the rational corpus of a scientific discipline — say, physics — we will suppose the statements in F to express the relevant parts of the personal experience of all the workers in the field, up to the time when we take our snapshot.

I might also mention here that there seem to be a number of problems connected with logic and the philosophy of science which may be greatly simplified when examined in connection with the concept of a rational corpus. Many types of counterfactuals, for example, seem to be reducible to the following kind of counterfactual: if the statement S were included in my rational corpus (and everything inconsistent with S deleted), then the statement P would (rationally) be included in my rational corpus also. We still have a 'counterfactual' to deal with, but it is on a metalinguistic level; if we wish to test it, all we have to do is to make the antecedent true — i.e., construct a rational corpus just like the one I actually have, except that S is added and everything inconsistent with S is deleted. Then we can ask very simply, 'ought P to be included in this rational corpus?'[5]

We may also be able to throw some light on questions of modality and propositional attitudes by relating them to the protosyntactical concept of a rational corpus. Quine's researches already seem to lead in this direction.[6]

A similar approach may even be quite fruitful in investigating concepts quite foreign to rational belief; we might want to formalize the concept of a non-rational corpus, which would be a body of beliefs for which there is no evidence, but which are nevertheless

5. Suggestions leading in this direction have been made by various scholars: N. Goodman, *Fact, Fiction, and Forecast*, Cambridge, 1955; and R. Chisholm, "Law Statements and Counterfactual Inference," *Analysis* 15, 1955, who provides an analysis begging for the formalization of rational corpora.

6. Quine, "Quantifiers and Propositional Attitudes," *Journal of Philosophy* 53, 1956.

meaningful and may be accepted or rejected; that is to say, the body of beliefs which might be called metaphysical. We might also consider an ethical corpus, containing ethical assertions standing in certain relations to each other, and in this way formulate intelligibly the relation of priority which some ethical assertions seem to bear to others.

There is one problem which arises in many applications of the concept of a rational corpus — this is the problem of being able to specify that such and such a statement does *not* belong to a given rational corpus. It is obvious from what I have already said that a rational corpus will have to contain an infinite number of statements. How are are to go through this infinite list of statements to make sure that the statement S is not among them? We might find the denial of S in this set of statements, but it might still happen that S also belongs to it. This is sure to be the case if either ML or the original set of statements are inconsistent.

The answer is that we shall try to arrange matters so that those statements about rational corpora in which we are interested can be made without having to go through the whole list of statements, subject only to restrictive clauses of the type, "... unless S belongs to the rational corpus." Thus (only as an example) we might say that the statements in F, and the axioms of ML, and the ponentials of these statements, are to constitute a rational corpus, *unless* among these statements there is a self-contradictory statement S. This form of assertion allows us to put the *onus probandi* on the person who would deny that this set of statements is a rational corpus: until he manages to produce such a self-contradictory statement S, we will feel free to ignore his complaints. This is only reasonable; we can't prove that there is no such S belonging to the rational corpus, but our opponent may be able to prove that there is such an S.

3. So much for preliminaries. Now for the formal development. I have already supposed that F is an expression that may be spelled out in Quine's protosyntax, and whose framed ingredients are the statements we are accepting as protocol statements. Since I wish to restrict myself to the paraphernalia of protosyntax, I cannot talk about all the statements in a rational corpus at once; instead I shall talk about partial rational corpora. Each of these partial rational corpora will contain a finite number of framed ingredients, which may include framed ingredients of F, axioms of ML, and statements which are ingredients of an expression containing only ingredients of F, axioms of ML, and ponentials of earlier ingredients. The proof of a theorem, for example, will be a partial rational corpus. I shall thus talk about the (non-finite) set of (finite) rational corpora based on F.

It is obvious that certain expressions must be included in rational corpora which have nothing but their probability to recommend them — e.g., the statement asserting that the sun will rise tomorrow. To get such statements into a rational corpus, we must stipulate that any expression whose probability, relative to such and such a rational corpus exceeds (say) p, is to be included in such and such another rational corpus. What shall we pick for p? It would be rather difficult to justify any single choice; but we can reduce the element of arbitrariness by picking n such p's, and defining n *levels* of rational corpora to which a statement may belong. These different levels would correspond (in practise, not in principle) to the confidence coefficients used by statisticians—but we should also want much more demanding levels. They would correspond to different degrees of 'practical certainty'.

Why do we bother with this? Why can't we simply take the contents of rational corpora as ingredients of F, axioms, etc., leaving probable statements to be *believed* but not directly *included* in rational corpora? The answer is that probability must be defined relative to rational corpora, and many of the statements relative to which an evaluation of probability must be made are themselves only probable. Thus, on my view, we assign a probability of (about) '1/2' to the statement, "Heads will appear on the next toss of this coin," only because we have excellent grounds for supposing that this coin falls heads half the time — i.e., because a certain statistical statement is highly probable. If we do not include this highly probable statistical statement in some form of rational corpus, we will be hard put to it to find any justification in the logic of rational belief for the assignment of probability we make to the statement in question.

In order to set up a useful sequence of rational corpora, let us pick n rational numbers, and let fractions denoting these numbers in order of increasing magnitude be $r_1, r_2, \ldots r_n$. We can now stipulate that if an expression has a probability of p, relative to a rational corpus of level r_i, and if there is a theorem to the effect that the rational number denoted by p is greater than the rational number denoted by r_{i-1}, then the expression is to be included in the rational corpus of level r_{i-1}.

The numbers we pick will have an effect on what we ought to believe, and the degree to which we ought to believe it; the effect is not a very great one, but in order to have something definite to think about (and for the sake of later examples), I shall pick the fractions: "8/10", "90/100", "95/100", "96/100", "97/100", "98/100", "99/100", "995/1000", "998/1000", and "1/1".

An expression x will be said to be a rational corpus of the highest level (level r_n, where $r_n =$ "1/1"), based on F, symbolically, $r_n \text{RC}_F x$, if x begins with $S_6 \frown S_7$, and ends with $S_6 \frown S_7$, and if every framed ingredient of x is an ingredient of some expression each of whose ingredients is either an ingredient of F, an axiom, or a ponential of earlier ingredients in the expression.

An expression x will be said to be a rational corpus of level $r_i (r_i \neq r_n)$ based on F, symbolically $r_i \text{RC}_F x$, if x begins and ends with $S_6 \frown S_7$, and if, for every framed ingredient w of x there is a pair of fractions y and z, such that the probability of w, relative to the rational corpora of basis F and level r_{i+1}, is this pair of fractions, and such that $y \,_s\text{gr}\, r_i$ is a theorem.[7]

$\Delta 95$ $\ulcorner r_n \text{RC}_F \overline{\theta} \urcorner for \ulcorner S_6 \frown S_7 \text{ B } \theta \cdot S_6 \frown S_7 \text{ E } \theta \cdot (\alpha)(\alpha \text{ Ing } \theta \supset$

$$(\exists \beta)(\alpha \text{ Ing } \beta \cdot (\gamma)(\gamma \text{ Ing } \beta \supset \gamma \text{ Ing F v Ax } \gamma \text{ v}$$

$$(\exists \delta)(\delta \text{ Pr}_\beta \gamma \cdot \delta cd \, \gamma \text{ Pr}_\beta \, \gamma))))\frown \urcorner$$

$\Delta 95a$ $\ulcorner r_i \text{RC}_F \overline{\theta} \urcorner for \ulcorner S_6 \frown S_7 \text{ B } \theta \cdot S_6 \frown S_7 \text{ E } \theta \cdot (\alpha)(\alpha \text{ Ing } \theta \supset$

$$(\exists \beta)(\exists \gamma)(\alpha \, r_{i+1} \text{Prob}_F (\beta;\gamma) \cdot \text{Thm } \beta \,_s\text{gr} \, r_i))\urcorner$$

The above definition allows us to eliminate any protosyntactical expression '$r_i \text{RC}_F x$' in favor of a statement which involves only rational corpora of the next higher level (r_{i+1}) and probability statements. Finally, in virtue of the protosyntactical definability of probability, we come to an expression containing statements of the form $\ulcorner r_n \text{RC}_F \, \theta \urcorner$ (among other forms), which can be eliminated (by $\Delta 95$) in favor of statements involving only the ordinary protosyntactical expressions 'Ax', 'F', 'Pr', 'Thm', and so on.

It should be noted that the requirement that the probability of a certain statement exceed a certain degree is interpreted *protosyntactically* in the last clause of $\Delta 95a$. We must remember that 'Thm $x \,_s\text{gr} \, y$' states that a certain expression is a theorem, not that one rational number is greater than another. We can be sure — as sure as we are of the consistency of ML and of F — that if the expression in question is a theorem, then the rational number denoted by x is greater than the rational number denoted by y. Curiously enough, it will turn out that the consistency of the rational corpora of all but the highest level is assured, regardless of the consistency of F and of ML. (I must quickly admit that this consistency is assured only because, should F and ML be inconsistent, no probability statements will be valid, and all the other levels of rational corpora will simply be empty.)

---

7. But compare $\Delta 95a^*$, p. 274.

The second part of the definition, involving probability, is not intelligible to us yet, for we have not yet defined probability. But already we can decide whether or not a given complex expression is a rational corpus of the level r_n based on F; and this gives us a foothold for defining probability.

CHAPTER EIGHT

Rational Matrices and Statistical Statements

1. The first task in defining probability is to pick out, of all those matrices which can be formed in our supplemented version of ML, those to which the honorific epithet 'rational' may be applied. The reason for restricting our attentions to rational matrices—or to rational classes, if we wish so to designate the classes denoted by the abstracts of rational matrices—is brought out by the following example. (It is also suggested by the example employed by Nelson Goodman to illustrate what he calls 'the paradox of confirmation.'[1])

Consider a particular toss of a coin—say, the next toss, or the fifteenth toss. It is clear that we will often want to be able to say that the probability that this toss belongs to the class of tosses resulting in heads is 1/2. It is also clear that this statement will often be based on the knowledge that the coin lands heads about half the time. Now consider, as an alternative, the class which is the union of the class of all tosses resulting in heads with the unit class of the next toss (or the fifteenth toss). The next toss (or the fifteenth toss) is a member of this class; the proportion of the members of this class which result in heads is very close to 1. Why doesn't this lead us to assign a probability of 1 (or close to 1) to the statement that the next toss (or the fifteenth toss) will result in heads? Or if we wish to maintain a frequency theory of probability, what is the matter with using this class as a reference class (or fundamental probability set) in which to evaluate the probability in question?

The answer is that to employ suoh a peculiar class is absurd; in order for a statement about the proportion of A's which are B's to be reasonably relevant to a probability statement, we must demand that the A's be a rational class, and not an odd class such as the one described above. It is not merely that we do not want to say that the next toss of the coin is a *random* member of this class; for under *no* circumstances will we want to say that *any* toss is a random member of this peculiar class.

Equally important, we must demand that in order for a statement about the proportion of A's which are B's to be reasonably relevant to a probability statement, the intersection of A and B be a rational

---

1. Goodman, *Fact, Fiction, and Forecast*, Cambridge (Mass.), 1955.

class. This requirement, and its relevance to the problem of primitive statistical generalization, is illustrated by the following example. Let A and B be rational classes, and let us suppose that we have drawn a sample S consisting of n A's, of which m are also B's. We shall suppose that the class of all n-fold samples of A's is a rational class. Consider the general property, applicable to n-fold samples, of 'representing' the parent population in a certain respect. We may say that a sample has this property, or rather, a particular property of this general class of properties, if a class-ratio in the sample bears a definite relationship to the corresponding class ratio in the parent population. There are any number of such relationships, each determining a sense of 'representative', which are such that in this sense of 'representative', the proportion of representative samples, among the class of all n-fold samples of A's, is very high.

Many of these senses of 'representative' are quite as absurd as the class of coin-tosses proposed above. Thus, if the true value of the relative frequency in which we are interested is p, we may define 'representative' samples as those in which the corresponding class-ratio falls between the limits $p - d_1$ and $p - d_2$ or between the limits $p + d_3$ and $p + d_4$. This has the undesirable consequence that a sample is representative only if the class-ratio in the sample *differs* from the class-ratio in the parent population. We may also define 'representative' samples as those in which the class-ratio falls between the limits $p - d_5$ and $p + d_6$, where both d_5 and d_6 are positive. This seems more reasonable, but we may still have $d_5 = d_6$, or $d_5 = 0$, or $d_6 = 0$, or any number of other arrangements.

It will simplify things greatly to demand that only one sense of 'representative' be considered rational. We could stipulate that a class is to be *rationally representative* if its class-ratio lies between limits of the form $p - d_5$ and $p + d_6$, where $d_5 = d_6$. But for classes in which the class-ratio is known to be very large or very small, even this is counter-intuitive: $p - d_5$ might turn out to be less than 0, or $p + d_6$ might turn out to be more than 1. What finally seems to be the best sense of *rationally representative* is this: d_5 and d_6 must both be positive, and their sum must be a minimum for that value of p closest to $1/2$ among the values of p possible to the parent population in the rational corpus about which we are talking, among all such pairs of parameters d' and d'' for which the proportion of representative samples is the same as that for d_5 and d_6.

All of this could be formalized, but since I do not have a complete definition which will cover all of the other kinds of rational

matrices, there seems to be little point in doing so. I shall merely
suppose that there is one, writing $r_i \operatorname{RepMat_F} x$ to mean that x is
a rationally representative matrix, relative to the rational corpora
of level r_i and basis F.

Δ96a $\ulcorner r_i \operatorname{RepMat_F} \zeta \urcorner$ *for* ...

There are a number of other matrices which we shall surely
want to call rational. We may plausibly demand that each of the
atomic non-logical formulae be a rational matrix, whether the
primitive predicate in question denotes a simple property, or a re-
relation, or an n-fold relationship, or whatever. The conjunction
of any two rational matrices is to be a rational matrix, as well as
the conjunction of one rational matrix with the negation of another.
The conjunction of a rational matrix with a matrix expressing
membership in a number (e.g., "x ∈ 17") is to be rational. Any
matrix which is satisfied by only one object may be considered rational. The class of all subclasses of a primitive rational class
(one, not itself a class of classes of a rational class, designated by
the abstract of a rational matrix) is to be a rational class. If x is
a rational matrix, then there must be a theorem to the effect that
every object belonging to a class denoted by an abstract of x also
belongs to 1 (or to 2, or to 3, as the case may be). If x is a rational
matrix and y is a statement, then x al y and x cj y are to be rational matrices. Finally, if x is a rational matrix, we must have a
theorem to the effect that the class of objects satisfying x belongs
to some number smaller than two to the googolplex—i.e., smaller
than $2^{(10)^{10^{100}}}$. And of course is x is a rationally representative
matrix, then x is rational.[2]

Let us suppose that all of this is compounded in the following
definition, and that the following explanatory metatheorems[3] follow
directly from Δ96b. $r_i \operatorname{RMat_F} x$ is to be read, x is a rational matrix for the rational corpora of level r_i and basis F.

2. Discussion of these odd classes has mainly occurred in connection with subjunctive
   conditionals and the distinction between law and non-law statements. See, for example,
   H. Reichenbach, *Experience and Prediction*, Chicago, 1938, and *Nomological Statements
   and Admissible Operations*, Amsterdam, 1954; R. Chisholm, "Law Statements and Counterfactual Inference," *Analysis* 15, 1955. So far no generally satisfactory characterization
   of them has been proposed. I think a formal characterization is possible but that it will
   have to be phrased in terms of rational corpora.
3. I have called the protosyntactical statements about probability, rational corpora, and
   so on, 'metatheorems,' because, like the metatheorems in ML, they express protosyntactical relationships that hold among any expressions having a given form. Since they are
   not (like Quine's metatheorems) about theoremhood, but about other equally protosyntactical concepts, I have given them all numbers over 1000, and preceded each of them with
   a double asterisk.

Δ96b $\ulcorner r_i \, \text{RMat}_F \ \zeta \urcorner$ *for* ... [the gist of the foregoing paragraph]

**1010 $\ulcorner \text{P}_0\text{Fmla} \ \zeta \supset r_i \, \text{RMat}_F \ \zeta \urcorner$

**1011 $\ulcorner r_i \, \text{RMat}_F \ \zeta \cdot r_i \, \text{RMat}_F \ \eta \cdot \supset \cdot r_i \, \text{RMat}_F \ \zeta \ \text{cj} \ \eta \cdot$

$r_i \, \text{RMat}_F \ \zeta \ \text{cj} \ \text{n} \ \eta \urcorner$

**1012 $\ulcorner r_i \, \text{RMat}_F \ \zeta \cdot \text{Stat} \ \eta \cdot \supset \cdot r_i \, \text{RMat}_F \ \zeta \ \text{cj} \ \eta \cdot r_i \, \text{Mat}_F \ \zeta \ \text{al} \ \eta \urcorner$

Quine[4] defines Vbl x to mean that x is a variable (Δ26); $x \ \text{F} \ y$ to mean that x is free in y (Δ36); and where x and y are variables and z and w are formulae $x a z$ e $y a w$ is to be the formula whose abbreviation in ML is formed by putting x and y under the respective circumflexes and w and z in the respective blanks of '(^ ϵ ^)' (Δ69). I shall also suppose that Num x has been defined to designate the formula whose abbreviation in ML is formed by putting x in the blank of '(ϵ Nn)'.

**1013 $\ulcorner r_i \, \text{RMat}_F \ \zeta \cdot \alpha \ \text{F} \ \zeta \supset \alpha = \gamma \cdot \text{Vbl} \ \eta \cdot \supset r_i \, \text{RMat}_F \ \eta \ \text{id} \ \gamma \ \text{a} \ \zeta \urcorner$

**1014 $\ulcorner (\exists \theta)(r_i \, \text{RC}_F \ \theta \cdot \text{Vbl} \ \eta \cdot \eta \ \text{a} \ \zeta \ \text{e} \ \text{'l'} \ \text{Ing} \ \theta) \supset r_i \, \text{RMat}_F \ \zeta \urcorner$

**1015 $\ulcorner \alpha \ \text{F} \ \zeta \supset \alpha = \gamma \cdot \text{Vbl} \ \eta \cdot \supset r_i \, \text{RMat}_F \ \eta \ \text{id} \ \gamma \ \text{a} \ \zeta \urcorner$

(i.e., all unit classes are rational)

**1016 $\ulcorner r_i \, \text{RMat}_F \ \zeta \cdot \alpha \ \text{F} \ \zeta \supset \alpha = \gamma \cdot \gamma \ \text{F} \ \zeta \cdot \text{Vbl} \ \eta \cdot$

$\text{Thm} \ (\text{Num} \ \beta) \cdot \supset r_i \, \text{RMat}_F \ \eta \ \text{incl} \ \gamma \ \text{a} \ \zeta \ \text{cj} \ \eta \ \text{e} \ \beta \urcorner$

If we write GNum x to designate the expression whose abbreviation in ML is formed by writing x in the blank of '($\leqslant 2^{(10)^{10^{100}}}$)', we have also,

**1017 $\ulcorner r_i \, \text{RMat}_F \ \zeta \cdot \alpha \ \text{F} \ \zeta \supset \alpha = \gamma \cdot \gamma \ \text{F} \ \zeta \cdot \supset \text{Thm} \ \eta \ \text{qu} \ (\text{Num} \ \eta \cdot$

$\gamma \ \text{a} \ \zeta \ \text{e} \ \eta \cdot \supset \text{GNum} \ \eta) \urcorner$

**1018 $\ulcorner r_i \, \text{RMat}_F \ \zeta \cdot \text{Thm} \ \text{cl} \, (\zeta \ \text{b} \ \eta) \cdot \supset r_i \, \text{RMat}_F \ \eta \urcorner$

(Quine defines cl x as the formula which is the *closure* of x; Δ45.) The final metatheorems show that it is possible to replace a rational matrix containing any number of free variables with a rational matrix containing one (or two, or three, etc.) free variables.

**1019 $\ulcorner r_i \, \text{RMat}_F \ \zeta \cdot \text{Vbl} \ \eta' \cdot (\exists \alpha)(\eta' \ \text{id} \ \eta \ \text{Ing} \ \alpha \cdot$

$(\gamma)(\eta' \ \text{id} \ \gamma \ \text{Ing} \ \alpha \supset \cdot \text{Vbl} \ \gamma \ \text{v} \ (\exists \beta)(\exists \gamma')(\text{Vbl} \ \gamma' \cdot$

---

4. Quine, *Mathematical Logic*, p. 298ff. The later references to Quine in this chapter also come from this section of ML.

$$\eta' \text{ id } \beta \text{ Pr}_\alpha \eta' \text{ id } \gamma \cdot \eta' \text{ id } \gamma = \eta' \text{ id } (\gamma' \text{ pr } \beta)))) \cdot$$
$$\supset r_i \text{RMat}_F (\eta' \text{ id } \eta \text{ cj } \zeta)^\rceil$$

**1020 $^\lceil r_i \text{RMat}_F \zeta \cdot \text{Vbl } \eta \cdot \supset . \; r_i \text{RMat}_F \eta \text{ qe } \zeta . \; r_i \text{RMat}_F \eta \text{ qu } \zeta^\rceil$

(Quine defines x qe y as the formula which is also described by n(x qu ny) in Δ64).

The above definitions Δ96a and Δ96b—or rather the above suggestions as to the lines along which such definitions might be developed—may or may not be adequate. There may be matrices that are required for the reconstruction of many inductive arguments which cannot be expressed as rational matrices in the above sense; and it may also be possible to show that there are classes just as strange as those which started us on this investigation, that are designated by abstracts of matrices that turn out to be rational under Δ96a and Δ96b. This is why I have not provided explicit formulations of these definitions. I have stated the metatheorems **1010-**1020 explicitly because they seem innocuous enough, and they suffice for future developments.

It would seem to be ultimately more advantageous—at any rate it would be more elegant—to start from the other end of the problem: to concentrate on defining *irrational* matrices. This would have the decided advantage that we would not have to suppose that the atomic non-logical formulas were rational matrices: if they were not we would (or could) know it.

Given an adequate definition of rational matrices (or of the other kind of matrix) I should still imagine that the foregoing metatheorems would hold. In particular, I should still suppose that there would be one sense of representative (corresponding to Neyman's 'shortest confidence interval') which is applicable in a given context, and no more.

2.   The next project is to set down some definitions concerning those statistical statements that will be of particular interest to us. First I shall define what it is to mean to say that a certain expression is a statistical statement about[5] two other expressions[6] in a rational corpus of given level and basis. It is here that we introduce the restriction to rational matrices; and it is here also that we restrict ourselves to 'ordinary' fractions. If A and A $\cap$ B aren't both rational classes, or if p and q are not both ordinary fractions,

---

5. Or better: "about the classes denoted by the expressions ..."
6. In ML abstracts are defined only contextually; this carries over to protosyntactical nomenclature, but no difficulty arises in the present connection due to the fact that the abstracts (and the description of the part of the statement in which they occur) occur in suitably eliminable contexts.

we may know the statement "$\%\,(A,B,(p\,;q))$" without knowing a statement about "A" and "B". An ordinary fraction is one with an ordinary numeral as a numerator and an ordinary numeral as a denominator: "0/1", "1/1", "1/2", "1/3", "2/3", etc.; we may define a special 'successor relation generating ratios in this order, on the basis of the successor relation for natural numbers. (The new relation would hold for ratios, not fractions.) On the basis of this sequence of ratios in the object language, we may define a sequence of fraction-matrices in protosyntax, corresponding to: "$x = 0/1$", "$x = 1/1$", "$x = 1/2$", "$x = 2/2$", "$x = 1/3$", etc. The point of this convention is that if p and q are fractions appearing in statistical statements we have either Thm p $_s$gr q, or Thm q $_s$gr p, or Thm p id q. All three of these expressions may be theorems, too, but that is something we shall worry about later.

Δ97a $\ulcorner$ RM ζ $\urcorner$ *for* ζ is "$x = 0/1$" or ζ is "$x = 1/1$" or etc., as above

Now to say that x is a statistical statement about y and z in a rational corpus of level r_i and basis F, in symbols, x r_iSA$_F(y,z)$, is to say that there is a pair of fractions, w and w', such that x is pct$(y,z,(w;w'))$ and x is included in some rational corpus of level r_i and basis F, and also that there is a y' and a z' which are rational matrices and a y'' and z'' that are variables, such that y'' qu $(y''$ e y b $y')$ and z'' qu $(z''$ e y int z b $z')$ are theorems, and that there is w'' and a w''' that are ratio-matrices (as defined in Δ97a) such that w e S_2a w'' and w' e S_2a w''' are theorems.

Δ97b $\ulcorner$ θ r_iSA$_F(\eta,\zeta)$ $\urcorner$ *for* $\ulcorner$ ($\exists\alpha$)($\exists\alpha'$)($\theta =$ pct $(\eta,\zeta, (\alpha;\alpha'))$) ·

($\exists\varphi$)(r_iRC$_F$ φ · θ Ing φ) · ($\exists\eta'$)($\exists\zeta'$)($\exists\eta''$)($\exists\zeta''$)

(Vbl η'' · Vbl ζ'' · r_iRMat$_F$ η' · r_iRMat$_F$ ζ' ·

Thm η'' qu $(\eta''$ e η b $\eta')$ ·

Thm ζ'' qu $(\zeta''$ e ζ int η b $\zeta')$) · ($\exists\gamma$)($\exists\gamma'$)(RM γ ·

RM γ' · Thm α e S_2 a γ · Thm α' e S_2 a γ')) $\urcorner$

According to my definition of a rational corpus of a given level and basis, it will turn out that if there is a statement y which belongs to some rational corpus of this level and basis, and y cd z is a theorem, then there will be a rational corpus of the same level and basis containing z as a framed ingredient. This is certainly a necessary feature of a logic of rational belief; but one confusing consequence of it is that if we have the statement "$\%(A,B,(.4;.6))$" in a rational corpus of given level and basis, we will also have the statement "%(A,B, (.3;.7))" in some rational corpus of the same level and basis. We want some way of singling out the statistical statement about a given subject matter which is of the greatest interest to us—namely, the statement which is in some sense the (or a) strongest statement acceptable in that context.

First I shall define the relation 'stronger than' between two statistical statements, relative to a given level and basis of rational corpus: I shall say that the statement x is stronger than the statement y in the rational corpora of level r_i and basis F, in symbols $x \, r_i \mathrm{Str_F} \, y$, if they are both statistical statements about some subject matter in the rational corpora of level r_i and basis F and if the interval associated with the ratios mentioned in the first statement falls properly within (i.e., includes at most one endpoint of) the interval associated with the ratios mentioned in the second. Protosyntactically, this latter requirement will be expressed by demanding that a certain statement, preceded and followed by $\widehat{S_6} S_7$, be a rational corpus of level r_i and basis F.

$$\Delta 98 \quad \ulcorner \zeta \, r_i \mathrm{Str_F} \, \eta \urcorner \quad for \quad \ulcorner (\exists \zeta')(\exists \zeta'')(\exists \eta')(\exists \eta'')(\exists \alpha)(\exists \alpha')$$

$$(\exists \beta)(\exists \beta')(\zeta \, r_i \mathrm{SA_F}(\zeta',\zeta'') \cdot \eta \, r_i \mathrm{SA_F}(\eta',\eta'') \cdot$$

$$\zeta = \mathrm{pct}(\zeta',\zeta'',(\alpha;\alpha')) \cdot \eta = \mathrm{pct}(\eta',\eta'',(\beta;\beta')) \cdot$$

$$r_i \mathrm{RC_F} \, \widehat{S_6} \widehat{S_7} ((\alpha_s \mathrm{gr}\beta \text{ cj } \beta'_s \mathrm{gr}\alpha') \text{ al}(\alpha \text{ id } \beta \text{ cj } \beta'_s \mathrm{gr}\alpha')$$

$$\text{al } (\alpha_s \mathrm{gr}\beta \text{ cj } \beta' \text{ id } \alpha'))\widehat{} \widehat{S_6} S_7) \urcorner$$

This definition looks rather complicated, but it's not really so bad; it says that one statement is to be considered stronger than another statement, if the two statements have the required form, described in the definition, and if, in addition, a certain expression is a rational corpus of a specified type.

Now we can define what it is to be a strongest statement about a given subject matter. The statement x is a strongest statement about y and z in the rational corpus of level r_i and basis F, symbolically, $x \, r_i \mathrm{S^*A_F}(y,z)$, if x is a statistical statement about y and z, and there is no statement in any rational corpus of this level and basis, about the same subject matter, which is stronger than x.

$$\Delta 99 \quad \ulcorner \zeta \, r_i \mathrm{S^*A_F}(\eta,\eta') \urcorner \quad for \quad \ulcorner \zeta \, r_i \mathrm{SA_F}(\eta,\eta') \cdot (\alpha)(\alpha \, r_i \mathrm{SA_F}(\eta,\eta')$$

$$\supset \sim \alpha \, r_i \mathrm{Str_F} \, \zeta) \urcorner$$

Here, for the first time, we have what appears to be a patently non-constructive definition: given a statement x about (using) abstracts y and z, and given the level and basis of the rational corpus with which we are concerned, it is still not clear how we are supposed to go about finding out whether or not this is a 'strongest' statistical statement about y and z. It is obvious that we cannot generally list all of the ingredients of rational corpora of level r_i and basis F, and hence that we cannot check through all the statements that occur in these rational corpora to see if there is a stronger one than x about y and z. Nevertheless, once we have defined probability, certain metatheorems can be stated which will be of help. In particular, it will turn out that frequently there is, after all, a definite procedure for finding a strongest statement about a given subject matter. This procedure is far too tedious for everyday use; but in everyday use we are satisfied with statements that are only approximately strongest.

It is also worth noting that there may be any number of strongest statistical statements—e.g., if "%(A,B,(8/10;9/10))" is a strongest statement about "A" and "B", then so may "%(A,B,(80/100;90/100))" and "%(A,B,(16/20;36/40))" be strongest statements. Furthermore, it may be that both "%(A,B,(8/10;9/10))" and "%(A,B,(7/10;8/10))" are strongest statements, since neither is stronger than the other. It will be seen later that this is a genuine possibility.

The next definition is that of equality of strength between two statistical statements. To say that one statistical statement x is exactly as strong as another statistical statement y in the rational corpora of level r_i and basis F, in symbols, $x\ r_i S{=}_F\ y$, is to say, of course, that x and y are about some subject matters, and that the ratios mentioned in x are known to be equal to the ratios mentioned in y.

$\Delta 100$ $\ulcorner \zeta\ r_i S{=}_F\ \eta \urcorner$ *for* $\ulcorner (\exists\zeta')(\exists\zeta'')(\exists\eta')(\exists\eta'')(\exists\alpha)(\exists\alpha')(\exists\beta)$

$(\exists\beta')(\zeta\ r_i SA_F (\zeta',\zeta'') \cdot \eta\ r_i SA_F (\eta',\eta'') \cdot$

$\zeta = pct (\zeta',\zeta'',(\alpha;\alpha')) \cdot \eta = pct (\eta',\eta'',(\beta;\beta'')) \cdot$

$r_i RC_F\ \widehat{S_6 S_7}((\alpha\ id\ \beta)\ cj\ (\alpha'\ id\ \beta'))\widehat{S_6 S_7}) \urcorner$

The final important relation between statistical statements is that of difference. I shall say that x differs from y in the rational corpora of level r_i and basis F, in symbols, $x\ r_i Dif_F\ y$, if x and y are about some subject matters, and there is a rational corpus asserting that the ratios mentioned in x are both greater than the ratios mentioned in y, or that the ratios mentioned in y are both greater than the corresponding ratios mentioned in x.

$\Delta 101$ $\ulcorner \zeta\ r_i Dif_F\ \eta \urcorner$ *for* $\ulcorner (\exists\zeta')(\exists\zeta'')(\exists\eta')(\exists\eta'')(\exists\alpha)(\exists\alpha')(\exists\beta)$

$(\exists\beta')(\zeta\ r_i SA_F (\zeta',\zeta'') \cdot \eta\ r_i SA_F (\eta',\eta'') \cdot$

$$\zeta = \text{pct}\,(\,\zeta',\zeta'',(\alpha;\alpha'))\,\eta = \text{pct}\,(\eta',\eta'',(\beta;\beta''))\,\cdot$$

$$r_i\,\text{RC}_\text{F}\;\widehat{\text{S}_6\,\text{S}_7}\,((\alpha\,_\text{s}\text{gr}\beta\;\text{cj}\;\alpha'\,_\text{s}\text{gr}\beta')\;\text{al}$$

$$(\beta\,_\text{s}\text{gr}\alpha\;\text{cj}\;\beta'\,_\text{s}\text{gr}\alpha'))\widehat{\;\;}\overline{\text{S}_6\,\text{S}_7)}$$

On the hypothesis, which will be proved later, that if there is any ingredient at all of a rational corpus of level r_i and basis F, then if x is a theorem, $\widehat{\text{S}_6\,\text{S}_7}x\widehat{\;\;}\widehat{\text{S}_6\,\text{S}_7}$ is a rational corpus of level r_i and basis F, the following sequence of statements hold as metatheorems.

Since there is a decision procedure for ordinary fractions, we have, where ψ and ξ are ordinary fractions,

$$\overline{\ulcorner\text{Thm}\;\xi\;_\text{s}\text{gr}\;\psi\;\text{v}\;\text{Thm}\,\psi\;_\text{s}\text{gr}\;\xi\;\text{v}\;\text{Thm}\;\psi\;\text{id}\;\xi\;}$$

On the above hypothesis, this establishes the exhaustiveness of the relationships defined by the above three definitions:

**1021 $\ulcorner(\exists\zeta')(\exists\zeta'')(\exists\eta')(\exists\eta'')(\zeta\;r_i\,\text{SA}_\text{F}(\zeta',\zeta'')\cdot\eta\;r_i\,\text{SA}_\text{F}(\eta',\eta''))$

$\supset\cdot\zeta\;r_i\,\text{Str}_\text{F}\;\eta\;\text{v}\;\eta\;r_i\,\text{Str}_\text{F}\;\zeta\;\text{v}\;\zeta\;r_i\,\text{Dif}_\text{F}\;\eta\;\text{v}\;\zeta\;r_i\,\text{S}=_\text{F}\;\overline{\eta}\;$

On the same hypothesis, these relationships are also exclusive in any consistent rational corpus of given level and basis; the requirement of consistency may be expressed by saying that no rational corpus of the given level and basis contains both a statement x and its negation nx.

**1022 $\ulcorner(\,r_i\,\text{RC}_\text{F}\;\theta\cdot\alpha\;\text{Ing}\;\theta\cdot\supset\sim\text{n}\alpha\;\text{Ing}\;\theta\,)\supset(\eta\;r_i\,\text{Str}_\text{F}\;\zeta\supset\sim$

$\zeta\;r_i\,\text{Str}_\text{F}\;\overline{\eta}\,)$

**1023 $\ulcorner(\,r_i\,\text{RC}_\text{F}\;\theta\cdot\alpha\;\text{Ing}\;\theta\cdot\supset\sim\text{n}\alpha\;\text{Ing}\;\theta\,)\supset(\eta\;r_i\,\text{Str}_\text{F}\;\zeta\supset\sim$

$\zeta\;r_i\,\text{Dif}_\text{F}\;\overline{\eta}\,)$

**1024 $\ulcorner(\,r_i\,\text{RC}_\text{F}\;\theta\cdot\alpha\;\text{Ing}\;\theta\cdot\supset\sim\text{n}\alpha\;\text{Ing}\;\theta\,)\supset(\eta\;r_i\,\text{Str}_\text{F}\;\zeta\supset\sim$

$\zeta\;r_i\,\text{S}=_\text{F}\;\overline{\eta}\,)$

**1025 $\ulcorner(\,r_i\,\text{RC}_\text{F}\;\theta\cdot\alpha\;\text{Ing}\;\theta\cdot\supset\sim\text{n}\alpha\;\text{Ing}\;\theta\,)\supset(\eta\;r_i\,\text{Dif}_\text{F}\;\zeta\supset\sim$

$\eta\;r_i\,\text{Str}_\text{F}\;\overline{\zeta}\,)$

**1026 $\ulcorner(\,r_i\,\text{RC}_\text{F}\;\theta\cdot\alpha\;\text{Ing}\;\theta\cdot\supset\sim\text{n}\alpha\;\text{Ing}\;\theta\,)\supset(\eta\;r_i\,\text{Dif}_\text{F}\;\zeta\supset\sim$

$\zeta\;r_i\,\text{S}=_\text{F}\;\overline{\eta}\,)$

**1027 $\ulcorner(\,r_i\,\text{RC}_\text{F}\;\theta\cdot\alpha\;\text{Ing}\;\theta\cdot\supset\sim\text{n}\alpha\;\text{Ing}\;\theta\,)\supset(\zeta\;r_i\,\text{S}=_\text{F}\;\eta\supset\sim$

$\zeta\;r_i\,\text{Str}_\text{F}\;\overline{\eta}\,)$

On the same hypothesis, the following relationships also hold:

**1028 $\ulcorner\zeta\;r_i\,\text{S}=_\text{F}\;\eta\cdot\eta\;r_i\,\text{S}=_\text{F}\;\zeta'\cdot\supset\zeta\;r_i\,\text{S}=_\text{F}\;\overline{\zeta'}\;$

**1029 ⌜$\zeta \, r_i S{=}_F \, \eta \, \cdot \equiv \cdot \, \eta \, r_i S{=}_F \, \zeta$⌝

**1030 ⌜$\zeta \, r_i S{=}_F \, \eta \cdot \eta \, r_i S{=}_F \, \zeta' \cdot \supset \zeta \, r_i S{=}_F \, \zeta'$⌝

**1031 ⌜$\zeta \, r_i S{=}_F \, \zeta' \cdot \zeta' \, r_i \mathrm{Str}_F \, \eta \cdot \supset \zeta \, r_i \mathrm{Str}_F \, \eta$⌝

**1032 ⌜$\zeta \, r_i S{=}_F \, \zeta' \cdot \zeta' \, r_i \mathrm{Dif}_F \, \eta \cdot \supset \zeta \, r_i \mathrm{Dif}_F \, \eta$⌝

**1033 ⌜$\zeta \, r_i S{=}_F \, \zeta' \supset \cdot \zeta \, r_i \mathrm{Dif}_F \, \eta \equiv \zeta' \, r_i \mathrm{Dif}_F \, \eta$⌝

**1034 ⌜$\zeta \, r_i S{=}_F \, \zeta' \supset \cdot \zeta \, r_i \mathrm{Str}_F \, \eta \equiv \zeta' \, r_i \mathrm{Str}_F \, \eta$⌝

**1035 ⌜$\zeta \, r_i S{=}_F \, \zeta' \supset \cdot \eta \, r_i \mathrm{Str}_F \, \zeta \equiv \eta \, r_i \mathrm{Str}_F \, \zeta'$⌝

**1036 ⌜$\zeta \, r_i \mathrm{Dif}_F \, \eta \cdot \equiv \cdot \, \eta \, r_i \mathrm{Dif}_F \, \zeta$⌝

**1037 ⌜$\zeta \, r_i \mathrm{Str}_F \, \eta \cdot \eta \, r_i \mathrm{Str}_F \, \zeta' \cdot \supset \zeta \, r_i \mathrm{Str}_F \, \zeta'$⌝

**1038 ⌜$\zeta \, r_i \mathrm{Str}_F \, \zeta' \cdot \eta \, r_i \mathrm{Dif}_F \, \zeta' \cdot \supset \cdot \zeta \, r_i \mathrm{Dif}_F \, \eta \, \mathrm{v} \, \zeta \, r_i \mathrm{Str}_F \, \eta$⌝

**1039 ⌜$\zeta \, r_i \mathrm{Str}_F \, \zeta' \cdot \eta \, r_i \mathrm{Dif}_F \, \zeta \cdot \supset \cdot \eta \, r_i \mathrm{Dif}_F \, \zeta' \, \mathrm{v} \, \eta \, r_i \mathrm{Str}_F \, \zeta'$⌝

(If the last two metatheorems are not immediately obvious, they can be made obvious with a little algebra in the object language; or even more simply, they can be made obvious by a consideration of the intervals whose endpoints are the ratios mentioned in ζ, ζ', and η.)

There are a number of metatheorems concerning strongest statistical statements which are very important. Although they could already be established for the statements appearing in rational corpora of level r_n, they cannot be established in their full generality until probability has been defined. It is to this latter task that I now turn.

CHAPTER NINE

Probability Defined

1. As I mentioned earlier, one of the oddities of my theory is that probability is defined in terms of randomness, rather than vice versa. But what does it mean to apply the adjective 'random' to an object or group of objects? What is a random cigarette smoker, or a random selection of college students, or a random potato? In the first place it is clear that there is always a substantive to which the adjective is applied, so that in general we are concerned with a random *member* of a *class*. This suggests that there is an ambiguity in the phrase 'random selection'. Do we mean, for example, a group of college students each of which is a random member of the class of college students? Or do we mean a random member of the class of groups of college students?

On the frequency theory of probability, the former sense of 'random selection' seems most often to be intended. A selection is a random one if the probability that any given member of the parent population belong to this selection is the same as the probability that any other member of the parent population belong to the selection. Let us consider this proposal in some detail.

Suppose a sociologist begins to describe an experiment he has performed by saying, "Well, I took a random selection of college students, and..." On the basis of the above proposal, he will find himself in hot water almost immediately. He must be interpreted as saying that each student in his sample is a random member of the class of college students; or, defining random in terms of the frequency theory of probability, he is saying that the probability that any given college student belongs to his sample is the same as the probability that any other college student belongs to his sample; or finally, he must be saying that the relative frequency with which any given college student belongs to his sample is the same as the relative frequency with which any other college student belongs to his sample. But since he selects his sample only once, and every college student either belongs to it once and for all, or does not belong to it once and for all, this last claim is absurd.

If he attempts to escape by taking the other side of the above ambiguity, he must claim to be saying that the group of students in his sample is a random member of the class of groups of college students; or, defining probability by reference to relative frequency, he is saying that the relative frequency with which groups of college students are the group which constitutes his sample is the same for every group. Again his statement turns out to be patently false.

The most plausible alternative to take on the frequency theory is to eschew the temptation to define randomness directly, and to define a *random selection* in the following way: a random selection is to be a selection obtained by a *method* which is such that if it were to be applied over and over again, then, in the long run, every member of the class in question would be selected about equally often. This definition of a random selection eliminates the need to consider the ambiguity mentioned above; but it still does not seem quite plausible. The hypothesis that the particular group of college students considered by the sociologist is a random selection of college students remains a material hypothesis — it may be that the method by which he selected them is a method such that if it were applied over and over again it would select each college student equally often; but, on the other hand, this may not be the case. In general it seems rather unlikely that such a method could actually be employed in such a situation. It should be noticed that the method of selecting college students employed by the sociologist can be tested for its statistical impartiality only in the same way in which we test any other statistical hypothesis on this theory by testing a random selection of the selections made by the method in question. But this new occurrence of the expression 'random selection' requires a new consideration of 'method' which in turn must be justified by a new statistical hypothesis; the regression is potentially endless.[1]

Again, even if we are willing to accept the hypothesis that the method employed by the sociologist will, in the long run, select each college student equally often, we may question the *relevance* of randomness in this sense to the inferences he is trying to draw. Let us suppose that he has before him a list of all college students, arranged alphabetically by last name. Suppose he has a bag with 26 balls in it, each one marked with a different letter of the alphabet. Now the method this sociologist employs is the following: He allows himself to be blindfolded, puts his hand in the bag, stirs the balls around, and draws out one. The group of college students he will use in his investigation will be the group of those whose last names begin with the letter marking the ball he has drawn. It is obvious that this method meets the requirement that in the long run each

1. G. S. Brown, who accepts a frequency interpretation of probability, argues that the frequency interpretation of randomness is self-contradictory. *Probability and Scientific Inference*, New York, 1957.

college student will be selected by it equally often, if we have reason to believe that each ball will be selected equally often.

Let us suppose that this is what he has done, and that his sample consists of all those college students whose last names begin with the letter M. If he says, "On the basis of my random selection, I conclude such and so about the sexual habits of the college population," we *might* be inclined to accept his results. If he says, "On the basis of my random selection, I conclude that about 62% of the college population is of Scottish ancestry," we might be a bit sceptical. But if he says, "On the basis of my random selection, I conclude that 100% of the college population have last names beginning with the letter M," we would be sure he was joking.

All this goes to show is that on the frequency theory of a random selection, we may sometimes want to deny the plausibility of using a certain sample as the basis for an inference, even though it does meet all the requirements of being a random selection in the only sense in which this can be explained by reference to frequency. It also suggests that if we want to find a conception of randomness or random selection which is intuitively more plausible than that suggested above, we must take account not only of the object and the class of which it is supposed to be a random member, but also of the property or class *with respect to which* it is supposed to be a random member of this class. In the example, the group selected by the sociologist seems (intuitively) to be a random one with respect to the property of reflecting the sexual habits of the college population; but it is certainly not a random one with respect to the property of reflecting the proportion of the college population whose last names begin with the letter M.

Consider a bag of counters. Under certain circumstances you would doubtless be willing to agree that the next counter I draw is a random member of the class of counters in the bag. (It is one definite counter; this counter is (now) in the bag.) But while this counter is a random member of the class of counters in the bag with respect to being red or green or having a certain number of dots, it is definitely not a random counter with respect to the perfectly legitimate properties of 'being drawn by me', 'being drawn by an American male', etc. It may very well be the case that some of the counters are drawn by other people, but the description of the counter with which we are concerned precludes this possibility in this particular case. On the other hand, suppose that we come into a room in which there has just been a large cocktail party, and see a bag of counters on a table with one red counter lying beside it. It is conceivable that we might say that this red counter is a random member of the class of counters drawn from the bag with respect to the property of being drawn by a male; although it is certainly not (for us) a random member of this class with respect to the property of being red. To be clear about what we mean in any given case, we must therefore refer to the property with respect to which the given entity is a random member of the given class.

But why is it that the property with which we are concerned is relevant? In the example of the sociologist sampling the college population to discover the proportion which are of Scottish ancestry, we felt that his sample consisting of all those students whose last names begin with the letter M was hardly random in the appropriate sense. Why? The most straightforward answer is simply that we *know* that the proportion of people of Scottish descent among those whose last names begin with M is greater than that among the population as a whole. The randomness of the selection in question seems to depend not only on the property with which we are concerned, but also upon our body of factual knowledge.

Still another example may help to make this dependence clear. Let a coin be tossed ten times in another room; consider the sixth toss. It seems plausible to suppose that this toss is a random member of the class of tosses of this coin, with respect to the property of landing heads. (The fact that the coin has already been tossed constitutes no difficulty — 'the next toss' is just as definite a description as 'the sixth toss', and the object described definitely has or definitely has not the property in question in either case.) But now suppose that some honest fellow who has watched the tossing tells us that 8 of these ten tosses resulted in heads, while we know that in general it is practically certain that about half of all the tosses of this coin will have resulted in heads. Now it no longer seems plausible to consider the sixth toss a random member of the class of *all* tosses of this coin with respect to the property of resulting in heads; but we can plausibly consider it a random member of the class of the ten tosses under discussion with respect to this property. Relative to what we know *now*, it is a random member of a class in which the relative frequency of heads is 8/10. Finally, suppose that the same honest fellow tells us that the first five tosses all resulted in heads; now we will be inclined to say that the sixth toss is a random member of the class composed only of the last five tosses (with respect to the property of resulting in heads), in which the relative frequency of heads is 3/5.

"The sixth toss" is a definite description; the object it describes may or may not have the property of resulting in heads. But the class of which this object is a random member, with respect to this property, will be one particular class or another according to the information we have about this object and about the various classes to which we know this object belongs. This information will be represented in our rational corpus, and must be referred to if we are to judge the plausibility of an assertion of randomness.

A complete statement about randomness will therefore require reference to four things: the object concerned; the class of which it is said to be a random member; the property or class with respect to which it is a random member of this class; and, finally, the rational corpus relative to which it is a random member of this class with respect to this property.

We have thus reached the point reached by Keynes in his *Treatise on Probability,* when he suggested that in its most common sense, randomness must require reference to these four things.[2] But what is the specific form of the dependence of randomness on our body of knowledge? The most obvious aspect of this dependence is that we will wish to *deny* that A is a random member of B with respect to C, when our rational corpus includes the knowledge that (a) A is a member of some subclass D of B, and (b) the proportion C's in D is p, while the proportion of C's in B has some different definite value, q. These two conditions are sufficient to cause us to deny the randomness in question; for the time being, let us suppose that they are necessary as well. In later developments we shall have to broaden (a) to include classes other than subclasses of B, and we shall have to make precise what it means to say that we know that the two proportions differ.

Given a definition of randomness along the lines suggested above, the definition of probability presents no problem at all. We shall say that the probability that A belongs to C is p, if and only if (a) A is a random member of some class B with respect to membership in C, relative to our rational corpus, and (b) we know that the proportion of B's which are also C's is p. We must be sure, of course, that our definition of randomness is such that if A is a random member of two different classes, B and D, in the required sense, then the proportion of each of these classes which is included in C is known to be the same.

The definitions of 'known difference in proportion', 'random member', 'probability', and so on, will, like the definition of 'rational corpus' on which they depend, be protosyntactical definitions. This means that a statement about randomness or about probability will always be construed as a purely formal statement; that is, a statement whose validity or invalidity depends only upon its notational features, or, what amounts to the same thing, a statement which could be expected to turn out to be a protosyntactical theorem (or the denial of a theorem) on the basis of a suitable selection of axi-

2. Keynes, *A Treatise on Probability*, pp. 291-292.

oms governing the protosyntactical primitive M.

At first sight it may seem questionable to interpret 'random' as a purely logical predicate in the face of the use which is made of the term in statistical investigations. This use often seems to be empirical, and to be quite independent of our 'knowledge' and 'ignorance' and the syntactical features of our language. If you are conducting a statistical investigation, and you claim that your samples are random, while I assert that they are not random, how is this conflict between us to be resolved? According to the above conception of randomness it is to be resolved by logical procedures; but in such cases don't people usually attempt to resolve the conflict by reference to facts? But 'reference to facts' is itself a somewhat vague phrase: it may mean direct reference to facts (events, possession of properties by objects, etc.) by the *use* of statements of the object language; but it may also mean an indirect reference to (perhaps only probable) facts by the mention of (factual) statements in the object language. If we interpret our body of knowledge as a set of statements in the object language, as I have done, then the second interpretation is perfectly plausible: the only really persuasive basis for denying the randomness of a sample is *knowledge* of bias (or probable bias), and this in turn means that the denial must be based on certain factual statements that are included among the statements in my rational corpus.

When I refer to facts to support my denial of the randomness of your sample, I do so with two things in mind: if your rational corpus contains the same material as mine, I am merely reminding you of the relevant part of this material in order that I may point out your *logical* error; if your rational corpus does not contain the material that mine does, then my object may not be to point out your logical error (since you may have made none) but simply to enlarge your rational corpus, and to *this* end I will cite evidence, call upon the authority of experts, and so on. Your rebuttal will be in the first instance an argument designed to show that the facts to which I referred (indirectly) are not (known to be) relevant after all — i.e., that it is I who have committed the logical blunder. In the second instance, your rebuttal will consist in the rejection of the proposed addition to your rational corpus; if the rejection is rational (as it must be if it is to save your original assertion of randomness), the grounds of the rejection will be such as to cause me to reject the factual statement in question too. I hope to be able to show that in general such a conflict can always be resolved in this way, provided that the rules of the game are made explicit and provided that the combatants are willing to learn from each other's experience.

There is one possible difficulty with this conception of randomness which should perhaps be mentioned here. This is that randomness may not turn out to be constructive. We will want to define 'the object A is a random member of the class B with respect to membership in the class C, relative to the rational corpora of level r_i and basis F,' as meaning roughly that there is some rational corpus of this level and basis which contains the statement "A ϵ B", and that there is no other class D such that "A ϵ D" belongs to a rational corpus of this level and basis, and such that there is also a statement in this rational corpus expressing the fact that the proportion of B's which are C's differs from the proportion of D's which are C's.

Now it may be easy enough to exhibit a rational corpus containing the statement "A ϵ B", but it may be quite another matter to be sure that there is *no* rational corpus containing such and such other statements. This may not be as serious as it sounds; the denial of an assertion of randomness — the assertion that there is a rational corpus containing such and such statements — is constructive. We can thus achieve agreement concerning randomness in the same way that we can achieve agreement concerning non-theoremhood. If X is a theorem, we are surely free, in the absence of proof to the contrary, to suppose that the denial of X is not a theorem. In the same way it seems quite plausible to put the *onus probandi* on the person who would deny a particular assertion of randomness; an assertion of randomness is to be presumed valid until proven invalid. This is rendered even more plausible by the reflection that we need not restrict ourselves to simple properties: it will be a property of some samples, for example, that they are selected by a poor method — that is, a method which often leads to samples which, while random at the time they are selected, turn out to be non-random in the face of future additions to our rational corpus.

2.   This conception of randomness, even in its unformalized roughness, leads to a number of interesting philosophical considerations, of which I shall give two here. The first might be entitled, "The Refutation of Stace's Refutation of Moore's Refutation of Idealism." The second is a rebuttal of Broad's argument that postulates about the universe are required for the justification of induction.

The thesis of Stace's paper, "The Refutation of Realism," is that we "... have not the slightest reason for believing that ... [unexperienced entities] exist."[3] Professor Stace asks us to consider a piece of paper: "I am at this moment experiencing it, and at this moment it exists, but how can I know that it existed last night in my desk when, so far as I know, no mind was experiencing it?"[4] Ac-

---

3. W. T. Stace, "Refutation of Realism," *Mind* 53, 1934; Reprinted in Feigl and Sellars, *Readings in Philosophical Analysis*, New York, 1949, p. 364.
4. *Ibid.*, p. 366.

cording to Stace, we cannot arrive at the conclusion that it existed when it was not being observed by an inductive argument, for inductive arguments proceed from observed cases to unobserved cases, and, "... by hypothesis, its existence when it is not being experienced cannot be observed."[5]

Now it is admitted that the piece of paper exists when it *is* being observed; unless 'exists' in this context is to *mean* 'is being perceived' we must suppose either that existence is an observable sort of property in itself, or (more plausibly) that anything that has some of the more usual observable properties (a certain weight, texture, color, etc.) exists. In either of these last two cases, there is no difficulty in constructing an inductive argument to show that unexperienced pieces of paper exist. I assert, first, that the times during which I observed the piece of paper last week are a random sample of the set of time intervals which make up the past week, with respect to the property that the piece of paper exists then, or has a certain weight, texture, color, etc., relative to my rational corpus. I assert, second, that if the piece of paper exists or has these properties during *all* of a random sample of the times between t_1 and t_2, then it is rationally obligatory to give a high degree of credence to the statement that it existed (or had these properties) during *all* of the times in this interval.

The second assertion can hardly be doubted without doubting all inductive inferences; such inferences are made constantly, and although the mechanics of these inductive inferences are greatly in need of clarification, it would be folly to deny their possibility. The first assertion is the one that leaves an opening (in this context) for counter-argument. According to my conception of randomness, it may be difficult for me to *show* that the sample in question is random in the appropriate sense; but the *onus probandi* is on Professor Stace — he cannot simply deny that the sample is a random one; he must *show* that it is not random. That is, he must name some property possessed by the sample or by the times of which it is composed, and he must also state some highly credible hypothesis connecting this property with the property with respect to which the sample was alleged to be random.

The property he would name is obvious enough — all the times which compose the sample are times during which the piece of paper was being perceived. But he would also have to claim that his rational corpus contained a statement to the effect that things exist more often when they are being perceived than when they are not, or that the properties of weight and color, etc. belong to things more often when they are being perceived than when they are not.

5. *Ibid.*, p. 367.

And if Stace does claim to have such statements in his rational corpus, he should be able to show why it is *rational* to have them there. In short, so far as Stace's argument is concerned, the burden of proof is on the idealist: he must show that we have reason to suppose that things are different when they are not being perceived.

Broad accepts a logical theory of probability according to which a given object is a random member of a class if it is as likely to be any one member as any other. But on this conception of randomness, even with the help of the notorious principle of indifference, we are rarely entitled to assert that a particular sample is random. In particular, the parts of the universe which we have observed are not a random sample of the whole, for, as Broad points out, we are not as likely to encounter instances remote in space or time as we are those close to hand.[6] For this reason in particular, Broad feels obligated to postulate a strong principle of the uniformity of nature. In my theory, on the other hand, where probability is defined by reference to randomness rather than vice versa, there is no difficulty at all in supposing that that part of the universe which we have observed is a random sample of the whole universe (including those parts remote in space and time) with respect to the property of being fairly representative of such traits and uniformities as may exist in the universe and are the subject matter of scientific inquiry.

3.   The major problem in providing a formal definition of randomness is that of formalizing the expression 'is known to differ' as it occurs in such contexts as, "The proportion of people of Scottish descent among people whose last names begin with M is known to differ from the proportion among people in general." The material with which we have to work consists of statistical statements and statements about membership, and the context in which we shall operate is that of the rational corpora of a given level and basis.

As my earlier discussion, and Keynes' discussion in 1921, have indicated, a statement about randomness must have the following general form: an object A is a random member of a class C, with respect to membership in a class B, relative to our rational corpora of a given level and basis. The major difference between the informal characterization of randomness and the formal characterization that follows, is that the informal characterization will be phrased in terms of classes and objects in the world, while the prosyntactical definition refers only to notational features of statements (often about the world) in the object language.

Before attempting to describe the character of the rational corpus relative to which we will be entitled to claim that "A" is a random member of "B" with respect to "C", it will help to make things

C. D. Broad, "Problematic Induction," *Proceedings of the Aristotelian Society*, 1928.

clear if we consider instead, in more detail than before, the grounds on which we would be led to deny this. Let us consider a concrete example: suppose that I assert that 'the next toss of this coin' ('A') is a random member of 'the class of all coin tosses' ('B'), with respect to membership in 'the class of coins landing heads up' ('C'). ('Object', 'class', 'member', and 'membership' must in this context be given a somewhat elliptical meaning; e.g., 'object' must mean, 'expression denoting an object', 'member' must mean 'is connected by 'ε' in a rational corpus', etc.)

Another person might dispute my assertion of randomness on the grounds that the coin is known to be biassed, landing heads far more often than the general run of coins. (But not on the grounds that, for all we know, the coin *might* be biassed!) Thus we may plausibly be forced to deny that 'A' is a random member of 'B' with respect to 'C', when (a) we know that 'A' is a member of some other class 'B*'(here B* is the class of tosses performed with *this* coin), and (b) we know that the proportion of objects in 'B*' which belong to 'C' differs from the proportion of objects in 'B' which belong to 'C'. But that (a) and (b) are not sufficient is indicated by the fact that the argument can be turned around in such a way that its form remains but its plausibility vanishes. Thus if 'B*' is the class of tosses performed with this coin, and if the proportion of these tosses which land heads is known to differ from the proportion of coin tosses in general which land heads, it is clear that our knowledge about 'A' and 'B' will not lead us to deny that 'A' is a random member of 'B*' with respect to 'C'. Thus the third condition that must be satisfied before we can deny the randomness in question is that (c) we do *not* know that 'B*' is included in 'B'.

Again, suppose we know that the object 'A' belongs to 'C' if and only if the object 'A*' belongs to 'C*'. Suppose further that 'A*' belongs to 'B*' and we know that the proportion of objects belonging to 'C*' among the objects belonging to 'B*' differs from the proportion of objects belonging to 'C' among the objects belonging to 'B'. Then this somewhat indirect information will suffice to cause us to deny (if certain other conditions are satisfied) that, relative to our rational corpus, 'A' is a random member of 'B' with respect to 'C'.

The 'certain other conditions' may be clarified by an example. Suppose we are drawing balls from two bags connected by an infernal machine. We are informed that this infernal machine operates in such a way that a certain ball (A*) drawn from the first bag (B*) is red (C*) if and only if a certain other ball (A**) drawn from the second bag (B**) is black (C**). If our knowledge about the proportion of red balls in bag number one and of black balls in bag number two is the same — i.e., if we know that the proportions are the same, or if the strongest statistical statements we have about the two proportions are equally strong — we may be willing to say that 'A*' is a random member of 'B*' with respect to 'C*' and that 'A**' is a random member of 'B**' with respect to 'C**'. On the other hand, if our knowledge about these two proportions is different, we shall want to deny both these statements about randomness.

Now consider the class (B) of all pairs of draws consisting first of a draw from bag number one, and second of a draw from bag number two, such that the first object belongs to C* and the second to C**, or the first object does not belong to C* and the second does not belong to C**, and the class (C) of all pairs of draws such that the first belongs to C* and the second to C**. The proportion of objects in B belonging to C will in general be different from the proportion of objects in B* belonging to C* and from the proportion of objects in B** belonging to C**. Furthermore we know that (A*;A**) belongs to B, and that (A*;A**) belongs to C if and only if A* belongs to C*. While we are happy enough to have our knowledge about (A*;A**), B, and C prevent the randomness of 'A*' in 'B*' with respect to 'C*', we would be most unhappy to have the converse hold.

We do not want the fact that (a) we know that (A*;A**) belongs to B, and that (A*;A**) belongs to C if and only if A* belongs to C*, and (b) we know that the proportion of objects in B which belong to C differs from the proportion of objects in B* which belong to C*, to preclude our saying that '(A*;A**)' is a random member of 'B' with respect to 'C'. But obviously it is not true that we know that B is included in B* — in fact we know that B is not included in B* — so that in order to save the randomness of '(A*;A**)' in 'B' with respect to 'C', we must expand the clause (c) on page 109 to include not only the demand that we do not know that the preventing class B is included in the prevented class B*, but also the demand that we do not know that the prevented class B* is included in a cartesian product of B with some other class. In the present example, B* does not prevent '(A*;A**)' from being a random member of 'B' with respect to 'C', because we know that B is included in the cartesian product of B* with B**.

Finally, it will be convenient to confine our attention to the class not conflicting in the above sense with another class, about which we have the greatest amount of information; thus we shall deny that 'A' is a random member of its unit class with respect to the class 'C', on the grounds that (unless we know that A does (or does not) belong to C) we have stronger information about some other class to which A is known to belong. If it is otherwise possible for 'A' to be a random member of 'B' with respect to 'C', and for 'A' to be a random member of 'D' with respect to 'C', but the strongest statistical statement we know about B and C is stronger than the strongest statistical statement we know about D and C, we shall say that 'A' is *not* a random member of 'D' with respect to 'C', but that it is a random member of 'B' with respect to 'C'.

In general and roughly, then, we deny that 'A' is a random member of 'B' with respect to 'C' (1) when we know that A (or some other object A*) belongs to some other class in which the relevant proportion *differs* from that in B, and the randomness of 'A' in 'B' with respect to 'C' is not saved by one of the gambits indicated above; or (2) when we know that A (or A*) belongs to some other class about which we have stronger relevant statistical information, and which is not itself prevented from being the class of which 'A' is a random member with respect to 'C' by considerations of the first sort. When there is no reason in the rational corpora of the basis and level with which we are concerned to deny that 'A' is a random member of 'B' with respect to 'C', we shall say that 'A' *is* a random member of 'B' with respect to 'C'.[7]

It would be possible to present a definition of randomness embodying all these factors; but it will obviously be much simpler— and more expedient from the point of view of later metatheorems— to define separately the senses in which knowledge about one class can prevent an object from being a random member of another class with respect to a third class. The confusing relationships between use and mention of expressions denoting classes will also be eliminated in the formal definitions. This too will help to make things clearer.

Two preliminary concepts, which are required for reasons that will only become apparent later, must be introduced before we proceed to the definitions of randomness and probability. The first of these is that of a biconditional chain. We shall say that the expression x is connected with the expression y by a biconditional chain in the rational corpora of level r_i and basis F—in symbols, $x r_i B_F y$— if there is an expression z such that x b y is an ingredient of z, and for every x' and y', if x' b y' is an ingredient of z, then either there is a rational corpus of level r_i and basis F of which x' b y' is an ingredient, or there is an x'' such that x' b x'' and x'' b y' are ingredients of z prior to x' b y'.

Δ102 $\ulcorner \xi \, r_i B_F \eta \urcorner$ *for* $\ulcorner (\exists \alpha)(\xi$ b η Ing $\alpha \cdot (\beta)(\gamma)(\beta$ b γ Ing $\alpha \supset \cdot$

        $(\exists\theta)(r_i RC_F \theta \cdot \beta$ b γ Ing $\theta)$ v $(\exists\gamma')(\beta$ b γ' $Pr_\alpha \beta$ b $\gamma \cdot$

        γ' b γ $Pr_\alpha \beta$ b $\gamma)))\urcorner$

---

7. The material from here to the end of the chapter may be skimmed by the reader unfamiliar
    with the notation.

There follow three useful metatheorems:

**1041 $\ulcorner (\exists\theta)\ (r_i \mathrm{RC_F}\ \theta\ \cdot\ \zeta\ \mathrm{b}\ \eta\ \mathrm{Ing}\ \theta) \supset \zeta\ r_i \mathrm{B_F}\ \eta \urcorner$ Δ102

**1042 $\ulcorner (\exists\theta)\ (r_n \mathrm{RC_F}\ \theta\ \cdot\ \zeta\ \mathrm{b}\ \eta\ \mathrm{Ing}\ \theta) \equiv \zeta\ r_n \mathrm{B_F}\ \eta \urcorner$ Δ95, Δ102

**1043 $\ulcorner \zeta\ r_i\ \mathrm{B_F}\ \eta\ \cdot\ \eta\ r_i \mathrm{B_F}\ \zeta'\ \cdot \supset \zeta\ r_i \mathrm{B_F}\ \zeta' \urcorner$

The other preliminary concept is that of rational membership. We need to be sure that if x e y is an ingredient of our rational corpus, and if x' e y' is an ingredient of it, then we are free to act in certain respects as if x pr x' e y cp y' were an ingredient of our rational corpus — though in point of fact it may not be. Thus we shall say that x is a rational member of y in the rational corpus of level r_i and basis F- in symbols, $x\ r_i$ Mem$_F$ y — if x e y is an ingredient of some expression z each of whose framed ingredients of the form x' e y' is either an ingredient of some rational corpus of level r_i and basis F, or has the form x'' pr x''' e y'' cp y''' where x'' e y'' and x''' e y''' occur earlier in the sequence.

Δ103 $\ulcorner \zeta\ r_i \mathrm{Mem_F}\ \eta \urcorner$ for $\ulcorner (\exists\gamma)\ (\zeta\ \mathrm{e}\ \eta\ \mathrm{Ing}\ \gamma\ \cdot\ (\alpha)\ (\beta)\ (\alpha\ \mathrm{e}\ \beta\ \mathrm{Ing}\ \gamma \supset\ \cdot$

$(\exists\ \theta)\ (r_i \mathrm{RC_F}\ \theta\ \cdot\ \alpha\ \mathrm{e}\ \beta\ \mathrm{Ing}\ \theta)\ \mathrm{v}\ (\exists\alpha')\ (\exists\beta')\ (\exists\alpha'')\ (\exists\beta'')$

$(\alpha'\ \mathrm{e}\ \beta'\ \mathrm{Pr}_\gamma\ \alpha\ \mathrm{e}\ \beta\ \cdot\ \alpha''\ \mathrm{e}\ \beta''\ \mathrm{Pr}_\gamma\ \alpha\ \mathrm{e}\ \beta\ \cdot\ \mathrm{Thm}\ \alpha\ \mathrm{id}\ \alpha'\ \mathrm{pr}\ \alpha''\ \cdot$

$(\exists\gamma')\ (\exists\theta)\ (r_i \mathrm{RC_F}\theta\ \cdot\ \mathrm{Thm}\ \beta\ \mathrm{id}\ (\beta'\ \mathrm{cp}\ \beta'')\ \mathrm{int}\ \gamma'\ \cdot\ \alpha\ \mathrm{e}\ \beta'$

$\mathrm{cp}\ \beta''\ \mathrm{cd}\ \alpha\ \mathrm{e}\ \beta\ \mathrm{Ing}\ \theta\ )))) \cdot \sim (\exists\theta)\ (r_i \mathrm{RC_F}\ \theta\ \cdot\ \mathrm{n}\ \zeta\ \mathrm{e}\ \eta\ \mathrm{Ing}\ \theta) \urcorner$

There follow three useful metatheorems analogous to those that hold for biconditional chains.

**1044 $\ulcorner (\exists\theta)\ (r_i \mathrm{RC_F}\ \theta\ \cdot\ \zeta\ \mathrm{e}\ \eta\ \mathrm{Ing}\ \theta) \supset \zeta\ r_i \mathrm{Mem_F}\ \eta \urcorner$ Δ103

**1045 $\ulcorner (\exists\theta)\ (r_n \mathrm{RC_F}\ \theta\ \cdot\ \zeta\ \mathrm{e}\ \eta\ \mathrm{Ing}\ \theta) \equiv \zeta\ r_n \mathrm{Mem_F}\ \eta \urcorner$ Δ103, Δ95

**1046 $\ulcorner \zeta\ r_i \mathrm{Mem_F}\eta\ \cdot\ \zeta'\ r_i \mathrm{Mem_F}\eta'\ \cdot \supset \zeta\ \mathrm{pr}\ \zeta' r_i \mathrm{Mem_F}\ \eta\ \mathrm{cp}\ \eta'$ Δ103

v $(\exists\theta)\ (r_i \mathrm{RC_F}\ \theta\ \cdot\ \mathrm{n}\ \zeta\ \mathrm{pr}\ \zeta'\ \mathrm{e}\ \eta\ \mathrm{cp}\ \eta'\ \mathrm{Ing}\ \theta) \urcorner$

It is obvious that there is an intimate connection between $(x_1;$ $(x_2;\ x_3))\ r_i$Mem$_F$ $(y_1\ \mathrm{cp}\ (y_2\ \mathrm{cp}\ y_3))$ and $(x_3;\ (x_1;\ x_2))\ r_i$Mem$_F$ $(y_3\ \mathrm{cp}\ (y_1\ \mathrm{cp}\ y_2))$. We shall say that one is a membership permutation of the other. The following three definitions, which may be construed as parts of Δ103, will make this subsidiary concept precise.

We shall say that x e v (this is the statement saying that the object designated by x is an element; it is defined in Quine's Δ70) is a member element of y e y', if there is an expression z, such that x e v is an ingredient of z and y e v is not an ingredient of z, and for every x', if x' e v is an ingredient of z, there is a w and a w'

such that w id w' pr x' is a theorem or w id x' pr w' is a theorem, and w e v is the same as y e v, or w e v is prior in z to x' e v. In symbols we shall express this by x e v ME y e y'.

Δ103a $\ulcorner \eta$ e v ME ζ e ζ' $\urcorner$ for $\ulcorner (\exists \gamma) (\eta$ e v Ing $\gamma \cdot \sim \zeta$ e v Ing $\gamma \cdot$

$(\alpha) (\alpha$ e v Ing $\gamma \supset (\exists \beta) (\exists \beta') ($ Thm β id β' pr α v

Thm β id α pr $\beta' \cdot (\beta$ e v $= \zeta$ e v) v $(\beta$ e v Pr$_\gamma$ α e v)))) $\urcorner$

We shall say that x e v is an ultimate member element of y e y' — in symbols, x e v UME y e y' — if x e v is a member element of y e y', and there is no x' such that x' e v is a member element of x e v.

Δ103b $\ulcorner \eta$ e v UME ζ e ζ' $\urcorner$ for $\ulcorner \eta$ e v ME ζ e $\zeta' \cdot \sim (\exists \alpha)(\alpha$ e v ME η e v)$\urcorner$

Finally, we shall say that x' e y' is a membership permutation of x e y — in symbols, x' e y' MP x e y — if x e y b x' e y' is a theorem, and for every z, z e v is an ultimate member element of x e y if and only if z e v is an ultimate member element of x' e y'.

Δ103c $\ulcorner \eta'$ e ζ' MP η e ζ $\urcorner$ for $\ulcorner$ Thm η' e ζ' b η e ζ $\cdot$

$(\alpha)(\alpha$ e v UME η e $\zeta \equiv \alpha$ e v UME η' e $\zeta')\urcorner$

The membership permutation defined by Δ103c is somewhat more general than the relation between two complex membership statements which can be obtained from one another by simply changing around the constituent symbols; it allows for notational and immaterial logical changes as well.

Let us write y' $r_i \mathrm{DP_F}(x,y,z)$ to mean that y' prevents x from being a random member of y with respect to z by difference, relative to the rational corpora of level r_i and basis F. On the basis of a slight and obvious generalization of the preceding analysis of randomness, to say that y' $r_i \mathrm{DP_F}(x,y,z)$ will be to say, first, that there are expressions x', z', and w', such that for every w, if w is a strongest statistical statement about y and z in the rational corpora of level r_i and basis F, then w' is a strongest statement about y' and z', w differs from w', x e z and x' e z' are connected by a biconditional chain, and x' is a rational member of y', all in the rational corpora of level r_i and basis F. Second, it is to say that there are no expressions x'', y'', and y''', such that x'' e y'' is a membership permutation of x e y and x'' is a rational member of y'' in the rational corpora of level r_i and basis F, and there is a rational corpus of this level and basis containing the statement x' e y' cd y'' incl y' cp y''', and that there are no expressions y'', z'', w'', such that there is a rational corpus of level r_i and basis F containing the statement x' e y' cd y'' incl y' and

x' is a rational member of y'' and x' e z' and x' e z'' are connected by a biconditional chain, and w'' is a strongest statement about y'' and z'' and is exactly as strong as w, and, finally, such that there is no subset of y'' to which x' is known to belong in which the frequency of objects belonging to z is known to differ from the frequency in y''.

$\Delta104$ $\ulcorner \beta' r_i \mathrm{DP_F}(\alpha, \beta, \gamma) \urcorner$ for $\ulcorner (\exists \alpha')(\exists \gamma')(\exists \eta')(\exists \eta)(\alpha$ e γ $r_i \mathrm{B_F}$ α' e γ' ·

η' $r_i \mathrm{S^*A_F}(\beta', \gamma')$ · $\eta r_i \mathrm{S^*A_F}(\beta, \gamma)$ · α' $r_i \mathrm{Mem_F}$ β' · η $r_i \mathrm{Dif_F}$ η' ·

$\sim (\exists \alpha'')(\exists \beta'')(\exists \beta''')(\alpha''$ $r_i \mathrm{Mem_F}$ β'' · α e β MP α'' e β'' ·

$(\exists \theta)(r_i \mathrm{RC_F}$ θ · α' e β' cd β'' incl β' cp β''' Ing θ)) ·

$\sim (\exists \beta'')(\exists \gamma'')(\exists \eta'')$ $(\alpha'$ $r_i \mathrm{Mem_F}$ β'' · α' e $\gamma' r_i \mathrm{B_F}$ α' e γ'' ·

η'' $r_i \mathrm{S^*A_F}(\beta'', \gamma'')$ · $(\exists \theta)(r_i \mathrm{RC_F}$ θ · α' e β' cd β'' incl β' Ing θ)·

$(\eta''')(\beta''')(\gamma''')(\alpha'$ $r_i \mathrm{Mem_F}$ β''' · α' e $\gamma'' r_i \mathrm{B_F}$ α' e γ''' ·

η''' $r_i \mathrm{S^*A_F}(\beta''', \gamma''')$ · $(\exists \theta)(r_i \mathrm{RC_F}$ θ · α' e β'' cd β''' incl β'') ·

$\supset \sim \eta''' r_i \mathrm{Dif_F}$ η''))) $\urcorner$

I shall write y' $r_i \mathrm{SP_F}(x, y, z)$ to mean that y' prevents x from being a random member of y with respect to z, relative to the rational corpora of level r_i and basis F, in virtue of stronger knowledge in these rational corpora about y' and a suitable z' than about y and z. To say that $y' r_i \mathrm{SP_F}(x, y, z)$ is to say that there are expressions x', z', and w', such that for every w, if w is a strongest statement in the rational corpora of level r_i and basis F about y and z, then w' is a strongest statement about y' and z', x' is a rational member of y', x e z and x' e z' are connected by a biconditional chain, and w' is stronger than w, all in the rational corpora of level r_i and basis F, and furthermore, that there is no y'' such that y'' prevents x' from being a random member of y' with respect to z', relative to the rational corpora of level r_i and basis F, by difference.

$\Delta105$ $\ulcorner \beta' r_i \mathrm{SP_F}(\alpha, \beta, \gamma) \urcorner for \ulcorner (\exists \alpha')(\exists \gamma')(\exists \eta')(\eta)(\eta r_i \mathrm{S^*A_F}(\beta, \gamma) \supset$·

$\eta' r_i \mathrm{S^*A_F}(\beta', \gamma')$ · α e $\gamma r_i \mathrm{B_F}$ α' e γ' · $\eta' r_i \mathrm{Str_F}$ η ·

$\alpha' r_i \mathrm{Mem_F}$ β' · $\sim (\exists \beta'')(\beta'' r_i \mathrm{DP_F}(\alpha', \beta', \gamma'))) \urcorner$

On the basis of the foregoing analysis, we may say that x is a random member of y with respect to z, relative to the rational corpora of level r_i and basis F, symbolically x $r_i \mathrm{Ran_F}(y, z)$, if nothing prevents it. Thus x $r_i \mathrm{Ran_F}(y, z)$ if there is a w which is a strongest statement about y and z in the rational corpora of level

r_i and basis F, and x is a rational member of y in the rational corpora of level r_i and basis F, and there is no expression y' which either prevents x from being a random member of y with respect to z by difference or prevents x from being a random member of y with respect to z by excess strength, relative to the rational corpora of level r_i and basis F.

Δ106 $\ulcorner \alpha\, r_i \operatorname{Ran}_F (\beta, \gamma)\urcorner$ for $\ulcorner (\exists \eta)(\eta\, r_i \mathrm{S^*A_F}\, (\beta, \gamma)) \cdot \alpha\, r_i \operatorname{Mem}_F \beta \cdot$

$\sim(\exists \beta')(\beta'\, r_i \mathrm{DP_F}\, (\alpha, \beta, \gamma)\ v\ \beta'\, r_i \mathrm{SP_F}\, (\alpha, \beta, \gamma))\urcorner$

The definition of probability is now obvious; two things, however, deserve comment. When we say that the probability of a statement S is $(p;p')$, we are relating a pair of fractions, not a pair of ratios, to the statement S. If it seems odd to take a pair of fractions as legislative for rational belief, it is only a little bit odder than taking rational numbers as legislative for it. If we want to *test* the rationality of the actual degree of belief a given person has in a given statement, then we must use ratios — namely those ratios *mentioned* in the probability statement indicating the degree of belief he ought to have. The oddity of having a pair of fractions rather than a single fraction will be dealt with in some detail when I come to compare my view of probability with those of the personalists and other betting enthusiasts. The other thing that deserves comment is that probability is defined only for statements equivalent to a statement of the form '... ∈---'. But in the framework of ML there is no limitation in this fact, as will be seen in the next chapter.

To say that the probability of the expression x, relative to the rational corpora of level r_i and basis F, is the pair of expressions $(y; y')$, in symbols, $x\, r_i \operatorname{Prob}_F (y; y')$, is simply to say that there are expressions x', w', and z', such that x and x' e z are biconditionally connected in the rational corpora of level r_i and basis F, x' is a random member of w' with respect to z' in the rational corpora of level r_i and basis F, and that pct $(w', z', (y; y'))$ is a strongest statement about w' and z' in the rational corpora of this basis.

Δ107 $\ulcorner \eta\, r_i \operatorname{Prob}_F (\psi; \xi)\urcorner$ for $\ulcorner (\exists \alpha)(\exists \beta)(\exists \gamma)(\eta\, r_i \mathrm{B_F}\, \alpha\ \mathrm{e}\ \gamma \cdot$

$\alpha\, r_i \operatorname{Ran}_F (\beta, \gamma) \cdot \operatorname{pct} (\beta, \gamma, (\psi; \xi))\ r_i \mathrm{S^*A_F}\, (\beta, \gamma))\urcorner$

CHAPTER TEN

Rational Inheritance

1. Many of the metatheorems in this chapter are complicated enough to deserve proof. Some of them even surprised me. A few words about the nature of these proofs are therefore in order. We have no axioms governing the logical behavior of the protosyntactical primitive M; but in general, no proof will depend upon the peculiar properties of this predicate. Just as the notation of joint denial and quantification has been introduced into protosyntax, so, we shall suppose, will the corresponding metatheorems appear among the protosyntactical truths; we shall suppose that the axioms of quantification of ML apply to protosyntactical formulas. Any metatheorem of Part Two of ML is therefore fair game for the justification of a line of a proof.

But we shall have another occasion to cite theorems and metatheorems from the body of ML; any of these theorems may be cited to justify a line of a proof of the form Thm x, where x is an expression in protosyntax designating an expression in ML which is a theorem. Thus we shall cite *100 to justify Thm x al nx, as well as to justify Thm x v ~ Thm x. Theorems and metatheorems in ML numbered 200 and higher may of course be cited only to justify lines of the form Thm x.

A metatheorem in ML establishes that there is always a proof for an expression of a certain form, i.e., that any expression of this form is a theorem. The protosyntactical metatheorems in this and subsequent chapters may be construed in the same way—as establishing the existence of a proof of any *protosyntactical* statement of a given form. In the same way, the metatheorems of ML could be translated into protosyntax and established as protosyntactical theorems, and whole classes of these could be established at once by protosyntactical metatheorems. But what really interests us is not the protosyntactical theoremhood of a protosyntactical statement saying that such and such a statement in ML is a theorem, but the theoremhood in ML of the statement in ML. Similarly, what interests us about the metatheorems in this and subsequent chapters is not the fact there is a proof for protosyntactical statements of a certain type, but the fact that a certain set of statements in ML bears certain relations (such as those defined in the preceding chapter) to certain other statements. To say that a statement x has a probability of so and so, relative to the set of statements F, is to make a statement about the object language—just as to say that a statement y is a theorem is to make a statement about the object language. In the latter case there will be a *proof* of y; metatheorems are useful merely because they enable us to establish the existence of proofs for whole classes of statements at once. In the former case there is generally nothing analogous to a proof. We are completely dependent upon metatheorems when it comes to establishing probability relationships. But these metatheorems may nevertheless ensure practical agreement with respect to particular cases; and in certain circumstances—perhaps in the majority of ordinary situations—the probability relation will turn out to be constructive after all, in the sense that *for all practical purposes* the non-theoremhood of x is constructive when nx is a theorem.

The techniques of proof that I shall employ in this and the following chapter are mainly borrowed from Quine. Square brackets indicate the deletion of an antecedent whose closure has been shown to be a theorem, in accordance with *111. Every line of a proof is a statement whose closure is a theorem. A one or two digit numeral appearing in the line of a proof is to be taken as standing for all the material, exclusive of any bracketed material, appearing in the line of that proof bearing that numeral. A three or four digit numeral is to be taken as standing for the metatheorem labelled with that numeral, or one of its alphabetic variants. A three digit numeral stands, of course, for a metatheorem in protosyntax having the same form as the one bearing that numeral in ML, not the metatheorem of that number in ML.

New protosyntactical notation will be introduced *ad libitum*, not only on the basis of definitions given by Quine, but also on the basis of hypothetical analogues of these definitions. These expressions, often introduced to serve very limited functions, will be introduced informally, as they have been in the past.

The prime object of the present chapter is to establish that if x is an ingredient of some rational corpus of level r_i and basis F, and if x cd y is an ingredient of some rational corpus of level r_{i+1} and basis F, then y is an ingredient of some rational corpus of level r_i and basis F. This is important as establishing the *rationality* of inferring a probable conclusion from premises that are themselves only probable. A long sequence of metatheorems is required to establish this for the rational corpora of level r_n and r_{n-1}, and it must be established for the rational corpora of level r_i and r_{i-1} before it can be established, by the same long sequence of metatheorems, for the rational corpora of level r_{i-1} and r_{i-2}. It would be possible to prove the metatheorem in question by induction, but the proof would be intolerably long, and we would miss many interesting sidelights. Instead, I shall prove a sequence of metatheorems leading to the special case of this metatheorem applied to the rational corpora of level r_n and of level r_{n-1}. The proofs will be constructed in such a way that they will also hold for the application of the metatheorem to the rational corpora of level r_i and r_{i-1}, if the metatheorem holds for rational corpora of level r_{i+1} and r_i, when we replace one justification of a line by another justification. I hope this rather spread-out form of mathematical induction won't confuse anyone—it would be possible, at any rate, to prove each metatheorem for each level of rational corpus separately.[1]

2. Some of the metatheorems in this chapter must be prefaced with the condition that ML and F are jointly consistent—i.e., that there is no rational corpus of the highest level containing both the statement x and its negation nx. The following definition will allow us to shorten the hypothesis; it is stated for all levels generally.

$\Delta 108$ $\ulcorner r_i C_F \urcorner$ for $\ulcorner \sim (\exists \eta)(\exists \Theta)(r_i RC_F \Theta \cdot \eta \ \mathrm{Ing} \ \Theta \cdot n\eta \ \mathrm{Ing} \ \Theta) \urcorner$

The following metatheorem depends directly on the properties of the protosyntactical primitive M.

**1101 $\ulcorner S_6 \widehat{\ } S_7 \ E \ \eta \cdot S_6 \widehat{\ } S_7 \ B \ \zeta \cdot \supset : \alpha \ \mathrm{Ing} \ \eta \ v \ \alpha \ \mathrm{Ing} \ \zeta \cdot \equiv \alpha \ \mathrm{Ing} \ \eta \widehat{\ } \zeta \urcorner$

**1102 $\ulcorner \sim S_6 \widehat{\ } S_7 \ P \ \eta \supset \eta \ \mathrm{Ing} \ S_6 \widehat{\ } S_7 \eta \widehat{\ } S_6 \widehat{\ } S_7 \urcorner$

Proof.

*100, $\Delta 29$, $\ulcorner [\Delta 29 \supset \cdot] \sim S_6 \widehat{\ } S_7 \ P \ \eta \supset \eta \ \mathrm{Ing} \ S_6 \widehat{\ } S_7 \eta \widehat{\ } S_6 \widehat{\ } S_7 \urcorner$

**1103 $\ulcorner r_i RC_F \ S_6 \widehat{\ } S_7 \eta \widehat{\ } S_6 \widehat{\ } S_7 \cdot \sim S_6 \widehat{\ } S_7 \ P \ \eta \cdot \supset (\exists \zeta)(r_i RC_F \ \zeta \cdot$
$\eta \ \mathrm{Ing} \ \zeta) \urcorner$

Proof.

*100 $\ulcorner [1102 \cdot \supset :] r_i RC_F \ S_6 \widehat{\ } S_7 \eta \widehat{\ } S_6 \widehat{\ } S_7 \cdot \sim S_6 \widehat{\ } S_7 \ P \ \eta \cdot \supset$
$r_i RC_F \ S_6 \widehat{\ } S_7 \eta \widehat{\ } S_6 \widehat{\ } S_7 \cdot \eta \ \mathrm{Ing} \ S_6 \widehat{\ } S_7 \eta \widehat{\ } S_6 \widehat{\ } S_7 \urcorner$ (1)

*232 $\ulcorner r_i RC_F \ S_6 \widehat{\ } S_7 \eta \widehat{\ } S_6 \widehat{\ } S_7 \cdot \eta \ \mathrm{Ing} \ S_6 \widehat{\ } S_7 \eta \widehat{\ } S_6 \widehat{\ } S_7 \cdot \supset \cdot (\exists \zeta)$
$(r_i RC_F \ \zeta \cdot \eta \ \mathrm{Ing} \ \zeta) \urcorner$ (2)

*100 $\ulcorner [1 \cdot 2 \cdot \supset :] 1103 \urcorner$

The citation of *232 in this proof is not quite cricket; it is only jus-

---

[1]. The rest of this chapter is devoted to proofs of theorems; most of these theorems will be stated in more general form in Chapter Twelve, where their significance will be discussed.

tified because, given axioms governing the protosyntactical primitive M, there will be an analogue of *232 holding for definite descriptions, but not for abstracts, which can be proved within protosyntax.

**1104 $\ulcorner r_n \mathrm{RC_F} \ \zeta \cdot \eta \ \mathrm{Ing} \ \zeta \cdot \supset (\exists \beta)(\eta \ \mathrm{Ing} \ \beta \cdot (\gamma)(\gamma \ \mathrm{Ing} \ \beta \supset \cdot$

$\gamma \ \mathrm{Ing} \ \mathrm{F} \ \mathrm{v} \ \mathrm{Ax} \ \gamma \ \mathrm{v} \ (\exists \delta)(\delta \ \mathrm{Pr}_\beta \ \gamma \cdot \delta \ \mathrm{cd} \ \gamma \ \mathrm{Pr}_\beta \ \gamma)))\urcorner$

Proof.

*100 $\ulcorner [\Delta 95 \supset \cdot] \ r_n \mathrm{RC_F} \ \zeta \supset (\alpha)(\alpha \ \mathrm{Ing} \ \zeta \supset (\exists \beta)(\alpha \ \mathrm{Ing} \ \beta \cdot$

$(\gamma)(\gamma \ \mathrm{Ing} \ \beta \supset \cdot \gamma \ \mathrm{Ing} \ \mathrm{F} \ \mathrm{v} \ \mathrm{Ax} \ \gamma \ \mathrm{v} \ (\exists \delta)(\delta \ \mathrm{Pr}_\beta \ \gamma \cdot$

$\delta \ \mathrm{cd} \ \gamma \ \mathrm{Pr}_\beta \ \gamma)))\urcorner$ (1)

*159 $\ulcorner [1 \equiv :] \ (\alpha)(r_n \mathrm{RC_F} \ \zeta \supset \cdot \alpha \ \mathrm{Ing} \ \zeta \supset (\exists \beta)(\alpha \ \mathrm{Ing} \ \beta \cdot (\gamma)$

$(\gamma \ \mathrm{Ing} \ \beta \supset \cdot \gamma \ \mathrm{Ing} \ \mathrm{F} \ \mathrm{v} \ \mathrm{Ax} \ \gamma \ \mathrm{v} \ (\exists \delta)(\delta \ \mathrm{Pr}_\beta \ \gamma \cdot$

$\delta \ \mathrm{cd} \ \gamma \ \mathrm{Pr}_\beta \ \gamma)))\urcorner$ (2)

*103 $\ulcorner [2 \supset :] \ r_n \mathrm{RC_F} \ \zeta \supset \cdot \eta \ \mathrm{Ing} \ \zeta \supset (\exists \beta)(\eta \ \mathrm{Ing} \ \beta \cdot (\gamma)$

$(\gamma \ \mathrm{Ing} \ \beta \supset \cdot \gamma \ \mathrm{Ing} \ \mathrm{F} \ \mathrm{v} \ \mathrm{Ax} \ \gamma \ \mathrm{v} \ (\exists \delta)(\delta \ \mathrm{Pr}_\beta \ \gamma \cdot$

$\delta \ \mathrm{cd} \ \gamma \ \mathrm{Pr}_\beta \ \gamma)))\urcorner$ (3)

*100 $\ulcorner [3 \supset :] \ 1104\urcorner$

**1105 $\ulcorner r_n \mathrm{RC_F} \ \zeta \equiv (\alpha)(\mathrm{S}_6\widehat{\ }\mathrm{S}_7 \ \mathrm{B} \ \zeta \cdot \mathrm{S}_6\widehat{\ }\mathrm{S}_7 \ \mathrm{E} \ \zeta \cdot \alpha \ \mathrm{Ing} \ \zeta \supset (\exists \beta)$

$(\alpha \ \mathrm{Ing} \ \beta \cdot (\gamma)(\gamma \ \mathrm{Ing} \ \beta \supset \cdot \gamma \ \mathrm{Ing} \ \mathrm{F} \ \mathrm{v} \ \mathrm{Ax} \ \gamma \ \mathrm{v} \ (\exists \delta)$

$(\delta \ \mathrm{Pr}_\beta \ \gamma \cdot \delta \ \mathrm{cd} \ \gamma \ \mathrm{Pr}_\beta \ \gamma))))\urcorner$

Proof.

*157 $\ulcorner (\alpha) (\mathrm{S}_6\widehat{\ }\mathrm{S}_7 \ \mathrm{B} \ \zeta \cdot \mathrm{S}_6\widehat{\ }\mathrm{S}_7 \ \mathrm{E} \ \zeta \cdot \alpha \ \mathrm{Ing} \ \zeta \supset (\exists \beta)(\alpha \ \mathrm{Ing} \ \beta \cdot$

$(\gamma)(\gamma \ \mathrm{Ing} \ \beta \supset \gamma \ \mathrm{Ing} \ \mathrm{F} \ \mathrm{v} \ \mathrm{Ax} \ \gamma \ \mathrm{v} \ (\exists \alpha ')(\alpha ' \ \mathrm{Pr}_\beta \ \gamma \cdot$

$\alpha ' \ \mathrm{cd} \ \gamma \ \mathrm{Pr}_\beta \ \gamma)))) \equiv r_n \mathrm{RC_F} \ \zeta\urcorner$ (1)

*100 $\ulcorner [1 \supset \cdot] 1105\urcorner$

**1106 $\ulcorner \eta \ \mathrm{Ing} \ \mathrm{S}_6\widehat{\ }\mathrm{S}_7\widehat{\ }\eta\widehat{\ }\mathrm{S}_6\widehat{\ }\mathrm{S}_7 \cdot (\exists \beta)(\eta \ \mathrm{Ing} \ \beta \cdot (\gamma)(\gamma \ \mathrm{Ing} \ \beta \supset$

$\gamma \ \mathrm{Ing} \ \mathrm{F} \ \mathrm{v} \ \mathrm{Ax} \ \gamma \ \mathrm{v} \ (\exists \delta)(\delta \ \mathrm{Pr}_\beta \ \gamma \cdot \delta \ \mathrm{cd} \ \gamma \ \mathrm{Pr}_\beta \ \gamma))) \cdot \supset$

$r_n \mathrm{RC_F} \ \mathrm{S}_6\widehat{\ }\mathrm{S}_7\widehat{\ }\eta\widehat{\ }\mathrm{S}_6\widehat{\ }\mathrm{S}_7\urcorner$

Proof.

*100, Δ29 $\ulcorner \eta \ \mathrm{Ing} \ \mathrm{S}_6\widehat{\ }\mathrm{S}_7\widehat{\ }\eta\widehat{\ }\mathrm{S}_6\widehat{\ }\mathrm{S}_7 \supset \sim \mathrm{S}_6\widehat{\ }\mathrm{S}_7 \ \mathrm{P} \ \eta\urcorner$ (1)

*100, Δ29 $\ulcorner \sim S_6\frown S_7\ P\ \eta \supset \cdot\ \alpha\ Ing\ S_6\frown S_7\frown \eta\frown S_6\frown S_7 \supset \alpha = \eta \urcorner$ (2)

*223 $\ulcorner \alpha = \eta \supset \cdot\ (\exists\beta)(\eta\ Ing\ \beta \cdot (\gamma)(\gamma\ Ing\ \beta \supset \cdot\ \gamma\ Ing\ F\ v\ Ax\ \gamma\ v$

$(\exists\delta)(\delta\ Pr_\beta\ \gamma \cdot \delta\ cd\ \gamma\ Pr_\beta\ \gamma))) \equiv (\exists\beta)(\alpha\ Ing\ \beta \cdot$

$(\gamma)(\gamma\ Ing\ \beta \supset \cdot\ \gamma\ Ing\ F\ v\ Ax\ \gamma\ v\ (\exists\delta)(\delta\ Pr_\beta\ \gamma \cdot$

$\delta\ cd\ \gamma\ Pr_\beta\ \gamma)))\urcorner$ (3)

*100 $\ulcorner[1 \cdot 2 \cdot 3 \cdot \supset:]\ \eta\ Ing\ S_6\frown S_7\frown \eta\frown S_6\frown S_7 \cdot (\exists\beta)(\eta\ Ing\ \beta \cdot (\gamma)$

$(\gamma\ Ing\ \beta \supset \cdot\ \gamma\ Ing\ F\ v\ Ax\ \gamma\ v\ (\exists\delta)(\delta\ Pr_\beta\ \gamma \cdot$

$\delta\ cd\ \gamma\ Pr_\beta\ \gamma))) \cdot \supset \cdot\ \alpha\ Ing\ S_6\frown S_7\frown \eta\frown S_6\frown S_7 \supset (\exists\beta)$

$(\alpha\ Ing\ \beta \cdot (\gamma)(\gamma\ Ing\ \beta \supset \cdot\ \gamma\ Ing\ F\ v\ Ax\ \gamma\ v\ (\exists\delta)$

$(\delta\ Pr_\beta\ \gamma \cdot \delta\ cd\ \gamma\ Pr_\beta\ \gamma)))\urcorner$ (4)

*134, *100, Δ19,

$\ulcorner S_6\frown S_7\ B\ S_6\frown S_7\frown \eta\frown S_6\frown S_7 \urcorner$ (5)

*134, *100, Δ20,

$\ulcorner S_6\frown S_7\ E\ S_6\frown S_7\frown \eta\frown S_6\frown S_7 \urcorner$ (6)

*100 $\ulcorner[4 \cdot 5 \cdot 6 \cdot \supset:]\ \eta\ Ing\ S_6\frown S_7\frown \eta\frown S_6\frown S_7 \cdot (\exists\beta)(\eta\ Ing\ \beta \cdot$

$(\gamma)(\gamma\ Ing\ \beta \supset \cdot\ \gamma\ Ing\ F\ v\ Ax\ \gamma\ v\ (\exists\delta)(\delta\ Pr_\beta\ \gamma \cdot$

$\delta\ cd\ \gamma\ Pr_\beta\ \gamma))) \cdot \supset \cdot\ S_6\frown S_7\ B\ S_6\frown S_7\frown \eta\frown S_6\frown S_7 \cdot$

$S_6\frown S_7\ E\ S_6\frown S_7\frown \eta\frown S_6\frown S_7 \cdot \alpha\ Ing\ S_6\frown S_7\frown \eta\frown S_6\frown S_7 \supset$

$(\exists\beta)(\alpha\ Ing\ \beta \cdot (\gamma)(\gamma\ Ing\ \beta \supset \cdot\ \gamma\ Ing\ F\ v\ Ax\ \gamma\ v$

$(\exists\delta)(\delta\ Pr_\beta\ \gamma \cdot \delta\ cd\ \gamma\ Pr_\beta\ \gamma)))\urcorner$ (7)

*159 $\ulcorner[(\alpha)\ 7 \supset::]\ \eta\ Ing\ S_6\frown S_7\frown \eta\frown S_6\frown S_7 \cdot (\exists\beta)(\eta\ Ing\ \beta \cdot (\gamma)$

$(\gamma\ Ing\ \beta \supset \cdot\ \gamma\ Ing\ F\ v\ Ax\ \gamma\ v\ (\exists\delta)(\delta\ Pr_\beta\ \gamma \cdot$

$\delta\ cd\ \gamma\ Pr_\beta\ \gamma))) \cdot \supset \cdot (\alpha)(S_6\frown S_7\ B\ S_6\frown S_7\frown \eta\frown S_6\frown S_7 \cdot$

$S_6\frown S_7\ E\ S_6\frown S_7\frown \eta\frown S_6\frown S_7 \cdot \alpha\ Ing\ S_6\frown S_7\frown \eta\frown S_6\frown S_7 \supset$

$(\exists\beta)(\alpha\ Ing\ \beta \cdot (\gamma)(\gamma\ Ing\ \beta \supset \cdot\ \gamma\ Ing\ F\ v\ Ax\ \gamma\ v$

$(\exists\delta)(\delta\ Pr_\beta\ \gamma \cdot \delta\ cd\ \gamma\ Pr_\beta\ \gamma)))\urcorner$ (8)

*123 $\ulcorner[1105 \cdot 8 :]\ 1106\urcorner$

In line (3) above I used a substitutivity-of-identity principle; although *223 comes from the part of ML which employs the concept of membership, a similar principle would have to be forthcoming in a fully formalized protosyntax.

**1107 $\ulcorner r_n\text{RC}_\text{F}\ \zeta\cdot\eta\ \text{Ing}\ \zeta\cdot\supset r_n\text{RC}_\text{F}\ \widehat{S_6\ S_7}\ \eta\ \widehat{\ }\ \widehat{S_6\ S_7}\urcorner$

Proof.

*100, Δ29, $\ulcorner\eta\ \text{Ing}\ \zeta\supset\sim\widehat{S_6\ S_7}\ \text{P}\ \eta\urcorner$ (1)

*100, Δ29, $\ulcorner\sim\widehat{S_6\ S_7}\ \text{P}\ \eta\supset\eta\ \text{Ing}\ \widehat{S_6\ S_7}\ \eta\ \widehat{\ }\ \widehat{S_6\ S_7}\urcorner$ (2)

*100, $\ulcorner[1\cdot2\cdot1104\cdot1106\cdot\supset:]1107\urcorner$

**1108 $\ulcorner(\exists\zeta)(r_n\text{RC}_\text{F}\ \zeta\cdot\eta\ \text{Ing}\ \zeta)\equiv r_n\text{RC}_\text{F}\ \widehat{S_6\ S_7}\ \eta\ \widehat{\ }\ \widehat{S_6\ S_7}\cdot\sim\widehat{S_6\ S_7}\ \text{P}\ \eta\urcorner$

Proof.

*161 $\ulcorner[(\zeta)\ 1107\cdot\equiv\cdot](\exists\zeta)(r_n\text{RC}_\text{F}\ \zeta\cdot\eta\ \text{Ing}\ \zeta)\supset$
$r_n\text{RC}_\text{F}\ \widehat{S_6\ S_7}\ \eta\ \widehat{\ }\ \widehat{S_6\ S_7}\urcorner$ (1)

*100 $\ulcorner[1\cdot1103\cdot\supset\cdot]1108\urcorner$

**1109 $\ulcorner r_n\text{RC}_\text{F}\ \zeta\cdot r_n\text{RC}_\text{F}\ \eta\cdot\supset r_n\text{RC}_\text{F}\ \widehat{\zeta\ \eta}\urcorner$

Proof.

*100 $\ulcorner[\Delta95\supset\cdot]\ r_n\text{RC}_\text{F}\ \zeta\supset\widehat{S_6\ S_7}\ \text{E}\ \zeta\urcorner$ (1)

*100 $\ulcorner[\Delta95\supset\cdot]\ r_n\text{RC}_\text{F}\ \eta\supset\widehat{S_6\ S_7}\ \text{B}\ \eta\urcorner$ (2)

*100 $\ulcorner[1\cdot2\cdot1101\cdot\supset:\cdot]\ r_n\text{RC}_\text{F}\ \zeta\cdot r_n\text{RC}_\text{F}\ \eta\cdot\supset:\alpha\ \text{Ing}\ \zeta\ \text{v}$
$\alpha\ \text{Ing}\ \eta\cdot\equiv\alpha\ \text{Ing}\ \widehat{\zeta\ \eta}\urcorner$ (3)

*122 $\ulcorner\alpha\ \text{Ing}\ \zeta\ \text{v}\ \alpha\ \text{Ing}\ \eta\cdot\equiv\alpha\ \text{Ing}\ \widehat{\zeta\ \eta}:\supset:\cdot\alpha\ \text{Ing}\ \zeta\ \text{v}$
$\alpha\ \text{Ing}\ \eta\cdot\supset(\exists\beta)(\alpha\ \text{Ing}\ \beta\cdot(\gamma)(\gamma\ \text{Ing}\ \beta\supset\cdot\gamma\ \text{Ing}\ \text{F}\ \text{v}$
$\text{Ax}\ \gamma\ \text{v}\ (\exists\delta)(\delta\ \text{Pr}_\beta\ \gamma\cdot\delta\ \text{cd}\ \gamma\ \text{Pr}_\beta\ \gamma))):\equiv\cdot$
$\alpha\ \text{Ing}\ \widehat{\zeta\ \eta}\supset(\exists\beta)(\alpha\ \text{Ing}\ \beta\cdot(\gamma)(\gamma\ \text{Ing}\ \beta\supset\cdot$
$\gamma\ \text{Ing}\ \text{F}\ \text{v}\ \text{Ax}\ \gamma\ \text{v}\ (\exists\delta)(\delta\ \text{Pr}_\beta\ \gamma\cdot\delta\ \text{cd}\ \gamma\ \text{Pr}_\beta\ \gamma)))\urcorner$ (4)

*100 $\ulcorner1104\supset:\ r_n\text{RC}_\text{F}\ \zeta\cdot r_n\text{RC}_\text{F}\ \eta\cdot\supset\cdot\alpha\ \text{Ing}\ \zeta\supset(\exists\beta)$
$(\alpha\ \text{Ing}\ \beta\cdot(\gamma)(\gamma\ \text{Ing}\ \beta\supset\cdot\gamma\ \text{Ing}\ \text{F}\ \text{v}\ \text{Ax}\ \gamma\ \text{v}\ (\exists\delta)$
$(\delta\ \text{Pr}_\beta\ \gamma\ \text{v}\ \delta\ \text{cd}\ \gamma\ \text{Pr}_\beta\ \gamma)))\urcorner$ (5)

*100 $\ulcorner[1104\supset:]\ r_n\text{RC}_\text{F}\ \zeta\cdot r_n\text{RC}_\text{F}\ \eta\cdot\supset\cdot\alpha\ \text{Ing}\ \eta\supset(\exists\beta)$
$(\alpha\ \text{Ing}\ \beta\cdot(\gamma)(\gamma\ \text{Ing}\ \beta\supset\cdot\gamma\ \text{Ing}\ \text{F}\ \text{v}\ \text{Ax}\ \gamma\ \text{v}\ (\exists\delta)$
$(\delta\ \text{Pr}_\beta\ \gamma\cdot\delta\ \text{cd}\ \gamma\ \text{Pr}_\beta\ \gamma)))\urcorner$ (6)

*100 $\ulcorner[3 \cdot 4 \cdot 5 \cdot 6 \cdot \supset :] r_n RC_F \ \zeta \cdot r_n RC_F \ \eta \cdot \supset \cdot \alpha \ \mathrm{Ing} \ \zeta \frown \eta \supset$

$(\exists \beta)(\alpha \ \mathrm{Ing} \ \beta \cdot (\gamma)(\gamma \ \mathrm{Ing} \ \beta \supset \cdot \gamma \ \mathrm{Ing} \ F \ v \ Ax \ \gamma \ v$

$(\exists \delta)(\delta \ Pr_\beta \ \gamma \cdot \delta \ cd \ \gamma \ Pr_\beta \ \gamma)))\urcorner$ (7)

*159 $\ulcorner[(\alpha) \ 7 \supset :] r_n RC_F \ \zeta \cdot r_n RC_F \ \eta \cdot \supset (\alpha)(\alpha \ \mathrm{Ing} \ \zeta \frown \eta \supset$

$(\exists \beta)(\alpha \ \mathrm{Ing} \ \beta \cdot (\gamma)(\gamma \ \mathrm{Ing} \ \beta \supset \cdot \gamma \ \mathrm{Ing} \ F \ v \ Ax \ \gamma \ v$

$(\exists \delta)(\delta \ Pr_\beta \ \gamma \cdot \delta \ cd \ \gamma \ Pr_\beta \ \gamma))))\urcorner$ (8)

*100 $\ulcorner[\Delta 95 \supset :] r_n RC_F \ \zeta \cdot r_n RC_F \ \eta \cdot \supset S_6 \frown S_7 \ B \ \zeta \urcorner$ (9)

*100 $\ulcorner[\Delta 95 \supset :] r_n RC_F \ \zeta \cdot r_n RC_F \ \eta \cdot \supset S_6 \frown S_7 \ E \ \eta \urcorner$ (10)

*100, $\Delta 19$, $\ulcorner S_6 \frown S_7 \ B \ \zeta \cdot S_6 \frown S_7 \ E \ \eta \cdot \supset \cdot S_6 \frown S_7 \ B \ \zeta \frown \eta \cdot$

$S_6 \frown S_7 \ E \ \zeta \frown \eta \urcorner$ (11)

*100,$\Delta 20$ $\ulcorner[8 \cdot 9 \cdot 10 \cdot 11 \cdot \supset :] 1109 \urcorner$
($\Delta 95$)

**1110 $\ulcorner (\exists \theta)(r_n RC_F \ \theta \cdot \eta \ \mathrm{Ing} \ \theta) \cdot (\exists \theta')(r_n RC_F \ \theta' \cdot \zeta \ \mathrm{Ing} \ \theta') \cdot$

$\supset (\exists \varphi)(r_n RC_F \ \varphi \cdot \eta \ \mathrm{Ing} \ \varphi \cdot \zeta \ \mathrm{Ing} \ \varphi) \urcorner$

Proof.

**1108 $\ulcorner (\exists \theta)(r_n RC_F \ \theta \cdot \eta \ \mathrm{Ing} \ \theta) \equiv r_n RC_F \ S_6 \frown S_7 \eta \frown S_6 \frown S_7 \cdot$

$\sim S_6 \frown S_7 \ P \ \eta \urcorner$ (1)

**1108 $\ulcorner (\exists \theta')(r_n RC_F \ \theta' \cdot \zeta \ \mathrm{Ing} \ \theta') \equiv r_n RC_F \ S_6 \frown S_7 \zeta \frown S_6 \frown S_7 \cdot$

$\sim S_6 \frown S_7 \ P \ \zeta \urcorner$ (2)

*100, $\Delta 29$ $\ulcorner \eta \ \mathrm{Ing} \ \theta \supset \sim S_6 \frown S_7 \ P \ \eta \urcorner$ (3)

*100, $\Delta 29$ $\ulcorner \zeta \ \mathrm{Ing} \ \theta' \supset \sim S_6 \frown S_7 \ P \ \zeta \urcorner$ (4)

*100, $\Delta 29$ $\ulcorner \sim S_6 \frown S_7 \ P \ \eta \supset \eta \ \mathrm{Ing} \ S_6 \frown S_7 \eta \frown S_6 \frown S_7 \urcorner$ (5)

*100, $\Delta 29$ $\ulcorner \sim S_6 \frown S_7 \ P \ \zeta \supset \zeta \ \mathrm{Ing} \ S_6 \frown S_7 \zeta \frown S_6 \frown S_7 \urcorner$ (6)

*100 $\ulcorner[5 \cdot 3 \cdot \supset :] r_n RC_F \ \theta \cdot \eta \ \mathrm{Ing} \ \theta \cdot \supset \eta \ \mathrm{Ing} \ S_6 \frown S_7 \eta \frown S_6 \frown S_7 \urcorner$ (7)

*100 $\ulcorner[4 \cdot 6 \cdot \supset :] r_n RC_F \ \theta' \cdot \zeta \ \mathrm{Ing} \ \theta' \cdot \supset \zeta \ \mathrm{Ing} \ S_6 \frown S_7 \zeta \frown S_6 \frown S_7 \urcorner$ (8)

*161 $\ulcorner[(\theta) \ 7 : \equiv :] (\exists \theta)(r_n RC_F \ \theta \cdot \eta \ \mathrm{Ing} \ \theta) \supset$

$\eta \ \mathrm{Ing} \ S_6 \frown S_7 \eta \frown S_6 \frown S_7 \urcorner$ (9)

*161 $\ulcorner[(\theta') \ 8 : \equiv \cdot] (\exists \theta')(r_n RC_F \ \theta' \cdot \zeta \ \mathrm{Ing} \ \theta') \supset$

$\zeta \ \mathrm{Ing} \ S_6 \frown S_7 \zeta \frown S_6 \frown S_7 \urcorner$ (10)

*100, Δ29 $\quad \ulcorner [9 \cdot 10 \cdot \supset :] \, (\exists \theta)(r_n RC_F \, \theta \cdot \eta \, \text{Ing} \, \theta) \cdot$

$\qquad\qquad (\exists \theta')(r_n RC_F \, \theta' \cdot \zeta \, \text{Ing} \, \theta') \cdot \supset \cdot$

$\qquad\qquad \eta \, \text{Ing} \, S_6 \frown S_7 \frown \eta \frown S_6 \frown S_7 \, S_6 \frown S_7 \, \zeta \frown S_6 \frown S_7 \cdot$

$\qquad\qquad \zeta \, \text{Ing} \, S_6 \frown S_7 \frown \eta \frown S_6 \frown S_7 \, S_6 \frown S_7 \, \zeta \frown S_6 \frown S_7 \urcorner$ $\qquad$ (11)

**1109 $\quad \ulcorner r_n RC_F \, S_6 \frown S_7 \frown \eta \frown S_6 \frown S_7 \cdot r_n RC_F \, S_6 \frown S_7 \, \zeta \frown S_6 \frown S_7 \cdot \supset$

$\qquad\qquad r_n RC_F \, S_6 \frown S_7 \frown \eta \frown S_6 \frown S_7 \, S_6 \frown S_7 \, \zeta \frown S_6 \frown S_7 \urcorner$ $\qquad$ (12)

*100 $\quad \ulcorner [1 \cdot 2 \cdot 11 \cdot 12 \cdot \supset :] \, (\exists \theta)(r_n RC_F \, \theta \cdot \eta \, \text{Ing} \, \theta) \cdot$

$\qquad\qquad (\exists \theta')(r_n RC_F \, \theta' \cdot \zeta \, \text{Ing} \, \theta') \cdot \supset$

$\qquad\qquad r_n RC_F \, S_6 \frown S_7 \frown \eta \frown S_6 \frown S_7 \, S_6 \frown S_7 \, \zeta \frown S_6 \frown S_7 \cdot$

$\qquad\qquad \eta \, \text{Ing} \, S_6 \frown S_7 \frown \eta \frown S_6 \frown S_7 \, S_6 \frown S_7 \, \zeta \frown S_6 \frown S_7 \cdot$

$\qquad\qquad \zeta \, \text{Ing} \, S_6 \frown S_7 \frown \eta \frown S_6 \frown S_7 \, S_6 \frown S_7 \, \zeta \frown S_6 \frown S_7 \urcorner$ $\qquad$ (13)

*232 $\quad \ulcorner [13 : \supset :] \, (\exists \varphi)((\exists \theta)(r_n RC_F \, \theta \cdot \eta \, \text{Ing} \, \theta) \cdot (\exists \theta)(r_n RC_F \, \theta' \cdot$

$\qquad\qquad \zeta \, \text{Ing} \, \theta') \cdot \supset r_n RC_F \, \varphi \cdot \eta \, \text{Ing} \, \varphi \cdot \zeta \, \text{Ing} \, \varphi) \urcorner$ $\qquad$ (14)

*160 $\quad \ulcorner [14 \equiv :] \, 1110 \urcorner$

Again, strictly speaking, we have used an improper principle; but we may suppose that an analogue of *232 holds for all the terms (i.e., abstracts) allowable in protosyntax.

**1111 $\quad \ulcorner \text{Thm} \, \zeta \supset r_n RC_F \, S_6 \frown S_7 \, \zeta \frown S_6 \frown S_7 \urcorner$

Proof.

*100 $\quad \ulcorner \gamma \, \text{Ing} \, \beta \supset \cdot \text{Ax} \, \gamma \, v \, (\exists \delta)(\delta \, \text{Pr}_\beta \, \gamma \cdot \delta \, \text{cd} \, \gamma \, \text{Pr}_\beta \, \gamma) : \supset :$

$\qquad\qquad \gamma \, \text{Ing} \, \beta \supset \cdot \gamma \, \text{Ing} \, F \, v \, \text{Ax} \, \gamma \, v \, (\exists \delta)(\delta \, \text{Pr}_\beta \, \gamma \cdot$

$\qquad\qquad \text{cd} \, \gamma \, \text{Pr}_\beta \, \gamma) \urcorner$ $\qquad$ (1)

*101 $\quad \ulcorner [(\gamma) \, 1 \supset :] \, (\gamma)(\gamma \, \text{Ing} \, \beta \supset \cdot \text{Ax} \, \gamma \, v \, (\exists \delta)(\delta \, \text{Pr}_\beta \gamma \cdot$

$\qquad\qquad \delta \, \text{cd} \, \gamma \, \text{Pr}_\beta \gamma)) \supset (\gamma)(\gamma \, \text{Ing} \, \beta \supset \cdot \gamma \, \text{Ing} \, F \, v \, \text{Ax} \, \gamma \, v$

$\qquad\qquad (\exists \delta)(\delta \, \text{Pr}_\beta \gamma \cdot \delta \, \text{cd} \, \gamma \, \text{Pr}_\beta \gamma)) \urcorner$ $\qquad$ (2)

*100 $\quad \ulcorner [2 \supset :] \, \zeta \, \text{Ing} \, \beta \cdot (\gamma)(\gamma \, \text{Ing} \, \beta \supset \text{Ax} \, \gamma \, v \, (\exists \delta)(\delta \, \text{Pr}_\beta \gamma \cdot$

$\qquad\qquad \delta \, \text{cd} \, \gamma \, \text{Pr}_\beta \gamma)) \cdot \supset \cdot \zeta \, \text{Ing} \, \beta \cdot (\gamma)(\gamma \, \text{Ing} \, \beta \supset$

$\qquad\qquad \gamma \, \text{Ing} \, F \, v \, \text{Ax} \, \gamma \, v \, (\exists \delta)(\delta \, \text{Pr}_\beta \, \gamma \cdot \delta \, \text{cd} \, \gamma \, \text{Pr}_\beta \, \gamma)) \urcorner$ $\qquad$ (3)

*149, Δ77 $\quad \ulcorner [(\beta) \, 3 \supset \cdot] \, \text{Thm} \, \zeta \supset (\exists \beta)(\zeta \, \text{Ing} \, \beta \cdot (\gamma)(\gamma \, \text{Ing} \, \beta \supset \cdot$

$$\gamma \text{ Ing F v Ax } \gamma \text{ v } (\exists\delta)(\delta \text{ Pr}_\beta \gamma \cdot$$

$$\overline{\delta \text{ cd } \gamma \text{ Pr}_\beta \gamma)))}^\rceil \tag{4}$$

*100 $\ulcorner [4 \cdot 1106 \cdot \supset] \text{ Thm } \zeta \supset r_n\text{RC}_\text{F} \ \overline{S_6\widehat{\ }S_7\widehat{\ }\zeta\widehat{\ }S_6\widehat{\ }S_7}^\rceil$

**1112 $\ulcorner r_n\text{RC}_\text{F} \ \theta \cdot \eta \text{ Ing } \theta \cdot \eta \text{ cd } \zeta \text{ Ing } \ \theta \supset r_n\text{RC}_\text{F} \ \overline{S_6\widehat{\ }S_7\widehat{\ }\zeta\widehat{\ }S_6\widehat{\ }S_7}^\rceil$

Proof.

**1104 $\ulcorner r_n\text{RC}_\text{F} \ \theta \cdot \eta \text{ Ing } \theta \cdot \supset (\exists\beta)(\eta \text{ Ing } \theta \cdot (\gamma)(\gamma \text{ Ing } \beta \supset \cdot$

$$\gamma \text{ Ing F v Ax } \gamma \text{ v } (\exists\delta)(\delta \text{ Pr}_\beta \gamma \cdot \delta \text{ cd } \gamma \text{ Pr}_\beta \gamma)))\overline{}^\rceil \tag{1}$$

**1104 $\ulcorner r_n\text{RC}_\text{F} \ \theta \cdot \eta \text{ cd } \zeta \text{ Ing } \theta \cdot \supset (\exists\beta')(\eta \text{ cd } \zeta \text{ Ing } \beta' \cdot$

$$(\gamma)(\gamma \text{ Ing } \beta' \supset \cdot \gamma \text{ Ing F v Ax } \gamma \text{ v } (\exists\delta)(\delta \text{ Pr}_{\beta'}\gamma \cdot$$

$$\overline{\delta \text{ cd } \gamma \text{ Pr}_{\beta'} \gamma)))}^\rceil \tag{2}$$

Here again we come to a step which depends on the intuitive properties of the primitive protosyntactical matrix M. It is clear that any plausible formalization of protosyntax will allow us to assert the conditional whose antecedent is the conjunction of the consequent of (1) with the consequent of (2), and whose consequent is:

$\ulcorner (\exists\beta'')(\zeta \text{ Ing } \beta'' \cdot (\gamma)(\gamma \text{ Ing } \beta'' \supset \gamma \text{ Ing F v Ax } \gamma \text{ v}$

$(\exists\delta)(\delta \text{ Pr}_{\beta''} \gamma \cdot \delta \text{ cd } \gamma \text{ Pr}_{\beta''}\gamma))).\overline{}^\rceil$

That this is so, may be seen from the fact that given any two expressions fulfilling the antecedent, we may construct an expression fulfilling the consequent by simply lopping off everything after the last occurrence of $S_6\widehat{\ }S_7$ in the first expression, and everything before the first occurrence of $S_6\widehat{\ }S_7$ in the second expression, and everything after the last occurrence of $S_6\widehat{\ }S_7$ in the second expression, concatenating these two expressions in the order indicated, and adding to the right hand end of this new expression, $\zeta\widehat{\ }S_6\widehat{\ }S_7$. Let us call the conditional described above 'A', and suppose that it already appears as a metatheorem.

*100 $\ulcorner [1 \cdot 2 \cdot \text{A} \cdot \supset :] r_n\text{RC}_\text{F} \ \theta \cdot \eta \text{ Ing } \theta \cdot \eta \text{ cd } \zeta \text{ Ing } \theta \cdot \supset$

$$(\exists\beta'')(\zeta \text{ Ing } \beta'' \cdot (\gamma)(\gamma \text{ Ing } \beta'' \supset \cdot \gamma \text{ Ing F v Ax } \gamma \text{ v}$$

$$(\exists\delta)(\delta \text{ Pr}_{\beta''} \gamma \cdot \delta \text{ cd } \gamma \text{ Pr}_{\beta''} \gamma)))\overline{}^\rceil \tag{3}$$

*100, $\Delta 29$ $\ulcorner \eta \text{ cd } \zeta \text{ Ing } \theta \supset \sim \overline{S_6\widehat{\ }S_7 \text{ P } \zeta}^\rceil$ (4)

*100, $\Delta 29$ $\ulcorner \sim \overline{S_6\widehat{\ }S_7 \text{ P } \zeta \supset \zeta \text{ Ing } S_6\widehat{\ }S_7\widehat{\ }\zeta\widehat{\ }S_6\widehat{\ }S_7}^\rceil$ (5)

*100 $\ulcorner [3 \cdot 4 \cdot 5 \cdot 1106 \cdot \supset] \overline{1112}^\rceil$

**1113 $\ulcorner(\exists\theta)(r_n\mathrm{RC_F}\ \theta\cdot\eta\ \mathrm{Ing}\ \theta\cdot\eta\ \mathrm{cd}\ \zeta\ \mathrm{Ing}\ \theta)\supset$

$\qquad r_n\mathrm{RC_F}\ \widehat{S_6}\widehat{S_7}\ \zeta\ \widehat{S_6}\widehat{S_7}\urcorner$

Proof.

*161 $\ulcorner[(\ \theta\ )112\equiv]\ 1113\urcorner$

**1114 $\ulcorner\mathrm{Thm}\ \eta\ \mathrm{cd}\ \zeta\cdot r_n\mathrm{RC_F}\ \widehat{S_6}\widehat{S_7}\eta\ \widehat{S_6}\widehat{S_7}\cdot\supset r_n\mathrm{RC_F}\ \widehat{S_6}\widehat{S_7}\zeta\ \widehat{S_6}\widehat{S_7}\urcorner$

Proof.

**1111 $\ulcorner\mathrm{Thm}\ \eta\ \mathrm{cd}\ \zeta\supset r_n\mathrm{RC_F}\ \widehat{S_6}\widehat{S_7}\eta\ \mathrm{cd}\ \zeta\ \widehat{S_6}\widehat{S_7}\urcorner$ (1)

Once more we must have recourse to the protosyntactical properties of the primitive matrix M:

$\ulcorner\mathrm{Thm}\ \eta\ \mathrm{cd}\ \zeta\supset\ \sim\widehat{S_6}S_7\ \mathrm{P}\ \eta\urcorner$ (2)

$\ulcorner\mathrm{Thm}\ \eta\ \mathrm{cd}\ \zeta\supset\ \sim\widehat{S_6}S_7\ \mathrm{P}\ \eta\ \mathrm{cd}\ \zeta\urcorner$ (3)

*100 $\ulcorner[1\cdot2\cdot3\cdot1108\cdot\supset:]\ \mathrm{Thm}\ \eta\ \mathrm{cd}\ \zeta\cdot r_n\mathrm{RC_F}\ \widehat{S_6}\widehat{S_6}\eta\ \widehat{S_6}S_7\cdot\supset$

$\qquad(\exists\theta)(r_n\mathrm{RC_F}\ \theta\cdot\eta\ \mathrm{Ing}\ \theta)\cdot(\exists\theta')(r_n\mathrm{RC_F}\ \theta'\cdot$

$\qquad\eta\ \mathrm{cd}\ \zeta\ \mathrm{Ing}\ \theta')\urcorner$ (4)

*100 $\ulcorner[4\cdot1110\cdot\supset:]\ \mathrm{Thm}\ \eta\ \mathrm{cd}\ \zeta\cdot r_n\mathrm{RC_F}\ \widehat{S_6}\widehat{S_7}\eta\ \widehat{S_6}S_7\cdot\supset$

$\qquad(\exists\theta'')(r_n\mathrm{RC_F}\ \theta''\cdot\eta\ \mathrm{Ing}\ \theta''\cdot\eta\ \mathrm{cd}\ \zeta\ \mathrm{Ing}\ \theta'')\urcorner$ (5)

*100 $\ulcorner[5\cdot1113\cdot\supset:]\ 1114\urcorner$

**1115 $\ulcorner\mathrm{Thm}\ \eta\ \mathrm{cd}\ \zeta\cdot(\exists\theta)(r_n\mathrm{RC_F}\ \theta\cdot\eta\ \mathrm{Ing}\ \theta)\cdot\supset$

$\qquad(\exists\Phi)(r_n\mathrm{RC_F}\ \varphi\cdot\zeta\ \mathrm{Ing}\ \varphi)\urcorner$

Proof.

As in the preceding proof, we have,

$\ulcorner\mathrm{Thm}\ \eta\ \mathrm{cd}\ \zeta\supset\cdot\sim\widehat{S_6}S_7\ \mathrm{P}\ \eta\cdot\sim\widehat{S_6}S_7\ \mathrm{P}\ \zeta\urcorner$ (1)

*100 $\ulcorner[1108\supset:]\sim\widehat{S_6}S_7\ \mathrm{P}\ \eta\supset\cdot r_n\mathrm{RC_F}\ \widehat{S_6}\widehat{S_7}\eta\ \widehat{S_6}S_7\equiv$

$\qquad(\exists\theta)(r_n\mathrm{RC_F}\ \theta\cdot\eta\ \mathrm{Ing}\ \theta)\urcorner$ (2)

*100 $\ulcorner[110\supset:]\sim\widehat{S_6}S_7\ \mathrm{P}\ \zeta\supset\cdot r_n\mathrm{RC_F}\ \widehat{S_6}\widehat{S_7}\ \zeta\ \widehat{S_6}S_7\equiv$

$\qquad(\exists\varphi)(r_n\mathrm{RC_F}\ \varphi\cdot\zeta\ \mathrm{Ing}\ \varphi)\urcorner$ (3)

*100 $\ulcorner[1\cdot2\cdot3\cdot1114\cdot\supset:]\ 1115\urcorner$

**1116 ⌜Thm $\zeta \supset (\exists \eta)(r_n RC_F\ \eta \cdot \zeta\ \text{Ing}\ \eta)$⌝

Proof.

As before, ⌜Thm $\zeta \supset\ \sim S_6\frown S_7\ P\ \zeta$⌝ (1)

**1111 ⌜Thm $\zeta \supset r_n RC_F\ S_6\frown S_7\frown \zeta\frown S_6\frown S_7$⌝ (2)

*100 ⌜[1 ⵯ 2 · ⊃] Thm $\zeta \supset \cdot r_n RC_F\ S_6\frown S_7\frown \zeta\frown S_6\frown S_7\ \cdot \sim S_6\frown S_7\ P\ \zeta$⌝ (3)

*123 ⌜[3 · 1108 · ⊃] **1116⌝

**1117 ⌜$(\exists \theta)(r_n RC_F\ \theta \cdot \zeta\ \text{Ing}\ \theta \cdot \eta\ \text{Ing}\ \theta) \supset \cdot (\exists \theta)(r_n RC_F\ \theta \cdot$

$\zeta\ \text{Ing}\ \theta) \cdot (\exists \theta)(r_n RC_F\ \theta \cdot \eta\ \text{Ing}\ \theta)$⌝

Proof.

*100 ⌜$r_n RC_F\ \theta \cdot \zeta\ \text{Ing}\ \theta \cdot \eta\ \text{Ing}\ \theta \cdot \supset r_n RC_F\ \theta \cdot \zeta\ \text{Ing}\ \theta \cdot$

$r_n RC_F\ \theta \cdot \eta\ \text{Ing}\ \theta$⌝ (1)

*149 ⌜$[(\ \theta\ )\ 1 \supset]\ (\exists \theta)(r_n RC_F\ \theta \cdot \zeta\ \text{Ing}\ \theta \cdot \eta\ \text{Ing}\ \theta) \supset$

$(\exists \theta)(r_n RC_F\ \theta \cdot \zeta\ \text{Ing}\ \theta \cdot r_n RC_F\ \theta \cdot \eta\ \text{Ing}\ \theta)$⌝ (2)

*156 ⌜$(\exists \theta)(r_n RC_F\ \theta \cdot \zeta\ \text{Ing}\ \theta \cdot r_n RC_F\ \theta \cdot \eta\ \text{Ing}\ \theta) \equiv \cdot$

$(\exists \theta)(r_n RC_F\ \theta \cdot \zeta\ \text{Ing}\ \theta) \cdot (\exists \theta)(r_n RC_F\ \theta \cdot$

$\eta\ \text{Ing}\ \theta)$⌝ (3)

*100 ⌜[2 · 3 · ⊃] 1117⌝

*1118 ⌜$(\exists \eta)(r_i RC_F\ \eta \cdot \zeta\ \text{Ing}\ \eta) \supset \text{Stat}\ \zeta$⌝

Proof.

As Ax z is defined (in △76) by Quine,

⌜Ax $\zeta \supset \text{Stat}\ \zeta$⌝ (1)

Since F is to contain only statements as ingredients,

⌜$\zeta\ \text{Ing}\ F \supset \text{Stat}\ \zeta$⌝ (2)

If ⌜ζ' cd ζ⌝ is a statement, i.e., contains no free variables, then ζ is a statement, i.e., contains no free variables.

⌜Stat ζ' cd $\zeta \supset \text{Stat}\ \zeta$⌝ (3)

Thus the sequence of expressions which justifies the inclusion of ζ in a rational corpus can contain only statements; and since ζ is included in this sequence, ζ is a statement. If $r_i \leqslant r_{n-1}$, we know there is an α, and γ, such that ⌜Stat ζ b α e γ⌝.

If ML and F are not consistent, then every statement is an ingredient of a rational corpus of the highest level:

**1119 $\ulcorner \sim r_n C_F \supset \cdot \text{Stat } \zeta \supset r_n RC_F \ S_6 \widehat{\ } S_7 \widehat{\ } \zeta \widehat{\ } S_6 \widehat{\ } S_7 \urcorner$

Proof.

*1117, Δ108 $\ulcorner \sim r_n C_F \supset (\exists \theta)(r_n RC_F \ \theta \cdot \eta \text{ Ing } \theta)\urcorner$ (1)

Δ77 (*100) $\ulcorner \text{Stat } \eta \cdot \text{Stat } \zeta \cdot \supset \text{Thm } \eta \text{ cd } (n\eta \text{ cd } \zeta)\urcorner$ (2)

*100 $\ulcorner [1 \cdot 2 \cdot 1118 \cdot \supset] \sim r_n C_F \supset (\exists \theta)(r_n RC_F \ \theta \cdot \eta \text{ Ing } \theta) \cdot$
   $\text{Stat } \zeta \supset \text{Thm } \eta \text{ cd } (n\eta \text{ cd } \zeta)\urcorner$ (3)

*100 $\ulcorner [1115 \cdot 3 \cdot \supset] \sim r_n C_F \supset \cdot \text{Stat } \zeta \supset (\exists \theta)(r_n RC_F \ \theta \cdot$
   $n\eta \text{ cd } \zeta \text{ Ing } \theta)\urcorner$ (4)

*1117, Δ108 $\ulcorner \sim r_n C_F \supset (\exists \theta)(r_n RC_F \ \theta \cdot n\eta \text{ Ing } \theta)\urcorner$ (5)

*100 $\ulcorner [4 \cdot 5 \cdot 1110 \cdot \supset :] \sim r_n C_F \cdot \supset \text{Stat } \zeta \supset (\exists \theta)(r_n RC_F \ \theta \cdot$
   $n\eta \text{ Ing } \theta \cdot n\eta \text{ cd } \zeta \text{ Ing } \theta)\urcorner$ (6)

*100 $\ulcorner [6 \cdot 1112 \cdot \supset] 1119\urcorner$

**1120 $\ulcorner r_n C_F \supset \cdot (\exists \zeta)(r_n RC_F \ \zeta \cdot \eta \text{ Ing } \zeta) \supset \sim (\exists \zeta)(r_n RC_F \ \zeta \cdot$
   $n\eta \text{ Ing } \zeta)\urcorner$

Proof.

**1110 $\ulcorner (\exists \zeta)(r_n RC_F \ \zeta \cdot \eta \text{ Ing } \zeta) \cdot (\exists \zeta)(r_n RC_F \ \zeta \cdot n\eta \text{ Ing } \zeta) \cdot \supset$
   $(\exists \zeta)(r_n RC_F \ \zeta \cdot \eta \text{ Ing } \zeta \cdot n\eta \text{ Ing } \zeta)\urcorner$ (1)

*100, Δ108 $\ulcorner [1 : \supset] 1120\urcorner$

Now we come to a more interesting group of metatheorems. Let
us suppose that there is a metatheorem to the effect that if x' and
y' are ordinary ratio-matrices, i.e., if RM x' and RM y', as defined
hypothetically in Δ97a, and if $x \text{ e } S_2 \text{ a } x'$ and $y \text{ e } S_2 \text{ a } y'$ are theorems, then either $x \ _s\text{gr } y$ or $y \ _s\text{gr } x$ or $y \text{ id } x$ is a theorem. This
is not a far fetched supposition, since given any fractions such as
'1/1', '4/7', '3/8', etc., there is a mechanical procedure for deciding which of the above three relationships hold.

**1121 $\ulcorner \text{RM}\alpha' \cdot \text{RM}\beta' \cdot \text{Thm } \alpha \text{ e } S_2 a \ \alpha' \cdot \text{Thm } \beta \text{ e } S_2 a \ \beta' \cdot \supset \cdot$
   $\text{Thm } \alpha \text{ id } \beta \text{ v Thm } \alpha \ _s\text{gr } \beta \text{ v Thm } \beta \ _s\text{gr } \alpha\urcorner$

(This metatheorem would follow from the somewhat simpler metatheorem which states that if RM x and RM y, then one of the above mentioned expressions is a theorem.)

The next metatheorem merely states a few of the ordinary properties of theoremhood.

**1122a ⌜Thm ζ · Thm η · ⊃ Thm η cj ζ⌝

Proof. *100 and ⌜Stat ζ · Stat η · ⊃ Thm ζ cd (η cd η cj ζ)⌝, and *104

**1122b ⌜Thm ζ b η ⊃ · Thm ζ ≡ Thm η⌝

Proof. *104 and D5

*1122c ⌜Thm ζ · Thm nη · ⊃ Thm ζ al η⌝

Proof. *100 and ⌜Stat nη ⊃ Stat η⌝, ⌜Stat ζ · Stat η ⊃ Thm ζ cd ζ al η⌝, and *104

The following metatheorem establishes a necessary and sufficient condition for a statement ⌜pct(β,γ,(α;α'))⌝ to be a statistical statement about β and γ in the rational corpora of level r_i and basis F. It will be more useful than Δ97b itself.

**1123 ⌜pct (β,γ,(α;α')) r_i SA$_F$(β,γ) ≡ (∃ θ)(r_i RC$_F$ θ ·

pct (β,γ,(α;α')) Ing θ) · (∃β')(∃γ')(∃η)(∃η')

(Vbl η · Vbl η' · r_i RMat$_F$ β' · r_i RMat$_F$ γ' ·

Thm η qu (η e β b β') · Thm η' qu (η' e β int γ b γ')) ·

(∃ζ)(∃ζ')(RM ζ · RM ζ' · Thm α e S$_2$aζ ·

Thm α' e S$_2$aζ')⌝

Proof.

By a series of obvious and tedious applications of *100 and *123, and by a change of variables and a few applications of *158, we have:

⌜[Δ97b ≡ ·] φ r_i SA$_F$(β,γ) ≡ (∃ θ)(r_i RC$_F$ θ · φ Ing θ) ·

(∃β')(∃γ')(∃η)(∃η')(Vbl η · Vbl η' · r_i RMat$_F$ β' ·

r_i RMat$_F$ γ' · Thm η qu (η e β b β') ·

Thm η' qu (η' e β int γ b γ') · (∃β'')(∃γ'')(φ =

pct (β,γ,(β'';γ'')) · (∃ζ)(∃ζ')(RM ζ · RM ζ' ·

Thm β'' e S$_2$aζ · Thm γ'' e S$_2$aζ'))⌝   (1)

In virtue of the presumptive properties of the protosyntactical primitive M, we will have also,

$$\ulcorner \text{pct}(\beta,\gamma,(\alpha;\alpha')) = \text{pct}(\beta,\gamma,(\beta'';\gamma'')) \cdot \equiv \cdot \alpha = \beta'' \cdot \alpha' = \gamma'' \urcorner \quad (2)$$

*123 $\ulcorner [2 \supset :](\exists\beta'')(\exists\gamma'')(\text{pct}(\beta,\gamma,(\beta,\gamma,(\alpha',\alpha')) =$

$$\text{pct}(\beta,\gamma,(\beta'';\gamma'')) \cdot (\exists\zeta)(\exists\zeta')(\text{RM }\zeta \cdot \text{RM }\zeta' \cdot$$

$$\text{Thm }\beta'' \text{ e } S_2\text{a}\zeta \cdot \text{Thm }\gamma'' \text{ e } S_2\text{a}\zeta')) \cdot \equiv \cdot (\exists\beta'')(\exists\gamma'')$$

$$(\alpha = \beta'' \cdot \alpha' = \gamma'' \cdot (\exists\zeta)(\exists\zeta')(\text{RM }\zeta \cdot \text{RM }\zeta' \cdot$$

$$\text{Thm }\beta'' \text{ e } S_2\text{a}\zeta \cdot \text{Thm }\gamma'' \text{ e } S_2\text{a}\zeta')) \urcorner \quad (3)$$

By employing a version of *234, modified to fit protosyntax and to enable us to apply it to two variables at once, we finally achieve:

*100 $\ulcorner [3 \cdot \text{modified} *234 \cdot \supset \cdot](\exists\beta'')(\exists\gamma'')(\text{pct}(\beta,\gamma,(\alpha;\alpha')) =$

$$\text{pct}(\beta,\gamma,(\beta'';\gamma'')) \cdot (\exists\zeta)(\exists\zeta')(\text{RM }\zeta \cdot \text{RM }\zeta' \cdot$$

$$\text{Thm }\beta'' \text{ e } S_2\text{a}\zeta \cdot \text{Thm }\gamma'' \text{ e } S_2\text{a}\zeta')) \cdot \equiv \cdot (\exists\zeta)(\exists\zeta')$$

$$\text{RM }\zeta \cdot \text{RM }\zeta' \cdot \text{Thm }\beta'' \text{ e } S_2\text{a}\zeta \cdot \text{Thm }\gamma'' \text{ e } S_2\text{a}\zeta')) \urcorner \quad (4)$$

Writing $\ulcorner \text{pct}(\beta,\gamma,(\alpha;\alpha'))$ for φ in line (1) to yield (1'), $\urcorner$

*123, (4) $\ulcorner [1' \cdot \equiv \cdot] 1123 \urcorner$

**1124 $\ulcorner \text{pct}(\beta,\gamma,(\psi;\xi))r_i\text{SA}_F(\beta,\gamma) \cdot \text{pct}(\beta',\gamma',$

$$(\psi';\xi')) r_i\text{SA}_F(\beta',\gamma') \cdot \supset \cdot \text{Thm}(\psi \text{ id } \psi' \text{ cj}$$

$$\xi \text{ id } \xi') \text{ v Thm}((\psi \text{ }_s\text{gr }\psi' \text{ cj } \xi \text{ }_s\text{gr }\xi') \text{ al}$$

$$(\psi' \text{}_s\text{gr }\psi \text{ cj } \xi'\text{}_s\text{gr }\xi)) \text{ v Thm}((\psi \text{}_s\text{gr }\psi' \text{ cj } \xi'\text{}_s\text{gr }\xi) \text{ al}$$

$$(\psi' \text{ id } \psi \text{ cj } \xi'\text{}_s\text{gr }\xi) \text{ al }(\psi \text{}_s\text{gr }\psi' \text{ cj } \xi' \text{ id } \xi)) \text{ v}$$

$$\text{Thm}((\psi'\text{}_s\text{gr }\psi \text{ cj } \xi \text{ }_s\text{gr }\xi') \text{ al }(\psi' \text{ id } \psi \text{ cj } \xi \text{ }_s\text{gr }\xi')$$

$$\text{al }(\psi'\text{}_s\text{gr }\psi \text{ cj } \xi \text{ id } \xi')) \urcorner$$

Proof.

*100 $\ulcorner [1123 \cdot \supset \cdot] \text{pct}(\beta,\gamma,(\psi;\xi)) r_i\text{SA}_F(\beta,\gamma) \cdot \supset \cdot (\exists\eta)(\exists\eta')$

$$(\text{RM }\eta \cdot \text{RM }\eta' \cdot \text{Thm }\psi \text{ e } S_2\text{a}\eta \cdot \text{Thm }\xi \text{ e } S_2\text{a}\eta') \urcorner \quad (1)$$

*100 $\ulcorner [1123 \cdot \supset \cdot] \text{pct}(\beta',\gamma',(\psi';\xi')) r_i\text{SA}_F(\beta',\gamma') \supset$

$$(\exists\zeta)(\exists\zeta')(\text{RM }\zeta \cdot \text{RM }\zeta' \cdot \text{Thm }\psi' \text{ e } S_2\text{a}\zeta \cdot$$

$$\text{Thm }\xi' \text{ e } S_2\text{a}\zeta') \urcorner \quad (2)$$

*100, *158 $\ulcorner[1 \cdot 2 \cdot \supset :]$ pct $(\beta,\gamma,(\psi;\xi))\, r_i \mathrm{SA_F}(\beta,\gamma) \cdot$ pct $(\beta',\gamma',$

$\qquad\qquad (\psi',\xi'))\, r_i \mathrm{SA_F}(\beta',\gamma') \cdot \supset \cdot (\exists\zeta')(\exists\zeta)(\exists\eta)(\exists\eta')$

$\qquad\qquad (\mathrm{RM}\ \eta \cdot \mathrm{RM}\ \eta' \cdot \mathrm{Thm}\ \psi\ \mathrm{e}\ \mathrm{S_2 a}\eta \cdot \mathrm{Thm}\ \xi\ \mathrm{e}\ \mathrm{S_2 a}\eta' \cdot$

$\qquad\qquad \mathrm{RM}\ \zeta \cdot \mathrm{RM}\ \zeta' \cdot \mathrm{Thm}\ \psi'\ \mathrm{e}\ \mathrm{S_2 a}\zeta \cdot$

$\qquad\qquad \mathrm{Thm}\ \xi'\ \mathrm{e}\ \mathrm{S_2 a}\zeta')\ulcorner$ (3)

*100, *123, *158 $\ulcorner[3 \equiv\, :$pct $(\beta,\gamma,(\psi;\xi))\, r_i \mathrm{SA_F}(\beta,\gamma) \cdot$ pct $(\beta',\gamma',$

  *138 $\qquad\qquad (\psi';\xi'))\, r_i \mathrm{SA_F}(\beta',\gamma') \cdot \supset \cdot (\exists\zeta')(\exists\eta')$

$\qquad\qquad (\mathrm{RM}\ \eta' \cdot \mathrm{RM}\ \zeta' \cdot \mathrm{Thm}\ \xi\ \ \mathrm{e}\ \mathrm{S_2 a}\eta' \cdot$

$\qquad\qquad \mathrm{Thm}\ \xi'\ \mathrm{e}\ \mathrm{S_2 a}\zeta') \cdot (\exists\zeta)(\exists\eta)(\mathrm{RM}\ \zeta \cdot$

$\qquad\qquad \mathrm{RM}\ \eta \cdot \mathrm{Thm}\ \psi\ \mathrm{e}\ \mathrm{S_2 a}\eta \cdot$

$\qquad\qquad \mathrm{Thm}\ \psi'\ \mathrm{e}\ \mathrm{S_2 a}\zeta)\urcorner$ (4)

**1121, *161 $\ulcorner(\exists\zeta')(\exists\eta')(\mathrm{RM}\ \eta' \cdot \mathrm{RM}\ \zeta' \cdot \mathrm{Thm}\ \xi\ \mathrm{e}\ \mathrm{S_2 a}\eta' \cdot$

$\qquad\qquad \mathrm{Thm}\ \xi'\ \mathrm{e}\ \mathrm{S_2 a}\zeta') \supset (\mathrm{Thm}\ \xi\ \mathrm{id}\ \xi'\ \mathrm{v}$

$\qquad\qquad \mathrm{Thm}\ \xi\ _\mathrm{s}\mathrm{gr}\ \xi'\ \mathrm{v}\ \mathrm{Thm}\ \xi'\ _\mathrm{s}\mathrm{gr}\ \xi)\urcorner$ (5)

**1121, *161 $\ulcorner(\exists\zeta)(\exists\eta)(\mathrm{RM}\ \zeta \cdot \mathrm{RM}\ \eta \cdot \mathrm{Thm}\ \psi\ \mathrm{e}\ \mathrm{S_2 a}\eta \cdot$

$\qquad\qquad \mathrm{Thm}\ \psi'\ \mathrm{e}\ \mathrm{S_2 a}\zeta) \supset (\mathrm{Thm}\ \psi\ \mathrm{id}\ \psi'\ \mathrm{v}$

$\qquad\qquad \mathrm{Thm}\ \psi\ _\mathrm{s}\mathrm{gr}\ \psi'\ \mathrm{v}\ \mathrm{Thm}\ \psi'\ _\mathrm{s}\mathrm{gr}\ \psi)\urcorner$ (6)

*100 $\ulcorner[4 \cdot 5 \cdot 6 \cdot \supset :]$ pct $(\beta,\gamma,(\psi;\xi))\, r_i \mathrm{SA_F}(\beta,\gamma) \cdot$ pct $(\beta',\gamma',$

$\qquad\qquad (\psi';\xi'))\, r_i \mathrm{SA_F}(\beta',\gamma') \cdot \supset \cdot (\mathrm{Thm}\ \xi\ \mathrm{id}\ \xi'\ \mathrm{v}$

$\qquad\qquad \mathrm{Thm}\ \xi\ _\mathrm{s}\mathrm{gr}\ \xi'\ \mathrm{v}\ \mathrm{Thm}\ \xi'\ _\mathrm{s}\mathrm{gr}\ \xi) \cdot (\mathrm{Thm}\ \psi\ \mathrm{id}\ \psi'\ \mathrm{v}$

$\qquad\qquad \mathrm{Thm}\ \psi\ _\mathrm{s}\mathrm{gr}\ \psi'\ \mathrm{v}\ \mathrm{Thm}\ \psi'\ _\mathrm{s}\mathrm{gr}\ \psi)\urcorner$ (7)

*100 $\ulcorner[1122\mathrm{a}, 1122\mathrm{b}, 1122\mathrm{c}\ \text{ad lib.} \cdot 7 \cdot \supset\,]\ 1124\urcorner$

**1125 $\ulcorner\mathrm{Thm}\ \zeta \supset (\exists\eta)(r_i \mathrm{RC_F}\ \eta \cdot \zeta\ \mathrm{Ing}\ \eta) \cdot \supset (1021 \cdot$

$\qquad\qquad 1022 \ldots 1039)\urcorner$

Proof.

*100 $\ulcorner[1124 \supset\,]\ 1125\urcorner$

Note that the 'i' in **1125 acts like a free variable. We have not established **1021 $-$ **1039 in general, but only hypothetically. So far, we can only eliminate the hypothesis for the rational corpora of level r_n, as shown by the following metatheorem.

**1126 $\ulcorner r_i = r_n \cdot \supset 1021 \cdot 1022 \cdot 1023 \cdot \ldots \cdot 1039\urcorner$

Proof.

*100 $\ulcorner [1116 \cdot 1125 \cdot \supset] 1126\urcorner$

**1127 $\ulcorner r_n C_F \supset \sim \eta\, r_n Str_F\, \eta\urcorner$

Proof.

(ML) $\ulcorner$Thm n$((\psi\, _s gr\, \psi\, cj\, \xi\, _s gr\, \xi)$ al $(\psi\, id\, \psi\, cj\, \xi\, _s gr\, \xi)$ al

$\quad\quad (\psi\, _s gr\, \psi\, cj\, \xi\, id\, \xi))\urcorner$ (1)

*100 $\ulcorner [1116 \cdot 1 \cdot \supset] (\exists\zeta)(r_n RC_F\, \zeta \cdot n((\psi\, _s gr\, \psi\, cj\, \xi\, _s gr\, \xi)$ al

$\quad\quad (\psi\, id\, \psi\, cj\, \xi _s gr\, \xi)$ al $(\psi\, _s gr\, \psi\, cj\, \xi\, id\, \xi))\, Ing\, \zeta)\urcorner$ (2)

*100, Δ98 $\ulcorner r_n C_F \cdot [2 \cdot] \supset \sim \eta\, r_n Str_F\, \eta\urcorner$

**1128 $\ulcorner \sim r_n C_F \supset \cdot \eta\, r_n SA_F(\eta',\eta'') \supset \eta\, r_n Str_F\, \eta\urcorner$

Proof.

Let the statement whose denial is said to be a theorem in the first line of the last proof be abbreviated $\ulcorner$S.$\urcorner$

(ML) $\ulcorner$Thm nS$\urcorner$ (1)

*100 $\ulcorner [1 \cdot 1116 \cdot 1118 \cdot \supset]$ Stat nS$\urcorner$ (2)

Δ38, Δ47 $\ulcorner [2 \supset]$ Stat S$\urcorner$ (3)

*100 $\ulcorner [1119 \cdot 3 \cdot \supset \cdot] \sim r_n C_F \supset r_n RC_F\, S_6 \widehat{\ } S_7 \widehat{\ } S \widehat{\ } S_6 \widehat{\ } S_7\urcorner$ (4)

$\ulcorner [1 \supset] \sim S_6 \widehat{\ } S_7\, P\, S\urcorner$ (5)

*100, Δ98 $\ulcorner [5 \cdot 1103 \cdot 4 \cdot \supset] 1128\urcorner$

**1129 $\ulcorner \sim r_n C_F \supset \sim \eta\, r_n S^* A_F(\beta,\gamma)\urcorner$

Proof.

*100, Δ99 $\ulcorner [1128 \supset] 1129\urcorner$

Metatheorem **1128 has shown that if F and ML are not jointly consistent, then any statistical statement is stronger than itself; an immediate consequence of this, expressed in **1129, is that there is no strongest statistical statement about a given subject matter. From this in turn, it follows that no statement has a probability, if ML and F are jointly inconsistent; and this leads to the conclusion that in this situation no rational corpus other than that of the highest level will have any ingredients. In this sense, inconsistency in the rational corpora of the highest level is not hereditary. The following three metatheorems establish this curious fact.

**1130 $\ulcorner \sim r_n C_F \supset \sim \eta \ r_n \mathrm{Prob}_F(\psi;\xi)\urcorner$

Proof: *100, Δ107, $\ulcorner[1129 \supset] \ 1130\urcorner$

**1131 $\ulcorner \sim r_n C_F \supset \sim (r_{n-1} RC_F \ \eta \cdot \zeta \ \mathrm{Ing} \ \eta)\urcorner$

Proof: *100, Δ95a $\ulcorner[1130 \supset] \ 1131\urcorner$

**1132 $\ulcorner r_i \neq r_n \supset : \sim r_n C_F \supset \cdot \sim (r_i RC_F \ \zeta \cdot \eta \ \mathrm{Ing} \ \zeta)\urcorner$

Proof:

for $r_i = r_{n-1},$ $\ulcorner 1132 \urcorner$

for $r_i = r_{n-2}$

*100, Δ99, $\ulcorner[1131 \supset] \sim r_n C_F \supset \sim \eta \ r_{n-1} S^* A_F(\beta,\gamma)\urcorner$ (1)

*100, Δ107 $\ulcorner[1 \supset] \sim r_n C_F \supset \sim \zeta \ r_{n-1} \mathrm{Prob}_F(\psi,\xi)\urcorner$ (2)

*100, Δ95b $\ulcorner[2 \supset] \sim r_n C_F \supset \cdot \sim (r_{n-2} RC_F \ \eta \cdot \zeta \ \mathrm{Ing} \ \eta)\urcorner$ (3)

And so on, to,

$\ulcorner \sim r_n C_F \supset \cdot \sim (r_1 RC_F \ \zeta \cdot \eta \ \mathrm{Ing} \ \zeta)\urcorner$

An obvious corollary is:

**1133 $\ulcorner r_i \neq r_n \supset \cdot \sim r_n C_F \supset r_i C_F \urcorner$

Proof.

*100 $\ulcorner \sim (r_i RC_F \eta \cdot \zeta \ \mathrm{Ing} \ \eta) \cdot \supset \cdot \sim (r_i RC_F \ \eta \cdot \zeta \ \mathrm{Ing} \ \eta \cdot$

$n \zeta \ \mathrm{Ing} \ \eta)\urcorner$ (1)

*100, *159, Δ8, $\ulcorner[1132 \cdot 1 \cdot \supset] \ 1133\urcorner$

3.   The next group of metatheorems will establish that if ML and F are jointly consistent, then every ingredient of a rational corpus of level r_n will also be an ingredient of a rational corpus of level r_{n-1}. From now on reference to the theoremhood in ML of statements answering to certain descriptions in the protosyntax of ML will be increasingly frequent. A line in a proof,

    Thm'....'

will be justified on the left by a citation such as 'ML*100', if *100 in ML justifies '...'; the argument being that if '...' is an instance of *100, then 'Thm'...'' will be a theorem in protosyntax. If several theorems or metatheorems are required to lead to '...' by a fairly obvious route, the reference to the left of the line will cite all of them.

The first really interesting theorem of this section is that if a given level of rational corpus is consistent; and if x cd y is a theorem, and there is a rational corpus of this level and basis containing x, then there is one containing y; then there is no statement stronger in this level and basis of rational corpus than any statement pct $(z,w,(t;t))$.

**1142 $\quad \ulcorner r_i C_F \cdot (\eta)(\zeta)(\text{Thm } \eta \text{ cd } \zeta \cdot (\exists \theta)(r_i RC_F \ \theta \cdot \eta \text{ Ing } \theta) \cdot \supset$

$(\exists \theta)(r_i RC_F \ \theta \cdot \zeta \text{ Ing } \theta)) \cdot \supset \sim \eta \ r_i Str_F \text{ pct }(\beta,\gamma,(\alpha;\alpha))\urcorner$

Proof.

Ratio extension
of ML; D 72 $\quad \ulcorner \text{Thm pct }(\beta',\gamma',(\alpha';\alpha'')) \text{ cd }(\alpha'' \ _s\text{gr } \alpha' \text{ al}$

$\alpha'' \text{ id } \alpha')\urcorner$ $\hfill (1)$

Ratio extension
of ML $\quad \ulcorner \text{Thm }(\alpha'' \ _s\text{gr } \alpha' \text{ al } \alpha'' \text{ id } \alpha') \text{ cd n }((\alpha' \ _s\text{gr } \alpha \text{ cj}$

$\alpha'' \text{ id } \alpha) \text{ al }(\alpha' \text{ id } \alpha \text{ cj } \alpha \ _s\text{gr } \alpha'') \text{ al}$

$(\alpha' \ _s\text{gr } \alpha \text{ cj } \alpha \ _s\text{gr } \alpha'')\urcorner$ $\hfill (2)$

*100, Δ98 $\ulcorner r_i C_F \cdot (\eta)(\zeta)(\text{Thm } \eta \text{ cd } \zeta \cdot (\exists \theta)(r_i RC_F \ \theta \cdot$
*158, (1),(2)

$\eta \text{ Ing } \theta) \cdot \supset (\exists \theta)(r_i RC_F \cdot \zeta \text{ Ing } \theta)) \cdot \supset :$

$[1120 \supset : \cdot] (\exists \beta')(\exists \gamma')(\exists \alpha')(\exists \alpha'')(\eta =$

$\text{pct }(\beta',\gamma',(\alpha';\alpha'')) \cdot \eta \ r_i SA_F(\beta',\gamma')) \cdot \supset$

$\sim \eta \ r_i Str_F(\text{pct }(\beta,\gamma,(\alpha;\alpha))) \cdot \urcorner$ $\hfill (3)$

*100, Δ98 $\ulcorner \sim (\exists \beta')(\exists \gamma')(\exists \alpha')(\exists \alpha'')(\eta = \text{pct }(\beta',\gamma',(\alpha';\alpha''))) \cdot$
*158

$\eta \ r_i SA_F(\beta',\gamma')) \cdot \supset \sim \eta \ r_i Str_F \text{ pct }(\beta,\gamma,$

$(\alpha;\alpha))\urcorner$ $\hfill (4)$

*100 $\ulcorner [3 \cdot 4 \cdot \supset] 1142 \urcorner$

If x is a variable foreign to y, and y is a statement and an ingredient of some rational corpus of level r_i and basis F, then (subject to the same general hypotheses as set down for **1142) the statement that the x abstract of y belongs to the unit class of the universal class will be an ingredient of some rational corpus of level r_i and basis F. The statement saying that the x abstract of

y belongs to the unit class of the universal class will be expressed after the fashion of Quine's Δ71 as x a y e unt v. Quine's Δ65 defines 'fx' as the alphabetically earliest variable foreign to x.

**1143 $\ulcorner (\eta)(\zeta)(\text{Thm } \eta \text{ cd } \zeta \cdot (\exists \theta)(r_i \text{RC}_\text{F} \ \theta \cdot \eta \text{ Ing } \theta) \cdot \supset$

$(\exists \theta)(r_i \text{RC}_\text{F} \ \theta \cdot \zeta \text{ Ing } \theta)) \supset : (\exists \theta)(r_i \text{RC}_\text{F} \ \theta \cdot$

$\beta \text{ Ing } \theta) \supset (\exists \theta)(r_i \text{RC}_\text{F} \ \theta \cdot \text{f}\beta\text{a}\beta \text{ e unt v Ing } \theta)\urcorner$

Proof.

ML (*102,*193) $\ulcorner \text{Thm } \beta \text{ cd f}\beta\text{a}\beta \text{ id v}\urcorner$ (1)

ML (†345,†210, $\ulcorner \text{Thm f}\beta\text{a}\beta \text{ id v cd f}\beta\text{a}\beta \text{ e unt v} \cdot \urcorner$ (2)
      *100)

ML (*100,*104) $\ulcorner [1 \cdot 2 \cdot \supset] \text{ Thm } \beta \text{ cd f}\beta\text{a}\beta \text{ e unt v}\urcorner$ (3)

**231 $\ulcorner [3 \supset] 1143 \urcorner$

The double star beside the reference to Quine's metatheorem 231, serves here and in later proofs to indicate that the metatheorem in question is to be considered modified to apply to protosyntactical terms (denoting expressions) rather than to logical terms (denoting classes).

**1144 $\ulcorner (\eta)(\zeta)(\text{Thm } \eta \text{ cd } \zeta \cdot (\exists \theta)(r_i \text{RC}_\text{F} \ \theta \cdot \eta \text{ Ing } \theta) \cdot \supset$

$(\exists \theta)(r_i \text{RC}_\text{F} \theta \cdot \zeta \text{ Ing } \theta)) \supset (\exists \theta)(r_i \text{RC}_\text{F} \ \theta \cdot$

$\beta \text{ Ing } \theta) \supset (\exists \theta)(r_i \text{RC}_\text{F} \ \theta \cdot \text{pct (unt f}\beta\text{a}\beta,\text{unt v},$

$(\text{``}_s1\text{''};\text{``}_s1\text{''})) \text{ Ing } \theta)\urcorner$

Proof.

ML (ι x ϵ 1, $_s1 = 1/1$) $\ulcorner \text{Thm } \beta \text{ cd pct (unt f}\beta\text{a}\beta,\text{unt v},$

$(\text{``}_s1\text{''};\text{``}_s1\text{''}))\urcorner$ (1)

**231, *100 $\ulcorner [1 \cdot \supset] 1144 \urcorner$

Here, for the first time, I have employed quotation marks within protosyntactical contexts; it would be possible to spell out the entire statistical statement in terms of the allowable notation of protosyntax, but the resulting expression would be more complex and not nearly so clear. This practise will lead to no trouble so long as we remember that while $_s1$ is a ratio, "$_s1$" is a fraction which can be eliminated from any protosyntactical context in which it occurs— it is not, however, even the name of an expression—it is *part* of the name of a complex expression.

**1145 $\ulcorner r_i C_F \cdot (\eta)(\zeta)(\text{Thm } \eta \text{ cd } \zeta \cdot (\exists \theta)(r_i RC_F \; \theta \cdot \eta \text{ Ing } \theta) \cdot \supset$
$(\exists \theta)(r_i RC_F \; \theta \cdot \zeta \text{ Ing } \theta)) \cdot \supset \cdot (\exists \theta)(r_i RC_F \; \theta \cdot$
$\beta \text{ Ing } \theta) \supset \text{pct}(\text{unt } f\beta a\beta, \text{unt } v, (\text{"}_s 1, \text{"}; \text{"}_s 1\text{"}))$
$r_i S^*A_F (\text{unt } f\beta a\beta, \text{ unt } v)\urcorner$

Proof.

**1015 $\ulcorner r_i \text{RMat}_F f (\text{unt } v) \text{ e v cj f} (\text{unt } v) \text{ id } v \cdot$
$r_i \text{RMat}_F f (f\beta a\beta) \text{ e v cj f} (f\beta a\beta) \text{id } f\beta a\beta \urcorner$ (1)

ML x ϵ y $\equiv \cdot$ x ϵ V $\cdot \iota$x $\subset$ y
$\vert$ Thm f (unt v) qu (f (unt v) e unt v b (f (unt v) e v cj
$\quad$ f (unt v) id v))$\urcorner$ (2)

$\ulcorner$Thm f (fβaβ) qu (f (fβaβ) e v b (f (fβaβ) e v cj f (fβaβ) id
$\quad$ fβaβ))$\urcorner$ (3)

**234b, *100, Δ97b, $\ulcorner [1 \cdot 2 \cdot 3 \cdot \supset]$ $r_i RC_F \cdot (\eta)(\zeta)(\text{Thm } \eta \text{ cd } \zeta \cdot$
$(\exists \theta)(r_i RC_F \; \theta \cdot \eta \text{ Ing } \theta) \cdot \supset (\exists \theta)(r_i RC_F \; \theta \cdot \zeta \text{ Ing } \theta)) \cdot$
$\supset \cdot (\exists \theta)(r_i RC_F \; \theta \cdot \beta \text{ Ing } \theta) \supset (\exists \beta')(\exists \gamma')(\exists \eta')(\exists \eta'')$
$(\text{Vbl } \eta' \cdot \text{Vbl } \eta'' \cdot r_i \text{RMat}_F \; \beta' \cdot r_i \text{RMat}_F \; \gamma' \cdot$
$\text{Thm } \eta' \text{qu} (\eta \text{ e unt } f\beta a\beta \text{ b } \beta') \cdot \text{Thm } \eta'' \text{qu} (\eta'' \text{ e unt } f\beta a\beta$
$\text{int unt v b } \gamma'))\urcorner$ (4)

Δ97a $\ulcorner$RM S$_2$ id "$_s$1"$\urcorner$ (5)

*100, ML: $_s$1 ϵ $\hat{x}(x = {}_s 1)$ $\ulcorner$Thm "$_s$1" e S$_2$a(S$_2$ id "$_s$1")$\urcorner$ (6)

**234b, *158, *100: $\ulcorner [6 \cdot \supset] (\exists \zeta')(\exists \zeta'')(\text{RM } \zeta' \cdot \text{RM } \zeta'' \cdot$
$\text{Thm "}_s 1\text{" e S}_2 a\zeta' \cdot \text{Thm "}_s 1\text{" e}$
$S_2 a\zeta'')\urcorner$ (7)

*100 $\ulcorner [4 \cdot 7 \cdot 1144 \cdot \supset]$ $r_i C_F \cdot (\eta)(\zeta)(\text{Thm } \eta \text{ cd } \zeta \cdot (\exists \theta)$
$(r_i RC_F \; \theta \cdot \eta \text{ Ing } \theta) \cdot \supset (\exists \theta)(r_i RC_F \; \theta \cdot \zeta \text{ Ing } \theta)) \cdot$
$\supset \cdot (\exists \theta)(r_i RC_F \; \theta \cdot \beta \text{ Ing } \theta) \supset \text{pct} (\text{unt } f\beta a\beta b,$
$\text{unt } v, (\text{"}_s 1\text{"}; \text{"}_s 1\text{"})) r_i SA_F (\text{unt } f\beta a\beta, \text{unt } v)\urcorner$ (8)

*100, Δ99 $\ulcorner [8 \cdot 1142 \cdot \supset] 1145\urcorner$

**1146　$\ulcorner r_i C_F \cdot (\eta)(\zeta)(\text{Thm } \eta \text{ cd } \zeta \cdot (\exists \theta)(r_i RC_F \ \theta \cdot \eta \text{ Ing } \theta) \cdot$

$$\supset (\exists \theta)(r_i RC_F \ \theta \cdot \zeta \text{ Ing } \theta)) \cdot \supset$$

$$\sim \beta'' r_i SP_F \ \text{f}\beta\text{a}\beta, \text{unt f}\beta\text{a}\beta, \text{unt v})$$

Proof.

*100　$\ulcorner [1142 \supset] \ \eta'' \ r_i S^*A_F(\beta'',\gamma'') \supset \sim \eta'' \ r_i Str_F \text{ pct (unt f}\beta\text{a}\beta, \text{unt}$

$$\text{v}; (``_s 1''; ``_s 1'')) \urcorner \tag{1}$$

ML, D 72　$\ulcorner \text{Thm pct (unt f}\beta\text{a}\beta, \text{unt v}, (``_s 1''; ``_s 1'')) \text{ cd}$

$$\text{n (pct (unt f}\beta\text{a}\beta, \text{ unt v}, (\alpha; \alpha')) \text{ cj n} (\alpha' \text{ id} ``_s 1'')) \urcorner \tag{2}$$

*100, Δ101,　$\ulcorner [2 \supset :] \ r_i C_F \cdot (\eta)(\zeta)(\text{Thm } \eta \text{ cd } \zeta \cdot (\exists \theta)(r_i RC_F \ \theta \cdot$

$$\eta \text{ Ing } \theta) \cdot \supset (\exists \theta)(r_i RC_F \ \theta \cdot \zeta \text{ Ing } \theta)) \cdot \supset :$$

$$\eta \ r_i S^*A_F (\text{unt f}\beta\text{a}\beta, \text{unt v}) \cdot \supset \sim \eta \ r_i Dif_F$$

$$\text{pct (unt f}\beta\text{a}\beta, \text{unt v}, (``_s 1''; ``_s 1'')) \urcorner \tag{3}$$

*100, Δ98, Δ99　$\ulcorner \eta \ r_i S^*A_F (\text{unt f}\beta\text{a}\beta, \text{unt v}) \cdot$

$$\eta' r_i S^*A_F (\text{unt } \beta\text{a}\beta, \text{unt v}) \cdot \supset$$

$$\sim \eta \ r_i Str_F \ \eta' \urcorner \tag{4}$$

*100　$\ulcorner [3 \cdot 4 \cdot 1031 \cdot 1032 \cdot \supset :] \ r_i C_F \cdot (\eta)(\zeta)(\text{Thm } \eta \text{ cd } \zeta \cdot$

$$(\exists \theta)(r_i RC_F \ \theta \cdot \eta \text{ Ing } \theta) \cdot \supset (\exists \theta)(r_i RC_F \ \theta \cdot \zeta \text{ Ing } \theta)) :$$

$$(\exists \theta)(r_i RC_F \ \theta \cdot \beta \text{ Ing } \theta) : \supset \cdot \eta' r_i S^*A_F (\text{unt f}\beta\text{a}\beta, \text{unt v}) \supset$$

$$\eta' r_i S=_F \text{ pct (unt f}\beta\text{a}\beta, \text{unt v}, (``_s 1''; ``_s 1'')) \urcorner \tag{5}$$

*100, Δ101,　$\ulcorner [1 \cdot 5 \cdot 1034 \cdot \supset] \ 1146 \urcorner$

**1147　$\ulcorner (\eta)(\zeta)(\text{Thm } \eta \text{ cd } \zeta \cdot (\exists \theta)(r_i RC_F \ \theta \cdot \eta \text{ Ing } \theta) \cdot \supset$

$$(\exists \theta)(r_i RC_F \ \theta \cdot \zeta \text{ Ing } \theta)) \cdot \supset \cdot \eta \ r_i B_F \ \zeta \supset$$

Proof.　$$\zeta \ r_i B_F \ \eta \urcorner$$

Let the links of the biconditional chain connecting η and ζ be:

$$\ulcorner \eta \text{ b } \eta_1 \urcorner; \ulcorner \eta_1 \text{ b } \eta_2 \urcorner; \ulcorner \eta_2 \text{ b } \eta_3 \urcorner; \ldots \ulcorner \zeta_3 \text{ b } \zeta_2 \urcorner; \ulcorner \zeta_2 \text{ b } \zeta_1 \urcorner; \ulcorner \zeta_1 \text{ b } \zeta \urcorner$$

Each of these links is an ingredient of some rational corpus of level r_i and basis F:

Δ102　$\ulcorner (\exists \theta)(r_i RC_F \ \theta \cdot \zeta_1 \text{ b } \zeta \text{ Ing } \theta) \urcorner$

ML (*100)　$\ulcorner \text{Thm } \zeta_1 \text{ b } \zeta \text{ cd } \zeta \text{ b } \zeta_1 \urcorner$

By the hypothesis of **1147, we thus have,

$\ulcorner(\exists\theta.)(r_i\,\mathrm{RC_F}\ \theta\cdot\zeta\ \mathrm{b}\ \zeta_1\ \mathrm{Ing}\ \theta\,)\urcorner$

But if we apply this argument to each link of the chain connecting η and ζ, we can construct a new chain connecting ζ and η:

$\ulcorner\zeta\ \mathrm{b}\ \zeta_1\urcorner;\ \ulcorner\zeta_1\ \mathrm{b}\ \zeta_2\urcorner;\ \ulcorner\zeta_2\ \mathrm{b}\ \zeta_3\urcorner;\ \dots\ \ulcorner\eta_3\ \mathrm{b}\ \eta_2\urcorner;\ \ulcorner\eta_2\ \mathrm{b}\ \eta_1\urcorner;\ \ulcorner\eta_1\ \mathrm{b}\ \eta\urcorner$

**1148 $\ulcorner(\eta)(\zeta)(\mathrm{Thm}\ \eta\ \mathrm{cd}\ \zeta\cdot(\exists\theta)(r_i\,\mathrm{RC_F}\ \theta\cdot\eta\ \mathrm{Ing}\ \theta)\cdot\supset$

$(\exists\theta)(r_i\,\mathrm{RC_F}\ \theta\cdot\zeta\ \mathrm{Ing}\ \theta))\supset:\eta\ r_i\,\mathrm{B_F}\ \zeta\cdot$

$\eta\ r_i\,\mathrm{B_F}\ \zeta'\cdot\supset\eta\ r_i\,\mathrm{B_F}\ \zeta\ \mathrm{cj}\ \zeta'\urcorner$

Proof.

Let the links of the biconditional chain connecting η and ζ be:

$\ulcorner\eta\ \mathrm{b}\ \zeta_1\urcorner;\ \ulcorner\zeta_1\ \mathrm{b}\ \zeta_2\urcorner;\ \dots\ \ulcorner\zeta_n\ \mathrm{b}\ \zeta\urcorner$

Each of these links is an ingredient of a rational corpus of level r_i and basis F, and corresponding to each of these links is a statement about theoremhood:

$\ulcorner\mathrm{Thm}\,(\eta\ \mathrm{b}\ \zeta_1)\ \mathrm{cd}\,(\eta\ \mathrm{b}\,(\eta\ \mathrm{cj}\ \zeta_1))\urcorner;\ \ulcorner\mathrm{Thm}\,(\zeta_1\ \mathrm{b}\ \zeta_2)\,\mathrm{cd}\,((\eta\ \mathrm{cj}\ \zeta_1)$

$\mathrm{b}\,(\eta\ \mathrm{cj}\ \zeta_2))\urcorner;\ \dots\ \ulcorner\mathrm{Thm}\,(\zeta_n\ \mathrm{b}\ \zeta)\ \mathrm{cd}\,((\eta\ \mathrm{cj}\ \zeta_n)\ \mathrm{b}\,(\eta\ \mathrm{cj}\ \zeta))\urcorner$

We are thus assured (by an argument analogous to that of the preceding proof) of the existence of a biconditional chain connecting η and $\ulcorner\eta\ \mathrm{cj}\ \zeta\urcorner$.

Now let the links of the biconditional chain connecting η and ζ' be:

$\ulcorner\eta\ \mathrm{b}\ \zeta'_1\urcorner;\ \ulcorner\zeta'_1\ \mathrm{b}\ \zeta'_2\urcorner;\ \dots\ \ulcorner\zeta'_m\ \mathrm{b}\ \zeta'\urcorner$

Each of these links is an ingredient of a rational corpus of level r_i and basis F, and corresponding to each of them is a statement about theoremhood:

$\ulcorner\mathrm{Thm}\,(\eta\ \mathrm{b}\ \zeta'_1)\ \mathrm{cd}\,((\hat\eta\ \mathrm{cj}\ \zeta)\ \mathrm{b}\,(\zeta\ \mathrm{cj}\ \zeta'_1))\urcorner;\ \ulcorner\mathrm{Thm}\,(\zeta'_1\ \mathrm{b}\ \zeta'_2)\ \mathrm{cd}$

$((\zeta\ \mathrm{cj}\ \zeta'_1)\ \mathrm{b}\,(\zeta\ \mathrm{cj}\ \zeta'_2))\urcorner;\ \dots\ \ulcorner\mathrm{Thm}\,(\zeta'_m\ \mathrm{b}\ \zeta')\ \mathrm{cd}$

$((\zeta\ \mathrm{cj}\ \zeta'_m)\ \mathrm{b}\,(\zeta\ \mathrm{cj}\ \zeta'))\urcorner$

These theorems, together with the hypothesis of **1148, assure us of the existence of a biconditional chain connecting $\ulcorner\eta\ \mathrm{cj}\ \zeta\urcorner$ with $\ulcorner\zeta\ \mathrm{cj}\ \zeta'\urcorner$. But,

**1043 $\ulcorner\eta\ r_i\,\mathrm{B_F}\ \eta\ \mathrm{cj}\ \zeta\cdot\eta\ \mathrm{cj}\ \zeta\ r_i\,\mathrm{B_F}\ \zeta\ \mathrm{cj}\ \zeta'\cdot\supset\eta\ r_i\,\mathrm{B_F}\ \zeta\ \mathrm{cj}\ \zeta'\urcorner$

then yields the desired conclusion.

**1049 $\ulcorner$ ζ pr ζ' r_i Mem$_F$ η cp η' · (η)(ζ)(Thm η cd ζ ·

$\qquad$ (∃ θ)(r_i RC$_F$ θ · η Ing θ) · ⊃ (∃ θ)(r_i RC$_F$ θ ·

$\qquad$ ζ Ing θ)) · ⊃ ζ' pr ζ r_i Mem$_F$ η' cp η $\urcorner$

Proof.

ML(†460) $\ulcorner$ Thm ((ζ pr ζ' e η cp η') cd (ζ' pr ζ e η' cp η)) $\urcorner$ $\qquad$ (1)

*103 $\ulcorner$ (η)(ζ)(Thm η cd ζ · (∃ θ)(r_i RC$_F$ θ · η Ing θ) · ⊃

$\qquad$ (∃ θ)(r_i RC$_F$ θ · ζ Ing θ)) ⊃ : [1 ·] (∃ θ)(ζ pr ζ' e

$\qquad$ η cp η' Ing θ · r_i RC$_F$ θ) · ⊃ (∃ θ)(r_i RC$_F$ θ ·

$\qquad$ ζ' pr ζ e η' cp η Ing θ) $\urcorner$ $\qquad$ (2)

ML(†417) $\ulcorner$ Thm ζ pr ζ' id α ' pr α '' ⊃ Thm ζ' pr ζ id

$\qquad$ α '' pr α ' $\urcorner$ $\qquad$ (3)

ML(D 27) $\ulcorner$ Thm η cp η' id (β' cp β'') int γ' · ⊃ · Thm η' cp

$\qquad$ η id (β'' cp β') int (converse of γ') $\urcorner$ $\qquad$ (4)

ML(*100, D 27) $\ulcorner$ Thm ((ζ pr ζ' e β' cp β'') cd (ζ pr ζ' e η cp η'))

$\qquad$ cd ((ζ' pr ζ e β'' cp β') cd (ζ' pr ζ e

$\qquad$ η' cp η)) $\urcorner$ $\qquad$ (5)

*103 $\ulcorner$ (η)(ζ)(Thm η cd ζ · (∃ θ)(r_i RC$_F$ θ · η Ing θ) · ⊃

$\qquad$ (∃ θ)(r_i RC$_F$ θ · ζ Ing θ)) ⊃ : [1 ·] (∃ θ)(r_i RC$_F$ θ ·

$\qquad$ ((ζ pr ζ' e β' cp β'') cd (ζ pr ζ' e η cp η')) Ing θ) ·

$\qquad$ ⊃ (∃ θ)(r_i RC$_F$ θ · ((ζ' pr ζ e β'' cp β') cd

$\qquad$ (ζ' pr ζ e η' cp η)) Ing θ) $\urcorner$ $\qquad$ (6)

Lines (2), (3), (4), and (6), (with the help of **232 applied to (4), and
*158 applied to the conjunction of (4) and (6)), show that, subject to
the hypothesis of **1049, it is possible to construct a sequence jus-
tifying $\ulcorner$ ζ' pr ζ r_i Mem$_F$ η' cp η $\urcorner$, by simply adding one ingredient
to the sequence justifying $\ulcorner$ ζ pr ζ' r_i Mem$_F$ η cp η' $\urcorner$; the ingredient
is simply $\ulcorner$ ζ' pr ζ e η' cp η $\urcorner$.

The following metatheorem is a very important one; it states
that if a level of rational corpus is consistent, and if any logical
consequence of an ingredient of some rational corpus of that level
and basis is also an ingredient of some rational corpus of that level
and basis, then it is not the case that any β'' prevents by difference

in this rational corpus the randomness of $\ulcorner$fβaβ $\urcorner$ in $\ulcorner$untfβaβ $\urcorner$, with respect to $\ulcorner$unt v $\urcorner$, when β is an ingredient of some rational corpus of this level and basis. It is the counterpart to **1146.

**1150 $\ulcorner r_i$C$_F$ · (η)(ζ)(Thm η cd ζ · ($\exists\theta$)(r_iRC$_F$ θ · η Ing θ) ·

$\supset$ ($\exists\theta$)(r_iRC$_F$ θ · ζ Ing θ)) · $\supset$ · ($\exists\theta$)(r_iRC$_F$ θ ·

β Ing θ) $\supset$ ~ β'' r_iDP$_F$(fβaβ,unt fβaβ,unt v)$\urcorner$

Proof.

Let γ be a variable foreign to γ'' and β. In virtue of the fact that any class having one or no members is a rational class, we may establish the first line of the following proof by an argument analogous to that used to support **1145.

$\ulcorner r_i$C$_F$ · (η)(ζ)(Thm η cd ζ · ($\exists\theta$)(r_iRC$_F$ θ · η Ing θ) · $\supset$

($\exists\theta$)(r_iRC$_F$ θ · ζ Ing θ)) · $\supset$ · ($\exists\theta$)(r_iRC$_F$ θ ·

β Ing θ) $\supset$ pct (unt α'',γa (γ e γ'' al β),(" ,1" ; " ,1"))

r_iS*A$_F$(α'',γa (γ e γ'' al β)) $\urcorner$ (1)

ML(*100) $\ulcorner$Thm β b η cd β b η al β $\urcorner$ (2)

By an argument analogous to that for **1148, we have:

$\ulcorner r_i$C$_F$ · (η)(ζ)(Thm η cd ζ · ($\exists\theta$)(r_iRC$_F$ θ · η Ing θ) · $\supset$

($\exists\theta$)(r_iRC$_F$ θ · ζ Ing θ)) · $\supset$: β r_iB$_F$ α'' e γ'' · [2 · $\supset$]

β r_iB$_F$ α'' e γa (γ e γ'' al β) $\urcorner$ (3)

ML(†342) $\ulcorner$Thm α'' e β'' cd unt α'' incl β'' $\urcorner$ (4)

ML(†182) $\ulcorner$Thm β cd (" ,1" id " ,1") $\urcorner$ (5)

ML,(4) $\ulcorner$Thm β cd (α'' e β'' cd unt α'' incl β'') $\urcorner$ (6)

ML(†344) $\ulcorner$Thm α'' e v cd α'' e unt α'' $\urcorner$ (7)

ML(†190,†359)∆103, $\ulcorner$(η)(ζ)(Thm η cd ζ · ($\exists\theta$)(r_iRC$_F$ θ ·
*103

η Ing θ) · $\supset$ ($\exists\theta$)(r_iRC$_F$ θ ·

ζ Ing θ)) $\supset$ · α'' r_iMem$_F$ β'' $\supset$

($\exists\theta$)(r_iRC$_F$ θ · α'' e v Ing θ) $\urcorner$ (8)

Finally, by an argument analogous to that used to support line (5), with the help of **1028 and *117, we have:

$\ulcorner$(η)(ζ)(Thm η cd ζ · ($\exists\theta$)(r_iRC$_F$ θ · η Ing θ) · $\supset$ ($\exists\theta$)

$(r_i \mathrm{RC_F} \ \theta \cdot \zeta \ \mathrm{Ing} \ \theta)) \supset : \mathrm{pct}\,(\mathrm{unt}\ \mathrm{f}\beta a\beta, \mathrm{unt}\ \mathrm{v},(\text{``}_s1\text{''};\text{``}_s1\text{''}\,))$

$r_i \mathrm{S}^*\mathrm{A_F}\,(\mathrm{unt}\ \mathrm{f}\beta a\beta, \mathrm{unt}\ \mathrm{v})\cdot \mathrm{pct}\,(\mathrm{unt}\ \alpha'', \gamma a\,(\gamma\ \mathrm{e}\ \gamma''\ \mathrm{al}\ \beta),$

$(\text{``}_s1\text{''};\text{``}_s1\text{''}\,))\,r_i \mathrm{S}^*\mathrm{A_F}\ (\mathrm{unt}\ \alpha'', \gamma a\,(\gamma\ \mathrm{e}\ \gamma''\ \mathrm{al}\ \beta))\cdot \supset$

$(\eta)(\zeta)(\eta\ r_i\mathrm{S}^*\mathrm{A_F}(\mathrm{unt}\ \mathrm{f}\beta a\beta, \mathrm{unt}\ \mathrm{v})\cdot \zeta r_i \mathrm{S}^*\mathrm{A_F}(\mathrm{unt}\ \alpha'',$

$\gamma a\,(\gamma\ \mathrm{e}\ \gamma''\ \mathrm{al}\ \beta))\cdot \supset \eta\ r_i \mathrm{S}=_F \zeta)^\urcorner$ \hfill (9)

*100 $\ulcorner 1\cdot 3\cdot 6\cdot 7\cdot 8\cdot 9\cdot \supset]\ r_i\mathrm{C_F}\cdot (\eta)(\zeta)(\mathrm{Thm}\ \eta\ \mathrm{cd}\ \zeta\cdot$

$\qquad (\exists\theta)(r_i\mathrm{RC_F}\ \theta\cdot\eta\ \mathrm{Ing}\ \theta)\cdot \supset (\exists\theta)(r_i\mathrm{RC_F}\ \theta\cdot$

$\qquad \zeta\ \mathrm{Ing}\ \theta))\cdot \supset\cdot (\exists\theta)(r_i\mathrm{RC_F}\ \theta\cdot\beta\ \mathrm{Ing}\ \theta)\supset :$

$\qquad \alpha''\ \mathrm{e}\ \gamma''\ r_i\mathrm{B_F}\ \beta\cdot\eta\ r_i\mathrm{S}^*\mathrm{A_F}(\mathrm{unt}\ \mathrm{f}\beta a\beta, \mathrm{unt}\ \mathrm{v})\cdot$

$\qquad \alpha''\ r_i\mathrm{Mem_F}\ \beta''\cdot \supset\cdot (\exists\theta)(r_i\mathrm{RC_F}\ \theta\cdot\alpha''\ \mathrm{e}\ \beta''\ \mathrm{cd}$

$\qquad \mathrm{unt}\ \alpha''\ \mathrm{incl}\ \beta''\ \mathrm{Ing}\ \theta)\cdot\alpha''\ r_i\mathrm{Mem_F}\ \mathrm{unt}\ \alpha''\cdot$

$\qquad \mathrm{pct}\,(\mathrm{unt}\ \alpha'', \gamma a\,(\gamma\ \mathrm{e}\ \gamma''\ \mathrm{al}\ \beta),(\text{``}_s1\text{''};\text{``}_s1\text{''}\,))$

$\qquad r_i\mathrm{S}^*\mathrm{A_F}(\mathrm{unt}\ \alpha'',\ \gamma a\,(\gamma\ \mathrm{e}\ \gamma''\ \mathrm{al}\ \beta))\cdot \mathrm{pct}\,(\mathrm{unt}\ \alpha'',$

$\qquad \gamma a\,(\gamma\ \mathrm{e}\ \gamma''\ \mathrm{al}\ \beta),(\text{``}_s1\text{''};\text{``}_s1\text{''}\,))\,r_i\mathrm{S}=_F \eta^\urcorner$ \hfill (10)

*100 to match (10) with △104; then ****234**:

$\ulcorner r_i\mathrm{C_F}\cdot (\eta)(\zeta)(\mathrm{Thm}\ \eta\ \mathrm{cd}\ \zeta\cdot(\exists\theta)(r_i\mathrm{RC_F}\ \theta\cdot\eta\ \mathrm{Ing}\ \theta)\cdot\supset$

$\quad (\exists\theta)(r_i\mathrm{RC_F}\ \theta\cdot\zeta\ \mathrm{Ing}\ \theta))\cdot\supset\cdot(\exists\theta)(r_i\mathrm{RC_F}\ \theta\cdot$

$\quad \beta\ \mathrm{Ing}\ \theta)\supset :\eta\ r_i\mathrm{S}^*\mathrm{A_F}(\mathrm{unt}\ \mathrm{f}\beta a\beta, \mathrm{unt}\ \mathrm{v})\cdot\eta''r_i\mathrm{S}^*\mathrm{A_F}(\beta'',\gamma'')\cdot$

$\quad \mathrm{f}\beta a\beta\ \mathrm{e}\ \mathrm{v}\ r_i\mathrm{B_F}\ \alpha''\ \mathrm{e}\ \gamma''\cdot\alpha''\ r_i\mathrm{Mem_F}\ \beta''\cdot\supset$

$\quad (\exists\alpha')(\exists\beta')(\exists\gamma')(\exists\eta')(\exists\beta''')(\alpha'\ r_i\mathrm{Mem_F}\ \beta'\cdot\mathrm{f}\beta a\beta\ \beta\ \mathrm{unt}$

$\quad \mathrm{f}\beta a\beta\ \mathrm{MP}\ \alpha'\ \mathrm{e}\ \beta'\cdot(\exists\theta)(r_i\mathrm{RC_F}\ \theta\cdot\beta'\ \mathrm{incl}\ \beta''\ \mathrm{cp}\ \beta'''$

$\quad \mathrm{Ing}\ \theta):\mathrm{v}:(\exists\theta)(r_i\mathrm{RC_F}\ \theta\cdot\alpha''\ \mathrm{e}\ \beta''\ \mathrm{cd}\ \beta'\ \mathrm{incl}\ \beta''$

$\quad \mathrm{Ing}\ \theta)\cdot\alpha''\ r_i\mathrm{Mem_F}\ \beta'\cdot\eta'\ r_i\mathrm{SA_F}(\beta',\gamma')\cdot\eta'$

$\quad \cdot\eta'\ r_i\mathrm{S}=_F \eta\cdot\alpha''\ \mathrm{e}\ \gamma''\ r_i\mathrm{B_F}\alpha''\ \mathrm{e}\ \gamma')^\urcorner$ \hfill (11)

*100, D8, *159 $\ulcorner[(\alpha'')(\gamma'')(\eta'')(\eta)\ 1\supset]\ 1150^\urcorner$

$\qquad$ (△104)

**1151 $\ulcorner r_i\mathrm{C_F}\cdot(\eta)(\zeta)(\mathrm{Thm}\ \eta\ \mathrm{cd}\ \zeta\cdot(\exists\theta)(r_i\mathrm{RC_F}\ \theta\cdot\eta\ \mathrm{Ing}\ \theta)\cdot$

$\qquad \supset(\exists\theta)(r_i\mathrm{RC_F}\ \theta\cdot\zeta\ \mathrm{Ing}\ \theta))\cdot\supset\cdot(\exists\theta)$

$\qquad (r_i\mathrm{RC_F}\ \theta\cdot\beta\ \mathrm{Ing}\ \theta)\supset\mathrm{f}\beta a\beta\ r_i\mathrm{Ran_F}(\mathrm{unt}\ \mathrm{f}\beta a\beta, \mathrm{unt}\ \mathrm{v})^\urcorner$

Proof.

*100, **234, *157, $\ulcorner [1145 \cdot (\beta'')(1150 \cdot 1146) \cdot \supset] 1051 \urcorner$

(via: Thm β cd f$\beta a\beta$ e unt f$\beta a\beta$)

**1152 $\ulcorner r_i C_F \cdot (\eta)(\zeta)(\text{Thm } \eta \text{ cd } \zeta \cdot (\exists\theta)(r_i RC_F \ \theta \cdot \eta \text{ Ing } \theta) \cdot$
$$\supset (\exists\theta)(r_i RC_F \ \theta \cdot \zeta \text{ Ing } \theta)) \cdot \supset \cdot (\exists\theta)$$
$$(r_i RC_F \ \theta \cdot \beta \text{ Ing } \theta) \supset \beta \ r_i \text{Prob}_F(\text{``}_s1\text{''};\text{``}_s1\text{''}) \urcorner$$

Proof.

*100,ML(*253,†210,†345) $\ulcorner$Thm β cd (β b f$\beta a\beta$ e unt v)$\urcorner$ (1)

**233 $\ulcorner(\eta)(\zeta)(\text{Thm } \eta \text{ cd } \zeta \cdot (\exists\theta)(r_i RC_F \ \theta \cdot \eta \text{ Ing } \theta) \cdot \supset$
$$(\exists\theta)(r_i RC_F \ \theta \cdot \zeta \text{ Ing } \theta)) \cdot \supset : (\exists\theta)(r_i RC_F \ \theta \cdot$$
$$\beta \text{ Ing } \theta)[\cdot 1 \cdot \supset](\exists\theta)(r_i RC_F \ \theta \cdot \beta \text{ b f}\beta a\beta \text{ e}$$
$$\text{unt v Ing } \theta)\urcorner \tag{2}$$

*100 $\ulcorner[2 \cdot 1041 \cdot \supset :](\eta)(\zeta)(\text{Thm } \eta \text{ cd } \zeta \cdot (\exists\theta)(r_i RC_F \ \theta \cdot$
$$\eta \text{ Ing } \theta) \cdot \supset (\exists\theta)(r_i RC_F \ \theta \cdot \zeta \text{ Ing } \theta)) \cdot \supset \cdot$$
$$(\exists\theta)(r_i RC_F \ \theta \cdot \beta \text{ Ing } \theta) \supset \beta \ r_i B_F \text{ f}\beta a\beta \text{ e unt v}\urcorner \tag{3}$$

*100, **232 $\ulcorner[3 \cdot 1151 \cdot 1145 \cdot \supset] 1152\urcorner$
Δ107

**1153 $\ulcorner r_i C_F \cdot (\eta)(\zeta)(\text{Thm } \eta \text{ cd } \zeta \cdot (\exists\theta)(r_i RC_F \ \theta \cdot \eta \text{ Ing } \theta) \cdot \supset$
$$(\exists\theta)(r_i RC_F \ \theta \cdot \zeta \text{ Ing } \theta)) \cdot \supset : (\exists\theta)(r_i RC_F \ \theta \cdot$$
$$\beta \text{ Ing } \theta) \supset \cdot r_i \neq r_1 \supset (\exists\theta)(r_{i-1} RC_F \ \theta \cdot \beta \text{ Ing } \theta)\urcorner$$

Proof.

Ratio extension of ML: $\ulcorner$Thm $\text{``}_s1\text{''} \ _s\text{gr } r_{i-1}\urcorner$ (1)

**232, (Δ95) $\ulcorner[1152 \cdot 1 \cdot 1103 \cdot \supset] 1153\urcorner$
*100

This last theorem expresses the fact that if the rational corpora of a given level and basis are consistent, and if the 'theorematic conditional hypothesis', $\ulcorner(\eta)(\zeta)(\text{Thm } \eta \text{ cd } \zeta \cdot (\exists\theta)(r_i RC_F \ \theta \cdot \eta \text{ Ing } \theta) \cdot \supset (\exists\theta)(r_i RC_F \ \theta \cdot \zeta \text{ Ing } \theta))\urcorner$, holds, then if a statement x is an ingredient of a rational corpus of this level, it is also an ingredient of a rational corpus of the next lower level, provided that there is a next lower level. This is not, by any means, the last word on rational inheritance. It will turn out, in the next two chapters, that for $r_i \neq r_n$, both of these hypotheses may be dropped; I have already shown that the theorematic conditional hypothesis can be dropped for the rational corpora of level r_n, in metatheorem **1115.

CHAPTER ELEVEN

Rational Inference

1. In this chapter I am not concerned with rational inference in any very general sense; I propose to concern myself only with those inferences of the form: If A then B, A, therefore B. In the rational corpora of the highest level, such inferences are forthcoming immediately from the definition of a rational corpus of this level. In the rational corpora of lower levels, the possibility of such inferences remains to be demonstrated; and it will turn out that they are only possible when one premise is an ingredient of the next higher level of rational corpus. A special case of this form of inference has already been mentioned in the last chapter, as the 'theorematic conditional hypothesis'.[1]

We must first pause to show that there are only a finite number of possibilities for the pair of parameters in a statistical statement. I have already supposed that all rational classes are finite, and even that the number of their members must be less than two to the googolplex. (**1017) This is a convention of the language. It merely means that if we have any reason to suppose that there are more objects than this in the class, we shall also have a means of ordering the objects, and will confine our attentions and our inferences to the *first* two to the googolplex of them.

Now suppose that I had suggested 100 instead of $2^{(10)^{10^{100}}}$ as the upper limit for the number of members allowed in a rational class. This would be implausible because we know of many classes much larger than this, but don't worry about that. The point is that if this is the upper limit for the number of members in a rational class, then the only ratio matrices which make sense are:

$$\text{``}x = {_s}0\text{''}, \text{``}x = {_s}1\text{''}, \text{``}x = 1/2\text{''}, \text{``}x = 1/3\text{''}, \text{``}x = 2/3\text{''}, \ldots$$
$$\text{``}x = 97/100\text{''}$$

The only possible class ratios, under these circumstances, would be those ratios between ${_s}0$ and ${_s}1$ inclusive that can be named by a fraction having a denominator less than 100. If it were alleged, then, that "%(A,B,(127/1000;157/1000))" were a strongest statis-

---

1. This chapter, like the preceding one, is devoted to technical developments which will be summarized in Chapter Twelve, and may therefore be skipped by all and only those who skipped Chapter Ten.

tical statement in our rational corpus about A and B, the allegation could be shown to be in error, subject to the plausible hypothesis that every theorematic consequence of an ingredient of a rational corpus is to be also an ingredient of a rational corpus, by the exhibition of the theorem: "% (A,B,(127/1000;157/1000)) ⊃ % (A,B, (13/100;15/100))". This will be a theorem by virtue of the conventional limitation of rational classes to classes containing only 100 members. (If A and B are not rational classes, the allegation is also in error.)

In precisely the same way, if every rational class is conventionally limited to having at most two to the googolplex members, there are only a finite number of ratios that can usefully be mentioned in a statistical statement: the ratios between $_s0$ and $_s1$, inclusive, which can be expressed as fractions having denominators less than $2^{(10)10^{100}}$.

Instead of speaking of fractions, let us, as before, speak of ratio-matrices. The ratio matrices that interest us, then, will be a special finite subclass of the class of all ratio matrices defined by Δ97a. Let there be N of these matrices:

$$\ulcorner S_2 \text{ id } f_1 \urcorner, \ulcorner S_2 \text{ id } f_2 \urcorner, \dots \ulcorner S_2 \text{ id } f_N \urcorner$$

We shall say that x is a *Normal Ratio Matrix*, if x is one or another of these N matrices:

Δ109 $\ulcorner RM_N \zeta \urcorner$ *for* $\ulcorner \zeta = S_2 \text{ id } f_1 \cdot v \cdot \zeta = S_2 \text{ id } f_2 \cdot v \cdot \cdots$

$\cdot v \cdot \zeta = S_2 \text{ id } f_N : RM \zeta \urcorner$

Statistical statements using parameters satisfying one or another of these matrices will be particularly interesting—although other kinds of statistical statements will also appear as ingredients of rational corpora. We shall say that x is a *Normal Statistical Statement*, if it is a statistical statement using parameters that are theorematically members of the S_2 abstracts of a pair of Normal Ratio Matrices:

Δ110 $\ulcorner RM_N Stat \zeta \urcorner$ for $\ulcorner (\exists \beta)(\exists \gamma)(\exists \alpha)(\exists \alpha')(\zeta = pct(\beta, \gamma, (\alpha'\alpha')) \cdot$

$(\exists \eta)(\exists \eta')(RM_N \eta' \cdot Thm \alpha e S_2 a \eta \cdot$

$Thm \alpha' e S_2 a \eta')) \urcorner$

If $pct(w, x, (y;z))$ is a statement about w and x in the rational corpus of level r_i and basis F, then the following is a theorem in ML, where $pct(w, x, (y';z'))$ is a normal statistical statement: $pct(w, x, (y;z)) \text{ cd } (pct(w, x, (y';z')) \text{ cj } (y' _sgr y \text{ al } y' \text{ id } y) \text{ cj } (z _sgr z' \text{ al } z \text{ id } z'))$.

**1160 $\ulcorner$ pct $(\beta,\gamma,(\alpha;\alpha'))$ r_i SA$_F(\beta,\gamma) \supset (\exists\zeta)(\exists\zeta')(RM_N$Stat

pct $(\beta,\gamma,(\zeta;\zeta')) \cdot$ Thm pct $(\beta,\gamma,(\alpha;\alpha'))$ cd

(pct $(\beta,\gamma,(\zeta';\zeta'))$ cj $(\zeta$ $_s$gr α al ζ id α) cj

$(\alpha'$ $_s$gr ζ' al α' id $\zeta'))) \urcorner$

Proof.

*100, Δ97b, Δ110; (ML ratio extension, D 72)

$\ulcorner$ [1017 $\cdot$ $\supset$] 1160 $\urcorner$

The following metatheorem shows that if every theorematic consequence of an ingredient of a rational corpus of level r_i and basis F is also an ingredient of some rational corpus of this level and basis, then a strongest statistical statement about given subject matter is a normal statistical statement.

**1161 $\ulcorner(\eta)(\zeta)($ Thm η cd $\zeta \cdot (\exists\theta)(r_iRC_F$ $\theta \cdot \eta$ Ing θ) $\cdot \supset$

$(\exists\theta)(r_i$RC$_F$ $\theta \cdot \zeta$ Ing θ)) $\supset \cdot$ pct $(\beta,\gamma,(\alpha;\alpha'))$

r_iS*A$_F(\beta,\gamma) \supset (\exists\zeta)(\exists\zeta')(RM_N$ $\zeta \cdot$ RM$_N$ $\zeta' \cdot$

Thm α e S$_2$a $\zeta \cdot$ Thm α' e S$_2$a $\zeta' \urcorner$

Proof.

*100,Δ99, $\ulcorner$ pct $(\beta,\gamma,(\alpha;\alpha'))$ r_iS*A$_F(\beta,\gamma) \supset (\eta)(\eta$ r_iSA$_F(\beta,\gamma) \supset$

$\sim \eta$ r_iStr$_F$ pct $(\beta,\gamma,(\alpha;\alpha')) \urcorner$ (1)

*100,Δ99, **234b, $\ulcorner$ pct $(\beta,\gamma,(\alpha;\alpha'))$ r_iS*A$_F(\beta,\gamma) \supset$ pct $(\beta,\gamma,$

$(\alpha';\alpha'))$ r_iSA$_F(\beta,\gamma) \urcorner$ (2)

ML(*100,*104) $\ulcorner$ Thm η cj $\zeta \supset \cdot$ Thm $\eta \cdot$ Thm $\zeta \urcorner$ (3)

**1160 $\ulcorner$ pct $(\beta,\gamma,(\alpha;\alpha'))$ r_iSA$_F(\beta,\gamma) \supset [\exists \supset \cdot] (\exists\eta)(\exists\eta')$
*100
(RM$_N$Stat pct $(\beta,\gamma,(\eta;\eta')) \cdot$ Thm pct $(\beta,\gamma,(\alpha;\alpha'))$

cd pct $(\beta,\gamma,(\eta;\eta')) \cdot$ Thm η $_s$gr α al η id $\alpha \cdot$

Thm α' $_s$gr η' al α' id $\eta') \urcorner$ (4)

*100,Δ97a,Δ109,Δ97b, $\ulcorner(\eta)(\zeta)($ Thm η cd $\zeta \cdot (\exists\theta)(r_iRC_F$ $\theta \cdot$

η Ing θ) $\cdot \supset (\exists\theta)(r_iRC_F$ $\theta \cdot \zeta$ Ing θ)) $\cdot \supset :$

pct $(\beta,\gamma,(\alpha;\alpha'))$ r_iSA$_F(\beta,\gamma) \cdot$ RM$_N$Stat

pct $(\beta,\gamma,(\eta;\eta')) \cdot$ Thm pct $(\beta,\gamma,(\alpha;\alpha'))$ cd

pct $(\beta,\gamma,(\eta;\eta')) \cdot \supset$ pct $(\beta,\gamma,(\eta;\eta'))$ r_iSA$_F(\beta,\gamma) \urcorner$ (5)

Ratio extension $\ulcorner(\exists\beta)(\exists\beta')(\exists\gamma)(\exists\gamma')(\text{Thm }\alpha \text{ e } S_2 a\beta \cdot$
of ML, Δ97a

Thm α' e $S_2 a\beta' \cdot$ Thm η e $S_2 a\gamma \cdot$

Thm η' e $S_2 a\gamma' \cdot$ RM $\beta \cdot$ Rm $\beta' \cdot$ RM $\gamma \cdot$

RM $\gamma') \supset :$ Thm η ${}_s$gr α al η id $\alpha \cdot$ Thm α'

${}_s$gr η' al α' id $\eta' \cdot \supset \cdot$ Thm η ${}_s$gr α v Thm η

id $\alpha \cdot$ Thm α' ${}_s$gr η' v Thm α' id $\overline{\eta'}\ ^\urcorner$ (6)

ML(*100, *104)(Δ97a) $\ulcorner$pct$(\beta,\gamma,(\alpha;\alpha')\,r_i SA_F(\beta,\gamma) \cdot$ Thm $\eta'' \cdot \supset$

Thm pct$(\beta,\gamma,(\alpha;\alpha'))$ cd $\overline{\eta''}\ ^\urcorner$ (7)

**233,*100 $\ulcorner(\eta)(\zeta)(\text{Thm }\gamma$ cd $\zeta \cdot (\exists\theta)(r_i RC_F\ \theta \cdot \gamma$ Ing $\theta) \cdot \supset$

$(\exists\theta)(r_i RC_F\ \theta \cdot \zeta$ Ing $\theta)) \cdot$ pct$(\beta,\gamma,(\alpha;\alpha'))$

$r_i SA_F(\beta,\gamma) \cdot [\,7 \supset :\,]$ Thm η'' v Thm $\zeta'' \cdot$

$\sim(\exists\theta)(r_i RC_F\ \theta \cdot \eta''$ Ing $\theta) \cdot \supset$ Thm $\overline{\zeta''}\ ^\urcorner$ (8)

**233,*100(Δ99,Δ98) $\ulcorner[\,1 \cdot 2 \cdot 5 \cdot 6 \cdot 8 \cdot \supset \cdot :](\eta)(\zeta)(\text{Thm }\eta$ cd $\zeta \cdot$

$(\exists\theta)(r_i RC_F\ \theta \cdot \eta$ Ing $\theta) \cdot \supset (\exists\theta)(r_i RC_F\ \theta \cdot \zeta$ Ing $\theta)) \cdot$

pct$(\beta,\gamma,(\alpha;\alpha'))\,r_i S*A_F(\beta,\gamma) \cdot \supset :$ RM$_N$Stat pct$(\beta,\gamma,(\eta;\eta')) \cdot$

Thm pct$(\beta,\gamma,(\alpha;\alpha'))$ cd pct$(\beta,\gamma;(\eta';\eta')) \cdot$ Thm η ${}_s$gr α al

η id $\alpha \cdot$ Thm α' ${}_s$gr η' al α' id $\eta' \cdot \supset$ Thm η id $\alpha \cdot$

Thm η' id $\overline{\alpha'}\ ^\urcorner$ (9)

Ratio extension of ML, Δ110. $\ulcorner$RM$_N$Stat pct$(\beta,\gamma,(\eta;\eta')) \supset$
*100

$(\exists\zeta)(\exists\zeta')(\text{RM}_N\ \zeta \cdot \text{RM}_N\ \zeta' \cdot$ Thm α e$_2$S a$\zeta \cdot$

Thm α' e $S_2 a \overline{\zeta'})\ ^\urcorner$ (10)

*100,*159,*161 $\ulcorner[\,9 \cdot 10 \cdot \supset \cdot :]\ (\eta)(\zeta)(\text{Thm }\eta$ cd $\zeta \cdot (\exists\theta)$

$(r_i RC_F\ \theta \cdot \eta$ Ing $\theta) \cdot \supset (\exists\theta)(r_i RC_F\ \theta \cdot \zeta$ Ing $\theta)) \cdot \supset :$

pct$(\beta,\gamma,(\alpha';\alpha'))\,r_i S*A_F(\beta,\gamma) \cdot \supset \cdot (\exists\eta)(\exists\eta')(\text{RM}_N$Stat

pct$(\beta,\gamma,(\eta;\eta')) \cdot$ Thm pct$(\beta,\gamma,(\alpha;\alpha'))$ cd pct$(\beta,\gamma,(\eta;\eta')) \cdot$

Thm η ${}_s$gr α al η id $\alpha \cdot$ Thm α' ${}_s$gr η' al α' id $\eta') \supset$

$(\exists\zeta)(\exists\zeta')(\text{RM}_N\ \zeta \cdot \text{RM}_N\ \zeta' \cdot$ Thm α e $S_2 a \zeta \cdot$

Thm α' e $S_2 a\ \overline{\zeta'})\ ^\urcorner$ (11)

*100 $\ulcorner[\,2 \cdot 11 \cdot 4 \cdot \supset]\ 1161\ ^\urcorner$

The next metatheorem, subject to the usual hypothesis concerning consistency and the theorematic conditional, establishes that if there is any normal statistical statement satisfying a given condition, then there is a strongest statistical statement satisfying that condition, in the sense that there is no stronger normal statistical statement satisfying the same condition.

**1162   If θ is like φ except for containing free occurrences of η wherever φ contains free occurrences of ζ, then,

$$\ulcorner r_i \, C_F \cdot (\eta)(\zeta)(\text{Thm } \eta \text{ cd } \zeta \cdot (\,\exists\,\theta)(r_i RC_F \; \theta \cdot \eta \text{ Ing } \theta) \cdot \supset$$

$$(\,\exists\,\theta)(r_i RC_F \; \theta \cdot \zeta \text{ Ing } \theta)) \cdot \supset \cdot (\,\exists\,\eta)(RM_N Stat \, \eta \cdot \theta) \supset$$

$$(\,\exists\,\zeta)(\eta)(RM_N Stat \, \zeta \cdot \varphi : RM_N Stat \, \eta \cdot \theta \cdot \supset \sim \eta \; r_i Str_F \; \zeta)\urcorner$$

Proof.

*100 $\ulcorner \sim (\,\exists\,\eta)(RM_N Stat \, \eta \cdot \theta) \supset 1162\urcorner$ (1)

*100, *157, *159; $\ulcorner (\triangle 98) \; (\,\exists\,\eta)(RM_N Stat \, \eta \cdot \theta \cdot \sim (\,\exists\,\beta)(\,\exists\,\gamma)$

            $(\eta \; r_i SA_F(\beta,\gamma))) \supset 1162\urcorner$ (2)

*100 *159 $\ulcorner (\,\exists\,\eta)(RM_N Stat \, \eta \cdot \theta \cdot (\,\exists\,\beta)(\,\exists\,\gamma)(\eta \; r_i SA_F(\beta,\gamma)) \cdot$

     $(\zeta)(RM_N Stat \, \zeta \cdot \varphi \cdot \supset \sim \zeta \, r_i Str_F \, \eta)) \supset 1162\urcorner$ (3)

Suppose that $\ulcorner (\,\exists\,\eta)(RM_N Stat \, \eta \cdot \theta \cdot (\,\exists\,\beta)(\,\exists\,\gamma)(\eta \; r_i SA_F(\beta,\gamma)) \cdot$

$(\,\exists\,\zeta)(RM_N Stat \, \zeta \cdot \varphi \cdot \zeta \, r_i Str_F \, \eta))\urcorner$. Let $\zeta_1, \zeta_2, \zeta_3, \ldots$ be a sequence of statements such that for every ζ_k, $\ulcorner RM_N Stat \, \zeta_k \cdot (\zeta)(\zeta = \zeta_k \supset \varphi)\urcorner$, and such that for every ζ_k and ζ_{k+1}, $\ulcorner \zeta_{k+1} r_i Str_F \, \zeta_k \urcorner$. Under the hypothesis of 1162, this sequence has a last member ζ_n. The hypothesis concerning the theorematic conditional allows us to apply **1037 to show that if ζ_j is earlier in the sequence than ζ_k, then $\ulcorner \zeta_k \, r_i Str_F \, \zeta_j \urcorner$. Furthermore, the hypothesis $\ulcorner r_i C_F \urcorner$ allows us to apply **1022 to show that if ζ_j is earlier in the sequence than ζ_k, then $\ulcorner \sim \zeta_j \, r_i Str_F \, \zeta_k \urcorner$, so that no statement can appear in the sequence more than once. And in view of **1034, no two statements occurring in the sequence can be equally strong. But since there are only a finite number of normal statistical statements which are not (given the hypothesis of **1162, and the fact that there is some ingredient of a rational corpus of level r_i and basis F) equally strong in this rational corpus, the sequence in question must be finite in length—i.e., have a last member ζ_n, such that $\ulcorner (\eta)$ $(RM_N Stat \, \eta \cdot \theta \cdot \supset \sim \eta \, r_i Str_F \, \zeta_n)\urcorner$. In virtue of the assumed properties of the sequence, this entails $\ulcorner (\,\exists\,\zeta)(\eta)(RM_N Stat \, \zeta \cdot \varphi \cdot$

$RM_N Stat\ \eta \cdot \theta \cdot \supset \sim \eta\ r_i Str_F\ \zeta)^\urcorner$. Thus we have,

*100 $\ulcorner r_i C_F \cdot (\eta)(\zeta)(Thm\ \eta\ cd\ \zeta \cdot (\exists\theta)(r_i RC_F\ \theta \cdot \eta\ Ing\ \theta) \cdot \supset$

$\qquad (\exists\theta)(r_i RC_F\ \theta \cdot \zeta\ Ing\ \theta)) \cdot \supset : (\exists\eta)(RM_N Stat\ \eta \cdot$

$\qquad \theta \cdot (\exists\beta)(\exists\gamma)(\eta\ r_i SA_F(\beta,\gamma)) \cdot (\exists\zeta)(RM_N Stat\ \zeta \cdot \varphi \cdot$

$\qquad \zeta\ r_i Str_F\ \eta)) \supset 1162^\urcorner$ (4)

*100 $\ulcorner [1 \cdot 2 \cdot 3 \cdot 4 \cdot \supset]\ 1162^\urcorner$

**1163 $\ulcorner r_i C_F \cdot (\eta)(\zeta)(Thm\ \eta\ cd\ \zeta \cdot (\exists\theta)(r_i RC_F\ \theta \cdot \eta\ Ing\ \theta) \cdot \supset$

$\qquad (\exists\theta)(r_i RC_F\ \theta \cdot \zeta\ Ing\ \theta)) \cdot pct(\beta,\gamma,(\alpha;\alpha'))$

$\qquad r_i SA_F(\beta,\gamma) \cdot \supset (\exists\eta)(\eta\ r_i S*A_F(\beta,\gamma))^\urcorner$

Proof.

Ratio exten- $\quad \ulcorner Thm\ pct(\beta,\gamma,(\alpha';\alpha'))\ cd\ pct(\beta,\gamma,(``_s0";``_s1"))^\urcorner$ (1)
sion of ML

*100, **233 $\quad \ulcorner r_i C_F \cdot (\eta)(\zeta)(Thm\ \eta\ cd\ \zeta \cdot (\exists\theta)(r_i RC_F\ \theta \cdot$
(Δ97a, Δ97b)
$\qquad \eta\ Ing\ \theta) \cdot \supset (\exists\theta)(r_i RC_F\ \theta\ , \zeta\ Ing\ \theta)) \cdot$

$\qquad pct(\beta,\gamma,(\alpha;\alpha'))\ r_i SA_F(\beta,\gamma) \cdot [1123 \cdot 1] \cdot \supset$

$\qquad pct(\beta,\gamma,(``_s0";``_s1"))\ r_i SA_F(\beta,\gamma)^\urcorner$ (2)

**232, *100, Δ108, Δ109; $\ulcorner RM_N Stat(\beta,\gamma,(``_s0";``_s1"))^\urcorner$ (3)

*100, **232, $\ulcorner [2 \cdot 3 \cdot]\ r_i C_F \cdot (\eta)(\zeta)(Thm\ \eta\ cd\ \zeta \cdot (\exists\theta)$

$\qquad (r_i RC_F\ \theta \cdot \eta\ Ing\ \theta) \cdot \supset (\exists\theta)(r_i RC_F\ \theta \cdot$

$\qquad \zeta\ Ing\ \theta)) \cdot pct(\beta,\gamma,(\alpha;\alpha'))\ r_i SA_F(\beta,\gamma) \cdot \supset$

$\qquad (\exists\zeta)(RM_N Stat\ \zeta \cdot \zeta\ r_i SA_F(\beta,\gamma))^\urcorner$ (4)

**1162 $\ulcorner r_i C_F \cdot (\eta)(\zeta)(Thm\ \eta\ cd\ \zeta \cdot (\exists\theta)(r_i RC_F\ \theta \cdot \eta\ Ing\ \theta) \cdot \supset$

$\qquad (\exists\theta)(r_i RC_F\ \theta \cdot \zeta\ Ing\ \theta)) \cdot \supset \cdot (\exists\zeta)(RM_N Stat\ \zeta \cdot$

$\qquad \zeta\ r_i SA_F(\beta,\gamma)) \supset (\exists\eta)(\zeta)(RM_N Stat\ \zeta \cdot$

$\qquad \zeta\ r_i SA_F(\beta,\gamma) \cdot RM_N Stat\ \eta \cdot \eta\ r_i SA_F(\beta,\gamma) \cdot \supset$

$\qquad \sim \zeta\ r_i Str_F\ \eta)^\urcorner$ (5)

*100, *157 $\ulcorner [4 \cdot 5 \cdot \supset :]\ r_i C_F \cdot (\eta)(\zeta)(Thm\ \eta\ cd\ \zeta \cdot (\exists\theta)$

$\qquad (r_i RC_F\ \theta \cdot \eta\ Ing\ \theta) \cdot \supset (\exists\theta)(r_i RC_F\ \theta \cdot$

$\qquad \zeta\ Ing\ \theta)) \cdot pct(\beta,\gamma,(\alpha;\alpha'))\ r_i SA_F(\beta,\gamma) \cdot \supset$

$$(\exists \eta)(\text{RM}_N \text{Stat } \eta \cdot \eta \, r_i \text{SA}_F(\beta,\gamma) \cdot (\zeta)(\zeta \, r_i \text{SA}_F(\beta,\gamma) \cdot$$
$$\text{RM}_N \text{Stat } \zeta \cdot \supset \sim \zeta \, r_i \text{Str}_F \, \eta)) \overline{)} \tag{6}$$

*100, **233, Δ98, $\ulcorner r_i \text{C}_F \cdot (\eta)(\zeta)(\text{Thm } \eta \text{ cd } \zeta \cdot (\exists \theta)(r_i \text{RC}_F \, \theta \cdot$

$\eta \text{ Ing } \theta) \cdot \supset (\exists \theta)(r_i \text{RC}_F \, \theta \cdot \zeta \text{ Ing } \theta)) \cdot \supset : [1160 \supset \cdot]$

$(\exists \eta)(\text{RM}_N \text{Stat } \eta \cdot \eta \, r_i \text{SA}_F(\beta,\gamma) \cdot (\zeta)(\zeta \, r_i \text{SA}_F(\beta,\gamma) \cdot$

$\text{RM}_N \text{Stat } \zeta \cdot \supset \sim \zeta \, r_i \text{Str}_F \, \eta)) \supset (\exists \eta)(\eta \, r_i \text{SA}_F(\beta,\gamma) \cdot$

$$(\zeta)(\zeta \, r_i \text{SA}_F(\beta,\gamma) \supset \sim \zeta \, r_i \text{Str}_F \, \eta)) \overline{)} \tag{7}$$

*100, Δ99 $\ulcorner [6 \cdot 7 \cdot \supset] \, 1163 \overline{)}$

**1164 $\ulcorner r_i \text{C}_F \cdot (\eta)(\zeta)(\text{Thm } \eta \text{ cd } \zeta \cdot (\exists \theta)(r_i \text{RC}_F \, \theta \cdot \eta \text{ Ing } \theta) \cdot$

$\supset (\exists \theta)(r_i \text{RC}_F \, \theta \cdot \zeta \text{ Ing } \theta)) \cdot (\exists \theta)(r_i \text{RC}_F \, \theta \cdot$

$\eta \text{ cd } \eta \text{ Ing } \theta) \cdot \supset (\exists \alpha)(\exists \beta)(\exists \gamma)(\exists \eta)(\alpha \, r_i \text{Mem}_F \, \beta \cdot$

$\zeta \, r_i \text{B}_F \, \alpha \text{ e } \gamma \cdot \eta \, r_i \text{S*A}_F(\beta,\gamma) \cdot$

$(\beta')(\sim \beta' \, r_i \text{DP}_F(\alpha,\beta,\gamma))) \overline{)}$

ML(*253,*254; $\ulcorner \text{Thm} \, (\zeta \text{ cd } \zeta) \text{cd} (f\zeta a\zeta \text{ e unt v b } \zeta) \overline{)}$ $\quad$ (1)
†210,†211,†345)

*100 $\ulcorner r_i \text{C}_F \cdot (\eta)(\zeta)(\text{Thm } \eta \text{ cd } \zeta \cdot (\exists \theta)(r_i \text{RC}_F \, \theta \cdot \eta \text{ Ing } \theta) \cdot \supset$
**253 $\quad (\exists \theta)(r_i \text{RC}_F \, \theta \cdot \zeta \text{ Ing } \theta)) \cdot (\exists \theta)(r_i \text{RC}_F \, \theta \cdot$

$\zeta \text{ cd } \zeta \text{ Ing } \theta) \cdot [1 \cdot 1041 \cdot \supset] \, f\zeta a\zeta \text{ e unt v } r_i \text{B}_F \, \zeta \overline{)}$ (2)

ML(*253,*254; $\ulcorner \text{Thm} \, (\zeta \text{ cd } \zeta) \text{ cd } f\zeta a\zeta \text{ e unt } f\zeta a\zeta \overline{)}$ $\quad$ (3)
†210,†211,†344)

*100,**233 $\ulcorner r_i \text{C}_F \cdot (\eta)(\zeta)(\text{Thm } \eta \text{ cd } \zeta \cdot (\exists \theta)(r_i \text{RC}_F \, \theta \cdot$

$\eta \text{ Ing } \theta) \cdot \supset (\exists \theta)(r_i \text{RC}_F \, \theta \cdot \zeta \text{ Ing } \theta)) \cdot$

$(\exists \theta)(r_i \text{RC}_F \, \theta \cdot \zeta \text{ cd } \zeta \text{ Ing } \theta) \cdot [3 \cdot 1044 \cdot \supset]$

$f\zeta a\zeta \, r_i \text{Mem}_F \text{ unt } f\zeta a\zeta \overline{)}$ (3)

*100 $\ulcorner [1145 \cdot 1150 \cdot \supset :] \, r_i \text{C}_F \cdot (\eta)(\zeta)(\text{Thm } \eta \text{ cd } \zeta \cdot (\exists \theta)$

$(r_i \text{RC}_F \, \theta \cdot \eta \text{ Ing } \theta) \cdot \supset (\exists \theta)(r_i \text{RC}_F \, \theta \cdot \zeta \text{ Ing } \theta)) \cdot$

$(\exists \theta)(r_i \text{RC}_F \, \theta \cdot \zeta \text{ cd } \zeta \text{ Ing } \theta) \cdot (\exists \theta)(r_i \text{RC}_F \, \theta \cdot$

$\zeta \text{ Ing } \theta) \cdot \supset \cdot \text{pct} (\text{unt } f\zeta a\zeta, \text{unt v}, (\text{``}_s 1\text{''};\text{``}_s 1\text{''}))$

$r_i \text{S*A}_F (\text{unt } f\zeta a\zeta, \text{unt v}) \cdot \sim \beta' \, r_i \text{DP}_F (f\zeta a\zeta, \text{unt }$

$f\zeta a\zeta, \text{unt v}) \overline{)}$ (4)

Similarly, $\ulcorner r_i C_F \cdot (\eta)(\zeta)(\text{Thm } \eta \text{ cd } \zeta \cdot (\exists\theta)(r_i RC_F \ \theta \cdot \eta \text{ Ing } \theta) \cdot$
$\supset (\exists\theta)(r_i RC_F \ \theta \cdot \zeta \text{ Ing } \theta)) \cdot (\exists\theta)(r_i RC_F \ \theta \cdot$
$\zeta \text{ cd } \zeta \text{ Ing } \theta) \cdot (\exists\theta)(r_i RC_F \ \theta \cdot \text{n}\zeta \text{ Ing } \theta) \cdot \supset \cdot$
$\text{pct (unt f}\zeta\text{a}\zeta,\text{unt v},(\text{``}_s0\text{''};\text{``}_s0\text{''})) r_i S*A_F (\text{unt}$
$\text{f}\zeta\text{a}\zeta,\text{unt v}) \cdot \sim \beta' \ r_i DP_F(\text{f}\zeta\text{a}\zeta,\text{unt f}\zeta\text{a}\zeta,\text{unt v})\urcorner$(5)

By an argument analogous to that leading to line (8) of **1145, we can establish:

**233, $\ulcorner \text{Thm } (\zeta \text{ cd } \zeta) \text{ cd pct (unt f}\zeta\text{a}\zeta,\text{unt v},(\text{``}_s0\text{''};\text{``}_s1\text{''})) \supset :$
$r_i C_F \cdot (\eta)(\zeta)(\text{Thm } \eta \text{ cd } \zeta \cdot (\exists\theta)(r_i RC_F \ \theta \cdot$
$\eta \text{ Ing } \theta) \cdot \supset (\exists\theta)(r_i RC_F \ \theta \cdot \zeta \text{ Ing } \theta)) \cdot (\exists\theta)$
$(r_i RC_F \ \theta \cdot \zeta \text{ cd } \zeta \text{ Ing } \theta) \cdot \supset \text{pct (unt f}\zeta\text{a}\zeta,$
$\text{unt v},(\text{``}_s0\text{''};\text{``}_s1\text{''})) r_i SA_F (\text{unt f}\zeta\text{a}\zeta,\text{unt v})\urcorner$ (6)

Ratio exten- $\ulcorner \text{Thm } (\zeta \text{ cd } \zeta) \text{ cd pct (unt f}\zeta\text{a}\zeta,\text{unt v},(\text{``}_s0\text{''};\text{``}_s1\text{''}))\urcorner$ (7)
sion of ML

*100 $\ulcorner [6 \cdot 7 \cdot \supset :] \ r_i C_F \cdot (\eta)(\zeta)(\text{Thm } \eta \text{ cd } \zeta \cdot (\exists\theta)(r_i RC_F \ \theta \cdot$
$\eta \text{ Ing } \theta) \cdot \supset (\exists\theta)(r_i RC_F \ \theta \cdot \zeta \text{ Ing } \theta)) \cdot (\exists\theta)$
$(r_i RC_F \ \theta \cdot \zeta \text{ cd } \zeta \text{ Ing } \theta) \cdot \supset \text{pct (unt f}\zeta\text{a}\zeta,\text{unt v},$
$(\text{``}_s0\text{''};\text{``}_s1\text{''})) r_i SA_F (\text{unt f}\zeta\text{a}\zeta,\text{unt v})\urcorner$ (8)

Ratio exten- $\ulcorner \text{Thm n (pct (unt f}\zeta\text{a}\zeta,\text{unt v},(\text{``}_s0\text{''};\text{``}_s0\text{''}))) \text{cd}$
sion of ML. $\text{pct (unt f}\zeta\text{a}\zeta,\text{unt v},(\text{``}_s1\text{''};\text{``}_s1\text{''}))\urcorner$ (9)

Ratio exten- $\ulcorner \text{Thm n (pct (unt f}\zeta\text{a}\zeta,\text{unt v},(\text{``}_s1\text{''};\text{``}_s1\text{''}))) \text{cd}$
sion of ML. $\text{pct (unt f}\zeta\text{a}\zeta,\text{unt v},(\text{``}_s0\text{''};\text{``}_s0\text{''}))\urcorner$ (10)

Ratio exten- $\ulcorner \text{Thm pct (unt f}\zeta\text{a}\zeta,\text{unt v},(\text{``}_s0\text{''};\text{``}_s0\text{''})) \text{ cd n}\zeta\urcorner$ (11)
sion of ML.

Ratio exten- $\ulcorner \text{Thm pct (unt f}\zeta\text{a}\zeta,\text{unt v},(\text{``}_s1\text{''};\text{``}_s1\text{''})) \text{ cd } \zeta\urcorner$ (12)
sion of ML.

*100 $\ulcorner \text{Thm } \eta \text{ cd } \zeta \cdot (\exists\theta)(r_i RC_F \ \theta \cdot \eta \text{ Ing } \theta) \cdot \supset (\exists\theta)$
$(r_i RC_F \ \theta \cdot \zeta \text{ Ing } \theta) : \supset : \text{Thm } \eta \text{ cd } \zeta \cdot \sim (\exists\theta)$
$(r_i RC_F \ \theta \cdot \zeta \text{ Ing } \theta) \cdot \supset \sim (\exists\theta)(r_i RC_F \ \theta \cdot$
$\eta \text{ Ing } \theta)\urcorner$ (13)

*100,**233 $\ulcorner[(\eta)(\zeta)\ 13\cdot101\cdot9\cdot10\cdot11\cdot12\cdot\supset:]\ r_i\,C_F\cdot(\eta)(\zeta)$

$(\text{Thm }\eta\text{ cd }\zeta\cdot(\exists\theta)(r_i\,RC_F\ \theta\cdot\eta\text{ Ing }\theta)\cdot\supset$

$(\exists\theta)(r_i\,RC_F\ \theta\cdot\zeta\text{ Ing }\theta))\cdot(\exists\theta)(r_i\,RC_F\ \theta\cdot$

$\zeta\text{ cd }\zeta\text{ Ing }\theta)\cdot\sim(\exists\theta)(r_i\,RC_F\ \theta\cdot\zeta\text{ Ing }\theta)\cdot$

$\sim(\exists\theta)(r_i\,RC_F\ \theta\cdot n\zeta\text{ Ing }\theta)\cdot\supset\cdot\sim(\exists\theta)$

$(r_i\,RC_F\ \theta\cdot n\text{ pct}(\text{unt }f\zeta a\zeta,\text{unt }v,(\text{``}_s0\text{''};\text{``}_s0\text{''}))$

$\text{Ing }\theta)\cdot\sim(\exists\theta)(r_i\,RC_F\ \theta\cdot n\text{ pct}(\text{unt }f\zeta a\zeta,$

$\text{unt }v,(\text{``}_s1\text{''};\text{``}_s1\text{''}))\text{ Ing }\theta)\urcorner$ (14)

*100 $\ulcorner\text{Thm }\eta\text{ cd }\zeta\cdot(\exists\theta)(r_i\,RC_F\ \theta\cdot\eta\text{ Ing }\theta)\cdot\supset(\exists\theta)(r_i\,RC_F\ \theta\cdot$

$\zeta\text{ Ing }\theta):\supset:\sim(\exists\theta)(r_i\,RC_F\ \theta\cdot\zeta\text{ Ing }\theta)\supset$

$\sim(\text{Thm }\eta\text{ cd }\zeta\cdot(\exists\theta)(r_i\,RC_F\ \theta\cdot\eta\text{ Ing }\theta))\urcorner$ (15)

Ratio exten- $\ulcorner\eta\ r_i\,SA_F(\text{unt }f\zeta a\zeta,\text{unt }v)\cdot\eta\ r_i\,Str_F\text{ pct}(\text{unt }f\zeta a\zeta,$
sion of ML, $\Delta 98$

$\text{unt }v,(\text{``}_s0\text{''};\text{``}_s1\text{''}))\cdot\supset:\text{Thm }\eta\text{ cd}$

$n(\text{pct}(\text{unt }f\zeta a\zeta,\text{unt }v,(\text{``}_s0\text{''};\text{``}_s0\text{''})))\cdot$

$(\exists\theta)(r_i\,RC_F\ \theta\cdot\eta\text{ Ing }\theta)\cdot v\cdot\text{Thm }\eta\text{ cd}$

$n(\text{pct}(\text{unt }f\zeta a\zeta,\text{unt }v,(\text{``}_s1\text{''};\text{``}_s1\text{''})))\cdot$

$(\exists\theta)(r_i\,RC_F\ \theta\cdot\eta\text{ Ing }\theta)\urcorner$ (16)

*100,**233 $\ulcorner[(\eta)(\zeta)\ 15\cdot101\cdot8\cdot14\cdot16\cdot\supset:]\ r_i\,C_F\cdot(\eta)(\zeta)$

$(\text{Thm }\eta\text{ cd }\zeta\cdot(\exists\theta)(r_i\,RC_F\ \theta\cdot\eta\text{ Ing }\theta)\cdot\supset(\exists\theta)$

$(r_i\,RC_F\ \theta\cdot\zeta\text{ Ing }\theta))\cdot(\exists\theta)(r_i\,RC_F\ \theta\cdot\zeta\text{ cd }\zeta\text{ Ing }\theta)\cdot$

$\sim(\exists\theta)(r_i\,RC_F\ \theta\cdot\zeta\text{ Ing }\theta)\cdot\sim(\exists\theta)(r_i\,RC_F\ \theta\cdot n\zeta$

$\text{Ing }\theta)\cdot\supset\cdot\text{pct}(\text{unt }f\zeta a\zeta,\text{unt }v,(\text{``}_s0\text{''};\text{``}_s1\text{''}))$

$r_i\,SA_F(\text{unt }f\zeta a\zeta,\text{unt }v)\cdot\eta\ r_i\,SA_F(\text{unt }f\zeta a\zeta,\text{unt }v)\supset$

$\sim\eta\ r_i\,Str_F(\text{pct}(\text{unt }f\zeta a\zeta,\text{unt }v,(\text{``}_s0\text{''};\text{``}_s1\text{''})))\urcorner$ (17)

Ratio exten- $\ulcorner\text{pct}(\beta',\gamma,(\alpha;\alpha'))\,r_i\,S^*A_F(\beta',\gamma)\cdot(\exists\theta)(r_i\,RC_F\ \theta\cdot$
sion of ML,

$\zeta\text{ cd }\zeta\text{ Ing }\theta)\cdot\supset\cdot\text{Thm}(\zeta\text{ cd }\zeta)\text{ cd}$

$n\alpha'\,_s\text{gr ``}_s1\text{''}\cdot\text{Thm}(\zeta\text{ cd }\zeta)\text{ cd }n\text{``}_s0\text{''}\,_s\text{gr }\alpha\urcorner$ (18)

*100,**233,$\Delta101$, $\ulcorner[(\eta)\ 17\cdot18\cdot\supset:]\ r_i\,C_F\cdot(\eta)(\zeta)(\text{Thm }\eta\text{ cd }\zeta\cdot$
*157,*159,$\Delta108$

$(\exists\theta)(r_i\,RC_F\ \theta\cdot\eta\text{ Ing }\theta)\cdot\supset(\exists\theta)$

$$(r_i \text{RC}_\text{F} \ \theta \cdot \zeta \ \text{Ing} \ \theta)) \cdot (\exists \theta)(r_i \text{RC}_\text{F} \ \theta \cdot$$

$$\zeta \ \text{cd} \ \zeta \ \text{Ing} \ \theta) \cdot \sim (\exists \theta)(r_i \text{RC}_\text{F} \ \theta \cdot \zeta \ \text{Ing} \ \theta) \cdot$$

$$\sim (\exists \theta)(r_i \text{RC}_\text{F} \ \theta \cdot \text{n} \zeta \ \text{Ing} \ \theta) \cdot \supset \cdot$$

$$\text{pct} (\text{unt} \ f\zeta a\zeta, \text{unt} \ v, (\text{``}_s0\text{''};\text{``}_s1\text{''}))$$

$$r_i \text{S*A}_\text{F} (\text{unt} \ f\zeta a\zeta, \text{unt} \ v) \cdot \sim \beta' \ r_i \text{DP}_\text{F}$$

$$(f\zeta a\zeta, \text{unt} \ f\zeta a\zeta, \text{unt} \ v)^\top \tag{19}$$

*100, **233 $\ulcorner [2 \cdot 3 \cdot 4 \cdot 5 \cdot 19 \cdot \supset \cdot] \ 1164^\urcorner$
*157, *159

**1165 $\ulcorner r_i \text{C}_\text{F} \cdot (\eta)(\zeta)(\text{Thm} \ \eta \ \text{cd} \ \zeta \cdot (\exists \theta)(r_i \text{RC}_\text{F} \ \theta \cdot \eta \ \text{Ing} \ \theta) \cdot \supset$

$$(\exists \theta)(r_i \text{RC}_\text{F} \ \theta \cdot \zeta \ \text{Ing} \ \theta)) \cdot (\exists \theta)(r_i \text{RC}_\text{F} \ \theta \cdot \zeta \ \text{cd} \ \zeta$$

$$\text{Ing} \ \theta) \cdot \supset (\exists \alpha)(\exists \beta)(\exists \gamma)(\alpha \ r_i \text{Ran}_\text{F}(\beta, \gamma) \cdot$$

$$\zeta \ r_i \text{B}_\text{F} \ \alpha \ \text{e} \ \gamma)^\urcorner$$

Proof.

*100, *158, *160 $\ulcorner [1161 \cdot 1164 \cdot \supset :] \ r_i \text{C}_\text{F} \cdot (\eta)(\zeta)(\text{Thm} \ \eta \ \text{cd} \ \zeta \cdot$

$$(\exists \theta)(r_i \text{RC}_\text{F} \ \theta \cdot \eta \ \text{Ing} \ \theta) \cdot \supset (\exists \theta)(r_i \text{RC}_\text{F} \ \theta \cdot \zeta \ \text{Ing} \ \theta)) \cdot$$

$$(\exists \theta)(r_i \text{RC}_\text{F} \ \theta \cdot \zeta \ \text{cd} \ \zeta \ \text{Ing} \ \theta) \cdot \supset (\exists \eta)(\text{RM}_\text{N}\text{Stat} \ \eta \cdot (\exists \alpha)$$

$$(\exists \beta)(\exists \gamma)(\alpha \ r_i \text{Mem}_\text{F} \ \beta \cdot \zeta r_i \text{B}_\text{F} \ \alpha \ \text{e} \ \gamma \cdot \eta \ r_i \text{S*A}_\text{F}(\beta, \gamma) \cdot$$

$$(\beta')(\sim \beta' \ r_i \text{DP}_\text{F}(\alpha, \beta, \gamma))))^\urcorner \tag{1}$$

**1162 $\ulcorner r_i \text{C}_\text{F} \cdot (\eta)(\zeta)(\text{Thm} \ \eta \ \text{cd} \ \zeta \cdot (\exists \theta)(r_i \text{RC}_\text{F} \ \theta \cdot \eta \ \text{Ing} \ \theta) \cdot \supset$

$$(\exists \theta)(r_i \text{RC}_\text{F} \ \theta \cdot \zeta \ \text{Ing} \ \theta)) \cdot \supset \cdot (\exists \eta)(\text{RM}_\text{N}\text{Stat} \ \eta \cdot$$

$$(\exists \alpha)(\exists \beta)(\exists \gamma)(\alpha \ r_i \text{Mem}_\text{F} \ \beta \cdot \zeta \ r_i \text{B}_\text{F} \ \alpha \ \text{e} \ \gamma \cdot$$

$$\eta \ r_i \text{S*A}_\text{F}(\beta, \gamma) \cdot (\beta')(\sim \beta' \ r_i \text{DP}_\text{F}(\alpha, \beta, \gamma)))) \supset (\exists \eta)$$

$$(\eta')(\text{RM}_\text{N}\text{Stat} \ \eta \cdot (\exists \alpha)(\exists \beta)(\exists \gamma)(\alpha \ r_i \text{Mem}_\text{F} \ \beta \cdot$$

$$\zeta \ r_i \text{B}_\text{F} \ \alpha \ \text{e} \ \gamma \cdot \eta \ r_i \text{S*A}_\text{F}(\beta, \gamma) \cdot (\beta')(\sim \beta'$$

$$r_i \text{DP}_\text{F}(\alpha, \beta, \gamma)) : \text{RM}_\text{N}\text{Stat} \ \eta' \cdot (\exists \alpha)(\exists \beta)(\exists \gamma)$$

$$\alpha \ r_i \text{Mem}_\text{F} \ \beta \cdot \zeta \ r_i \text{B}_\text{F} \ \alpha \ \text{e} \ \gamma \cdot \eta' \ r_i \text{S*A}_\text{F}(\beta, \gamma) \cdot$$

$$(\beta')(\sim \beta' \ r_i \text{DP}_\text{F}(\alpha, \beta, \gamma)) \cdot \supset \sim \eta' \ r_i \text{Str}_\text{F} \ \eta))^\urcorner \tag{2}$$

*100,*158,*160 $\ulcorner [1 \cdot 2 \cdot \supset :] \ r_i \text{C}_\text{F} \cdot (\eta)(\zeta)(\text{Thm} \ \eta \ \text{cd} \ \zeta \cdot (\exists \theta)$

$$(r_i \text{RC}_\text{F} \ \theta \cdot \eta \ \text{Ing} \ \theta) \cdot \supset (\exists \theta)(r_i \text{RC}_\text{F} \ \theta \cdot \zeta \ \text{Ing} \ \theta)) \cdot (\exists \theta)$$

$$(r_i \text{RC}_\text{F} \ \theta \cdot \zeta \ \text{cd} \ \zeta \ \text{Ing} \ \theta) \cdot \supset (\exists \eta)(\exists \alpha)(\exists \beta)(\exists \gamma)(\text{RM}_\text{N}\text{Stat} \ \eta \cdot$$

$\eta \ r_i \text{S*A}_\text{F}(\beta,\gamma) \cdot \alpha \ r_i \text{Mem}_\text{F} \ \beta \cdot \zeta \ r_i \text{B}_\text{F} \ \alpha \ \text{e} \ \gamma \cdot (\beta')$

$(\sim \beta' \ r_i \text{DP}_\text{F}(\alpha,\beta,\gamma)) \cdot \eta \ r_i \text{S*A}_\text{F}(\beta,\gamma) \cdot (\eta')(\text{RM}_\text{N} \text{Stat} \ \eta' \cdot$

$(\exists \alpha'')(\exists \beta'')(\exists \gamma'')(\alpha'' \ r_i \text{Mem}_\text{F} \ \beta'' \cdot \zeta \ r_i \text{B}_\text{F} \ \alpha'' \ \text{e} \ \gamma'' \cdot$

$\eta' \ r_i \text{S*A}_\text{F}(\beta''\gamma'') \cdot (\beta')(\sim \beta' \ r_i \text{DP}_\text{F}(\alpha'',\beta'',\gamma''))) \cdot \supset$

$\sim \eta' \ r_i \text{Str}_\text{F} \ \eta \,)) \overline{}$ $\hfill (3)$

*156 $\overline{}(\exists \eta)(\exists \alpha)(\exists \beta)(\exists \gamma)(\text{RM}_\text{N} \text{Stat} \ \eta \cdot \eta \ r_i \text{S*A}_\text{F}(\beta,\gamma) \cdot$
*100
*158 $\qquad \alpha \ r_i \text{Mem}_\text{F} \ \beta \cdot \zeta \ r_i \text{B}_\text{F} \ \alpha \ \text{e} \ \gamma \cdot (\beta')(\sim \beta' \ r_i \text{DP}_\text{F}(\alpha,\beta,\gamma)) \cdot$
*160
$\qquad (\eta')(\text{RM}_\text{N} \text{Stat} \ \eta' \cdot (\exists \alpha'')(\exists \beta'')(\exists \gamma'')(\alpha'' \ r_i \text{Mem}_\text{F} \ \beta'' \cdot$

$\qquad \zeta \ r_i \text{B}_\text{F} \ \alpha'' \ \text{e} \ \gamma'' \cdot \eta' r_i \text{S*A}_\text{F}(\beta'',\gamma'') \cdot (\beta')(\sim \beta' \ r_i \text{DP}_\text{F}$

$\qquad (\alpha'',\beta'',\gamma''))) \cdot \supset \sim \eta' \ r_i \text{Str}_\text{F} \ \eta)) \supset \cdot (\exists \alpha)(\exists \beta)(\exists \gamma)(\exists \eta)$

$\qquad (\eta \ r_i \text{S*A}_\text{F}(\beta,\gamma) \cdot \alpha \ r_i \text{Mem}_\text{F} \ \beta \cdot \zeta \ r_i \text{B}_\text{F} \ \alpha \ \text{e} \ \gamma \cdot (\beta')$

$\qquad (\sim \beta' \ r_i \text{DP}_\text{F}(\alpha,\beta,\gamma))) \cdot (\exists \eta)(\eta \ r_i \text{S*A}_\text{F}(\beta,\gamma) \cdot (\eta')((\exists \alpha'')$

$\qquad (\exists \beta'')(\exists \gamma'')(\text{RM}_\text{N} \text{Stat} \eta' \cdot \eta' r_i \text{S*A}_\text{F}(\beta'',\gamma'') \cdot \zeta \ r_i \text{B}_\text{F} \ \alpha'' \text{e} \ \gamma''$

$\qquad \cdot \alpha'' \ r_i \text{Mem}_\text{F} \ \beta'' \cdot (\beta')(\sim \beta' \ r_i \text{DP}_\text{F}(\alpha'',\beta'',\gamma''))) \cdot \supset$

$\qquad \sim \eta' \ r_i \text{Str}_\text{F} \ \eta)) \overline{}$ $\hfill (4)$

*158 $\overline{}(\exists \eta)(\eta \ r_i \text{S*A}_\text{F}(\beta,\gamma) \cdot (\eta')((\exists \alpha'')(\exists \beta'')(\exists \gamma'')(\text{RM}_\text{N} \text{Stat} \ \eta' \cdot$
*162
$\qquad \eta' \ r_i \text{S*A}_\text{F}(\beta'',\gamma'') \cdot \zeta \ r_i \text{B}_\text{F} \ \alpha'' \ \text{e} \ \gamma'' \cdot \alpha'' \ r_i \text{Mem}_\text{F} \ \beta'' \cdot$

$\qquad (\beta')(\sim \beta' \ r_i \text{DP}_\text{F} (\alpha'',\beta'',\gamma''))) \cdot \supset \sim \eta' \ r_i \text{Str}_\text{F} \eta)) \equiv$

$\qquad (\exists \eta)(\eta')(\alpha'')(\beta'')(\gamma'')(\eta \ r_i \text{S*A}_\text{F}(\beta,\gamma) : \text{RM}_\text{N} \text{Stat} \ \eta' \cdot$

$\qquad \eta' \ r_i \text{S*A}_\text{F}(\beta'',\gamma'') \cdot \zeta \ r_i \text{B}_\text{F} \ \alpha'' \ \text{e} \ \gamma'' \cdot \alpha'' \ r_i \text{Mem}_\text{F} \ \beta'' \cdot$

$\qquad (\beta')(\sim \beta' \ r_i \text{DP}_\text{F}(\alpha'',\beta'',\gamma'')) \cdot \supset \sim \eta' \ r_i \text{Str}_\text{F} \ \eta) \overline{}$ $\hfill (5)$

*100 $\overline{}[5 \supset :] \ (\exists \eta)(\eta \ r_i \text{S*A}_\text{F}(\beta,\gamma) \cdot (\eta')((\exists \alpha'')(\exists \beta'')(\exists \gamma'')$
*139
D8 $\qquad (\text{RM}_\text{N} \text{Stat} \ \eta' \cdot \eta' \ r_i \text{S*A}_\text{F}(\beta'',\gamma'') \cdot \zeta \ r_i \text{B}_\text{F} \ \alpha'' \ \text{e} \ \gamma'' \cdot$
*119
$\qquad \alpha'' \ r_i \text{Mem}_\text{F} \ \beta'' \cdot (\beta')(\sim \beta' \ r_i \text{DP}_\text{F}(\alpha'',\beta'',\gamma''))) \cdot \supset$

$\qquad \sim \eta' \ r_i \text{Str}_\text{F} \ \eta)) \supset (\beta'')(\sim (\exists \alpha'')(\exists \gamma'')(\exists \eta')(\eta)$

$\qquad (\eta \ r_i \text{S*A}_\text{F}(\beta,\gamma) \supset \cdot \text{RM}_\text{N} \text{Stat} \ \eta' \cdot \eta' \ r_i \text{S*A}_\text{F}(\beta'',\gamma'') \cdot$

$\qquad \zeta \ r_i \text{B}_\text{F} \ \alpha'' \ \text{e} \ \gamma'' \cdot \alpha'' \ r_i \text{Mem}_\text{F} \ \beta'' \cdot (\beta')(\sim \beta'$

$\qquad r_i \text{DP}_\text{F}(\alpha'',\beta'',\gamma'')) \cdot \eta' \ r_i \text{Str}_\text{F} \ \eta)) \overline{}$ $\hfill (6)$

*122
Δ105
$\ulcorner$ RM$_N$Stat $\eta' \cdot \eta'$ r_iS*A$_F(\beta'',\gamma'') \cdot \equiv \eta'$ r_iS*A$_F(\beta'',\gamma'')$:

ζ r_iB$_F$ α'' e $\gamma'' \equiv \alpha$ e γ r_iB$_F$ α'' e γ'' : $\supset$: [6 $\equiv \cdot$]

$(\exists\eta)(\eta$ r_iS*A$_F(\beta,\gamma) \cdot (\eta')((\exists\alpha'')(\exists\beta'')(\exists\gamma'')$

(RM$_N$Stat $\eta' \cdot \eta'$ r_iS*A$_F(\beta'',\gamma'') \cdot \zeta$ r_iB$_F$ α'' e $\gamma'' \cdot$

α'' r_iMem$_F$ $\beta'' \cdot (\beta')(\sim \beta'$ r_iDP$_F(\beta'',\gamma''))) \cdot \supset$

$\sim \eta'$ r_iStr$_F$ $\eta)) \supset (\beta'')(\sim \beta''$ r_iSP$_F(\alpha,\beta,\gamma))$ $\urcorner$ (7)

*100
*232
$\ulcorner r_i$C$_F \cdot (\eta)(\zeta)($Thm η cd $\zeta \cdot (\exists\theta)(r_iRC_F$ $\theta \cdot \eta$ Ing $\theta) \cdot \supset$

$(\exists\theta)(r_i$RC$_F$ $\theta \cdot \zeta$ Ing $\theta)) \cdot [1161 \cdot]$: RM$_N$Stat $\eta' \cdot$

η' r_iS*A$_F(\beta'',\gamma'') \cdot \equiv \eta'$ r_iS*A$_F(\beta'',\gamma'')$ $\urcorner$ (8)

*100
$\ulcorner r_i$C$_F \cdot (\eta)(\zeta)($Thm η cd $\zeta \cdot (\exists\theta)(r_iRC_F$ $\theta \cdot \eta$ Ing $\theta) \cdot \supset$

$(\exists\theta)(r_i$RC$_F$ $\theta \cdot \zeta$ Ing $\theta)) \cdot [1147 \cdot 1043 \cdot] \supset$:

ζ r_iB$_F$ α e $\gamma \supset \cdot \zeta$ r_iB$_F$ α'' e $\gamma'' \equiv \alpha$ e γ r_iB$_F$

α'' e γ'' $\urcorner$ (9)

*100
$\ulcorner [8 \cdot 9 \cdot \supset:]$ r_iC$_F \cdot (\eta)(\zeta)($Thm η cd $\zeta \cdot (\exists\theta)(r_iRC_F$ $\theta \cdot$

η Ing $\theta) \cdot \supset (\exists\theta)(r_iRC_F$ $\theta \cdot \zeta$ Ing $\theta)) \cdot (\exists\theta)$

$(r_i$RC$_F$ $\theta \cdot \zeta$ cd ζ Ing $\theta) \cdot \supset \cdot (\exists\eta)(\eta$ r_iS*A$_F(\beta,\gamma)) \cdot$

α r_iMem$_F$ $\beta \cdot \zeta$ r_iB$_F$ α e $\gamma \cdot (\beta')(\sim \beta'$ r_iDP$_F$

$(\alpha,\beta,\gamma)) \cdot (\exists\eta)(\eta$ r_iS*A$_F(\beta,\gamma) \cdot (\eta')((\exists\alpha'')(\exists\beta'')$

$(\exists\gamma'')($RM$_N$Stat $\eta' \cdot \eta'$ r_iS*A$_F(\beta'',\gamma'') \cdot \zeta$ r_iB$_F$ α'' e

$\gamma'' \cdot \alpha''$ r_iMem$_F$ $\beta'' \cdot (\beta')(\sim \beta'$ r_iDP$_F(\alpha'',\beta'',\gamma''))) \cdot$

$\supset \sim \eta'$ r_iStr$_F$ $\eta)) : \supset :: \cdot r_iC_F \cdot (\eta)(\zeta)($Thm η cd $\zeta \cdot$

$(\exists\theta)(r_i$RC$_F$ $\theta \cdot \eta$ Ing $\theta) \cdot \supset (\exists\theta)(r_iRC_F$ $\theta \cdot$

ζ Ing $\theta)) \cdot (\exists\theta)(r_iRC_F$ $\theta \cdot \zeta$ cd ζ Ing $\theta) \cdot \supset : (\exists\eta)$

$(\eta$ r_iS*A$_F(\beta,\gamma)) \cdot \alpha$ r_iMem$_F$ $\beta \cdot \zeta$ r_iB$_F$ α e $\gamma \cdot (\beta')$

$(\sim \beta'$ r_iDP$_F(\alpha,\beta,\gamma))$: RM$_N$Stat $\eta' \cdot \eta'$ r_iS*A$_F(\beta'',\gamma'') \cdot$

$\equiv \eta'$ r_iS*A$_F(\beta'',\gamma'')$: ζ r_iB$_F$ α'' e $\gamma'' \equiv \alpha$ e γ r_iB$_F$ α'' e

γ'' : $(\exists\eta)(\eta$ r_iS*A$_F(\beta,\gamma) \cdot (\eta')((\exists\alpha'')(\exists\beta'')(\exists\gamma'')$

(RM$_N$Stat $\eta' \cdot r_i$S*A$_F(\beta'',\gamma'') \cdot \zeta$ r_iB$_F$ α'' e $\gamma'' \cdot$

α'' r_iMem$_F$ $\beta'' \cdot (\beta')(\sim \beta'$ r_iDP$_F(\alpha'',\beta'',\gamma''))) \cdot \supset$

$\sim \eta'$ r_iStr$_F$ $\eta))$ $\urcorner$ (10)

*100 $\ulcorner[10 \cdot 7 \cdot \supset : \cdot] r_i C_F \cdot (\eta)(\zeta)(\text{Thm } \eta \text{ cd } \zeta \cdot (\exists \theta)(r_i RC_F \ \theta \cdot$

$\eta \text{ Ing } \theta) \cdot \supset (\exists \theta)(r_i RC_F \ \theta \cdot \zeta \text{ Ing } \theta)) \cdot (\exists \theta)$

$(r_i RC_F \ \theta \cdot \zeta \text{ cd } \zeta \text{ Ing } \theta) \cdot \supset \cdot (\exists \eta)(\eta \ r_i S^*A_F(\beta,\gamma)) \cdot$

$\alpha \ r_i \text{Mem}_F \ \beta \cdot \zeta \ r_i B_F \ \alpha \text{ e } \gamma \cdot (\beta')(\sim \beta' \ r_i DP_F(\alpha,\beta,\gamma)) \cdot$

$(\exists \eta)(\eta \ r_i S^*A_F(\beta,\gamma) \cdot (\eta')((\exists \alpha'')(\exists \beta'')(\exists \gamma'')$

$(\text{RM}_N \text{Stat } \eta' \cdot \eta' \ r_i S^*A_F(\beta'',\gamma'') \cdot \zeta \ r_i B_F \ \alpha'' \text{ e } \gamma'' \cdot$

$\alpha'' \ r_i \text{Mem}_F \ \beta'' \cdot (\beta')(\sim \beta' \ r_i DP_F(\alpha'',\beta'',\gamma''))) \cdot \supset$

$\sim \eta' \ r_i \text{Str}_F \ \eta)) : \supset : r_i C_F \cdot (\eta)(\zeta)(\text{Thm } \eta \text{ cd } \zeta \cdot (\exists \theta)$

$(r_i RC_F \ \theta \cdot \eta \text{ Ing } \theta) \cdot \supset (\exists \theta)(r_i RC_F \ \theta \cdot \zeta \text{ Ing } \theta)) \cdot$

$(\exists \theta)(r_i RC_F \ \theta \cdot \zeta \text{ cd } \zeta \text{ Ing } \theta) \cdot \supset \cdot (\exists \eta)(\eta \ r_i S^*A_F$

$(\beta,\gamma)) \cdot \alpha \ r_i \text{Mem}_F \ \beta \cdot \zeta \ r_i B_F \ \alpha \text{ e } \gamma \cdot (\beta')(\sim \beta'$

$r_i DP_F(\alpha,\beta,\gamma)) \cdot (\beta'')(\sim \beta'' \ r_i DP_F(\alpha,\beta,\gamma))\urcorner$ (11)

*100 $\ulcorner[(\alpha)(\beta)(\gamma) \ 11 \cdot 149 \cdot 160 \cdot 3 \cdot 4 \cdot \supset :] \ r_i C_F \cdot (\eta)(\zeta)$

$(\text{Thm } \eta \text{ cd } \zeta \cdot (\exists \theta)(r_i RC_F \ \theta \cdot \eta \text{ Ing } \theta) \cdot \supset (\exists \theta)$

$(r_i RC_F \ \theta \cdot \zeta \text{ Ing } \theta)) \cdot (\exists \theta)(r_i RC_F \ \theta \cdot \zeta \text{ cd } \zeta$

$\text{Ing } \theta) \cdot \supset (\exists \alpha)(\exists \beta)(\exists \gamma)((\exists \eta)(\eta \ r_i S^*A_F(\beta,\gamma)) \cdot (\beta')$

$(\sim \beta' \ r_i DP_F(\alpha,\beta,\gamma)) \cdot (\beta'')(\sim \beta'' \ r_i SP_F(\alpha,\beta,\gamma)) \cdot$

$\zeta \ r_i B_F \ \alpha \text{ e } \gamma \cdot \alpha \ r_i \text{Mem}_F \ \beta)\urcorner$ (12)

*100, *140 (Δ106) $\ulcorner[12 \supset] \ 1165\urcorner$

**1166 $\ulcorner r_i C_F \cdot (\eta)(\zeta)(\text{Thm } \eta \text{ cd } \zeta \cdot (\exists \theta)(r_i RC_F \ \theta \cdot \eta \text{ Ing } \theta) \cdot \supset$

$(\exists \theta)(r_i RC_F \ \theta \cdot \zeta \text{ Ing } \theta)) \cdot (\exists \theta)(r_i RC_F \ \theta \cdot \zeta \text{ cd } \zeta$

$\text{Ing } \theta) \cdot \supset (\exists \psi)(\exists \xi)(\zeta \ r_i \text{Prob}_F(\psi;\xi))\urcorner$

Proof.

*100 $\ulcorner \alpha \ r_i \text{Ran}_F(\beta,\gamma) \cdot \zeta \ r_i B_F \ \alpha \text{ e } \gamma \cdot \supset (\exists \eta)(\eta \ r_i S^*A_F(\beta,\gamma))\urcorner$ (1)

*100, **234b, Δ99, Δ97b;

$\ulcorner(\exists \eta)(\eta \ r_i S^*A_F(\beta,\gamma) \supset (\exists \psi)(\exists \xi)(\text{pct}(\beta,\gamma,(\psi;\xi))r_i S^*A_F$

$(\beta,\gamma))\urcorner$ (2)

*100 $\ulcorner[1 \cdot 2 \cdot \supset :] \ \alpha \ r_i \text{Ran}_F(\beta,\gamma) \cdot \zeta \ r_i B_F \ \alpha \text{ e } \gamma \cdot \supset \cdot \zeta \ r_i B_F \ \alpha \text{ e }$

$\gamma \cdot \alpha \ r_i \text{Ran}_F(\beta,\gamma) \cdot (\exists \psi)(\exists \xi)(\text{pct}(\beta,\gamma,(\psi;\xi))$

$r_i S^*A_F(\beta,\gamma))\urcorner$ (3)

*149 $\ulcorner[(\alpha)(\beta)(\gamma)\,3\cdot\supset\cdot]\,(\exists\alpha)(\exists\beta)(\exists\gamma)(\alpha\,r_i\,\mathrm{Ran_F}(\beta,\gamma)\cdot$

$\qquad\zeta\,r_i\mathrm{B_F}\,\alpha\,\mathrm{e}\,\gamma)\supset(\exists\alpha)(\exists\beta)(\exists\gamma)(\zeta\,r_i\mathrm{B_F}\,\alpha\,\mathrm{e}\,\gamma\cdot$

$\qquad\alpha\,r_i\,\mathrm{Ran_F}(\beta,\gamma)\cdot(\exists\psi)(\exists\xi)(\mathrm{pct}\,(\beta,\gamma,(\psi;\xi))$

$\qquad r_i\mathrm{S^*A_F}(\beta,\gamma)))\urcorner$ (4)

*158, *138　$\ulcorner(\exists\alpha)(\exists\beta)(\exists\gamma)(\zeta\,r_i\mathrm{B_F}\,\alpha\,\mathrm{e}\,\gamma\cdot\alpha\,r_i\,\mathrm{Ran_F}(\beta,\gamma)\cdot$
(Δ107)

$\qquad(\exists\psi)(\exists\xi)(\mathrm{pct}\,(\beta,\gamma,(\psi;\xi))\,r_i\mathrm{S^*A_F}(\beta,\gamma))\supset$

$\qquad(\exists\psi)(\exists\xi)(\zeta\,r_i\,\mathrm{Prob_F}(\psi;\xi))\urcorner$ (5)

*100　$\ulcorner[1165\cdot4\cdot5\cdot\supset]\,1166\urcorner$

**1167　$\ulcorner(\eta)(\zeta)(\mathrm{Thm}\,\eta\,\mathrm{cd}\,\zeta\cdot(\exists\theta)(r_i\mathrm{RC_F}\,\theta\cdot\eta\,\mathrm{Ing}\,\theta)\cdot\supset(\exists\theta)$

$\qquad(r_i\mathrm{RC_F}\,\theta\cdot\zeta\,\mathrm{Ing}\,\theta))\cdot r_i\mathrm{C_F}\cdot\alpha\,\mathrm{e}\,\gamma\,r_i\mathrm{B_F}\,\alpha'\,\mathrm{e}\,\gamma'\cdot$

$\qquad\alpha\,r_i\,\mathrm{Ran_F}(\beta,\gamma)\cdot\alpha'\,r_i\,\mathrm{Ran_F}(\beta',\gamma')\cdot\eta\,r_i\mathrm{S^*A_F}(\beta,\gamma)\cdot$

$\qquad\eta'\,r_i\mathrm{S^*A_F}(\beta',\gamma')\cdot\supset\cdot\sim\eta\,r_i\mathrm{Str_F}\,\eta'\cdot\sim\eta'\,r_i\mathrm{Str_F}\,\eta\urcorner$

Proof.

*100, Δ106,　$\ulcorner\alpha\,r_i\,\mathrm{Ran_F}(\beta,\gamma)\cdot\alpha'\,r_i\,\mathrm{Ran_F}(\beta',\gamma')\cdot\supset\cdot\sim(\exists\beta'')$

$\qquad(\beta''\,r_i\mathrm{DP_F}(\alpha,\beta,\gamma))\cdot\sim(\exists\beta''')(\beta'''\,r_i\mathrm{DP_F}$

$\qquad(\alpha',\beta',\gamma'))\urcorner$ (1)

**233, *100, Δ106,　$\ulcorner\alpha\,r_i\,\mathrm{Ran_F}(\beta,\gamma)\cdot\alpha'\,r_i\,\mathrm{Ran_F}(\beta',\gamma')\cdot\supset\cdot$

$\qquad\sim\beta\,r_i\mathrm{SP_F}(\alpha',\beta',\gamma')\cdot\sim\beta'\,r_i\mathrm{SP_F}$

$\qquad(\alpha,\beta,\gamma)\urcorner$ (2)

*100, **233, Δ105;　$\ulcorner[1\cdot2\cdot3\cdot\supset\cdot]\,1167\urcorner$

**1168　$\ulcorner r_i\mathrm{C_F}\cdot(\eta)(\zeta)(\mathrm{Thm}\,\eta\,\mathrm{cd}\,\zeta\cdot(\exists\theta)(r_i\mathrm{RC_F}\,\theta\cdot\eta\,\mathrm{Ing}\,\theta\cdot\supset$

$\qquad(\exists\theta)(r_i\mathrm{RC_F}\,\theta\cdot\zeta\,\mathrm{Ing}\,\theta))\cdot\alpha\,\mathrm{e}\,\gamma\,r_i\mathrm{B_F}\,\alpha'\,\mathrm{e}\,\gamma'\cdot$

$\qquad\alpha\,r_i\,\mathrm{Ran_F}(\beta,\gamma)\cdot\alpha'\,r_i\,\mathrm{Ran_F}(\beta',\gamma')\cdot\eta\,r_i\mathrm{S^*A_F}(\beta,\gamma)\cdot$

$\qquad\eta'\,r_i\mathrm{S^*A_F}(\beta',\gamma')\cdot\supset\sim\eta\,r_i\mathrm{Dif_F}\,\eta'\urcorner$

Proof.

*131　$\ulcorner\sim(\exists\beta')(\beta'\,r_i\mathrm{DP_F}(\alpha,\beta,\gamma)\,\mathrm{v}\,\beta'\,r_i\mathrm{SP_F}(\alpha,\beta,\gamma))\supset(\beta')\sim$

$\qquad(\beta'\,r_i\mathrm{DP_F}(\alpha,\beta,\gamma)\,\mathrm{v}\,\beta'\,r_i\mathrm{SP_F}(\alpha,\beta,\gamma))\urcorner$ (1)

*110　$\qquad\supset\sim(\beta'\,r_i\mathrm{DP_F}(\alpha,\beta,\gamma)\,\mathrm{v}\,\beta'\,r_i\mathrm{SP_F}(\alpha,\beta,\gamma))\urcorner$ (2)

*131(Δ104) $\ulcorner \sim \beta' r_i \mathrm{DP_F}(\alpha,\beta,\gamma) \supset (\alpha')(\gamma')(\eta')(\eta) \sim (\alpha \ \mathrm{e} \ \gamma$

$r_i \mathrm{B_F} \ \alpha' \ \mathrm{e} \ \gamma' \cdot \eta' \ r_i \mathrm{S^*A_F}(\beta',\gamma') \cdot \eta \ r_i \mathrm{S^*A_F}(\beta,\gamma) \cdot$

$\alpha' \ r_i \mathrm{Mem_F} \ \beta' \cdot \eta \ r_i \mathrm{Dif_F} \ \eta' \cdot \sim (\exists \alpha'')(\exists \beta'')$

$(\exists \beta''')(\alpha'' r_i \mathrm{Mem_F} \ \beta'' \cdot \alpha \ \mathrm{e} \ \beta \ \mathrm{MP} \ \alpha'' \ \mathrm{e} \ \beta'' \cdot$

$(\exists \theta)(r_i \mathrm{RC_F} \ \theta \cdot \alpha' \ \mathrm{e} \ \beta' \ \mathrm{cd} \ \beta'' \ \mathrm{incl} \ \beta' \ \mathrm{cp} \ \beta'''$

$\mathrm{Ing} \ \theta)) \cdot \sim (\exists \beta'')(\exists \gamma'')(\exists \eta'')(\alpha' r_i \mathrm{Mem_F} \beta'' \cdot$

$\alpha' \ \mathrm{e} \ \gamma' \ r_i \mathrm{B_F} \ \alpha' \ \mathrm{e} \ \gamma'' \cdot \eta'' \ r_i \mathrm{S^*A_F}(\beta'',\gamma'') \cdot$

$\eta'' \ r_i \mathrm{S^=_F} \ \eta \cdot (\exists \theta)(r_i \mathrm{RC_F} \ \theta \cdot \alpha' \ \mathrm{e} \ \beta' \ \mathrm{cd} \ \beta''$

$\mathrm{incl} \ \beta' \ \mathrm{Ing} \ \theta) \cdot (\eta''')(\beta''')(\gamma''')(\alpha' \ r_i \mathrm{Mem_F} \ \beta''' \cdot$

$\alpha' \ \mathrm{e} \ \gamma'' \ r_i \mathrm{B_F} \ \alpha' \ \mathrm{e} \ \gamma''' \cdot \eta''' \ r_i \mathrm{S^*A_F}(\beta''',\gamma''') \cdot$

$(\exists \theta)(r_i \mathrm{RC_F} \ \theta \cdot \alpha' \ \mathrm{e} \ \beta'' \ \mathrm{cd} \ \beta''' \ \mathrm{incl} \ \beta'' \ \mathrm{Ing} \ \theta) \cdot$

$\supset \sim \eta''' \ r_i \mathrm{Dif_F} \ \eta''))) \urcorner$ \hfill (3)

*110 $\supset \sim (\alpha \ \mathrm{e} \ \gamma \ r_i \mathrm{B_F} \ \alpha' \ \mathrm{e} \ \gamma' \cdot \eta' \ r_i \mathrm{S^*A_F}(\beta',\gamma') \cdot$

$\eta \ r_i \mathrm{S^*A_F}(\beta,\gamma) \cdot \alpha' \ r_i \mathrm{Mem_F} \ \beta' \cdot \eta \ r_i \mathrm{Dif_F} \ \eta' \cdot$

$\sim (\exists \alpha'')(\exists \beta'')(\exists \beta''')(\alpha'' r_i \mathrm{Mem_F} \ \beta'' \cdot \alpha \ \mathrm{e} \ \beta \ \mathrm{MP} \ \alpha'' \ \mathrm{e}$

$\beta'' \cdot (\exists \theta)(r_i \mathrm{RC_F} \ \theta \cdot \alpha' \ \mathrm{e} \ \beta' \ \mathrm{cd} \ \beta'' \ \mathrm{incl} \ \beta' \ \mathrm{cp} \ \beta'''$

$\mathrm{Ing} \ \theta)) \cdot \sim (\exists \beta'')(\exists \gamma'')(\exists \eta'')(\alpha' r_i \mathrm{Mem_F} \beta'' \cdot \alpha' \ \mathrm{e} \ \gamma'$

$r_i \mathrm{B_F} \ \alpha' \ \mathrm{e} \ \gamma'' \cdot \eta'' \ r_i \mathrm{S^*A_F}(\beta'',\gamma'') \cdot \eta'' \ r_i \mathrm{S^=_F} \ \eta \cdot (\exists \theta)$

$(r_i \mathrm{RC_F} \ \theta \cdot \alpha' \ \mathrm{e} \ \beta' \ \mathrm{cd} \ \beta'' \ \mathrm{incl} \ \beta' \ \mathrm{Ing} \ \theta) \cdot (\eta''')(\beta''')$

$(\gamma''')(\alpha' \ r_i \mathrm{Mem_F} \ \beta''' \cdot \alpha' \ \mathrm{e} \ \gamma'' \ r_i \mathrm{B_F} \ \alpha' \ \mathrm{e} \ \gamma''' \cdot \eta'''$

$r_i \mathrm{S^*A_F}(\beta''',\gamma''') \cdot (\exists \theta)(r_i \mathrm{RC_F} \ \theta \cdot \alpha' \ \mathrm{e} \ \beta'' \ \mathrm{cd} \ \beta'''$

$\mathrm{incl} \ \beta'' \ \mathrm{Ing} \ \theta) \cdot \supset \sim \eta''' r_i \mathrm{Dif_F} \ \eta''))) \urcorner$ \hfill (4)

*100 $\ulcorner [2 \cdot 4 \cdot \supset :]$ Hyp $1168 \cdot \eta \ r_i \mathrm{Dif} \ \eta' \cdot \supset \cdot (\exists \alpha'')(\exists \beta'')(\exists \beta''')$

$(\alpha'' \ r_i \mathrm{Mem_F} \ \beta'' \cdot \alpha \ \mathrm{e} \ \beta \ \mathrm{MP} \ \alpha'' \ \mathrm{e} \ \beta'' \cdot (\exists \theta)$

$(r_i \mathrm{RC_F} \ \theta \cdot \alpha' \ \mathrm{e} \ \beta' \ \mathrm{cd} \ \beta'' \ \mathrm{incl} \ \beta' \ \mathrm{cp} \ \beta''' \ \mathrm{Ing} \ \theta)) \ \mathrm{v}$

$(\exists \beta'')(\exists \gamma'')(\exists \eta'')(\alpha' \ r_i \mathrm{Mem_F} \ \beta'' \cdot \alpha' \ \mathrm{e} \ \gamma' \ r_i \mathrm{B_F} \ \alpha' \ \mathrm{e} \ \gamma'' \cdot$

$\eta'' \ r_i \mathrm{S^*A_F}(\beta'',\gamma'') \cdot \eta'' \ r_i \mathrm{S^=_F} \ \eta \cdot (\exists \theta)(r_i \mathrm{RC_F} \ \theta \cdot$

$\alpha' \ \mathrm{e} \ \beta' \ \mathrm{cd} \ \beta'' \ \mathrm{incl} \ \beta' \ \mathrm{Ing} \ \theta) \cdot (\eta''')(\beta''')(\gamma''')$

$(\alpha' \ r_i \mathrm{Mem_F} \ \beta''' \cdot \alpha' \ \mathrm{e} \ \gamma'' \ r_i \mathrm{B_F} \ \alpha' \ \mathrm{e} \ \gamma''' \cdot$

$$\eta''' \, r_i S \, A_F(\beta''',\gamma''') \cdot (\exists \theta)(r_i RC_F \ \theta \cdot \alpha' e \beta'' \text{ cd } \beta'''$$

$$\text{incl } \beta'' \text{ Ing } \theta) \cdot \supset \sim \eta''' \, r_i Dif_F \ \eta'')) \ \rceil \qquad (5)$$

In a similar manner, we may obtain, using **1147 and *123:

$$\lceil \text{Hyp } 1168 \cdot \eta' \, r_i Dif_F \ \eta \cdot \supset \cdot (\exists \alpha'')(\exists \beta'')(\exists \beta''')$$

$$(\alpha'' \, r_i Mem_F \ \beta'' \cdot \alpha' e \beta' \text{ MP } \alpha'' e \beta'' \cdot (\exists \theta)$$

$$(r_i RC_F \ \theta \cdot \alpha' e \beta \text{ cd } \beta'' \text{ incl } \beta \text{ cp } \beta''' \text{ Ing } \theta)) \text{ v}$$

$$(\exists \beta'')(\exists \gamma'')(\exists \eta'')(\alpha \, r_i Mem_F \ \beta'' \cdot \alpha e \gamma \, r_i B_F \ \alpha e \gamma'' \cdot$$

$$\eta'' \, r_i S^*A_F(\beta'',\gamma'') \cdot \eta'' \, r_i S=_F \eta' \cdot (\exists \theta)(r_i RC_F \ \theta \cdot$$

$$\alpha e \beta \text{ cd } \beta'' \text{ incl } \beta \text{ Ing } \theta) \cdot (\eta''')(\beta''')(\gamma''')$$

$$(\alpha \, r_i Mem_F \ \beta''' \cdot \alpha e \gamma'' \, r_i B_F \ \alpha e \gamma''' \cdot \eta'''$$

$$r_i S^*A_F(\beta''',\gamma''') \cdot (\exists \theta)(r_i RC_F \ \theta \cdot \alpha e \beta'' \text{ cd } \beta'''$$

$$\text{Incl } \beta'' \text{ Ing } \theta) \cdot \supset \sim \eta''' \, r_i Dif_F \ \eta'')) \ \rceil \qquad (6)$$

I shall now establish that $\lceil$ R6 $\supset \sim$ R5 $\rceil$ is a matrix whose closure is a protosyntactical theorem. We may, without loss of generality, suppose that the number of ultimate membership elements of $\lceil \alpha \text{ e } \beta \rceil$ is less than or equal to the number of ultimate membership elements of $\lceil \alpha' \text{ e } \beta' \rceil$. Of course any membership permutation of $\lceil \alpha \text{ e } \beta \ \rceil$ will have the same number of ultimate membership elements; and we have (inasmuch as having a certain number of ultimate membership elements may be supposed, in this language, to be determined by syntactical rules governing the primitive predicates),

$$\lceil \alpha \text{ e } \beta \text{ MP } \alpha'' e \beta'' \supset \text{Thm n } \beta'' \text{ incl } \beta' \text{ cp } \beta''' \rceil \qquad (7)$$

*100 $\lceil$ Thm n β'' incl β' cp $\beta''' \supset$ Thm $(\alpha' e \beta' \text{ cd } \beta'' \text{ incl } \beta''')$ cd

$$\text{n } \alpha' e \beta' \rceil \qquad (8)$$

Δ103, Δ106, *100. $\lceil$ Hyp 1168 $\supset \sim (\exists \theta)(r_i RC_F \ \theta \cdot \text{n} \alpha' e \beta'$

$$\text{Ing } \theta) \rceil \qquad (9)$$

**231 $(\eta)(\zeta)(\text{Thm } \eta \text{ cd } \zeta \cdot (\exists \theta)(r_i RC_F \ \theta \cdot \eta \text{ Ing } \theta) \cdot \supset (\exists \theta)$

$$(r_i RC_F \ \theta \cdot \zeta \text{ Ing } \theta)) \supset : \text{Thm } (\alpha' e \beta'' \text{ incl } \beta' \text{ cp}$$

$$\beta''') \text{ cd n} \alpha' e \beta' \cdot (\exists \theta)(r_i RC_F \ \theta \cdot \alpha' e \beta' \text{ cd } \beta'' \text{ incl}$$

$$\beta' \text{ cp } \beta''' \text{ Ing } \theta) \cdot \supset (\exists \theta)(r_i RC_F \ \theta \cdot \text{n } \alpha' e \beta' \text{ Ing } \theta) \rceil$$

$$(10)$$

*100 $\ulcorner[7 \cdot 8 \cdot 9 \cdot 10 \cdot \supset :]$ Hyp 1168 $\cdot \supset \cdot \alpha$ e β MP α'' e $\beta'' \supset$

$\sim (\exists\theta)(r_i \text{RC}_\text{F} \ \theta \cdot \alpha'$ e β'cd β incl β'cp β''' Ing $\theta)\overline{)}^{\rfloor}$ (11)

*100 $\supset \sim (\alpha'' r_i \text{Mem}_\text{F}\beta'' \cdot \alpha$ e β MP α'' e $\beta'' \cdot (\exists\theta)$

$(r_i \text{RC}_\text{F} \ \theta \cdot \alpha'$ e β' cd β'' incl β' cp β''' Ing $\theta))^{\rfloor}$ (12)

*159, *131 $\ulcorner[(\alpha'')(\beta'')(\beta''') \ 12 \supset :]$ Hyp 1168 $\supset \sim (\exists\alpha'')(\exists\beta'')$

$(\exists\beta''')(\alpha'' r_i \text{Mem}_\text{F} \ \beta'' \cdot \alpha$ e β MP α'' e $\beta'' \cdot$

$(\exists\theta)(r_i \text{RC}_\text{F} \ \theta \cdot \alpha'$ e β' cd β'' incl β' cp

β''' Ing $\theta))^{\rfloor}$ (13)

Lines similar to lines (1)–(5) may be used to establish:

$\ulcorner$Hyp 1168 $\cdot \alpha'$ e $\gamma' \ r_i \text{B}_\text{F} \ \alpha'$ e $\gamma'' \cdot \eta'' r_i \text{S*A}_\text{F}(\beta'',\gamma'') \cdot$

$\alpha' r_i \text{Mem}_\text{F} \ \beta'' \cdot \eta' r_i \text{Dif}_\text{F}\eta'' \cdot \supset \cdot (\exists\alpha)(\exists\beta)(\exists\beta''')$

$(\alpha \ r_i \text{Mem}_\text{F} \ \beta \cdot \alpha'$ e β' MP α e $\beta \cdot (\exists\theta)(r_i \text{RC}_\text{F} \ \theta \cdot$

α' e β'' cd β incl β'' cp β''' Ing $\theta))$ v $(\exists\beta_4)(\exists\gamma_4)(\exists\eta_4)$

$(\alpha' r_i \text{Mem}_\text{F}\beta_4 \cdot \alpha'$ e $\gamma'' r_i \text{B}_\text{F} \ \alpha'$ e $\gamma_4 \cdot \eta_4 \ r_i \text{S*A}_\text{F}(\beta_4,\gamma_4) \cdot$

$\eta_4 \ r_i \text{S=}_\text{F} \ \eta' \cdot (\exists\theta)(r_i \text{RC}_\text{F} \ \theta \cdot \alpha'$ e β'' cd β_4

incl β'' Ing $\theta) \cdot (\eta_6)(\beta_6)(\gamma_6)(\alpha' \ r_i \text{Mem}_\text{F} \ \beta_6 \cdot \alpha'$ e γ_4

$r_i \text{B}_\text{F} \ \alpha'$ e $\gamma_6 \cdot \eta_6 \ r_i \text{S*A}_\text{F}(\beta_6 \cdot \gamma_6) \cdot (\exists\theta)(r_i \text{RC}_\text{F} \ \theta \cdot$

α' e β_4 cd β_6 incl β_4 Ing $\theta) \cdot \supset \sim \eta_6 \ r_i \text{Dif}_\text{F} \ \eta_4))^{\rfloor}$ (14)

I have supposed that the number of ultimate membership elements of $\ulcorner\alpha$ e $\beta\urcorner$ is less than or equal to the number of ultimate membership elements of $\ulcorner\alpha'$ e $\beta'\urcorner$. Clearly the number of ultimate membership elements of $\ulcorner\alpha'$ e $\beta''\urcorner$ must be the same as the number of ultimate membership elements of $\ulcorner\alpha'$ e $\beta'\urcorner$. Thus we must have, as in line (7),

$\ulcorner\alpha'$ e β' MP α e $\beta \supset$ Thm n βincl β'' cp $\beta'''\urcorner$ (15)

With the addition of $\ulcorner\alpha' \ r_i \text{Mem}_\text{F} \ \beta''\urcorner$ to the hypotheses of 1168, we may obtain by an argument strictly parallel to that embodied in lines (7)–(13):

$\ulcorner$Hyp 1168 $\cdot \alpha' \ r_i \text{Mem}_\text{F} \ \beta'' \cdot \supset \sim (\exists\alpha)(\exists\beta)(\exists\beta''')(\alpha r_i \text{Mem}_\text{F} \ \beta \cdot$

α' e β' MP α e $\beta \cdot (\exists\theta)(r_i \text{RC}_\text{F} \ \theta \cdot \alpha'$ e β'' cd β

incl β'' cp β''' Ing $\theta))^{\rfloor}$ (16)

*103 $\ulcorner(\eta''')(\beta''')(\gamma''')(\alpha'\ r_i\,\mathrm{Mem_F}\ \beta''' \cdot \alpha'\ \mathrm{e}\ \gamma''\ r_i\mathrm{B_F}\ \alpha'\ \mathrm{e}\ \gamma''' \cdot$

$\eta'''\ r_i\mathrm{S*A_F}(\beta''',\gamma''') \cdot (\exists\theta)(r_i\mathrm{RC_F}\ \theta \cdot \alpha'\ \mathrm{e}\ \beta''\ \mathrm{cd}$

$\beta'''\ \mathrm{incl}\ \beta''\ \mathrm{Ing}\ \theta) \cdot \supset \sim \eta'''\ r_i\mathrm{Dif_F}\ \eta'') \supset :$

$\alpha'\ r_i\,\mathrm{Mem_F}\ \beta_4 \cdot \alpha'\ \mathrm{e}\ \gamma''\ r_i\mathrm{B_F}\ \alpha'\ \mathrm{e}\ \gamma_4 \cdot \eta_4\ r_i\mathrm{S*A_F}$

$(\beta_4,\gamma_4) \cdot (\exists\theta)(r_i\mathrm{RC_F}\ \theta \cdot \alpha'\ \mathrm{e}\ \beta''\ \mathrm{cd}\ \beta_4\ \mathrm{incl}\ \beta''\ \mathrm{Ing}\ \theta)$

$\cdot \supset \eta_4\ r_i\mathrm{Dif_F}\ \eta''\urcorner$ (17)

**1032 $\ulcorner\eta_4\ r_i\mathrm{S=_F}\ \eta' \cdot \eta'\ r_i\mathrm{Dif_F}\ \eta'' \cdot \supset \eta_4\ r_i\mathrm{Dif_F}\ \eta''\urcorner$ (18)

**1036 $\ulcorner\eta'\ r_i\mathrm{Dif_F}\ \eta \equiv \eta\ r_i\mathrm{Dif_F}\ \eta'\urcorner$ (19)

**1032 $\ulcorner\eta''\ r_i\mathrm{S=_F}\ \eta \cdot \eta\ r_i\mathrm{Dif_F}\ \eta' \cdot \supset \eta''\ r_i\mathrm{Dif_F}\ \eta'\urcorner$ (20)

**1036 $\ulcorner\eta''\ r_i\mathrm{Dif_F}\ \eta' \equiv \eta'\ r_i\mathrm{Dif_F}\ \eta''\urcorner$ (21)

*100 $\ulcorner[17 \cdot 18 \cdot 19 \cdot 20 \cdot 21 \cdot \supset :]\eta\ r_i\mathrm{Dif_F}\ \eta' \cdot \alpha'\ r_i\mathrm{Mem_F}\ \beta'' \cdot$

$\alpha'\ \mathrm{e}\ \gamma'\ r_i\mathrm{B_F}\ \alpha'\ \mathrm{e}\ \gamma'' \cdot \eta''\ r_i\mathrm{S*A_F}(\beta'',\gamma'') \cdot \eta''\ r_i\mathrm{S=_F}\ \eta \cdot$

$(\exists\theta)(r_i\mathrm{RC_F}\ \theta \cdot \alpha'\ \mathrm{e}\ \beta'\ \mathrm{cd}\ \beta''\ \mathrm{incl}\ \beta'\ \mathrm{Ing}\ \theta) \cdot (\eta''')$

$(\beta''')(\gamma''')(\alpha'\ r_i\mathrm{Mem_F}\ \beta''' \cdot \alpha'\ \mathrm{e}\ \gamma''\ r_i\mathrm{B_F}\ \alpha'\ \mathrm{e}\ \gamma''' \cdot$

$\eta'''\ r_i\mathrm{S*A_F}(\beta''',\gamma''') \cdot (\exists\theta)(r_i\mathrm{RC_F}\ \theta \cdot \alpha'\ \mathrm{e}\ \beta''\ \mathrm{cd}\ \beta'''$

$\mathrm{incl}\ \beta''\ \mathrm{Ing}\ \theta) \cdot \supset \sim \eta'''\ r_i\mathrm{Dif_F}\ \eta'') \cdot \supset \cdot \alpha'\ r_i\,\mathrm{Mem_F}$

$\beta_4 \cdot \alpha'\ \mathrm{e}\ \gamma''\ r_i\mathrm{B_F}\ \alpha'\ \mathrm{e}\ \gamma_4 \cdot \eta_4\ r_i\mathrm{S*A_F}(\beta_4,\gamma_4) \cdot$

$(\exists\theta)(r_i\mathrm{RC_F}\ \theta \cdot \alpha'\ \mathrm{e}\ \beta''\ \mathrm{cd}\ \beta_4\ \mathrm{incl}\ \beta''\ \mathrm{Ing}\ \theta) \cdot \supset$

$\sim \eta_4\ r_i\mathrm{S=_F}\ \eta'\urcorner$ (22)

*100 $\ulcorner[22 \supset : \cdot]\ \mathrm{Hyp}\ 1168 \cdot \eta\ r_i\mathrm{Dif_F}\ \eta' \cdot \supset : \alpha'\ r_i\mathrm{Mem_F}\ \beta'' \cdot$

$\alpha'\ \mathrm{e}\ \gamma'\ r_i\mathrm{B_F}\ \alpha'\ \mathrm{e}\ \gamma'' \cdot \eta''\ r_i\mathrm{S*A_F}(\beta'',\gamma'') \cdot \eta''r_i\mathrm{S=_F}\ \eta \cdot$

$(\exists\theta)(r_i\mathrm{RC_F}\ \theta \cdot \alpha'\ \mathrm{e}\ \beta'\ \mathrm{cd}\ \beta''\ \mathrm{incl}\ \beta'\ \mathrm{Ing}\ \theta) \cdot (\eta''')$

$(\beta''')(\gamma''')(\alpha'\ r_i\mathrm{Mem_F}\ \beta''' \cdot \alpha'\ \mathrm{e}\ \gamma''\ r_i\mathrm{B_F}\ \alpha'\ \mathrm{e}\gamma''' \cdot$

$\eta'''\ r_i\mathrm{S*A_F}(\beta''',\gamma''') \cdot (\exists\theta)(r_i\mathrm{RC_F}\ \theta \cdot \alpha'\ \mathrm{e}\ \beta''\ \mathrm{cd}\ \beta'''$

$\mathrm{incl}\beta''\ \mathrm{Ing}\ \theta) \cdot \supset \sim \eta'''\ r_i\mathrm{Dif_F}\ \eta'') \cdot \supset \sim (\alpha'r_i\mathrm{Mem_F}\ \beta_4 \cdot$

$\cdot \alpha'\ \mathrm{e}\ \gamma''\ r_i\mathrm{B_F}\ \alpha'\ \mathrm{e}\ \gamma_4 \cdot \eta_4\ r_i\mathrm{S*A_F}(\beta_4,\gamma_4) \cdot$

$(\exists\theta)(r_i\mathrm{RC_F}\ \theta \cdot \alpha'\ \mathrm{e}\ \beta''\ \mathrm{cd}\ \beta_4\ \mathrm{incl}\ \beta''\mathrm{Ing}\ \theta) \cdot$

$\eta_4\ r_i\mathrm{S=_F}\ \eta' \cdot (\eta_6)(\beta_6)(\gamma_6)(\alpha'\ r_i\mathrm{Mem_F}\ \beta_6 \cdot \alpha'\ \mathrm{e}\ \gamma_4\ r_i\mathrm{B_F}$

$\alpha'\ \mathrm{e}\ \gamma_6 \cdot \eta_6 r_i\mathrm{S*A_F}(\beta_6,\gamma_6) \cdot (\exists\theta)(r_i\mathrm{RC_F}\ \theta \cdot \alpha'\ \mathrm{e}\ \beta_4$

$\mathrm{cd}\ \beta_6\ \mathrm{incl}\ \beta_4\ \mathrm{Ing}\ \theta) \cdot \supset \sim \eta_6\ r_i\mathrm{Dif_F}\ \eta_4))\urcorner$ (23)

*159,*131 $\ulcorner[(\beta_4)(\gamma_4)(\eta_4)$ 23 $\supset : \cdot]$ Hyp 1168 $\cdot \eta \; r_i \mathrm{Dif_F} \; \eta' \cdot \supset :$

$\alpha' \; r_i \mathrm{Mem_F} \; \beta'' \cdot \alpha' \; e \; \gamma' \; r_i \mathrm{B_F} \; \alpha' \; e \; \gamma'' \cdot$

$\eta'' \; r_i \mathrm{S^*A_F}(\beta'',\gamma'') \cdot \eta'' \; r_i \mathrm{S=_F} \; \eta \cdot (\exists \theta)(r_i \mathrm{RC_F} \; \theta \cdot$

$\alpha' \; e \; \beta' \; \mathrm{cd} \; \beta'' \; \mathrm{incl} \; \beta' \; \mathrm{Ing} \; \theta) \cdot (\eta''')(\beta''')(\gamma''')$

$(\alpha' \; r_i \mathrm{Mem_F} \; \beta''' \cdot \alpha' \; e \; \gamma'' \; r_i \mathrm{B_F} \; \alpha' \; e \; \gamma''' \cdot \eta'''$

$r_i \mathrm{S^*A_F}(\beta''',\gamma''') \cdot (\exists \theta)(r_i \mathrm{RC_F} \; \theta \cdot \alpha' \; e \; \beta'' \; \mathrm{cd}$

$\beta''' \; \mathrm{incl} \; \beta'' \; \mathrm{Ing} \; \theta) \cdot \supset \sim \eta''' \; r_i \mathrm{Dif_F} \; \eta'') \cdot \supset \sim (\exists \beta_4$

$(\exists \gamma_4)(\exists \eta_4)(\alpha' \; r_i \mathrm{Mem_F} \; \beta_4 \cdot \alpha' \; e \; \gamma'' \; r_i \mathrm{B_F} \; \alpha' \; e \; \beta_4 \cdot$

$\eta_4 \; r_i \mathrm{S^*A_F}(\beta_4,\gamma_4) \cdot (\exists \theta)(r_i \mathrm{RC_F} \; \theta \cdot \alpha' \; e \; \beta''$

$\mathrm{cd} \; \beta_4 \; \mathrm{incl} \; \beta'' \; \mathrm{Ing} \; \theta) \cdot \eta_4 \; r_i \mathrm{S=_F} \; \eta' \cdot (\eta_6)(\beta_6)(\gamma_6)$

$(\alpha' \; r_i \mathrm{Mem_F} \; \beta_6 \cdot \alpha' \; e \; \gamma_4 \; r_i \mathrm{B_F} \; \alpha' \; e \; \gamma_6 \cdot \eta_6 \; r_i \mathrm{S^*A_F}$

$(\beta_6,\gamma_6) \cdot (\exists \theta)(r_i \mathrm{RC_F} \; \theta \cdot \alpha' \; e \; \beta_4 \; \mathrm{cd} \; \beta_6 \; \mathrm{incl} \; \beta_4$

$\mathrm{Ing} \; \theta) \cdot \supset \sim \eta_6 \; r_i \mathrm{Dif_F} \; \eta_4))\urcorner$ (24)

*100 $\ulcorner[14 \cdot 16 \cdot 20 \cdot 24 \cdot \supset :]$ Hyp 1168 $\cdot \eta \; r_i \mathrm{Dif_F} \eta' \cdot \supset$

$\sim (\alpha' \; r_i \mathrm{Mem_F} \; \beta'' \cdot \alpha' \; e \; \gamma' \; r_i \mathrm{B_F} \; \alpha' \; e \; \gamma'' \cdot \eta'' \; r_i \mathrm{S^*A_F}$

$(\beta'',\gamma'') \cdot \eta'' \; r_i \mathrm{S=_F} \; \eta \cdot (\exists \theta)(r_i \mathrm{RC_F} \; \theta \cdot \alpha' \; e \; \beta' \; \mathrm{cd}$

$\beta'' \; \mathrm{incl} \; \beta' \; \mathrm{Ing} \; \theta) \cdot (\eta''')(\beta''')(\gamma''')(\alpha' \; r_i \mathrm{Mem_F} \; \beta''' \cdot$

$\alpha' \; e \; \gamma'' \; r_i \mathrm{B_F} \; \alpha' \; e \; \gamma''' \cdot \eta''' \; r_i \mathrm{S^*A_F}(\beta''',\gamma''') \cdot (\exists \theta)$

$(r_i \mathrm{RC_F} \; \theta \cdot \alpha' \; e \; \beta'' \; \mathrm{cd} \; \beta''' \; \mathrm{incl} \; \beta'' \; \mathrm{Ing} \; \theta) \cdot \supset$

$\sim \eta''' \; r_i \mathrm{Dif_F} \; \eta''))\urcorner$ (25)

*159,*131 $\ulcorner[(\beta'')(\gamma'')(\eta'')$ 25 $\cdot \supset :]$ Hyp 1168 $\cdot \eta \; r_i \mathrm{Dif_F} \; \eta' \cdot \supset$

$\sim (\exists \beta'')(\exists \gamma'')(\exists \eta'')(\alpha' \; r_i \mathrm{Mem_F} \; \beta'' \cdot \alpha' \; e \; \gamma'$

$r_i \mathrm{B_F} \; \alpha' \; e \; \gamma'' \cdot \eta'' \; r_i \mathrm{S^*A_F}(\beta'',\gamma'') \cdot \eta'' \; r_i \mathrm{S=_F} \; \eta \cdot$

$(\exists \theta)(r_i \mathrm{RC_F} \; \theta \cdot \alpha' \; e \; \beta' \; \mathrm{cd} \; \beta'' \; \mathrm{incl} \; \beta' \; \mathrm{Ing} \; \theta) \cdot$

$(\eta''')(\beta''')(\gamma''')(\alpha' \; r_i \mathrm{Mem_F} \; \beta''' \cdot \alpha' \; e \; \gamma'''$

$r_i \mathrm{B_F} \; \alpha' \; e \; \gamma''' \cdot \eta''' \; r_i \mathrm{S^*A_F}(\beta''',\gamma''') \cdot (\exists \theta)$

$(r_i \mathrm{RC_F} \; \theta \cdot \alpha' \; e \; \beta'' \; \mathrm{cd} \; \beta''' \; \mathrm{incl} \; \beta'' \; \mathrm{Ing} \; \theta) \cdot \supset$

$\sim \eta''' \; r_i \mathrm{Dif_F} \; \eta''))\urcorner$ (26)

*100 $\ulcorner[13 \cdot 26 \cdot \supset :]$ 1168 $\urcorner$

**1169 $\ulcorner r_i C_F \cdot (\eta)(\zeta)(\text{Thm } \eta \text{ cd } \zeta \cdot (\exists \theta)(r_i RC_F \ \theta \cdot \eta \text{ Ing } \theta) \cdot \supset$
$(\exists \theta)(r_i RC_F \ \theta \cdot \zeta \text{ Ing } \theta)) \cdot \alpha \text{ e } \gamma \ r_i B_F \ \alpha' \text{ e } \gamma' \cdot$
$\alpha \ r_i \text{Ran}_F(\beta, \gamma) \cdot \alpha' \ r_i \text{Ran}_F(\beta', \gamma') \cdot \eta \ r_i S^*A_F(\beta, \gamma) \cdot$
$\eta' \ r_i S^*A_F(\beta', \gamma') \cdot \supset \eta \ r_i S=_F \eta'\urcorner$

Proof.

*100 $\ulcorner [1125 \cdot 1021 \cdot \supset :] r_i C_F \cdot (\eta)(\zeta)(\text{Thm } \eta \text{ cd } \zeta \cdot (\exists \theta)$
$(r_i RC_F \ \theta \cdot \eta \text{ Ing } \theta) \cdot \supset (\exists \theta)(r_i RC_F \ \theta \cdot \zeta \text{ Ing } \theta)) \cdot$
$\eta \ r_i S^*A_F(\beta, \gamma) \cdot \eta' \ r_i S^*A_F(\beta', \gamma') \cdot \supset \cdot \eta \ r_i \text{Str}_F \ \eta' \text{ v}$
$\eta' \ r_i \text{Str}_F \ \eta \text{ v } \eta \ r_i S=_F \eta' \text{ v } \eta \ r_i \text{Dif}_F \ \eta'\urcorner$ (1)

*100 $\ulcorner [1167 \cdot 1168 \cdot 1 \cdot \supset] \ 1169\urcorner$

**1170 $\ulcorner r_i C_F \cdot (\eta)(\zeta)(\text{Thm } \eta \text{ cd } \zeta \cdot (\exists \theta)(r_i RC_F \ \theta \cdot \eta \text{ Ing } \theta) \cdot \supset$
$(\exists \theta)(r_i RC_F \ \theta \cdot \zeta \text{ Ing } \theta)) \cdot \eta \ r_i B_F \ \zeta \cdot \eta \ r_i \text{Prob}_F$
$(\psi; \xi) \cdot \supset \zeta \ r_i \text{Prob}_F(\psi; \xi)\urcorner$

Proof.

*100,**232, $\ulcorner \eta \ r_i B_F \ \zeta \supset (\exists \theta)(\exists \beta)(r_i RC_F \theta \cdot \beta \text{ Ing } \theta)\urcorner$ (1)

ML(*100) $\ulcorner \eta \ r_i B_F \ \zeta \cdot r_i RC_F \ \theta \cdot \beta \text{ Ing } \theta \cdot \supset \text{Thm } \beta \text{ cd } (\zeta \text{ cd } \zeta)\urcorner$ (2)

**233 $\ulcorner r_i C_F \cdot (\eta)(\zeta)(\text{Thm } \eta \text{ cd } \zeta \cdot (\exists \theta)(r_i RC_F \theta \cdot \eta \text{ Ing } \theta) \cdot \supset$
$(\exists \theta)(r_i RC_F \ \theta \cdot \zeta \text{ Ing } \theta)) \cdot \eta \ r_i B_F \ \zeta \cdot$
$\eta \ r_i \text{Prob}_F(\psi; \xi) \cdot [1 \cdot 2 \cdot] \supset (\exists \theta)(r_i RC_F \ \theta \cdot \zeta \text{ cd}$
$\zeta \text{ Ing } \theta)\urcorner$ (3)

*100 $\ulcorner [1166 \cdot 3 \cdot \supset :] r_i C_F \cdot (\eta)(\zeta)(\text{Thm } \eta \text{ cd } \zeta \cdot (\exists \theta)$
$(r_i RC_F \ \theta \cdot \eta \text{ Ing } \theta) \cdot \supset (\exists \theta)(r_i RC_F \ \theta \cdot \zeta \text{ Ing } \theta)) \cdot$
$\eta \ r_i B_F \ \zeta \cdot \eta \ r_i \text{Prob}_F(\psi; \xi) \cdot \supset (\exists \psi')(\exists \xi')$
$(\zeta \ r_i \text{Prob}_F(\psi'; \xi'))\urcorner$ (4)

*100, △107, *160 $\ulcorner [4 \supset :] r_i C_F \cdot (\eta)(\zeta)(\text{Thm } \eta \text{ cd } \zeta \cdot (\exists \theta)$
$(r_i RC_F \ \theta \cdot \eta \text{ Ing } \theta) \cdot \supset (\exists \theta)(r_i RC_F \ \theta \cdot \zeta \text{ Ing } \theta)) \cdot$
$\eta \ r_i B_F \ \zeta \cdot \eta \ r_i \text{Prob}_F(\psi; \xi) \cdot \supset (\exists \alpha)(\exists \beta)(\exists \gamma)(\exists \alpha')$
$(\exists \beta')(\exists \gamma')(\exists \psi')(\exists \xi')(\eta \ r_i B_F \ \alpha \text{ e } \gamma \cdot \zeta \ r_i B_F \ \alpha' \text{ e } \gamma' \cdot$

$$\alpha \; r_i \, \mathrm{Ran_F}(\beta,\gamma) \cdot \alpha' \; r_i \, \mathrm{Ran_F}(\beta',\gamma') \cdot \mathrm{pct}\,(\beta,\gamma,(\psi;\xi))$$

$$r_i \mathrm{S}^* \mathrm{A_F}(\beta,\gamma) \cdot \mathrm{pct}\,(\beta',\gamma',(\psi';\xi')) \, r_i \mathrm{S}^* \mathrm{A_F}(\beta',\gamma')) \qquad (5)$$

*100 $\ulcorner [\,1043 \cdot 1147 \cdot \supset\,] \; r_i \mathrm{C_F} \cdot (\eta)(\zeta)(\mathrm{Thm}\; \eta \; \mathrm{cd}\; \zeta \cdot (\exists \theta\,)$

$(r_i \mathrm{RC_F}\; \theta \cdot \eta \; \mathrm{Ing}\; \theta\,) \cdot \supset (\exists \theta\,)(r_i \mathrm{RC_F}\; \theta \cdot \zeta \; \mathrm{Ing}\; \theta\,)) \cdot$

$\supset : \eta \; r_i \mathrm{B_F}\; \zeta \cdot \eta \; r_i \mathrm{B_F}\; \alpha \; \mathrm{e}\; \gamma \cdot \zeta \; r_i \mathrm{B_F}\; \alpha' \; \mathrm{e}\; \gamma' \cdot \supset$

$\alpha \; \mathrm{e}\; \gamma \; r_i \mathrm{B_F}\; \alpha' \; \mathrm{e}\; \gamma'\urcorner \qquad (6)$

*100 (combined with a judicious manipulation of quantifiers)

$\ulcorner [\,5 \cdot 6 \cdot 1169 \cdot \supset :\,] \; r_i \mathrm{C_F} \cdot (\eta)(\zeta)(\mathrm{Thm}\; \eta \; \mathrm{cd}\; \zeta \cdot (\exists \theta\,)$

$(r_i \mathrm{RC_F}\; \theta \cdot \eta \; \mathrm{Ing}\; \theta\,) \cdot \supset (\exists \theta\,)(r_i \mathrm{RC_F}\; \theta \cdot \zeta \; \mathrm{Ing}\; \theta\,)) \cdot$

$\eta \; r_i \mathrm{B_F}\; \zeta \cdot \eta \; r_i \, \mathrm{Prob_F}(\psi;\xi) \cdot \supset (\exists \psi')(\exists \xi')(\exists \alpha)(\exists \beta)$

$(\exists \gamma)(\exists \alpha')(\exists \beta')(\exists \gamma')(\eta \; r_i \mathrm{B_F}\; \alpha \; \mathrm{e}\; \gamma \cdot \zeta \; r_i \mathrm{B_F}\; \alpha' \; \mathrm{e}\; \gamma' \cdot$

$\alpha \; r_i \, \mathrm{Ran_F}(\beta,\gamma) \cdot \alpha' \, r_i \, \mathrm{Ran_F}(\beta',\gamma') \cdot \mathrm{pct}\,(\beta,\gamma,(\psi;\xi))$

$r_i \mathrm{S}^* \mathrm{A_F}(\beta,\gamma) \cdot \mathrm{pct}\,(\beta',\gamma',(\psi';\xi')) \, r_i \mathrm{S}^* \mathrm{A_F}(\beta',\gamma') \cdot$

$\mathrm{pct}\,(\beta,\gamma,(\psi;\xi)) \; r_i \mathrm{S}=_F \mathrm{pct}\,(\beta',\gamma',(\psi';\xi')))\urcorner \qquad (7)$

In view of the fact that in a rational corpus which is consistent, the statements relating the fractions that appear in statistical statements are either theorems or the negations of theorems,

$\ulcorner r_i \mathrm{C_F} \cdot \mathrm{pct}\,(\beta,\gamma,(\psi;\xi)) \; r_i \mathrm{S}=_F \mathrm{pct}\,(\beta',\gamma',(\psi';\xi')) \cdot \supset \cdot$

$\mathrm{Thm}\; \psi \; \mathrm{id}\; \psi' \cdot \mathrm{Thm}\; \xi \; \mathrm{id}\; \xi'\urcorner \qquad (8)$

ML (D 72) $\ulcorner \mathrm{Thm}\; \psi \; \mathrm{id}\; \psi' \cdot \mathrm{Thm}\; \xi \; \mathrm{id}\; \xi' \cdot \supset \mathrm{Thm}\; \mathrm{pct}\,(\beta',\gamma',(\psi';\xi'))$

$\mathrm{cd}\; \mathrm{pct}\,(\beta',\gamma',(\psi;\xi))\urcorner \qquad (9)$

Ratio exten- $\ulcorner \mathrm{Thm}\; \psi \; \mathrm{id}\; \psi' \cdot \mathrm{Thm}\; \xi \; \mathrm{id}\; \xi' \cdot \supset \cdot \mathrm{Thm}\; \mathrm{n}\,(\alpha \;_s \mathrm{gr}\; \psi')$
sion of ML
$\mathrm{cd}\; \mathrm{n}\,(\alpha \;_s \mathrm{gr}\; \psi) \cdot \mathrm{Thm}\; \mathrm{n}\,(\xi' \;_s \mathrm{gr}\; \gamma) \; \mathrm{cd}$

$\bar{\mathrm{n}}\,(\xi \;_s \mathrm{gr}\; \gamma)\urcorner \qquad (10)$

**233,*100 $\ulcorner [\,7 \cdot 8 \cdot 9 \cdot 10 \cdot \supset :\,] \; r_i \mathrm{C_F} \cdot (\eta)(\zeta)(\mathrm{Thm}\; \eta \; \mathrm{cd}\; \zeta \cdot$

$(\exists \theta\,)(r_i \mathrm{RC_F}\; \theta \cdot \eta \; \mathrm{Ing}\; \theta\,) \cdot \supset (\exists \theta\,)(r_i \mathrm{RC_F}\; \theta \cdot$

$\zeta \; \mathrm{Ing}\; \theta\,)) \cdot \eta \; r_i \mathrm{B_F}\; \zeta \cdot \eta \; r_i \, \mathrm{Prob_F}(\psi;\xi) \cdot \supset$

$(\exists \psi')(\exists \xi')(\exists \alpha)(\exists \beta)(\exists \gamma)(\exists \alpha')(\exists \beta')(\exists \gamma')$

$(\eta \; r_i \mathrm{B_F}\; \alpha \; \mathrm{e}\; \gamma \cdot \zeta \; r_i \mathrm{B_F}\; \alpha' \; \mathrm{e}\; \gamma' \cdot \alpha \; r_i \, \mathrm{Ran_F}(\beta,\gamma) \cdot$

$\alpha' \; r_i \, \mathrm{Ran_F}(\beta',\gamma') \cdot \mathrm{pct}\,(\beta,\gamma,(\psi;\xi)) \, r_i \mathrm{S}^* \mathrm{A_F}(\beta,\gamma) \cdot$

$$\text{pct}\,(\beta',\gamma',(\,\psi';\xi'))\,r_i\,\mathrm{S*A_F}(\beta',\gamma')\cdot\text{pct}\,(\beta',\gamma')$$
$$(\psi;\xi))\,r_i\,\mathrm{S*A_F}(\beta',\gamma'))\,^\rceil \qquad\qquad (11)$$

*158, *100, Δ107, $^\lceil[\,11\cdot\supset]\;1170\,^\rceil$

**1171 $^\lceil r_i\,\mathrm{C_F}\cdot(\eta)(\zeta)(\mathrm{Thm}\;\eta\;\mathrm{cd}\;\zeta\cdot(\,\exists\theta\,)(\,r_i\,\mathrm{RC_F}\;\theta\cdot\eta\;\mathrm{Ing}\;\theta\,)\cdot\supset$
$(\,\exists\theta\,)(\,r_i\,\mathrm{RC_F}\;\theta\cdot\zeta\;\mathrm{Ing}\;\theta\,))\cdot\zeta\;r_i\mathrm{B_F}\;\alpha\;\mathrm{e}\;\gamma\cdot$
$\text{pct}\,(\beta,\gamma,(\psi;\xi))\,r_i\,\mathrm{S*A_F}(\beta,\gamma)\cdot\alpha\;r_i\,\mathrm{Mem_F}\;\beta\cdot$
$\sim(\,\exists\beta''\,)(\beta''\;r_i\mathrm{DP_F}(\alpha,\beta,\gamma))\cdot\supset(\,\exists\psi'\,)(\,\exists\xi'\,)$
$(\zeta\;r_i\mathrm{Prob_F}(\,\psi';\xi'\,)\cdot\mathrm{Thm}\;\psi'\;_{,}\mathrm{gr}\;\psi\;\mathrm{al}\;\psi'\;\mathrm{id}\;\psi\,)^\rceil$

Proof.

By a complicated argument analogous to that pursued in the proof of
**1168, we may show that,

$^\lceil r_i\,\mathrm{C_F}\cdot(\eta)(\zeta)(\mathrm{Thm}\;\eta\;\mathrm{cd}\;\zeta\cdot(\,\exists\theta\,)(\,r_i\,\mathrm{RC_F}\;\theta\cdot\eta\;\mathrm{Ing}\;\theta\,)\cdot\supset$
$(\,\exists\theta\,)(\,r_i\,\mathrm{RC_F}\;\theta\cdot\zeta\;\mathrm{Ing}\;\theta\,))\cdot\zeta\;r_i\mathrm{B_F}\;\alpha\;\mathrm{e}\;\gamma\cdot$
$\text{pct}\,(\beta,\gamma,(\psi;\xi))\,r_i\,\mathrm{S*A_F}(\beta,\gamma)\cdot\alpha\;r_i\,\mathrm{Mem_F}\;\beta\cdot\sim(\,\exists\beta''\,)$
$(\beta''r_i\mathrm{DP_F}(\alpha,\beta,\gamma))\cdot\zeta\;r_i\mathrm{B_F}\;\alpha'\;\mathrm{e}\;\gamma'\cdot\alpha'\;r_i\,\mathrm{Ran_F}(\beta',\gamma')\cdot$
$\text{pct}\,(\beta',\gamma',(\psi';\xi'))\,r_i\mathrm{S*A_F}(\beta',\gamma')\cdot\supset\sim\text{pct}\,(\beta,\gamma,(\psi;\xi))$
$r_i\mathrm{Dif_F}\;\text{pct}\,(\beta',\gamma',(\,\psi';\xi'))^\rceil \qquad\qquad (1)$

*100, **233 $^\lceil\alpha'\;r_i\,\mathrm{Ran_F}(\beta',\gamma')\supset(\,\exists\eta'\,)(\eta'\;r_i\mathrm{S*A_F}(\beta',\gamma')\,:$
Δ106, Δ105 $\sim\text{pct}\,(\beta,\gamma,(\psi;\xi))\,r_i\mathrm{S*A_F}(\beta,\gamma)\;\mathrm{v}\sim\alpha'\;\mathrm{e}\;\gamma'\;r_i\mathrm{B_F}$
$\alpha\;\mathrm{e}\;\gamma\;\mathrm{v}\sim\alpha\;r_i\,\mathrm{Mem_F}\;\beta\;\mathrm{v}\sim\text{pct}\,(\beta,\gamma,(\psi;\xi))$
$r_i\mathrm{Str_F}\;\eta'\;\mathrm{v}\sim\sim(\,\exists\beta''\,)(\beta''\;r_i\mathrm{DP_F}(\alpha,\beta,\gamma)))^\rceil \qquad (2)$

*100, Δ106 $^\lceil[\,1\cdot1147\cdot1043\cdot\supset:]\;r_i\,\mathrm{C_F}\cdot(\eta)(\zeta)(\mathrm{Thm}\;\eta\;\mathrm{cd}\;\zeta\cdot$
$(\,\exists\theta\,)(\,r_i\,\mathrm{RC_F}\;\theta\cdot\eta\;\mathrm{Ing}\;\theta\,)\cdot\supset(\,\exists\theta\,)(\,r_i\,\mathrm{RC_F}\;\theta\cdot$
$\zeta\;\mathrm{Ing}\;\theta\,))\cdot\zeta\;r_i\mathrm{B_F}\;\alpha\;\mathrm{e}\;\gamma\cdot\text{pct}\,(\beta,\gamma,(\psi;\xi))$
$r_i\mathrm{S*A_F}(\beta,\gamma)\cdot\alpha\;r_i\,\mathrm{Mem_F}\;\beta\cdot\sim(\,\exists\beta''\,)(\beta''\;r_i\mathrm{DP_F}$
$(\alpha,\beta,\gamma))\cdot\zeta\;r_i\mathrm{B_F}\;\alpha'\;\mathrm{e}\;\gamma'\cdot\alpha'\;r_i\,\mathrm{Ran_F}(\beta',\gamma')\cdot$
$\text{pct}\,(\beta',\gamma',(\,\psi';\xi'))\,r_i\mathrm{S*A_F}(\beta',\gamma')\cdot\supset\cdot$
$\sim\text{pct}\,(\beta,\gamma,(\psi;\xi))\,r_i\mathrm{Dif_F}\;\text{pct}\,(\beta',\gamma',(\,\psi';\xi'))\cdot$

$$(\exists \eta')(\eta' \ r_i S^* A_F (\beta', \gamma') \cdot \sim \text{pct} (\beta, \gamma, (\psi; \xi))$$

$$r_i \text{Str}_F \ \eta') \tag{3}$$

*100 (using **1021,1022,1023) $^\ulcorner \alpha \ r_i \text{Ran}_F (\beta, \gamma) \cdot \eta \ r_i S^* A_F (\beta, \gamma) \cdot$
(Δ99, Δ98)
$$\eta' \ r_i S^* A_F (\beta, \gamma) \cdot \supset \eta \ r_i S^* A_F \ \eta'^\urcorner \tag{4}$$

*100,*158,*160. $^\ulcorner [4 \cdot 1034 \cdot \supset :] \alpha' \ r_i \text{Ran}_F (\beta', \gamma') \cdot \text{pct} (\beta', \gamma',$

$$(\psi'; \xi')) \ r_i S^* A_F (\beta', \gamma') \cdot \supset \cdot (\exists \eta')(\eta' \ r_i S^* A_F (\beta', \gamma') \cdot$$

$$\sim \text{pct} (\beta, \gamma, (\psi; \xi)) \ r_i \text{Str}_F \ \eta') \equiv \sim \text{pct} (\beta, \gamma, (\psi; \xi))$$

$$r_i \text{Str}_F \ \text{pct} (\beta', \gamma', (\psi'; \xi'))^\urcorner \tag{5}$$

*100, $^\ulcorner [5 \cdot 3 \cdot 1021 \cdot \supset :] r_i C_F \cdot (\eta)(\zeta)(\text{Thm} \ \eta \ \text{cd} \ \zeta \cdot (\exists \theta)$

$$(r_i RC_F \ \theta \cdot \eta \ \text{Ing} \ \theta) \cdot \supset (\exists \theta)(r_i RC_F \ \theta \cdot \zeta \ \text{Ing} \ \theta)) \cdot$$

$$\zeta \ r_i B_F \ \alpha \ e \ \gamma \cdot \text{pct} (\beta, \gamma, (\psi; \xi)) \ r_i S^* A_F (\beta, \gamma) \cdot$$

$$\alpha \ r_i \text{Mem}_F \ \beta \cdot \sim (\exists \beta'')(\beta'' \ r_i DP_F (\alpha, \beta, \gamma)) \cdot \zeta \ r_i B_F$$

$$\alpha' \ e \ \gamma' \cdot \alpha' \ r_i \text{Ran}_F (\beta', \gamma') \cdot \text{pct} (\beta', \gamma', (\psi'; \xi'))$$

$$r_i S^* A_F (\beta', \gamma') \cdot \supset \cdot \text{pct} (\beta, \gamma, (\psi; \xi)) \ r_i S=_F \text{pct} (\beta', \gamma',$$

$$(\psi'; \xi')) \ \text{v} \ \text{pct} (\beta', \gamma', (\psi', \xi')) \ r_i \text{Str}_F \ \text{pct} (\beta, \gamma, (\psi, \xi))^\urcorner \tag{6}$$

In virtue of the definitions of ordinary ratio matrices and ordinary statistical statements in Δ97a and 97b, we have as an instance of *100,

$^\ulcorner [1124 \cdot \supset :] \text{pct} (\beta, \gamma, (\psi; \xi)) \ r_i S^* A_F (\beta, \gamma) \cdot \text{pct} (\beta', \gamma', (\psi', \xi'))$

$$r_i S^* A_F (\beta', \gamma') \cdot \supset \cdot \text{Thm} \ \psi \ \text{id} \ \psi' \ \text{v} \ \text{Thm} \ \psi \ _s \text{gr} \ \psi' \ \text{v}$$

$$\text{Thm} \ \psi' \ _s \text{gr} \ \psi^\urcorner \tag{7}$$

*100, **233, Δ98, Δ100, Δ102, $^\ulcorner r_i C_F \cdot (\eta)(\zeta)(\text{Thm} \ \eta \ \text{cd} \ \zeta \cdot (\exists \theta)) \cdot$

$$(r_i RC_F \ \theta \ \vdots \ \eta \ \text{Ing} \ \theta) \cdot \supset (\exists \theta)(r_i RC_F \ \theta \cdot \zeta \ \text{Ing} \ \theta)) \cdot$$

$$\text{pct} (\beta, \gamma, (\psi; \xi)) \ r_i S^* A_F (\beta, \gamma) \cdot \text{pct} (\beta', \gamma', (\psi'; \xi'))$$

$$r_i S^* A_F (\beta', \gamma') : \text{pct} (\beta, \gamma, (\psi; \xi)) \ r_i S=_F \text{pct} (\beta', \gamma',$$

$$(\psi'; \xi')) \ \text{v} \ \text{pct} (\beta', \gamma'; (\psi'; \xi')) \ r_i \text{Str}_F \ \text{pct} (\beta, \gamma, (\psi; \xi)) \cdot$$

$$[7 \cdot] \supset \cdot \text{Thm} \ \psi \ \text{id} \ \psi' \ \text{v} \ \text{Thm} \ \psi' \ _s \text{gr} \ \psi^\urcorner \tag{8}$$

*100 $^\ulcorner [6 \cdot 8 \cdot \exists \supset :] r_i C_F \cdot (\eta)(\zeta)(\text{Thm} \ \eta \ \text{cd} \ \zeta \cdot (\exists \theta)(r_i RC_F \ \theta \cdot$

$$\eta \ \text{Ing} \ \theta) \cdot \supset (\exists \theta)(r_i RC_F \ \theta \cdot \zeta \ \text{Ing} \ \theta)) \cdot \zeta \ r_i B_F \ \alpha \ e \ \gamma \cdot$$

$$\text{pct} (\beta, \gamma, (\psi; \xi)) \ r_i S^* A_F (\beta, \gamma) \cdot \alpha \ r_i \text{Mem}_F \ \beta \cdot$$

$$\sim (\exists\beta'')(\beta''r_i\mathrm{DP_F}(\alpha,\beta,\gamma)) \cdot \zeta \, r_i\mathrm{B_F} \; \alpha' \; \mathrm{e} \; \gamma' \cdot$$

$$\alpha' \; r_i\mathrm{Ran_F}(\beta',\gamma') \cdot \mathrm{pct}\,(\beta',\gamma' \cdot (\psi';\xi')) \, r_i\mathrm{S^*A_F}$$

$$(\beta',\gamma') \cdot \supset \cdot \mathrm{Thm} \; \psi' \; {}_\mathrm{s}\mathrm{gr} \; \psi \; \mathrm{al} \; \psi' \; \mathrm{id} \; \psi^\urcorner \qquad (9)$$

*100, *135, *158 $\ulcorner[9 \cdot \supset :] \; r_i\mathrm{C_F} \cdot (\eta)(\zeta)(\mathrm{Thm} \; \eta \; \mathrm{cd} \; \zeta \cdot (\exists\theta)$

(Δ107) $(r_i\mathrm{RC_F} \; \theta \cdot \eta \; \mathrm{Ing} \; \theta) \cdot \supset (\exists\theta)(r_i\mathrm{RC_F} \; \theta \cdot \zeta \; \mathrm{Ing} \; \theta)) \cdot$

$$\zeta \, r_i\mathrm{B_F} \; \alpha \; \mathrm{e} \; \gamma \cdot \mathrm{pct}\,(\beta,\gamma,(\psi;\xi)) \, r_i\mathrm{S^*A_F}(\beta,\gamma) \cdot$$

$$\alpha \; r_i\mathrm{Mem_F} \; \beta \cdot \sim (\exists\beta'')(\beta''r_i\mathrm{DP_F}(\alpha,\beta,\gamma)) \cdot$$

$$\zeta \, r_i\mathrm{Prof_F}(\psi';\xi') \cdot \supset \cdot \zeta \, r_i\mathrm{Prob_F}(\psi';\xi') \cdot \mathrm{Thm} \; \psi'$$

$${}_\mathrm{s}\mathrm{gr} \; \psi \; \mathrm{al} \; \psi' \; \mathrm{id} \; \psi^\urcorner \qquad (10)$$

*158,*149 $\ulcorner[10 \cdot \supset :] \; r_i\mathrm{C_F} \cdot (\eta)(\zeta)(\mathrm{Thm} \; \eta \; \mathrm{cd} \; \zeta \cdot (\exists\theta)$

$$(r_i\mathrm{RC_F} \; \theta \cdot \eta \; \mathrm{Ing} \; \theta) \cdot \supset (\exists\overset{\circ}{\theta})(r_i\mathrm{RC_F} \; \theta \cdot$$

$$\zeta \; \mathrm{Ing} \; \theta)) \cdot \zeta \, r_i\mathrm{B_F} \; \alpha \; \mathrm{e} \; \gamma \cdot \mathrm{pct}\,(\beta,\gamma,(\psi;\xi))$$

$$r_i\mathrm{S^*A_F}(\beta,\gamma) \cdot \alpha \; r_i\mathrm{Mem_F} \; \beta \cdot \sim (\exists\beta'')(\beta''r_i\mathrm{DP_F}$$

$$(\alpha,\beta,\gamma)) \cdot (\exists\psi')(\exists\xi')(\zeta \, r_i\mathrm{Prob_F}(\psi',\xi')) \cdot \supset \cdot$$

$$(\exists\psi')(\exists\xi')(\zeta \, r_i\mathrm{Prob_F}(\psi';\xi') \cdot \mathrm{Thm} \; \psi' \; {}_\mathrm{s}\mathrm{gr} \; \psi \; \mathrm{al}$$

$$\psi' \; \mathrm{id} \; \psi)^\urcorner \qquad (11)$$

ML(*100) $\ulcorner \zeta \, r_i\mathrm{B_F} \; \alpha \; \mathrm{e} \; \gamma \cdot (\eta)(\zeta)(\mathrm{Thm} \; \eta \; \mathrm{cd} \; \zeta \cdot (\exists\theta)(r_i\mathrm{RC_F} \; \theta \cdot$

$$\eta \; \mathrm{Ing} \; \theta) \cdot \supset (\exists\theta)(r_i\mathrm{RC_F} \; \theta \cdot \zeta \; \mathrm{Ing} \; \theta)) \cdot \supset (\exists\theta)$$

$$(r_i\mathrm{RC_F} \; \theta \cdot \zeta \; \mathrm{cd} \; \zeta \; \mathrm{Ing} \; \theta)^\urcorner \qquad (12)$$

*100 $\ulcorner[1166 \cdot 11 \cdot 12 \cdot \supset :] \; 1171^\urcorner$

**1172 $\ulcorner r_i\mathrm{C_F} \cdot (\eta)(\zeta)(\mathrm{Thm} \; \eta \; \mathrm{cd} \; \zeta \cdot (\exists\theta)(r_i\mathrm{RC_F} \; \theta \cdot \eta \; \mathrm{Ing} \; \theta) \cdot \supset$

$$(\exists\theta)(r_i\mathrm{RC_F} \; \theta \cdot \zeta \; \mathrm{Ing} \; \theta)) \cdot \zeta \; \mathrm{cj} \; \eta \; r_i\mathrm{Prob_F}(\psi;\xi) \cdot$$

$$\eta \; r_i\mathrm{Prob_F}(\psi';\xi') \cdot \supset \mathrm{Thm} \; \psi' \; {}_\mathrm{s}\mathrm{gr} \; \psi \; \mathrm{al} \; \psi' \; \mathrm{id} \; \psi^\urcorner$$

Proof.

We must first introduce one new protosyntactical definition; $\ulcorner(\eta \; \mathrm{e}$ $\gamma\gamma'\mathrm{a\,a}\zeta)^\urcorner$ *for* the expression whose abbreviation in ML consists of the expression η, followed by 'ϵ' followed by the expression γ, under a circumflex, the expression γ' under a circumflex, ' (', the matrix ζ, and ') '. The formal definition would be quite analogous to the definition (Δ67) of $\ulcorner(\zeta \, \mathrm{e} \, \eta \, \mathrm{a} \, \theta)^\urcorner$.

*100 $\ulcorner[1152 \cdot \supset : \cdot (\exists \theta)(r_i \, \text{RC}_\text{F} \ \theta \cdot \eta \ \text{Ing} \ \theta) \cdot \supset : (\eta)(\zeta)$

(Thm η cd $\zeta \cdot r_i \, \text{C}_\text{F} \cdot (\exists \theta)(r_i \, \text{RC}_\text{F} \ \theta \cdot \eta \ \text{Ing} \ \theta) \cdot \supset$

$(\exists \theta)(r_i \, \text{RC}_\text{F} \ \theta \cdot \zeta \ \text{Ing} \ \theta)) \cdot \zeta$ cj $\eta \ r_i \, \text{Prob}_\text{F}(\psi;\xi) \cdot$

$\eta \ r_i \, \text{Prob}_\text{F}(\psi';\xi') \cdot [1169] \cdot \supset \text{Thm} \ \psi' \ \text{id} \ _s1\urcorner$ \hfill (1)

*100, Δ97a, Δ97b, Δ99, Δ107, $\ulcorner \zeta$ cj $\eta \ r_i \, \text{Prob}_\text{F}(\psi;\xi) \cdot \supset \cdot$

Thm ψ' id $_s1 \supset$ Thm $\psi' \ _s\text{gr} \ \psi$ al ψ' id $\psi\urcorner$ \hfill (2)

*100 $\ulcorner[1 \cdot 2 \cdot \supset :] \ (\exists \theta)(r_i \, \text{RC}_\text{F} \ \theta \cdot \eta \ \text{Ing} \ \theta) \supset 1172\urcorner$ \hfill (3)

ML(*100) $\ulcorner \text{Stat} \ \eta \cdot \text{Stat} \ \zeta \cdot \supset \text{Thm} \ \text{n}\eta \ \text{cd} \ \text{n}(\zeta \ \text{cj} \ \eta)\urcorner$ \hfill (4)

**233 $\ulcorner(\exists \theta)(r_i \, \text{RC}_\text{F} \ \theta \cdot \text{n}\eta \ \text{Ing} \ \theta) \supset : r_i \, \text{C}_\text{F} \cdot (\eta)(\zeta)(\text{Thm} \ \eta \ \text{cd} \ \zeta \cdot$

$(\exists \theta)(r_i \, \text{RC}_\text{F} \ \theta \cdot \eta \ \text{Ing} \ \theta) \cdot \supset (\exists \theta)(r_i \, \text{RC}_\text{F} \ \theta \cdot$

$\zeta \ \text{Ing} \ \theta)) \cdot [4 \cdot] \cdot \zeta$ cj $\eta \ r_i \, \text{Prob}_\text{F}(\psi;\xi) \cdot \eta \ r_i \, \text{Prob}_\text{F}$

$(\psi';\xi') \cdot \supset (\exists \theta)(r_i \, \text{RC}_\text{F} \ \theta \cdot \text{n}(\zeta \ \text{cj} \ \eta) \ \text{Ing} \ \theta)\urcorner$ \hfill (5)

Making use of the obvious analogue of 1152, we have,

*100 $\ulcorner 1152$ Analogue $\cdot 5 \cdot \supset : \cdot] \ (\exists \theta)(r_i \, \text{RC}_\text{F} \ \theta \cdot \text{n}\eta \ \theta) \supset : r_i \, \text{C}_\text{F} \cdot$

$(\eta)(\zeta)(\text{Thm} \ \eta \ \text{cd} \ \zeta \cdot (\exists \theta)(r_i \, \text{RC}_\text{F} \ \theta \cdot \eta \ \text{Ing} \ \theta) \cdot \supset$

$(\exists \theta)(r_i \, \text{RC}_\text{F} \ \theta \cdot \zeta \ \text{Ing} \ \theta)) \cdot \zeta$ cj $\eta \ r_i \, \text{Prob}_\text{F}(\psi;\xi) \cdot$

$\eta \ r_i \, \text{Prob}_\text{F}(\psi';\xi') \cdot [1169 \cdot] \supset \cdot \text{Thm} \ \psi \ \text{id} \ ``_s0" \cdot$

Thm ψ' id $``_s0"\urcorner$ \hfill (6)

ML(*100, †184) $\ulcorner \text{Thm} \ \psi \ \text{id} \ ``_s0" \cdot \text{Thm} \ \psi' \ \text{id} \ ``_s0" \cdot \supset \text{Thm} \ \psi' \ \text{id}$

ψ al $\psi' \ _s\text{gr} \ \psi\urcorner$ \hfill (7)

*100 $\ulcorner[6 \cdot 7 \cdot \supset :] \ (\exists \theta)(r_i \, \text{RC}_\text{F} \ \theta \cdot \text{n}\eta \ \text{Ing} \ \theta) \supset 1172\urcorner$ \hfill (8)

By an argument analogous to that embodied in lines (6)–(17) of **1165, we have,

$\ulcorner \sim(\exists \theta)(r_i \, \text{RC}_\text{F} \ \theta \cdot \eta \ \text{Ing} \ \theta) \cdot \sim (\exists \theta)(r_i \, \text{RC}_\text{F} \ \theta \cdot \text{n}\eta \ \text{Ing} \ \theta) \cdot \supset :$

$r_i \, \text{C}_\text{F} \cdot (\eta)(\zeta)(\text{Thm} \ \eta \ \text{cd} \ \zeta \cdot (\exists \theta)(r_i \, \text{RC}_\text{F} \ \theta \cdot \eta \ \text{Ing} \ \theta) \cdot$

$\supset (\exists \theta)(r_i \, \text{RC}_\text{F} \ \theta \cdot \zeta \ \text{Ing} \ \theta)) \cdot \supset \text{pct}(\text{unt} \ \text{f}\eta \text{a}\eta, \text{untv},$

$(``_s0";``_s1")) \ r_i \, \text{S*A}_\text{F}(\text{unt} \ \text{f}\eta \ \text{a}\eta, \text{unt} \ \text{v})\urcorner$ \hfill (9)

The following line may be established by a proof similar to that offered for **1148:

$\ulcorner(\eta)(\zeta)(\operatorname{Thm}\eta\ \operatorname{cd}\ \zeta\cdot(\exists\theta)(r_i\operatorname{RC_F}\theta\cdot\eta\ \operatorname{Ing}\theta)\cdot\supset(\exists\theta)$

$\zeta\ \operatorname{Ing}\theta\ ))\supset:\alpha'\ e\ \gamma'\ r_i\operatorname{B_F}\zeta\ \operatorname{cj}\eta\cdot\supset\alpha'\ e\ \gamma'\ al$

$\eta\cdot r_i\operatorname{B_F}\eta\urcorner$ (10)

Ratio extension $\ulcorner(\eta)(\zeta)(\operatorname{Thm}\eta\ \operatorname{cd}\ \zeta\cdot(\exists\theta)(r_i\operatorname{RC_F}\theta\cdot\eta\ \operatorname{Ing}\theta)\cdot\supset$
of ML, **233 $(\exists\theta)(r_i\operatorname{RC_F}\theta\cdot\zeta\ \operatorname{Ing}\theta))\cdot\operatorname{pct}(\beta',\gamma',(\psi;\xi))r_i\operatorname{S*A_F}$

$(\beta',\gamma')\cdot\supset\operatorname{pct}(\beta',\alpha a\,(\alpha\ e\ \gamma'\ al\ \eta),(\psi;``_s1"))$

$r_i\operatorname{SA_F}(\beta',\alpha a\,(\alpha\ e\ \gamma'\ al\ \eta))\urcorner$ (11)

Ratio exten- $\ulcorner(\eta)(\zeta)(\operatorname{Thm}\eta\ \operatorname{cd}\ \zeta\cdot(\exists\theta)(r_i\operatorname{RC_F}\theta\cdot\eta\ \operatorname{Ing}\theta)\cdot$
sion of ML $\supset(\exists\theta)(r_i\operatorname{RC_F}\theta\cdot\zeta\ \operatorname{Ing}\theta))\cdot\operatorname{pct}(\beta',\gamma',(\psi',\xi))$
**233

$r_i\operatorname{S*A_F}(\beta',\gamma')\cdot\operatorname{pct}(\beta',\alpha a\,(\alpha\ e\ \gamma'\ al\ \eta),(\psi';\xi''))$

$r_i\operatorname{SA_F}(\beta',\alpha a\,(\alpha\ e\ \gamma'\ al\ \eta))\cdot(\exists\theta)(r_i\operatorname{RC_F}\theta\cdot$

$\psi''\ _s\operatorname{gr}\psi\ \operatorname{Ing}\theta)\cdot\supset(\exists\theta)(r_i\operatorname{RC_F}\theta\cdot\eta\ \operatorname{Ing}\theta)\urcorner$ (12)

Similarly, $\ulcorner(\eta)(\zeta)(\operatorname{Thm}\eta\ \operatorname{cd}\ \zeta\cdot(\exists\theta)(r_i\operatorname{RC_F}\theta\cdot\eta\ \operatorname{Ing}\theta)\cdot$

$\supset(\exists\theta)(r_i\operatorname{RC_F}\theta\cdot\zeta\ \operatorname{Ing}\theta))\cdot\operatorname{pct}(\beta',\gamma',(\psi;\xi))$

$r_i\operatorname{S*A_F}(\beta',\gamma')\cdot\operatorname{pct}(\beta',\alpha a\,(\alpha\ e\ \gamma'\ al\ \eta),(\psi'';\xi''))$

$r_i\operatorname{SA_F}(\beta',\alpha a\,(\alpha\ e\ \gamma'\ al\ \eta))\cdot(\exists\theta)(r_i\operatorname{RC_F}\theta\cdot``_s1"$

$_s\operatorname{gr}\xi''\ \operatorname{Ing}\theta)\cdot\supset(\exists\theta)(r_i\operatorname{RC_F}\theta\cdot n\eta\ \operatorname{Ing}\theta)\urcorner$ (13)

*100,*157,*159 $\ulcorner[11\cdot12\cdot13\cdot\supset:\cdot]\sim(\exists\theta)(r_i\operatorname{C_F}\theta\cdot\eta\ \operatorname{Ing}\theta)\cdot$

$\sim(\exists\theta)(r_i\operatorname{RC_F}\theta\cdot n\eta\ \operatorname{Ing}\theta)\cdot\supset:r_i\operatorname{C_F}\cdot(\eta)(\zeta)$

$(\operatorname{Thm}\eta\ \operatorname{cd}\ \zeta\cdot(\exists\theta)(r_i\operatorname{RC_F}\theta\cdot\eta\ \operatorname{Ing}\theta)\cdot\supset(\exists\theta)$

$(r_i\operatorname{RC_F}\theta\cdot\zeta\ \operatorname{Ing}\theta))\cdot\operatorname{pct}(\beta',\gamma',(\psi;\xi))r_i\operatorname{S*A_F}(\beta',\gamma')\cdot$

$\supset\operatorname{pct}(\beta',\alpha a\,(\alpha\ e\ \gamma'\ al\ \eta),(\psi;``_s1"))\ r_i\operatorname{S*A_F}(\beta',\alpha a$

$(\alpha\ e\ \gamma'\ al\ \eta))\urcorner$ (14)

*100,Δ106,Δ107, $\ulcorner[10\cdot14\cdot\supset:\cdot\sim(\exists\theta)(r_i\operatorname{RC_F}\theta\cdot\eta\ \operatorname{Ing}\theta)\cdot$

$\sim(\exists\theta)(r_i\operatorname{RC_F}\theta\cdot n\eta\ \operatorname{Ing}\theta)\cdot\supset:r_i\operatorname{C_F}\cdot(\eta)(\zeta)$

$(\operatorname{Thm}\eta\ \operatorname{cd}\ \zeta\cdot(\exists\theta)(r_i\operatorname{RC_F}\theta\cdot\eta\ \operatorname{Ing}\theta)\cdot\supset(\exists\theta)$

$(r_i\operatorname{RC_F}\theta\cdot\zeta\ \operatorname{Ing}\theta))\cdot\zeta\ \operatorname{cj}\eta\ r_i\operatorname{B_F}\alpha'\ e\ \gamma'\cdot$

$\alpha'\ r_i\operatorname{Ran_F}(\beta',\gamma')\cdot\operatorname{pct}(\beta',\gamma',(\psi;\xi))\ r_i\operatorname{S*A}(\beta',\gamma')\cdot\supset\cdot$

$\eta\ r_i\operatorname{B_F}\alpha'\ e\ \alpha a\,(\alpha\ e\ \gamma'\ al\ \eta)\cdot\alpha'\ r_i\operatorname{Mem_F}\beta'\cdot$

$$\text{pct}\,(\beta',\alpha a\,(\alpha\ e\ \gamma'\ \text{al}\ \eta),(\psi;``_s1"\,))\,r_i\,S*A_F(\beta',\alpha a$$

$$(\alpha\ e\ \gamma'\ \text{al}\ \eta)) \tag{15}$$

In any actual rational corpus, it is doubtful that there will be any-
thing preventing $\ulcorner\alpha'\ r_i\,\text{Ran}_F(\beta',\alpha a\,(\alpha\ e\ \gamma'\ \text{al}\ \eta))\urcorner$ by difference; but
we cannot prove this directly. We can show, however, that there
are expressions which are not prevented by difference, and which
will otherwise function precisely as α, β', and $\ulcorner\alpha a\,(\alpha\ e\ \gamma'\ \text{al}\ \eta)\urcorner$
would presumably function in an actual rational corpus. Consider
a sequence of expressions (or a long expression with these expressions as framed ingredients),

$$\ulcorner\alpha_1\ e\ \beta_1\ \text{cj}\ \alpha_1\ e\ \gamma_1\urcorner,\ulcorner\alpha_2\ e\ \beta_2\ \text{cj}\ \alpha_2\ e\ \gamma_2\urcorner,\ \cdots$$

$$\ulcorner\alpha_j\ e\ \beta_j\ \text{cj}\ \alpha_j\ e\ \gamma_j\urcorner\cdots,$$

such that for every j,

$$\ulcorner\alpha_j\ r_i\,\text{Mem}_F\ \beta_j\urcorner$$
$$\ulcorner\eta\ r_i\text{B}_F\ \alpha_j\ e\ \gamma_j\urcorner$$
$$\ulcorner\beta_j\ r_i\text{DP}_F(\alpha',\beta',\alpha\,a\,(\alpha\ e\ \gamma'\ \text{al}\ \eta))\urcorner$$

And such that no expression meeting these requirements fails to be
included in the sequence of expressions.

Let A be the pair: $\ulcorner\alpha_1\ \text{pr}\ (\alpha_2\ \text{pr}\ (\alpha_3\ \text{pr}\ (\cdots)))\urcorner$

Let B be the cross product, $\ulcorner\text{unt}\ \alpha_1\ \text{cp}\,(\text{unt}\ \alpha_2\ \text{cp}\,(\text{unt}\ \alpha_3$

$$\text{cp}\,(\cdots)))\urcorner$$

Let C be the cross product, $\ulcorner\gamma_1\ \text{cp}\,(\gamma_2\ \text{cp}\,(\gamma_3\ \text{cp}\,(\cdots)))\urcorner$

ML($\dagger$190,$\dagger$344) $\ulcorner\text{Thm}\ \alpha\ e\ \beta\ \text{cd}\ \alpha\ e\ \text{unt}\ \alpha\urcorner$ $\tag{16}$

**233 $\ulcorner(\eta)(\zeta)(\text{Thm}\ \eta\ \text{cd}\ \zeta\cdot(\exists\theta)(r_i\text{RC}_F\ \theta\cdot\eta\ \text{Ing}\ \theta)\cdot\supset(\exists\theta)$

$\quad\quad(r_i\text{RC}_F\ \theta\dot{}\zeta\ \text{Ing}\ \theta))\supset:[16\cdot]\,(\exists\theta)(r_i\text{RC}_F\ \theta\cdot$

$\quad\quad\alpha\ e\ \beta\ \text{Ing}\ \theta)\cdot\supset(\exists\theta)(r_i\text{RC}_F\ \theta\cdot$

$\quad\quad\alpha\ e\ \text{unt}\ \alpha\ \text{Ing}\ \theta)\urcorner$ $\tag{17}$

*100, $\triangle$103, [17 $\cdot\supset$:] $\ulcorner(\eta)(\zeta)(\text{Thm}\ \eta\ \text{cd}\ \zeta\cdot(\exists\theta)(r_i\text{RC}_F\ \theta\cdot$
(etc.)
$\quad\quad\eta\ \text{Ing}\ \theta)\cdot\supset(\exists\theta)(r_i\text{RC}_F\ \theta\cdot\zeta\ \text{Ing}\ \theta))\supset\cdot$

$\quad\quad\alpha\ r_i\,\text{Mem}_F\ \beta\supset\alpha\ r_i\,\text{Mem}_F\ \text{unt}\ \alpha\urcorner$ $\tag{18}$

*100 $\ulcorner[\,1046\cdot18\cdot\supset]$ Hyp 18 $\supset$ A $r_i\,\text{Mem}_F$ B$\urcorner$ $\tag{19}$

*100 $\ulcorner[\,1148\cdot\supset]$ Hyp 18 $\supset\eta\ r_i\text{B}_F$ A e C$\urcorner$ $\tag{20}$

By the argument of line (10),

*100 $\ulcorner[20 \supset :] (\eta)(\zeta)(\text{Thm } \eta \text{ cd } \zeta \cdot (\exists\theta)(r_i\text{RC}_F \theta \cdot \eta \text{ Ing } \theta) \cdot \supset$

$(\exists\theta)(r_i\text{RC}_F \theta \cdot \zeta \text{ Ing } \theta)) \cdot \zeta \text{ cj } \eta \ r_i\text{B}_F \alpha' \text{ e } \gamma' \cdot \supset$

$\eta \ r_i\text{B}_F \alpha' \text{ pr A e } \delta\delta'\text{aa}(\delta \text{ e } \gamma' \text{ al } \delta' \text{ e C})\urcorner$ (21)

*100 $\ulcorner[1152 \cdot 1170 \cdot 1169 \cdot 2 \cdot \supset] (\exists\theta)(r_i\text{RC}_F \theta \cdot \text{A e C Ing } \theta) \supset$

$1172\urcorner$ (22)

ML(*100) $\ulcorner\text{Thm n(A e C) cd (n(A e C) al } n\zeta)\urcorner$ (23)

**233,(ML *122) $\ulcorner(\eta)(\zeta)(\text{Thm } \eta \text{ cd } \zeta \cdot (\exists\theta)(r_i\text{RC}_F \theta \cdot$

$\eta \text{ Ing } \theta) \cdot \supset (\exists\theta)(r_i\text{RC}_F \theta \cdot \zeta \text{ Ing } \theta)) \cdot$

$\eta \ r_i\text{B}_F \text{ A e C} \cdot \supset \text{n(A e C) al } n\zeta \ r_i\text{B}_F \text{ n}(\zeta \text{ cj } \eta)\urcorner$

(24)

**233 $\ulcorner(\eta)(\zeta)(\text{Thm } \eta \text{ cd } \zeta \cdot (\exists\theta)(r_i\text{RC}_F \theta \cdot \eta \text{ Ing } \theta) \cdot \supset (\exists\theta)$

$(r_i\text{RC}_F \theta \cdot \zeta \text{ Ing } \theta)) \cdot (\exists\theta)(r_i\text{RC}_F \theta \cdot \text{n(A e B)}$

$\text{Ing } \theta) \cdot [23 \cdot] \supset (\exists\theta)(r_i\text{RC}_F \theta \cdot \text{n(A e C) al } n\zeta$

$\text{Ing } \theta)\urcorner$ (25)

*100 $\ulcorner[1152 \text{ Analogue} \cdot 25 \cdot 1169 \cdot 1170 \cdot 7 \cdot \supset \cdot] (\exists\theta)$

$(r_i\text{RC}_F \theta \cdot \text{n(A e C) Ing } \theta) \cdot \supset 1172\urcorner$ (26)

By a chain of argument analogous to that leading from (9) to (14),
we can show that,

$\ulcorner\sim (\exists\theta)(r_i\text{RC}_F \theta . \text{A e C Ing } \theta) \cdot \sim (\exists\theta)(r_i\text{RC}_F \theta \cdot$

$\text{n(A e C) Ing } \theta) \cdot \supset : (\eta)(\zeta)(\text{Thm } \eta \text{ cd } \zeta \cdot (\exists\theta)$

$(r_i\text{RC}_F \theta \cdot \eta \text{ Ing } \theta) \cdot \supset (\exists\theta)(r_i \text{ RC}_F \theta \cdot \zeta \text{ Ing } \theta)) \cdot$

$\text{pct }(\beta',\gamma',(\psi;\xi)) r_i\text{S*A}_F(\beta',\gamma') \cdot \supset \text{pct }(\beta' \text{ cp B},\delta\delta'\text{aa}$

$(\delta \text{ e } \gamma' \text{ al } \delta' \text{ e C}),(\psi;``_s1")) r_i\text{S*A}_F(\beta' \text{ cp B},$

$\delta\delta'\text{aa}(\delta \text{ e } \gamma' \text{ al } \delta' \text{ e C}))\urcorner$ (27)

Now we must show that, subject to the appropriate conditions,

$\ulcorner\sim (\exists\beta'')(\beta'' \ r_i\text{DP}_F(\alpha' \text{ pr A},\beta' \text{ cp B},\delta\delta'\text{aa}(\delta \text{ e } \gamma' \text{ al } \delta' \text{ e C})))\urcorner$

First of all, none of the β_j prevents the randomness assertion in
question; for there will always be a membership permutation of
$\ulcorner\alpha'\text{pr A e } \beta' \text{ cp B}\urcorner$, having the form $\ulcorner\alpha_j \text{ pr A' e unt } \alpha_j \text{ cp B'}\urcorner$. By
**1149,

⌜α' pr A e β' cp B MP α_j pr A' e unt α_j cp B' $\supset$ $\cdot$ α' pr A

r_i Mem$_F$ β' cp B $\supset$ α_j pr A' r_i Mem$_F$ unt α_j cp B'⌝ (28)

ML(*100,†190,†344) ⌜Thm pct $(\beta',\gamma',(\psi;\xi))$ cd $((\alpha_j$ e $\beta_j)$ cd

(unt α_j cp B' incl β_j cp B'))⌝ (29)

With suitable applications of **232 and *100, we thus have, for each α_j and β_j,

⌜$(\eta)(\zeta)($ Thm η cd ζ $\cdot$ $(\exists\theta)(r_i$ RC$_F$ θ $\cdot$ η Ing θ) $\cdot$ $\supset$ $(\exists\theta)$

$(r_i$ RC$_F$ θ $\cdot$ ζ Ing θ)) $\cdot$ pct $(\beta',\gamma',(\psi;\xi))$ r_i S*A$_F$

(β',γ') $\cdot$ $\supset$ $(\exists\alpha'')(\exists\beta''')(\exists\beta'')(\alpha''$ r_i Mem$_F$ β'' $\cdot$

α' pr A e β' cp B MP α'' e β'' $\cdot$ $(\exists\theta)(r_i$ RC$_F$ θ $\cdot$

α_j e β_j cd β'' incl β_j cp β''' Ing θ))⌝ (30)

Similarly, no expression which fails to prevent ⌜α' r_i Ran$_F(\beta',\alpha$a $(\alpha$ e γ' al $\eta))$⌝ will prevent the randomness expression in question. For, let $\beta^*, \alpha^*, \gamma^*$, be such that ⌜$\alpha^*$ r_i Mem$_F$ β^*⌝, ⌜α^* e γ^* r_i B$_F$ η⌝, and such that there is an η^* satisfying ⌜η^* r_i S*A$_F(\beta^*,\gamma^*)$⌝ and ⌜η^* r_i Dif$_F$ pct $(\beta',\alpha$a$(\alpha$ e γ' al $\eta),(\psi;``_s1''))$⌝. Since β^* is distinct from the β_j,

⌜$\sim\beta^*$ r_i DP$_F(\alpha',\beta',\alpha$a $(\alpha$ e γ' al $\eta))$⌝ (31)

*100, *141, Δ104 ⌜[31 $\cdot$ $\supset$:] $(\exists\alpha'')(\exists\beta'')(\exists\beta''')(\alpha''$ r_i Mem$_F$ β'' $\cdot$

α' e β' MP α'' e β'' $\cdot$ $(\exists\theta)(r_i$ RC$_F$ θ $\cdot$ α^* e β^* cd

β'' incl β^* cp β''' Ing θ)) v $(\exists\beta'')(\exists\gamma'')(\exists\eta'')$

$(\alpha^*$ r_i Mem$_F$ β'' $\cdot$ η'' r_i S*A$_F(\beta'',\gamma'')$ $\cdot$ η r_i S$=_F$

pct $(\beta',\alpha$a $(\alpha$ e γ' al $\eta),(\psi;``_s1''))$ $\cdot$ α^* e γ^* r_iB$_F$

α^* e γ'' $\cdot$ $(\exists\theta)(r_i$ RC$_F$ θ $\cdot$ α^* e γ^* cd β'' incl β^*

Ing θ) $\cdot$ $(\eta''')(\beta''')(\gamma''')(\alpha^*$ r_i Mem$_F$ β''' $\cdot$ α^* e γ''

r_iB$_F$ α^* e γ''' $\cdot$ η''' r_i S*A$_F(\beta''',\gamma''')$ $\cdot$ $(\exists\theta)(r_i$ RC$_F$ θ $\cdot$

α^* e β'' cd β''' incl β'' Ing θ) $\cdot$ $\supset$ $\sim$ η''' r_iDif$_F$ η''))⌝ (32)

ML(various possible theorems) ⌜α' e β' MP α'' e β'' $\supset$ α' pr A e

β' cp B MP α'' pr A e β'' cp B⌝ (33)

**1046 ⌜A r_i Mem$_F$ B $\cdot$ α'' r_i Mem$_F$ β'' $\cdot$ $\supset$ α'' pr A r_i Mem$_F$

β'' cp B⌝ (34)

ML(possibility, again) $\ulcorner$ Thm $((\alpha* \text{ e } \beta*) \text{ cd } (\beta'' \text{ incl } \beta* \text{ cp } \beta'''))$ cd

$\qquad ((\alpha* \text{ e } \beta*) \text{ cd } (\beta'' \text{ cp } B \text{ incl } (\beta* \text{ cp } \beta''') \text{ cp } B))\urcorner$ (35)

*100 $\ulcorner [\,33 \cdot 34 \cdot 35 \cdot \supset :\,] (\eta)(\zeta)(\text{Thm } \eta \text{ cd } \zeta \cdot (\exists\theta)(r_i \text{RC}_\text{F} \ \theta \ \cdot$
**233
**232 $\qquad \eta \text{ Ing } \theta) \cdot \supset (\exists\theta)(r_i \text{RC}_\text{F} \ \theta \cdot \zeta \text{ Ing } \theta)) \supset \cdot (\exists\alpha'')$

$\qquad (\exists\beta'')(\exists\beta''')(\alpha'' \ r_i \text{Mem}_\text{F} \ \beta'' \cdot \alpha' \text{ e } \beta' \text{ MP } \alpha'' \text{ e } \beta'' \cdot$

$\qquad (\exists\theta)(r_i \text{RC}_\text{F} \ \theta \ \cdot \alpha* \text{ e } \beta* \text{ cd } \beta'' \text{ incl } \beta* \text{ cp } \beta'''$

$\qquad \text{Ing } \theta))\urcorner$ (36)

*100 $\ulcorner (\eta)(\zeta)(\text{Thm } \eta \text{ cd } \zeta \cdot (\exists\theta)(r_i \text{RC}_\text{F} \ \theta \cdot \eta \text{ Ing } \theta) \cdot \supset (\exists\theta)$

$\qquad (r_i \text{RC}_\text{F} \ \theta \cdot \zeta \text{ Ing } \theta)) \cdot [\text{Thm } \psi \text{ id } \psi \cdot \text{Thm } ``_s 1'' \text{ id }$

$\qquad ``_s 1'' \cdot ] \supset \cdot \eta \ r_i \text{S} =_\text{F} \text{ pct } (\beta', \alpha\text{a} (\alpha \text{ e } \gamma' \text{ al } \eta),(\psi; ``_s 1''))$

$\qquad \equiv \eta \ r_i \text{S} =_\text{F} \text{ pct } (\beta' \text{ cp } B, \delta\delta' \text{aa} (\delta \text{ e } \gamma' \text{ al } \delta' \text{ e } C),$

$\qquad (\psi, ``_s 1''))\urcorner$ (37)

*100,*122 $\ulcorner [\,37 \cdot \supset :\,] (\eta)(\zeta)(\text{Thm } \eta \text{ cd } \zeta \cdot (\exists\theta)(r_i \text{RC}_\text{F} \ \theta \ \cdot$

$\qquad \eta \text{ Ing } \theta) \cdot \supset (\exists\theta)(r_i \text{RC}_\text{F} \ \theta \cdot \zeta \text{ Ing } \theta)) \cdot \supset \cdot$

$\qquad (\exists\beta'')(\exists\gamma'')(\exists\eta'')(\alpha* \ r_i \text{Mem}_\text{F} \ \beta'' \cdot \eta'' \ r_i \text{S*A}_\text{F}$

$\qquad (\beta'', \gamma'') \cdot \eta \ r_i \text{S} =_\text{F} \text{ pct } (\beta', \alpha\text{a} (\alpha \text{ e } \gamma' \text{ al } \eta),$

$\qquad (\psi; ``_s 1'')) \cdot \alpha* \text{ e } \gamma* \ r_i \text{B}_\text{F} \ \alpha* \text{ e } \gamma'' \cdot (\exists\theta)$

$\qquad (r_i \text{RC}_\text{F} \ \theta \cdot \alpha* \text{ e } \gamma* \text{ cd } \beta'' \text{ incl } \beta* \text{ Ing } \theta) \cdot$

$\qquad (\eta''')(\beta''')(\gamma''')(\alpha* \ r_i \text{Mem}_\text{F} \ \beta''' \cdot \alpha* \text{ e } \gamma* r_i \text{B}_\text{F}$

$\qquad \alpha* \text{ e } \gamma''' \cdot \eta''' \ r_i \text{S*A}_\text{F} (\beta''', \gamma''') \cdot (\exists\theta)(r_i \text{RC}_\text{F} \ \theta \cdot$

$\qquad \alpha* \text{ e } \beta'' \text{ cd } \beta''' \text{ incl } \beta'' \text{ Ing } \theta) \cdot \supset \sim \eta'''$

$\qquad r_i \text{Dif}_\text{F} \ \eta'')) \supset (\exists\beta'')(\exists\gamma'')(\exists\eta'')(\alpha* \ r_i \text{Mem}_\text{F} \ \beta'' \cdot$

$\qquad \eta'' \ r_i \text{S*A}_\text{F} (\beta'', \gamma'') \cdot \eta \ r_i \text{S} =_\text{F} \text{ pct } (\beta' \text{ cp } B, \delta\delta' \text{aa}$

$\qquad (\delta \text{ e } \gamma' \text{ al } \delta' \text{ e } C),(\psi; ``_s 1'')) \cdot \alpha* \text{ e } \gamma* \ r_i \text{B}_\text{F} \ \alpha* \text{ e }$

$\qquad \gamma'' \cdot (\exists\theta)(r_i \text{RC}_\text{F} \ \theta \ \cdot \alpha* \text{ e } \gamma* \text{ cd } \beta'' \text{ incl } \beta*$

$\qquad \text{Ing } \theta))\urcorner$ (38)

*100,*141,Δ104 $\ulcorner [\,36 \cdot 38 \cdot \supset :\,] (\eta)(\zeta)(\text{Thm } \eta \text{ cd } \zeta \cdot (\exists\theta)$

$\qquad (r_i \text{RC}_\text{F} \ \theta \cdot \eta \text{ Ing } \theta) \cdot \supset (\exists\theta)(r_i \text{RC}_\text{F} \ \theta \cdot \zeta \text{ Ing } \theta)) \supset$

$\qquad \cdot \sim \beta'' \ r_i \text{DP}_\text{F} \ (\alpha', \beta', \alpha\text{a} (\alpha \text{ e } \gamma' \text{ al } \eta)) \supset \sim \beta'' \ r_i \text{DP}_\text{F}$

$\qquad (\alpha' \text{ pr } A, \beta' \text{ cp } B, \delta\delta' \text{ aa} (\delta \text{ e } \gamma' \text{ al } \delta' \text{ e } C))\urcorner$ (39)

*100,*141,Δ104 $\ulcorner$[30 ⊃ :] $(\eta)(\zeta)($Thm η cd $\zeta \cdot ($∃$\theta)(r_i$RC$_F$ $\theta \cdot$

η Ing $\theta) \cdot \supset ($∃$\theta)(r_i$RC$_F$ $\theta \cdot \zeta$ Ing $\theta)) \supset \cdot$

$\beta'' \ r_i$DP$_F(\alpha',\beta',\alpha$a$(\alpha$ e γ' al $\eta)) \supset \sim \beta'' \ r_iDP_F(\alpha'$ pr

A,β' cp B,$\delta\delta'$aa$(\delta$ e γ' al δ' e C$))\urcorner$ (40)

*100,*159 $\ulcorner$[39 $\cdot$ 40 $\cdot \supset$:] $(\eta)(\zeta)($Thm η cd $\zeta \cdot ($∃$\theta)(r_i$RC$_F$ $\theta \cdot$

η Ing $\theta) \cdot \supset ($∃$\theta)(r_i$RC$_F$ $\theta \cdot \zeta$ Ing $\theta)) \supset \sim$

(∃β'')($\beta'' \ r_i$DP$_F(\alpha'$ pr A,β' cp B, $\delta\delta'$aa$(\delta$ e

γ' al δ' e C$)))\urcorner$ (41)

**1046 $\ulcorner$[19 $\cdot$] $\alpha' \ r_i$Mem$_F$ $\beta' \cdot \supset \alpha'$ pr A r_iMem$_F$ β' cp B$\urcorner$ (42)

*100 $\ulcorner$[21 $\cdot$ 27 $\cdot$ 41 $\cdot$ 42 $\cdot \supset$] $\sim ($∃$\theta)(r_i$RC$_F$ $\theta \cdot \eta$ Ing $\theta) \cdot$

$\sim ($∃$\theta)(r_i$RC$_F$ $\theta \cdot$nη Ing $\theta) \cdot \sim ($∃$\theta)(r_i$RC$_F$ $\theta \cdot$

A e C Ing $\theta) \cdot \sim ($∃$\theta)(r_i$RC$_F$ $\theta \cdot$ n A e C Ing $\theta) \cdot \supset :$

$(\eta)(\zeta)($Thm η cd $\zeta \cdot ($∃$\theta)(r_i$RC$_F$ $\theta \cdot \eta$ Ing $\theta) \cdot \supset$

(∃$\theta)(r_i$RC$_F$ $\theta \cdot$nη Ing $\theta)) \cdot \alpha' \ r_iMem_F$ $\beta' \cdot \eta$ cj ζ

r_iB$_F$ α' e $\gamma' \cdot$ pct $(\beta',\gamma',(\psi;\xi))r_i$S*A$_F$ $(\beta',\gamma') \cdot \supset$

α' pr A r_iMem$_F$ β' cp B $\cdot$ $\not\eta$ r_iB$_F$ α' pr A e $\delta\delta'$aa

$(\delta$ e γ' al δ' e C$) \cdot$ pct $(\beta'$ cp B,$\delta\delta'$aa$(\delta$ e γ' al δ' eC),

$(\psi;$"$_s$1"$)r_i$S*A$_F$ $(\beta'$ cp B,$\delta\delta'$aa$(\delta$ e γ' al δ' e C$)) \cdot$

$\sim ($∃β'')($\beta'' \ r_i$DP$_F$ $(\alpha'$ pr A,β' cp B,$\delta\delta'$aa$(\delta$ e γ' al

δ' e C$))\urcorner$ (43)

*100 $\ulcorner$[43 $\cdot$ 1171 $\cdot \supset$:$\cdot$] $\sim ($∃$\theta)(r_i$RC$_F$ $\theta \cdot \eta$ Ing $\theta) \cdot \sim ($∃$\theta)$

$(r_i$RC$_F$ $\theta \cdot$nη Ing $\theta) \cdot \sim ($∃$\theta)(r_i$RC$_F$ $\theta \cdot$ A e C

Ing $\theta) \cdot \sim ($∃$\theta)(r_i$RC$_F$ $\theta \cdot$ n A e C Ing $\theta) \cdot \supset :$

$(\eta)(\zeta)($Thm η cd $\zeta \cdot ($∃$\theta)(r_i$RC$_F$ $\theta \cdot \eta$ Ing $\theta) \cdot \supset$

(∃$\theta)(r_i$RC$_F$ $\theta \cdot \zeta$ Ing $\theta)) \cdot \alpha' \ r_iMem_F$ $\beta' \cdot \eta$ cj ζ

r_iB$_F$ α' e $\gamma' \cdot$ pct $(\beta',\gamma',(\psi;\xi))r_i$S*A$_F(\beta',\gamma') \cdot \supset$

(∃ψ'')(∃ξ'')(η r_iProb$_F(\psi'';\xi'') \cdot$ Thm ψ'' $_s$gr ψ al

ψ'' id $\psi)\urcorner$ (44)

*161,$\triangle$107 $\ulcorner[(\alpha')(\beta')(\gamma') 44 \supset : \cdot] \sim (\exists\theta)(r_i\mathrm{RC_F} \ \theta \cdot \eta \ \mathrm{Ing} \ \theta) \cdot$
$\sim (\exists\theta)(r_i\mathrm{RC_F} \ \theta \cdot \mathrm{n}\eta \ \mathrm{Ing} \ \theta) \cdot \sim (\exists\theta)$
$(r_i\mathrm{RC_F} \ \theta \cdot \mathrm{A \ e \ C \ Ing} \ \theta) \cdot \sim (\exists\theta)(r_i\mathrm{RC_F} \ \theta \cdot$
$\mathrm{n \ A \ e \ C \ Ing} \ \theta) \cdot \supset : \cdot (\eta)(\zeta)(\mathrm{Thm} \ \eta \ \mathrm{cd} \ \zeta \cdot$
$(\exists\theta)(r_i\mathrm{RC_F} \ \theta \cdot \eta \ \mathrm{Ing} \ \theta) \cdot \supset (\exists\theta)(r_i\mathrm{RC_F} \ \theta \cdot$
$\zeta \ \mathrm{Ing} \ \theta)) \cdot \eta \ \mathrm{cj} \ \zeta \ r_i\mathrm{Prob_F}(\psi;\zeta) \cdot \supset (\exists\psi'')$
$(\exists\xi'')(\eta \ r_i\mathrm{Prob_F}(\psi'';\xi'') \cdot \mathrm{Thm} \ \psi'' \ _\mathrm{s}\mathrm{gr} \ \psi \ \mathrm{al}$
$\psi'' \ \mathrm{id} \ \psi)\urcorner$ (45)

*100,$\triangle$107 $\ulcorner[1169 \supset :] r_i\mathrm{C_F} \cdot (\eta)(\zeta)(\mathrm{Thm} \ \eta \ \mathrm{cd} \ \zeta \cdot (\exists\theta)$
$(r_i\mathrm{RC_F} \ \theta \cdot \eta \ \mathrm{Ing} \ \theta) \cdot \supset (\exists\theta)(r_i\mathrm{RC_F} \ \theta \cdot$
$\zeta \ \mathrm{Ing} \ \theta)) \cdot \supset : \eta \ r_i\mathrm{Prob_F}(\psi'';\xi'') \cdot \mathrm{Thm} \ \psi''$
$_\mathrm{s}\mathrm{gr} \ \psi \ \mathrm{al} \ \psi'' \ \mathrm{id} \ \psi \cdot \supset \cdot \eta \ r_i\mathrm{Prob_F}(\psi';\xi') \supset$
$\mathrm{Thm} \ \psi'' \ \mathrm{id} \ \psi'\urcorner$ (46)

ML $\ulcorner\mathrm{Thm} \ \psi'' \ \mathrm{id} \ \psi' \cdot \mathrm{Thm} \ \psi'' \ _\mathrm{s}\mathrm{gr} \ \psi \ \mathrm{al} \ \psi'' \ \mathrm{id} \ \psi \cdot \supset \mathrm{Thm} \ \psi'$
$_\mathrm{s}\mathrm{gr} \ \psi \ \mathrm{al} \ \psi' \ \mathrm{id} \ \psi\urcorner$ (47)

*100, *159, *161 $\ulcorner[46 \cdot 47 \cdot \supset :] r_i\mathrm{C_F} \cdot (\eta)(\zeta)(\mathrm{Thm} \ \eta \ \mathrm{cd} \ \zeta \cdot$
$(\exists\theta)(r_i\mathrm{RC_F} \ \theta \cdot \eta \ \mathrm{Ing} \ \theta) \cdot \supset (\exists\theta)(r_i\mathrm{RC_F} \ \theta \cdot$
$\zeta \ \mathrm{Ing} \ \theta)) \cdot \supset : (\exists\psi'')(\exists\xi'')(\eta \ r_i\mathrm{Prob_F}(\psi'';\xi'') \cdot$
$\mathrm{Thm} \ \psi'' \ _\mathrm{s}\mathrm{gr} \ \psi \ \mathrm{al} \ \psi'' \ \mathrm{id} \ \psi) \supset \eta \ r_i\mathrm{Prob_F}(\psi';\xi') \supset$
$\mathrm{Thm} \ \psi' \ _\mathrm{s}\mathrm{gr} \ \psi \ \mathrm{al} \ \psi' \ \mathrm{id} \ \psi\urcorner$ (48)

*100 $\ulcorner[45 \cdot 48 \cdot \supset :] \sim (\exists\theta)(r_i\mathrm{RC_F} \ \theta \cdot \eta \ \mathrm{Ing} \ \theta) \cdot \sim (\exists\theta)$
$(r_i\mathrm{RC_F} \ \theta \cdot \mathrm{n}\eta \ \mathrm{Ing} \ \theta) \cdot \sim (\exists\theta)(r_i\mathrm{RC_F} \ \theta \cdot \mathrm{A \ e \ C}$
$\mathrm{Ing} \ \theta) \cdot \sim (\exists\theta)(r_i\mathrm{RC_F} \ \theta \cdot \mathrm{n \ A \ e \ C \ Ing} \ \theta) \cdot \supset \cdot$
$1172\urcorner$ (49)

*100 $\ulcorner[3 \cdot 8 \cdot 22 \cdot 28 \cdot 49 \cdot \supset \cdot] 1172\urcorner$

**1173 $\ulcorner r_i \neq r_n \supset : r_{i+1}\mathrm{C_F} \cdot (\eta)(\zeta)(\mathrm{Thm} \ \eta \ \mathrm{cd} \ \zeta \cdot (\exists\theta)$
$(r_{i+1}\mathrm{RC_F} \ \theta \cdot \eta \ \mathrm{Ing} \ \theta) \cdot \supset (\exists\theta)(r_{i+1}\mathrm{RC_F} \ \theta \cdot$
$\zeta \ \mathrm{Ing} \ \theta)) \cdot (\exists\theta)(r_i\mathrm{RC_F} \ \theta \cdot \eta \ \mathrm{cj} \ \zeta \ \mathrm{Ing} \ \theta) \cdot \supset$
$(\exists\theta)(r_i\mathrm{RC_F} \ \theta \cdot \eta \ \mathrm{Ing} \ \theta)\urcorner$

Proof.

**233,*100,Δ95a $\ulcorner r_i \neq r_n \supset : (\exists\theta)(r_i \mathrm{RC_F}\ \theta \cdot \eta\ \mathrm{cj}\ \zeta\ \mathrm{Ing}\ \theta) \supset$

$(\exists\psi)(\exists\xi)(\eta\ \mathrm{cd}\ \zeta\ r_{i+1}\mathrm{Prob_F}(\psi;\xi)) \cdot$

$\mathrm{Thm}\ \psi\ _\mathrm{s}\mathrm{gr}\ r_i)\urcorner$ (1)

*100 $\ulcorner[\,1172 \supset : \cdot\,]\ r_{i+1}\mathrm{C_F} \cdot (\eta)(\zeta)(\mathrm{Thm}\ \eta\ \mathrm{cd}\ \zeta \cdot (\exists\theta)$

$(r_{i+1}\mathrm{RC_F}\ \theta \cdot \eta\ \mathrm{Ing}\ \theta) \cdot \supset (\exists\theta)(r_{i+1}\mathrm{RC_F}\ \theta \cdot$

$\zeta\ \mathrm{Ing}\ \theta)) \cdot \eta\ \mathrm{cj}\ \zeta\ r_{i+1}\mathrm{Prob_F}(\psi;\xi) \cdot \mathrm{Thm}\ \psi_\mathrm{s}\mathrm{gr}\ r_i \cdot$

$\eta\ r_{i+1}\mathrm{Prob_F}(\psi';\xi') \cdot \supset \cdot \mathrm{Thm}\ \psi'\ _\mathrm{s}\mathrm{gr}\ \psi\ \mathrm{al}\ \psi'\ \mathrm{id}\ \psi \cdot$

$\mathrm{Thm}\ \psi\ _\mathrm{s}\mathrm{gr}\ r_i\urcorner$ (2)

ML $\ulcorner \mathrm{Thm}\ \psi'\ _\mathrm{s}\mathrm{gr}\ \psi\ \mathrm{al}\ \psi'\ \mathrm{id}\ \psi \cdot \mathrm{Thm}\ \psi\ _\mathrm{s}\mathrm{gr}\ r_i \cdot \supset \mathrm{Thm}\ \psi'$

$_\mathrm{s}\mathrm{gr}\ r_i\urcorner$ (3)

*100,*161,*158 $\ulcorner[\,2 \cdot 3 \cdot \supset :\,]\,\vert\ r_{i+1}\mathrm{C_F} \cdot (\eta)(\zeta)(\mathrm{Thm}\ \eta\ \mathrm{cd}\ \zeta \cdot$

$(\exists\theta)(r_{i+1}\mathrm{RC_F}\ \theta \cdot \eta\ \mathrm{Ing}\ \theta) \cdot \supset (\exists\theta)(r_{i+1}\mathrm{RC_F}\ \theta \cdot$

$\zeta\ \mathrm{Ing}\ \theta)) \cdot (\exists\psi)(\exists\xi)(\eta\ \mathrm{cj}\ \zeta\ r_{i+1}\mathrm{Prob_F}(\psi;\xi) \cdot$

$\mathrm{Thm}\ \psi_\mathrm{s}\mathrm{gr}\ r_i) \cdot \supset \cdot \eta\ r_{i+1}\mathrm{Prob_F}(\psi';\xi') \supset \mathrm{Thm}\ \psi'$

$_\mathrm{s}\mathrm{gr}\ r_i\urcorner$ (4)

*159,*149 $\ulcorner[(\psi')(\xi')\ 4 \cdot 1 \cdot \supset : \cdot\,]\ r_i \neq r_n \supset : r_{i+1}\mathrm{C_F} \cdot$
*100 $(\eta)(\zeta)(\mathrm{Thm}\ \eta\ \mathrm{cd}\ \zeta \cdot (\exists\theta)(r_{i+1}\mathrm{RC_F}\ \theta \cdot \eta\ \mathrm{Ing}\ \theta) \cdot \supset$

$(\exists\theta)(r_{i+1}\mathrm{RC_F}\ \theta \cdot \eta\ \mathrm{cj}\ \zeta\ \mathrm{Ing}\ \theta)) \cdot \supset \cdot (\exists\psi')(\exists\xi')$

$(\eta\ \mathrm{cj}\ \zeta\ r_{i+1}\mathrm{Prob_F}(\psi';\xi') \cdot \mathrm{Thm}\ \psi'\ _\mathrm{s}\mathrm{gr}\ r_i) \supset (\exists\psi')$

$(\exists\xi')(\eta\ r_{i+1}\mathrm{Prob_F}(\psi';\xi') \cdot \mathrm{Thm}\ \psi'\ _\mathrm{s}\mathrm{gr}\ r_i)\urcorner$ (5)

ML(*100) $\ulcorner \mathrm{Stat}\ \eta\ \mathrm{cj}\ \zeta \supset \mathrm{Thm}\ (\eta\ \mathrm{cj}\ \zeta)\ \mathrm{cd}\ (\eta\ \mathrm{cd}\ \eta)\urcorner$ (6)

**233,*100 $\ulcorner[\,1118 \cdot 6 \cdot \supset : \cdot\,]\ r_{i+1}\mathrm{C_F} \cdot (\eta)(\zeta)(\mathrm{Thm}\ \eta\ \mathrm{cd}\ \zeta \cdot$

$(\exists\theta)(r_{i+1}\mathrm{RC_F}\ \theta \cdot \eta\ \mathrm{Ing}\ \theta) \cdot \supset (\exists\theta)$

$(r_{i+1}\mathrm{RC_F}\ \theta \cdot \zeta\ \mathrm{Ing}\ \theta)) \cdot (\exists\theta)(r_i\mathrm{RC_F}\ \theta \cdot$

$\eta\ \mathrm{cj}\ \zeta\ \mathrm{Ing}\ \theta) \cdot \supset (\exists\theta)(r_{i+1}\mathrm{RC_F}\ \theta \cdot \eta\ \mathrm{cd}\ \eta$

$\mathrm{Ing}\ \theta)\urcorner$ (7)

*100 $\ulcorner[5 \cdot 7 \cdot 1166 \cdot \supset : \cdot] \; r_i \neq r_n \supset : r_{i+1}C_F \cdot (\eta)(\zeta)$

(Thm η cd $\zeta \cdot (\exists\theta)(r_{i+1}RC_F \; \theta \cdot \eta$ Ing $\theta) \cdot \supset$

$(\exists\theta)(r_{i+1}RC_F \; \theta \cdot \zeta$ Ing $\theta)) \cdot (\exists\theta)(r_i RC_F \; \theta \cdot$

η cj ζ Ing $\theta) \cdot \supset (\exists\psi')(\exists\xi')(\eta \; r_{i+1}Prob_F(\psi';\xi') \cdot$

Thm $\psi' \; {}_sgr \; r_i)\urcorner$ (8)

*100 (and properties of ingredienthood) $\ulcorner(\exists\psi')(\exists\xi')$

$(\eta \; r_{i+1}Prob_F(\psi':\xi') \cdot$ Thm $\psi' \; {}_sgr \; r_i) \supset r_i RC_F$

$S_6\widehat{\;}S_7\widehat{\;}\eta\widehat{\;}S_6\widehat{\;}S_7 \cdot \sim S_6\widehat{\;}S_7 \; P \; \eta\urcorner$ (9)

*100 $\ulcorner[8 \cdot 9 \cdot 1104 \cdot \supset :] \; 1173\urcorner$

**1174 $\ulcorner r_i \neq r_n \supset : r_{i+1}C_F \cdot (\eta)(\zeta)($Thm η cd $\zeta \cdot (\exists\theta)$

$(r_{i+1}RC_F \; \theta \cdot \eta$ Ing $\theta) \cdot \supset (\exists\theta)(r_{i+1}RC_F \; \theta \cdot$

ζ Ing $\theta)) \cdot (\exists\theta)(r_i RC_F \; \theta \cdot \eta$ Ing $\theta) \cdot \eta \; r_{i+1}B_F \; \zeta \cdot$

$\supset (\exists\theta)(r_i RC_F \; \theta \cdot \zeta$ Ing $\theta)\urcorner$

Proof.

*100 $\ulcorner[1170 \supset] \; r_i \neq r_n \supset : \cdot (\eta)(\zeta)($Thm η cd $\zeta \cdot (\exists\theta)$

$(r_{i+1}RC_F \; \theta \cdot \eta$ Ing $\theta) \cdot \supset (\exists\theta)(r_{i+1}RC_F \; \theta \cdot \zeta$ Ing $\theta)) \cdot$

$\eta \; r_{i+1}B_F \; \zeta \cdot \supset : \eta \; r_{i+1}Prob_F(\psi;\xi) \cdot$ Thm $\psi {}_sgr \; r_i \cdot$

$\supset \cdot \zeta \; r_{i+1}Prob_F(\psi;\xi) \cdot$ Thm $\psi \; {}_sgr \; r_i\urcorner$ (1)

*157,*149 $\ulcorner[(\psi)(\xi) \; 1 \cdot \supset ::] \; r_i \not\equiv r_n \supset : \cdot (\eta)(\zeta)($Thm η cd $\zeta \cdot$

$(\exists\theta)(r_{i+1}RC_F \; \theta \cdot \eta$ Ing $\theta) \cdot \supset (\exists\theta)$

$(r_{i+1}RC_F \; \theta \cdot \zeta$ Ing $\theta)) \cdot \eta \; r_{i+1}B_F \; \zeta \cdot \supset :$

$(\exists\psi)(\exists\xi)(\eta \; r_{i+1}Prob_F(\psi;\xi) \cdot$ Thm $\psi \; {}_sgr \; r_i) \supset$

$(\exists\psi)(\exists\xi)(\zeta \; r_{i+1}Prob_F(\psi;\xi) \cdot$ Thm $\psi \; {}_sgr \; r_i)$ (2)

**233,*100,$\triangle$95a $(\exists\theta)(r_i RC_F \; \theta \cdot \eta$ Ing $\theta) \cdot r_i \neq r_n \cdot \supset$

$(\exists\psi)(\exists\xi)(\eta \; r_{i+1}Prob_F(\psi;\xi) \cdot$

Thm $\psi \; {}_sgr \; r_i)$ (3)

*100 $[2 \cdot 3 \cdot \supset ::] \; r_i \neq r_n \supset : \cdot (\eta)(\zeta)($Thm η cd $\zeta \cdot (\exists\theta)$

$(r_{i+1}RC_F \; \theta \cdot \eta$ Ing $\theta) \cdot \supset (\exists\theta)(r_{i+1}RC_F \; \theta \cdot$

$$\zeta \text{ Ing } \theta)) \cdot \eta \ r_{i+1}\text{B}_\text{F} \ \zeta \cdot (\exists \theta)(r_i \text{RC}_\text{F} \ \theta \cdot \eta \text{ Ing } \theta) \cdot \supset$$

$$(\exists \psi)(\exists \xi)(\zeta \ r_{i+1}\text{Prob}_\text{F}(\psi;\xi) \cdot \text{Thm } \psi \ _\text{s}\text{gr } r_i)^{\urcorner} \tag{4}$$

*100 (and properties of ingredienthood) $^{\ulcorner}(\exists \psi)(\exists \xi)$

$$(\zeta \ r_{i+1}\text{Prob}_\text{F}(\psi;\xi) \cdot \text{Thm } \psi \ _\text{s}\text{gr } r_i) \supset \cdot r_i \text{RC}_\text{F}$$

$$\text{S}_6\widehat{\ }\text{S}_7\widehat{\ }\zeta\widehat{\ }\text{S}_6\widehat{\ }\text{S}_7 \cdot \sim \text{S}_6\widehat{\ }\text{S}_7 \ \text{P} \ \zeta^{\urcorner} \tag{5}$$

*100 $^{\ulcorner}[4 \cdot 5 \cdot 1104 \cdot \supset :] \ 1174^{\urcorner}$

**1175 $^{\ulcorner}r_i \neq r_n \supset : r_{i+1}\text{C}_\text{F} \cdot (\eta)(\zeta)(\text{Thm } \eta \text{ cd } \zeta \cdot (\exists \theta)$

$$(r_{i+1}\text{RC}_\text{F} \ \theta \cdot \eta \text{ Ing } \theta) \cdot \supset (\exists \theta)(r_{i+1}\text{RC}_\text{F} \ \theta \cdot$$

$$\zeta \text{ Ing } \theta)) \cdot (\exists \theta)(r_{i+1}\text{RC}_\text{F} \ \theta \cdot \eta \text{ cd } \zeta \text{ Ing } \theta) \cdot$$

$$(\exists \theta)(r_i \text{RC}_\text{F} \ \theta \cdot \eta \text{ Ing } \theta) \cdot \supset (\exists \theta)(r_i \text{RC}_\text{F} \ \theta \cdot$$

$$\zeta \text{ Ing } \theta)^{\urcorner}$$

Proof.

ML (*100) $^{\ulcorner}\text{Stat } \eta \text{ cd } \zeta \supset \text{Thm } (\eta \text{ cd } \zeta) \text{ cd } (\eta \text{ b}(\eta \text{ cj } \zeta))^{\urcorner} \tag{1}$

**233 $^{\ulcorner}(\eta)(\zeta)(\text{Thm } \eta \text{ cd } \zeta \cdot (\exists \theta)(r_{i+1}\text{RC}_\text{F} \ \theta \cdot \eta \text{ Ing } \theta) \cdot \supset$

$$(\exists \theta)(r_{i+1}\text{RC}_\text{F} \ \theta \cdot \zeta \text{ Ing } \theta)) \cdot (\exists \theta)(r_{i+1}\text{RC}_\text{F} \ \theta \cdot$$

$$\eta \text{ cd } \zeta \text{ Ing } \theta) \cdot \supset (\exists \theta)(r_{i+1}\text{RC}_\text{F} \ \theta \cdot$$

$$\eta \text{ b}(\eta \text{ cd } \zeta) \text{Ing } \theta)^{\urcorner} \tag{2}$$

**1041 $^{\ulcorner}(\exists \theta)(r_{i+1}\text{RC}_\text{F} \ \theta \cdot \eta \text{ b}(\eta \text{ cj } \zeta) \text{Ing } \theta) \supset \eta \ r_{i+1}\text{B}_\text{F}$

$$\eta \text{ cj } \zeta^{\urcorner} \tag{3}$$

*100 $^{\ulcorner}[2 \cdot 3 \cdot 1174 \cdot \supset ::] \ r_i \neq r_n \supset : r_{i+1}\text{C}_\text{F} \cdot (\eta)(\zeta)$

$$(\text{Thm } \eta \text{ cd } \zeta \cdot (\exists \theta)(r_{i+1}\text{RC}_\text{F} \ \theta \cdot \eta \text{ Ing } \theta) \cdot \supset$$

$$(\exists \theta)(r_{i+1}\text{RC}_\text{F} \ \theta \cdot \zeta \text{ Ing } \theta)) \cdot (\exists \theta)(r_{i+1}\text{RC}_\text{F} \ \theta \cdot$$

$$\eta \text{ cd } \zeta \text{ Ing } \theta) \cdot (\exists \theta)(r_i \text{RC}_\text{F} \ \theta \cdot \eta \text{ Ing } \theta) \cdot \supset$$

$$(\exists \theta)(r_i \text{RC}_\text{F} \ \theta \cdot \eta \text{ cj } \zeta \text{ Ing } \theta)^{\urcorner} \tag{4}$$

*100 $^{\ulcorner}[4 \cdot 1173 \cdot \supset :] \ 1175^{\urcorner}$

**1176 $^{\ulcorner}r_i \neq r_n \cdot r_{i+1}\text{C}_\text{F} \cdot (\eta)(\zeta)(\text{Thm } \eta \text{ cd } \zeta \cdot (\exists \theta)(r_{i+1}\text{RC}_\text{F} \ \theta \cdot$

$$\eta \text{ Ing } \theta) \cdot \supset (\exists \theta)(r_{i+1}\text{RC}_\text{F} \ \theta \cdot \zeta \text{ Ing } \theta)) \cdot \supset :$$

$$\text{Thm } \eta \text{ cd } \zeta \cdot (\exists \theta)(r_i \text{RC}_\text{F} \ \theta \cdot \eta \text{ Ing } \theta) \cdot \supset$$

$$(\exists \theta)(r_i \text{RC}_\text{F} \ \theta \cdot \zeta \text{ Ing } \theta)^{\urcorner}$$

Proof.

ML(*100) $\ulcorner$ Thm η cd ζ · Stat β · ⊃ Thm $(\eta$ b $\beta)$ cd $(\eta$ cd ζ $)\urcorner$ (1)

**233,*100,Δ95a $\ulcorner$ $(\exists\theta)(r_i \text{RC}_\text{F}\ \theta \cdot \eta\ \text{Ing}\ \theta) \cdot r_i \neq r_n \cdot$ ⊃

$\qquad\qquad (\exists\psi)(\exists\xi)(\eta\ r_{i+1}\text{Prob}_\text{F}(\psi;\xi) \cdot \text{Thm}\ \psi\ {}_\text{s}\text{gr}\ r_i)\urcorner$ (2)

*156,*100,Δ107 $\ulcorner$ $\eta\ r_{i+1}\text{Prob}_\text{F}(\psi;\xi) \cdot \text{Thm}\ \psi\ {}_\text{s}\text{gr}\ r_i \cdot$ ⊃

$\qquad\qquad (\exists\alpha)(\exists\gamma)(\eta\ r_{i+1}\text{B}_\text{F}\ \alpha\ \text{e}\ \gamma)\urcorner$ (3)

From Δ102 and the protosyntactical meaning of x Pr_yz, we have,

$\ulcorner$ $(\exists\alpha)(\exists\gamma)(\eta\ r_{i+1}\text{B}_\text{F}\ \alpha\ \text{e}\ \gamma) \supset (\exists\beta)(\exists\theta)(r_i\text{RC}_\text{F}\ \theta \cdot \eta\ \text{b}\ \beta$

$\qquad \text{Ing}\ \theta)\urcorner$ (4)

*161,*100 $\ulcorner$ $[(\psi)(\xi)(3 \cdot 4) \cdot \supset :]\ (\exists\psi)(\exists\xi)(\eta\ r_{i+1}\text{Prob}_\text{F}(\psi;\xi) \cdot$

$\qquad \text{Thm}\ \psi\ {}_\text{s}\text{gr}\ r_i) \supset (\exists\beta)(\exists\theta)(r_{i+1}\text{RC}_\text{F}\ \theta \cdot$

$\qquad \eta\ \text{b}\ \beta\ \text{Ing}\ \theta)\urcorner$ (5)

**233 $\ulcorner$ $(\eta)(\zeta)(\text{Thm}\ \eta\ \text{cd}\ \zeta \cdot (\exists\theta)(r_{i+1}\text{RC}_\text{F}\ \theta \cdot \eta\ \text{Ing}\ \theta) \cdot \supset$

$\qquad (\exists\theta)(r_{i+1}\text{RC}_\text{F}\ \theta \cdot \zeta\ \text{Ing}\ \theta)) \supset : \text{Thm}\ (\eta\ \text{b}\ \beta)\ \text{cd}$

$\qquad (\eta\ \text{cd}\ \zeta) \cdot (\exists\theta)(r_{i+1}\text{RC}_\text{F}\ \theta \cdot \eta\ \text{b}\ \beta\ \text{Ing}\ \theta) \cdot \supset$

$\qquad (\exists\theta)(r_{i+1}\text{RC}_\text{F}\ \theta \cdot \eta\ \text{cd}\ \zeta\ \text{Ing}\ \theta)\urcorner$ (6)

*100 $\ulcorner$ $[1 \cdot 6 \cdot \supset : \cdot]\ (\eta)(\zeta)(\text{Thm}\ \eta\ \text{cd}\ \zeta \cdot (\exists\theta)(r_{i+1}\text{RC}_\text{F}\ \theta \cdot$

$\qquad \eta\ \text{Ing}\ \theta) \cdot \supset (\exists\theta)(r_{i+1}\text{RC}_\text{F}\ \theta \cdot \zeta\ \text{Ing}\ \theta)) \supset :$

$\qquad \text{Thm}\ \eta\ \text{cd}\ \zeta \cdot (\exists\theta)(r_{i+1}\text{RC}_\text{F}\ \theta \cdot \eta\ \text{b}\ \beta\ \text{Ing}\ \theta) \cdot \supset$

$\qquad (\exists\theta)(r_{i+1}\text{RC}_\text{F}\ \theta \cdot \eta\ \text{cd}\ \zeta\ \text{Ing}\ \theta)\urcorner$ (7)

*161,*159,*158 $\ulcorner$ $[(\beta)\ 7 \supset : \cdot]\ (\eta)(\zeta)(\text{Thm}\ \eta\ \text{cd}\ \zeta \cdot (\exists\theta)$

$\qquad (r_{i+1}\text{RC}_\text{F}\ \theta \cdot \eta\ \text{Ing}\ \theta) \cdot \supset (\exists\theta)(r_{i+1}\text{RC}_\text{F}\ \theta \cdot$

$\qquad \zeta\ \text{Ing}\ \theta)) \supset : \text{Thm}\ \eta\ \text{cd}\ \zeta \cdot (\exists\beta)(\exists\theta)(r_{i+1}\text{RC}_\text{F}\ \theta \cdot$

$\qquad \eta\ \text{b}\ \beta\ \text{Ing}\ \theta) \cdot \supset (\exists\theta)(r_{i+1}\text{RC}_\text{F}\ \theta \cdot \eta\ \text{cd}\ \zeta\ \text{Ing}\ \theta)\urcorner$ (8)

*100 $\ulcorner$ $[2 \cdot 5 \cdot 8 \cdot \supset : \cdot]\ (\eta)(\zeta)(\text{Thm}\ \eta\ \text{cd}\ \zeta \cdot (\exists\theta)(r_{i+1}\text{RC}_\text{F}\ \theta \cdot$

$\qquad \eta\ \text{Ing}\ \theta) \cdot \supset (\exists\theta)(r_{i+1}\text{RC}_\text{F}\ \theta \cdot \zeta\ \text{Ing}\ \theta)) \supset :$

$\qquad \text{Thm}\ \eta\ \text{cd}\ \zeta \cdot (\exists\theta)(r_i\text{RC}_\text{F}\ \theta \cdot \eta\ \text{Ing}\ \theta) \cdot r_i \neq r_n \cdot \supset$

$\qquad (\exists\theta)(r_{i+1}\text{RC}_\text{F}\ \theta \cdot \eta\ \text{cd}\ \zeta\ \text{Ing}\ \theta)\urcorner$ (9)

*100 $\ulcorner$ $[9 \cdot 1175 \cdot \supset ::]\ 1176\urcorner$

**1177 $\ulcorner r_i \neq r_n \supset r_{i+1}C_F : \supset :$ Thm η cd $\zeta \cdot (\exists\theta)(r_i RC_F \, \theta \cdot$

η Ing $\theta) \cdot \supset (\exists\theta)(r_i RC_F \, \theta \cdot \zeta$ Ing $\theta)\urcorner$

Proof.

for $r_i = r_n$, **1115

for $r_i = r_{n-1}$, **1115 and **1176

for $r_i = r_{n-2}$, **1177 for $r_i = r_{n-1}$ and **1176,

etc.

It is obvious that metatheorem **1177 will enable us to simplify the preceding metatheorems enormously—most of them have had the closure of the consequent of **1177 as an antecedent; this could now be replaced by $\ulcorner r_i \neq r_n \supset r_{i+1}C_F\urcorner$. But a further simplification can be made, and I shall postpone the restatement of some of the more important of the foregoing theorems until this has been done.

Subject to the hypothesis $\ulcorner r_i \neq r_n \supset r_{i+1}C_F\urcorner$, the statement pct$(w,x,(y;z))$ will be an ingredient of a rational corpus of level r_i if and only if the statement pct$(w,\text{compl } x,(\text{``}_s1\text{''}_s\min z;\text{``}_s1\text{''}_s\min y))$ is an ingredient of a rational corpus of this level. To know something about the proportion of A's that are B's is to know something about the proportion of A's that are not B's.

**1178 $\ulcorner r_i \neq r_n \supset r_{i+1}C_F \cdot \supset \cdot$ pct$(\beta,\gamma,(\psi{:}\xi)) \, r_i SA_F(\beta,\gamma) \equiv$

pct$(\beta,\text{compl } \gamma,(\text{``}_s1\text{''}_s\min \xi;\text{``}_s1\text{''}_s\min \psi))$

$r_i SA_F(\beta,\text{compl } \gamma)\urcorner$

Proof.

Ratio exten- $\ulcorner$ Thm pct$(\beta,\gamma,(\psi;\xi))$ b pct$(\beta,\text{compl } \gamma,(\text{``}_s1\text{''}_s\min \xi;$
sion of ML $\text{``}_s1\text{''}_s\min \psi))\urcorner$ (1)

*100 $\ulcorner[1 \cdot 1177 \cdot \supset :] \, r_i \neq r_n \supset r_{i+1}C_F \cdot \supset \cdot (\exists\theta)(r_i RC_F \, \theta \cdot$

pct$(\beta,\gamma,(\psi;\xi))$ Ing $\theta) \equiv (\exists\theta)(r_i RC_F \, \theta \cdot$ pct$(\beta,\text{compl}$

$\gamma,(\text{``}_s1\text{''}_s\min \xi;\text{``}_s1\text{''}_s\min \psi))$ Ing $\theta)\urcorner$ (2)

(Δ96b—presumably) $\ulcorner(\exists\beta')(\exists\gamma')(\exists\eta)(\exists\eta')($Vbl $\eta \cdot$ Vbl $\eta' \cdot$

r_iRMat$_F \, \beta' \cdot r_i$RMat γ' . Thm η qu$(\eta$ e β b $\beta') \cdot$

Thm η'qu $(\eta'$ e β int γ b $\gamma')) \equiv (\exists\beta')(\exists\gamma')(\exists\eta)(\exists\eta')$

Vbl $\eta \cdot$ Vbl $\eta' \cdot r_i$RMat$_F \, \beta' \cdot r_i$RMat$_F \, \gamma'$. Thm η qu

$(\beta$ b $\beta') \cdot$ Thm η' qu $(\eta'$ e β int compl γ b $\gamma'))\urcorner$ (3)

(Δ97a) $\ulcorner (\exists\zeta)(\exists\zeta')(\mathrm{RM}\ \zeta \cdot \mathrm{RM}\ \zeta' \cdot \mathrm{Thm}\ \psi\ \mathrm{e}\ S_2\mathrm{a}\zeta \cdot \mathrm{Thm}\ \xi\ \mathrm{e}$

$\qquad S_2\mathrm{a}\zeta') \equiv (\exists\zeta)(\exists\zeta')(\mathrm{RM}\ \zeta \cdot \mathrm{RM}\ \zeta' \cdot \mathrm{Thm}\ ``_s1''_s\mathrm{min}\ \xi$

$\qquad \mathrm{e}\ S_2\mathrm{a}\zeta \cdot \mathrm{Thm}\ ``_s1''_s\mathrm{min}\ \xi\ \mathrm{e}\ S_2\mathrm{a}\zeta \cdot \mathrm{Thm}\ ``_s1''_s\mathrm{min}\ \psi$

$\qquad \mathrm{e}\ S_2\mathrm{a}\zeta')\urcorner$ (4)

*100 $\ulcorner [2 \cdot 3 \cdot 4 \cdot \supset :]\ 1178\urcorner$

**1179 $\ulcorner r_i \neq r_n \supset r_{i+1}C_F \cdot \supset \cdot \mathrm{pct}\,(\beta,\gamma,(\psi;\xi))\ r_i\mathrm{Str}_F$

$\qquad \mathrm{pct}\,(\beta',\gamma',(\psi';\xi')) \equiv \mathrm{pct}\,(\beta,\mathrm{compl}\ \gamma,(``_s1''_s\mathrm{min}\ \xi;$

$\qquad ``_s1''_s\mathrm{min}\ \psi))\ r_i\mathrm{Str}_F\ \mathrm{pct}\,(\beta',\mathrm{compl}\ \gamma',(``_s1''_s\mathrm{min}\ \xi';$

$\qquad ``_s1''_s\mathrm{min}\ \psi'))\urcorner$

Proof.

Ratio-extension of ML. $\ulcorner \mathrm{Thm}\ ((\psi\ _s\mathrm{gr}\ \psi'\ \mathrm{cj}\ \xi'\ _s\mathrm{gr}\ \xi)\ \mathrm{al}$

$\qquad (\psi\ \mathrm{id}\ \psi'\ \mathrm{cj}\ \xi'\ _s\mathrm{gr}\ \xi)\ \mathrm{al}\ (\psi\ _s\mathrm{gr}\ \psi'\ \mathrm{cj}\ \xi'\ \mathrm{id}\ \xi))\ \mathrm{b}$

$\qquad ((``_s1''_s\mathrm{min}\ \xi\ _s\mathrm{gr}\ ``_s1''\ _s\mathrm{min}\ \xi'\ \mathrm{cj}\ ``_s1''\ _s\mathrm{min}\ \psi'$

$\qquad _s\mathrm{gr}\ ``_s1''\ _s\mathrm{min}\ \psi)\ \mathrm{al}\ (``_s1''\ _s\mathrm{min}\ \xi\ _s\mathrm{gr}\ ``_s1''_s\mathrm{min}\ \xi'\ \mathrm{cj}$

$\qquad ``_s1''_s\mathrm{min}\ \psi'\ \mathrm{id}\ ``_s1''_s\mathrm{min}\ \psi)\ \mathrm{al}\ (``_s1''_s\mathrm{min}\ \xi\ \mathrm{id}$

$\qquad ``_s1''_s\mathrm{min}\ \xi'\ \mathrm{cj}\ ``_s1''_s\mathrm{min}\ \psi'\ _s\mathrm{gr}\ ``_s1''_s\mathrm{min}\ \psi))\urcorner$ (1)

*100, etc. $\ulcorner [1 \cdot 1177 \cdot 1178 \cdot \supset :]\ 1179\urcorner$

**1180 $\ulcorner r_i \neq r_n \supset r_{i+1}C_F \cdot \supset \cdot \mathrm{pct}\,(\beta,\gamma,(\psi;\xi))\ r_i S^*A_F(\beta,\gamma) \equiv$

$\qquad \mathrm{pct}\,(\beta,\mathrm{compl}\ \gamma,(``_s1''\ _s\mathrm{min}\ \xi;``_s1''\ _s\mathrm{min}\ \psi))$

$\qquad r_i S^*A_F(\beta,\mathrm{compl}\ \gamma)\urcorner$

Proof.

*100, etc. $\ulcorner [1178 \cdot 1179 \cdot \supset :]\ 1180\urcorner$

**1181 $\ulcorner r_i \neq r_n \supset r_{i+1}C_F \cdot \supset \cdot \mathrm{pct}\,(\beta,\gamma,(\psi;\xi))\ r_i\mathrm{Dif}_F$

$\qquad \mathrm{pct}\,(\beta',\gamma',(\psi';\xi')) \equiv \mathrm{pct}\,(\beta,\mathrm{compl}\ \gamma,(``_s1''_s\mathrm{min}\ \xi;$

$\qquad ``_s1''_s\mathrm{min}\ \psi))\ r_i\mathrm{Dif}_F\ \mathrm{pct}\,(\beta',\mathrm{compl}\ \gamma',(``_s1''_s\mathrm{min}\ \xi';$

$\qquad ``_s1''_s\mathrm{min}\ \psi'))\urcorner$

Proof.

Similar to the proof of **1179

**1182 $\ulcorner r_i \neq r_n \supset r_{i+1}C_F \cdot \supset \cdot \text{pct}(\beta,\gamma,(\psi;\xi)) r_i S =_F$

$\qquad \text{pct}(\beta',\gamma',(\psi';\xi')) \equiv \text{pct}(\beta,\text{compl } \gamma,(\text{``}_s1\text{''},\min \xi;$

$\qquad \text{``}_s1\text{''},\min \psi)) r_i S =_F \text{pct}(\beta',\text{compl } \gamma',(\text{``}_s1\text{''},\min \xi';$

$\qquad \text{``}_s1\text{''},\min \psi'))\urcorner$

Proof.

Similar to the proof of ****1179**

**1183 $\ulcorner r_i \neq r_n \supset r_{i+1}C_F \cdot \supset \cdot \zeta r_i B_F \eta \equiv n\zeta r_i B_F n\eta\urcorner$

Proof.

ML(*100) $\ulcorner (\text{Stat } \zeta \cdot \text{Stat } \eta) \supset \text{Thm} (\zeta \text{ b } \eta) \text{ b } (n\zeta \text{ b } n\eta)\urcorner$ \hfill (1)

*100 $\ulcorner [1 \cdot 1177 \cdot \supset :] r_i \neq r_n \supset r_{i+1}C_F \cdot \supset \cdot (\exists \theta)(r_i RC_F \theta \cdot$

$\qquad \zeta \text{ b } \eta \text{ Ing } \theta) \equiv (\exists \theta)(r_i RC_F \theta \cdot n\zeta \text{ b } n\eta \text{ Ing } \theta)\urcorner$ \hfill (2)

Thus every link of the one biconditional chain will be mirrored by a statement forming a link of the other.

**1184 $\ulcorner r_i \neq r_n \supset r_{i+1}C_F \cdot \alpha r_i \text{Mem}_F \beta \cdot \supset \cdot \beta' r_i DP_F(\alpha,\beta,\gamma) \equiv$

$\qquad \beta' r_i DP_F(\alpha,\beta,\text{compl } \gamma)\urcorner$

Proof.

*100,****1177**, $\ulcorner r_i \neq r_n \supset r_{i+1}C_F \cdot \alpha r_i \text{Mem}_F \beta \cdot \alpha' r_i \text{Mem}_F \beta' \supset \cdot$
ML(†190,†411) $\qquad (\exists \theta)(r_i RC_F \theta \cdot \alpha \text{ e v Ing } \theta) \cdot$

$\qquad (\exists \theta)(r_i RC_F \theta \cdot \alpha' \text{ e v Ing } \theta)\urcorner$ \hfill (1)

ML(*230,D20) $\ulcorner \text{Thm} (\alpha' \text{ e v}) \text{ cd } (n \alpha' \text{ e } \gamma' \text{ b } \alpha' \text{ e compl } \gamma')\urcorner$ \hfill (2)

Similarly, $\ulcorner \text{Thm} (\alpha \text{ e v}) \text{ cd } (n \alpha \text{ e } \gamma \text{ b } \alpha \text{ e compl } \gamma)\urcorner$ \hfill (3)

**1183 $\ulcorner r_i \neq r_n \supset r_{i+1}C_F \cdot \supset \cdot \alpha' \text{ e } \gamma' r_i B_F \alpha \text{ e } \gamma \equiv n(\alpha' \text{ e } \gamma')$

$\qquad r_i B_F n(\alpha \text{ e } \gamma)\urcorner$ \hfill (4)

*100 $\ulcorner [1177 \cdot 2 \cdot 3 \cdot 1041 \cdot 1147 \cdot 4 \cdot 1043 \cdot 1 \cdot \supset :] r_i \neq r_n \supset$

$\qquad r_{i+1}C_F \cdot \alpha r_i \text{Mem}_F \beta \cdot \supset : \alpha' r_i \text{Mem}_F \beta' \cdot \alpha' \text{ e } \gamma'$

$\qquad r_i B_F \alpha \text{ e } \gamma \cdot \equiv \cdot \alpha' r_i \text{Mem}_F \beta' \cdot \alpha' \text{ e compl } \gamma'$

$\qquad r_i B_F \alpha \text{ e compl } \gamma\urcorner$ \hfill (5)

Similarly, $\ulcorner r_i \neq r_n \supset r_{i+1}C_F \cdot \supset : \alpha' r_i \text{Mem}_F \beta'' \cdot \alpha' \text{ e } \gamma' r_i B_F$

$\qquad \alpha' \text{ e } \gamma'' \cdot \equiv \cdot \alpha' r_i \text{Mem}_F \beta'' \cdot \alpha' \text{ e compl } \gamma'$

$\qquad r_i B_F \alpha' \text{ e compl } \gamma''\urcorner$ \hfill (6)

*100, Δ99, Δ100, and sufficient juggling of quantifiers,

$$\ulcorner[\,1180 \cdot 1181 \cdot 5 \cdot 6 \cdot \supset :]\ 1184\ \urcorner$$

**1185 $\ulcorner r_i \neq r_n \supset r_{i+1}C_F \cdot \alpha\ r_i \text{Mem}_F\ \beta \cdot \supset \cdot \beta'\ r_i \text{SP}_F(\alpha,\beta,\gamma) \equiv$

$\qquad\qquad \beta'\ r_i \text{SP}_F(\alpha,\beta,\text{compl}\ \gamma)\urcorner$

Proof.

*100,*116,*159 $\ulcorner[\,(\beta'')\ 1184 \supset :]\ r_i \neq r_n \supset r_{i+1}C_F\ \cdot$

$\qquad\qquad \alpha'\ r_i \text{Mem}_F\ \beta' \cdot \supset \cdot \sim (\exists\beta'')(\beta''\ r_i \text{DP}_F$

$\qquad\qquad (\alpha',\beta',\gamma')) \equiv \sim (\exists\beta'')(\beta''\ r_i\,\text{DP}_F(\alpha',\beta',\text{compl}\ \gamma'))\urcorner$ (1)

From here on the proof is like that of **1184.

**1186 $\ulcorner r_i \neq r_n \supset r_{i+1}C_F \cdot \supset \cdot \alpha\ r_i \text{Ran}_F(\beta,\gamma) \equiv \alpha\ r_i \text{Ran}_F$

$\qquad\qquad (\beta,\text{compl}\ \gamma)\urcorner$

Proof.

*100 $\ulcorner[\,1184 \cdot 1185 \cdot \supset :]\ r_i \neq r_n \supset r_{i+1}C_F \cdot \supset : \alpha\ r_i \text{Mem}_F\ \beta \cdot$

$\qquad\qquad \sim \beta'\ r_i \text{DP}_F(\alpha,\beta,\gamma) \cdot \sim \beta'\ r_i \text{SP}_F(\alpha,\beta,\gamma) \cdot \equiv \cdot$

$\qquad\qquad \alpha\ r_i \text{Mem}_F\ \beta \cdot \sim \beta'\ r_i \text{DP}_F(\alpha,\beta,\text{compl}\ \gamma) \cdot \sim \beta'$

$\qquad\qquad r_i \text{SP}_F(\alpha,\beta,\text{compl}\ \gamma)\urcorner$ (1)

**1180, Δ99 $\ulcorner r_i \neq r_n \supset r_{i+1}C_F \cdot \supset \cdot (\exists\eta)(\eta\ r_i\text{S*A}_F(\beta,\gamma)) \equiv$

$\qquad\qquad (\exists\eta)(\eta\ r_i\text{S*A}_F(\beta,\text{compl}\ \gamma))\urcorner$ (2)

*100,*159,*116,D 8, $\ulcorner[\,1 \cdot 2 \cdot \supset :]\ 1186\urcorner$
Δ106

**1187 $\ulcorner r_i \neq r_n \supset r_{i+1}C_F \cdot \supset \cdot \eta\ r_i \text{Prob}_F(\psi;\xi) \equiv \text{n}\ \eta$

$\qquad\qquad r_i \text{Prob}_F(``_s1",_s\min \xi; ``_s1",_s\min \psi)\urcorner$

Proof.

*100 $\ulcorner[\,1177 \supset :]\ r_i \neq r_n \supset r_{i+1}C_F \cdot \alpha\ r_i \text{Mem}_F\ \beta \cdot \supset (\exists\theta)$

$\qquad\qquad (r_i \text{RC}_F\ \theta \cdot \alpha\ \text{e v Ing}\ \theta)\urcorner$ (1)

ML(*230,D 20) $\ulcorner[\,1177 \cdot 1 \cdot 1183\ \supset :]\ r_i \neq r_n \supset r_{i+1}C_F\ \cdot$

$\qquad\qquad \alpha\ r_i \text{Mem}_F\ \beta \cdot \supset \cdot \eta\ r_i\text{B}_F\ \alpha\ \text{e}\ \gamma \equiv$

$\qquad\qquad \text{n}\ \eta\ r_i\text{B}_F\ \alpha\ \text{e compl}\ \gamma\urcorner$ (2)

*100 $\ulcorner[2 \cdot 1186 \cdot 1180 \cdot \supset :] \ r_i \neq r_n \supset r_{i+1}C_F \cdot \supset : \eta \ r_iB_F \ \alpha \ e \ \gamma \cdot$
$\alpha \ r_i\text{Ran}_F(\beta,\gamma) \cdot \text{pct}(\beta,\gamma,(\psi;\xi))r_iS^*A_F(\beta,\gamma) \cdot \equiv \cdot$
$n\eta \ r_iB_F \ \alpha \ e \ \text{compl} \ \gamma \cdot \alpha \ r_i \text{Ran}_F(\beta,\text{compl} \ \gamma) \cdot$
$\text{pct}(\beta,\text{compl} \ \gamma,(\text{"}_s1\text{"}_s\text{min} \ \xi;\text{"}_s1\text{"}_s\text{min} \ \psi))$
$r_iS^*A_F(\beta,\text{compl} \ \gamma)\overline{}\ulcorner$ (3)

*159,*116,*140,*149, $\ulcorner[(\alpha)(\beta)(\gamma) 3 \cdot \supset] \ 1187\urcorner$

**1188 $\ulcorner r_i \neq r_n \supset r_iC_F\urcorner$

Proof.

Since $\ulcorner r_i \ _s\text{gr} \ \text{"1/2"}\urcorner$ is a theorem,

$\ulcorner\text{Thm} \ (\psi \ _s\text{gr} \ r_i) \ \text{cd n}(\text{"}_s1\text{"}_s\text{min} \ \psi \ _s\text{gr} \ r_i)\urcorner$ (1)

*100 $\ulcorner[1169 \cdot 1177 \cdot 1147 \cdot 1043 \cdot \supset :] \ r_nC_F \cdot \eta \ r_nB_F \ \alpha \ e \ \gamma \cdot$
Δ101 $\eta \ r_nB_F \ \alpha' e \ \gamma' \cdot \alpha \ r_n\text{Ran}_F(\beta,\gamma) \cdot \alpha' \ r_n\text{Ran}_F(\beta',\gamma') \cdot$
$\text{pct}(\beta,\gamma,(\psi;\xi))r_nS^*A_F(\beta,\gamma) \cdot \text{pct}(\beta',\gamma',(\psi';\xi'))$
$r_nS^*A_F(\beta',\gamma') \cdot \supset (\exists\theta)(r_n\text{RC}_F \ \theta \cdot \psi \ \text{id} \ \psi' \ \text{Ing} \ \theta)\urcorner$ (2)

Since any statement in a rational corpus relating fractions appearing in statistical statements is a theorem,

*100, Δ107 $\ulcorner[2 \cdot \supset :] \ r_nC_F \cdot \eta \ r_n\text{Prob}_F(\psi,\xi) \cdot \eta \ r_n\text{Prob}_F(\psi';\xi') \cdot$
$\supset \text{Thm} \ \psi \ \text{id} \ \psi'\urcorner$ (3)

ML $\ulcorner\text{Thm} \ \psi \ \text{id} \ \psi' \cdot \text{Thm} \ \psi' \ _s\text{gr} \ r_{n-1} \cdot \supset \text{Thm} \ \psi \ _s\text{gr} \ r_{n-1}\urcorner$ (4)

*100 $\ulcorner[1187 \cdot 3 \cdot 1 \cdot \supset :] \ r_nC_F \cdot \eta \ r_n\text{Prob}_F(\psi';\xi') \cdot$
$\text{Thm} \ \psi' \ _s\text{gr} \ r_{n-1} \cdot \supset \cdot n \ \eta \ r_n\text{Prob}_F(\text{"}_s1\text{"}_s\text{min} \ \xi;$
$\text{"}_s1\text{"}_s\text{min} \ \psi) \supset \text{Thm} \ n(\text{"}_s1\text{"}_s\text{min} \ \psi \ _s\text{gr} \ r_{n-1})\urcorner$ (5)

*157,*161,Δ95a $\ulcorner r_nC_F \cdot (\exists\theta)(r_{n-1}\text{RC}_F \ \theta \cdot \eta \ \text{Ing} \ \theta) \cdot \supset \cdot$
$n \ \eta \ r_n\text{Prob}_F(\text{"}_s1\text{"}_s\text{min} \ \xi;\text{"}_s1\text{"}_s\text{min} \ \psi) \supset$
$\text{Thm} \ n(\text{"}_s1\text{"}_s\text{min} \ \psi \ _s\text{gr} \ r_{n-1})\urcorner$ (6)

For the fractions that appear in statistical statements, again,

$\ulcorner n \ \eta \ r_n\text{Prob}_F(\text{"}_s1\text{"}_s\text{min} \ \xi;\text{"}_s1\text{"}_s\text{min} \ \psi) \cdot r_nC_F \cdot$
$\text{Thm} \ n(\text{"}_s1\text{"}_s\text{min} \ \psi \ _s\text{gr} \ r_{n-1}) \cdot \supset$
$\sim \text{Thm} \ \text{"}_s1\text{"}_s\text{min} \ \xi \ _s\text{gr} \ r_{n-1}\urcorner$ (7)

*159,*131 $\ulcorner[(\psi)(\xi) 5 \cdot 7 \cdot \supset:] r_n C_F \cdot (\exists \theta)(r_{n-1} RC_F \theta \cdot$

$\eta \ \mathrm{Ing} \ \theta) \cdot \supset \cdot \sim (\exists \psi)(\exists \xi)(n \ \eta \ r_n \mathrm{Prob}_F$

$(``_s1", _s\min \xi; ``_s1", _s\min \psi) \cdot \mathrm{Thm} \ ``_s1", _s\min \xi$

$_s\mathrm{gr} \ r_{n-1})\urcorner$ (8)

In view of the unlimited number of 'ordinary' fractions,

$\ulcorner(\exists \psi)(\exists \xi)(n \ \eta \ r_n \mathrm{Prob}_F (``_s1", _s\min \xi; ``_s1", _s\min \psi) \cdot$

$\mathrm{Thm} \ ``_s1", _s\min \xi \ _s\mathrm{gr} \ r_{n-1}) \equiv (\exists \psi)(\exists \xi)(n \ \eta \ r_n \mathrm{Prob}_F$

$(\psi; \xi) \cdot \mathrm{Thm} \ \psi \ _s\mathrm{gr} \ r_{n-1})\urcorner$ (9)

*100,Δ95a $\ulcorner[8 \cdot 9 \cdot \supset:] r_n C_F \supset \cdot (\exists \theta)(r_{n-1} RC_F \theta \cdot \eta \ \mathrm{Ing} \ \theta) \supset$

$\sim (\exists \theta)(r_{n-1} RC_F \theta \cdot n \ \eta \ \mathrm{Ing} \ \theta)\urcorner$ (10)

*100,Δ108 $\ulcorner[10 \cdot 1117 \cdot \supset:] r_n C_F \supset r_{n-1} C_F\urcorner$ (11)

In a similar manner, we may prove, with the help of line (11),

$\ulcorner r_n C_F \supset r_{n-2} C_F \urcorner$ (12)

$\ulcorner r_n C_F \supset r_{n-3} C_F \urcorner$ (13)

and so on. Thus in general, we have,

$\ulcorner r_i \neq r_n \supset \cdot r_n C_F \supset r_i C_F \urcorner$ (14)

*100 $\ulcorner[14 \cdot 1133 \cdot \supset:] 1188\urcorner$

This final metatheorem allows us to simplify our earlier metatheorems still more; it shows that under my definition of probability, a direct contradiction can never appear in a rational corpus of
level lower than r_n—so that we may replace the specific hypothesis
$\ulcorner r_i C_F \urcorner$ by the general conventional demand, $\ulcorner r_n C_F \urcorner$. Furthermore,
since many of the theorems will hold vacuously (e.g., **1187) if F
and ML should turn out to be jointly inconcistent, we may sometimes drop even the hypothesis $\ulcorner r_n C_F \urcorner$.

CHAPTER TWELVE

Properties of Rational Corpora

1. First I shall summarize the important results of the preceding two chapters.[1] It will be noticed that many of the metatheorems subdivide to yield a statement concerning rational corpora in general which depends on the joint consistency of ML and F, and a statement concerning rational corpora of level other than r_n which is independent of the joint consistency of ML and F.

**1210a $\ulcorner r_n C_F \cdot (\exists \theta)(r_i RC_F \ \theta \cdot \zeta \ \mathrm{Ing} \ \theta) \cdot \supset$

$$\zeta \ r_i \, \mathrm{Prob}_F(\text{``}_s 1\text{''};\text{``}_s 1\text{''})\urcorner$$

**1210b $\ulcorner r_i \ne r_n \supset : (\exists \theta)(r_i RC_F \ \theta \cdot \zeta \ \mathrm{Ing} \ \theta) \supset$

$$\zeta \ r_i \, \mathrm{Prob}_F(\text{``}_s 1\text{''};\text{``}_s 1\text{''})\urcorner$$

These two metatheorems state that the probability of any statement, relative to a rational corpus of given level and basis that includes that statement, is as high as possible, provided ML and F are jointly consistent. It holds regardless of the consistency of ML and F for levels other than r_n, since if ML and F are not consistent no other level of rational corpus than the highest will have any ingredients at all.

The next metatheorem states that if there is a rational corpus of level r_i and basis F containing the statement y as a framed ingredient, then if there is a rational corpus of level r_{i-1} containing any ingredients at all, there will be one containing y. If $r_i = r_1$, then there is no rational corpus of level r_{i-1}; and if ML and F are not jointly consistent, then there will be no ingredients at all in any rational corpus of level r_{i-1}. By **1177 and **1188, if there are any ingredients in the rational corpus of level r_{i-1}, then there will be an ingredient of the form $\ulcorner \eta \ \mathrm{al} \ n\eta \urcorner$.

**1211 $\ulcorner (\exists \theta)(r_i RC_F \ \theta \cdot \zeta \ \mathrm{Ing} \ \theta) \supset \cdot (\exists \theta)(r_{i-1} RC_F \ \theta \cdot$

$$\zeta \ \mathrm{al} \ n\zeta \ \mathrm{Ing} \ \theta) \supset (\exists \theta)(r_{i-1} RC_F \ \theta \cdot \zeta \ \mathrm{Ing} \ \theta)\urcorner$$

---

1. The first section of this chapter is worth struggling through, even for the non-logician; it summarizes the results of the preceding technical chapters. The second section and the third concern further technical matters, and may be skimmed or skipped. The final section is an informal discussion of a few of the more curious properties of rational corpora.

A consequence of this is that, if ML and F are jointly consistent, then every ingredient of the rational corpus of the highest level— i.e., all theorems, all ingredients of F, and everything deducible from the theorems of ML and the ingredients of F—will be included in every other rational corpus.

**1212 $\ulcorner r_n C_F \cdot (\exists \theta)(r_n RC_F \; \theta \cdot \zeta \; \text{Ing} \; \theta) \cdot \supset$

$(\exists \theta)(r_i RC_F \; \theta \cdot \zeta \; \text{Ing} \; \theta)\urcorner$

Due to the fact that we have restricted rational classes in such a way that they can contain no more than two to the googolplex members, we may be sure that if there is a statement about y and z at all in a rational corpus, there is a strongest statement about y and z—subject, in the rational corpus of the highest level, to the condition that ML and F be jointly consistent.

**1213a $\ulcorner r_n C_F \cdot (\exists \eta)(\eta \; r_i SA_F(\beta,\gamma)) \cdot \supset (\exists \eta)(\eta \; r_i S^*A_F(\beta,\gamma))\urcorner$

**1213b $\ulcorner r_i \neq r_n \cdot (\exists \eta)(\eta \; r_i SA_F(\beta,\gamma)) \cdot \supset (\exists \eta)(\eta \; r_i S^*A_F(\beta,\gamma))\urcorner$

If y is a statement, and if there is a rational corpus of level r_i and basis F containing any ingredients at all, then the probability of y relative to this level and basis of rational corpus exists, provided that r_i is distinct from r_n or provided that ML and F are jointly consistent. If y al ny is an ingredient of a rational corpus of level r_i and basis F, then y is a statement, and there is a rational corpus of this level and basis containing an ingredient.

**1214a $\ulcorner r_n C_F \cdot (\exists \theta)(r_i RC_F \; \theta \cdot \zeta \; \text{al} \; n\zeta \; \text{Ing} \; \theta) \cdot \supset$

$(\exists \psi)(\exists \xi)(\zeta \; r_i \text{Prob}_F(\psi;\xi))\urcorner$

**1214b $\ulcorner r_i \neq r_n \cdot (\exists \theta)(r_i RC_F \; \theta \cdot \zeta \; \text{al} \; n\zeta \; \text{Ing} \; \theta) \cdot \supset$

$(\exists \psi)(\exists \xi)(\zeta \; r_i \text{Prob}_F(\psi;\xi))\urcorner$

If two statements are connected in a rational corpus of given level and basis by a biconditional chain, then their probabilities are the same.

**1215 $\ulcorner \eta \; r_i B_F \; \zeta \supset \cdot \eta \; r_i \text{Prob}_F(\psi;\xi) \equiv \zeta \; r_i \text{Prob}_F(\psi;\xi)\urcorner$

The following is a metatheorem of some practical interest. (Others will follow later in the chapter.) If x is a random member of y with respect to z in the rational corpora of level r_i and basis F, unless it turns out that this expression of randomness is prevented by strength by some expression y'', and if pct $(y,z(w;w'))$ is a strongest statistical statement about y and z in this rational corpus, then the probability of x e z is not less than w.

**1216 $\ulcorner \zeta\, r_i\, \mathrm{B_F}\ \alpha\ \mathrm{e}\ \gamma \cdot \alpha\ r_i\, \mathrm{Mem_F}\ \beta \cdot {\sim} (\exists\beta')(\beta'\, r_i\, \mathrm{DP_F}(\alpha,\beta,\gamma)) \cdot$

$\mathrm{pct}\,(\beta,\gamma,(\psi;\xi))\, r_i\, \mathrm{S^*A_F}(\beta,\gamma) \cdot \supset \cdot \zeta\, r_i\, \mathrm{Prob_F}(\,\psi';\xi') \supset$

$\mathrm{Thm}\ \psi\ {}_{s}\mathrm{gr}\ \psi'\ \mathrm{al}\ \psi\ \mathrm{id}\ \psi'\ \urcorner$

The minimum probability of a conjunction of two statements is not greater than the minimum probability of either of the two statements taken by itself.

**1217 $\ulcorner \zeta\ \mathrm{cj}\ \eta\ r_i\, \mathrm{Prob_F}(\psi;\xi) \cdot \zeta\, r_i\, \mathrm{Prob_F}(\,\psi';\xi') \cdot \supset$

$\mathrm{Thm}\ \psi'\ {}_{s}\mathrm{gr}\ \psi\ \mathrm{al}\ \psi'\ \mathrm{id}\ \psi\ \urcorner$

If a conjunction of two statements is an ingredient of a rational corpus of level r_i and basis F, then each of these statements will appear by itself as an ingredient of a rational corpus of this level and basis.

**1218 $\ulcorner (\exists\theta)(r_i\, \mathrm{RC_F}\ \theta \cdot \eta\ \mathrm{cj}\ \zeta\ \mathrm{Ing}\ \theta) \supset (\exists\theta)(r_i\, \mathrm{RC_F}\ \theta \cdot \zeta\ \mathrm{Ing}\ \theta)\ \urcorner$

If two statements are connected by a biconditional chain in the rational corpora of level r_i and basis F, and if one of them appears as an ingredient of a rational corpus of level r_{i-1}, then so will the other.

**1219 $\ulcorner \eta\ r_i\, \mathrm{B_F}\ \zeta \cdot (\exists\theta)(r_{i-1}\mathrm{RC_F}\ \theta \cdot \eta\ \mathrm{Ing}\ \theta) \cdot \supset$

$(\exists\theta)(r_{i-1}\mathrm{RC_F}\ \theta \cdot \zeta\ \mathrm{Ing}\ \theta)\ \urcorner$

If there is a rational corpus of level r_i and basis F containing the conditional y cd z, and a rational corpus of level r_{i-1} containing the statement y, then there will be a rational corpus of level r_{i-1} and basis F containing the statement z as a framed ingredient.

**1220 $\ulcorner (\exists\theta)(r_i\, \mathrm{RC_F}\ \theta \cdot \eta\ \mathrm{cd}\ \zeta\ \mathrm{Ing}\ \theta) \cdot (\exists\theta)(r_{i-1}\mathrm{RC_F}\ \theta \cdot$

$\eta\ \mathrm{Ing}\ \theta) \cdot \supset (\exists\theta)(r_{i-1}\mathrm{RC_F}\ \theta \cdot \zeta\ \mathrm{Ing}\ \theta)\ \urcorner$

An even more important principle, which, in virtue of **1212, is merely a special case of **1220, is that if y cd z is a theorem, and there is a rational corpus of level r_i and basis F containing y, then there is a rational corpus of this level and basis containing z.

**1221 $\ulcorner \mathrm{Thm}\ \eta\ \mathrm{cd}\ \zeta \cdot (\exists\theta)(r_i\, \mathrm{RC_F}\ \theta \cdot \eta\ \mathrm{Ing}\ \theta) \cdot \supset$

$(\exists\theta)(r_i\, \mathrm{RC_F}\ \theta \cdot \zeta\ \mathrm{Ing}\ \theta)\ \urcorner$

Finally, for completeness, I shall set down **1188, which states that every rational corpus, with the possible exception of that of the highest level, is consistent.

**1188 $\ulcorner r_i \neq r_n \supset r_i\, \mathrm{C_F}\ \urcorner$

2. Many of the metatheorems that appear in Quine's ML can be generalized to yield interesting results in connection with the logic of rational belief. Two of these—the substitutivity of identity and the substitutivity of the biconditional—are of particular interest, and I shall give below two metatheorems corresponding to Quine's *123 and *224.

Quine's *123 reads, "If $\vdash \ulcorner \varphi \equiv \varphi' \urcorner$, and ψ' is formed from ψ by putting φ' for some occurrences of φ, then $\vdash \ulcorner \psi \equiv \psi' \urcorner$." The antecedent here requires that the closure of $\ulcorner \varphi \equiv \varphi' \urcorner$ be a theorem, and the consequent assures us that the closure of $\ulcorner \psi \equiv \psi' \urcorner$ will be a theorem. In the generalized version applicable to rational corpora, we need demand only that $\ulcorner \varphi \equiv \varphi' \urcorner$ be known (it is then its own closure), but the conclusion will correspondingly be weakened to the assurance that $\ulcorner \psi \equiv \psi' \urcorner$ will be known. What is even more important and interesting is that if $\ulcorner \varphi \equiv \varphi' \urcorner$ is an ingredient of a rational corpus of level r_i and basis F, and if ψ is an ingredient of a rational corpus of level r_{i-1} and basis F, and if ψ' is like ψ except for containing occurrences of φ' where ψ contains occurrences of φ, then ψ' will also be an ingredient of a rational corpus of level r_{i-1} and basis F. Let us write (following Quine's $\Delta 57$) $y' S ?_z^{z'} y$ to mean that y' is like y except for containing one or more occurrences of z' where y contains z.

**1230 $\ulcorner (\exists \theta)(r_i \text{RC}_\text{F} \; \theta \cdot \zeta \text{ b } \zeta' \text{ Ing } \theta) \cdot \eta' \, S ?_\zeta^{\zeta'} \eta \cdot \supset$

$(\exists \theta)(r_i \text{RC}_\text{F} \; \theta \cdot \eta' \text{ b } \eta \text{ Ing } \theta) \urcorner$

Proof.   1221 and ML(*122)

**1231 $\ulcorner (\exists \theta)(r_i \text{RC}_\text{F} \; \theta \cdot \zeta \text{ b } \zeta' \text{ Ing } \theta) \cdot \eta' \, S ?_\zeta^{\zeta'} \eta \cdot (\exists \theta)$

$(r_{i-1} \text{RC}_\text{F} \; \theta \cdot \eta \text{ Ing } \theta) \cdot \supset (\exists \theta)(r_{i-1} \text{RC}_\text{F} \; \theta \cdot$

$\eta' \text{ Ing } \theta) \urcorner$

Proof. $[1230 \cdot 1219 \cdot \supset \cdot] \; 1231$

These metatheorems may be generalized still further; we need not demand that the biconditional in question be known, itself; it is sufficient if the two statements are connected in the rational corpora of given level and basis by a biconditional chain. If y and y' are connected by a biconditional chain, and z' is like z except for containing occurrences of y' in some places where z contains occurrences of y, then z and z' are connected by a biconditional chain.

**1232 $\ulcorner \zeta \, r_i \, B_F \, \zeta' \cdot \eta' \, S?^{\zeta'}_{\zeta} \, \eta \cdot \supset \eta' \, r_i \, B_F \, \eta \urcorner$

Proof. Each link in the biconditional chain in question may be shown to exist by **1230.

If y and y' are connected by a biconditional chain, and z' is like z except for containing occurrences of y' in some places where z contains occurrences of y, then the probability of z is the same as that of z'.

**1233 $\ulcorner \zeta \, r_i \, B_F \, \zeta' \cdot \eta' S?^{\zeta'}_{\zeta} \, \eta \cdot \supset \cdot \eta \, r_i \, \mathrm{Prob}_F(\psi;\xi) \equiv$
$\eta' \, r_i \, \mathrm{Prob}_F(\psi;\xi) \urcorner$

Proof. [1232 · 1215 · $\supset$:] 1233

Under the same circumstances, there will be a rational corpus of level r_{i-1} containing z only if there is one containing z'.

**1234 $\ulcorner \zeta \, r_i \, B_F \, \zeta' \cdot \eta' \, S?^{\zeta'}_{\zeta} \, \eta \cdot \supset \cdot (\exists \theta)(r_{i-1} \mathrm{RC}_F \, \theta \cdot \eta \, \mathrm{Ing} \, \theta) \supset$
$(\exists \theta)(r_{i-1} \mathrm{RC}_F \, \theta \cdot \eta' \, \mathrm{Ing} \, \theta) \urcorner$

Proof. [1232 · 1219 · $\supset$:] 1234

In the same way we may establish a somewhat more general version of the principle of the substitutivity of identity. In lieu of demanding that the closure of y id y' be a theorem, it suffices merely to know the statement y id y' in order to know the equivalence of two expressions, of which one is obtained from the other by replacing occurrences of y by occurrences of y'. Again, we may say also that if the identity in question is known in the rational corpus of level r_i, and if $z' S?^{y'}_{y} z$, and z is an ingredient of the rational corpus of level r_{i-1}, then z' will also be an ingredient of this rational corpus.

**1235 $\ulcorner (\exists \theta)(r_i \mathrm{RC}_F \, \theta \cdot \zeta \, \mathrm{id} \, \zeta' \, \mathrm{Ing} \, \theta) \cdot \eta' S?^{\zeta'}_{\zeta} \eta \cdot \supset$
$(\exists \theta)(r_i \mathrm{RC}_F \, \theta \cdot \eta' \, \mathrm{b} \, \eta \, \mathrm{Ing} \, \theta) \urcorner$

Proof. 1221 and ML(*223)

**1236 $\ulcorner (\exists \theta)(r_i \mathrm{RC}_F \, \theta \cdot \zeta \, \mathrm{id} \, \zeta' \, \mathrm{Ing} \, \theta) \cdot \eta' S?^{\zeta'}_{\zeta} \eta \cdot \supset \cdot (\exists \theta)$
$(r_{i-1} \mathrm{RC}_F \, \theta \cdot \eta \, \mathrm{Ing} \, \theta) \supset (\exists \theta)(r_{i-1} \mathrm{RC}_F \, \theta \cdot$
$\eta' \, \mathrm{Ing} \, \theta) \urcorner$

It would also be possible to define an 'identity chain' analogous to the biconditional chain defined in $\triangle 102$, and to establish three further metatheorems corresponding to **1232, **1233, and **1234.

There are any number of metatheorems in ML which can be transferred in somewhat broadened form to the logic of rational belief. All of these statements, including those presented above, merely formalize the common sense requirements of any *application* of formal logic to arguments in actual discourse. ML, as it stands, does not suffice for this; it does not say that anyone who believes that all men are mortal and that Socrates is a man should also believe that Socrates is mortal. But the whole function of logic, when it is applied to ordinary discourse, is to enable us to demand in point of rationality that if a person accepts certain premises he should also accept the conclusions entailed by them. This demand can be expressed formally through the definition of a rational corpus, and characterized in any desired degree of detail by means of statements such as **1230-**1236 above, which parallel the metatheorems of ML.

These statements are interesting ones in the logic of rational belief, since ignorance of the principles they express (caused, perhaps, by overzealous attention to the semantic problems surrounding identity) sometimes leads to difficulty. For example, if someone were to believe that the morning star were obscured by haze, but not that the evening star were obscured by haze, would we want to call him irrational? Some writers give the impression that we would always want to call him irrational—on the grounds that the two statements are contradictory, there being only one object that serves as the subject of both statements. But it seems fairer to call him irrational only if he has rational grounds for believing that the morning star is the same as the evening star. It is only then that he ought, in point of rationality, attach the same degree of belief to both statements. And I might point out that it is only 'highly probable' that the two expressions in question designate the same object.

3.   This section will be devoted to establishing a final selection of metatheorems. If the logic of rational belief is to function as it is intended to function in resolving disputes concerning the credibility of given conclusions, relative to given evidence, among people who agree to be rational and to share the same rational corpus, we must find some more practical way of discovering probabilities than that indicated in the last chapter. It is to this end that the following metatheorems may be considered 'useful'.

The first and major difficulty that lies in the way of many of the metatheorems in this sequence is that there is no general way of establishing the uniqueness of a strongest statistical statement about a given subject matter. (It has been established in so far as it bears on probability statements, but this merely means that if there are two differing strongest statements about y and z, no object can ever be a random member of y with respect to z.) Barring the establishment of conventions concerning the possible contents of F, there is no reason why, for example, "%(A,B,(.4;.6))" and "%(A,B,(.5;.7))" should not both be strongest statements about "A" and "B" in the rational corpus of level r_i. It will doubtless be objected that as "%(A,B,(.4;.6)) · %(A,B,(.5;.7)) · ⊃ %(A,B,(.5;.6))" is a theorem, "%(A,B,(.5;.6))" ought to be the strongest statement in the rational corpus in question. But this will only be so if the *conjunction* of the two first-mentioned statistical statements is an ingredient of the rational corpus of level r_i, and this by no means follows from the fact that the two statements individually are ingredients.

On the other hand, the conjunction of the two statements will appear as an ingredient of the rational corpus of the next-lower level, according to the following metatheorem.

**1240 $\ulcorner$($\exists \theta$)(r_i RC$_F$ $\theta \cdot \eta$ Ing θ) · ($\exists \theta$)(r_{i-1}RC$_F$ $\theta \cdot \zeta$ Ing θ) · ⊃

($\exists \theta$)(r_{i-1}RC$_F$ $\theta \cdot \eta$ cj ζ Ing θ)$\urcorner$

Proof. **1221 and $\ulcorner$Thm η cd((η cj ζ) b ζ)$\urcorner$; **1219

This means that "%(A,B,(.5;.6))" will appear in the next lower level rational corpus, in the circumstances at hand; but then we have no way of being sure that we will not suddenly also have "%(A, B,(.2;.55))" is an ingredient of a rational corpus of level r_{i-1}. For the sake of convenience, then, we shall stipulate in some of the following metatheorems that the rational corpus in question be *uniform*, in the sense that there is no subject matter about which there are differing strongest statistical statements. In practise we need only be sure that there is uniformity with regard to those statistical statements that are relevant to the statement under investigation; and ultimately, as Chapter Eighteen will suggest, we will be able to show on the simplest of epistemological grounds, that every rational corpus based on experience is uniform.

To say that a rational corpus of level r_i and basis F is uniform, in symbols, $\ulcorner r_i \, U_F \urcorner$, is simply to say that for every expressions y, z, w, and w', if w is a strongest statistical statement about y and z, and w' is a strongest statistical statement about y and z, then w is exactly as strong as w'.

Δ111 $\ulcorner r_i \, U_F \urcorner$ *for* $\ulcorner$(β)(γ)(η)(ζ)($\eta \, r_i$ S*A$_F$(β,γ) · $\zeta \, r_i$ S*A$_F$(β,γ) · ⊃

$\eta \, r_i$ S=$_F$ ζ)$\urcorner$

The highest level rational corpus is uniform, since at this level we may use as many ingredients as we wish as premises in deriving new ingredients.

**1241 $\ulcorner r_n U_F \urcorner$

The usefulness of the requirement of uniformity is indicated by the following metatheorem.

**1242 $\ulcorner r_i U_F \cdot (\exists \eta)(\eta \ r_i SA_F(\beta, \gamma)) \cdot \supset :$

$$(\exists \eta)(\eta \ r_i S^*A_F(\beta, \gamma) \cdot \eta \ r_i Str_F \ \zeta) \equiv$$
$$(\eta)(\eta \ r_i S^*A_F(\beta, \gamma) \supset \eta \ r_i Str_F \ \zeta) \cdot$$
$$(\exists \eta)(\eta \ r_i S^*A_F(\beta, \gamma) \cdot \eta \ r_i Dif_F \ \zeta) \equiv$$
$$(\eta)(\eta \ r_i S^*A_F(\beta, \gamma) \supset \eta \ r_i Dif_F \ \zeta) \cdot$$
$$(\exists \eta)(\eta \ r_i S^*A_F(\beta, \gamma) \cdot \zeta \ r_i Str_F \ \eta) \equiv$$
$$(\eta)(\eta \ r_i S^*A_F(\beta, \gamma) \supset \zeta \ r_i Str_F \ \eta) \cdot$$
$$(\exists \eta)(\eta \ r_i S^*A_F(\beta, \gamma) \cdot \eta \ r_i S=_F \ \zeta) \equiv$$
$$(\eta)(\eta \ r_i S^*A_F(\beta, \gamma) \supset \eta \ r_i S=_F \ \zeta)^\urcorner$$

Proof. $\triangle 111$, **1033, **1034, and **1035

I showed that if ML and F are jointly consistent, then the probability of any statement exists. The proof of this, however, did not give us any usable method for finding the probability of a given statement—unless the statement happened to be an ingredient of the rational corpus relative to which its probability was wanted.

The following metatheorem suggests a definite procedure for finding the probability of a statement S—or what is the same thing, for finding a triplet of expressions A;(B;C) such that A is a random member of B with respect to C, relative to the rational corpus in question, and such that A e C is connected to S by a biconditional chain in this rational corpus. This procedure is only definite if there is a definite procedure for finding a strongest (or a strong-enough) statistical statement about any two rational classes. Such a definite procedure (for ordinary circumstances) is suggested in chapter 19; but it is anyway doubtful if any practical difficulties can arise in this connection, while they obviously can, and do, in the former connection.

The hypothesis of the metatheorem requires that we need concern ourselves with only a finite number of triplets $(A_j;(B_j;C_j))$. Metatheorem **1236 shows that if $(A_j;(B_j;C_j))$ id $(A_k;(B_k;C_k))$ is an ingredient of our rational corpus, we need not concern ourselves with $(A_j;(B_j;C_j))$ and $(A_k;(B_k;C_k))$ separately; it is also clear that we need not concern ourselves about mere changes in type—e.g., we need not generally concern ourselves with both $(A_j;(B_j;C_j))$ and (unt $A;(xa(x$ incl B_j cj x e "1"); $xa(x$ incl $C_j)))$. It is therefore not absurd to suppose that the hypothesis can be satisfied

**1243 $\ulcorner r_i U_F \cdot (\alpha)(\beta)(\gamma)(\alpha \ r_i \mathrm{Mem}_F \ \beta \cdot \alpha$ e $\gamma \ r_i B_F \ \zeta \cdot (\exists \eta)$

$(\eta \ r_i S^* A_F(\beta,\gamma)) \cdot \supset (\exists \theta)(r_i RC_F \ \theta \cdot (\alpha$ id α_1 cj

β id β_1 cj γ id $\gamma_1)$ Ing θ v $(\alpha$ id α_2 cj β id β_2 cj

γ id $\gamma_2)$ Ing θ v ... v $(\alpha$ id α_n cj β id β_n cj γ id $\gamma_n)$

Ing θ v $(\alpha$ id unt α_1 cj $\delta a(\delta$ incl β_1 cj δ e "1")

incl β cj $\delta a(\delta$ incl $\gamma_1)$ incl $\gamma)$ Ing θ v ...)) $\cdot (\exists \eta_1)$

$(\exists \eta_2)...(\exists \eta_n)(\eta_1 \ r_i S^* A_F(\beta_1,\gamma_1) \cdot \eta_2 \ r_i S^* A_F$

$(\beta_2,\gamma_2) \cdots \eta_n \ r_i S^* A_F(\beta_n,\gamma_n)) \cdot \supset \cdot \alpha_1 \ r_i \mathrm{Ran}_F(\beta_1,\gamma_1)$

v $\alpha_2 \ r_i \mathrm{Ran}_F(\beta_2,\gamma_2)$ v $\cdots \alpha_n \ r_i \mathrm{Ran}_F(\beta_n,\gamma_n)\urcorner$

Proof.

Consider the expression $\ulcorner ST_1 \urcorner$ defined in (1):

(1) $\ulcorner ST_1 \urcorner$ *for* $\ulcorner S_6 \frown S_7 \frown \eta_1 \frown S_6 \frown S_7 \frown \eta_2 \frown S_6 \frown S_7 \cdots \frown S_6 \frown S_7 \frown \eta_n \frown S_6 \frown S_7 \urcorner$

I.   If there is an ingredient η_k of $\ulcorner ST_1 \urcorner$ such that,

(2) $\ulcorner (\eta)(\eta$ Ing $ST_1 \supset \cdot \eta_k \ r_i \mathrm{Str}_F \ \eta$ v $\eta_k \ r_i S=_F \eta)\urcorner$

then clearly $\ulcorner \alpha_k \ r_i \mathrm{Ran}_F(\beta_k,\gamma_k)\urcorner$.

II.   If there is no such ingredient in $\ulcorner ST_1 \urcorner$—that is to say, if

(3) $\ulcorner (\eta)(\eta$ Ing $ST_1 \supset (\exists \eta')(\eta'$ Ing $ST_1 \cdot \eta' \ r_i \mathrm{Str}_F \ \eta$ v $\eta' \ r_i \mathrm{Dif}_F \ \eta))\urcorner$

then we have,

(4) $\ulcorner (\exists \eta)(\exists \eta')(\eta$ Ing $ST_1 \cdot \eta'$ Ing $ST_1 \cdot \eta \ r_i \mathrm{Dif}_F \ \eta' \cdot (\eta'')$

$(\eta'')(\eta''$ Ing $ST_1 \supset \cdot \sim \eta'' \ r_i \mathrm{Str}_F \ \eta \cdot \sim \eta'' \ r_i \mathrm{Str}_F \ \eta'))\urcorner$

We may thus form the non-empty expression defined by (5):

(5) $\ulcorner D_1 \urcorner$ for $\ulcorner (\jmath \alpha)(\beta)(\gamma)(\beta$ Ing $\alpha \equiv \cdot \beta$ Ing $ST_1 \cdot \sim (\exists \gamma)$

$(\gamma$ Ing $ST_1 \cdot \gamma \ r_i \mathrm{Str}_F \ \beta)$: $\beta \ \mathrm{Pr}_\alpha \ \gamma \supset$

$\beta \ \mathrm{Pr}_{ST_1} \ \gamma$: γ Ing $\alpha \cdot \beta$ Ing $\alpha \cdot \supset \beta \neq \gamma)\urcorner$

III.   No ingredient η_k in $\ulcorner D_1 \urcorner$ corresponds to a triplet $\alpha_k, \beta_k, \gamma_k$ such that $\ulcorner (\exists \beta)(\beta \ r_i SP_F(\alpha_b,\beta_b,\gamma_b))\urcorner$. We thus need only examine the triplets corresponding to each ingredient of $\ulcorner D_1 \urcorner$ in order to ascertain whether or not they are prevented by difference. Let us make sure that this is possible. We must be able to tell whether or not there is a β' such that we know $\ulcorner \beta_j$ incl β_k cp $\beta' \urcorner$; but this seems easy enough. We must also be able to tell whether or not there is a β' such that we know $\ulcorner \beta'$ incl $\beta_j \urcorner$ and such that a number of other conditions are satisfied. But since there can be such a β' only if it is known to be identical with one of the β's associated with the ingredients of $\ulcorner D_1 \urcorner$, even this poses no problems. In short, if there is an ingredient η_k in $\ulcorner D_1 \urcorner$ such that $\ulcorner \sim (\exists \beta)(\beta \ r_i \mathrm{DP_F}(\alpha_k, \beta_k, \gamma_k)) \urcorner$, then we can tell that there is without undue difficulty—and then we have,

$$\ulcorner \alpha_k \ r_i \mathrm{Ran_F}(\beta_k, \gamma_k) \urcorner$$

IV. If there is no η_k in $\ulcorner D_1 \urcorner$ such that $\ulcorner \alpha_k \ r_i \mathrm{Ran_F}(\beta_k, \gamma_k) \urcorner$, then we form the expression $\ulcorner ST_2 \urcorner$ defined in (6):

(6) $\ulcorner ST_2 \urcorner$ for $\ulcorner (\exists \alpha)(\beta)(\gamma)(\beta \ \mathrm{Ing} \ \alpha \equiv \cdot \ \beta \ \mathrm{Ing} \ ST_1 \sim \beta \ \mathrm{Ing} \ D_1$:

$$\beta \ \mathrm{Pr}_\alpha \ \gamma \supset \beta \ \mathrm{Pr}_{ST_1} \ \gamma : \beta \ \mathrm{Ing} \ \alpha \cdot \gamma \ \mathrm{Ing} \ \alpha \cdot \supset$$

$$\gamma \neq \beta) \urcorner$$

Since $\ulcorner D_1 \urcorner$ is not empty—in fact, it has at least two ingredients—$\ulcorner ST_2 \urcorner$ has less ingredients than $\ulcorner ST_1 \urcorner$. Again we go through the process we went through with $\ulcorner ST_1 \urcorner$; if there is an ingredient of $\ulcorner ST_2 \urcorner$, η_k, such that,

(7) $\ulcorner (\eta)(\eta \ \mathrm{Ing} \ ST_2 \supset \eta_k \ r_i \mathrm{Str_F} \ \eta \ \mathrm{v} \ \eta_k \ r_i \mathrm{S=}_F \ \eta) \urcorner$

then we have $\ulcorner \alpha_k \ r_i \mathrm{Ran_F}(\beta_k, \gamma_k) \urcorner$.

V. Otherwise, we form an expression $\ulcorner D_2 \urcorner$ analogous to $\ulcorner D_1 \urcorner$, but defined on the basis of $\ulcorner ST_2 \urcorner$ instead of $\ulcorner ST_1 \urcorner$.

We continue this way until we have found the expressions α_k, β_k, and γ_k that we have been seeking. We know that the process will terminate, because each expression $\ulcorner ST_1 \urcorner$ to which we come during the procedure will contain at least two less ingredients than the expression $\ulcorner ST_{i-1} \urcorner$. And because we know that the probability of ζ, relative to this level and basis of rational corpus, exists, we know that the procedure will terminate successfully.

The procedure outlined above, though gratifyingly mechanical and guaranteed to lead to success, is often more unwieldy than necessary. It will often happen that there are an enormous number of triplets that must be mentioned in the hypothesis of **1243; and it may even happen (for example, when ζ is an ingredient of the rational corpus of level r_i and basis F) that there are an infinite number of these triplets, so that **1243 is not applicable at all. It will be convenient, therefore, to have a number of metatheorems that can be used to cut down the number of expressions that have to be considered. The following metatheorems, presented without proof, are intended to provide a more or less practical framework in which to discuss the question of randomness.

**1244 $\ulcorner \alpha' \, e \, \gamma' \, r_i B_F \, \alpha \, e \, \gamma \supset \, \sim \alpha' \, r_i \text{Mem}_F \, \beta' \cdot \supset \cdot$

$\qquad \sim \beta' \, r_i \text{DP}_F(\alpha,\beta,\gamma) \cdot \sim \beta' \, r_i \text{SP}_F(\alpha,\beta,\gamma) \cdot$

$\qquad \sim \alpha' \, r_i \text{Ran}_F(\beta',\gamma') \urcorner$

**1245 $\ulcorner \alpha' \, e \, \gamma' \, r_i B_F \, \alpha \, e \, \gamma \cdot \alpha \, r_i \text{Mem}_F \, \beta \cdot \alpha' \, r_i \text{Mem}_F \, \beta \cdot \supset$

$\qquad (\exists \varphi)(r_i \text{RC}_F \, \varphi \cdot \gamma \, \text{id} \, \gamma' \, \text{Ing} \, \varphi) : \supset$

$\qquad \sim \beta \, r_i \text{SP}_F(\alpha,\beta,\gamma) \urcorner$

**1246 $\ulcorner r_i U_F : \alpha' \, e \, \gamma' r_i B_F \, \alpha \, e \, \gamma \cdot \alpha' r_i \text{Mem}_F \, \beta \cdot \alpha \, r_i \text{Mem}_F \, \beta \cdot \supset$

$\qquad (\exists \theta)(r_i \text{RC}_F \, \theta \cdot \gamma \, \text{id} \, \gamma' \, \text{Ing} \, \theta) : \supset$

$\qquad \sim \beta \, r_i \text{DP}_F(\alpha,\beta,\gamma) \urcorner$

**1247 $\ulcorner (\exists \theta)(r_i \text{RC}_F \, \theta \cdot \beta' \, \text{id} \, \beta'' \, \text{Ing} \, \theta) \supset : \beta' \, r_i \text{DP}_F(\alpha,\beta,\gamma) \equiv$

$\qquad \beta'' \, r_i \text{DP}_F(\alpha,\beta,\gamma) \cdot \beta' \, r_i \text{SP}_F(\alpha,\beta,\gamma) \equiv$

$\qquad \beta'' \, r_i \text{SP}_F(\alpha,\beta,\gamma) \cdot \alpha \, r_i \text{Ran}_F(\beta',\gamma) \equiv$

$\qquad \alpha \, r_i \text{Ran}_F(\beta'',\gamma) \urcorner$

**1248 $\ulcorner (\alpha')(\gamma')(\eta')(\eta)(\alpha \, e \, \gamma \, r_i B_F \, \alpha' \, e \, \gamma' \cdot \alpha \, r_i \text{Mem}_F \, \beta \cdot$

$\qquad \alpha' \, r_i \text{Mem}_F \, \beta' \cdot \eta \, r_i S^* A_F(\beta,\gamma) \cdot \eta' \, r_i S^* A_F$

$\qquad (\beta',\gamma') : \supset \cdot \eta \, r_i S=_F \eta' \, v \, \eta \, r_i \text{Str}_F \, \eta') \supset \cdot$

$\qquad \sim \beta' \, r_i \text{DP}_F(\alpha,\beta,\gamma) \cdot \sim \beta' \, r_i \text{SP}_F(\alpha,\beta,\gamma) \urcorner$

**1249 $\ulcorner \alpha \, r_i \text{Mem}_F \, \beta \cdot \eta \, r_i S^* A_F(\beta,\gamma) \cdot \sim (\exists \beta')(\beta' \, r_i \text{DP}_F(\alpha,\beta,\gamma)) \cdot$

$\qquad \supset : \alpha' \, e \, \gamma' \, r_i B_F \, \alpha \, e \, \gamma \cdot \eta' \, r_i S^* A_F(\beta'\gamma') \cdot$

$\qquad \sim \eta' \, r_i \text{Str}_F \, \eta \cdot \sim \eta' \, r_i S=_F \eta \cdot \supset \sim \alpha' \, r_i \text{Ran}_F(\beta',\gamma') \urcorner$

**1250 $\ulcorner (\exists \theta)(r_i \text{RC}_F \, \theta \cdot \beta \, \text{incl} \, \beta' \, \text{Ing} \, \theta \cdot n \, \beta \, \text{id} \, \beta' \, \text{Ing} \, \theta) \supset$

$\qquad \sim \beta' \, r_i \text{DP}_F(\alpha,\beta,\gamma) \urcorner$

**1251 $\ulcorner (\exists \theta)(r_i RC_F \ \theta \cdot \beta \ \text{incl} \ \beta' \ cp \ \beta'' \ \text{Ing} \ \theta) \supset$

$\sim \beta' \ r_i DP_F(\alpha,\beta,\gamma)\urcorner$

**1252 $\ulcorner (\alpha')(\beta')(\gamma')(\eta')(\eta)(\alpha \ r_i \text{Mem}_F \ \beta : \alpha' \ e \ \gamma' \ r_i B_F \ \alpha \ e \ \gamma \cdot$

$\alpha' \ r_i \text{Mem}_F \ \beta' \cdot \eta \ r_i S*A_F(\beta,\gamma) \cdot \eta' r_i S*A_F(\beta',\gamma') \cdot \supset \cdot$

$\eta \ r_i \text{Str}_F \ \eta' \ v \ \eta \ r_i S=_F \ \eta') \supset \cdot \alpha \ r_i \text{Ran}_F(\beta,\gamma) \equiv$

$\sim (\exists \beta'')(\beta'' \ r_i DP_F(\alpha,\beta,\gamma))\urcorner$

**1253 $\ulcorner \alpha \ r_i \text{Mem}_F \ \beta \cdot \eta \ r_i S*A_F(\beta,\gamma) \cdot \sim (\exists \eta')(\eta' \ r_i \text{Str}_F \ \eta) \cdot \supset$

$\alpha \ r_i \text{Ran}_F(\beta,\gamma) \equiv \sim (\exists \beta')(\beta'' r_i DP_F(\alpha,\beta,\gamma))\urcorner$

4. The first thing which requires discussion is the applicability of my definition of randomness. Although we can be sure that the statement about randomness for which we are looking exists, if ML and F are jointly consistent, and although we even have, under most circumstances, a definite procedure for finding it, the search for it can be a tedious one. Furthermore, since the number of rational corpora of a given level and basis is, provided ML and F are consistent, infinite, how can we be sure that we have taken account of *all* of the possibilities?

We can't be sure of this, any more than we can be sure that ML and F are consistent. But although this puts a statement of the form $x \ r_i \text{Ran}_F(y, z)$ in the same category as a statement of the form $\sim$ Thm x, the system can nevertheless provide a technique and a framework within which to discuss constructively alternatives with respect to randomness. This is important, if, as I maintain, much of the dispute about the soundness of inductive conclusions is reducible to a dispute about randomness. The way in which my definition provides a framework within which to settle disputes about randomness will be exhibited by means of an example in Chapter Twenty. It is already clear that two people sharing the same rational corpus who disagree concerning an assertion of randomness will be able to proceed *toward* agreement; and it is furthermore clear that they may be able to come to agreement in a finite number of steps of argument.

One of the most curious things about the system as presented so far, is that the ordinary rules of logic do not seem to hold *within* a rational corpus of a given level and basis. We can have a rational corpus of level r_i and basis F containing the statement A, and containing the statement A cd B, without having one of this level and basis containing the statement B. Another way of expressing this is to say that from the fact that there is a rational corpus of level

r_i and basis F containing A, and one containing B, we can infer that there is one containing both A and B, but not that there is one containing the conjunction of A and B.

This may seem a little odd until we recall that there are several levels of rational corpora, and that it is only when the highest level of rational corpus in which either A or B appears is r_i that the conjunction of A and B may fail to appear in a rational corpus of level r_i. Under these circumstances, it is not at all surprising that the probability of the conjunction of A and B is less than the probability of A, and less than the probability of B; and hence that while either A or B, by itself, is sufficiently credible to be merely 'accepted', their conjunction is not.

We *could* introduce a special convention to the effect that if A and B are ingredients of a rational corpus, then the conjunction of A and B is to be an ingredient of a rational corpus of this same level and basis. This has the effect of reinstituting the conventional logical rules concerning derivation from premises within the rational corpus of a given level. On the other hand, it would have seriously counter intuitive consequences. Consider, for example, a lottery of a million tickets, of which one will be the winner. In advance of a fair drawing, the chances are a million to one against a given ticket being the winner. It seems reasonable then to include the statement, "ticket number j (for every j from 1 to 1,000,000) will not win the lottery," in a rational corpus of level r_i. If it is objected that this is not reasonable, on the grounds that there is a finite probability that ticket j will, after all, win the lottery, we can answer by pointing out that according to the same line of reasoning, there is a finite probability that *any* statistical hypothesis of the sort that everyone simply accepts, is false. But if we accept into the rational corpus of level r_i the statement (for every j) "Ticket number j will not win the lottery," and if we allow the conjunction of any two ingredients of a rational corpus to be also an ingredient of it, then the conjunction of the whole million of these statements will be an ingredient of our rational corpus, and this millionfold conjunction, together with the statement that there are only a million tickets, logically entails the statement, "None of the tickets will win the lottery." This statement, too, will therefore appear in a rational corpus of the given level and basis. Since we have in this rational corpus the statement that there is a ticket that will win the lottery, we may conjoin these two statements and derive any statement at all in the rational corpus of level r_i.

This would be intolerable. If, however, we forego the privilege of including A cj B in a rational corpus of level r_i and basis F merely because both A and B are ingredients of rational corpora of this

level and basis, (and hence if we forego the derivation of consequences from more than one premise at a time in a given rational
corpus) then we not only avoid the above problem, but the rational
corpora of level lower than r_n are demonstrably consistent, as
**1188 shows.

The sense in which the rational corpora of lower levels are consistent deserves some clarification. What I showed in **1188 was
merely that if there is a rational corpus of a given level (other than
r_n) containing a statement A, then there is no rational corpus of
that level and basis containing a statement nA. This is not to say,
as the above discussion of the lottery will have made clear, that no
contradictory statements can be *derived* from the ingredients of a
rational corpus. The point is that this form of derivation is not a
legitimate way of arriving at new ingredients, so that we shall
never be directed to 'accept' both a statement and its negation in a
rational corpus of given basis and level.

It is noteworthy that this form of consistency applies to rational
corpora in spite of the fact that (so far as I know) there is no reason why a statement A and its negation nA could not be connected
by a biconditional chain in a rational corpus of level r_i and basis
F. If this is so, however, we shall still not have both A and nA in a
lower rational corpus; in fact if a e c and a e compl c are connected by a biconditional chain, and we have a r_i Ran$_F$(b,c), then
any strongest statement about b and c in the rational corpora of
level r_i and basis F must be exactly as strong as any strongest
statement in the rational corpora of this level and basis about b
and compl c; i.e., the two pairs of parameters must be symmetrical about the fraction "1/2"—or better, the ratios denoted by the
parameters must be symmetrical about 1/2.

Metatheorem **1221 states that if the conditional A cd B is a
theorem, and if A is an ingredient of a rational corpus of level r_i
and basis F, then B is to be an ingredient of some rational corpus
of level r_i and basis F. This is tantamount to using the theoremtic
conditional, A cd B, as a principle of inference, allowing us to pass
from belief in A to belief in B. This kind of principle of inference
has always been considered useful and legitimate. Metatheorem
**1220 states more generally that we can make the same transition
whenever the conditional A cd B is known—i.e., when it is included
in a rational corpus of level r_{i+1}—whether or not it happens to be
a theorem. Suppose that this conditional is not merely logical—that
it expresses a fact about the world, and that it is included in our
rational corpora on the basis of the evidence in its favor. It still
enables us to pass from (rational) belief in A to (rational) belief in
B. Is this not the phenomenon that has led some philosophers

(Pierce, for example) to speak of 'material rules of inference'? Employing a non-logical conditional as a principle of inference may lead to results which, in the light of our limitation to arguments containing only one non-logical premise, no purely logical conditionals could support. The same results could, of course, be justified by a direct evaluation of probability; the applicability of non-logical conditionals as rules of inference is a result of the earlier definitions, not an addition to them.

CHAPTER THIRTEEN

Probability and Frequency

1. I have already shown that the ordinary axioms of probability employed in statistical texts apply directly to proportions, so that 'the probability of an A being a B' *can* be interpreted as 'the proportion of A's which are B's.' I have also indicated reasons which seem to me sufficient to reject 'proportion' as an explicatum for probability. But there is also an important sense in which the axioms of the classical probability calculus apply to probability statements defined as I have defined them in the preceding chapters.

Neyman's lucid and careful discussion of the foundations of (what I should prefer to call) the theory of proportions, in *Lectures and Conferences on Probability and Mathematical Statistics* will serve admirably as a starting point. He says, "... the probability of an object A having the property B is defined as the proportion of objects A having the property B."[1] I shall now show that when this is raised to the metalinguistic level, and a couple of very simple and obvious interpretations are made, it becomes a special case of Δ107. To begin with, consider the indefinite article 'an'. It is a pervasive characteristic of texts of probability written by statisticians that the concept of probability is almost invariably introduced by means of a statement involving an indefinite article: the probability of *an* A being a B, the probability of *an* experiment E having a certain result, etc.

When the expression, 'the probability of an A being a B' is defined as a whole, in terms of frequencies, the indefinite article can simply drop out of sight. But there is no need to ignore it; it can be interpreted as follows: '*an* A' is to be interpreted as 'all x such that x is a random member of A'. Instead of accepting an assertion about 'an A' as an irreducible form of expression (and one which seems to have been overlooked by logicians — a surprising matter, since they have been so particular about the definite article) I shall suppose that a formal explication of the locution can be given in terms of randomness. The level and basis of the rational corpus relative to which, and the expression with respect to which, the assertion of randomness is made, remain to be determined by the

1. Jerzy Neyman, *Lectures and Conferences on Probability and Mathematical Statistics*, Second (revised) Edition, Washington, 1952, p. 4.

context. (This interpretation of the indefinite article also seems to be suitable to other contexts than those involving probability.)

We may now reformulate Neyman's definition as follows:

(1) x e B_ Prob_$(p;p)$ $\equiv \cdot x$_ Ran_(A,B) $\cdot$ pct(A,B,$(p;p)$)_ S*A_(A,B)

A and B now denote the names of classes, rather than the classes themselves, as they do in Neyman's definition; similarly, p is now a fraction rather than a ratio. To show that Neyman's conception is essentially a special case of mine, it now suffices to fill in the blanks in line (1) in such a way that the conventional probability laws hold.

Let us consider the level and basis of the rational corpus relative to which these assertions may be made. Neyman talks about 'unknown probabilities', so it is clear that no actual rational corpus will do; this is also indicated by the fact that the proportion mentioned on the right hand side of (1) is supposed to be completely precise. It thus seems reasonable to take as the basis of this ideal rational corpus a consistent set of statistical statements of the form pct(A,x,($y;y$)), where y is an ordinary fraction, and x is B_1, B_2, ... or B_n, where the B_i are the names of subclasses of the class denoted by A, such that for every B_i and B_j, there is an expression B_k such that B_k id B_i int B_j is a theorem, and there is an expression B_k such that B_k id B_i un B_j is a theorem, and there is a B_k such that B_k un B_i id A is a theorem. We demand that this set of statistical statements be complete — i.e., that for every B_i there is a statement pct(A,B_i($y;y$)) in the basis of this rational corpus — and we may also demand that each of these statistical statements be true — though this is inessential, since the whole system is hypothetical anyway. Since these statements are about proportions, we know that if they are consistent, they will satisfy the rules (theorems) of the class-ratio calculus.

The level of the rational corpus in which we are operating is irrelevant, since it has this ideal basis, let us take the level as r_n. Finally, since we must include reference to the fundamental probability set denoted by A in the probability assertion itself, let us abbreviate the basis of this ideal rational corpus by IA. Thus we have, corresponding to Neyman's definition,

N-1 'x e B r_nProb$_{IA}$($p;p$)' for 'x r_nRan$_{IA}$(A,B) $\cdot$

pct(A,B,$(p;p)$)r_nS*A$_{IA}$ (A,B)'

The conditional probability of B, given B', is simply defined:

N-2 'x e B, B' r_nProb$_{IA}$ ($p;p$)' for 'x e Br_nProb $_{IAB'}$($p;p$)'

Before proceeding to show that the special form of probability statement defined in N-1 obeys the ordinary probability laws, we must make the added stipulation that the basis IA of the rational corpus in question contains *only* such statements as were described earlier — in particular that it contains no statement pct $(x, y, (z;z))$ where x is different from A or where y is different from the B_i.

NT-1   'x e B r_nProb$_{IA}(p;p) \supset$ n $(x$ e B$)$ r_nProb$_{IA}("_s 1"_s$ min p;

   "$_s 1"_s$ min p $)$'

Proof. **1187, if $r_n C_F$; otherwise, NT-1 holds by the falsity of the antecedent.

NT-2   'x e B r_nProb$_{IA}(p;p) \cdot x$ e B', B r_nProb$_{IA}(q;q) \cdot \supset \cdot$

   x e B cj x e B' r_nProb$_{IA}(p$ tms $q;p$ tms q $)$'

Proof.

Ratio-extension of ML   'pct $(A, B, (p;p)) r_n S^*A_{IA}(A, B) \cdot$

   pct $(A$ int $B, B', (q;q))$ $r_n S^*A_{IA}(A$ int $B, B') \cdot \supset$

   pct $(A, B$ int $B', (p$ tms $q;p$ tms $q))$ $r_n S^*A_{IA}(A, B$ int $B')$'

The problem is now to establish the following general statement about randomness:

(1)   'x r_nRan$_{IA}(A, B) \cdot x$ r_nRan$_{IAB}(A$ int $B, B') \cdot \supset$

   x r_nRan$_{IA}(A, B$ int $B')$'

Since all of the statistical statements with which we are concerned here are maximally strong, we have,

(2)   ' $\sim x$ r_nRan$_{IA}(A, B$ int $B') \equiv (\exists y)(y$ r_nDP$_{IA}(x, A, B$ int $B'))$'

Suppose that there is such an expression preventing 'x r_nRan$_{IA}(A, B$ int $B')$' by difference, and suppose the expression is K. By the conventions concerning the basis of our ideal rational corpus, K must be one of the B_i. Let the following statistical statements belong to to the rational corpus in question; if the rational corpus is consistent (i.e., if ML is consistent) they will be strongest statistical statements; if the rational corpus is not consistent, we have NT-2 anyway.

(3)   'pct $(K, B, ("n'/n"; "n'/n"))$'

(4)   'pct $(A, B, ("m'/m"; "m'/m"))$'

(5)   'pct $(K, B$ int $B', ("n''/n"; "n''/n"))$'

(6)   'pct (A, B int B', ("m''/m"; "m''/m'"))'

(7)   'pct (K int B, B', ("n''/n'"; "n''/n'"))'

(8)   'pct (A int B, B', ("m''/m'"; "m''/m'"))'

Since neither A incl K and n A id K, nor A incl K cp J, can be known in this rational corpus

(9)   '$x\, r_n \mathrm{Mem}_{IA} K \cdot x\, r_n \mathrm{Ran}_{IA}(A,B) \cdot \supset \sim \mathrm{pct}(K,B, ($ "n'/n";

       "n'/n")) $r_n \mathrm{Dif}_{IA}$ pct (A, B, ("m'/m"; "m'/m"))'

Similarly,

(10) $x\, r_n \mathrm{Mem}_{IAB} K$ int B $\cdot x\, r_n \mathrm{Ran}_{IAB}$ (A int B, B') $\cdot \supset$

        $\sim$ pct (K int B, B', ("n''/n'"; "n''/n'"))

        $r_n \mathrm{Dif}_{IAB}$ pct (A, int B, B', ("m''/m'"; "m''/m'"))

(11) $x\, r_n \mathrm{Mem}_{IA} K \cdot x\, r_n \mathrm{Mem}_{IAB}$ A int B $\cdot \supset x\, r_n \mathrm{Mem}_{IAB}$ K int B

From (9), (10), and (11), we obtain (remembering Δ101),

(12) $x\, r_n \mathrm{Mem}_{IA} K \cdot x\, r_n \mathrm{Ran}_{IA}(A,B) \cdot x\, r_n \mathrm{Ran}_{IAB}$ (A int B, B') $\cdot \supset$

        Thm "$m''/m' = n''/n' \cdot n'/n = m'/m$"

(13)   Thm "$m''/m' = n''/n' \cdot n'/n = m'/m$" $\supset$ Thm "$(n''/n =$

        $m''/m)$"

From (12) and (13), with Δ101, we get,

(14) $x\, r_n \mathrm{Ran}_{IA}(A,B) \cdot x\, r_n \mathrm{Ran}_{IAB}$ (A int B, B') $\cdot \supset \cdot x\, r_n \mathrm{Mem}_{IA} K \supset$

        $\sim$ pct (K, B int B', ("n''/n"; "n''/n")) $r_n \mathrm{Dif}_{IA}$ pct (A, B int B',

        ("m''/m"; "m''/m"))

Lines (14) and (2), with Δ104, give T-2.

The third and final theorem I shall prove here is the general addition theorem; in my notation, this will run:

NT-3 x e B $r_n \mathrm{Prob}_{IA}(p;p) \cdot x$ e B' $r_n \mathrm{Prob}_{IA}(q;q) \cdot x$ e B cj x e B'

        $r_n \mathrm{Prob}_{IA}(r;r) \cdot \supset x$ e B al x e B' $r_n \mathrm{Prob}_{IA}(p$ pls $q)$ min r;

        $(p$ plus $q)$ min r)

Proof.

Again the problem is to show that a conditional connecting statements of randomness holds. The conditional is:

(1) $x \, r_n \mathrm{Ran}_{IA}(A,B) \cdot x \, r_n \mathrm{Ran}_{IA}(A,B') \cdot x \, r_n \mathrm{Ran}_{IA}(A,B \text{ int } B') \cdot \supset$

$x \, r_n \mathrm{Ran}_{IA}(A,B \text{ un } B')$

Let us deny the consequent by supposing that K is an expression such that,

(2) $x \, r_n \mathrm{Mem}_{IA} \, K \cdot K \, r_n \mathrm{DP}_{IA}(x,A,B \text{ un } B')$

As before, let m'/m, m''/m, and m'''/m be the ratios mentioned in the strongest statements about K and B, K and B', and K and B int B', respectively; and n'/n, n''/n, and n'''/n be the ratios mentioned in strongest statements about A and B, A and B', and A and B int B', respectively. By hypothesis, K is such that:

(3)   Thm "$(m'/m + m''/m - m'''/m \neq n'/n + n''/n - n'''/n)$"

But this implies either,

(4)   Thm "$m'/m \neq n'/n$" v Thm "$m''/m \neq n''/n$" v

Thm "$m'''/m \neq n'''/n$"

Thus we obtain, contrary to hypothesis, (in view of $x \, r_n \mathrm{Mem}_{IA} \, K$)

(5) $\sim x \, r_n \mathrm{Ran}_{IA}(A,B)$ v $\sim x \, r_n \mathrm{Ran}_{IA}(A,B')$ v

$\sim x \, r_n \mathrm{Ran}_{IA}(A,B \text{ int } B')$

There cannot, therefore, be a K for which (2) holds, if the hypothesis of (1) is to hold; but if there is no such K, then the consequent of (1) must also hold. And (1), together with a suitable theorem from the class-ratio calculus, establishes NT-3.

Theorems NT-1, NT-2, and NT-3 suffice to show that the whole classical system of probability, as it bears on finite probability sets, can be construed as a special (if hypothetical) case of my conception of probability. How useful this special conception of probability is, is still open to doubt — although the usefulness of the class-ratio calculus, which it merely reflects on a metalinguistic level, is obvious enough. But there are at any rate two important facts indicated by the above three theorems. First, they show that probability, in a sense leading to the classical calculus and in a sense suitable to statistical investigations, is protosyntactically definable; and in fact they show that probability in this sense is merely a special idealized species of probability in the sense in which probability may be taken as a guide in life. Second, these three theorems show that, subject to certain conditions, it is possible to argue directly from one probability to another without considering questions of randomness and relative frequency on the way. These conditions are often met, for example, in games of chance; in tossing coins, under ordinary circumstances, any future toss is a random member of the class of tosses with respect to landing heads; and the relevant proportion is known quite precisely. It is thus often possible to infer 'directly' from the fact that the probability of heads on a toss of a coin is '1/2' that the probability of a pair of heads on a pair of tosses of the coin is '1/4'. But the limitations indicated by the ideality of the basis of the rational corpus relative to which this simplified probability calculus holds come to the fore when we deal with large groups of tosses, for then the slight uncertainty in our knowledge of the proportion of tosses which land heads becomes transformed into a large uncertainty in our knowledge about the proportion of 1000-fold sets of tosses containing between 450 and 500 heads.

I have dealt only with probability as defined by Neyman on the basis of finite probability sets. Obviously enough I cannot reduce his more general definition to mine. Equally obviously, however, we are not forced to deal with infinite probability sets at all; we choose to do so for the sake of convenience, generality, and elegance. In the classical problem of the probability that a chord of a circle of radius r will have a length greater than $2k$ ($\leq 2r$), for example, we could choose any number of finite probability sets, according to what we consider the 'smallest measurable angle' and the 'smallest measurable length.' But all this is silly when by the simple assumptions (a) that there is no smallest angle, and (b) that there is no smallest length, we can arrive at a simple and elegant solution — and indeed several solutions. There may be theories in the physical sciences according to which we are obligated to take infinite probability sets literally; if this is so, still, the interpretation of 'probability' in such theories must either be taken as a purely mathematical problem, coordinate with the theory itself; or it must at least wait for the detailed examination of the role played by theories in the logic of rational belief.

2. Although the concept of probability defined by Neyman is reducible to a special case of mine, it is the general form given by Δ107 which is required whenever we have to do with applications of our knowledge of class ratios, or with the actual testing of statistical hypotheses.

The procedure of testing a statistical hypothesis is described briefly and clearly by Neyman.[2] If H is a statistical hypothesis concerning the random variables x_i, we choose some function T of the x_i's such that T is a statistical hypothesis about a set of objects constituting a test sample — or, in my terminology, such that T is a property that a certain object (namely, the sample as a whole) may possess. Now if H is true, then presumably, a very small pro-

2. *Ibid.*, p. 43 ff.

portion of all possible samples meeting certain criteria (e.g., of being n-fold) will possess the property T. Thus if we actually obtain a sample with the property T, we infer that since we have observed something which would be very improbable if H were true, we ought not to believe the hypothesis H.

This description of the testing of a statistical hypothesis has one serious shortcoming: it minimizes the rather large (and often controversial) step involved in passing from a class ratio (or the corresponding ideal probability) to a definite legislative probability. It is one thing to say that for all x, if x is a random member of 'the class of samples of a certain sort', then the probability that x belongs to 'T' is very low — relative to a hypothetical rational corpus containing H — and it is quite another thing to say that if we were to include H in our rational corpus, the probability that A belongs to 'T' would be very low, where A is a definite description of some particular sample, and 'T' is the name of the class of objects having the property in question.

We can only argue from the former probability to the latter when A is a random member of 'the class of samples of a certain sort' with respect to membership in 'T'. And this is a matter which is often actually in dispute in the discussion of statistical hypothesis — a matter distinct from that of choosing a test criterion. The choice of a test criterion can be discussed in the framework of a class-ratio calculus — or in a generalization of this to any sets having a probability measure — but the randomness of a description of a particular sample, with respect to membership in 'T', can only be discussed intelligibly and rationally within the framework provided by some concept of a rational corpus. Our object in sampling a population is to obtain a representative sample — or one from which we can *infer* something about the parent population. The proportion of fairly large samples drawn from a population, which reflect the composition of the population, is large; so that if the particular sample we draw in a statistical investigation is a random one with respect to the property of being representative, we may be entitled to include the statement that this particular sample *is* representative (and hence to include the corresponding statistical hypothesis) in our rational corpus.

The joker, as has been generally recognized, is the randomness of the sample. The most popular general solution, however, seems to me to be on the wrong track entirely. This solution is that the elements composing the sample should be selected by some procedure which gives each element of the population an 'equal chance' to be selected. But as Neyman himself points out, a possible result is that if, "... the population is formed by the inhabitants of 300 cities and if the unit of sampling is represented by a block, then unrestricted [equal-chance] sampling combined with bad luck can produce a sample composed of blocks from just one city with the complete omission of other cities."[3] The 'equal chance' criterion may (and generally does) insure that *before* the sample is selected, it is random with respect to being representative — and this is no doubt the theory behind the current passion for tables of random numbers as guides to sampling. But the use of any number of tables of random digits does not prove that a sample is random with respect to a given property after it has been selected, despite the prevalent theories to this effect; the theorists are saved from absurdity, not by their theories, but by informal and untheoretical common sense. It is clear that if our sampling method gives us a sample such as that described by Neyman, we will not accept our 'bad luck' with a fatalistic shrug of our shoulders, but will demand a new selection of a sample from the population.

Why? In the first place, because we may know something which indicates that the sample taken from the particular city in question will not be representative, or will probably not be representative — e.g., if we are investigating the national corn pone consumption, and the city selected is Memphis. In the second place, while we may have no knowledge concerning whether or not the characteristics under investigation are more or less frequent or have different distributions in the one-city sample than in the population as a whole, we may still (correctly) feel that since such information may turn up in the future, it would be a waste of time to use a sample which, while random at the time of use, will turn out to be non-random in the future when the contents of our collective rational corpus has increased. What is required is that the sample, *as a whole, after it* has been selected, must be a random member of the class of all such samples, relative to what we know, with respect to the property of being representative in the desired sense. We may also use samples which, while not random members of the class of *all* equi-numerous samples with respect to being representative, are random members of a subclass of the class of all equi-numerous samples, where the proportion of representative samples in the subclass is actually higher than in the original class. When a sample is a random member of one of these especially representative subclasses of the class of all equi-numerous samples, it is all to the good. Such a sample may happen to be drawn by unrestricted sampling, or it may be arranged deliberately. To arrange it deliberately is to use some form of stratified sampling. For example, instead of choosing a sample of blocks from the 300 cities considered in the lump, we may select a sample of blocks from *each* of the 300

3. *Ibid.*, p. 108.

cities. If there are differences between cities, the proportion of samples chosen in this way which are representative is higher than the proportion of samples chosen by the unrestricted method which are representative; and in addition, a sample chosen in this way may give us more information concerning differences among the cities than a sample chosen by the unrestricted method.

Sampling problems can be highly complex — especially when the major problem is to get the maximum amount of relevant information for a given amount of money. But the complexities may be rendered a little less confusing when we remember that the sample must be a random member of a certain class of samples, and that this randomness depends essentially on what we *know* about the sample and what we *know* about the class of samples to which it belongs. It is important to be clear that the randomness of a sample with respect to being representative neither entails nor is entailed by the possible randomness of each *member* of the sample with respect to the characteristics under investigation. The latter type of randomness, as I shall show in detail in a later chapter, is irrelevant to the former.

Curiously enough, it is one of the most recent approaches to statistical estimation that is the most pervasive and fundamental from the logical point of view; this approach is Neyman's theory of confidence intervals, and it is on this theory that the whole of inductive logic ultimately depends. Fortunately, in addition to being basic to the most primitive forms of induction, or of learning from experience, the theory in its elementary applications is exceedingly easy to formulate and to apply in the system I have presented.

Consider a sample space W of n dimensions, consisting of points representing possible observations $(x_1, x_2, \ldots x_n)$. Suppose that there is just one parameter θ which it is required to estimate. It is possible to show that there are functions $\underline{\theta}(x_1, \ldots, x_n)$, and $\overline{\theta}(x_1, \ldots, x_n)$ defined over the whole sample space W, such that *whatever* be the value of θ, the proportion of sample points $(X_1, X_2, \ldots, X_n)$ in W for which $\underline{\theta}(X_1, \ldots, X_n) \leqslant \theta \leqslant \overline{\theta}(X_1, \ldots, X_n)$ holds exceeds some fixed value near 1. There are any number of functions $\underline{\theta}$ and $\overline{\theta}$ which meet the above criteria. However, in the very simplest situation, which is all that I am concerned with here, it will be possible to pick a pair of functions $\underline{\theta}$ and $\overline{\theta}$ which give, in Neyman's terminology, a shortest confidence interval. This shortest confidence interval corresponds, in general, to the unique 'rationally representative' matrix mentioned earlier, and leads, in general, to a strongest statistical statement about the given subject matter. Since by the finitude of the classes with which we are concerned, θ does have *some* value, it is thus immediately clear that if we draw a sample $(Y_1, \ldots, Y_n)$ which is random with respect to this property, relative to our rational corpus, we will be entitled to say that the probability, relative to this rational corpus, that θ lies inside the limits indicated by $\underline{\theta}(Y_1, \ldots, Y_n)$ and $\bar{\theta}(Y_1, \ldots, Y_n)$ is at least as great as this fixed value near 1. If the preassigned number is greater than that denoted by r_{n-1}, we will be entitled (and obligated) to accept the statement that θ lies between these limits as an ingredient of our rational corpus of level r_{n-1}. In a later chapter I shall treat an example of this pervasive and primitive type of inductive inference in detail; here I have merely wanted to exhibit one more important connection between probability as defined on my theory, and probability as it is employed by statisticians.

3. I should make it clear, however, that I am not presuming to have interpreted the process of estimation by means of confidence intervals (or for that matter, to have interpreted probability itself) along lines with which Neyman would agree. Neyman seems to feel quite strongly that there is no such thing as inductive reasoning. The properties of confidence intervals are discovered by a process of deduction from premises; then, according to Neyman, we may draw a sample and decide, by an act of will, to behave as if the real value of an unknown parameter were in the interval indicated by the confidence limits. This is not reasoning (obviously), and Neyman suggests calling the whole process inductive behavior. We have, on the one hand, inductive behavior, and on the other, deductive reasoning.

The answer to this argument has an important bearing on my endeavor, since there are many people who seem to feel as Neyman does. Neyman's argument hinges on an ambiguity in the term 'deductive'. Clearly my whole system of rational corpora and probability and randomness is a deductive system, in the sense that it is formal, the concepts being defined in protosyntax, the statements obeying the ordinary rules of quantification theory. On the other hand, the system is equally clearly not deductive in the Kantian sense of analytic — although there are formal rules stipulating what may be included in a rational corpus of given level and basis, these rules are not necessarily truth-preserving; it is possible to get more out of a given basis than experience puts in — though of course we pay for this in uncertainty. Thus the relationship between a given ingredient of a rational corpus, and the basis on which that rational corpus is constructed, is formal, rationalizable, deductive, in the sense that the relationship is protosyntactically (and hence syntactically) definable; but it is not analytic in the sense that there is and can be 'nothing present' in the given ingredient which is not already 'present' in the basis of the rational corpus in which it appears.

The matter of behavior is something else again; all I have been maintaining is that a logic of rational belief is possible, and that this logic is perfectly formal; so that given a language meeting certain criteria, and given the basis of a rational corpus, the degree of belief in a given statement to which one is logically entitled and obligated, relative to the rational corpora of a given level, is determinate. What one decides to *do* on the basis of the beliefs to which he is logically entitled is quite another matter; and I would not dream of trying to maintain that a 'logic of rational *behavior*' is possible which would dictate a particular course of action to be taken on the basis of given evidence. A theory of right action, while it would depend in part on what we have grounds for believing, will clearly depend also on many factors which can be called 'rational' only by increasing the elasticity of the term beyong all plausible limits.

And this is precisely the fact I would cite to support the usefulness of my logic of rational belief; for while it is often enough a highly complex ethical matter to agree on what to do, given the 'facts' of the situation, there is no need for it to be further complicated by pushing our knowledge of the facts off into a vague limbo of non-existent 'inductive reasoning' so that we cannot even agree on what to believe until we have already come to an agreement on what is is desirable to do. While it is a truth of psychology that it often takes more evidence to make us believe what we don't want to believe, it is surely not a truth of logic that we ought not to believe what we don't want to believe. Our behavior will reflect our desires; our beliefs need not.

CHAPTER FOURTEEN

Probability and Betting Quotients

1.   In the preceding chapter, I discussed the relation between the logic of rational belief that I am suggesting and certain key concepts of statistics, taking J. Neyman's viewpoint as representing one of the most carefully formulated positions with respect to the relation between practical statistics and the foundations of probability. In this section I shall do the same thing for the personalistic and logical theories. In particular, I shall discuss Kemeny's proof[1] that the multiplication and addition axioms are required for any theory of probability that is to serve as a basis for a fair betting system.

I should like to postpone, until the following chapter, the question of whether and how my logic of rational belief can be practically applied to real persons or groups of persons—the question of determining the basis of a person's rational corpus, of representing changes in it, and so on. Let us suppose, instead, that individuals come equipped with tags, listing the ingredients of the bases of their rational corpora. Let us further suppose that each of the objects with which we are going to be concerned belongs only to a finite number of distinct rational classes, so that we may use the technique suggested in **1243 to determine, for any given object and class, the class of which the object is a random member with respect to the given class, and that we are to be concerned only with rational corpora of a given level. Finally, let us suppose that we have a way of measuring degrees of belief to any desired degree of precision, which does not involve bets, hypothetical or otherwise. In short, we suppose that we may, by examining a person's tag and testing his beliefs (or a random sample of them) on our special belief-o-meter, determine whether or not he fulfills the requirements of Aristotle's definition of man as a rational animal.

Now we may ask about the relationship between rationality as defined by me and rationality as defined by the requirements of 'coherence'. We may ask, first of all, if all people whose degrees of belief in related statements obey the rules of probability laid

---

1. Kemeny, "Fair Bets and Inductive Probabilities," *Journal of Symbolic Logic* 20, 1955. See also R. S. Lehman, "On Confirmation and Rational Betting," *Journal of Symbolic Logic* 20, 1955.

down by Savage,[2] Ramsey,[3] De Finetti,[4] *et al.*, are *rational* in the sense of my definition. (Shimony[5] and Kemeny[6] have approached the problem from this angle, but seem to feel that further criteria can be laid down; their views being incomplete on this score, this particular question cannot be asked of them.)

The answer, obviously, is no. For it is clear that on my definition of rationality only a limited range of degrees of belief in a given statement is permissible. And it is also clear that a person *may* have any degree of belief whatever in an uncertain statement and still have a 'consistent' or 'coherent' body of beliefs, provided that the degrees of belief he has in other, related, statements be adjusted accordingly. In this sense, my definition of rationality is more restrictive than that offered by the personalistic writers.

It has often been suggested that the way to find out about someone's degree of belief in a given statement is to discover the minimum odds at which he would bet on the statement. Ramsey[3] was, I believe, the first person to point out that unless, for a given person, the degrees of belief thus determined in a set of related statements obey the laws of probability, the person runs the risk of having a book made against him; in more recent terminology, his beliefs would be said to be not coherent.[5]

Now we may ask whether anyone who was rational, in my sense, would have beliefs that were coherent. Consider the rational corpora of level r_i and basis F belonging to a person who is rational in my sense. If the probability of a given statement, S, relative to the rational corpora of this level and basis, is the pair of fractions 'p'; 'q', then his degree of belief in the statement S will fall between the ratios p and q. Similarly, his degree of belief in the denial of the statement S, nS, will fall between the ratios $_s1_s- q$ and $_s1_s- p$. But if q is different from p, it is not necessarily true that his degree of belief in S and his degree of belief in nS will add up to unity. If they do not, then *if* these degrees of belief are to be taken as indicating the betting quotients at which any rational man would take either side of a bet, he could have a book made against him. This is sufficient to show that the set of degrees of belief of a man who is rational in my sense, need not be coherent in the personalistic sense.

2. Savage, *The Foundations of Statistics.*
3. F. P. Ramsey, *The Foundations of Mathematics.*
4. De Finetti, *La prevision: ses lois logique, ses sources subjectives.*
5. A. Shimony, "Coherence and the Axioms of Confirmation," *Journal of Symbolic Logic* 20, 1955.
6. Kemeny, *op. cit.*

Although it is obvious which antecedent I shall end up by denying, it will be interesting to examine the relation between my conception of probability and the conception which leads to fair betting quotients in more detail. For this purpose, I shall refer to J. Kemeny's paper, "Fair Bets and Inductive Probabilities", which is purported to show "... that the probability axioms are necessary and sufficient conditions to assure that the degrees of confirmation form a set of fair betting quotients." Since the multiplication and addition axioms do not hold in general in my system, what I must show is that the probability axioms mentioned by Kemeny are not necessary to assure that my conception of probability will lead to a set of fair betting quotients.

To begin with, my definition of probability does not lead to a unique set of betting quotients at all, due to the fact that it only legislates that the degrees of belief of the person lie in certain intervals; but we can discuss the question of whether or not every set of beliefs which are rational in my sense will lead to a set of betting quotients which are fair, and we can also discuss the question of whether or not any such set of degrees of belief will fulfill the requirement of being transformable into fair betting quotients.

Kemeny's description of the betting situation is this:[7] "Under certain circumstances, e, two people wager money on whether a certain event h will or will not take place. ... If a person offers to pay a sum qS if he is wrong, and is to receive $(1 - q)S$ if he is right, then he is giving the odds $q : (1 - q)$. We will say that q is the betting quotient and S is the stake." If the betting quotients for a set of e, h pairs is *fair*, there is no betting system (consisting of a choice of e, h pairs to bet on, a choice of the stake, and a choice of the side of the bet) which will guarantee a profit. The set of betting quotients is *strictly fair*, if there is no betting system which will guarantee that there will be no loss, and at the same time offer a possible profit.

The relation between degrees of confirmation and betting quotients is this: if $c(h, e)$ is the degree of confirmation of h on evi- e, then $c(h, e)$ gives the reasonable betting quotients for a bet on h in circumstances e. In terms of my definition of probability, what corresponds to this is that the betting quotient q, to be reasonable, must fall between r and s, when H describes the event h, the basis F of the rational corpus includes a description of the circumstances, and H r_i Prob_F ('r';'s').

Kemeny shows that any confirmation function $c(h, e)$ must fulfill the following conditions if it is to determine betting quotients which

7. *Ibid.*, p. 263.

are fair:

(1)[8] $0 \leqslant c(h, e) \leqslant 1$

Since neither qS nor $(1 - q)S$ can be negative, and S cannot be negative, q must be positive and not more than 1. This requirement is met by my definition of probability; since both r and s lie between 0 and 1, and any rational degree of belief must lie between r and s.

(2)[9]   If h and e are equivalent to h' and e', respectively, then

$$c(h, e) = c(h', e')$$

In one sense this requirement is met by my definition; from the definition of rational corpora, it is clear that equivalent bases will generate identical sets of rational corpora; so that we need not be concerned about the difference in form between e and e'. On the other hand, **1215 assures us that the probabilities of statements known to be equivalent will be the same. Thus the legislation for rational belief is the same for the equivalent statements H and H'; but since the requirements of rationality are met by any degree of belief falling between the legislated limits, it is perfectly possible that a rational man may have somewhat different degrees of belief in statements that are known to be equivalent. Condition (2) is therefore not fulfilled except fortuitously, or for probabilities based on statistical statements that are completely precise.

(3)[10]   If e implies h, then $c(h, e) = 1$

This requirement is clearly fulfilled in my system; if e implies h, then H will be an ingredient of some rational corpus of the required level and basis. Relative to this rational corpus, the probability of H is ($"_s1"; "_s1"$), and the only allowable degree of belief in H is 'certainty'.

(4)[11]   If e implies that h and h' cannot both be true, then

$$c(h \vee h', e) = c(h, e) + c(h', e)$$

(5)[12] $c(h \cdot h', e) = c(h, e) \times c(h', h \cdot e)$

While my conception of probability failed to fulfill (2) merely because it does not legislate precisely the degree of belief that a person ought to have in order to be rational, it fails to fulfill (4) in

8. *Ibid.*, p. 265.
9. *Ibid.*, p. 265.
10. *Ibid.*, p. 265.
11. *Ibid.*, p. 265.
12. *Ibid.*, p. 266.

a far more serious way; the same difficulties arise in connection with condition (5), so I shall examine (4) and (5) together.

The statements in my theory of probability which correspond to (4) and (5) for the special case of degenerate intervals in the relevant statistical statements follow. For future reference I add a statement corresponding to the general addition rule.

(4*) Thm "$\sim a \, \epsilon \, b \, \mathrm{v} \sim a' \, \epsilon \, b'$ " $\supset$: "$a \, \epsilon \, b$" $r_i \mathrm{Prob_F}$ ("p";"q") $\cdot$

"$a' \, e \, b'$" $r_i \mathrm{Prob_F}$ ("p'";"q'") $\cdot \supset$

"$a \, \epsilon \, b \, \mathrm{v} \, a' \, e \, b'$" $r_i \mathrm{Prob_F}$ ("$p \, {}_s{+}\, p'$";"$q \, {}_s{+}\, q'$")

(4**) "$a \, \epsilon \, b$" $r_i \mathrm{Prob_F}$ ("p";"q") $\cdot$ "$a \, \epsilon \, b \cdot a' \, \epsilon \, b'$"

$r_i \mathrm{Prob_F}$ ("p'''";"q'''") $\cdot$ "$a' \, \epsilon \, b'$"

$r_i \mathrm{Prob_F}$ ("p'";"q'") $\cdot \supset$ "$a \, \epsilon \, b \, \mathrm{v} \, a' \, \epsilon \, b'$"

$r_i \mathrm{Prob_F}$ ("$p \, {}_s{+}\, p' \, {}_s{-}\, p'''$";"$q \, {}_s{+}\, q' \, {}_s{-}\, q'''$")

(5*) "$a \, \epsilon \, b$" $r_i \mathrm{Prob_F}$ ("p";"q") $\cdot$

"$a' \, \epsilon \, b'$" $r_i \mathrm{Prob}_{F \, \mathrm{s}\widehat{6}\,\mathrm{s}\widehat{7}}$ "$a \, \epsilon \, b$" $\widehat{\mathrm{s}6}\widehat{\mathrm{s}}7$ ("p'";"q'") $\cdot \supset$

"$a \, \epsilon \, b \cdot a' \, \epsilon \, b'$" $r_i \mathrm{Prob_F}$ ("$p \, {}_s\mathrm{x} \, p'$";"$q \, {}_s\mathrm{x} \, q'$")

The conditionals relating statistical statements on which (4**), (4*), and (5*) would presumably be based are not hard to come by. Let A be the class of which a is a random member with respect to b, and let A″ be the class of which a' is a random member with respect to b' when "$a \, \epsilon \, b$" is added to the basis of our rational corpus. Let M, M″, N, N″, be natural numbers such that A ϵ N, A″ ϵ N″, A $\cap$ b ϵ M, and A″ $\cap$ b′ ϵ M″. Consider the class of all pairs, such that the first object belongs to A and the second to A″. The number of such pairs is clearly N x N″. Similarly, the number of these pairs of objects such that the first belongs to A $\cap$ b and the second to A″ $\cap$ b′ is M x M″. Since we have as a theorem about ratios,

$$p \, {}_s{\le} \, M/N \, {}_s{\le} \, q \cdot p' \, {}_s{\le} \, M''/N'' \, {}_s{\le} \, q' \cdot \supset$$

$$p \, {}_s\mathrm{x} \, p' \, {}_s{\le} \, M \, \mathrm{x} \, M''/N \, \mathrm{x} \, N'' \, {}_s{\le} \, q \, {}_s\mathrm{x} \, q'$$

whatever M, N, M″, and N″ may actually be, we also have,

(5*a) $\%(A,b,(p;q)) \cdot \%(A'',b',(p';q')) \cdot \supset \%(\hat{x}\hat{y}(x \, \epsilon \, A \cdot y \, \epsilon \, A''),$

$\hat{x}\hat{y}(x \, \epsilon \, b \cdot y \, \epsilon \, b'),(p \, {}_s\mathrm{x} \, p';q \, {}_s\mathrm{x} \, q'))$

A possible statistical basis of something corresponding to the general addition rule is almost as easy to construct. Let A′ be the class of which a' is a random member with respect to b', and let N' and M' be natural numbers such that $A' \in N'$ and $A' \cap b' \in M'$, and let A, N, and M be as above. Let us further suppose that the pair, $a; a'$, is a random member of the pair product of A and A' with respect to membership in the pair product of b and b'. The total number of pairs such that the first object of the pair belongs to A and the second to A' is N x N'; the number of pairs of objects such that either the first belongs to b, or the second to b', or both, among the first-mentioned pairs, is M x $(N' - M') + M'$ x $(N - M)$ $-$ M x M', which reduces to M x N' + M' x N $-$ M x M'. We must now show that

$$p \,_s\leq M/N \,_s\leq q \cdot p' \,_s\leq M'/N' \,_s\leq q' \cdot \supset p \,_s+p' \,_s- p \,_s\mathrm{x} p' \,_s\leq$$

$$(M \text{ x } N' + M' \text{ x } N - M \text{ x } M')/(N \text{ x } N') \,_s\leq$$

$$q \,_s+ q' \,_s- q \,_s\mathrm{x} q'$$

I shall give half the argument in detail; the other half is analogous. We must show:

(i) $p \,_s+p' \,_s- p \,_s\mathrm{x} p' \,_s\leq M/N + M'/N' \,_s- (M \text{ x } M')/(N \text{ x } N')$,

when $p \,_s\leq M/N$ and $p' \,_s\leq M'/N'$.

Let $p \,_s+ \epsilon = M/N$, and $p' \,_s+ \epsilon' = M'/N'$, so that,

(ii) $(p \,_s+ \epsilon) \,_s+ (p' \,_s+ \epsilon') \,_s- ((p \,_s+ \epsilon) \,_s\mathrm{x} (p' \,_s+ \epsilon')) =$

$$M/N \,_s+ M'/N' \,_s- M \text{ x } M'/N \text{ x } N'$$

Or, rearranging the terms,

(iii) $p \,_s+p' \,_s- p \,_s\mathrm{x} p' \,_s+ (\epsilon \,_s+ \epsilon') \,_s- p \,_s\mathrm{x} \epsilon' \,_s- \epsilon \,_s\mathrm{x} \epsilon' \,_s- p' \,_s\mathrm{x} \epsilon =$

$$M'/N' \,_s+ M/N \,_s- M \text{ x } M'/N \text{ x } N'$$

To establish (i), it suffices to show that,

(iv) $\epsilon \,_s+ \epsilon' \,_s\geq p \,_s\mathrm{x} \epsilon' \,_s+ \epsilon \,_s\mathrm{x} \epsilon' \,_s+ p' \,_s\mathrm{x} \epsilon$

Or,

(v) $\epsilon \,_s+ \epsilon' \,_s\geq \epsilon \,_s\mathrm{x} (\epsilon' \,_s+ p') \,_s+ p \,_s\mathrm{x} \epsilon'$

But since $p' \,_s+ \epsilon' = M'/N'$, and $M'/N' \,_s\leq 1$, and $p \,_s\leq 1$, we have,

(vi) $\epsilon \,_s\geq \epsilon \,_s\mathrm{x} (\epsilon' \,_s+ p')$

and

(vii) $\epsilon' \,_s\geq p \,_s\mathrm{x} \epsilon'$

From which (v), and hence (i), follows. Thus the theoremhood of (4**a) is established:

(4**a) $\%(A,b,(p;q)) \cdot \%(A',b',(p';q')) \cdot \supset \%(\hat{x}\hat{y}(x \in A \cdot y \in A'),$

$\hat{x}\hat{y}(x \in b \vee y \in b'),(p_s + p'_s - p_s \times p';q_s + q'_s - q_s \times q'))$

Finding a plausible statistical basis for a counterpart of the special addition rule, however, is somewhat more complicated. Let A, A', N, N', M, and M' be the same as before. If we suppose merely that "$\sim a \in b \vee \sim a' \in b'$" is known, and not that it is a theorem, then we merely rule out the pairs of objects such that the first belongs to A and b, and the second to A' and b'. The proportion of the pairs of objects, excluding these, such that the first belongs to A and the second to A', which are also pairs of objects such that the first belongs to b or the second belongs to b', is therefore (M x N' + N' x M − 2 x M x M')/(N x N' − M x M'). This obviously does not correspond to the ordinary special addition law at all; but in some circumstances it can nevertheless be applied.

We can apply this formula to a pair of coin tosses: let a coin be tossed behind a screen by a dealer who calls out the results of each game—HT, TH, or TT, as the case may be. The omission of HH is due to the fact that a game is to consist of not just any old pair of tosses, but only those pairs of tosses which do not both result in heads. The players thus know in advance that either the first toss of the pair, or the second toss of the pair, will fail to result in heads. The probability, given by the above formula, that either the first or the second toss of a game will result in heads is "2/3", under the usual conditions of ignorance as to the outcome of a future game. This is obviously correct, while the attempt to apply the special addition rule *directly* would be misguided.

There is one simple and obvious situation where the special addition rule can often be applied with no difficulties at all; this is when a and a' are the same object, and the intersection of b and b' is known to be empty. Then the theorem about statistical statements which might serve as a basis for a probability statement corresponding to the special addition law is,

(4*a) $b \cap b' \in 0 \cdot \supset : \%(A',b,(p;q)) \cdot \%(A',b',(p';q')) \cdot \supset$

$\%(A',b \cup b',(p_s + p'_s;q_s + q'))$

I said that there was more in the way of having Kemeny's conventions (4) and (5) hold in my system than the matter of having intervals of rational belief in lieu of degrees. This is evident from the fact that (5*) does not follow from (5*a), (4*) does not follow from (4*a), and (4**) does not follow from (4**a). Conditionals concerning randomness are also required, and these conditionals may perfectly well not hold. These three conditionals follow:

(4*b)   Thm "$b \cap b' \epsilon 0$" $\supset$: "a" r_i Ran$_F$("A'''","b") ·

"a" r_i Ran$_F$("A'''","b'''") · $\supset$ "a" r_i Ran$_F$

("A'''","$b \cup b'''$")

(4**b)   "a" r_i Ran$_F$ ("A","b") · "a'''" r_i Ran$_F$ ("A'''","b'''") ·

"$(a;a')$" r_i Ran$_F$("A" cp "A'''", "b"cp"b'''") · $\supset$

"$(a;a')$" r_i Ran$_F$ ("A" cp "A'''", "$\hat{x}\hat{y}(x \epsilon b$ v

$y \epsilon b')$")

(5*b)   "a" r_i Ran$_F$ ("A","b") · "a'''" r_i Ran$_{F \, \widehat{s_6 s_7} \, "a \, \epsilon \, b \, " \, \widehat{} \, s_6 s_7}$

("A'''","b'''") · $\supset$ "$(a;a')$" r_i Ran$_F$("A" cp "A'''",

"b" cp "b'''")

It is interesting to note that when we have to deal only with statistical statements which are completely strong—that is, when the interval into which the class ratio is asserted to fall is vanishing (or negligible)—(4*b), (4**b), and (5*b) do hold in general, so that we have, in accordance with Kemeny's statements (4) and (5), my statements (4*), (4**), and (5*). The argument in favor of (4**b) has already been presented in the preceding chapter; the arguments for (4*b) and (5*b) are analogous.

It is not difficult to construct an example for which (4*b), (4**b), and (5*b) fail to hold. Let us suppose that a couple of graduate students at Duke University have taken a day off, and, returning, intend to bet on the outcome of some drawings made in their absence from bags of counters. They examine a summary of the experiment before making their bets; the pay-off will be based on the detailed report of the experiment.

The drawings are made from two bags containing red, black, and green counters. Let B_1 be the class of all objects consisting of a counter in the first bag paired with a number from 1 to 100; let R be the class of all pairs of objects such that the first object is red, and let G be the class of all pairs of objects such that the first object is green. Similarly, let B_2 be the class of all objects consisting of a counter in the second bag paired with a number from 1 to 100. It is clear that if a fifth of the counters in the first bag are red, then a fifth of the objects belonging to B_1 will also belong to R. Thus we may plausibly let our knowledge about the bags in the rational corpora of level r_i and basis F (which is to serve as the context for the whole example) be represented by the following statistical statements which are to be strongest statements in this rational corpus.[13]

S-1 $\%(B_1, R, (.2; .3))$

S-2 $\%(B_1, G, (.3; .4))$

S-3 $\%(B_2, G, (.4; .6))$

The experiment performed in the absence of the two students is to have consisted of 100 draws from the first bag, and 100 draws from the second bag. Let DB_1 be the class of all objects consisting of a counter drawn from the first bag in the experiment, paired with a number corresponding to the ordinal number of the draw, and let DB_2 be the class of all objects consisting of a counter drawn during the experiment from the second bag, paired with a number corresponding to the ordinal number of the draw on which it was drawn. Thus DB_1 and DB_2 will both have 100 members, even if the same counter is drawn a number of times during the experiment; and DB_1 and DB_2 will be subclasses of B_1 and B_2, respectively.

Let us suppose that the summary of the experiment in question consists of the three statistical statements:

S-4 $\%(\hat{x}\hat{y}(x \in DB_1 \cdot y \in DB_2), \hat{x}\hat{y}(x \in R \vee y \in G), (.6; .6))$

S-5 $\%(\hat{x}\hat{y}(x \in DB_1 \cdot y \in DB_2), \hat{x}\hat{y}(x \in R \cdot y \in G), (.2; .2))$

S-6 $\%(DB_1, R \cup G, (.6; .6))$

There are, of course, other statistical statements that may be included in the rational corpus in question; those which bear an asterisk require that we know the conjunction of two of the above statements, as well as that we know the two statements individually.

S-7* $\%(\hat{x}\hat{y}(x \in B_1 \cdot y \in B_2), \hat{x}\hat{y}(x \in R \cdot y \in G), (.08; .18))$ S1,S3

S-8* $\%(\hat{x}\hat{y}(x \in B_1 \cdot y \in B_2), \hat{x}\hat{y}(x \in R \vee y \in G), (.52; .72))$ S1,S3

S-9* $\%(B_1, R \cup G, (.5; .7))$ S1,S2

S-10* $\%(B_1, R, (.08; 1.0))$ S7

S-11* $\%(B_2, G, (.08; 1.0))$ S7

S-12* $\%(B_1, R, (0.0; .72))$ S8

S-13* $\%(B_2, G, (0.0; .72))$ S8

S-14 $\%(DB_1, R, (0.0; 0.6))$ S4

13. C_7 is to be the 7'th counter drawn from the first bag; C_{10} is to be the 10'th counter drawn from the second bag.

S-15 $\%(DB_2,G,(0.0;0.6))$ S4

S-16 $\%(DB_1,R,(0.2;1.0))$ S5

S-17 $\%(DB_2,G,(0.2;1.0))$ S5

S-18* $\%(B_1,R,(0.0;0.7))$ S9

S-19* $\%(B_1,G,(0.0;0.7))$ S9

S-20* $\%(DB_1,R,(.2;.6))$ S14,S16

S-21* $\%(DB_2,G,(.2;.6))$ S15,S17

S-22* $\%(B_1,R,(.08;.70))$ S10,S18

S-23* $\%(B_2,G,(.08;.70))$ S11,S19

S-24 $\%(\ C_7,R,(0.0;1.0))$ ML

S-25 $\%(\ C_{10},G,(0.0;1.0))$ ML

S-26 $\%(\ C_7,G,(0.0;1.0))$ ML

S-27 $\%(\ (C_7;C_{10}),\hat{x}\hat{y}(x \in R \cdot y \in G),(0.0;1.0))$ ML

S-28 $\%(\ (C_7;C_{10}),\hat{x}\hat{y}(x \in R \vee y \in G),(0.0;1.0))$ ML

R-1, R-2, R-3, and R-4 below may be seen to hold, since, among the possibilities open to us, there is no class (in the case of R-1) to which C_7 is known to belong, about which our knowledge is either different or stronger than our knowledge about B_1. The case is analogous with respect to R-2 and R-3, and since, if we add "$C_7 \in$ R" to the basis F of our rational corpus, the case is analogous with respect to R-4.

R-1   "C_7" $r_i \text{Ran}_F($ "B_1", "R" $)$

R-2   "C_7" $r_i \text{Ran}_F($ "B_1", "G" $)$

R-3   "C_{10}" $r_i \text{Ran}_F($ "B_2", "G" $)$

R-4   "C_{10}" $r_i \text{Ran}_{F\,S_6S_7\text{"}C_7 \in R\text{"}\,S_6S_7}($ "B_2"; "G" $)$

Since "R ∩ G ∈ 0" is a plausible enough theorem, we may suppose that the assertion that this is a theorem, R-1, and R-2, together constitute an instance of the antecedent of (4*b). But the corresponding conclusion, R-5, is clearly false.

R-5   "C_7" $r_i \text{Ran}_F($ "B_1", "R ∪ G" $)$

Similarly, the conjunction of R-1 and R-4 constitutes an instance of the antecedent of (5*b); but the corresponding conclusion, R-6, is false.

R-6   "$(C_7;C_{10})$" $r_i \mathrm{Ran_F}$ ("$\hat{x}\hat{y}(x \in B_1 \cdot y \in B_2)$", "$\hat{x}\hat{y}(x \in R \cdot$

     $y \in G)$")

Finally, if we eliminate S-5, so that we do have R-6, then R-6, in conjunction with R-1 and R-3, is an instance of the antecedent of (4**b); but again the consequent, R-7, is false:

R-7   "$(C_7;C_{10})$" $r_i \mathrm{Ran_F}$ ("$\hat{x}\hat{y}(x \in B_1 \cdot y \in B_2)$", "$\hat{x}\hat{y}(x \in R \text{ v}$

     $y \in G)$")

(If we do not eliminate S-5, (4**b holds by virtue of the falsity of the antecedent.)

The randomness-statements that do hold in these three cases are:

R-8   "C_7" $r_i \mathrm{Ran_F}$ ("DB_1", "$R \cup G$")

R-9   "$(C_7;C_{10})$" $r_i \mathrm{Ran_F}$ ("$\hat{x}\hat{y}(x \in DB_1 \cdot y \in DB_2)$",

     "$\hat{x}\hat{y}(x \in R \cdot y \in G)$")

R-10   "$(C_7;C_{10})$" $r_i \mathrm{Ran_F}$ ("$\hat{x}\hat{y}(x \in DB_1 \cdot y \in DB_2)$",

     "$\hat{x}\hat{y}(x \in R \text{ v } y \in G)$")

It will be interesting, as long as I am involved with this lengthy Counter instance, to consider the effect of a slight change in our knowledge from F to F*. Let us replace S-5 by S-5':

S-5' $\%(\hat{x}\hat{y}(x \in DB_1 \cdot y \in DB_2), \hat{x}\hat{y}(x \in R \cdot y \in G), (.25;.25))$

This allows us to replace S-16, S-17, S-20*, and S-21*, by slightly stronger statements:

S-16' $\%(DB_1, R, (.25;1.0))$		S5'
S-17' $\%(DB_2, G, (.25;1.0))$		S5'
S-20*' $\%(DB_1, R, (.25;0.6))$		S16',S14
S-21*' $\%(DB_2, G, (.25;0.6))$		S17',S15

Now the situation is different; S-20*' *differs* from S-1, so that in lieu of R-1, we have, (since DB_1 is included in B_1)

R-11   "C_7" $r_i \mathrm{Ran_F}$ ("DB_1", "R")

Since S-21*' does not differ from S-3, and the corresponding statement about DB_1 and G does not differ from S-2, R-2 and R-3 (and R-4) hold as is. Similarly, R-8, R-9, and R-10 remain valid. The interesting point now, is that the slight change suggested in our knowledge about DB_1 and the intersection of R and G makes a far greater range of belief concerning "$C_7 \epsilon R$" *rational*. From ("$.2$"; "$.3$") the probability changes to ("$.25$";"$.60$").

This is not necessarily very odd; since the proportion of objects belonging to R in DB_1 does, after all, seem to differ from the proportion of objects belonging to R in B_1, we might very well have some doubts about whether or not red counters are *drawn* more often than the other kinds. Further discussion of this sort of thing will be found in the next chapter.

The above considerations suffice to show that Kemeny's conditions (4) and (5) for 'degree of confirmation' are not fulfilled by my concept of probability. On the other hand, it is obvious that there is some distribution of degrees of belief, which is rational in my sense, and which in addition fulfills Kemeny's requirements. As my discussion of Neyman's theory will have showed, Kemeny's requirements (1)–(5) are met by my concept of probability when we are concerned with an ideally based rational corpus. Since the statistical statements in a set of rational corpora of level r_i must be consistent, if we are to have any probability statements at all, they must be consistent with some set of statistical statements about the universal class V and some of its subclasses, where this set of statistical statements constitutes the basis of an ideal rational corpus. Thus the probability statements based on F must be consistent —i.e., not *differ* from— the probability statements based on this ideal rational corpus. The latter probability statements must mention ratios which fall within the intervals demarcated by the ratios mentioned in the probability statements made relative to the rational corpora of level r_i and basis F. Hence there will be some distribution of degrees of belief which both conforms to Kemeny's requirements and is rational in my sense.

To sum up the results so far: a set of beliefs which is 'coherent' in Shimony's sense, need not be rational in my sense; furthermore, a set of beliefs which are 'rational' in my sense, need not be 'coherent—i.e., need not correspond to a set of fair betting quotients, in Kemeny's sense. On the other hand, there is always some distribution of degrees of belief which is rational in my sense, and which is also coherent, or which may serve as the basis of a set of fair betting quotients.

How is it possible to maintain that a given distribution of degrees of belief is 'rational', when this distribution of degrees of belief is incoherent, in the sense that anyone having these degrees of belief, and basing a set of betting quotients on them, could have a book made against him?

In the first place, it is obvious that a rational man will not have a book made against him, if he prefers not to lose money. If he offers odds of 4 : 1 against the next counter from the first bag (described above) being green, then he will not simultaneously offer odds of 3 : 7 in favor of this counter being green. It is not that either offer by itself is irrational, and it is not the theory of probability which tells him not to make these offers simultaneously, but the simple certainty that if someone puts up two dollars on his first offer, and seven dollars on his second offer, he stands to lose regardless of the color of the next counter. He loses one dollar if it is green, and one dollar if it isn't. So it is silly, regardless of your beliefs, not to have the odds of bets you offer conform to the axioms of confirmation set forth by Kemeny, unless you want to lose money. And the rational bettor who does not want to lose money will not be silly in this way.

But we may still ask whether or not these requirements must be met by the *degrees of belief* of a rational man. Suppose for the moment that degrees of belief can be measured precisely. Then either the degrees of belief of the rational man conform to Kemeny's requirements (1)—(5), (and the corresponding betting quotients do too) or, since the betting quotients must conform to (1)—(5) in any case, the degrees of belief of the rational man do not conform to (1)—(5) and the betting quotients offered actually differ from his degrees of belief. The latter alternative is rather odd; it could result in an offer of odds of 3 : 1 against an occurrence which is believed in to the degree 0.2. So if degrees of belief can be measured precisely—or even, if they are precise—then we must demand that in addition to the requirements of the logic of rational belief, the degrees of belief of a rational man must also conform to the requirements (1)—(5) laid down by Kemeny.

But these additional requirements seem gratuitous. We already know that the rational man is not going to have a book made against him—and this is the general condition originally laid down by Ramsey—and the further requirements seen to be needed only on the assumption that degrees of belief fall on determinate points in a continuous scale from 0 to 1. Now it is true, as Savage has pointed out, that you can force a person to choose between alternatives in such a way that you can 'determine', with any required degree of precision, his 'degree of belief' in a given statement (or state of affairs). But the procedure of forcing him to choose between alternatives is somewhat artificial; the point comes when the person has no real preference, but shrugs his shoulders and says, "What the hell, I'll pick this one." Choosing between alternatives is a clear-cut yes or no affair; just as a bet on an event requires clear-cut well defined betting quotients. But in many cases, the passage from the 'degree' of belief the person has to the expression of a preference or to the acceptance of certain odds, is accompanied by a shrug of the shoulders. I find nothing odd about the possibility that under some circumstances I might be willing to take either side of a 1 : 3 bet on a given event, or under the same circumstances of knowledge, either side of a 1 : 4 bet on the same event.

In short, I would suggest that 'degrees' of belief are not precise quantities of belief; that there is a certain element of vagueness involved in belief. This vagueness has been accepted by Keynes[14] and Koopman[15] as evidence that 'degrees' of belief are not simply ordered, as are degrees of other things, and that preferences and betting quotients are simply ordered only because of the circumstances that surround them, not because they reveal or reflect precisely determinate degrees of belief. To this extent, I think that it is all to the good that the axioms of the personalistic theories of probability are not in general fulfilled by my conception of probability.

2.   In the preceding section, I showed that since probability is related, on my theory, to a pair of fractions, the ordinary axioms of the probability calculus do not apply (as they ought to apply on either a degree-of-confirmation theory or a personalistic theory) to all rational degrees of belief. If the ratios mentioned in a given probability statement were always the same—i.e., corresponded to a degenerate interval—then the ordinary axioms would apply; but as matters stand, we cannot in general be sure that 'degrees of belief' statements will obey the ordinary addition and multiplication laws.

This oddity is not without its advantages as compared with the characteristics of the prevailing logical theories of probability. In my discussion of these theories, I mentioned the fact that some other concept than that of probability is invariably required to indicate the full nature of what our belief in a given statement ought to be, if we are to call ourselves rational. Keynes suggested the concept of weight; Carnap, in discussing the interpretation of degree of confirmation as an estimate of a relative frequency, suggested distinguishing between more and less reliable estimates, and hence, implicitly, between more and less reliable degrees of confirmation.

It is obvious that some such distinction is required in any theory of probability for which the ordinary axioms hold: the degree of confirmation of h on evidence e may have a certain value p; and the degree of confirmation of h on evidence e' may also have the

14. J. M. Keynes, *A Treatise on Probability.*

15. B. O. Koopman, "The Axioms and Algebra of Intuitive Probability," *Annals of Mathematics* 41, 1940.

value p, in spite of vast differences between e and e'. In fact, the degree of confirmation of h on the null evidence t may also be p. Thus, for example, the probability that the next counter drawn from a bag containing red and black counters in unknown proportions is black, may be $1/2$; and after collecting the evidence of a million draws (presumably with replacement) from the bag, we may discover that the probability that the next counter drawn from the bag is black is still $1/2$. And yet our state of mind in the two situations, before and after the millionfold sample, is decidedly different. Keynes[16] would say that we attach more *weight* to the latter probability; Carnap[17] would say that the degree of confirmation, treated as an estimate of the relative frequency, is far more *reliable* in the second case than in the first.

On my theory, the probability will not be the same in the two cases, although the odds at which a rational man might be willing to bet on the occurrence of a black counter on the next draw might perfectly well *happen* to be the same. The probability relative to no knowledge at all about the proportion will be the pair of fractions ("$_s0$";"$_s1$"), while after a million draws from the bag, our knowledge of the proportion will be quite precise, so that the probability in question will be, say, (".4995";".5005"). Before the collection of evidence, any degree of belief is perfectly rational—or perhaps it would be better to say that then perfectly rational belief is perfectly indeterminate—and after the collection of the evidence, only a degree of belief in a very narrow range is rational.

Thus on my theory, the weight of a probability, or its reliability, when it is considered an estimate of a relative frequency, which on Carnap's and Keynes' theory is a separate number, is embodied directly in the probability expression itself. It should be noted that the inclusion of 'e' in the symbol for degree of confirmation, no more than the inclusion of 'F' in my symbolic rendering of the probability relation, suffices practically to indicate the quantity of evidence. This is no doubt why Keynes and Carnap have suggested a supplementary concept to that of probability. Different kinds of evidence may have different degrees of evidential weight, and an enormous amount and variety of evidence is relevant to those commonly accepted but still uncertain statements which in turn provide much of the evidence for more genuinely and generally doubtful statements. To write down all of the evidence that may be accepted as indubitable which, directly or indirectly, bears on the high probability for me (or anyone else) that the sun will rise tomorrow, would be a monumental undertaking.

16. Keynes, *op. cit.*, p. 312.
17. R. Carnap, *The Logical Foundations of Probability*, pp. 533 ff., 554.

The distinction between different levels of rational corpora also seems to have something to do with weight. If the probability of H relative to the rational corpora of level r_i and basis F is the pair of fractions ("p";"q"), and that relative to the rational corpora of level r_{i-1} is the pair of fractions ("r";"s"), we know that in general the interval determined by r and s will fall properly within the interval determined by p and q. This corresponds to the assignment of greater weight to the second probability than to the first.

This may seem odd, since the evidence is the same in either case. But the explanation is simply that in choosing a level of rational corpus to serve as a standard for 'acceptance' in a given context, we are also choosing a standard for the weight of the evidence; so that relative to the lower-level rational corpus, the evidence that we have goes a longer way, and allows us to accept a more precise statistical assertion. Relative to the higher-level rational corpus (to adopt which is to adopt a more rigorous standard), the evidence does not go as far; it does not prove as much when our standard of cogency is more demanding.

Another distinction, already alluded to in the discussion of weight, between my theory and those of Carnap and Keynes, lies in the treatment of the evidence e; consider an hypothesis h and the evidence e, relative to which we are supposed to evaluate its degree of confirmation. It is supposed that the evidence is certain, indubitable. In actually evaluating the credibility of hypotheses, however, we often appear to take into account not only evidence which is indubitable in itself, but also evidence which, though only probable, is both highly probable and highly relevant to the hypothesis in question. Thus to support the hypothesis that the sun will rise tomorrow, we would not begin by citing evidence to support the fact that our physics instructor was an honest and clear-headed man, but would cite (perhaps among other things) the law of gravity, the existence of the earth and sun as heavenly bodies obeying this law within close limits, etc.

The theories of Keynes and Carnap provide no means of short-circuiting this process by simply accepting, once and for all, things that are overwhelmingly probable. What this means in practise, if it should ever come to that, is that the evidence relevant to h will have to include all of the evidence which is relevant to anything which, if true, would be relevant to h; all of the evidence which is relevant to anything which is relevant to anything which is relevant to anything which is relevant to h, and so on. If, for example, we consider previously confirmed hypotheses which are similar to h, or which are in some other way related to h, to be relevant to h, then our catalogue of evidence relevant to h must include all of the evidence relevant to these other hypotheses.

Obviously this is impractical. What we want is some sort of procedure for coming to agreement with respect to the credibility of controversial hypotheses. For this purpose, what anyone would do is simply accept as part of the evidence relevant to h, those similar well-confirmed hypotheses. How well confirmed must these hypotheses be? It depends on the context of our inquiry. But this whole procedure is merely what is formalized in my distinction between the levels of rational corpora. Thus it is only the highest level rational corpus that corresponds to the evidence e in Carnap's expression, "$c(h, e)$". But most contexts do not require this high degree of rigor.

There are a number of other differences between my logical conception of probability and that of Carnap and those who have been working along the same lines. One difference is that I have been working in a very rich language from the start, while Carnap has so far only considered relatively simple languages. While Carnap's requirement of logical independence among the atomic sentences can be waived, it is difficult to see how the requirement of completeness can be waived or weakened in any theory that depends on logical ranges. Above all, the practical difficulties of constructing a formal language meeting these requirements which is adequate to the needs of any particular branch of science seem overwhelming. Against this, my system does not require either logical completeness or logical independence.

Finally, there is the matter of induction. Keynes, to justify induction, had to fall back on a principle of the limitation of natural variety. Carnap admits that in a universe containing a large number of individuals, the probability of any general statement is close to 0. But in my theory of probability, it turns out that general statistical statements can indeed be rendered probable; and in fact can be accepted into the rational corpora of any level but the highest on the basis of ordinary instantial evidence. It is also possible to show how a rather slight change in one of the earlier definitions will lead to the inclusion of universal generalizations—such as 'all crows are black'—on the basis of this same type of evidence.

CHAPTER FIFTEEN

Further Discussion

1. There is one type of oddity in my system which is not brought out by comparison with other systems. There are two subtypes of it and they are both best illustrated by examples.

Let A, B, and C, be rational classes, and let the following statements be ingredients of our rational corpora of basis F and level r_i.

"%(A,C,(.4;.5))"

"%(A ∩ B,C,(.4;.9))"

"%(B,C,(0.0;1.0))"

Let these be the strongest statistical statements about their respective subject-matters that we can include in our rational corpora of this level and basis, and let w be a definite description such that "$w \in A \cap B$" is the only non-logical statement about w in F. It will be seen easily that A prevents w from being a random member of the intersection of A and B, with respect to C, and also prevents w from being a random member of B with respect to C. Thus we have,

"w" r_i Ran$_F$ ("A";"C").

Consequently the probability that w belongs to C, on my interpretation, is (".4";".5"), and the degree of belief that it is rational to have in the statement expressing this state of affairs is determined accordingly. The oddity is that here we know that w belongs to the intersection of A and B, and that the proportion of C's in this intersection is not less than (and may well be more than) the proportion of C's in A. Intuitively we might feel that a higher degree of belief than that indicated by the theory in the statement '$w \in C$' would be rational. In other words, we might feel that when w is known to belong to both A and B, it is somewhat more likely that it will also belong to C than when it is known only to belong to A.

This intuitive feeling is not reflected in the theory of rational corpora of level r_i. But the oddity will not be inherited by lower levels of rational corpus, as is shown by the following considerations. In general, we are not certain that the proportions expressed in the statistical statements actually obtain; we accept the statistical statements because they are probable, not because we have observed that they are true. And in general, if the statement

"%(A,B,(0.4;0.5))" and the statement "((A ∩ B,C,(0.4;0.9))" are so probable as to be acceptable in the rational corpus of level r_i, there will be a couple of somewhat stronger statistical statements which are somewhat less probable, but still acceptable for a rational corpus of slightly lower level, or one which is slightly less demanding. Also, the wider interval will in general contract more than the narrower, so that the following two statements might be the strongest ones to be accepted in the rational corpus of level r_{i-1}:

"%(A,C,(.41;.49))"

"%(A ∩ B,C,(.45;.85))"

In this level of rational corpus, the two statements differ; since A ∩ B is known to be included in A, we have,

"w" r_{i-1}: Ran$_F$ ("A ∩ B","C")

In other words, in a less demanding sense of 'know', we do know that the proportion of C's in A differs from the proportion of C's in the intersection of A and B; and relative to our knowledge, in this less demanding sense, the probability is different.

The second subtype of this general form of oddity may be even more surprising. Suppose as before that A, B, and C, are rational classes, and that w is a definite description such that the only non-logical statement about w in F is "$w \in$ A ∩ B". Let the strongest statements in the rational corpora of level r_i and basis F about A and C, B and C, and A ∩ B and C, be:

"%(A,C,(.39;50))"

"%(B,C,(.40;.51))"

"%(A ∩ B,C,(0.1;0.9))"

Let our knowledge be such that A prevents w from being a random member of B with respect to C, and B prevents w from being a random member of A with respect to C. We then have:

"w" r_i Ran$_F$ ("A ∩ B","Ċ")

The corresponding probability that w belongs to C, relative to this rational corpus, is ("0.1";"0.9").

This again seems rather odd, since only a slight change in our knowledge about A and C or in our knowledge about B and C would lead to a much more closely determined degree of rational belief. But again, changing the context to a different level of rational corpus may enable us to avoid the oddity.

In more general terms, it should be noticed that these oddities only arise in connection with statistical statements that are only approximate; and while all statistical statements in any rational corpus (possibly with the exception of a few ball-in-bag statements) are only approximately known, the approximation is in general far more precise than that in the examples with which I have dealt. Furthermore, the requirements of rationality may for many practical purposes be met by approximately rational corpora, so that even though we may be entitled to accept "%(A,C,(.39;.50))" as a strongest statistical statement in the rational corpora of a given level, we may feel free to pretend that "%(A,C,(.4;5))" is a strongest statistical statement in this rational corpus.

2.   How serious a shortcoming is the fact that only finite classes can serve in my system as the reference classes for probability statements? First it should be noted that the classes with which we are concerned may be *practically* as large as we want them to be; for example, the class of particles which Eddington thinks makes up the universe is far smaller than a googoplex. And we need never get into a conflict over this matter, since we can never know in point of fact that a certain class is larger than a googoplex unless the class is one that we have defined ourselves; but then we may arbitrarily limit our considerations to the first googoplex of its members.

Continuous probability distributions, on the other hand, are very useful indeed; but this in itself is a sufficient reason for using them. It is easy to show that recourse to infinite classes and continuous distributions combines rational safety with the mathematical ease that leads us to them. They can be construed as idealizations which are approached as the classes with which we are dealing get bigger and bigger, though remaining smaller than a googoplex.

And this interpretation of continuous probability distributions even seems to be in accord with their practical use—they are as readily applied to patently finite, but large, classes as they are to classes with no specific limit or to classes which, like the class of all men ever to be born, are only wishfully infinite. Most people, for example, are willing to agree that the number of goldfish which have existed, which do exist, or which ever will exist, is finite. Thus a continuous probability distribution for the weight of goldfish is necessarily false, since there cannot be more weights than goldfish. A continuous distribution, however, is far more convenient than a discrete distribution, and even if it must be literally false, it leads to conclusions regarding intervals of weights which would match the conclusions of an acceptable discrete distribution so closely that there is no point in worrying about the difference; the difference is on the side of rational caution, anyway.

Another and more interesting example that comes readily to mind is that of the theory of measurement and error. We may explain a continuous error function in the same way in which we explained the continuous weight distribution for goldfish. Suppose we define a sequence of length-predicates in such a way that a given object may have any 'real number length'. Suppose also that we have a Euclidian right triangle, whose legs are (somehow) known to be exactly one foot long. Now we would like to be able to say that the limit of the average of the measurements of the hypoteneuse is $\sqrt{2}$ feet. But this can be the limit only if there are literally an infinite number of measurements.

The situation can be explained as follows: Suppose that the smallest length-divisions in which we are interested are tenths of a foot. Since the number of possible distinct measurements is now finite (we may suppose that the only admissible measurements are 1.0 feet, 1.1 feet, . . . 2.0 feet) we may employ a discrete error function. We may also arbitrarily limit the total (possible) number of measurements to a googoplex. Now we can calculate a number n, such that it is overwhelmingly probable (to be interpreted in terms of levels of rational corpora) that the average of a random n-fold sample of this googoplex of measurements is closer to the true length (i.e., 1.4) than to any other permissible length (e.g., 1.2, 1.3, 1.5).

We can go through an analogous process if we decide to work with subdivisions of one hundredth of a foot; and we can calculate a new number n' such that it is overwhelmingly probable that a random n'-fold sample of measurements is closer to the true length (now 1.41) than to any other length (e.g., 1.40 or 1.42). We can do this for any finite subdivision of a foot into smaller lengths; but the finer subdivisions lead to a larger n for the number of measurements required to yield the true length. But we may change our technique slightly so that we may, on the basis of a discrete error function defined for very small subdivisions of a foot, calculate the size of a sample of measurements required to make it overwhelmingly probable that the average of the sample of measurements will fall within an interval of given size about the true value.

But how small is 'very small'? We can skip this question by supposing that the number of lengths is the same as the number of real numbers, and by using a continuous error function. The results of this simplification in any practical context will merely be somewhat on the safe side of the results that we would obtain by using a true (or acceptable) discrete error function, defined for some small, finite, division of lengths. Again the net result is an enormous mathematical simplification, a gain in generality, and a gain in elegance, all combined with rational safety; in spite of the fact that the continuity-of-lengths hypothesis upon which it is based is patently false.

The relation of statements concerning infinite classes and continuous probability distributions to rational corpora is thus not simple. What happens is this: when we discover the (approximate) continuous distribution which 'corresponds' to the discrete distribution that actually obtains in the class with which we are concerned, we do not merely include it in our rational corpus of an appropriate level. Rather we include in our rational corpus a general *conditional* stating that for every useful and reasonable division of the varying quantity into intervals, the proportion of objects in the class falling into that interval is given by a function of the endpoints of the interval, where the function is determined by the *hypothetical* continuous distribution. The question of when and on what grounds we can include a conditional of this form in our rational corpus is a somewhat complex matter; but at least it is simpler than the question of how we can include a statement of a continuous distribution in our rational corpus without knowing that the class over which the distribution is defined is infinite.

3.   I have been supposing that a formal language adequate to the needs of science could be created by adding to Quine's ML a finite number of primitive predicates, together with axioms governing their logical relations. Perhaps I should say, axioms *reflecting* their logical relations. There are a number of questionable facets to this supposition, and although I have briefly defended some of them before, I would now like to pursue the matter a little further.

First, is it plausible to have a scientific language which contains no primitive names at all? Indeed it is, since, as Quine points out,[1] we can introduce all the names we want by abstraction after we accept the relevant predicates as primitive, or after we define them; and in fact this technique is superior to that of adopting primitive names at the outset, because of the control it gives us over existence statements. It does not, as H. Hochberg[2] points out, enable us to solve all ontological problems to everyone's satisfaction; but I do not see why it does not enable us to exclude ontological questions from the subject-matter of logic.

But this brings us to the second point; it has been assumed that only a finite number of primitive predicates are required, so that

1. Quine, *Mathematical Logic*, p. 149.
2. H. Hochberg, "On Pegasizing," *Philosophy and Phenomenological Research* 17, 1957.

the number of names that can be introduced by abstraction on the primitive predicates is necessarily also finite. Certainly the number of names that are in any sense primitive in a natural language is finite—to which any dictionary will attest—and to go to the other extreme, it is clear that a coordinate language needs only one primitive name (for the origin) and n (corresponding to the number of dimensions) primitive relations. Finally, if we bar numerical expressions such as those denoting lengths, temperatures, times, etc., no natural or scientific language employs more than a finite number of distinct expressions. Numbers, of course, will not bother us, since these are logically definable. But even these numerical expressions must be definable on the basis of a finite number of other expressions, or the poor student of science would never be able to understand its vocabulary. In an earlier chapter I suggested how one might go about setting up such sets of definitions; in general it could be done in much the same way as the definitions of natural numbers, ratios, and real numbers are formulated.

Third, it should be noticed (again) that the primitive predicates are not limited to the names of 'observable' properties. It seems to me absurd (and at any rate unnecessary) to attempt to reduce 'electric current' to a congeries of observable properties by means of a definition. But it is also clear that if we are to introduce 'electric current' as a primitive predicate, it must somehow be related to other predicates, and ultimately to predicates denoting observable properties. There are two types of connections concerned in any such analysis, logical connections and (for want of a better term) empirical connections. The distinction between them is simply that the logical connections are the ones that cannot be refuted by experience, while the empirical ones can; but it does not follow that any particular set of connections must be singled out as logical. To analyze the connections is a complex matter, and it seems reasonable to suppose that the resulting analysis is to some extent arbitrary.

This brings us to the fourth point. Since in my language the logical connections are represented by the axioms governing the primitive predicates, such an analysis is supposed to have already been performed. But since the axioms must be to some extent arbitrary, one is led to wonder what the difference is between one arbitrary set and another. In the first place, the arbitrariness is limited by ordinary usage: our special symbols must be related to ordinary language if they are to be comprehensible. It is further limited by semantic considerations: e.g., that no statement whose truth is (semantically speaking) observable, may be contradictory to any statement deducible from the axioms.

Roughly speaking, the difference between two acceptable but different sets of axioms governing the primitive predicates is the difference between two languages. But since the two languages are based on the same natural language, and designed to serve the same function, it will make no practical difference whether we select one set of axioms or another; if we define a bird as a feathered biped, it is a very highly confirmed and acceptable hypothesis that all creatures of such and such a structure are birds; if we define a bird as a creature having such and such a structure, it is a very will confirmed and rationally acceptable hypothesis that all birds are feathered bipeds. In ordinary usage we do not bother to decide which is the fact and which the definition; but if a creature appeared that had the physiological structure of a bird, but had scales in lieu of feathers, we would have to decide. In my hypothetical language I merely assume that such decisions have been made in advance.

Some decisions of this sort may be better than others, in the sense that they lead to simpler and more elegant statements of our knowledge. We cannot always know in advance which of a pair of proposed alternative axioms is going to be the best to accept. It may even be that, unknown to us, the axioms may lead to a contradiction; or that the axioms, in conjunction with an observation statement will lead to a contradiction. For that matter, it may be that Quine's axioms of membership lead to a contradiction. Suppose that in a rational corpus of the highest level and basis F we find two statements x and y, that are contradictory. If they are purely logical, then clearly we must alter the language by patching up the difficulty in the axioms of membership of ML. If they are purely logical in the weaker sense, being consequences of the axioms of the primitive predicates, it is these axioms we will patch up. And on rare occasions we will alter the axioms, not to save the system from inconsistency, but merely to save an old, familiar, and much loved generalization from refutation at the hands of an unexpected counter instance.

These changes in the axioms of the language constitute changes in the language—changes from one language to another. Well, why not? We feel free, always, to change from an inconsistent language to a consistent one; why should we not feel free to change from an inconvenient language to a convenient one? And this is precisely the nature of the change when we save an old generalization from a counter instance by changing the 'meaning' of an old term. But this is not at all to say that there is no difference between an axiom and a generalization. It is only to say that changing languages is a perfectly plausible gambit, though it does not, in itself, increase our body of knowledge an iota. And to say that we are free to change languages is not to say that we do not have to decide what language we are going to use.

As Hofstader says, "In science we want our language to be an efficient instrument of prediction and communication ... Language is efficient in this way if we know as clearly, precisely, determinately as possible, what to do with it in the linguistic circumstances relevant to science."[3] We can pick and choose among various formal languages, just as we can pick and choose among informal languages (English, French, Russian, etc.) but we cannot pretend to precision or clarity if we do not choose among them—that is, if we do not know what language we are speaking.

4. Another matter which may be considered questionable in my delineation of a language for science, is that the language is purely extensional. This extensionality has certain virtues and certain defects. The main virtue is that the only abstract entities which we need to suppose 'exist' (in Quine's logical sense) are classes. The rest of the panapoly of abstract entities can be ignored, with a resultant simplification in our language.[4] The degree of virtue which we attach to the rejection of all abstract entities but classes depends in part, however, on our attitude toward classes; it may be felt that in accepting the existence of classes we are already going too far.

The major difficulty in claiming that a purely extensional language is adequate to the needs of science, is that it is necessary to be able to show that statements (of science, not of logic, and in particular, not of semantics) which appear to involve 'meaning' or 'modality' or any form of referential opacity, are unnecessary in an object language suitable to the needs of scientific discourse, or can be paraphrased away. The difficulty in showing this is most severe in psychology; for psychology is surely admissible as a science, and many statements of psychology concern beliefs, meanings, and so on—what Russell and Quine have called 'propositional attitudes'.

In a psychological and educational study, we may encounter, (to use Quine's example) the statement:

(1)   Tom believes that Cicero denounced Cataline.

From (1) we clearly cannot infer,

(2)   Tom believes that Tully denounced Cataline.

3. A. Hofstadter, "The Myth of the Whole: A Consideration of Quine's View of Knowledge," *Journal of Philosophy* 51, 1954.

4. See Quine's papers "On What There Is," "Reference and Modality," "Logic and the Reification of Universals," etc., for an exposition of the difficulties involved in languages which admit entities beyond classes as values of bound variables.

And in fact from (1) we cannot even infer "Tom ought to believe that Tully denounced Cataline," unless we have grounds for supposing that Tom ought to believe that Cicero and Tully are the same.

The question which really concerns us is how we can know that (1) is true but that (2) is false—for if we cannot know this it is hard to see why we 'cannot infer' (2) from (1). The simplest way is to present Tom with a true-false test, in which the statement "Cicero denounced Cataline" and the statement "Tully denounced Cataline" both appear. If Tom marks the former true and the latter false, then, presumably, (1) is true and (2) is false. But a better way of expressing (1) and (2) under these circumstances, is,

(3)   Tom believes (marks as true) the statement (expression), "Cicero denounced Cataline."

(4)   Tom believes (marks as true) the statement (expression), "Tully denounced Cataline."

There is nothing at all peculiar about supposing that (3) is true and (4) false.

But while (3) and (4) correspond to the ordinary significance of (1) and (2), there are cases in which the correspondence breaks down. Suppose that Tom is a famous German classicist, whose command of English is limited to "Cicero denounced Cataline". For him, (1) and (2) would both be true, but while (3) would also be true, (4) might be false. But we can still use direct quotation; we can say that Tom believes (marks as true) a statement in German which describes the state of affairs described by the expression "Cicero denounced Cataline" in English. Since you and I know that Cicero is the same as Tully, we know that this state of affairs is the same as that described by the expression "Tully denounced Cataline" in English.[5]

The peculiarity that remains is that statements such as (3) and (4) are supposed to be statements in our psychological and scientific object language, yet they contain the names of other statements. Must we construe the psychological part of the object language as in turn being a metalanguage? This would cast new doubts on the possibility of keeping the object language extensional. Consider,

(5)   Tom accepts "Frrzzznk" as meaningful in English.

Statement (5) may perfectly well be true. The history of philosophy

5. Or, perhaps best of all, we could say: if Tom spoke English well, he *would* mark both statements as true. The argument here is similar to that which Alonzo Church has attacked ("On Carnap's Analysis of Statements of Assertion and Belief," *Analysis* 10, 1950), but the context is so much narrower here that I do not think his objections apply.

is full of analogous instances. Clearly our psychological object language is not a metalanguage in the ordinary sense, for in (5) we are not using the object language to talk about the expression "Frrzzznk" as a hypothetical part of the English language, but only in relation to Tom. And to point out that Tom is unconventional in his attitude toward "Frrzzznk", we surely do not have to say in our psychological object language, "Frrzzznk is not meaningful in English," but only,

(6)   No normal English speaking person accepts "Frrzzznk" as meaningful.

Again we need only express a relation between the expression in question and a person, or all persons of a certain class.

In short, then, when our *object* language is called upon to talk about meanings, propositional attitudes, and so on, it is in the context of an inquiry in which we are concerned with the linguistic habits of other people; and in such a situation we can often explicitly restrict our attention to the sounds and marks (as such) that they make.[6] A description of the marks and sounds is no more (and no less) metalinguistic than a description of the dances performed by bees to indicate where honey is. This form of metalanguage can be as extensional as we please. Our psychological object language is simply an extensional object language; it is not used for describing or discussing another language, *qua* language, but merely (among other things) for describing and discussing the marks and sounds to which the primary objects of our investigation (people) react in certain ways.

Finally, it must be observed that the above does not imply that a behavioristic psychology is the only logically permissible form of psychology on the assumption of a strictly extensional object language. It may perfectly well happen that in addition to considering the observable reactions of people to marks and sounds (among other things) we will find it fruitful and helpful to consider non-observable 'mental' reactions as well. Among these may be classified, for example, the apprehension of meanings, or the belief in matters of fact. But this no more requires a rejection of extensionality than the consideration of non-observable fields of forces in physics requires it.

5.   Although questions of meaning and of propositional attitudes can be transformed into questions of the relations between people and marks and sounds in the field of psychology, this does not imply that we need not be concerned with modality, meaning, and so on, in relation to our scientific object language. In order to use our

6. Or the sounds and marks they *would* make if they spoke our object language.

object language, we must know what the primitive predicates mean; and presumably the axioms of the primitive predicates will be true only by virtue of these meanings. But an ordinary translation of the primitive predicates into colloquial scientific English, while less elegant than a formal semantic interpretation of the object language (or object calculus), would allow us to *use* the formal language; and this would suffice for the application of the formal language as a framework in which to settle certain important types of logical dispute.

A more serious matter is that of modality. The analysis of counterfactual conditionals, which are alleged to be essential to the pursuit of scientific knowledge and to its expression, has lead directly to questions of modality, or law-likeness. The important modalities in this connection are necessity and possibility, since the important kinds of counterfactual in science have the form, "if such and such possibilities were realized, then such and such an outcome would necessarily follow." Such statements cannot occur within rational corpora, since we have accepted a purely extensional object language. If we can explain them at all, it must be in terms belonging to our metalanguage.

Let us first consider logical necessity and possibility. Logical necessity and possibility present insuperable problems for us in their ordinary sense; but we may substitute rational necessity and possibility for them in such a way that if ML and F are consistent, which we must at any rate suppose, rational necessity and possibility will function in roughly the same way that logical necessity and possibility function. Let us define $r_n RC_0$ as a rational corpus of level r_n based on an expression F containing no ingredients at all. To say that a statement x is rationally necessary, will be simply to say that it is a framed ingredient of some rational corpus of level r_n and basis 0. To say that x is rationally possible, is to say that nx is not rationally necessary. Of course if ML is inconsistent, everything will be rationally necessary, and nothing will be rationally possible.

Physical necessity and possibility are more complicated, in that they seem to admit of degrees. Ingredients of F, for example, will generally fall at the bottom of (or below) the scale of physical necessity, for we may easily replace the ingredients of the actual basis of our rational corpus without making serious changes in the more general ingredients of our rational corpora of lower levels.

Many counterfactuals can be handled by an alteration in the ingredients of the basis F of our rational corpus. We may often say that a counterfactual conditional is to count as true, when, if the actual basis of our rational corpus is altered from F to F* in the

simplest way sufficient to lead to the inclusion in the rational corpora of level r_i and basis F* of the antecedent of the conditional,
then the consequent of the conditional will also be an ingredient of
some rational corpus of this level and basis. Thus we may be able
to handle ordinary counterfactual conditionals by transforming them
into metalinguistic conditionals concerning hypothetical rational
corpora. These latter conditionals need not ever be counterfactual.

Consider the following two counterfactuals:

(1)   If the temperature had gone down to 0°F last night, the water
      in the wheelbarrow outside my window would have frozen.
(2)   If the temperature had gone down to 0°F last night, the water
      in the wheelbarrow outside my window would not have frozen.

Let the basis of my rational corpus be F, and let the context of the
discussion be the rational corpora of level r_i. Let t be a statement
in the supplemented version of ML corresponding to the statement
in English, "The temperature went to 0°F last night." Similarly,
let f be a statement in the supplemented version of ML corresponding to the statement in English, "The water in the wheelbar-
row froze." To test the two counter-factual conditionals (1) and (2),
we may construct an expression F*, such that t is an ingredient of
the rational corpus of level r_i based on F*, and which is otherwise
as like F as possible. Thus we must delete from F all (and only)
those statements which lead to the inclusion of nt in the rational
corpus of level r_i based on F. This means that not only the formal
analogues of statements such as "The thermometer read 65° last
night" must be deleted, but also the formal analogues of statements
such as "It rained all last night," and "Last night was the 14'th of
August," etc., since F contains ingredients which lead to the inclusion in the rational corpus of level r_i and basis F of such meteor-
ological statements as the analogues of, "If it rained all last night,
the temperature did not go down to 0°F," and "The temperature
never goes down to 0°F in August in Connecticut," etc. Now it is
easily seen that f, and not nf is an ingredient of some rational corpus of level r_i and basis F*. In some such fashion, I would suggest,
it would be possible to eliminate English counterfactual conditionals in favor of protosyntactical conditionals which can always be
tested simply by constructing the required hypothetical rational
corpus.[7]

6.   I shall wind up my informal discussion of what I have attempted

7. Those who have written on counterfactuals have come closer and closer to this form of
   analysis; see in particular, J. Cooley, "Goodman's 'Fact, Fiction, and Forecast,'"
   Journal of Philosophy 54, 1957; and R. Chisholm, "The Contrary-to-fact Conditional,"
   Mind 55, 1946.

to accomplish in the preceding chapters by a few still more general reflections. One of these, which is perhaps too obvious to mention, is that a rational corpus is not intended to represent everything that a person 'knows' or 'believes'. It is, as the adjective indicates, concerned only with *rational* matters. I may have a very strong hunch that the next card I draw from an ordinary 52 card pack, well shuffled, etc., will be the ace of spades. Regardless of how strongly I believe this, it is not the sort of thing which ordinarily *ought* to be included in my rational corpus. My belief in it is thus not rational, but irrational. It is not only impossible to show that the belief is rational (to rationalize it) but it is possible to show that some very different degree of belief would be rational.

On the other hand, we may also be concerned with non-rational beliefs, about which the logic of rational belief cannot have anything to say. Someone may well have a degree of belief p in the statement ''The next time Kyburg mails a letter, he will fail to put a stamp on it.'' And it may be that, relative to his rational corpus, this is a rational degree of belief. Now it is quite possible that I know of no relevant fact that can be formulated in my formal language—or in English—which will make the degree of belief in this statement which is rational, relative to my rational corpus, any different from p. And yet I may have a very different degree of belief in the statement concerned. It may be convenient to term my degree of belief non-rational on the grounds that while no precise basis for having this degree of belief can be given (i.e., it is not rationalizable), it is not the case that a different degree of belief, on my part, can be rationalized. Why? Because the obscure feelings and attitudes which lead me to assign a different degree of belief than p to the statement are in this case, as opposed to the former, quite relevant to the statement.

Even more important, and even more significant, is the fact that only statements of matters of fact can occur as ingredients of a rational corpus. Consideration of the Good and the Beautiful is put aside. This is not to say that we could not construct criteria for ethical corpora and aesthetic corpora; it is only to say that this is not what I have done. It is not even to say that ultimately the consideration of ethical corpora may not be of infinitely greater importance than the consideration of rational corpora. But since what we ought to do depends in large or small part on what we ought to know, the construction of criteria for rational corpora has priority.

This brings me to a point touched upon briefly in the recent discussions of personalistic theories of probability: the relation between what we know and what we do. The personalistic theory of probability, many forms of test criteria for statistical hypotheses,

and now game theory, have a tendency to ignore any question of belief divorced from overt action. I think it is fruitful to be able to
seperate matters of fact from matters of value, chiefly because it
is then possible to achieve agreement on matters of fact (i.e., on
what we ought to believe) without having also to agree on matters
of value (i.e., on what we ought to desire), which seem to be far
more open to honest dispute.

Matters of value, as well as matters of fact, are of course involved in behavior. But the term 'rational behavior', which is intended to take account of both of these factors, still seems rather
unfortunate. If behavior is called rational simply because it maximizes a gain or minimizes a loss of a certain kind, we are presup-
posing that gains and losses of that kind are respectively desired
and avoided, above all else. But a person with a different system
of values might consider the gains and losses from another point
of view, and for him another form of behavior, in precisely the
same situation, might be rational.

The rationality of a certain pattern of behavior depends (I think)
only on the rationality of the beliefs or degrees of belief, which, in
conjunction with a given set of values, determine that behavior. In
other words, to say that a person's behavior is rational is to say
no more than that his beliefs in matters of fact are rational; while
a person's beliefs may perfectly well be rational without ever having
come to the test of determining his behavior.

One difficulty which has often been felt to be the ruination of
logical theories of probability (among which mine must be counted)
is that a logical theory leads to the result that a certain statement
has a certain probability only for a certain person; i.e., for a logical theory, as for a personalistic theory, probability is 'subjective'
in the sense that two people faced with different amounts of evidence, may have to assign different probabilities to the same statement.

This sense of 'subjectivity' is not very distressing—what can be
more plausible than to suppose that, relative to different *evidence,*
the degree of belief we *ought* to have in a given statement is different? But Keynes' logical conception of probability was subjective in a more damaging sense as well: the probability relations
between given evidence and a given hypothesis were to be 'intuited'.
And there was no standard to which to refer in case two people
faced with the same evidence had intuitions which differed. In the
way in which I have defined probability, however, this situation cannot arise. Given the set of basic statements F, the probability of
any statement relative to the rational corpus of any level based on
F, is perfectly determinate.

The set of basic statements for one person may still differ from the set of statements basic to the rational corpus of another; the probability of the same statement may be different for each of them. But this does not mean that the two people cannot come to agreement concerning probabilities. If they disagree about the probability of some statement, their disagreement reflects either a difference of information between them, or faulty logic on the part of one or both of them. If they come to the conclusion that it is not faulty logic, but a difference of information (evidence), they will attempt to supplement each other's rational corpora until they come to some sort of agreement, i.e., until they share roughly the same relevant evidence. When they do share the same relevant information, the probability of the statement in question is the same for both of them. More cannot be expected of them in the name of rationality.

It is possible that they would not come to agreement if, e.g., one or both of them were determined to be irrational; it is also possible that one person might reject the information offered by the other—e.g., if the other were notoriously careless in his reading or experiments, or were a pathological liar.

In the context of most scientific fields of inquiry, there is little more than a time lag between the acquisition of some new piece of information, and the time when it becomes 'common knowledge' in the field. We could therefore consider the probability of statements relative not only to an individual's rational corpus of given level, but also relative to the rational corpus of that level representing the knowledge accumulated in a whole field of research. The basic statements in F would then come to consist mainly of experimental results, together, for the sake of common sense, with the typical F of an individual.

What is likely to be the effect of thus expanding the concept of a rational corpus—or rather construing it in such an extended fashion? It still answers to the same formal criteria as before. In many instances, with respect to statements which come under the domain of the field whose rational corpus we have constructed, there will be very little difference between the probability of the statement relative to the rational corpus of the whole field, and the probability of the statement relative to the rational corpus of a competent worker in the field.

The matter is still further simplified by the fact that, by and large, statistical information in one field of inquiry is irrelevant to randomness statements made in another field, and hence will not affect the probability of statements relevant to that other field. I suppose that the set of tosses made by me of a given coin is a random member of the set of all equinumerous sets of tosses with the given coin. It is highly doubtful that if I were more familiar with my biological characteristics I would be led to deny this. It is even more doubtful that I would be led to deny it by a fuller knowledge of the culture of precolumbian Indians. But this independence among fields does not always hold; it is conspicuously lacking, for example, in operations research.

I would like to make a few final remarks on the basis F of a rational corpus. I have not suggested any particular form or forms that the ingredients of F must have, but presumably we may demand that they be simply reports of experience; some philosophers would demand that they be simply phenomenological reports. But the epistemological priority of the phenomenalistic scheme seems to me to be an open question. I shall not take up the question here, beyond suggesting that in terms of the above theory of rational belief, there may be no particular *logical* priority at all. Whether we start with statements about the physical world (which seems much the most sensible thing to start with) or whether we start with statements about our sensations, we may end up with essentially the same rational corpora. If this is so, then those who share with me a prejudice in favor of bricks and tables as over against sensations, may feel free to include physical language statements in the basis of their rational corpora.

It is true that some of our observations about the physical world turn out to have been in error; so that there will be statements in F (if F includes physical language statements) that eventually have to be excised. Well, why not? If we should find it advisable to change our language in some way, then obviously there may be statements appearing in F which after the change, have to be rejected. And the same thing can happen with any but the most ardently phenomenalistic theory: "I just felt a burning sensation...Oh no, I was wrong, it was a piece of ice."

Still, the fact that physical language statements have to be rejected sometimes, even when they are of the sort to be included in F, does suggest that a generalization of the above conception of a rational corpus might be in order. Thus instead of simply having a single expression F serve as the basis for our rational corpus, we might have n expressions, F_1, F_2, $\ldots F_n$, the different expressions serving to differentiate the different degrees of confidence we feel in different sorts of observations. The definition of a rational corpus of a given level would then proceed on the basis that only ingredients of F_n can occur in rational corpora of level r_n; that only ingredients of F_{n-1} can occur in rational corpora of level r_{n-1}, etc. But the answer to this problem of 'rejected observations' must await a full-fledged epistemological study.

PART THREE: *Practise*

CHAPTER SIXTEEN

Analysis of Contexts I

1. The most difficult and most important test for a proposed explication to meet is that of providing a plausible analysis of the contexts in which the original expression (the explicandum) is used with a fair amount of confidence. Since any explication of probability is bound to be highly controversial, and since this is especially true when a logical explicatum is offered and applied to the 'empirical' contexts of Appendix II (1)—(6), I shall devote a perhaps excessive (in view of the results of Chapter Eleven) amount of attention to examining these contexts. The other contexts, although they more or less clearly require a logical explicatum, will also be examined in some detail, since the way in which a logical explicatum is to function in such contexts is also rather controversial.

The object of all this analysis is to show that the theory of probability which I have offered, in spite of its radical aspects, does not have any particularly radical consequences among the contexts in which probability is used. It will further be shown that the theory expresses formally what we intuitively feel, even in the vague contexts in which we refer to the probability of historical statements and the like.

The one really arbitrary element in my definition of probability—that is, the element which it would be hard to pinpoint in an actual discussion about a probability statement—is the level of the rational corpus relative to which the probability is assigned. Presumably this is fixed by the context, and may vary from context to context. If in a given context we are disposed to be very cautious about our assertions, we will employ rational corpora of level r_{n-1}; if we are disposed to be as cautious as it is possible to be, from a philosophical point of view, we will employ only the rational corpora of level r_n; in the ordinary round of living, we will often be content with rational corpora of level r_1. In short, the level of the rational corpora with which we are concerned in discussing a given probability statement is determined by the context; and in the final analysis, is a matter of agreement among the discussants. In the following examples I shall refer ambiguously to the level of rational corpus concerned as level r_i.

2. In this section I shall discuss the application of my theory to

the empirical contexts (1) through (3) of Appendix II. The major difficulty in the interpretation of such contexts is that of finding the intended basis of the rational corpus. In every case, an interpretation can be given involving an ideal rational basis, as suggested in Chapter Eleven; such a basis will only help to reproduce the intention of these contexts if we add the proviso that the ingredients of the ideal basis are all true; but then we must also add the proviso that the person who is making the probability statement have grounds for supposing that the corresponding statistical statement is in fact true. The rational corpus relative to which these so-called empirical probability statements are made, must therefore generally be construed as belonging to a person (or representing the body of acceptable knowledge in a field of inquiry), and as including a statistical statement corresponding to the probability assertion.

(1)   The probability of getting a head in a toss of this coin is 1/2.

This is one of the contexts in which a frequency theory of probability seems most plausible. The frequency theorist's assertion that if we knew that the relative frequency was different from 1/2, we would not make statement (1) is well founded. On my view, contrary to the usual logical view, the frequency theorist's converse assertion that if we did not know that the relative frequency was 1/2, we would not make statement (1) is also well founded. In fact, (1) may be paraphrased in terms of the theory of rational belief as follows:

(1) a For every x, if x is a description of a member of the class of tosses of this coin, and if C is a name of this class, and H a name of the class of tosses of coins resulting in heads, then if x is a random member of C with respect to H, the probability of x e H is ("1/2";"1/2"); Or, $x \, r_i \text{Ran}_F$ (C,H) $\supset$ x e H $r_i \text{Prob}_F$ ("1/2";"1/2").

The relation between (1) a and the frequency interpretation of probability is given by the following theorem in the logic of rational belief:

(1400) $(x) \, (x \, r_i \text{Ran}_F \, (C,H) \supset x$ e H $r_i \text{Prob}_F$ ("1/2";"1/2")) $\equiv$ pct $(C,H,("1/2";"1/2")) \, r_i S^* A_F \, (C,H)$

Thus the circumstances under which a person might be able to assert (1) are essentially the same for the frequency theorist as for me, the major difference being that I give an explanation for the word 'know' in the condition that you can only assert (1) when you know that the relative frequency is 1/2.

There are still differences, of course. On my view, (1) is logically true, if true at all; while on the frequency view (1) merely reproduces the statistical assertion on which it is based, and hence is an empirical assertion about the world. On the frequency interpretation (1) is true if and only if the world has a certain character, while on my view, (1) is true if and only if we have reason to believe that the world has this character. But there is no point at issue concerning the statistical statement upon which (1) is based, on either view. For the frequency theorist, (1) is essentially an unnecessary form of locution; we can always replace it by a statistical statement. Therefore I do not see where I am depriving the frequency theorist of anything relevant to his theory by pre-empting the term probability to mean something else.

It is certainly never necessary to interpret (1) as merely another form of statistical statement; and there are even some (perhaps not earth shaking) arguments against the sufficiency of interpreting (1) in this way. The most obvious is that we cannot interpret a probability statement concerning a singular statement (e.g., 'the probability of getting heads on the next toss of this coin is 1/2') in the same way, so that we must (unnecessarily) have two explications of the term 'probability' in lieu of one. Another hinges on the grammatical difference between (1) and the statistical interpretation that is often offered for it. Statement (1) makes use of the indefinite article 'a'; the statistical interpretation replaces this by 'all' in some such form as, "The proportion of all tosses of this coin which result in heads is 1/2." Presumably the transition from 'a' toss to 'all tosses' in this interpretation is analogous to the transition from 'a man' to 'all men' in interpreting "A man is a featherless biped," as "All men are featherless bipeds." But the last statement holds distributively, while the proposed interpretation of (1) must be understood as referring only collectively to the class of all tosses. It may be plausible to interpret a statement about 'a' member of a class as a statement about 'each' member of the class (this is what I have done in (1) a), but it does not seem plausible to interpret such a statement as a statement about the class itself, when the latter statement does not hold distributively.

In short, we generally suppose, what is indicated on my theory, that if (1) is asserted by a rational person, this person has good reason to believe the corresponding statistical assertion; i.e., that the statistical assertion which serves as the basis for (1) is included in his rational corpus, and that if we knew exactly what he knew, or if we were willing to take his word for what he knew, we would have good reason to include the statistical assertion in our rational corpus too.

But how about other contexts of (1): e.g., when someone says "I do not know whether (1) is true or not," or, "Suppose that (1) were true," or, "(1) is indicated by the evidence." What seems to be involved in all these cases is not (1) itself, but the statistical statement on which it is based. (But we may always retain the form of (1) by relating the probability to a hypothetical rational corpus, as I did in Chapter Eleven.) "I do not know what the probability is that this coin will fall heads," would then mean simply, "I do not have in my rational corpus any statistical statement about the behavior of this coin which is strong enough to bother about." "Suppose that (1) were true," would mean, "Suppose that the statistical statement on which (1) is based were true." "(1) is indicated by the evidence," would mean "The evidence-statements on which my rational corpus is based are such as to require the inclusion in the rational corpora of level r_i of the statistical statement on which (1) is based."

The question, "How do you know (1)?" on the frequency interpretation, would be answerable only by citing the evidence which supports the statistical assertion involved. On my interpretation, such a question would be construed in the same way, except that it is possible in addition to point out the protosyntactical relation between the evidence statements and the statistical statement which makes it rationally obligatory that if you accept the evidence statements you must also accept the statistical statement in question.

(2)   The probability that a human birth is the birth of a male is 0.51.

The analysis of this statement is analogous to that of the preceding one, although there is less chance that anyone would try to derive the value of this probability from *a priori* considerations. We mean, when we assert (2), that if anything is a random member of the class of human births with respect to being the birth of a male, relative to our rational corpus, then the probability that this birth is the birth of a male, relative to our rational corpus, is approximately (".51";".51"). And this holds only if we can accept the corresponding statistical statement.

As in the first example, the probability statement, on my interpretation, has no factual content at all; that is, it does not mention any facts, but only statements. The statements in turn mention facts, and one of the statements mentioned (implicitly) in the probability statement as belonging to my rational corpus, is a statement corresponding to the English statement: "About 51% of human births are the births of males." Furthermore, to say that this statement appears in my rational corpus, is to say that it is 'acceptable' relative to the evidence I have, in the sense made precise by the logic of rational belief. Thus when a person asserts (2), it is generally because he wishes to inform us that the required factual statement is included in his rational corpus, i.e., that it is 'highly probable' relative to the evidence that he has, and hence (generally) it jolly well ought to be included in our rational corpora too. We can either take his word for it, as evidence, or we can go out and collect statistical evidence for it on our own part.

With regard to this statement, even more than with regard to (1), we might hear someone say that they do not know the probability involved. Again, this is to be interpreted as meaning that they don't have in their rational corpora statistical statements on the subject which are strong enough to bother about. They may say this even if they know that the proportion in question (as who would not?) lies between .3 and .7, or even if they know that it lies between .4 and .6. But the explanation of the claim not to know the probability is the same as before: a statistical statement of the precision of those which they do know is hardly worth bothering about when they know that there are other people who know far more precise statistical statements about the same subject matter. If the matter were to become of interest to them, they would no doubt take the trouble to look up the evidence that has been collected and to find the strongest statistical statement which is justified (in appropriate rational sense) by this evidence.

(3)   The probability of an alpha particle striking the area A of the target, in this experiment, is 0.3476.

The statement will be interpreted in a way analogous to that in which the two above statements have been treated. The difference is that here the statistical statement on which the probability statement is based may be part of a physical theory. From the 'boundary' conditions of the experiment, together with a general physical theory, it may be possible to deduce the long run relative frequency with which alpha particles will strike the area A. The physicist, challenged on an assertion such as (3), will show that the relevant statistical statement *follows from* the conditions supposed to hold for the experiment, together with a general theory for which there is 'ample evidence'. The conditions too, will in general be believed to hold only on the grounds of other evidence.

There is also a difference between the way (1) and (3) function. Barring sporting graduate students in physics, no one is going to be very concerned about whether or not a single alpha particle hits the area A. We are not in general concerned with some definite alpha particle which is a random member of the class of those concerned in the experiment. Usually we are practically interested in the performance of some large number of alpha particles: n. I showed in Chapter Eleven how a statement of the form (3) can lead to a statement about the probability that an n-fold sample of alpha particles has the property that (say) between .3 and .4 of them will hit the target A. But this statement in turn must be interpreted as being about an n-fold sample—that is, about any n-fold sample which is random with respect to the property in question.

Now in the first place, it is quite consonant with (3) that we should never have occasion to find a given n-fold sample which is random in the required sense: e.g., the proportion may depend on a number of factors which, while they cancel each other out to produce (3), are nevertheless well within our control when we have to do with n-fold samples. This is to say that there may be some general statement in our rational corpus which prevents the use of the consequence drawn from (3) in any practical situation. For example, it might be that alpha particles run in schools, so that of any n-fold sample fired in a single experiment, the proportion that hit the area A of the target would be close to 0 or close to 1. The deduction from (3) would be quite all right; but it would not be relevant because of the knowledge we have that any n-fold sample we will consider will have been a sample of alpha particles shot in the same experiment.

It is an interesting fact that no such statement as that about the schoolishness of alpha particles is known, and it is this fact that makes statements like (3) useful. It is a fact about the world that no physicist knows about this schoolishness; it is a purely logical fact that no rational corpus based on a set of ingredients such as might appear as the basis of a contemporary physicist's rational corpus, will include as a framed ingredient a statement asserting the schoolishness of alpha particles. It is also worth noting that this fact about physicists and this logical fact about their rational corpora, need not reflect a physical fact: it may perfectly well be that alpha particles do interact; it is highly improbable, that's all. But even if it were not improbable, we might still be interested in (3); it suffices for (3) to be useful and interesting that there should be some actual groups of alpha particles which are random in the required sense.

3.   The probability statements (4)—(6) of Appendix II require a more detailed analysis in terms of use, than did the probability statements (1)—(3). I shall begin with (5), since that is the most straightforward.

(5)   The probability of 10 heads occurring in 10 tosses of this coin is $(1/2)^{10}$.

This statement is derivable from statement (1); if (1) holds, then there is a statistical statement saying that half the tosses of the coin result in heads, which is included in the rational corpus of the level and basis determined by the context. But if this statement is an ingredient of a rational corpus, then the statistical statement corresponding to (5) is an ingredient of the same rational corpus. From this, together with an analogue of theorem (1400), we arrive at (5) itself.

But let us go through the process in somewhat greater detail. Let C be the class of all tosses of this coin, and H the class of tosses resulting in heads. If (1) is true, the statement "$\%(C,H,(1/2;1/2))$" will be a strongest statement about C and H in my rational corpora of level r_i. The following statement is a theorem in the class-ratio calculus:

$$\text{``}\%(C,H,(1/2;1/2)) \cdot C \,\epsilon\, 10^{100} \cdot \supset \%(\hat{x}\,(x \subset C \cdot x\,\epsilon\,10),$$

$$\hat{x}\,(x \subset H \cdot x\,\epsilon\,10),\,(1/2^{10};\,1/2^{10}))\text{''}$$

Actually, the consequent of the theorem will state that the proportion in question is slightly (very slightly) less than $1/2^{10}$. But we will not in general have "$C\,\epsilon\,10^{100}$" in our rational corpus anyway. We will not know how many members C has; but we may suppose it to have a great many, and generally we will be dealing with larger classes of tosses than those made with a particular coin. At any rate, we shall suppose that the consequent of this statement will be included in our rational corpus, and this means that the following statement holds:

(5)a $x\;r_i\,\text{Ran}_F(\text{``}C_{10}\text{''},\text{``}H_{10}\text{''}) \supset x\;e\;\text{``}H_{10}\text{''}\;r_i\,\text{Prob}_F(\text{``}1/2\text{''};\text{``}1/2\text{''})$

where "C_{10}" is an abbreviation of "$\hat{x}(x \subset C . x\,\epsilon\,10)$" and "$H_{10}$" is an abbreviation of "$\hat{x}(x \subset H . x\,\epsilon\,10)$".

It should be noted that (5)a says nothing about the 'independence' of the elements that go to make up C. Whether any assertion of randomness corresponding to the antecedent of (5)a can ever be made is another matter entirely. It is not implausible to suppose that we have information about certain subclasses of the class of all 10-fold subclasses of C which will prevent most of the things with which we would naturally be concerned from being random in the required sense, while at the same time, our knowledge about these subclasses would not prevent a given toss, in general, from being a random member of C with respect to H. For example we might discover empirically that among ten-fold sets of tosses which are performed consecutively, sequences of all heads or all tails occur with undue frequency. Let CT_{10} be the class of ten-fold sets of consecutive tosses. CT_{10} is obviously known to be a subclass of C_{10}.

In general (but not always) we will be concerned with sets of consecutive tosses, rather than sets of non-consecutive tosses. If we know that the proportion of ten-fold sets of consecutive tosses resulting in heads among the members of CT_{10} differs from the corresponding proportion among the members of C_{10}, we will naturally not be as interested in $(5)\,a$ (though it will remain true), as we are in $(5)\,b$, below:

$(5)\,b$ $x\ r_i \operatorname{Ran}_F(\text{``}CT_{10}\text{''},\text{``}H_{10}\text{''}) \supset x\ e\ \text{``}H_{10}\text{''}\ r_i \operatorname{Prob}_F(p;q)$

where p and q are fractions representing our knowledge about CT_{10} and H_{10}.

(4)   The probability of an American male, of the professional class who is alive and 35 years old in 1954 being alive in 1955, is p.

(6)   The probability that 10 of the 50 men of age 35 and of the professional class who take out insurance with us in 1954 will die before 1955, is r.

The analysis of (4) is the same as that of the statements considered above: it is true (logically true) relative to any rational corpus which contains the statistical statement on which it is based. But as business men or stockholders we are really interested in (6). While we will recognize the truth of (4), or the credibility of the corresponding statistical statement (provided we have suitable evidence in our rational corpus about the class in question), there are additional requirements which our rational corpus must meet if (6) is to be true (and logically true) as well.

Let M be the class of American males of the professional class, who are alive and 35 years old in 1954. Let D be the class of things that die before 1955. If (4) holds, relative to our rational corpus, then our rational corpus contains the statistical statement, "$\%(M,D,(p;p))$"—or, more accurately, a statistical statement like "$\%(M,D,(p-d;p+d))$", where d is some small ratio.

Let M_{50} be the class of all 50-fold sub-classes of M, and D_{10} be the class of all classes containing 10 things that die before 1955. Let q be a ratio such that,

Thm "$\%(M,D,(p;p))$. M ϵ N . $\supset \%(M_{50},D_{10}(q;q))$"

where N is the total number of American males, of age 35, and of the professional class, who are alive in 1954. Our rational corpus will thus contain the latter statistical statement as well as the former.

Note that the inclusion of "$\%(M_{50},D_{10},(q;q))$" in our rational corpus is not sufficient to establish (6). What it does establish is (6'):

(6′)   The probability that 10 men of a group of 50, of age 35 and of the professional class, who are alive in 1954, will die before 1955, is q.

But this is not the same as (6), even if $q = r$. Statement (6) is not about just any group of 50 men, but about a particular group of men—namely the fifty who take out insurance with us in 1954. (6′) can be paraphrased as a conditional, after the fashion of (5), (6) cannot. Let us denote the 50-fold class of men with whom we are concerned by M^*. M^* is a member of M_{50}, and it is either a member of D_{10} or it is not: we don't know which. Statement (6) says that, relative to our rational corpus, the probability that M^* is a member of D_{10} is r. That is to say,

(6)a "$M^* \in D_{10}$"r_i Prob$_F$("r";"r")

which in turn is to say,

(6)b $(\exists x)(\exists y)(\exists z)(x \, e \, z \, r_i B_F$ "$M^* \in D_{10}$" . $x \, r_i \text{Ran}_F(y,z)$. pct$(y,z,($"r";"r"$))r_i S^* A_F(y,z))$

Now we can ask about the circumstances under which M^*, M_{50}, and D_{10}, will fulfil the requirements of (6)b. Clearly, the only requirement that must be met for M^*, M_{50}, and D_{10} to fulfil the requirements of (6), is that there be no class K^* such that,

"K^*"r_i DP$_F$("M^*","M_{50}","D_{10}").

This requirement may be met, but then again it may not be. For example let MI be the subclass of M which is composed of only those men who take out insurance. Now it is quite possible that we should have special information about this subclass. That is, it is quite possible that some statement, "%(MI,D,($s;s$))" should be an ingredient of our rational corpus, where s is a ratio differing from p. It might be greater than p if, as a matter of fact, we knew that people had a tendency to take out insurance when they felt the imminence of death; it might be less than p if only cautious people took out insurance, and if cautious people were less likely to be killed than incautious people.

If we know a strongest statistical statement about MI and D which differs from a strongest statement about M and D, then we also know a strongest statement about M_{50} and D_{10} which differs from that about M_{50} and D_{10}, where MI$_{50}$ is the class of 50-fold subclasses of MI. Since we also know that M^* is a member of MI$_{50}$, and that MI$_{50}$ is included in M_{50}, we have,

"MI$_{50}$" r_i DP$_F$("M^*","M_{50}","D_{10}")

(unless there is a proper sub-class of MI$_{50}$ in which the proportion of objects belonging to D_{10} is the same as that in M_{50} as a whole ... but then we might as well have dealt with this subclass from the start, and saved ourselves all this bother about MI_{50}.)

If M* is a random member of MI_{50}, relative to what we know, with respect to D_{10}, then the r in (6) will indeed be different from q. The relation between (4) and (6) is thus somewhat more complicated than is generally supposed. Neyman, and no doubt other statisticians, would explain that the 'reference class' called for in (4) is different from the reference class called for in (6); but the difficulty with this view is that in the first place, (6) does not 'call' for a reference class at all, in the way that (6') does; and in the second place, no general standard has been proposed hitherto for selecting the 'correct' reference class, or for adjudicating between conflicting claims as to the 'correct' reference class.

An insurance company will know a great deal about its policy holders—enough, actually, to render them distinguishable individuals in its records. (I never heard of an insurance company which couldn't tell which of its policy holders had died.) It also has, in its collective rational corpus, a huge number of statistical statements about the mortality rates in various classes. It knows, for example, that the mortality rate for 1954-1955 in the unit class of policy holder John Doe is (0;1). But this does not represent the probability, for the insurance company, that John Doe will die in the period in question, because there are many other classes to which the insurance company knows that John Doe belongs, about which they have much stronger information. In the same way, M* belongs to the unit class of M*, in which the proportion of objects belonging to D_{10} is known to be (0;1); but it also belongs to a number of other classes about which more is known. In general, it will be one of these of which M* will be a random member with respect to D_{10}, relative to the rational corpus of the insurance company.

(7)   The probability that the next 10 tosses of this coin will all yield heads is $1/2^{10}$.

(8)   The probability that the next toss of this coin will yield heads is $1/2$.

Let us examine (8) first. Let N be the next toss. (8) then states that relative to our rational corpus, N is a random member of some class, with respect to membership in the class of tosses resulting in heads, H. (This is true in general, but not universally—it may be that "N ϵ H" is connected by a biconditional chain to some other statement $p \epsilon q$, such that p is a random member of r with respect to q.) Furthermore, (8) states that the proportion of objects belonging to H in this class is rationally believed to be $1/2$.

It should be noticed that in general, (1) and (8) are independent. It is perfectly possible that while the class of all tosses of this coin contains only 40% heads, there is a special subclass, to which N belongs, which contains 50% heads. Under these circumstances, (1) would be false, and (8) true. As the preceding discussion should have amply indicated, (8) does not follow from (1).

The relation between (5) and (7) is analogous to that between (1) and (8). Let N* be the next ten tosses. If (5) is true, and if N* is a random member of C_{10} with respect to membership in H_{10}, then (7) will also hold. But this is all we can say.

Consider the following two statements:

(a) $"N" r_i \text{Ran}_F ("C"; "H")$
(b) $"N*" r_i \text{Ran}_F ("C_{10}"; "H_{10}")$

Even these are quite independent of each other. In view of the current theories concerning randomization, this is an important fact to note indeed. Suppose that (1) and (5) are both true. It is obvious that (a) may be true, and (b) may be false, if we know that the classes of consecutive tosses (CT_{10}) have a higher frequency of 'all heads' than 10-fold classes of tosses in general. (It would follow from this and (1) that the frequency of 'all tails' would be higher too.) (b) would be false, because we would know that N* was a member of CT_{10}, and that the frequency of H_{10} in this class is higher than the frequency of H_{10} in C_{10}, and that C_{10} is not included in CT_{10}. On the other hand, if we know nothing about the tosses immediately preceding N, (a) would remain valid.

On the other hand, if we knew that the first toss of a series more often resulted in heads than later tosses in the series, (a) could be false while (b) was true.

There are any number of possible states of knowledge relative to which neither (a) nor (b) would hold. If we were perfectly clairvoyant, of course, neither would ever hold. If we were partially clairvoyant—e.g., if it were a well confirmed hypothesis that we were right in predicting the behavior of coin tosses nine times out of ten—then knowledge of our prediction would be sufficient to cause the rejection of (a) and (b). Or the tosses might be performed by a person with known psycho-kinetic powers and a peculiar predilection for heads: if we knew all this, then (rationally!) we would have to reject both (a) and (b). And so on.

Again we see that the passage from a general probability statement like (1) to a definite probability statement like (8) is fraught with peril. But this is not to say that the transition must be made on an intuitive basis; the whole purpose of the logic of rational belief is to provide a *formal* basis for this transition which has hitherto been made intuitively.

CHAPTER SEVENTEEN

Analysis of Contexts II

1. Now we come to a somewhat more interesting group of contexts; those which are often encountered in the justification of what an old-fashioned philosopher like myself would call inductive arguments.

(9) Given an n-fold random sample of P's, m of which are Q's, the probability is t that between $m/n - d$ and $m/n + d$ of all the P's are Q's.

(10) Relative to the information that m P's out of n are also Q's, the probability is v that the next P to be examined is also a Q.

These statements are the kind of statements which are often encountered in the context of statistical inference. The analysis to be given here will be mainly concerned with removing the ambiguities in these statements as they stand, and in relating the statements to crude types of inductive inference. I say crude, because in most inquiries we have far more information than has been expressed by 'given' and 'relative' above, and, as is only rational, we do not hesitate to use it.

Let us begin with the ambiguities involved in (9). It might be paraphrased, "For all x, if x is a random n-fold sample of P's with respect to the property of being representative (in the sense that the proportion in the sample lies within an interval d about the true proportion, or what is the same thing, in the sense that the true proportion lies in an interval d about the sample proportion), then the probability is t that this sample is representative." Now if our rational corpus contains a statement S asserting that a certain proportion of the P's are Q's, then, in the manner discussed in connection with (5), (9) holds for appropriate values of t and d, given a value for n. On this interpretation, (9) is about 'an' indefinite n-fold sample, and not about any particular one.

But, as everybody knows, the proportion of representative samples only depends somewhat on the proportion of P's which are Q's; so that even if we have no knowledge concerning this proportion at all, we can still be sure that the proportion of n-fold samples which are representative in the sense required lies between $t_{1/2}$ and 1, where $t_{1/2}$ represents the proportion of n-fold samples which are representative, on the hypothesis that the proportion of P's which are Q's is $1/2$.

From the fact that the statistical statement just described ought, even in the absence of any information at all concerning the proportion of Q's among P's, to be included in our rational corpus, it is clear that in the absence of any more interesting statement about the proportion of representative samples, the following probability statement is valid:

(9)a. The probability that an n-fold subclass of P's will be representative (within the specified limits) is ($"t_{1/2}"; "_s 1"$)

provided only that we do not know that the number of P's is less than n. It is valid, though it means no more than that in the absence of any knowledge concerning the proportion of Q's among P's, we have *reason to suppose* that a certain statistical statement is true— that is, that we must include it in some rational corpus. In fact, this particular statement will generally be included in our highest level rational corpus, regardless of what we know (in a weaker sense) about the proportion of P's which are Q's.

But (9)a does not always reproduce the intent of (9); it says something about *all* random samples, not about some particular sample, some *given* sample, in which m of the n P's are also Q's. Let N be an n-fold sample of P's, and let m be the number of members of the intersection of N and Q. Now let all this be known in some rational corpus of level r_i and basis F, and, furthermore, let N be a random member of the class of all n-fold subclasses of P, with respect to the rationally representative property suitable to the case. Since we presumably have no knowledge concerning the proportion of P's that are Q's, N will be rationally representative only if the proportion of Q's in N falls within a symmetrical interval of width $2d$ about the true proportion of Q's in P. Finally, let the strongest statistical statement in the rational corpora of level r_i and basis F about P and Q be that upon which (9)a is based.

From all this it follows that with respect to this rational corpus the probability that N is actually rationally representative is ($"t_{1/2}"; "_s 1"$). Since to. say that N, consisting of m members of Q and $n-m$ members of P, has this property, is to say that the proportion of Q's among the whole class of P's lies within a distance d of m/n. Thus the probability of "%(P,Q,($m/n - d; m/n + d$))" is precisely ($t_{1/2}"; "_s 1"$) relative to this rational corpus.

The same considerations, restrictions, and complications are involved in saying that N is a random member of the class of all n-fold samples of P with respect to being rationally representative, as are involved in any other assertion of randomness. In particular, randomness of N in the sense required is quite independent of the randomness of any particular member of N with respect to the property of belonging to Q.

Statement (10) is somewhat more ambiguous than statement (9). The information that *"m* P's out of *n* are also Q's," may be considered a general statistical statement about the P's which has been confirmed to the degree necessary for inclusion in the rational corpus serving as context for the statement. If this is the sense of (10), then the analysis of (10) will correspond precisely to the analysis of (8).

A more common meaning of (10) is that we have examined *n* P's, found *m* of them to be Q's, and, on the basis of this information, want the probability that the *n* + 1'st P will also turn out to be Q. Such statements are often called upon in discussions of induction, and in systems such as Carnap's, they bear the brunt of almost all inductive argument, since general statistical statements cannot (in this system) become highly confirmed in the sense of c*.

One approach to the analysis of (10), intended in this latter sense, suggests itself immediately. The approach is this: we know, given the information mentioned in (10), that the proportion of the first $(n + 1)$ P's which are also Q's, lies between $m/(n + 1)$ and $(m + 1)/(n + 1)$. If, then, the $n + 1$'st P is a random member of this class, with respect to Q, then the probability that it will belong to Q is $("m/(n + 1)";"(m + 1)/(n + 1)")$. I suspect that this does not lead to the classical difficulties, because in the first place, these difficulties depend upon axioms of the calculus of probability which do not hold in my system; and in the second place, because this probability has the very plausible value $("_s0";"_s1")$ for $n = 0$.

Nevertheless, I am slightly suspicious of this approach. My suspicions center around the question of whether "the first $n + 1$ P's" is a rational class whenever (a) P is a rational class, and (b) we have in our rational corpus knowledge concerning whether or not each of the first *n* P's were or were not Q's. If "the first $n + 1$ P's" is not a rational class in this situation, then no object can be a random member of it with respect to membership in Q, and the above suggestion does us no good.

But we may always take the analysis of (10) through a stage corresponding to (9). Suppose, for example, that (9) holds for the rational corpora of level r_n and basis F. Suppose also that the ratio $t_{1/2}$ is greater than the ratio denoted by the fraction r_{n-1}. This means that the statistical statement, $"\%(P,Q,(m/n - d; m/n + d))"$ will be included in some rational corpus of level r_{n-1} based on F. Now if the next P happens to be a random member of the class of all P's, with respect to Q, relative to this rational corpus, then the probability that the next P will be a Q is clearly $("m/n - d";"m/n + d")$, relative to this rational corpus.

2. The next two probability statements are more general, and do not admit of such precise analyses. Nevertheless, even though a precise analysis cannot be given, an analysis in terms of the logic of rational belief may do much to clarify them, and to clarify statements of a more controversial nature which are like them.

(11) Relative to the evidence accumulated by biological and zoological studies, the probability is p that all mammals have hearts.

There are two ways in which this statement can be interpreted. In the first place, it is possible to take the 'evidence' of biology and zoology to include certain theories which are highly confirmed; relative to this evidence, the probability in question (p) may very well be unity. This approach will be considered later, in connection with statement (12).

We may also consider another and more direct interpretation of (11) which might, for example, have applied to Aristotle's rational corpus. Forgetting about theories, we may take the 'evidence' accumulated by biology and zoology to be simply statistical evidence concerning the proportion of mammals studied who have hearts. A great number of mammals have been studied in these areas of inquiry, and they have all been found to have hearts; none have been found to lack hearts. The question is, "How do we get from the knowledge that all examined mammals have hearts to the probability statement in question?"

It is clear that this cannot be simply a relatively special case of the situation outlined in the discussion of statement (9). Statement (9) only asserts that it is highly probable that a certain relative frequency falls within a certain interval. Here we are saying that it is highly probable that the relative frequency is precisely 1.0. Nevertheless, let us begin with an analogue of (9). We know what it means to say that the probability that between (say) 99.9% and 100% of mammals have hearts is $(``p_1"; ``p_2")$, relative to the rational corpora of basis F and level r_i. In general p_2 will be $_s1$, and since the 'evidence of biology and zoology' comprises a great many mammals, p_1 will also be large.

Suppose that p_1 is greater than the fraction denoted by r_{i-1}, so that the analogue of the statement that between 99.9% and 100% of mammals have hearts is to be included in the rational corpus of basis F and level r_{i-1}. Now suppose further that the number denoted by r_{i-2} is less than .999. This means that for all x, if x is is a random member of the class of mammals, with respect to heartiness, relative to the rational corpora of level r_{i-1}, then "x has a heart" is to be included in a rational corpus of level r_{i-2}.

If we can show,

(a) $(\exists y)(r_{i-1} \, \text{RC}_\text{F} \, y \cdot x \, e \,$ "Mammals" Ing $y) \supset$

   $\sim (\exists z)(z \, r_{i-1} \text{DP}_\text{F}(x,$ "Mammals", "Heart-having"))

Then we will have shown,

(b) $(\exists y)(r_{i-1} \, \text{RC}_\text{F} \, y \cdot x \, e \,$ "Mammals" Ing $y) \supset \cdot$

   $(\exists y)(r_{i-2} \, \text{RC}_\text{F} \, y \cdot x \, e \,$ "Heart-having" al n$(x \, e \,$ "Heart-

   having") Ing $y) \supset (\exists y)(r_{i-2} \, \text{RC}_\text{F} \, y \cdot$

   $x \, e \,$ "Heart-having" Ing $y)$

But this last statement is roughly equivalent to supposing that the general statement "$(x)(x \, \epsilon \,$ Mammals $\supset x \, \epsilon \,$ Heart-having)" is an ingredient of a rational corpus of level r_{i-1}.

I shall undertake to show in the following chapter that, given a slight change in the definition of a rational corpus, this rough equivalence does in fact hold precisely. Under the present circumstances, we can only say that we 'might as well' include the general conditional in the rational corpora of level r_{i-1}. If we are to include the general conditional in a rational corpus of level r_i, then it takes only a very slight extension of the concept of probability, as hitherto defined, to be able to say that the probability of this general conditional is as great as the probability of any other ingredient of this rational corpus.

Although I shall leave the details of this argument for the following chapter, there is one point that had best be made here; if we know that there is a mammal without a heart (which would follow from an observation statement to the effect that such and such a mammal lacked a heart, or which might be known otherwise), then statement (a) does not hold. The definite description of this mammal will not satisfy (a), for obvious reasons; it is only if (a) is satisfied by every expression x that we can include the general conditional in the rational corpora of level r_{i-1}.

(12)   Given the evidence of experiments performed on heredity, the probability is p that the genetic theory is true.

The technique I have applied to universal statements above can be extended almost directly to theories. To say that a theory is true means no more, so far as I can tell, then that all of its consequences are true. To phrase this in terms of rational belief, we might say that a theory is rationally credible if it is rationally obligatory to believe that all of its consequences are true.

Consider the theory T as expressed in a number of statements

S_1, S_2, ... S_n. The theory enables us to derive, by purely logical means, what 'will be the case' under certain specified conditions, called boundary conditions. (In order to be free to draw consequences from the theory, the theory had best be understood as the conjunction of $S_1 ... S_n$.) The theory is rationally credible if it is credible that for every set of boundary conditions, SB_i, the circumstances C_i predicted by the theory will actually obtain.

There remains one possible difference between the statement that everything satisfying the boundary conditions SB_i will also satisfy the prediction C_i of the theory, and the statement that every mammal has a heart. The difference is that while it is not implausible to suppose that the class of mammals is finite, it is not so plausible to suppose that the situations satisfying the boundary conditions of the theory are similarly limited. Nevertheless, there is an approach to the matter which seems reasonable enough. We may limit our attention to the predictions actually made with the help of the theory. Furthermore, it is often possible to divide the situations SB_i to which the theory applies into a finite class of broad types of situations, SB_i^1, SB_i^2, ... SB_i^m, such that the theory may be confirmed more or less independently for each of these types of application. This helps to explain, incidentally, our tendency in testing a theory to treat broad classes of situations distinctly. But it also leads to a further difficulty.

This difficulty arises when we try to consider what it is that can constitute a random sample of the consequences of the theory. The sense of randomness required is explained by the fact that we want the proportion of confirming instances among the test situations to represent the proportion of confirming instances among all situations to which the theory applies. But we often have good reason for believing that if the theory is going to fail, i.e., if the proportion of confirming instances is not unity, then it is going to fail only in some types of situation, and not in all. A class of confirming instances, all falling in the broad class SB_i^1 will therefore not be considered a random sample of consequences with respect reflecting the proportion of true predictions on the part of the theory. In effect, then, what we must do is to confirm the theory for situations of type SB_i^1, for situations of the type SB_i^2, and so on, the sum of these confirmations being in effect, the confirmation of the theory itself.

Now it may very well be that, due to other general statements in our rational corpus, one or a very few confirming instances of type SB_i^1 will render it highly probable that the theory holds for all those instances of this type to which the theory will ever be applied. It is even possible that, relative to what we know when the theory is first formulated, before it is tested at all, the probability is over-whelming that the theory will hold for instances of this type. Clearly what is required, then, is to examine random samples of the types of instances in which we do *not* (yet) have any reason to believe that the theory will hold. If we do not confirm the hypothesis that the theory will hold for *these* situations, we cannot consider the theory credible.

This analysis also leads to the plausible consequence that a theory which is refuted in one particular sort of application need not be altogether rejected. All that needs to be rejected, for example, is the application of the theory to situations of type SB_i^1; in effect what we shall do is to replace the theory $S_1 \cdot S_2 \cdot \ldots \cdot S_n$ by the rather less general theory, $S_1 \cdot \ldots S_n \cdot \sim SB_i^1$. The theory, even when restricted in its domain of application, may still be highly useful.

We may even have an old theory, T, which has had to be replaced in some uses by a new theory T′, but which is still useful. We have the statement nT in our rational corpus—the old theory is simply not true—and yet we want to use the old theory, say, for some calculations. Even this can be arranged; we merely need to take note of the fact that in a certain class of applications, predictions made by means of the old theory T will differ only trivially from predictions made by means of the new theory T′; thus the old theory may be retained if we add a clause restricting it to these applications, and mentioning the fact that its results are only approximate. Thus altered, T will not conflict with T′.

One more factor should be mentioned: the statement of the boundary conditions in a given experiment, and the statement of the observed consequences, are themselves only probable. They are said to hold, e.g., within the limits of experimental error. But with respect to a suitably selected level or rational corpus, they are not probable, but certain—that is, their probability relative to the next-higher level of rational corpus is so high that they may be 'accepted' into the rational corpus with which we are concerned in testing the theory.

To return to statement (12), we may suppose that the genetic theory is embodied in a number of statements $S_1 \ldots S_n$. Ordinarily the statements embodying a theory will include not only factual statements, but also statements which are true by definition: a gene, for example, may be postulated to have properties *per definitionem*. But I shall suppose that when the theory is translated into our formal language, these statements (or others from which they follow) are included among the axioms governing the primitive predicates—just as we may suppose that a term corresponding to 'gene' is included among the primitive predicates. It may be possible, though I don't believe it could be made plausible, that the term 'gene' can be defined in terms of 'observables'; but there is no necessity for attempting to do this—we need only assume what seems to be actually the case, that there is some logical connection between the term corresponding to 'gene' and other terms corresponding to words with which we are more familiar.   ·

The testing ground for the theory is the inheritance of certain observable (at least indirectly observable) characteristics. In particular, we may have reason for supposing that if the theory is true, then the relative frequency of red sweet peas in a population of sweet peas will be 0.75, provided certain specifiable conditions prevail. The latter is a statement that can be put to the test by the techniques mentioned earlier. If, relative to a rational corpus of given basis and level, the specified conditions may be accepted as prevailing, and the statement that the relative frequency of red sweet peas lies in a fairly small interval around 0.75 is also 'acceptable', then this counts as a confirmation of the theory. By performing a large number of such experiments, we may, depending on what else we know, arrive at a high degree of probability for the theory, so far as it applies to such characteristics.

On the other hand (and this is often pointed out), while the theory is well-confirmed indeed in this type of application, there are uses of the theory, such as concern the inheritance of 'mental' traits to which its application is open to rather more doubt. It should also be pointed out, however, that this doubt about the applicability of the theory to the inheritance of more complicated characteristics is a purely hypothetical doubt. The probability of the theory is determined by the fact that it is confirmed by what, *so far as we know*, is a random sample of its possible applications. It is only the fact that sometime in the future it may be that this sample of applications is no longer random, relative to what we know, that makes us wary of the theory in some of its more esoteric applications.

In connection with this theory, there is one point which deserves special comment. In conventional formulations of the gene theory, statements like the following are often encountered: ''The fertilization of ovules of the two different kinds, by the pollen of two different kinds, takes place at random.'' An examination of the contexts in which such statements appear makes it clear that 'random' is not used as I have defined it. It is used, on the contrary, as part of an empirical assertion, namely, that the various *kinds* of mating possible in the situation occur with approximately equal frequencies. This is a statistical statement (whose truth or falsity is quite

independent of our state of knowledge). Of course there is a probability statement corresponding to it, but even this probability does
not correspond to a statement of randomness.

In these contexts, even more than in other contexts, it is important to bear in mind that due to the fact that we all have available a
tremendous store of knowledge, much of which is relevant to statements of the kind considered here, things are much more complicated than I have made them appear. The 'confirmation' of a theory is often based on previously confirmed statistical statements,
on parts of our large fund of every-day, common-sense knowledge,
on the still-acceptable parts of discarded theories, on acceptable
universal generalizations, and on other theories which still stand.
Here I have only been considering the *reductio ad simplicitum*, as
it were. It is the not too easy task of a full blown inductive logic
(for which the theory of rational belief is offered as a basis) to ex-
plore in detail such contexts as I have touched upon in this section.

3.   After the perigrinations of the preceding section, the analysis
of the last two statements from Appendix II, though perhaps disap-
pointingly vague, is rather simple.

(13)   It is highly probable that Caesar crossed the Rubicon.
(14)   If you are wealthy, it is more likely that you will be caught
       if you cheat on your income tax, then if you are not wealthy.

The first statement says that it is highly probable that a certain
event took place in the past. Relative to my rational corpus, the
statement asserting that this event took place is highly probable
because (a) the consensus of opinion among competent historians
supports the statement, and (b) the relative frequency with which
competent historians have to eat their words is low.

Relative to the rational corpus of historical inquiry, however,
the situation is different. Here the evidence in favor of the statement in question consists mainly of certain pieces of paper (or
parchment) on which are written certain marks. Linguistics, cal-
ligraphy, etc., tell us that it is highly probable that these marks
correspond to the English statement "Caesar crossed the Rubicon." Psychological hypotheses can tell us that it is highly probable that the author of the text (physics substantiates the hypothesis
that there was one) intended to assert that Caesar did in fact cross
the Rubicon. Physical evidence can help to show that the documents
are not forgeries. We may have sociological evidence, which, combined with psychological evidence, makes it highly probable that
men such as the authors of these documents will not (simultaneously or following one another) invent a story such as this more

than one time out of ten, and so on.

This is all highly artifical, I know, but it nevertheless seems plausible to suppose that some such step by step treatment of the evidence in relation to rational corpora could well be employed. In general, of course, it will only be one or two steps in the argument which are controversial, and these steps can be discussed in the framework of the logic of rational belief far more simply than can the whole argument.

Some of the steps in arguments such as the above may seem similar to arguments of the much disputed form, if S were not so, P would be very improbable; P; therefore S. For example, "If the drawings in the lottery were not loaded, it would be very improbable for the premier's daughter-in-law to win the prize; she did win the prize; therefore the drawings were loaded."

The analogy does not hold. The arguments employed above that might be alleged to be similar to this one, have rather the form: P is incredible. Therefore, (and as usual, only until evidence to the contrary is forthcoming) we may include the denial of P, nP, in our rational corpus, of level r_i. In the rational corpus of level r_{i+1}, we have as an ingredient, nP cd S. Therefore we may include S in our rational corpus of level r_i. The lottery example becomes, "Before the drawing, it is incredible that if the lottery is not fixed, the premier's daughter-in-law will win the prize, after the drawing, we know that the daughter-in-law of the premier won the prize, whether or not the lottery was fixed." On my view, the probability of a faked lottery would depend not only on the direct evidence of who won the prize, but also on highly confirmed psychological statements concerning the motives and methods of faking lotteries; but on my view things turn out to be somewhat more plausible as well.

The analysis of (14) is somewhat simpler, in spite of the fact that the probabilities in question are (for me, at least) somewhat vaguer. 'You' in the statement may be intended in the general way, as 'a person'. The statement will then be analogous to statements (1)–(5). It will be true if and only if the rational corpus relative to which it is asserted contains a statement to the effect that the proportion of wealthy people who cheat on their income tax and who end up by getting caught, is greater than the corresponding proportion of poor people. This statistical statement may in turn be rendered acceptable to the rational corpus in question, by being rendered highly probable relative to a higher level rational corpus which contains a statistical psychological statement to the general effect that income tax inspectors will be more careful about checking large income tax returns than about checking small ones.

The 'you' may also refer to some specific individual—say, Alexander Q. Pettifog. The rational corpus relative to which (14) is asserted, then, may contain the above described statistical hypothesis and also be such that Al is a random member of the class of income-tax-filers with respect to the property of getting caught if he cheats. (We may not know whether or not he is rich, or we may be contemplating a hypothetical rational corpus in which this knowledge is absent.) Or the statement (on this second interpretation) may refer to a subclass of the class concerned in the general interpretation; e.g., it is perhaps only cheating of the sort that Al is contemplating that income tax inspectors catch more frequently in the returns of wealthy people than in those of poor people.

Incidentally, (13) and (14), and to some extent (12), indicate that although we are often able to restrict our considerations to a single field in the process of evaluating a probability, it is not always possible to do so. (13) and (14), at any rate, depend for their probability on psychological, sociological, and even (e.g., in establishing the age of a document) physical laws. In order to be able to discuss the probability of historical statements in our system, then, we need to have already discussed the question of what physical statements may be included in our rational corpus, as well as what psychological statements, what sociological statements, what statements from linguistics, etc. At the very least, we have to be *able* to discuss these questions. But to have done this, or even to be able to do it, is already to have established the unity of science. And even to hope that it may be done is to hope for a unity of scientific education, and at the very least to hope for a common language to express what is common knowledge in diverse specialties.

4.   At this point some readers may wonder whether I have defined randomness so liberally that all of the old paradoxes generated by the principle of indifference may not find their way back into the system. While I cannot show that the system I have outlined is free from contradictions or even free from unsuspected implausibilities, I can show that one paradox of probability, based on the principle of indifference, cannot occur in it. This paradox is found in the example discussed by Broad in his article on problematic induction.[1]

Suppose we have a bag of counters, each of which may be any one of n distinguishable colors. One of the questions asked by Broad is, "What is the probability, relative to only this evidence, that a counter drawn at random will be red?" Making use of the principle of indifference, and assuming that each counter is 'equally likely' to have any one of the n distinguishable colors, Broad gives the answer of $1/n$. But the reasoning which leads to this answer

1. C. D. Broad, "Problematic Induction," *Proceedings of the Aristotelian Society* 28, 1928.

leads also to some rather paradoxical conclusions. If we assume that a sample of the counters has been drawn at random, and the color of any one counter is independent of the color of any other counter, then, regardless of the size of the sample we draw, the probability that a given counter remaining in the bag is red is $1/n$. And this result holds good even if the bag had contained a thousand counters, and we had drawn 999 red counters, leaving only one in the bag.

What happens to this argument in the framework of my theory? We are supposed to have the perfectly good statistical hypothesis that the proportion of distinguishable colors which are red is $1/n$. Granting that this is the sort of statistical information we might have in the context of this argument, it might be maintained that the next counter which we draw is a random member of the class of counters with respect to belonging to the class of red objects. This might very well be true in such a situation. But the two statements do not add up to a probability statement. If, as seems only reasonable, we interpret 'red' as the class of red objects, the statistical statement says that the proportion of the classes of classes of indistinguishably colored objects which belong to the unit class of the class of red objects is $1/n$. The assertion about randomness concerns a counter, and says that a certain counter (the next one we draw) is a random member of a certain class of counters with respect to membership in the class of red objects, not that it is a random member of the class of colors with respect to membership in the unit of the class of red objects. If we could draw a color at random, the argument might hold up; but the counter is not a member of the class of colors (random or otherwise) since only colors can belong to a class of colors.

But in the absence of information about the counters in the bag, we might be able to construct an argument somewhat similar to Broad's. In the absence of any information in our rational corpus which would prevent it, we might be able to make the assertion that the next counter to be drawn is a random member of the class of all *colored counters* with respect to membership in the class of red objects. But the relevant statistical hypothesis then concerns the proportion of all colored counters which are red, not the proportion of all colors which are red. And we may, on the basis of our knowledge of poker and children's games, have some such vague hypothesis in our rational corpus as that the proportion of red counters among all colored counters lies somewhere between 0.1 and 0.7. Obviously the fact that there are n distinguishable colors is quite irrelevant to this. As we accumulate information by drawing counters out of the bag, this hypothesis will become irrelevant as well; we will confirm a stronger statistical hypothesis about a subclass of the class of all colored counters.

CHAPTER EIGHTEEN

Induction

1. "The theory of induction," Whitehead has said, "Is the despair of philosophy."[1] It is my object in this chapter to show that so far as I can tell at this stage, the logic of rational belief provides a plausible theory of induction. Some of the contexts in which probability is ordinarily used that were discussed in the last chapter may already have suggested that this is so; they may also have suggested that this theory is capable of providing a 'justification' of induction. But I should prefer to postpone the question of justification until the chapter after next. Here I want only to show that the logic of rational belief does provide a *theory* of induction.

I shall do this, first, by showing that induction, on my theory of probability and rational belief, is possible, i.e., that general empirical statements can occur in rational corpora which are based on statements concerning only particulars. That is the task of the present section. In the following section, I shall give a very brief outline of an inductive logic, an outline embracing only a few of the broad types of inference which are used in science. In the third section I shall give a very simplified illustration of how this theory of induction might work out in practise.

To show that my logic of rational belief provides a theory of induction requires, roughly, that I show that from a 'plausible' basis of a rational corpus, it follows that some statement of greater generality than any that occur in F must be included in the rational corpora of level r_{n-1}, (provided ML and F are consistent). What I shall do is this: I shall exhibit a basis F, containing only the sort of statements which most philosophers seem to accept as a suitable basis for knowledge. Then I will show that, given this basis F, we are (barring unforseen complications) obligated to include a certain statement of the sort that qualifies as general in the rational corpora of this basis and level r_{n-1}.

This shows that, taking the logic of rational belief as a theory of induction, induction is possible. But there remains the possibility that there are very few bases of rational corpora simple enough to lead to the inclusion of more general statements in the rational corpora of lower levels than are contained in the bases themselves.

---

1. A. N. Whitehead, *Science in the Modern World*, New York, 1925.

This possibility may be partially disposed of by showing that an increase in the basis F considered originally, such that the general statement which has originally to be included in the rational corpora of level r_{n-1} no longer appears there, leads to the inclusion in this rational corpus of a new and different but equally general statement.

Let F be:

$S_6 \frown S_7 \frown "\%(\hat{x}p'''(x), \hat{y}p''(y),(.75;.75))" \frown S_6 \frown S_7 "\hat{x}p'''(x) \epsilon 1000" \frown S_6 \frown S_7$

Let the following statement be a theorem, based on the axioms for the primitive predicates:

(1) $\hat{x} p'''(x) \subset \hat{z} p'(z)$

Let $\hat{z} p'(z) \epsilon$ N; from (1) in conjunction with the second ingredient of F, we can show that N $\leqslant$ 1000.

Let "K" and "R" be defined as follows:

(2) "K" for "$\hat{x}(x \subset \hat{z}(p'(z)) \cdot x \epsilon 1000)$"

(3) "R" for "$\hat{x}(w)(x \subset \hat{z}(p'(z)) \cdot \%(x, \hat{y}(p''(y)), (w;w)) \cdot \supset$

$\%(\hat{z}(p'(z)), \hat{y}(p''(y)), (f_1(w); f_u(w))))$"

where f is determined by the shortest interval requirement of rational representative matrices. For a thousand-fold sample of a class about which nothing is known in the rational corpora of level r_n, which is what we are interested in, $f_1(w)$ and $f_u(w)$ will be chosen as $w - .049$, and $w + .049$, respectively. This gives us the rationally representative matrix for the rational corpora of level r_n that leads to the strongest statistical statement that may (other things being equal) be included in a rational corpus of level ".998".

The following statement is a theorem, and hence should be included in every rational corpus, if ML and F are consistent. It will be included in the rational corpus of level r_n anyway.

(4) "$(z')(y')(z' \geqslant 1000 \cdot \hat{z}(p'(z)) \epsilon z' \cdot \%(\hat{z}(p'(z)), \hat{y}(p''(y)),$

$(y'; y')) \supset \%(K, R, (.998+;\ _s1))$"

Since the classes with which we are concerned are finite, we know that the antecedent of (4) holds for some z' and y'. Thus (by *161 and *100) we have:

(5) "$\%(K, R, (.998+;\ _s1))$"

as an ingredient of our rational corpus. There may be a stronger statement which is known in the rational corpora of level r_n—e.g., if it is known that $\hat{z} p'(z) \subset \hat{x} p'''(x)$, or that $\%(\hat{z} p'(z), \hat{y} p''(y),$

$(_s1;_s1)$). There will also be stronger ingredients of our rational corpus of level r_n and basis F, having the same subject matter, if ML and F are inconsistent. But the worst possible situation short of inconsistency (which would cause us to change the language) is where so far as we know, $\hat{z}\,p'(z)$ may have a googoplex of members, half of which are also members of $\hat{y}\,p''(y)$.

From (1) and the second ingredient of F, we have, also as an ingredient of F:

(6)   " $\hat{x}\,p'''(x) \in K$ "

Now the question which confronts us is whether or not the following statement holds:

(7)   " $\hat{x}\,p'''(x)$ " $r_n \mathrm{Ran}_F($"K";"R")

Or, since all we are concerned with is getting " $\hat{x}\,p'''(x) \in R$ " into our rational corpus, it suffices (if F and ML are consistent) to show that there is no expression 'E' such that,

(8)   "E" $r_n \mathrm{DP}_F($" $\hat{x}\,p'''(x)$ ", "K", "R")

In view of the limited nature of the basis of the rational corpus with which we are concerned, I shall suppose that there is no such expression; but one possibility concerning the existence of such an expression will be examined shortly in connection with the expanded rational corpus F'.

If there is no expression "E" for which (8) holds, we have,

(9)   "$_{.998}$" $RC_F\ \widehat{S_6}\widehat{S_7}$ " $\hat{x}\,p'''(x) \in R$ "$\widehat{S_6}\widehat{S_7}$

And in virtue of the fact that " $\%(\hat{x}\,p'''(x),\hat{y}\,p''(y),(.75;.75))$ " is an ingredient of F, we have,

(10)   "$_{.998}$" $RC_F\ \widehat{S_6}\widehat{S_7}$"$\%(\hat{z}\,p'(z^i),\hat{y}\,p''(y),(.701;.799))$ "$\widehat{S_6}\widehat{S_7}$

This shows that we have no reason to suppose that induction is not possible; if F and ML are consistent, (which, so far as we know, they are) a statement of greater factual content may be mentioned in a rational corpus of level ".998" than any that may be mentioned in F or in the rational corpora of level "$_s1$". So far so good. It now remains to be shown that if the addition of material to F leads to the rejection of (10), i.e., if for some F',

(11) $\sim(\exists x)($ "$_{.998}$" $RC_{F'}x$ · " $\%(\hat{z}\,p'(z),\hat{y}\,p''(y),$

        $(.701;.799))$ " $\mathrm{Ing}\ x)$

then there is some other statement in our rational corpus going beyond our experience.

Suppose that F' is just like F, except that it contains in addition to the first and second ingredients of F, two more ingredients, " $\hat{x}\ p''''(x) \in N$ ", and " $\%(\hat{x}\ p''''(x)$, $\hat{y}\ p''(y),(N_1/N;N_1/N))$ ". Let the following statement be a theorem:

(12) $\quad \hat{x}\ p''''(x) \subset \hat{z}\ p'(z)$

We define K' and R' as before:

(13) $\quad$ "K' " *for* $\hat{x}(x \subset \hat{z}\ p'(z) \cdot x \in 1000 + N)$

(14) $\quad$ "R' " *for* $\hat{x}(w)(x \subset \hat{z}\ p'(z) \cdot \%(x,\hat{y}\ p''(y),(w;w)) \cdot \supset$

$$\%(\hat{z}\ p'(z),\hat{y}\ p''(y),(f_1'(w);f_u'(w))))$$

where f' is selected in such a way that "R' " is a rationally representative matrix in the context with which we are concerned, and the following statement is an ingredient of the highest level rational corpus.

(15) $\quad$ " $\%(K', R', (.998;\ _s1))$ "

By an argument analogous to that on the preceding pages, we will presumably have,

(16) $\quad$ "$_{.998}$ " $RC_{F'}\ S_6\frown S_7\frown$ "$\%(\hat{z}\ p'(z),\hat{y}\ p''(y),(f_1'(N_1 + 750/N +$

$1000); f_u'(N_1 + 750/N + 1000)))$ "$\frown S_6\frown S_7$

Since the statistical statement mentioned in (16) may be quite different from that mentioned in (10), it is incumbent on us to show that if there is a difference between the two, then there is an expression "E" satisfying (8). This will also show that in general (but not always) there will be no sub-class of a sample which will prevent our using the sample as the basis for an inductive inference. (But often we can find much more efficient ways to utilize a sample than that discussed here.)

First we define "E_T":

(17) $\quad$ "E_T" *for* " $\hat{x}(x \in 1000 \cdot x \subset \hat{x}\ p'''(x) \cup \hat{x}\ p''''(x))$ "

Next we define a subclass of "E_T";

(18) $\quad$ "E_R" *for* " $\hat{x}\ (y)(z)(x \in E_T \cdot \%(x,\hat{y}\ p''(y),(y;z)) \cdot \supset$

$$y - .049 \geq f_1'(N_1 + 750/N + 1000) \cdot$$

$$z + .049 \leq f_u'(N_1 + 750/N + 1000))$$ "

Finally, we define "E_P":

(19) $\quad$ "E_P" *for* " $E_T \cap \overline{E}_R$ "

If $\hat{x}$ $p'''(x)$ belongs to E_R (if it does we will know it), it causes us no trouble—it merely leads to a weaker statistical statement than that to which the large sample leads.

But if $\hat{x}$ $p'''(x)$ belongs to E_P (and we will know this, too) it will cause us no trouble either. E_P is divided into two parts, in one of which high class ratios predominate, and in one of which low class ratios predominate. Whatever the real class ratio may be, the proportion of objects in E_P which belong to R must be relatively low, due to the exclusion of objects belonging to E_R. Furthermore, unless the class ratio in the large sample is very close to 0 or very close to 1, the upper limit p_2 in (20) cannot be $_s1$.

(20)   "$\%(E_P, R, (p_1; p_2))$"

The statement mentioned in (20) will be known, since it is inferrable from the ingredients of F'. Furthermore, (20) will be known to differ from (15); and since "$E_P \subset K$" is known,

(21)   "E_P" $r_n DP_F("\hat{x} \; p'''(x)"$, "K", "R")

The same will hold true for any 1000-fold sample belonging to E_P, as well as for $\hat{x}$ $p'''(x)$.

In addition to showing that an increase in statistical evidence will not rob our rational corpus of its general statement, this argument also shows that, at least under ordinary circumstances, our rational corpus will be uniform: we will not have two statistical statements in it which are strongest statements about the same subject matter, and which differ.

Finally, I shall show how a slight change in the definition of a rational corpus will allow us to include universal statements in it on the basis of empirical evidence. We replace $\Delta 95a$ by $\Delta 95a*$:

$\Delta 95a*$ $\ulcorner r_i RC_F \; \theta \; \urcorner$ for $\ulcorner S_6 \frown S_7$ B $\theta \cdot S_6 \frown S_7$ E $\theta \cdot (\alpha)(\alpha$ Ing $\theta \cdot \supset \cdot$

$(\exists \beta)(\exists \gamma)(\alpha \; r_{i+1} Prob_F(\beta; \gamma) \cdot$ Thm $\beta \; _s gr \; r_i)$ v $(\exists \beta)(\exists \gamma)$

$(\exists \alpha')(\alpha = \alpha'$ qu $(\alpha'$ e β cd α' e $\gamma) \cdot (\alpha'')((\exists \theta)$

$(r_{i+1} RC_F \; \theta \cdot \alpha''$ e β Ing $\theta) \supset (\exists \beta')(\exists \gamma')(\alpha''$ e $\gamma \; r_{i+1}$

$Prob_F(\beta'; \gamma') \cdot$ Thm $\beta' \; _s gr \; r_i)))) \; \urcorner$

Let (22) be an ingredient of our rational corpus of level ".998".

(22)   "$\%(z \; p'(z), \hat{y} \; p''(y), (.998; \; _s1))$"

Suppose that the statement "$(\exists w)(w \epsilon \; \hat{z} \; p'(z) \cdot \sim w \epsilon \; \hat{y} \; p''(y))$" is an ingredient of a rational corpus of level ".998". Then there will be an expression "E" such that,

(23) $(\exists x)($ "$_{.998}$" RC_F x $\cdot$ "E ϵ $\hat{z}$ $p'(z)$"Ing $x) \cdot \sim (\exists w')(\exists x)$

   ("E ϵ $\hat{y}$ $p''(y)$" "$_{.998}$" $Prob_F(w'; x') \cdot$

   Thm w' $_s$gr ".995")

"E" will be either a description of the (observed) object on which our knowledge of " $(\exists w)(w$ ϵ $\hat{z}$ $p'(z)$ $\cdot$ $\sim w$ ϵ $\hat{y}$ $p''(y))$" is based, or it will be a definite description of an object that some theory tells us exists. (23), therefore, will prevent us from including " (x) $(x$ ϵ $\hat{z}$ $p'(z)$ $\supset x$ ϵ $\hat{y}$ $p''(y))$" in our rational corpus of level ".995". But if (23) does not hold, and (22) is an ingredient of our rational corpus of level ".998", then we will include this general conditional in our rational corpus of level ".995". The change of definition which leads to this highly gratifying result, however, may raise difficulties with regard to consistency.

2. Inductive logic, on the theory presented here, is perfectly formal. It is concerned with showing that statements about the world going beyond our immediate experience, can be included in our rational corpora. This does not, however, constitute a 'reduction of induction to deduction'. The relation between a statement probable enough to be included in a rational corpus, and the statements already in that rational corpus (of a higher level) that serve as evidence for it, is obviously not the same as the relation between the premises and conclusion of a formally valid argument: as shown in the last section the statement can go beyond the evidence provided in the basis of a rational corpus. Furthermore, as I will show shortly, the existence of formal criteria for rational belief does not mean that the business of learning from experience is always mechanical: in the realm of theory, and particularly in the realm of concept-formation, one must go beyond the formal system, and perhaps even change the system itself. But the justification of the *results* of this imaginative leap will once more be mechanical (or semi-mechanical) and formal.

The fundamental type of induction is that exemplified in the preceding section—the argument from the constitution of a sample to the constitution of the parent population. C. Peirce,[2] Donald Williams,[3] and others, have also adopted this point of view, and based the 'validity' of induction on the fact that the majority of samples reflect the constitution of the parent population. This type of argument from experience is also very common in every-day life, the conclusions supported by this type of argument (validly or other-

2. Ch. Peirce, "The Probability of Induction," reprinted in Buchler (ed.), *The Philosophy of Peirce*, New York, 1950.
3. D. C. Williams, *The Ground of Induction*, Cambridge (Mass.), 1947.

wise) being of the kind: "Every time we plan a picnic it rains,"
"Count your change when you go to Brown's Store; half the time he
tries to short change you," "Most of the things the teacher says
are fairly sound," and so on.

But many of these conclusions may also be supported (if at all)
by arguments of a somewhat more sophisticated type; and there
are very few arguments—including, by the way, arguments supporting statistical hypotheses in the social sciences and the like—
which occur in scientific contexts and which cannot be cast in a
somewhat more persuasive form. Though simple statistical arguments are fundamental to the process of learning from experience,
is is also true that the more we learn, the less often do we need to
use these rather inefficient arguments. The following outline treats
of a number of types of inductive argument, more or less in order
of increasing sophistication.

(a)   Simple Statistical Generalizations.

An example was given in the last chapter of a simple statistical
generalization. Here I shall only point out that often the increase of
strength in the strongest statistical statement in a rational corpus
r_{i-1}, as opposed to a rational corpus of level r_i, is not merely
a result of decreasing demands in regard to probability. If, for example, the strongest statistical statement in a rational corpus of
level r_i states that a certain class ratio lies in an interval close to
$_s0$ or close to $_s1$, we can infer from this—by a purely logical principle of inference—that the proportion of representative samples is
much higher than it would be if the class ratio were $1/2$. (The ra-
tionally-representative matrix is also different.) This effect is very
pronounced when all of the objects in the sample have the property
in question.

(b)   Universal Generalizations.

Universal generalizations were also discussed in the last section. Even if we do not end up by replacing Δ95a with Δ95a*, there
is no practical difference between having "$\%(x,y(p;q))$" and "(w)
$(w \in x \supset w \in y)$" as ingredients of the rational corpus of level r_i,
provided that the ratio denoted by r_{i-1} is less than p, and there is
no rational corpus (of any level) containing the statement " $(\exists w)$
$(w \in x \cdot \sim w \in y)$".

(c)   Complex Statistical Generalizations.

It is only when we have already learned a certain amount about the world that we are prepared to consider complex statistical generalizations. Thus if we wish to discover the distribution of a certain variate in a population, we can confirm a number of statistical generalizations of the simple variety, whatever the state of our rational corpus. We can confirm the simple statistical generalization, saying that a proportion lying between p and p' of the population belongs to the class of objects to which values of the variate between X_i and X_j apply. But the matter is enormously simplified if we can find grounds for believing that the values of this variate are distributed *normally* in this population. And this, of course, can be achieved by finding out (in accordance with one of the standard inductive procedures listed here) that in all (or in a very high proportion) of the classes, of which the one we are interested in is a random member, the distribution of this variate is normal. For example, we have excellent grounds for supposing that the distribution of weights among a group of animals of a given species and age, living under given circumstances, will be well represented by a normal distribution, though we know perfectly well that no continuous distribution can be taken literally.

On the other hand, the more knowledge we have about the world, and the more general this knowledge, the more difficult it is to justify simple statistical generalizations directly; or rather, the statistical generalizations that we can justify directly become more and more trivial. It becomes easier and easier to think up reasons why a given sample is not random with respect to the representative property with which we are concerned. It is true that the sample is always a random sample (with respect to being representative of something) of some class—but the classes of which the samples are random samples become increasingly finely defined.

At the beginning, for example, we might be able to consider a series of tosses of a particular coin, made by a particular person, to be a random sample of all coin-tosses, with respect to being representative of the proportion of tosses resulting in heads. But we may subsequently discover that different coins fall heads with different frequencies, or that different people get different frequencies of heads with the same coin. With this new information in our rational corpus, the old sample becomes a random sample of the tosses of a particular coin, or a random sample of tosses by a particular person, rather than a random sample of coin-tosses in general, with respect to the property with which we are concerned. If we further discover that the number of heads is a function of the increasing entropy of the universe, then the sample is not even a random sample of the tosses of the given coin made by the given person—it is only a random sample of the tosses made by the given person, with the given coin, at the given time.

Situations of this kind will lead us to be even fussier about the samples we use than we are obligated to be in point of logic by the amount of knowledge we possess at the time. Even though we do not know that the relative frequency of heads in a sequence of tosses depends on who does the tossing, we may take a sample in which a number of people have tossed the coin—just to be on the safe side. We wish to guard against the possibility that some hypothesis about the influence of people on tossed coins will be confirmed in the future, which would, if we did not guard against it, make us go through the whole process again to arrive at an equally general conclusion concerning the behavior of the coin. We are concerned not only with the randomness of our samples now, but also with their randomness later, when we have added new information to our rational corpus. This is essentially the *raison d'etre* behind stratified sampling. And although we cannot ever be sure that no future information will cause us to reject the randomness of our samples, we can in some respects take experience as our guide in watching out for certain types of bias.

Here is one more example to illustrate this point. If we want to sample a shipload of beans with respect to the proportion of undersized beans, a sample from one particular part of the ship may very well be random relative to our rational corpus. But we draw our sample from different parts of the ship, not only to guard against the hypothesis that different parts of the ship may contain beans with different characteristics, but also so that we may use these smaller samples to confirm or disconfirm the hypothesis against which we are guarding.

(d)   **Arguments By Analogy.**

Argument by analogy is often given a fundamental place in inductive logic and in informal discussions of induction. I think this is a mistake, since it seems to me that a statistical argument can usually do the work of an analogical argument, and, in addition, can be rendered much more explicit in a formal system.

The general form of an argument by analogy—at least of the kind in which we are interested in induction—is this: things belonging to the class A are analogous to things belonging to the class B in such and such respects; things belonging to the class A also always belong to the class C; therefore it is reasonable to suppose that things belonging to the class B always belong to the class C too. For 'always' we may substitute 'sometimes', or 'never'.

We can reformulate the argument as follows: Let the objects belonging to A also belong to D, E, F, ... , and let the objects belonging to B also belong to D, E, F, ... This I shall take to be the sense of the statement that the A's and B's are analogous in such and such respects. Furthermore, we know that all of the objects belonging to A (or a certain proportion of them, or none of them) also belong to X. We do not have any information or evidence concerning the proportion of objects belonging to B which also belong to X—and in fact it may even be impossible for us to get any direct evidence concerning this latter proportion. Now consider the intersection of D, E, F, ... Both A and B are included in this intersection; they may or may not exhaust it. Call the intersection itself I. Clearly, under some circumstances, the objects belonging to A may be a random sample of the objects belonging to I with respect to the property of representing the proportion of all objects in I that also belong to X.

We may thus, as outlined under (a), (b), or (c), have excellent reasons for supposing that the proportion of the objects in I which also belong to X, lies within such and such limits. Any given member of B may also be a random member of I with respect to belonging to X, relative to our rational corpus. In this sense, the proportion of A's that are X's may determine the probability that a given B will belong to X. If all (or none) of the A's are X's, we may even infer, in accordance with (b), that all (or none) of the I's are X's, and hence that all (or none) of the B's are X's. This last is the situation that is most often contemplated when it is said that argument by analogy is a fundamental form of inductive argument.[4]

Arguments from analogy, then, are not only not fundamental, but are completely and simply reducible to arguments of other types. They are fundamental only in the sense that they can be paraphrased in terms of the statistical arguments which I take as fundamental, and perhaps also in the sense that the statistical arguments which I take as fundamental can be (with a considerable loss in clarity and precision) formulated in terms of analogical arguments.

---

4. Note that the analogical argument does not depend upon counting the number of *respects* in which the objects are analogous. Surely this would be an impossible task in any language adequate to the needs of empirical science; but even such a careful worker as Carnap seems to feel that it would be significant. (*Logical Foundations of Probability*, p. 569.)

(e)   Arguments From Natural Kinds.

As opposed to arguments from analogy, arguments based on hypotheses concerning natural kinds seem to be of fundamental and far reaching importance. The typical and most primitive kind of argument of this sort is illustrated by the following example: In biological or zoological investigations, we often confirm statements like 'All crows are black,'' or ''All ducks are web-footed'', quite sufficiently on the basis of a very small sample. But the argument could not be rationally persuasive if it took the form of arguments of the kind (a), (b), or (c). It is rationally persuasive because it is based on our knowledge that in practically all species of birds, the incidence of a certain type of characteristic, in birds of the same sex within that species, is either 0 or 1. If we know this, then, on the basis of a small sample (but one which includes both males and females) of the species, we can infer something about all members of the species; the only proviso is that the characteristic in question must be one of those covered in our law about natural kinds— web-footedness being an excellent example of such a characteristic.

To put the argument into somewhat more detailed form: We may suppose it a well confirmed hypothesis that all species of birds are (nearly) uniform with regard to major anatomical characteristics. (Actually, this hypothesis would in turn be based on a theory of inheritance.) Web-footedness is such a characteristic. It is incredible that a dozen ducks should all be freaks in this regard. This dozen ducks all have webbed feet. It is therefore rational to believe (to accept into the rational corpus of level immediately below that in which the hypothesis of natural kinds appears) that all ducks are web-footed. In a manner of speaking, as Pierce suggested, we use the general hypothesis about natural kinds as a *principle of inference* leading from the particular statement about the dozen normal ducks, to a general statement about all normal ducks.[5]

The power of statements concerning natural kinds is even more impressively displayed in the physical sciences. It is a very highly confirmed hypothesis indeed—and one that ought to be included in practically everybody's rational corpus—that every alloy has one melting point under standard conditions. That is, every metal and every alloy of metals is a natural kind with regard to melting point (and conductivity, specific heat, etc.). This rule is not only highly

---

5. Peirce refers to such principles, together with purely logical principles of inference, as 'guiding principles' or 'leading principles' of inference. See his well-known article "The Fixation of Belief," reprinted in Buchler, *op. cit.*

confirmed, but admits of no exceptions: it is a truly general statement. Thus while we may be slightly suspicious of our dozen ducks, we will not generally be suspicious of an alloy whose melting point we have carefully measured a dozen times.

In fact, to the extent that we can be sure that *one* sample of an alloy A melted under standard conditions at $T°K$, we can be sure that all samples of A will melt at this temperature. Actually, we can only be sure that the sample melts at $(T ± t)°K$, where t is not the conventional 'probable error', but an error that would be 'incredible' in the level of rational corpus with which we are concerned. It is to reduce t, mainly, that we repeat the experiment a number of times. The difficulty in confirming the general statement that all samples of A melt at $(T ± t)°K$ lies not in the generality of the statement (which follows directly from the generality of the above mentioned statement about natural kinds) but in the difficulty of determining the melting point of the given sample(s). This is something that cannot, presumably, be observed directly, unless we want to take the rather grandiose measure of identifying the melting point with the thermometer or galvanometer reading—but must be *inferred* from the thermometer or galvanometer readings.

Fortunately, we have another general statement in our rational corpus which enables us to infer from such readings, under specified conditions, that it is highly probable that the sample melted at a temperature in a small interval about the actual (corrected) observed reading.

Incidentally, the specification of the conditions in such situations as this is another matter which is clarified by considerations of randomness: it suffices that there is nothing about the conditions (like variations in pressure) which we *know* is connected statistically with errors in determination. The specification of the conditions merely assures us that this case of measurement is simply a random member of the class of all those cases about which we have some knowledge of the relative frequencies of different sorts of errors; i.e., that it is one to which the accepted theory of error for such cases applies. And this is related to the rationale for throwing out a determination which is greatly at variance with a respectable number of other determinations: it is incredible that such a large error could be due to the ordinary (expected) kinds of error that are taken account of in the relevant theory of error.

One of the major aims of natural science is to discover natural kinds, such that there is a well confirmed universal (or nearly universal) hypothesis to the effect that every instance of a given natural kind will have a great many of a specified list of properties in common with every other instance of the same natural kind. Here is another example of the need, in any plausible theory of induction, of a language employing predicates of a fairly large variety of types; a law about a natural kind is a law about a class which is a member of a certain class of classes of classes (instances), and about a class of classes of classes corresponding to properties. A simple predicate-individual language will clearly not do at all for this sort of thing.

But in spite of the pervasiveness of hypotheses concerning natural kinds as premises in much scientific argument, it must not be forgotten that the general hypotheses which provide the premises for these arguments are neither 'necessary laws of thought' nor 'synthetic a priori truths', nor 'postulates of the scientific method which must be accepted without evidence', but simply general statements included in our rational corpora on the basis—in most cases—of an overwhelming amount of evidence, direct and indirect.

These general statements concerning natural kinds are made credible by evidence of precisely the same sort that supports other inductive conclusions. Sometimes it may be reduced to the kind of evidence which provides the basis for arguments of type (a) or type (b). It is clear enough, no doubt, how arguments of these two types can be based on evidence consisting of an ennumeration of a sample of the sort that we can directly observe. But what can be the basis, in this sense, of an argument supporting the hypothesis that each alloy has one and only one melting point? We don't even know, it may be argued, that there is any alloy of which each sample has always the same melting point.

But the point is that in a very sound and useful sense we do know, for a large number of alloys, that every sample has melted, does melt, and will melt, (under standard conditions) at the same temperature. We know this in the same way and in the same sense that we know that all crows are black, or that all men are mortal. It is irrational, in the face of the evidence, not to believe it. But if there is evidence which makes it incumbent on us to believe of alloy A that it always and everywhere melts at the same temperature, and the same thing holds for alloy B, alloy C, alloy D, ... and alloy X, then the same sort of argument as that from the sample of beans to the characteristics of the parent population of beans applies to the sample of alloys A, B, ... X, and leads us to a conclusion about all alloys. There is no reason why, merely because we cannot directly observe that the instance (in this case, all samples of the alloy) has the property in question, we cannot both know that the instances do have these properties, and use this knowledge as the basis of further inferences. And the hypothesis which is inferred from this collection of instances may in turn be used to support an inference concerning the melting point of alloy Y without any sort of circularity.

(f)   Theories.

The inductive problem of thinking up and substantiating a theory is somewhat more complex than the problems considered above; I think this is partly due to the fact that the hallmark of a theory is that it introduces new terms into the language, and thus changes the language within which we are operating. The criteria which distinguish a good theory from a poor one—if there are any—are obscure; but the criteria which distinguish a rationally credible theory from an incredible one are precisely the same as those which apply to any other general hypothesis. The rules of evidence which apply to theories are precisely those rules which apply to such simple statements as "All the beans in this bag are black"—provided we haven't cheated by emptying the bag out onto the floor.

The complexity of argument that is found in connection with theories is not due to any peculiar character of the theory itself, but only to the wide variety of evidence that can be called upon to support any theory worthy of the name. For one thing, a theory is suggested only when we already have a great deal of information about the subject matter to which it applies: one of its prime functions is to make sense out of a wealth of seemingly but not explicitly related general empirical statements which have already been highly confirmed. If it does this, we already have good grounds for believing the theory, provided that the general facts on which the theory is based are, relative to what we know, a random sample of all the consequences of the theory.

This is perhaps not usually true—at least when we are first beginning to formulate theories about a subject—for then the facts are very unlikely to upset the theory, compared to facts which may be predicted on the basis of the theory, but which have not been investigated. Hence it is that the confirmation of predictions made by means of the theory in areas outside of that in regard to which the theory was first formulated, lend a greater degree of credibility to the theory than their number might suggest. It is somewhat difficult to talk about the grounds for believing a theory in the abstract, since there are so few theories that one is confronted by a genuine shortage of terminology, but it still seems safe to say that in general there will be different classes of consequences of the theory, whose standing in respect to confirmation is different. An entire class of consequences may often be confirmed by an argument from natural kinds.

All of this helps to explain the logical role of the 'crucial experiment'. Often it is not simply that there are two theories, one of which predicts one event under certain circumstances, and one of which predicts another; it might even be that there was only one theory that was being explicitly tested by the crucial experiment. But if the prediction being tested is one of a class of predictions which is the only class really open to doubt, and if this class of predictions (or the subject matter of the predictions) constitutes a natural kind, such that if one prediction of this class is vindicated, we have reason to suppose that all will be, then the outcome of the experiment will decide the fate of the theory.

A further complication in the confirmation of theories arises from the confusion which is possible between the non-logical postulates of the theory itself, and the logical postulates which are merely intended to govern the use of the novel terms that occur in the theory. It is not that there is only one right way of analyzing a given theory into a logical and a non-logical part; it is that often it is unclear what the *intended* analysis, on the part of the propounder of the theory, may have been. The very adequacy and familiarity of the theory may compound this confusion: the elementary laws of statics are a case in point. Again, when we reject one theory in favor of another one, we may retain in the new theory predicates which were invented for the sake of the old theory. These predicates may or may not have precisely the same meaning that they had on the old theory.

Just to add one less confusing consideration, it happens sometimes that one or a few very general, but nevertheless already explicit and highly confirmed statements can, under proper mathematical or logical treatment, be made to yield a whole elegant theory. In this situation, since the theory is simply a consequence of a few highly confirmed general statements, the theory will appear in any rational corpus that contains the logical product of these general statements.

(g)   Statistical Theories.

Statistical theories are not essentially different from other sorts of theories; often the consequences of the theory are so probable that they can be tested as directly as the consequences of non-statistical theories. An example is statistical mechanics. The statistical statements of the theory itself are not generally testable in the way that superficially similar statements which can be supported by an appeal to arguments of type (a) are. It is only more or less remote consequences of the theory that are directly testable in this way.

When we come to deal with complicated statistical hypotheses and theories with a statistical element in them, we already have so much information about the world that it is very hard not to make a mistake about randomness, even though it is simply a logical mistake. It is this, perhaps more than anything else, that explains the rare usefulness of tables of random numbers. It should also be noted that the problem of selecting a random sample for some purpose is often greatly simplified (in certain respects) by the theory itself. Statistical theories often contain a statement to the effect that certain events or things have one or another of a set of properties at random—which I would prefer to have expressed by saying that these different sorts of events happen with equal (or otherwise determinate) frequencies, but are not, within the context of the theory, determined in any other way. If this is so, then in the context of the theory, any sample of these events will be random with respect to, e.g., reflecting the relative frequency of certain consequences of these elementary events.

An argument which is intended to justify a statistical theory is still the same sort of argument we have been considering, but it will often be even more complicated. The point of an inductive logic, with regard to such complicated arguments, is not that it will enable the arguments to be put into irrefutable form, but that it will provide a framework within which the cogency of the argument can be discussed intelligibly, and within which interested parties, sharing the same evidence, can come to agreement.

In general, then, we see that very primitive statistical generalization of the kind mentioned in (a), and especially of the kind mentioned in (b), are very easy to make, although they require a great many instances to be worthy of a very high degree of belief. As we accumulate more and more knowledge about the world—that is, as more and more non-logical statements come to be included in our rational corpus—it becomes more and more difficult to make these generalizations without running into difficulties with the necessary statements of randomness; the subject matter of our generalizations must be more and more circumscribed. But at the same time, it becomes easier and easier to take advantage of what we have already learned in the way of general statements (and this applies especially to universal generalizations) to help to support new general statements. This is where arguments based on analogy and on membership of a class in a natural kind come in. When we have highly confirmed general statements it is often possible to arrive at a new general statement on the basis of a very small amount of new evidence. When we have highly confirmed theories, this form of inductive argument becomes even more important. Finally, when we get very sophisticated, we find ourselves coming back to statistical hypotheses and statistical theories. This time, in virtue of our increased knowledge and the complexities of the theories themselves, confirming them is no longer a simple matter of collecting vast quantities of evidence. Nevertheless, the complexity of the arguments supporting these statistical theories does not mean either that induction by simple enumeration does not play the very fundamental role that I have assigned to it, or that induction by simple enumeration is itself very complicated.

3. I shall now present, in some detail, a very hypothetical and simple illustrative example of the way in which the logic of rational belief works as a theory of induction. Let us imagine a Martian (or a computing machine) playing a slot machine. "Having an experience," for the Martian, consists in pulling the lever of the slot machine and noticing whether the color of the counter which pops out is red, green, or some other color. He is also capable of assigning an ordinal number to each experience—i.e., each pull of the lever. To make things even simpler, we shall suppose that he is infallible in his color judgements, and in keeping records of what he has observed.

ML, with four primitive predicates added, will suffice for his scientific language. Some axioms will also be required, and for the sake of clarity, a few definitions will be given as well.

$\ulcorner p'(\alpha) \urcorner$ is to be translated "α is a counter"

$\ulcorner p''(\alpha) \urcorner$ is to be translated "α is red"

$\ulcorner p'''(\alpha) \urcorner$ is to be translated "α is green"

$\ulcorner p''''(\alpha) \urcorner$ is to be translated "α is an ordered pair and the first object immediately succeeds the second"

Let us replace the p's by a more suggestive notation.

$\ulcorner C(\alpha) \urcorner$ for $\ulcorner p'(\alpha) \urcorner$

$\ulcorner R(\alpha) \urcorner$ for $\ulcorner p''(\alpha) \urcorner$

$\ulcorner G(\alpha) \urcorner$ for $\ulcorner p'''(\alpha) \urcorner$

$\ulcorner S(\alpha;\beta) \urcorner$ for $\ulcorner (\alpha;\beta) \,\epsilon\, \hat{\gamma}\, p''''(\gamma) \urcorner$

The color axiom will be:

$\vdash \ulcorner \sim R(\alpha) \,v \sim G(\alpha) \urcorner$

Some axioms governing the succession relation are:

$\vdash \ulcorner S(\alpha;\beta) \supset \cdot C(\alpha) \cdot C(\beta) \urcorner$

$\vdash \ulcorner p''''(\alpha) \supset (\exists \beta)(\exists \gamma)(\alpha = (\beta;\gamma)) \urcorner$

$\vdash \ulcorner S(\alpha;\beta) \supset {\sim}S(\beta;\alpha) \urcorner$

$\vdash \ulcorner {\sim}S(\alpha;\alpha) \urcorner$

$\vdash \ulcorner (\exists \alpha)(\beta)({\sim}S(\beta;\alpha)) \urcorner$

$\vdash \ulcorner S(\alpha;\beta) \cdot S(\alpha;\gamma) \cdot \supset \cdot \beta = \gamma \urcorner$

$\vdash \ulcorner S(\beta;\alpha) \cdot S(\gamma;\alpha) \cdot \supset \cdot \beta = \gamma \urcorner$

Suppose that the Martian pulls the lever a thousand times, and gets 400 green counters, 400 red ones, and 200 that are neither green nor red. He obviously has much more information than this, since he noted the order in which these various colors appeared as well as the simple fact that they did appear, but for the moment we shall ignore this supplementary information.

Let a number N be given, greater than or equal to 1000. Let a ratio r be given, such that $rN = N_1$ and $(1 - r)N = N_2$. Let a number k be given, lying between 0 and 1000. If we interpret r as the proportion of red counters, and k as the number of red counters in a 1000-fold sample, then we can calculate the proportion of *all* 1000-fold samples (subclasses) of the N counters, which have exactly k red counters in them, by means of the equation:

(1) $\quad \dfrac{C^k_{N_1} \, C^{n-k}_{N_2}}{C^n_N}$, where $n = 1000$, $C^i_j = \dfrac{j\,!}{i!(j-i)\,!}$

As N increases, the other numbers n, k, and r remaining constant, the value of (1) decreases toward (2) as a limit:

(2) $\quad C^k_{1000} \, r^k \, (1-r)^{1000-k}$

which is a function only of $n \, (= 1000)$, k, and r. Similarly, the proportion of 1000-fold subclasses of the class of all counters, that have a number of red counters lying between $1000 \, (r + m_1)$ and $1000 \, (r - m_2)$ will obviously be:

(3) $\quad \displaystyle\sum_{k \,=\, n\,(r \,-\, m_2)}^{k \,=\, n\,(r \,+\, m_1)} \dfrac{C^k_{N_1} \, C^{n-k}_{N_2}}{C^n_N}$

or, as N get larger, will approach:

(4) $\quad \displaystyle\sum_{k \,=\, n\,(r \,-\, m_2)}^{k \,=\, n\,(r \,+\, m_1)} C^k_n \, r^k (1-r)^{n-k}$

Take $m_1 = m_2$, both positive. (This will yield a rationally represent-ative matrix for the Martian in his state of ignorance with regard to the proportion of red counters.) Consider (3) as a function of both N and r; for suitably large N and n, (3) will be a minimum for r in the neighborhood of $1/2$. It will be a maximum (and $= 1$), if $r = 0$ or $r = 1$. However large N may be, and whatever r may be, the value of (3) will not be lower than that given by (4) for $r = 1/2$. Thus we may say that whatever value r may have, and however large N may be (greater than n) the proportion of n-fold samples containing be-tween $n(r + m_1)$ and $n(r - m_2)$ red counters lies between the value of (4) for $r = 1/2$ and $_s1$. To say that a given sample, containing k red counters, is one of these special samples, is to say that,

(5) $n(r + m_1) \geq k \geq n(r - m_2)$

or, what is precisely the same thing, to say that,

(6) $k/n + m_2 \geq r \geq k/n - m_1$

Since the Martian is starting from scratch, there is nothing in his (highest level) rational corpus to prevent his 1000-fold sample from being a random member of the class of all 1000-fold samples with respect to belonging to the subclass of all 1000-fold samples which is representative (in the m_1, m_2 sense) of the proportion of red counters among all the counters produced by the slot machine. The following statistical statements are the strongest ones that can appear in the two highest levels of his rational corpus:

"%($\hat{x}$C(x), $\hat{x}$R(x), $_s0$; $_s1$))" in his rational corpus of level "$_s1$"

"%($\hat{x}$C(x), $\hat{x}$R(x), (.351; .449))" in his rational corpus of level ".998"

His rational corpus of level ".995" will contain these statistical statements, but it will also contain a stronger one, since (a) the probability requirement is weaker, and (b) the minimum value for the proportion of representative samples will be given, not by $r = 1/2$ as before, but by $r = .449$. The shortest interval requirement for rationally representative matrices will also lead to a slightly different sense of 'representative'. Forgetting about the trivial skewness of the shortest representative interval, we may infer from the hypothesis that the proportion of red counters lies be-tween .351 and .449, that the proportion of 1000-fold samples which are representative in the sense of $m_1 = m_2 = .043$, lies between .995 and .9964. Thus in his rational corpus of level ".995" the Martian will include the statement:

"%($\hat{x}$C(x), $\hat{x}$R(x), (.357; .443))"

Below is a tabulation of the strongest statistical statements included in the Martian's rational corpora of each level, computed by applying the normal approximation, and by ignoring the skewness of the rational interval of representation.

Level	Strongest Statement
"$_s1$"	"%($\hat{x}$C(x), $\hat{x}$R(x), ($_s0$; $_s1$))"
".998"	"%($\hat{x}$C(x), $\hat{x}$R(x), (.351; .449))"
".995"	"%($\hat{x}$C(x), $\hat{x}$R(x), (.357; .443))"
".99"	"%($\hat{x}$C(x), $\hat{x}$R(x), (.360; .440))"
".98"	"%($\hat{x}$C(x), $\hat{x}$R(x), (.364; .436))"
".97"	"%($\hat{x}$C(x), $\hat{x}$R(x), (.366; .434))"
".96"	"%($\hat{x}$C(x), $\hat{x}$R(x), (.368; .432))"
".95"	"%($\hat{x}$C(x), $\hat{x}$R(x), (.370; .430))"
".90"	"%($\hat{x}$C(x), $\hat{x}$R(x), (.375; .425))"
".85"	"%($\hat{x}$C(x), $\hat{x}$R(x), (.378; .422))"
".80"	"%($\hat{x}$C(x), $\hat{x}$R(x), (.380; .420))"

It will be noticed that the strength of a strongest statistical statement that is included in a rational corpus of a given level depends not only on the evidence and the level, but on how many levels of rational corpus there are above the given level. The smaller the steps by which we descend from a rational corpus of level "$_s1$" to a rational corpus of level ".90", the stronger the hypothesis we are entitled to include in the rational corpora of the latter level. This seems rather unfortunate, but not impossible to put up with; perhaps a change in the definition of a rational corpus would eliminate the peculiarity, though I haven't been able to think of one.

Now let us suppose that every green counter has been followed immediately by a red one. Consider the class of all 400-fold samples of green counters, and the proportion of these which are representative of the relative frequency with which green counters are followed by red ones. Although the sample is much smaller (400 as opposed to 1000) than the previous sample, the fact that the observed ratio is unity leads to a series of strongest statements increasing much more rapidly in strength than before. Below I present a tabulation of strongest statements against level; as before, though with less justification, I have used the normal approximation, and with still less justification I have ignored the skewness of the interval of rational representation.

Level	Strongest Statement
".998"	"$\%(\hat{x}(\exists y)(G(y) \cdot S(x;y)), \hat{x}R(x), (.925;_s1))$"
".995"	"$\%(\hat{x}(\exists y)(G(y) \cdot S(x;y)), \hat{x}R(x), (.970;_s1))$"
".990"	"$\%(\hat{x}(\exists y)(G(y) \cdot S(x;y)), \hat{x}R(x), (.979;_s1))$"

If we adopt the change in definition of rational corpus suggested in the first section of this chapter, then, provided that there are no green counters that have been followed by red ones, the list ends here. The next level of rational corpus, under these circumstances, will contain the universal generalization:

$$(z)((\exists y)(G(y) \cdot S(z;y)) \supset R(z))$$

It should be noted that this does not conflict in any way with the series of statistical statements considered earlier that bear directly on the general relative frequency of red counters. On the other hand, if his object is to anticipate the sort of counter he is going to get from the slot machine on each pull of the lever, this universal statement is of far greater importance to him.

In regard to the first set of statistical statements, I ignored any possible significance of the order in which the various kinds of counters occurred; in regard to the second set of statistical statements, I paid attention to only one sort of order. In both cases I supposed that the sequence of counters provided no information which would jeopardize the randomness of his sample with respect to the properties under discussion. Now I shall remove this restriction, and suppose that when the order is taken into account (as, rationally, it must be) a statement is confirmed which leads to the rejection of some of the foregoing statements—in particular, those in the first table, with the exception of those in the two highest-level rational corpora.

Suppose that the evidence can be broken down in some such fashion as this:

first	100 counters	35 neither green nor red.
second	100 "	35 neither green nor red.
third	100 "	30 neither green nor red.
fourth	100 "	30 neither green nor red.
fifth	100 "	25 neither green nor red.
sixth	100 "	20 neither green nor red.
seventh	100 "	15 neither green nor red.

eighth   100   "   10 neither green nor red.

ninth   100   "   0 neither green nor red.

tenth   100   "   0 neither green nor red.

Without going into the matter in detail, we may suppose that this evidence justifies the inclusion, in the Martian's rational corpus of level ".998", of a hypothesis which states roughly that the proportion of counters of some color other than red or green decreases as more and more counters are observed. The hypothesis will be very weak, since there are few instances on which to base it: for 100-fold segments of the sequence, there are only 10 instances. But we may suppose that it will suffice to show that the counters he has observed are from an especially non-representative subclass of the class of all equinumerous subclasses of counters, with respect to revealing the proportion of red counters. The statements of randomness, on which his earlier inferences were based, no longer hold. The statement mentioned as an ingredient of his highest level rational corpus (in the first table) will still hold, of course: it is logically true. Furthermore, the statement mentioned in the first table as being an ingredient of his rational corpus of level ".998" will still be there—relative to the *highest* level of rational corpus, his thousand fold sample is still random. It is only relative to his rational corpus of level ".998" (or lower) that this sample is rendered non-random by the confirmation of the trend statement in question.

On the other hand, it should be noted that the second sequence of statistical statements remains unaffected; the hypothesis that other-colored counters get rarer and rarer has no bearing at all on the relative frequency with which green counters are followed by red ones. This suggests another virtue of statistical statements which involve parameters close to 0 or close to 1: they are less sensitive to discoveries about trends.

The trend statement mentioned above may suggest that the Martian may try a rather complicated theory: it is clear that there is a function (in fact, any number of functions) $f(i)$, such that if i is the ordinal number of one of the first thousand counters, $f(i)$ will have the value 1 if the counter is green, the value 2 if the counter is red, and the value 0 if the counter is some other color. The function $f(i)$ may be supposed to be defined for all values of i, so that the Martian may be tempted to wonder if it actually holds for all the counters beyond the first thousand. And it might even be suggested that he already has a thousand confirming instances of this theory, since he already knows that it applies to the first thousand counters.

But he does not have knowledge of a thousand-fold sample of counters which is *random* with respect to the property of representing the proportion of all counters which will confirm the theory. For the theory cannot spring entirely out of thin air—at least not this type of theory—and the instances *in view of which* the theory is formulated obviously constitute a special subclass of the class of all equally numerous instances, with respect to the property of including a member which will refute the theory. Suppose that it is the first m instances that are required to determine the function $f(i)$; if m is 1000, then the Martian has no confirming instances at all for his theory; if m is less than a thousand, the Martian has $1000 - m$ confirming instances for his theory. The last part of the 1000-fold sample may perfectly well be a random member of its class (the class of all $(1000 - m)$-fold subclasses of the class of counters) with respect to reflecting the proportion of counters for which the theory holds.

I hope I have shown in this chapter that a result of what is roughly called 'induction' can be represented by a statement which is highly probable relative to our body of knowledge, and which therefore may be included in that body of knowledge. Of course my discussion has been concerned only with a special formalized language (or even a 'calculus'), and has revolved around certain special groups of statements in that language. But I should maintain that the sense of 'probability' defined for these groups of statements is very close in meaning to the sense of 'probability' employed by people who are not devotees of any special interpretation of probability; and I should also maintain that the groups of statements which I have defined as rational corpora are analogous to the vague concept of a body of knowledge.

The example of the Martian at the slot machine may then, if all these things are true, be considered as a prototype of induction at work. Whether or not this should be construed as a 'justification' of induction, however, is still an open question; this question will be the subject of the last chapter.

CHAPTER NINETEEN

Statistical Inference

1. In view of the fundamental importance which attaches to statistical generalization on my theory, it will be interesting to compare the criteria embodied in this theory with the criteria suggested by various current theories of statistical inference or by the currently popular decision theories. It should be noted, however, that I am not offering a competitive theory of statistical inference, nor a competitive decision theory. The theory of statistical inference, decision theory, the theory of the most efficient design of experiments, and so on, are worked out by mathematical statisticians for definite purposes in situations in which we have a very respectable amount of information to go on. In particular, tests and decisions are made, not to determine beliefs, but to determine courses of action. The theory of probability I have presented above, and the distinction I have insisted upon between probabilities and ratios, will fit in perfectly well with these fancy theories and lead to no particularly surprising conclusions. But I also maintain that probability, in my sense, is involved in every application of these theories. Another reason for examining these theories is that there are philosophers who correctly see that induction by simple enumeration is fundamental, but who feel also that statistical decision theories and theories of statistical inference will prove to be the source and basis of any sound theory of induction. In this respect, I think they are in error.

I have already discussed the simplest form of Neyman's theory of confidence intervals, and shown that it is essentially the same as mine. The distinction rests primarily on the fact that for Neyman the selection of an 'appropriate' reference class is a matter of skill and intuition, while on my theory it is simply a matter of logic. Instead of beginning with a consideration of what it is to be a random member of a class, I could have begun by considering the criteria for a correct choice of reference class. It would have amounted to the same thing in the end, for the correct choice of a reference class, or fundamental probability set, clearly depends on what we know about the object we are concerned with, and what we know about the relations between the properties that we know this object to have, and the properties we are speculating about its having.

R. A. Fisher, in various of his publications, and particularly in *Statistical Methods for Research Workers,* and *The Design of Experiments,* shows most impressively the advantages to be gained from designing experiments in such a way as to take advantage of the knowledge we already possess—e.g., regarding the homogeneity or heterogeneity of different parts of the population we are investigating. The procedures he discusses are by and large altogether too sophisticated for mention here; but there is one procedure, about whose necessity Fisher is quite adamant, which does deserve mention here. I refer to randomization—a matter which I mentioned briefly before, and one which I feel is responsible for a significant amount of confusion in the gathering and application of statistical data.

Fisher's classical experiment about the lady tasting tea will provide an excellent framework in which to discuss randomization. The problem and the hypothetical experiment are described by Fisher as follows: "A lady declares that by tasting a cup of tea made with milk she can discriminate whether the milk or the tea infusion was first added to the cup." "Our experiment consists in mixing eight cups of tea, four in one way and four in the other, and presenting them to the subject for judgement in a random order..."[1]

It is easy to calculate that there are seventy ways of choosing four cups from eight, only one of which will divide the eight cups into two homogeneous groups (correctly) with regard to the method of preparation. The argument in favor of the proposed decision function—to reject the null hypothesis that the lady cannot after all discriminate only when she identifies all four cups correctly—rests on the supposition that if the lady lacks the ability to discriminate, she will choose the correct four cups only one time out of seventy in the long run. It is to insure that this supposition is correct that randomization is allegedly required. We need to "...justify the assumption that, if discrimination of the kind under test is absent, the result of the experiment will be wholly governed by the laws of chance."[2]

It is quite possible that under the conditions of the experiment the assumption in question might not be justified: "If all those cups made with the milk first had sugar added, while those made with the tea first had none, a very obvious difference in flavor would have been introduced which might well ensure that all those made with sugar should be classed alike."[3] Fisher points out that, on the other hand, it is totally impossible to meet the requirement that all

1. Ronald A. Fisher, *Design of Experiments* (Sixth Edition), Edinburgh, 1951, p. 11.
2. *Ibid.*, p. 17.
3. *Ibid.*, p. 17.

the cups must be *exactly* alike, "... because the uncontrolled causes which may influence the result are always strictly [*sic*] innumerable."[4] While the latter clause may be a pardonable exaggeration, Fisher's point is undoubtedly perfectly sound.

To insure that these differences among the cups will not impugn the validity of the experiment, we assign, strictly at random, four out of the eight cups to each treatment. That is to say, we pick the four cups to which milk will be added first by a procedure which will, in the long run, select each possible set of four cups equally often. We do not, speaking very strictly, *know* that our randomizing procedure will be such as to have this result, but, by employing random numbers or cards or some other mechanical system, we can have excellent grounds for *rationally believing* that it will. This is randomization, and according to Fisher, this "...simple precaution of randomization will suffice to guarantee the validity of the test of significance by which the result of the experiment is to be judged."[5]

I shall now argue that, in relation to perfectly possible and plausible states of our rational corpus, the simple precaution in question is neither a sufficient nor a necessary condition of the validity of the test of significance contemplated.

It is not a sufficient condition. Suppose that four of the eight cups were thinner than the others, and suppose that we have reason to believe that a cup with a thinner edge is more likely to be judged as having been made with the milk first than a cup with a thicker edge. Now if our randomization procedure is a suitable one, the four thin cups will receive the milk-first treatment one time out of seventy. But we perform the experiment only once; what do we do if our randomizing procedure does just happen to pick out these four cups for the milk-first treatment? Do we take another whirl with our randomizing apparatus? This will vitiate the sound frequency basis of our randomization, and will in general lead to the question of how biassed our randomization has to be, and in what respects it is biassed, before we reject a physically determined selection of cups. Or do we simply accept the rather odd result of our randomizing procedure, and admit that the experiment did not turn out well? In either case, it is clear that the mechanical randomization by itself is not sufficient to guarantee the reasonableness of the result of the experiment.

The randomization of the treatments is not necessary, either. Let us suppose that the eight cups are really quite indistinguishable to us. We arrange them in a linear order, and apply the milk-first treatment to cups numbered 1, 2, 5, and 7. This is a perfectly pos-

4. *Ibid.*, p. 17.
5. *Ibid.*, p. 17.

sible result of the randomizing procedure; if the test of significance is valid when this selection of cups is produced by a randomizing procedure, it is valid when this selection is made arbitrarily. The experiment is only performed once.

Since the test of the lady's ability is being made just once, the argument that if it were made an infinite (or very large) number of times, using a randomization procedure, the peculiarities of each cup would be cancelled out, is simply irrelevant. What we really require is that the actual selection of cups for treatment is random in my sense, with respect to providing an indication of the lady's tasting ability. Mechanical randomization is neither necessary nor sufficient for randomness in this sense.

Let us suppose that we seriously undertake such an experiment as this. Clearly it will be possible to find eight cups which are, to all intents and purposes, the same; it will be possible to make the various cups of tea so quickly that differences in temperature are trivial; and in fact it seems reasonable to suppose that there need be no physical characteristics of the cups of tea which could (so far as we know or can conceive) clew the lady as to which is which—no physical characteristics, that is, except one. This ineliminable characteristic, which might very well be related to her judgements, is the order in which the eight cups are presented for tasting. We can give the lady all eight cups simultaneously: but there will generally be a 'natural' order in which she will taste them: from left to right if the array is linear, or from left to right and from top to bottom, if the array is two-dimensional.

To simplify things, suppose that we present the cups in a linear array, and that we know the order in which the lady is going to taste the cups. Now it is clear that if we prepare the first four cups in the same way, the lady need only guess what we have done in order to make a perfect score. The experiment may thus easily be invalidated. Suppose that we prepare every other cup in the same way. Again it is not far-fetched to suppose that the lady will catch on and make a perfect score, even if her ability to discriminate is non-existent. The same difficulty arises in connection with any 'simple' arrangement. Even if we attempt deliberately to make the arrangement complicated—as I did in the 1, 2, 5, 7 arrangement suggested above—we may still happen to arrive at precisely the sort of arrangement that the lady expects. This then, is the real point of the randomizing procedure: to make sure that our subconscious—perhaps taken with the lady's great beauty—will not cause us to choose an arrangement which is precisely the sort of arrangement the lady would catch onto quickly. But if this is the point of randomization—to fool the lady—then clearly we will not accept an outcome of our randomizing machinery which leads to the first four cups being prepared in the same way, or every other cup, etc. The experiment is to be performed only once, and if there is anything wrong with deciding to prepare the first four cups in the same way, then the same thing will be wrong with letting your randomizing machine make that decision.

In experiments concerning agricultural plots, or in quality control experiments in industry, randomization is also often employed. Here there is no question of outwitting anyone. One reason for which randomization may be employed in such cases is similar to the reason given above, however. A scheme of physical randomization precludes the possibility that the experimenter may, in selecting objects for different treatments, or in picking a particular sample from a parent population, be influenced by his subconscious desire to achieve certain results. That this can happen is suggested by certain psychological facts; lacking these facts, it is doubtful that any empirical rationale could be given for randomization in such circumstances.

Some populations—e.g., a population of electric light bulbs, as they come off a production line—are ordered in such a way that any regular method of selecting a sample is likely to be biassed: if we pick the first n bulbs, our knowledge that in the process of production machines wear out will cause this sample not to be random with respect to revealing the proportion of defective bulbs; if we pick every i'th bulb, the desired assertion of randomness is prevented by our knowledge that quality will probably vary periodically. In this example, even more than in Fisher's illustration, it is difficult to see how an ordinary man could make a selection which was sufficiently irregular. The simplest method of getting a properly random sample is to use a table of random numbers—but if the use of the table results in a sample which is not random with respect to representing the property of the population in which we are interested, we are clearly obliged to try again.

What we require as a basis for inference, is not that the method be one which is as likely to select any one sample as any other, in the frequency sense and in the long run, but that the particular sample that we do in point of fact and once and for all select, be a random member of all such selections with respect to the property of being representative of the parent population. A mechanically selected sample is—often—unlikely to be representative. An intuitively selected sample—due to the machinations of the human subconscious, and perhaps for other reasons, such as the natural human desire for simplicity—is also unlikely to be representative. A randomized selection is often random with respect to being repre-

sentative, and it may be accepted as such unless we notice some debilitating feature of the particular selection which has resulted. But
the provisional clause must not be ignored on the basis of a 'long-
run' theory, since it is patently absurd to use a long-run theory to
justify beliefs about a particular statement when we have more directly relevant evidence concerning the statement. The frequency
statement that such and such a method will lead to such and such
results with a certain relative frequency is relevant to the results
of applying the method in a given case only when that application is
a random member of the class of all such applications, relative to
our total rational corpus, with respect to the property of leading
to a true conclusion.

There is another reason for the perhaps excessive use of randomizing techniques, which is pointed out by Neyman.[6] This is that
in discussing experimental procedures abstractly, we are concerned
with a large class of applications of a certain method, not with just
one application of it, and to say that among this large class there
will be a high frequency of successes is about all we can say. But
when we are concerned with a given application of the method, we
must take into account all of the factors that are relevant to that
particular experiment. The introduction of randomization makes it
possible to discuss the general theory abstractly and elegantly: but
this does not mean that we must follow some sort of randomizing
procedure in order to achieve valid results when we are concerned
not with the theory, nor with the general class of applications of the
theory, but with a concrete experiment about which we have a sup-
ply of detailed information, and from which we want to draw a definite, concrete conclusion.

These comments apply generally to theories of statistical inference which make use of randomization—whenever we employ randomization, it is, I maintain, irrational to accept the result of the
randomization unless this selection of objects is also random in
my sense. Similar considerations apply to the theory of statistical
decisions, when the justification of a particular decision function is
made to depend on certain long-run frequencies of the two kinds of
errors. In a given experiment, one or the other of these errors is
committed, or it is not; the long-run frequencies of these errors
are of interest to us only when (as is usually the case, of course)
the experiment is a random member (in my sense) of the class of
experiments to which the frequencies of errors apply.

2. This brings me to that most complete, fruitful, and elegant the-

6. J. Neyman, *Lectures and Conferences on Probability and Mathematical Statistics* (Second Edition), Washington, 1952.

ory of statistical decision functions recently developed by A. Wald.[7] For my own sake, as well as that of the reader, I shall consider only the very simplified example of the application of this theory used by R. B. Braithwaite;[8] but a few preliminary remarks are in order. The theory of statistical decision functions is designed to provide a framework in which to clarify and evaluate certain rules of inductive behavior. The term 'inductive behavior' was suggested by Neyman,[9] and I have already indicated that the standards of inductive behavior will necessarily go beyond what I have proposed as standards of rational belief. In the first place, these standards of inductive behavior must obviously take account of the desirability of different consequences of the behavior. The optimum form of inductive behavior for me and for you in a certain situation may very well be different, if we place different values on the possible outcomes of the situation. On the other hand, I would maintain that faced with the same evidence we should not only have roughly the same degree of belief in the occurrence of a particular outcome, but that this degree of belief should be *rational* in the sense that if we do disagree, we ought to be able to straighten out our disagreement.

One obvious way of arriving at a decision as to how to behave in a given situation, then, is to go through an ordinary process of induction, collecting evidence, evaluating it, and so on, until a statistical hypothesis about the relative frequencies of the different outcomes in such situations is highly confirmed. Then we need only apply our own standard of desirability to the various outcomes in order to discover that course of action which maximizes our rational expectation in terms of what we have sufficient grounds to believe and of what we desire.

Incidentally, this suggests that we distinguish between mathematical expectations and rational expectation—the relationship being analogous to that between relative frequency and probability. Rational expectation will apply to single events (including complex ones); mathematical (or average) expectation will apply to classes of events. It is in connection with rational expectation that the ordinary axioms of the probability calculus will apply; we will demand that rational expectation depend on a set of degrees of belief which is not only rational, but also coherent—since by definition we wish to maximize our rational expectation.

There is a way of short-cutting the process of arriving at inductive beliefs first, and then applying a scale of values to determine a course of action. It is with this short cut that most theories

7. A. Wald, *Statistical Decision Functions*, New York, 1950.
8. R. B. Braithwaite, *Scientific Explanation*, Cambridge, 1953.
9. J. Neyman, *First Course in Probability and Statistics*, New York, 1950.

of testing statistical hypotheses, as well as Wald's more general theory, are concerned. This can already be seen in the case of the lady tasting tea. If we wanted to acquire a usefully precise hypothesis concerning the relative frequency with which the lady will be able to discriminate correctly, we would require many more instances as evidence than the eight cups Fisher suggests. But we are satisfied to know that if we accept the criterion suggested by Fisher, we will falsely credit the lady with powers she does not possess only one time out of seventy—or rather, since we make the test but once, the probability of falsely crediting the lady with these powers is 1/70. (Our use of the test may therefore leave something to be desired from the point of view of chivalry.)

The short cuts analyzed by decision theory are important, because in many of those situations in which we call on statistical evidence to guide us in our actions, we are concerned mainly with avoiding certain well defined sorts of mistakes. It suffices in a particular situation to know that the probabilities of committing these mistakes are low. And this clearly requires both that the frequency with which samples leading to these mistakes be low, and that the sample at hand be a random one with respect to the property of leading to these mistakes.

But beyond these probabilities—the probabilities of making various sorts of mistakes—questions of rational belief need not (as these investigators have all pointed out) enter into the matter at all. In the same sense, however, the question of 'accepting' or 'rejecting' any hypothesis need not enter into the matter at all. The whole problem can be considered (as Wald considers it) as a problem of evaluating the rules for taking one or another course of action in given circumstances. It is interesting, but not startling, that such an evaluation can be given without knowing anything whatever about the probabilities of the physical hypotheses which might be true in the circumstances, and, even more impressive, that rules can be given which will lead to decision functions having very small risks and which still require far less data than would be required even for a rather weak confirmation that such and such a physical hypothesis is credible.

This all becomes clear if we consider a very simple case, such as that of deciding whether to put a batch of a certain drug on the market or to destroy it. When we test a sample of the drug for toxicity, we are not interested in confirming or disconfirming the hypothesis that the batch is toxic: we are not trying to find evidence such that we can include the statement "This batch is toxic" or the statement "This batch is not toxic" in our rational corpus. What we are interested in is being damned sure that we won't decide to put a toxic batch on the market. Given this practical certainty, moreover, we would also like to minimize the risk of destroying perfectly good batches. Instead of speaking of 'accepting' the hypothesis that the batch is toxic (since if we wanted to poison wolves with it, we would reject this hypothesis with respect to the same batch and on the same evidence) it seems more plausible to speak directly of withholding the drug from the market. If we were interested in the purely factual question of whether the drug was toxic or not, then we would not take risks and costs into account, and we would certainly not 'accept' the hypothesis that it was toxic without far more evidence than is required to keep us from putting it on the market

Somewhat more detailed discussion of a particular type of decision theory is important, I think, since there are some authors, notably R. B. Braithwaite and C. W. Churchman,[10] who have recently maintained that the problem of induction is irreducibly bound up with decision theory and with its attendant concern for values involved in accepting or rejecting hypotheses; they maintain that there is no problem of induction other than the problem of evaluating inductive behavior.

Braithwaite discusses at length a particular form of strategy which he calls 'the prudential policy.' It is similar to Wald's minimax policy. Wald himself devotes a great amount of attention to minimax solutions of the decision problem, on the grounds, " (1) a minimax solution seems, in general, to be a *reasonable* [my italics] solution of the decision problem when an *a priori* distribution in Ω does not exist or is unknown to the experimenter; (2) the theory of minimax solutions plays an important role in deriving basic results concerning complete classes of decision functions."[11] Braithwaite, on the other hand, believes that Wald's minimax policy "...raises a point of great philosophical interest..."[12] I shall maintain, as against Wald, that there are many situations in which, while we do not have a very accurate idea about the *a priori* distributions in Ω, we still have enough knowledge to render a minimax solution somewhat unreasonable under certain assignments of value; and as against Braithwaite, I shall maintain that the point which interests him—the necessity for a consideration of values in testing hypotheses—is of practical rather than philosophical interest, and in fact not of general, but only of instantial significance.

Braithwaite's example concerns the choice between two class-ratio hypotheses H_1 and H_2, about B and A, on the basis of a sample

10. C. W. Churchman, *Theory of Experimental Inference*, New York, 1948.
11. Wald, *op. cit.*, p. 18.
12. Braithwaite, *op. cit.*, p. 199.

of fixed size. A 'strategy' is a plan to 'prefer H_1' (or to prefer H_2) according to the composition of the sample. Thus if the sample consists of two members of B, and if s is the number of members of A in the sample, one possible strategy would be to prefer H_1 if $s = 0$, and to prefer H_2 if $s = 1$ or $s = 2$. H_1 is the hypothesis that the proportion of B's that are A's is .6; H_2 is the hypothesis that the proportion of B's that are A's is .3. It is clear that, on the basis of H_1, we can calculate the proportion x_i of all samples of the given size which will lead to a correct preference between H_1 and H_2 in accordance with a given strategy T_i. In the same way, we can calculate the corresponding proportion y_i on the assumption that H_2 is true.

Now suppose that if H_1 is true, and I prefer H_1, I gain a units of value; if H_1 is false, and I prefer H_1, I lose b units of value; similarly, c is the gain for choosing H_2 correctly, and d is the loss suffered by choosing H_2 incorrectly. We can now calculate the mathematical expectation of following each of the possible strategies T_i, in either of the two permissible cases: H_1 true, or H_2 true. Let $X_i = a\, x_i - d(1 - x_i)$, and $Y_i = c\, y_i - b(1 - y_i)$. X_i is the mathematical expectation of strategy T_i if H_1 is true, Y_i the mathematical expectation of strategy T_i if H_2 is true.

The prudential policy is simply to select, for every i, the lesser of X_i and Y_i, and then to adopt the strategy which renders this minimum expectation a maximum, or if there are several strategies that meet this criterion, to select one of those for which the greater of X_i or Y_i is a maximum.

The exceptional cases, when some of the $a, b, c,$ and d, values are 0, are of particular significance as illustrating certain oddities about the prudential policy. If either a or d (or both) is positive, and $b = c = 0$, i.e., if we gain by choosing H_1 correctly, and lose by choosing H_2 incorrectly, and otherwise neither gain nor lose, then, regardless of the evidence, the prudential policy is to choose H_1. Now it makes admirable good sense, in such a situation, always to *act* as if H_1 were true, however much we are persuaded by the evidence that H_2 is in point of fact true. But it is rather a different matter always to *believe* that H_1 is true in the face of any amount of evidence to the contrary. And it seems rather extreme to do away with 'beliefs' altogether.

It seems far more natural to say that under the circumstances, whatever degree of belief you are rationally obligated to have in H_2 by the evidence, you should always act on the basis of H_1, since you cannot lose by acting wrongly on the basis of H_1, and you cannot win by acting correctly on the basis of H_2.

A different type of exceptional case is suggested when both a and

b are positive, and both c and d are 0. Here the prudential policy directs us to prefer H_2, regardless of the evidence, on the grounds that in preferring H_2 we cannot lose, while in preferring H_1, although we *may* gain, we also may lose. It directs us to prefer H_2, not only in the face of any amount of evidence to the contrary, but regardless of the relative values of a and b. If we are to receive a million dollars for correctly preferring H_1, and lose a penny for incorrectly preferring H_1, we are still directed to prefer H_2.

Now if we were not as ignorant as is stipulated in the statement of the problem, so that we could, after all, assess the probabilities of H_1 and H_2, it is clear that the odds against H_1 would have to be 100,000, 000 to 1, on the assignment of values suggested, in order to render it rational to prefer H_2. Is it true that no amount of evidence in favor of H_2 can make it rationally obligatory to have a higher degree of belief than .00000001 in H_1? This is what Braithwaite seems to imply.

If the prudential policy were simply described as a possible basis for choosing between hypotheses, so that one could feel quite free to take it or leave it, all would be well and good, although one might be tempted to leave it rather often. But Braithwaite not only proposes it; he also goes on to defend it as a generally valid inductive policy. "This reasonableness [of the prudential policy] does not consist in the fact that any one particular action done in accordance with this general principle will produce consequences having greater utility than an action done in accordance with a different principle, but in the statistical fact, i.e., in the truth of the statistical hypothesis, that a number of actions done in accordance with the general principle will, by and large, yield more utility than an action done in accordance with a different principle."[13]

But the statistical fact referred to is simply false. For suppose we had only to make decisions in situations similar to the one described above, where a and b are both positive and c and d both 0. Is it possible to maintain as a statistical fact that the person who sticks to the prudential policy in preferring H_2 in the face of any amount of evidence will generally gain more (i.e., lose less, since he can gain nothing) than the person who risks a penny against a million dollars when there is every indication that he will probably win? I find it hard to believe that there is a statistical law from which it follows that the latter person will, over a large number of cases, lose—especially if he only prefers H_1 when there is much evidence in its favor.

One final example, which is intended once more to show the difficulty of treating a choice between actions as a choice between hypotheses, follows. Suppose that I am given a large bag, and told

13. *Ibid.*, p. 229.

that it contains black and white balls in the ratio of 1:2, 1:1, or 2:1. I am allowed to draw four balls, and then I must make a guess as to the ratio. If I guess correctly I am to receive one dollar; if I guess incorrectly, I am fined one dollar. I draw the four balls that I am allowed as evidence, and two of them turn out to be black. A prudential policy will presumably direct me to 'prefer the hypothesis' that the ratio is 1:1; and in the circumstances this is surely the most rational hypothesis to believe, although it is not worthy of a very high degree of rational belief.

But now suppose that, on the same evidence of four balls, I am presented with the choice of paying a one-dollar fine or accepting the long end of the following bet: 10 dollars to one dollar that the ratio is either 1:2 or 1:1, and also I must choose between paying a one dollar fine, and accepting the long end of this bet: ten dollars to one dollar that the ratio is either 2:1 or 1:1. It is difficult to see how the prudential policy can direct me to do anything but accept both bets—since I am not saving any money by refusing to bet, and since I *may* actually gain if I do accept one or both bets. This again is perfectly reasonable when we phrase the matter in terms of action—i.e., in terms of accepting or refusing bets. But in the terminology of choosing between hypotheses, we get this: on the basis of a sample containing two black balls and two white balls, accept the hypothesis that the ratio is 2:1, and accept the hypothesis that the ratio is 1:2. It is obvious that at most one of these hypotheses can be true (and the limited evidence available suggests that neither of them are true); but it is equally obvious that it is reasonable for us to act 'as if' both hypotheses were true.

In short, while values may be taken into account (as they are and must be) in choosing between actions, and statistical evidence may also be taken into account in choosing between actions, it is an obfuscation of the real issues involved in coming to an agreement about what it is that we have learned and can learn from experience to combine both considerations and call the resulting policy a policy of choosing between *hypotheses*, rather than between actions. As long as the elements of fact and the elements of value that enter into a decision can be kept straight, it is an aid to clear thinking to do so. The confusion between fact and value is an ancient and venerable one in theology, but it is new to science.

CHAPTER 20

Justification

1.   I shall consider here not only the justification of induction, but also the justification of the logic of rational belief that I have presented. Let us begin with a general examination of 'justification'. Consider the statement: "It will rain tomorrow." There is one obvious usage of 'justification' in accordance with which this statement will be justified only if, in point of fact, it does rain tomorrow. The rain, or the occurrence of rain, will justify the prediction of rain. In this sense a statement is justified only when it is (a) actually true, and (b) known to be true—in a very strict sense of 'know'.

In this sense of justification, it is obvious that no predictive statement can be justified while it is still predictive; "The sun will rise tomorrow," is, today, a prediction; it cannot be justified today. Tomorrow the statement will be justified (presumably); but translated into tomorrow's terminology, the statement is: "The sun rose today." When we deal with the far stronger statements which induction is often supposed to support, such as, "The sun will rise every morning for the next million years," it is clear that we *will* never have a justification for them. But of course we would like to have some grounds for believing these statements here and now—it is not possible simply to suspend judgement for a million years.

One suggestion is that while we do *believe* that the sun will continue to rise for a while, this belief cannot be justified now; it has no logical status, on this view, relative to the evidence we have for it. Reichenbach, for example, maintains that none of our beliefs about future occurrences are 'justified' before the events concerned have happened. My belief that the sun will rise tomorrow will only be justified when and if the sun does rise tomorrow. It follows immediately that none of our 'inductive' beliefs are justified. Reichenbach even goes so far as to state explicitly that he allows 'no form of rational belief'.[1]

This has one very strange consequence. It means that the belief that the sun will rise tomorrow is in exactly the same boat, has exactly the same *logical* status, as the belief that the sun will not

---

1. Reichenbach, "A Conversation Between Bertrand Russell and David Hume," *Journal of Philosophy* 46, 1949, p. 545.

rise tomorrow. Neither is justified today, neither is rational, and tomorrow either one may turn out to be justified. While 'justification' may be used in this narrow sense, and while we may be willing to admit that in this sense neither of the statements regarding tomorrow's sunrise is (today) justified, it still seems plausible and useful to make some kind of a distinction between the two statements.

The distinction which comes first to mind is that the belief that the sun will rise tomorrow will very probably turn out to be justified, while the belief that it will not rise will very probably turn out to be unjustified. G. H. von Wright suggests an interpretation of 'justification' along these lines. Induction will be 'justified' if predictions made in accordance with inductive procedures turn out to be justified by the actuality (or are true) very frequently. Or if we say that inductive conclusions are to be justified by reference to probability, "We must . . . be able to give some kind of guarantee that, in preferring the more probable to the less probable, we shall be more successful than in making the opposite preference."[2]

But as von Wright himself points out, there is no justification of induction in this sense. We cannot give a guarantee in advance that we shall be right more often than not, any more than we can give a guarantee that we shall always be right. Just as we have to wait until tomorrow to see whether or not our belief that the sun will rise is 'justified', according to Reichenbach, so we must wait until doomsday to see whether or not our 'probable' predictions lead to success more often than to failure. It is no good suggesting that our 'probable' predictions will *probably* lead to success: for to satisfy von Wright this second occurrence of 'probable' (if not nonsensical to start with) must, like the first occurrence, be interpreted factually.

It is thus clear that in neither the sense of justification that required known vindication in the future, nor in the sense of justification that requires a known high frequency of vindications in the future, can induction be justified. I do not think I need to present the argument supporting the thesis that there is no justification of induction in either of these senses in any greater detail; this thesis is one of the most cruelly beaten of contemporary horses, and details of the argument supporting it can be found in any philosophical periodical in various issues from 1910 to date.

But is there any other sense of justification that may be applied to the problem of elucidating the distinction between the statement, "The sun will rise tomorrow," and the statement, "The sun will

2. G. H. von Wright, *The Logical Problem of Induction*, Helsinki, 1941, p. 157.

not rise tomorrow''? There is the sense suggested by Heroditus: "There is nothing more profitable for a man than to take good counsel with himself; for even if the event turns out contrary to one's hopes, still one's decision was right, even though fortune has made it of no effect; whereas if a man acts contrary to good counsel, although by luck he gets what he had no right to expect, his decision was not any the less foolish.''[3]

In this sense, we may say that a belief is justified if it is the result of good counsel—regardless of how matters turn out in point of fact. Of course this is no direct help to us, for it leaves open the question of what good counsel is. But we may construe 'taking good counsel' as 'applying the rules of inductive inference'. Now what are the rules of inductive inference? It is the answer to this question, I think, that has been the concern of most writers who have taken the problems of induction seriously. The answers seem in general to have taken the form of suggestions as to postulates (e.g., the postulates in Russell's *Human Knowledge*, Keynes' postulate of limited variety) which, combined with experimental evidence, lead, by way of the ordinary rules of logic or certain axioms concerning probability, to a high degree of probability for those inductive conclusions to which (coincidentally, of course) we do in point of fact attribute a high degree of probability.

But there are two difficulties with this approach to the problem of induction. There is first of all the difficulty of accepting the postulates, since they cannot be justified inductively without assuming them to start with, and since they are supposed to be factual in nature rather than logical. This difficulty could be avoided by maintaining (not very plausibly, perhaps) that it is simply rational *per definitionem* to accept the postulates independently of any evidence in their favor. But there is a far more serious difficulty in the problem of applying these postulates to actual inductive situations. While it may be of philosophical interest to be able to show that the process of learning from experience is rationally justifiable, no one, I think, could seriously maintain that it is *not* rational to learn from experience without doing violence to ordinary usage. What is really important and interesting about the justification of induction is not that induction in general can be justified, but that there is a standard in terms of which we can evaluate the force of particular inductions. But no generally applicable method for evaluating the force of an induction (or the degree of rational belief which the evidence obligates us to have in the inductive conclusion) seems to be forthcoming on the postulate theory of induction.

3. Heroditus vii, 10. Quoted in Keynes, *Treatise on Probability*, New York, 1921.

This brings us to another sense of 'justification' which is closely related to the 'good counsel' sense. This is the sense in which one 'justifies a line of type'—that is, makes it come out even. When a line of type is justified, anybody can see that it is justified. In this sense, justification is required, and available, for the theorems of ML: you can say that a certain statement in ML is a theorem, but you are not *justified* in saying so unless you can produce a proof—and anybody can see that your assertion of the theoremhood of the statement is justified if you do produce a proof. In the same way, an inductive conclusion is justified if the relation between the evidence and the conclusion conforms to standard evidential rules, such that the rules and the evidence render the conclusion highly probable. We may also be satisfied by a slightly weaker sense of justification in which, while the inductive argument itself is not foolproof, the judgement of any particular objection offered against the argument is. It is this sort of thing that seems to be required by the adjective *rational* as applied to beliefs: it must be inevitable that two people accepting the same standard of rationality and the same body of evidence, will be able to come to agreement about the degree of belief in an inductive conclusion which is justified by this evidence.

The logic of rational belief I have been expounding is intended to be just such a standard. It is completely independent of the character of the world, and it is intended to be intuitively acceptable, to conform quite closely to ordinary usage, and to provide a framework within which disputes as to the force of an inductive conclusion, relative to given evidence, can be resolved. It is also possible that it may provide a framework in which it is possible to justify an inductive conclusion definitively—but this depends on the possibility of a strictly constructive assertion of randomness, and this, even if it is sometimes possible, is generally more trouble than it is worth.

The following two sections will be devoted to illustrating this claim by means of examples; in the final section I shall return to a question which may already be bothering some readers: "Granting that this is a somewhat plausible sense of 'rational justification', why, still, *ought* I to accept that which is rationally justified in this sense?"

2.   Let us examine, first of all, the way in which ML can be used to justify such statements as, "$2 + 3 = 5$." This statement is a theorem in ML, so that we can definitively justify it by exhibiting a proof—that is, a sequence of formulas each of which is an axiom or a ponential of earlier formulas in the sequence, and which ends with the statement in question. Such a proof would be enormously long (in primitive notation) and very complicated; but it would be a dif-

ficult student indeed who insisted on the fully detailed proof. It generally suffices to show (by metatheorems) that there is a proof. The important thing about the use of ML to justify such statements is not that we can write down a proof the minute someone questions the validity of the statement, but that (a) we know a proof exists, which could be exhibited if worst came to worst, and (b) we can therefore be sure that some argument (at the most tedious, a complete proof) will convince any doubter, provided, of course, that he accepts ML.

The proof, and any argument short of this, is designed merely to show that the statement in question is a theorem of ML. To show more than this, we must go beyond ML. Thus we may turn to semantics to show that the statement in question is not only a theorem in ML, but is also true. Or we may turn to my logic of rational belief, and show that the statement in question will be an ingredient of any rational corpus that has any ingredients at all. If we interpret ML legislatively, or if we interpret my logic of rational belief that way, then we can say that everyone *ought to know* that $2 + 3 = 5$, i.e., that everybody ought to know, "$2 + 3 = 5$".

The important thing to notice about this example is that ML provides a framework within which to discuss the theoremhood of logical and mathematical statements; we do not have to go back to the primitive notation and exhibit a formal proof in every case. A proof for a given statement is not always known, but we can often tell that there is one anyway, and an argument establishing this (as a metatheorem) will usually lead to agreement concerning the status of the statement.

Now consider a somewhat more interesting form of argument: that intended to justify a material statement. Suppose I ask for a justification of the statement, "All whales have hearts." I will be told, perhaps, that obviously, since all mammals have hearts, and all whales are mammals, all whales have hearts. Here we are confronted by a problem which faces all beginning students of logic. Granted that the conclusion 'follows from' the premises, so what? What is this peculiar expression 'follows from', and what is the argument supposed to convince me of, and how is it supposed to do it?

We can translate the argument into the terminology of ML, and show that the conclusion follows from the premises in the sense appropriate to ML. The difficult student will now say, "Very well, I accept your translation into the language of ML, and I now understand what 'follows from' is supposed to mean. Now why should I *accept* the conclusion?"

"If you accept the premises and the argument leading from the premises to the conclusion, you *have* to accept the conclusion!''

''Why?'' the student may ask.

And the student is perfectly correct. Why indeed *ought* he to accept the conclusion? Not because it is true; although he is willing to accept the premises, this does not mean that they are true; and if the premises may not be true, the conclusion may not be true either. We cannot even tell him that it would be inconsistent to accept the premises and not the conclusion—since it wouldn't be. It would only be inconsistent for him to accept the premises and also to accept the denial of the conclusion. When you come right down to it, what is there in logic that says you *ought* to be consistent? We can say that it is just not rational to be inconsistent; and perhaps this suffices to make our difficult student reject the denial of the conclusion. But of course the *tertium non datur* does not apply to beliefs: it is surely not the case that we must either believe *p* or believe the denial of *p*. There is nothing at all inconsistent about accepting the premises and suspending judgement about the conclusion.

This confusion about the status of premises and about the legislative function of logic is quite widespread. It is only due to the fog in which the status of the premises of their examples is concealed that the authors of many logical textbooks can get by without any concept corresponding to that of a rational corpus—unless, like Quine, they confine their attentions strictly to an analysis of the purely formal relationships that can hold between statements. The answer to the student's problem lies in a more complete specification of what it is to be rational, and a more detailed analysis of what it means to 'accept' a statement. If we adopt the terminology of the logic of rational belief, it becomes easier to explain the force of such arguments as the above. We say that the statement ''All whales have hearts,'' is justified by the argument in question if the person who is asking for a justification has in his rational corpus the required premises. The argument shows that if the conjunction of the premises is an ingredient of a rational corpus, then the conclusion must be an ingredient of that rational corpus. (See **1221.) Anyone who has reason to believe the conjunction of the premises has (at least) as much reason to believe the conclusion.

Things can now be allowed to get more complicated. It is not at all certain that a person who expresses some doubt about whether or not whales have hearts will be convinced by the above argument; he may very well doubt, for example, that all whales are mammals. We may first, then, be called upon to justify the statement ''All whales are mammals.'' We can do this by arguing that since whales are warm-blooded and suckle their young, they are (by definition) mammals. We can justify the statement that all whales are warm-blooded and suckle their young, by means of a 'natural-kinds' type of inductive argument: if some members of a species are warm-blooded, and some females of the species suckle their young, then all members of the species are warm-blooded, and all normal females of the species are capable of suckling their young. This conditional is highly acceptable; it could perhaps be supported in turn by reference to physiological theories. The antecedent of the conditional can be justified by reference to the experience (via verbal or written reports) of marine biologists, or by reference to the authority of Herman Melville.

Ultimately, the justification for the statement that all whales have hearts, whatever form it takes, will rest on premises whose grounds for inclusion in rational corpora consist of simple enumerative evidence. But it is a very rare event when it is necessary to go back this far in the chain of argument to convince someone of the rationality of believing a given inductive conclusion—just as it is a rare event when a mathematical statement must be justified by exhibiting a proof of it in the primitive notation of ML.

Most practical deductive argument, outside of mathematics and logic itself, is intended to justify inductive conclusions—that is, conclusions which, like the premises from which they are deduced, are at best highly probable. The logic of rational belief provides a framework in which these deductive arguments can be expressed, and in which the rational obligation to *believe* the conclusion, as well as the validity of the argument itself can be established. Formal logic, as expressed in ML, can do no more than establish the validity of the argument; the supplement to formal logic (but it is equally formal), as expressed in the logic of rational belief, finishes the job.

Most of the inductive arguments that occur in well-developed sciences have this 'deductive' form: the inductive conclusion follows validly from general premises (e.g., concerning natural kinds) together with particular premises about instances of the class with which the conclusion is concerned, (e.g., the statement that some whales have been found to be warm-blooded.) Ultimately, however, all of our empirical knowledge must rest on induction by simple enumeration; and there are many branches of inquiry (sociology, agriculture, medicine, etc.,) in which induction by simple enumeration, in more or less sophisticated form, is still the most common form of argument. And this is true in a limited way even in the more highly developed sciences, for it is only by virtue of statistical hypotheses that we can pass from the result of a measurement to the assignment of a magnitude.

It is in regard to arguments that depend in one way or another on statistical statements that the logic of rational belief is really essential. Most people are willing to accept the conclusion of a valid deductive argument when they are willing to accept the premises. (But when the number of premises is large, and when each premise is not overwhelmingly probable, this willingness may not be rational.) While the logic of rational belief may help to clarify what is going on, a straight-forward formal logic such as ML will generally suffice as a framework within which to achieve agreement with respect to the soundness of a deductive argument with an empirical (or inductive) conclusion. It is quite otherwise with explicitly statistical arguments, which rest always on some assertion of randomness. And in fact there is often a great deal of unresolved disagreement concerning such arguments: witness the arguments and counter-arguments, none of them publicly established once and for all, about the results of Kinsey's investigations, about the relationship between smoking and cancer, and about psychic research. I do not know enough to resolve the disagreements, but I still maintain that there is no excuse for having them remain unresolved among experts in the respective fields of inquiry.

The disputes about such controversial inductive conclusions as these generally center about the question of randomness. On my interpretation of probability, this is precisely what should be expected. It is unlikely that a competent scientific worker will make serious errors in reporting the composition of the sample on which his conclusion is based; it is also unlikely that he will make purely mathematical mistakes, and even more unlikely that he will get away with them for long, or that he will refuse to acknowledge them once they are pointed out. A more controversial matter is his analysis of his sample—that is, his selection of categories. This may even involve changes in the language, as in Thurston's factorial analyses, where the results of experiment are used to suggest new and fruitful terminology. But the selection of categories or the creation of new categories is entirely free. Some analyses may be rendered irrelevant by others—e.g., in the Martian example, the ordinal analysis of the sample supercedes the simple analysis into colors. But the former supercedes the latter, not because it is intrinsically a 'better' analysis, but because the former leads to the establishment of a statistical hypothesis which prevents the latter from establishing a statistical hypothesis; the matter boils down to one of randomness. The same thing applies to the well known shortcoming of an analysis of a sample into categories which admit of a purely logical correlation.[4] Here again, since we know on logical

4. J. Neyman, *Lectures and Conferences on Mathematical Statistics and Probability*, Washington, 1952. (Second Edition).

grounds alone that every sample will reveal this correlation, any other analysis will supercede the one in question: the analysis into logically related categories will not prevent the randomness of the sample with respect to any other property.

The importance of being able to come to a public agreement about what is a random member of what and with respect to which can hardly be overestimated. Is not the main source of dispute about Kinsey's findings the question as to whether or not his sample is a random one with respect to the property of reflecting the sexual habits of the population as a whole? May not the basic question about the relationship between smoking and cancer be the question of whether or not a given sample of smokers and non-smokers is a random member of the class of all such samples, with respect to the property of having a normal mean susceptibility to cancer? Is not the usual accusation leveled against Dr. Rhine that his published results are not a random sample of all his results?

The logic of rational belief provides a framework within which it is possible to come to agreement concerning assertions of randomness. The matter is usually somewhat more complicated than that of coming to an agreement about the validity of a deductive argument; this is so even if the assertions of randomness with which we are concerned are so simple that we may establish them definitively. But still, the form of argument and counter-argument is established by the logic of rational belief, so that disagreement about randomness reveals either a logical error (which can be uncovered), or a difference in the contents of the rational corpora of the participants to the argument. Generally the latter source of disagreement can be removed, too.

3. To see how this works, let us consider a hypothetical (and still oversimplified) discussion between two scientists, Grumbacher and O'Leary.

O'Leary: Say, Grumpy, old man, did you know that about $p\%$ of the P's are Q's?

Grumbacher: Are you sure? How do you know? What do you mean, 'about'? A most unprofessional expression, that!

O'Leary: Well, if you want to get technical, all right. I'm 99.8% sure that between p minus $d\%$ and p plus $d\%$ of the P's are Q s. I spent all last week sampling P's and $p\%$ of them were Q's. I'm just finishing up the report now, if you don't trust my math.

Grumbacher: How big was your sample? Where do you get this 99.8% pure stuff? You talk like a soap advertisement. I trust your mathematics, but...

O'Leary: [wishing he'd stayed in his own office] Well, I took a sample of n of them, and as you may easily verify, the proportion of n-fold samples which have the property that the ratio of Q's in them lies in an interval of $2d$ about the real ratio of Q's among P's is at least .998. And given that the proportion is close to p percent, the proportion of representative samples is slightly larger.

Grumbacher: Well, I can grant that last statistical hypothesis—after all, it's merely a mathematical truth. But I'm still in some doubt as to its relevance. How does it entitle you to infer that p (plus or minus d) % of *all* the P's are Q's?

O'Leary: As I said before, p% of this sample were Q's, and to say of such a sample that the proportion in it lies in the interval r plus or minus d, where r is the real ratio of Q's among P's, is to say that this real ratio r lies in the interval p plus or minus d.

Grumbacher: [writing thoughtfully on his scratch pad] Hmmm.

O'Leary: [with resignation] Since the sample I took last week was a random member of the class of all n-fold subclasses of P with respect to having a Q-ratio close to r, and since 99.8% of these samples have this property, the probability of the statistical statement that started this whole thing is at least .998; so I am justified in assigning a degree of belief of at least .998 to this statement. [O'Leary grins to himself mischievously as he continues.] And I am even justified in demanding, on rational grounds alone, that you give a high degree of credence to my result, too.

Grumbacher: [skeptically] That's all very well; if your sample was really a random one, the conclusion you've drawn does seem to follow. But, look here, how do you know that it *was* random?

O'Leary: [a little huffily] Well! As far as I am concerned—and I am not considered ignorant in my field—it was random with respect to the property of being representative. That is to say, I can think of no property which the sample has which would prevent it, by difference, at any rate, from being a random member of the class of all n-fold samples with respect to this property.

Grumbacher: [testily] Fiddlesticks! I can imagine how hard you looked for such a property...

O'Leary: Just a minute, now, Grump. Are you getting personal?

Grumbacher: I didn't mean to imply that you'd cheated; I just mean that if I'd been around when you took the sample, I might have been able to find a property preventing the randomness of your sample. You Irish are a bit hot-headed, you know. If you'd let me see the report of your experiment, maybe that would convince me that the sample was random.

O'Leary: [still piqued] All right, damn it, here are the records. See what you can trump up. [He hands a large manilla folder across the desk.]

Grumbacher: [Glances over the report, frowning slightly. Turns back to page one. Suddenly his face lights up and he slams the folder shut triumphantly.] There you are: all the members of your sample were R's as well as P's. You know as well as I do that not *all* P's are R's; and the proportion of Q's among the P's which are not R's may very well be different from that among the P's which are R's. And if it is, then your sample does belong to a special subclass of the class of all n-fold samples of P's—namely, those among which the relative frequency of R's is unity—and the proportion of representative samples in this subclass may be very different from that among the class as a whole. All you've proved—if you've proved this much—is that the proportion of Q's among members of the intersection of P and R is about p!

O'Leary: [undaunted] It's true that I've shown that too; but I've also shown the same thing for all the P's; this business about the ratio being different in the intersection of P and R and in the intersection of P and the complement of R is so much idle speculation. In order to prevent my sample from being random in precisely the sense that I said it was, you will have to show me that I have reason to believe, not that there *might* be such a difference, but that there actually is such a difference. So far as I know, there is no evidence to indicate that this is the case at all.

Grumbacher: It is true that I don't know of any evidence along these lines, though if you had taken some non-R's with your sample of P's, there might be such evidence; I can at least convict you of sloppiness. But someone else might perfectly well have such evidence. Then where would your fancy generalization be?

O'Leary: [daunted, this time] I guess you're right about the non-R's; if I'd thought of it, I'd have gotten some. But

it doesn't really affect the status of my generalization now; until someone produces evidence connecting
the presence or absence of R with the relative frequency of Q's among P's, I have a right to include my
generalization in my rational corpus of level .998;
and furthermore, until such evidence is forthcoming,
you cannot justify your lack of confidence in my generalization. Rationally, you are obligated to include
it in your rational corpus, too.

Grumbacher: [shrugs his shoulders] Well, when you put it that way,
I suppose I haven't a leg to stand on—yet. But I think
I'll look into the matter a bit more closely.

O'Leary: By all means do so—you have my best wishes, if not
my confidence in your ultimate success.

[A week passes. Grumbacher, with true teutonic persistance, spends
every night in the library. At the end of the week, Grumbacher calls
at O'Leary's office.]

Grumbacher: [Grinning jovially] Well, old man, I hate to be the one
to break the news; but you should have been a bit
more careful, O'Leary.

O'Leary: [groans and looks up from a page of computations]
Don't tell me you found something?

Grumbacher: Precisely. There's an article in the latest issue of
the JAR on the relative frequency of Q's among non-R
P's—evidently a big research project out West—and
the frequency is very different from that $p\%$ you were
talking about.

O'Leary: I guess that does it all right. Since I'm willing to accept the results published in that journal, I have to
reject the randomness of my sample with respect to
indicating the proportion of Q's among all P's. But I
guess my generalization holds good for the intersection of P and R, if not for all of P.

Grumbacher: Well, between you and this other guy, it seems like
you've got the problem pretty well under control anyway. He's taken care of the intersection of P and the
complement of R; you've taken care of the intersection of P and R.

O'Leary: [brightening] That's true. Well, I guess it's a good
thing you happened to catch that article; at least now
I won't claim more for my results than they're worth.

   The following points are involved in the application of the logic
of rational belief to controversial assertions of randomness. Let
the thesis be that the object O is a random member of a certain

class K, with respect to membership in another class C, relative to our joint rational corpus.

First: The object must be known to belong to K; and there must be a strongest statistical statement S in our rational corpus about K and C.

Second: There will be other classes, K_1, K_2, K_3, ... etc., to which the objects O_1, O_2, O_3, ... etc. (some or all of which may be the same as O) are known to belong.

Third: There will be strongest statistical statements S_1, S_2, S_3, ... etc., about K_1 and C_1, K_2 and C_2, ... etc., where '$O_1 \epsilon C_1$', '$O_2 \epsilon C_2$', etc., are biconditionally connected in the relevant rational corpus to '$O \epsilon C$'. If it is possible to agree on a finite list of K's, O's, and S's satisfying the second and third points, the process of discovering whether or not O is a random member of K with respect to C, relative to our rational corpus, is quite mechanical.

It will generally be possible to agree on whether or not any given quadruplet O_i, K_i, C_i, and S_i, fulfils the second and third conditions. There are thus only two forms of error that can be made in making an assertion of randomness. One form is to forget to include some significant quadruplet O_i, K_i, C_i, S_i among the list of things which may prevent the assertion of randomness in question; the other form is simply to be ignorant of a fact – as O'Leary was ignorant of a fact. Relative to his rational corpus, his argument was fine; but his rational corpus was out of touch with that of his science in a vital respect. Though this sort of mistake is often unavoidable, it is also very quickly corrected. The more familiar and widely read a person is with the subject matter under consideration the more quickly will he notice and correct such a mistake.

The first-mentioned form of mistake is a *logical* one, and is correspondingly rarer. But it is mistakes of this logical type that researchers who make use of direct statistical generalization are most often accused of having made. The accusation is often false: Grumbacher's initial objection of O'Leary's experiment was (at that point) entirely unjustified, just as W. T. Stace's objection to the inference from the perceptibility of perceived objects to the perceptibility of unperceived objects is entirely unjustified. These objections have the form of simply pointing out an O, K, and C, 'overlooked' by the person making the inference, and saying that there *might* be an S about K and C which would force him to reject the randomness of his sample. But this is not a *reason* to doubt the soundness of the argument. It becomes a reason only when the objector exhibits an S, which *ought* on the basis of sound empirical evidence, to be included in the rational corpus of the person making the inference, and which is such that its inclusion in his rational corpus prohibits him from making the assertion of randomness necessary to that inference.

Finally, even if the list of quadruplets is not finite, still, with respect to any finite part of the list, agreement can be reached within the framework. Therefore, I submit, the logic of rational belief provides a universal standard for the soundness of inductive conclusions, where by an inductive conclusion I understand any statement of fact going beyond recently observed concrete instances. It remains only to consider the justification of the standard itself.

4.   Granted that it is possible to justify many of our scientific beliefs by reference to the logic of rational belief and the coordinate theory of probability presented here, and also granted that the theory does not do violence to the customary meaning of 'probable', 'degree of rational belief', 'rational justification', 'practical certainty', and so on, one may still call for justification of the theory. The theory tells us, if we take it normatively, that relative to such and such statements that we already have reason to believe, we *ought* to have such and such a degree of belief in another statement; or that under certain conditions, such and such a statement *ought* to be included in our rational corpus of a given level. How can we justify this 'ought'? In short, why ought we to be rational, in the sense in which rationality is defined by the above theory?

The answer that comes to mind immediately (the arguments of Peirce, Dewey, and other empiricists—or for that matter, those of Hume—are quite sufficient to prevent us from trying to equate rationality with knowledge of the Truth) is that by being rational we are placing ourselves in a position to achieve our ends; that is, rationality is instrumental in achieving whatever ends we wish to achieve. But this cannot stand up without qualification. It is perfectly possible that our 'rational beliefs' about the world are mostly false, in spite of the fact that they are rational. It is perfectly possible that we should be far more successful in achieving our ends if we believe in and act on the basis of beliefs which would have to be designated as irrational on my theory.

What we can say, and about the strongest thing we can say, is that it is very *probable* (in the sense in which I have defined the word) that in basing our actions on rational beliefs, we shall be more successful than we would be if we employed some other basis. This can easily be defended on the grounds that rationality has usually paid off in the past; by and large those whose beliefs have been 'rational' in the sense defined by the theory, have received less unpleasant surprises than other people, and have been more successful in achieving their ends—other things being equal. But this in no way answers the question with which we started: for that question had to do with the very system of justification which is employed in justifying the statement that rationality is generally useful in achieving our ends.

In other words, the question can be repeated on a new level: "Granting that in the sense of probability that has been suggested, it is highly probable that we will be more successful if our beliefs are rational than if they are not, *why ought we to believe* that we shall be successful? And mind you, it is no answer to the question, 'Why ought we to believe what is probable?' to say, 'because it is probable and you ought to believe what is probable.'

We are in short led right back to the question, "Why ought we to be rational?" And it seems to me that this is really quite unanswerable except by, "Thou shalt!" But this is not a peculiarity unique to the logic of rational belief; it applies to purely logical statements as well: one might also ask, "Why ought I to pay any special attention to those particular logical expressions you happen to call 'theorems?" This ultimate lack of justification has been pointed out with admirable clarity and good humor by Feigl in his article, "De Principiis non disputandum . . . ?"[5]

Clearly any statement whose denial is self-contradictory is one which it is rational to believe. In the language of the logic of rational belief, any theorem in ML 'ought' to be believed (though this is a counsel of perfection) and ought to be included in a rational corpus of any level. This sense of 'ought' seems to be exactly that which is involved in the other parts of the theory of rational belief. You may offer as justification for it, the argument that if I were to believe some statement which is self contradictory, my body of beliefs would be inconsistent. Or you may say that if I am very confident of a very improbable thing, I shall very likely—very probably—turn out to be wrong in my expectation. But why *should* my beliefs be consistent? Why *shouldn't* I believe an 'improbable' thing? It is difficult to find any answer to the first question which does not presuppose that a set of beliefs ought to be consistent. Clearly, any *logical* argument, offered as a reason, would itself depend for its cogency on its consistency. The answer seems to be, "Thou shalt be consistent!" We have reached, in asking for a justification of this commandment, what Feigl terms the 'limits of justification'. In the same way, it is not surprising that in answering the second question we should be inclined to answer it with an imperative which lies beyond the limits of justification.

Now in either case it is obviously possible to bypass the problem

5. H. Feigl, "De Principiis non Disputandum . . . ?" Printed in *Philosophical Analysis*, (Ed. M. Black), Ithaca, 1950.

of ultimate justification in the formal development of the theory concerned. I did not introduce 'ought' into my formal characterization of a rational corpus. I simply said that a set of statements with such and such characteristics is, by definition, a rational corpus of such and such a level. In exactly the same way, a theorem may be defined in a calculus as an expression with such and such characteristics. Its definition makes no recommendations about what anyone ought to believe. Anybody can believe any damn thing they want to—consistently or otherwise—contradictions included—and it makes not a difference in the world to the calculus. I can believe all of Quine's axioms and that two and two are five; his system will be unaffected. In the same way, I can have any degree of belief in any proposition on any amount of evidence, and it does not affect my theory of probability.

There is only this rather tenuous connection between a formal system and actual beliefs: if the calculus employs certain expressions, such that my beliefs (or certain groups of them) can be expressed by means of these expressions, and if my beliefs, thus expressed, have certain properties defined in the metalanguage of the calculus, then they are called 'consistent'. Similarly, if groups of the statements thus expressed have certain properties defined in the metalanguage, then the statements are called collectively a rational corpus; and if my degrees of belief in other statements correspond to the fractions used in certain ingredients of my rational corpus, then these degrees of belief are called rational. From a strictly formal point of view, this is a matter of coincidence.

And yet the honorific character of 'rational', 'consistent', etc., is not entirely misleading. For if someone goes to the trouble of constructing a logical calculus, it is likely that he intends certain expressions not only to be theorems, but to be believed. I imagine he would be somewhat piqued if someone were to say, ''Well, I accept your axioms, and your rules of inference, and I admit that p is a theorem; but since I have no desire to be consistent, I really don't see why I should believe p—in fact, I am almost convinced that it is false.'' Not only are certain statements theorems, but these statements ought to be *believed* by anyone who accepts the axioms of the theory; when I show that p is a theorem, I feel that I have created some obligation on your part to believe it. In the same way, if I persuade you of the acceptability of certain evidence-statements, and show you that relative to a rational corpus based on those statements, a certain conclusion is highly probable, I feel that I have created an obligation for you either to have a high degree of confidence in the conclusion, or to give some rational justification for your lack of belief. The obligation in either case is something above and beyond the pure calculus, but it is nevertheless implicitly asserted by anyone who employs the calculus. If you know that a certain expression is a theorem, then you ought to believe that if the calculus in which it appears is consistent, it (the expression) is true in all possible worlds and under all possible interpretations; if you know that the probability of a certain statement is at least p, then you ought to have a degree of belief in the statement equal to or greater than the ratio denoted by p.

All this, and perhaps a little bit more, can be summed up by saying that it is a *duty* to be rational. If I didn't think that this were the case, I wouldn't have bothered presenting a calculus. At the point where we reach the limits of justification, we simply fall back on the moral command: Thou shalt be rational! The preceding chapters are, immodestly enough, intended as an amplification of this imperative.

APPENDICES AND BIBLIOGRAPHY

Possible Ramifications

I present below a few undeveloped ideas as to the connections between the foregoing, and related areas of inquiry, together with divers suggestions as to fruitful areas for further research.

1.   Man is, as Aristotle said, a rational animal. The essence of *rational* beliefs is that they can be communicated and shared. The logic of rational belief is intended to facilitate this process. Any man who can be taught the language of ML, with its supplementary primitive predicates, can be made amenable to persuasion by rational justification, and may therefore be said to be potentially rational, even though he is free to *decide* not to be rational.

2.   Thus rationality is a virtue that can be taught. Just as it has not been necessary for many years to 'intuit' such arithmetical theorems as '$2+2=4$', it is no longer necessary to intuit such rational truths as that in our present state of knowledge, it is highly probable that all whale's have hearts.

3.   "Probability," "Random," "Rational Corpus of level r_i," etc., are all protosyntactically definable. It does not seem implausible to suppose that not very restrictive conditions can be laid down under which these expressions will be constructive as well. If we can establish constructivity under the conditions that are met in inductive contexts, and important consequence follows:

4.   An induction machine is possible. Given constructivity within inductive contexts, we can construct a machine into which we can feed an electronic translation of a basis F of a rational corpus, and which will then perform the following functions: We can 'ask' for the relation between the classes A and B by feeding their electronic names (in order) into the machine; the machine will answer by typing a sequence of statistical statements, each of which is a strongest statement that can be included in the machine's rational corpus of given level. We may ask the machine for the probability of a given statement S, and the machine will respond by listing the probability of S for each level of its rational corpus. The machine corresponds to the head of a completely rational robot.

5.   The machine may also be constructed so as to gather its own set of basic statements F. But the method of coding the experience of the machine will have to be built into it, so that there is no theoretical gain in this modification. And we would have to give the

machine the equivalent of a good college education (or several) in order to prevent it from making horrible blunders due to ignorance.
6. The machine described would be capable of establishing statistical generalizations and universal generalizations, and such theories as embody no more information than is already contained in a number of already acceptable universal generalizations. Needless to say, there is more than this involved in the most highly developed parts of modern science. Here the scientist is often concerned, not only with making generalizations in the terms available in a given language, but with introducing far-reaching and elegant theories, and even with changing the language for the sake of the elegance and simplicity of the theory. It is very doubtful that standards of selection along these lines can be built into the machine—in particular, that the machine can be constructed so as to modify its own language. (And how would we understand what it is talking about then?) It is remotely possible that the machine can do these things, since people, after all, can do them; perhaps the machine can be built to spout a list of axioms governing the use of a new predicate that it had invented. But at any event, it is perfectly possible to modify the machine when we decide to modify our language, and to build into the machine the latest physical theories. It is also perfectly possible for the machine to report on the adequacy of a theory in any given area of application.
     So much for science fiction.
7. There is a special form of 'intuition' which, while not rational in itself, leads to rationalizable beliefs. A man in a machine shop picks up a piece of steel and says, "This is cold rolled." We ask, "How do you know? It is unlabelled; there are many kinds of steel in the shop; it looks just like any other piece of steel." He answers, "Well, it just looks like cold rolled steel to me." And it might very well happen that there is nothing about the piece of metal to which the man could point, or which he could describe, that would function as a sign that it was cold rolled steel. Anyone who has worked in a machine shop will know that there is nothing farfetched about this example, and will also be quite willing to agree that if the man is experienced, he will very probably be correct. There are doubtless characteristics of the piece of metal which lead him to his decision, but these characteristics cannot be *rationalized:* there is no way of talking about them. There is thus no way for the man rationally to justify his belief about the steel by reference to known properties of cold rolled steel.
     But it does not follow that his belief cannot be rationalized at all. If he is a very experienced machinist, his intuitions about steels will be very rarely in error. If this is a random instance of one of

his judgements, with respect to being confirmed in the future, we have every reason in the world to believe that he is correct this time. It is possible to substitute experience of the man and his judgments (which can be rationalized) for experience of steels (which cannot be rationalized.)

8.   What we can rationalize (in the honorific sense in which I have been using the term) is obviously limited by what we can say in our language; and in particular limited by what we can say in the supplemented version of ML. It would be not only interesting, but perhaps instructive and useful, to make some effort to create a formal language of science which would be capable of translation into the supplemented version of ML. It would at any rate show that the creation of such a language was possible, and in particular that an extensional language was adequate to the needs of science. It might further facilitate the application of the proposed standard of rational belief to the settlement of existing disputes concerning in-inductive conclusions of practical importance.

9.   The standard of rational belief presented here is not quite complete; the status of the ingredients of the basis F of the rational corpus has been left indeterminate. Clearly we require that if a person *observes* that such and such is the case, he should include the statement expressing this fact in his rational corpus. It may be that we can limit the statements that *can* belong to F by protosyntactical criteria—e.g., if C is the class of crows, and B the class of black things, it seems safe to say that nobody can *observe* that C is included in B. We may be able to formalize the requirement that the rational man take account of all of his experience by means of a new metalinguistic matrix $0(x, y,)$, which would be interpreted as expressing the fact that the person x has the experience which would be expressed by his saying that he had observed the state of affairs corresponding to the statement y. Or we might want to list a whole series of matrices analogous to this, of varying degrees of 'observational force', so that we may allow for the direct inclusion in in lower level rational corpora of relatively doubtful observations.

10.   The analysis of this metalinguistic matrix $0(x,y)$ constitutes an epistemological inquiry; we have not definitively answered the the question of "How do you know...?" until we can handle not only answers of the form "—renders...overwhelmingly probable," but also answers of the form, "I have seen it with my own eyes!" Incidentally, it should not be expected that this epistemological inquiry will be entirely independent of the logic of rational belief. It may be that there are several epistemological analyses which are equally sound insofar as they lead to plausible results. I have

suggested this already, by admitting my prejudice in favor of the epistemological priority of sticks and stones as opposed to sense data. Perhaps we may say that our observations of sticks and stones have been shown by inductive generalizations to be not completely infallible; or that our experience of sense data has led to inductive generalizations according to which sense data of certain sorts are highly dependable clues as to the state and nature of sticks and stones. There is much to be done in rational epistemology.

11.   I have pointed out that the logic of rational belief is a logic—that is, that it is concerned with what people ought to believe, and not with what they do believe. It is not a psychological theory. While it is the business of psychology to investigate whether or not a given person is in that state which we would call 'believing S to the degree p,' it is not the business of psychology, but of logic, to investigate whether a person *ought* to believe S to the degree p. And it is also clear that a person can satisfy the requirements of logic in this respect without being in the psychological state mentioned above; we would not call the person irrational if he merely didn't happen to be thinking about S. What we require (to call him rational) is that if he does think about S, he ought to have the logically appropriate degree of belief in S.

12.   In the same way, the analysis of the primitive metalinguistic matrix $0(x, y)$ is not the business of psychology; although here the connection may be closer than it is with respect to rational belief. To assert $0(x, y)$ is to make a psychological assertion—and no small portion of physiological psychology is concerned with just such assertions. The extent to which the epistemological analysis of this expression, however, needs to make use of psychological facts is open to question. Is the fact that we cannot now observe future events a psychological or a logical fact? If it is a psychological fact (which seems likely, in view of the contrary claims that are sometimes made), then this much psychology is surely required for our epistemological analysis. To the extent that epistemology makes use of psychological facts, epistemology is a factual inquiry. Yet, for philosophical purposes, the factual part should surely be minimized; the introduction of psychological facts stems merely from our desire, for the sake of simplicity and convenience, to *limit* the class of expressions y which can occur in the context $0(x,y)$.

13.   There may well be more to epistemology than the analysis of this matrix. Rational epistemology is concerned only with what can be directly said, and with what is factual. Intuitive knowledge of fact is beyond its scope. The same goes for ethical knowledge and aesthetic knowledge. Perhaps there is no aesthetic knowledge—

perhaps there is not even any ethical knowledge—but these are points which, if true, must be established. More work for the epistemologist.

14. There is another respect in which the logic of rational belief must be supplemented by further inquiry. An inductive logic is possible, as I have shown; but it is of interest and importance not only to show that it is possible, but to classify and analyze the major sorts of arguments which are employed in establishing inductive conclusions in actual scientific practise. This has been done with something approaching formality only with respect to very few situations, all of which are fairly trivial—*viz.*, those covered in essence by Mill's methods. Much has been written about statistical inference, but here formality is lacking. Logicians seem to have been more concerned with restating Mill's methods, or with showing that an inductive logic is impossible (in a certain sense, of course), than they have in producing a useful treatise on inductive logic.

15. Biologists, medical researchers, psychologists, sociologists, etc.,—not to mention students—might benefit from a full-fledged modern treatise on formal inductive logic. The questions answered by such a treatise would be of the form: "What things might you know which, together with experimental evidence of the type E, would support an inductive conclusion of the type C?" And not merely 'support', but support with a certain degree of rational cogency.

16. A treatise on epistemology would presumably answer (among other things) the questions concerning what can be said to be known 'immediately' or 'without inference.' In a like manner, a treatise on inductive logic would answer questions concerning the kinds of arguments which might be used in the defense of the rationality of certain beliefs which are not 'immediate' and are not 'known without inference.' The whole theory, of which the logic of rational belief forms one part, and of which epistemology and inductive logic form the other parts, might be considered a theory as to the basis and character of our factual knowledge. This subject has been of great interest to philosophers always, and has, with very good reason, been of particular interest during the last few hundred years. There has developed over this period a remarkable amount of agreement with respect to the content of our collective body of 'factual knowledge.' People being such cantankerous creatures as they are, such widespread agreement about anything so precisely defined as scientific knowledge is a matter deserving a great deal of attention. It is not enough to say that people are obligated by the evidence to agree, without specifying the nature of this obligation and the sort of thing that counts as 'evidence.' The logic of rational

belief, inductive logic, and epistemology, may serve to explain the rational obligation involved.

17. Semiotic, or the logical study of language, is conventionally divided, like Gaul, into three parts. Syntax (and hence also protosyntax) is concerned with the 'purely formal' relationships among symbols; semantics is concerned with the relationships between the symbols and what they symbolize: and pragmatics is concerned with the threefold relationship between a person who uses a symbol, the symbol, and a person who receives the symbolic communication.

My logic of rational belief is purely protosyntactical; the relationships discussed are merely relationships between groups of symbols; they are quite independent of what, if anything, the symbols designate, and also independent of how the symbols may be used, if at all, for communication. In Carnap's terminology, all that I have talked about (barring a few examples) is a calculus—not even a language. It becomes a language only when rules (formal or otherwise) are given concerning the interpretation of the primitive predicates.

18. But there is a direct relationship between the protosyntax of rational belief and the concerns of semantics and pragmatics; this is that the concept of randomness may be useful in these latter disciplines. Consider a typical assertion in semantics: "The expression 'P' designates the property P." This is all right if we are familiar with the property P. But suppose we are not; suppose we want to say, "The expression 'P' designates the property that *those things* all have." We might find it convenient to replace this by a statement like, "Those things are a random sample of the class of all things having the property designated by 'P', with respect to representing the range of variation of this property."

19. A more important use of concepts defined in the logic of rational belief might occur in pragmatics. It is a commonly observed phenomenon that people do not always understand each other as clearly as they should if they spoke exactly the same language. According to the conventional semantic analysis, if they speak the same language, they should designate the same class of objects by the same expression. But if we adopt the above formulation for certain of our rules of designation, it seems that it will not in general be the case that they designate exactly the same classes by the same expression.

Suppose that for A, 'P' designates the class X of entities and the class of all other entities like the X's in certain respects—i.e., A takes X as a random sample of P's, with respect to representing these 'certain respects'. Similarly, let 'P', for B, designate the class Y of entities, and the class of all other entities like the Y's in certain respects.

The classes X and Y will not, in general, be the same. It may thus happen that there are certain entities which A would say belong to the class designated by 'P', and which B would say do not belong to the class designated by 'P'. It would seem natural to say that the expression 'P' means exactly the same thing to A and B, if there is no object such that one of them would say that it belonged to the class designated by 'P' while the other would say that it did not. We could say that the expression 'P' meant 'just about' the same thing to A and to B, if there are relatively few objects such that this could happen. This may involve a factual question about the class of entities that A designates by 'P' and the class of entities that B designates by 'P', as well as a linguistic question. The factual question would be related to the existence of natural kinds.

We could even, on this analysis, speak of the probability of misunderstanding in a particular case. This probability would be reduced by the redundency of ordinary discourse, and would also depend on formal aspects of the context. We might also find that this conception explained the rather illusory nature of that 'far-reaching ethical agreement' among different cultures that has been cited as so highly significant by some philosophers.

20. This variation in meaning between one user and another of non-logical terms is one of the things which makes it seem doubtful to me that a formal interpretation of a calculus can add much to an informal interpretation. Even if axioms governing the primitive predicates are justified formally by reference to semantic rules, rather than informally by reference to ordinary usage, it still seems unlikely that the rules of our formalized language, as partly embodied in these axioms, will be truly vacuous for all users of the language. This vacuity of the rules of the language is rather in the nature of a goal; if we achieve it we shall never be forced by experience to change our language.

21. But it is not such an important goal: for experience may indicate the advisability of changing the language even when it does not force us to change it. And it is not a goal which must be achieved at all costs, for if you consider a certain statement an axiom—a rule of the language—while I consider it merely an exceptionally well-founded inductive generalization, we will nevertheless both agree that it should appear in a high-level rational corpus. We will never need to come to blows about it, unless we come across an apparently contrary instance; and even then we will not be disagreeing about matters of fact, but only about the relative desirability of different forms of usage. If, as I have suggested, there must always be a degree of ambiguity of denotation among some of the predicates of a formalized language of science, it is a good thing that absolute vacuousness of the formal rules of the language is not necessary.

Contexts

Typical contexts in which the word 'probability' occurs:

(1) The probability of getting a head on a toss of this well-tested coin is 1/2.

(2) The probability that a human birth will be the birth of a male is 0.52.

(3) The probability of an alpha ray striking the area A of the target, in experiment E, is 0.3476.

(4) The probability of an American male of the professional class who is alive at 35, being alive at 36, is p.

(5) The probability of 10 heads occurring in 10 tosses of this well-tested coin is $(1/2)^{10}$.

(6) The probability that 10 of the 50 men of age 35, belonging to the professional class, who take out insurance with us this year, will die before next year, is r.

(7) The probability that the next ten tosses of this coin will all yield heads is s.

(8) The probability that the next toss of this coin will result in heads is 1/2.

(9) Given an n-fold random sample of P's, m of which are Q's, the probability is t that between $m/n - d$ and $m/n + d$ of all P's are Q's.

(10) Relative to the evidence that m P's out of n are Q's, the probability is v that the next P to be examined is also a Q.

(11) Given the collective evidence of biology and zoology, the probability is very high that all mammals have hearts.

(12) Given the evidence of experiments performed on heredity, the probability is w that the genetic theory is true.

(13) It is highly probable that Caesar crossed the Rubicon.

(14) If you are wealthy, it is more probable that if you cheat on your income tax you will be caught that it is if you are not wealthy.

Selected Bibliography

1. Abruzzi, Adam. "Problems of Inference in the Socio-Physical Sciences," *Journal of Philosophy* 51, 1954.

2. Ambrose, Alice. "The Problem of Justifying Inductive Inference," *Journal of Philosophy* 44, 1947.

3. Anderson, Alan Ross. "A Note on Subjunctive and Counter-Factual Conditionals," *Analysis* 12, 1951-52.

4. Ayer, A. J. *Language, Truth and Logic.* New York Dover Publications. n.d.

5. —, "Individuals," *Mind* 61, 1952.

6. Baker, M. J., "Perceptual Claims and Certainties," *Analysis* 11, 1950-51.

7. Barker, S. F., *Induction and Hypothesis: A Study of the Logic of Confirmation.* Cornell University Press, Ithaca, New York, 1957.

8. —, Review of von Wright, *The Logical Problem of Induction. Journal of Philosophy* 55, 1958.

9. Barrett, W. "The Present State of the Problem of Induction," *Theoria* 6, 1940.

10. Beardsley, Elizabeth Lane. "Non-Accidental and Counterfactual Sentences," *Journal of Philosophy* 46, 1949.

11. Berg, Jan. "A Note on Dispositional Concepts," *Philosophy and Phenomenological Research* 16, 1955-56.

12. —, "On Defining Disposition Predicates," *Analysis* 15, 1954-55.

13. Bergmann, Gustav. "The Logic of Probability," *American Journal of Physics* 9, 1941.

14. —, "Frequencies, Probabilities, and Positivism," *Philosophy and Phenomenological Research* 6, 1945-46.

15. —, "Undefined Descriptive Predicates," *Philosophy and Phenomenological Research* 8, 1947-48.

16. —, "Comments on Storer's Definition of 'Soluble'," *Analysis* 12, 1951-52.

17. Black, Max. *Language and Philosophy*, Cornell University Press, Ithaca, New York, 1949.

18. —, *Problems of Analysis*, Cornell University Press, Ithaca, New York, 1954.

19. Braithwaite, R. B. "Jeffrey's Theory of Probability," *Mind* 40, 1931.

20. —, *Scientific Explanation.* Cambridge University Press, 1953.

21. Brandt, Richard. "The Languages of Realism and Nominalism," *Philosophy and Phenomenological Research* 17, 1956-57.

22. Broad, C. D. "On The Relation Between Induction and Probability (I)" *Mind* 27, 1918.

23. —, "The Relation Between Induction and Probability (II)," *Mind* 29, 1920.

24. —, "Johnson on the Logical Foundations of Science," *Mind* 33, 1924.

25. —, "The Principles of Problematic Induction," *Proceedings of the Aristotelian Society* 28, 1928.

26. —, "The Principles of Demonstrative Induction," *Mind* 39, 1930.

27. —, "Hr. von Wright on the Logic of Induction," *Mind* 53, 1944.

28. —, "Wahrscheinlichkeit, Statistic, und Wahrheit, by Richard von Mises," *Mind* 53, 1944.

29. Brodbeck, May. "An Analytic Principle of Induction?" *Journal of Philosophy* 49, 1952.

30. Bures, C. E. "The Concept of Probability," *Philosophy of Science* 5, 1938.

31. Burks, A. W. "Reichenbach's Theory of Probability and Induction," *Review of Metaphysics* 4, 1951.

32. —, "The Presupposition Theory of Induction," *Philosophy of Science* 20, 1954.

33. —, "Justification in Science," printed in *Academic Freedom, Logic, and Religion.* University of Pennsylvania Press, Philadelphia, 1953.

34. —, "On the Presuppositions of Induction," *Review of Metaphysics* 8, 1955.

35. Butler, Joseph. (Bishop Butler). *Works.* Gladstone, ed. Oxford 1896.

36. Campbell, Norman. *Physics, the Elements.* Cambridge University Press, 1920. Reprinted as *The Foundations of Science,* Dover Publications, New York, 1957.

37. Carlsson, Gösta. "Sampling, Probability, and Causal Inference," *Theoria* 18, 1952.

38. Carnap, Rudolf. *Foundations of Logic and Mathematics.* International Encyclopedia of Unified Science, University of Chicago Press, Chicago, 1939.

39. —, "Two Concepts of Probability," *Philosophy and Phenomenological Research* 5, 1944-45. Reprinted in Feigl and Sellars, *Readings . . .*

40. —, "On Inductive Logic," *Philosophy of Science* 12, 1945.

41. —, "Rejoinder to Mr. Kaufmann's Reply," *Philosophy and Phenomenological Research* 6, 1945-46.

42. —, "Remarks on Induction and Truth," *Philosophy and Phenomenological Research* 6, 1945-46.

43. —, *Meaning and Necessity:* A Study in Semantics and Modal Logic. University of Chicago Press, Chicago, 1947.

44. —, "Probability as a Guide in Life," *Journal of Philosophy,* 44, 1947.

45. —, "On the Application of Inductive Logic," *Philosophy and Phenomenological Research* 8, 1947-48.

46. —, *Logical Foundations of Probability,* University of Chicago Press, Chicago, 1950.

47. —, "Inductive Logic and Science," *Proceedings of the American Academy of Arts and Sciences* 80, 1951-54.

48. —, *The Continuum of Inductive Methods,* University of Chicago Press, Chicago, 1952.

49. —, "Meaning Postulates," *Philosophical Studies* 3, 1952.

50. —, "Remarks to Kemeny's Paper," *Philosophy and Phenomenological Research* 13, 1953.

51. —, "On Belief Sentences: Reply to Alonzo Church," *Philosophy and Analysis*, ed. Mcdonald.

52. —, "The Methodological Character of Theoretical Concepts," *Minnesota Studies in the Philosophy of Science* 1, 1956.

53. Chapman, H. Wallis. "Induction Again," *Analysis* 7, 1939-40.

54. Chatalian, George. "Probability: Inductive vs. Deductive," *Philosophical Studies* 3, 1952.

55. —, "Induction and the Problem of the External World," *Journal of Philosophy* 49, 1952.

56. Chisholm, Roderick. "The Contrary-to-fact Conditional," *Mind* 55, 1946. Reprinted in Feigl and Sellars, *Readings...*

57. —, "Epistemic Statements and the Ethics of Belief," *Philosophy and Phenomenological Research* 16, 1955-56.

58. —, "Law Statements and Counterfactual Inference," *Analysis* 15, 1954-55.

59. Church, Alonzo. "On the Concept of a Random Sequence," *Bulletin of the American Mathematical Society* 46, 1940.

60. —, "On Carnap's Analysis of Statements of Assertion and Belief," *Analysis*, 10, 1949-50. Reprinted in *Philosophy and Analysis*, ed. Mcdonald.

61. —, "Intensional Isomorphism and Identity of Belief," *Philosophical Studies* 5, 1954.

62. Churchman, C. W. "Statistics, Pragmatics, Induction," *Philosophy of Science* 15, 1948.

63. —, *Theory of Experimental Inference*, Macmillan, New York, 1948.

64. —, and Ackoff, *Methods of Inquiry*, Educational Publishers, Saint Louis, 1950.

65. Cohen, L. J., and Lloyd, A. C., "Assertion-Statements," *Analysis* 15, 1954-55.

66. Cohen, L. J., "Can the Logic of Indirect Discourse be Formalized?" *Journal of Symbolic Logic* 22, 1957.

67. Cohen, Morris R., and Nagel, Ernest. *An Introduction to Logic and Scientific Method*, Harcourt Brace and Co., New York, 1934.

68. Cooley, John C., "Goodman's 'Fact, Fiction and Forecast'," *Journal of Philosophy* 54, 1957.

69. —, "A Somewhat Adverse Reply to Professor Goodman," *Journal of Philosophy* 55, 1958.

70. Copeland, A. H. "Prediction and Probabilities," *Erkenntnis* 6, 1936.

71. Craik, Kenneth J. *The Nature of Explanation*, Cambridge University Press, 1943.

72. Cramér, Harald. *Mathematical Methods of Statistics*, Princeton University Press, Princeton, 1951.

73. Crawshay-Williams, R. "Equivocal Confirmation," *Analysis* 11, 1950-51.

74. Creed, Isabel. "The Justification of the Habit of Induction," *Journal of Philosophy* 37, 1940.

75. Cunningham, M. A. "The Justification of Induction," *Analysis* 7, 1940.

76. de Finetti, Bruno. *La prevision: ses lois logiques, ses sources subjectives,* Annales de l'Institut Henri Poincare 7, 1937.

77. Dewey, John. *Logic, The Theory of Inquiry.* Henry Holt and Co. New York, 1938.

78. Dewey, John. *Essays in Experimental Logic,* Dover Publications, New York, 1953.

79. Doob, J. L. "Probability and Statistics," *Transactions of the American Mathematical Society* 36, 1934.

80. Ducasse, C. J. "A Neglected Interpretation of Probability," *Proceedings of the VI'th International Congress on Philosophy,* 1926.

81. —, "Some Observations Concerning the Nature of Probability," *Journal of Philosophy* 37, 1941.

82. Ellis, Leslie. "On the Foundations of the Theory of Probabilities," *Transactions of the Cambridge Philosophical Society* 8, 1844.

83. Feibleman, James. "Pragmatism and Inverse Probability," *Philosophy and Phenomenological Research* 5, 1944-45.

84. Feigl, Herbert. "Validation and Vindication: The Nature and Limits of Ethical Argument," reprinted in Sellars and Hospers, *Readings in Ethical Theory.*

85. —, "Wahrscheinlichkeit und Erfahrung," *Erkenntnis* 1, 1930-31.

86. —, "The Logical Character of the Principle of Induction," *Philosophy of Science* 1, 1934. Reprinted in Feigl and Sellars, *Readings...*

87. —, "De Principiis Non Disputandum...?" in *Philosophical Analysis,* ed. M. Black.

88. —, "Confirmability and Configuration," *Revue Internationale de Philosophie* 5, 1951.

89. —, "Scientific Method without Metaphysical Presuppositions," *Philosophical Studies* 5, 1954.

90. —, "Some Major Issues and Developments in the Philosophy of Science," in *Minnesota Studies in the Philosophy of Science* 1, 1956.

91. Finch, Henry Albert. "An Explanation of Counterfactuals by Probability Theory," *Philosophy and Phenomenological Research* 18, 1958.

92. Fisher, Ronald A. "Theory of Statistical Estimation," *Proceedings of the Cambridge Philosophical Society* 22, 1923-25.

93. —, "Probability, Liklihood, and Quantity Of Information in the Logic of Uncertain Inference," *Proceedings of the Royal Society,* series A, 146, 1934.

94. —, *The Design of Experiments.* Oliver and Boyd Ltd., Edinburgh, (sixth ed.) 1951.

95. —, *Statistical Methods for Research Workers,* Oliver and Boyd Ltd., Edinburgh, 1925.

96. —, "The Logic of Inductive Inference," *Journal of the Royal Statistical Society* 98, 1935.

97. Gardiner, Martin. *In the Name of Science,* G. P. Putnam's Sons, New York, 1952. Revised edition: *Fads and Fallacies,* Dover Publications, New York, 1957.

98. Good, I. J., *Probability and the Weighing of Evidence*, London, 1950.

99. Goodman, Nelson. "A Query on Confirmation" *Journal of Philosophy* 43, 1946.

100. —, "On Infirmities of Confirmation-Theory," *Philosophy and Phenomenological Research* 8, 1947.

101. —, "The Problem of Counterfactual Conditionals," *Journal of Philosophy* 44, 1947. Reprinted in Linsky, *Semantics* . . . and in Goodman, *Fact, Fiction, and Forecast.*

102. —, "Sense and Certainty," *Philosophical Review* 61, 1952.

103. —, *Fact, Fiction and Forecast.* Harvard University Press, Cambridge (Mass.) 1955.

104. —, "Reply to an Adverse Ally," *Journal of Philosophy* 54, 1957.

105. Hailperin, Theodore. "Foundations of Probability in Mathematical Logic," *Philosophy of Science* 4, 1936-37.

106. Hampshire, Stuart. "Subjunctive Conditionals," *Analysis* 9, 1948-49.

107. Harrod, Roy. *Foundations of Inductive Logic*, Harcourt Brace and Co., New York, 1957.

108. Helmer, Olaf, and Oppenheim, Paul. "A Syntactical Definition of Probability and Degree of Confirmation," *Journal of Symbolic Logic* 10, 1945.

109. Hempel, Carl G. "Uber den Gehalt von Wahrscheinlichkeitsaussagen," *Erkenntnis* 5, 1935.

110. —, "On the Logical Form of Probability-Statements," *Erkenntnis* 7, 1937.

111. —, "Le probleme de la verite," *Theoria* 3, 1937.

112. —, "A Purely Syntactical Definition of Confirmation," *Journal of Symbolic Logic* 8, 1943.

113. —, "Studies in the Logic of Confirmation," *Mind* 54, 1945.

114. —, review of Reichenbach, *Nomological Statements and Admissible Operations*, Journal of Symbolic Logic 20, 1955.

115. —, and Oppenheim, Paul. "A Definition of 'Degree of Confirmation'," *Philosophy of Science* 12, 1945.

116. —, "Studies in the Logic of Explanation," *Philosophy of Science* 15, 1948. Reprinted in Feigl and Brodbeck, *Readings* . . .

117. Hochberg, Herbert. "On Pegasizing," *Philosophy and Phenomenological Research* 17, 1957.

118. Hofstadter, Albert. "The Myth of the Whole: A Consideration of Quine's View of Knowledge," *Journal of Philosophy* 51, 1954.

119. Hopf, E. "On Casuality, Statistics, and Probability," *Journal of Mathematics and Physics* 12, 1934.

120. Hosiasson, Janina. "Why do We Prefer Probabilities Relative to Many Data?" *Mind* 40, 1931.

121. —, "On Confirmation," *Journal of Symbolic Logic* 5, 1940.

122. —, "Induction et analogie," *Mind* 50, 1941.

123. Hume, David. *An Inquiry Concerning Human Understanding;* Open Court, La Salle, Ill. 1949.

124. Hutten, Ernest. "Induction as a Semantic Problem," *Analysis* 10, 1949-50.

125. Jeffreys, H. *Scientific Inference*, Cambridge University Press, 1931.

126. –, *Theory of Probability*, Oxford University Press, 1939.

127. Johnson, W. E. "Probability," *Mind* 41, 1932.

128. Jourdain, P. E. B. "Causality Induction, and Probability," *Mind* 28, 1919.

129. Juhos, Bela. "Deduktion, Induktion, und Wahrscheinlichkeit." *Methodos* 6, 1954.

130. Kaufmann, Felix. "The Logical Rules of Scientific Procedure," *Philosophy and Phenomenological Research* 2, 1941-42.

131. –, "Verification, Meaning, and Truth," *Philosophy and Phenomenological Research* 4, 1943-44.

132. –, "Concerning Mr. Nagel's Critical Comments," *Philosophy and Phenomenological Research*, 5, 1944-45.

133. –, "Discussion of Mr. Nagel's Rejoinder," *Philosophy and Phenomenological Research* 5, 1944-45.

134. –, "On the Nature of Inductive Inference," *Philosophy and Phenomenological Research* 6, 1945-46.

135. –, "Scientific Procedure and Probability," *Philosophy and Phenomenological Research* 6, 1945-46.

136. Kemble, Edwin C. "Is the Frequency Theory of Probability Adequate for all Scientific Purposes?" *American Journal of Physics*. 10, 1942.

137. –, "The Probability Concept," *Philosophy of Science* 8, 1941.

138. Kemeny, John G. "Carnap on Probability," *Review of Metaphysics* 5, 1951.

139. –, review of Carnap, *Logical Foundations of Probability*, *Journal of Symbolic Logic* 16, 1951.

140. –, "A Contribution to Inductive Logic," *Philosophy and Phenomenological Research* 13, 1952-53.

141. –, "Extension of the Methods of Inductive Logic," *Philosophical Studies* 3, 1952.

142. –, "A Logical Measure Function," *Journal of Symbolic Logic* 18, 1953.

143. –, "The Use of Simplicity in Induction," *Philosophical Review* 62, 1953.

144. –, "Fair Bets and Inductive Probabilities," *Journal of Symbolic Logic* 20, 1955.

145. –, "A New Approach to Semantics," *Journal of Symbolic Logic* 21, 1956.

146. –, and Oppenheim, Paul. "Degree of Factual Support." *Philosophy of Science* 19, 1952.

147. Keynes, John Maynard. *A Treatise on Probability*. Macmillan and Co., London, 1921.

148. Kneale, William. *Probability and Induction*, Oxford University Press, 1949.

149. Kyburg, Henry. "The Justification of Induction," *Journal of Philosophy* 53, 1956.

150. –, "The Justification of Deduction" *Review of Metaphysics*, 12, 1958.

151. –, "Demonstrative Induction," *Philosophy and Phenomenological Research*, 21, 1960.

152. –, "Braithwaite on Probability and Induction," *British Journal for the Philosophy of Science*, 11, 1958.

153. Leblanc, Hughes. "Two Probability Concepts," *Journal of Philosophy* 53, 1956.

154. Lehman, R. Sherman. "On Confirmation and Rational Betting," *Journal of Symbolic Logic* 20, 1955.

155. Lenz, John W. "Carnap on Defining 'Degree of Confirmation'," *Philosophy of Science* 23, 1956.

156. Lewis, C. I. *An Analysis of Knowledge and Valuation*, Open Court, La Salle, Ill., 1946.

157. Lewy, Casimir. "On the Justification of Induction," Analysis 7, 1939..

158. Lloyd, A. C. "The Logical Form of Law Statements," *Mind* 64, 1955.

159. Madden, Edward H. "Chance and Counterfacts in Wright and Peirce," *Review of Metaphysics* 9, 1956.

160. –, "Aristotle's Treatment of Probability and Signs," *Philosophy of Science* 24, 1957.

161. Margenau, H. "Probability, Many-Valued Logics, and Physics," *Philosophy of Science* 6, 1939.

162. –, "The Role of Definitions in Physical Science, with Remarks on the Frequency Definition of Probability," *American Journal of Physics*, 10, 1942.

163. –, "Physical versus Historical Reality," *Philosophy of Science*, 19, 1952. Reprinted in Wiener, *Readings...*

164. McLendon, H. J. "Has Russell Answered Hume?" *Journal of Philosophy* 49, 1952.

165. Meckler, Lester. "An Analysis of Belief-Sentences," *Philosophy and Phenomenological Research* 16, 1955-56.

166. Mill, John Stuart. *A System of Logic*, Longmans, Green and Co., New York, 1949.

167. Mises, R. von. Probability, Statistics, and Truth, New York, 1939. (translation of *Wahrscheinlichkeit, Statistik, und Wahrheit*, Wein, 1928.)

168. –, *Positivism*, Harvard University Press, Cambridge (Mass.) 1951.

169. –, "On the Foundations of Probability and Statistics," *Annals of Mathematical Statistics* 12, 1941.

170. –, "Comments on D. Williams Paper," *Philosophy and Phenomenological Research* 6, 1945-46.

171. –, "Comments on Donald Williams' Reply," *Philosophy and Phenomenological Research* 6, 1945-46.

172. Moore, Ashley. "The Principle of Induction," *Journal of Philosophy* 49, 1952.

173. –, "Induction (II), a Rejoinder to Miss Brodbeck," *Journal of Philosophy* 49, 1952.

174. Nagel, Ernest. "Logic Without Ontology," in Krikorian, *Naturalism and the Human Spirit*.

175. –, "Measurement," *Erkenntnis* 2, 1934.

176. –, "The Frequency Theory of Probability," *Journal of Philosophy* 30, 1933.

177. –, "The Meaning of Probability," *Journal of the American Statistical Association*, 1936.

178. –, *Principles of the Theory of Probability*, Vol. 1, no. 6, of the International Encyclopedia of Unified Science. University of Chicago Press, Chicago, 1939.

179. –, "Probability and the Theory of Knowledge," *Philosophy of Science* 6, 1939.

180. –, "Probability and Non-Demonstrative Interference," *Philosophy and Phenomenological Research* 5, 1945.

181. –, "Rejoinder to Mr. Kaufmann's Reply," *Philosophy and Phenomenological Research* 5, 1944-45.

182. –, "Some Reflections on the Use of Language in the Natural Sciences," *Journal of Philosophy* 42, 1945.

183. –, "Is the LaPlacean Theory of Probability Tenable?" *Philosophy and Phenomenological Research* 6, 1945-46.

184. –, "Reichenbach's Theory of Probability," *Journal of Philosophy* 47, 1950.

185. –, *Logic Without Metaphysics*, The Free Press, Glencoe, Ill. 1956.

186. Nelson, E. J. "Professor Reichenbach on Induction," *Journal of Philosophy* 33, 1936.

187. –, "The Inductive Argument for an External World," *Philosophy of Science* 3, 1936.

188. Neyman, Jerzy. "On the Problem of Confidence Intervals," *Annals of Mathematical Statistics* 6, 1935.

189. –, "Outline of a Theory of Statistical Estimation Based on the Classical Theory of Probability," *Philosophical Transactions of the Royal Society*, Series A, 236, 1937.

190. –, *First Course in Probability and Statistics*, Henry Holt and Company, New York, 1950.

191. –, *Lectures and Conferences on Mathematical Statistics and Probability*, Graduate School of the U. S. Department of Agriculture, Washington, 1952.

192. Nicod, Jean. *Foundations of Geometry and Induction*, The Humanities Press, New York, 1950.

193. Nochlin, Philip. "Reducibility and Intentional Words," *Journal of Philosophy* 50, 1953.

194. Oliver, James Willard. "Deduction and the Statistical Syllogism," *Journal of Philosophy* 50, 1953.

195. Oliver, W. Donald. "A Re-examination of the Problem of Induction," *Journal of Philosophy* 49, 1952.

196. Oppenheim, Paul. see: Helmer, Hempel, Kemeny.

197. Pap, Arthur. *The A Priori in Physical Theory*, Kings Crown Press, New York, 1946.

198. –, *Elements of Analytical Philosophy*, Macmillan, New York, 1949.

199. –, "Extensional Logic and the Laws of Nature," *Proceedings of the International Congress for Philosophy of Science*, Zurich, 1954.

200. –, "Belief, Synonymity, and Analysis," *Philosophical Studies* 6, 1955.

201. Parry, William T. "Re-examination of the Problem of Counterfactual Conditionals," *Journal of Philosophy* 54, 1957.

202. Pearson, E. S., and Clopper, C. J. "The Use of Confidence or Fiducial Limits Illustrated in the Case of a Binomial," *Biometrika* 26, 1934.

203. Pearson, Karl. *The Grammar of Science*, Meridian Books, New York 1957.

204. Peire, Charles. *The Philosophy of Peirce: Selected Writings*, Edited by Justus Buchler. Harcourt Brace and Co., New York, 1950.

205. Poincaré, Henri. *The Foundations of Science*. Science Press, New York, 1929.

206. —, *Science and Hypothesis*, Dover Publications, New York, 1952.

207. Polya, G. *Mathematics and Plausible Reasoning*. Princeton University press, Princeton, 1954.

208. Popper, Karl R. "A Set of Independent Axioms for Probability," *Mind* 47, 1938.

209. —, "A Note on Natural Laws and So-Called Contrary-to-fact Conditionals," *Mind* 58, 1949.

210. —, "Degree of Confirmation," *British Journal for the Philosophy of Science* 5, 1954-55.

211. —, "Two Autonomous Axiom Systems," *British Journal for the Philosophy of Science* 6, 1955-56

212. —, "Probability Magic," *Dialectica* 11, no's. 3, 4.

213. Putnam, Hilary. "Synonymity and the Analysis of Belief Sentences," *Analysis* 14, 1954.

214. Quine, W. V. O. "Designation and Existence," *Journal of Philosophy* 33, 1936.

215. —, "Truth by Convention," in *Philosophical Essays for A. N. Whitehead*, Longmans Green Co., New York, 1936.

216. —, "Notes on Existence and Necessity," *Journal of Philosophy* 40, 1943. Reprinted in Linsky, *Semantics. . .*

217. —, "On Universals," *Journal of Symbolic Logic* 12, 1947.

218. —, "On What There Is," *Review of Metaphysics* 2, 1948.

219. —, "The Problem of Interpreting Modal Logic," *Journal of Symbolic Logic* 14, 1949.

220. —, "On Mental Entities," *Proceedings of the American Academy of Arts and Sciences* 80, 1951-54.

221. —, "Semantics and Abstract Objects," *Proceedings of the American Academy of Arts and Sciences* 80, 1951-54.

222. —, *Mathematical Logic*, Harvard U. Press, Cambridge, 1951. (Revised Edition).

223. —, *From a Logical Point of View*. Harvard University Press, Cambridge (Mass.), 1953.

224. —, "Quantifiers and Propositional Attitudes," *Journal of Philosophy* 53, 1956.

225. Ramsey, Frank P. "Mr. Keynes on Probability," *The Cambridge Magazine*, 11, 1922.

226. –, *The Foundations of Mathematics*, Routledge and Kegan Paul, London, 1931.

227. Reichenbach, Hans. "Axiomatik der Wahrscheinlichkeitsrechnung," *Mathematische Zeitschrift* 34, 1932.

228. –, "Die logischen Grundlagen des Wahrscheinlichkeitsbegriffs," *Erkenntnis* 3, 1933. An English translation appears in Feigl and Sellars, *Readings...* and in Feigl and Brodbeck, *Readings...*

229. –, reply to Nelson. *Journal of Philosophy* 33, 1936.

230. –, *Experience and Prediction*, The University of Chicago Press, Chicago, 1938.

231. –, "On Probability and Induction," *Philosophy of Science* 5, 1938.

232. –, "On the Justification of Induction," *Journal of Philosophy* 37, 1940. Reprinted in Feigl and Sellars, *Readings...*

233. –, "Reply to Donald C. Williams' Criticism of the Frequency View of Probability," *Philosophy and Phenomenological Research* 5, 1945.

234. –, "The Theory of Probability," University of California Press, Berkeley and Los Angeles, 1949. Translation of Wahrscheinlichkeitslehre, Leiden, 1935.

235. –, "A Conversation Between Russell and Hume," *Journal of Philosophy* 46, 1949.

236. –, "Are Phenomenal Reports Absolutely Certain," *Philosophical Review* 61, 1952.

237. –, *Nomological Statements and Admissible Operations*, Studies in Logic and the Foundations of Mathematics, Amsterdam, North-Holland Publishing Co., 1954.

238. Rescher, Nicholas. "Translation as a Tool of Philosophical Analysis," *Journal of Philosophy* 53, 1956.

239. Russell, Bertrand. *The Problems of Philosophy*. The Home University Library, Oxford University Press, London, 1951.

240. –, "Descriptions," from *Introduction to Mathematical Philosophy*, Allen and Unwin, London, 1920. Reprinted in Linsky, *Semantics...*

241. –, *Human Knowledge, Its Scope and Limits*. Simon and Schuster, New York, 1948.

242. Salmon, Wesley C. "The Uniformity of Nature," *Philosophy and Phenomenological Research* 14, 1953-54.

243. –, "Regular Rules of Induction," *Philosophical Review* 65, 1956.

244. Scheffler, Israel. "On Justification and Commitment," *Journal of Philosophy* 51, 1954.

245. –, "An Inscriptional Approach to Indirect Quotation," *Analysis* 14, 1954.

246. –, "On Synonomy and Indirect Discourse," *Philosophy of Science* 22, 1955.

247. Schon, Donald. "Procedural and Material Rules," *Journal of Philosophy* 54, 1957.

248. Sellars, Wilfrid. "Inference and Meaning," *Mind* 62, 1953.

249. –, "Putnam on Synonymity and Belief," *Analysis* 15, 1955.

250. Shimony, Abner. "Coherence and the Axioms of Confirmation," *Journal of Symbolic Logic* 20, 1955.

251. Smullyan, Arthur. "The Concept of Empirical Knowledge," *Philosophical Review* 65, 1956.

252. Stace, W. T. "The Refutation of Realism," *Mind* 53, 1934. Reprinted in Feigl and Sellars, *Readings...*

253. Stanley, Robert L. "A Theory of Subjunctive Conditionals," *Philosophy and Phenomenological Research* 17, 1956-57.

254. Storer, Thomas. "On Defining 'Soluble'," *Analysis* 11, 1950-51.

255. Struik, D. J. "Foundations of the Theory of Probabilities," *Philosophy of Science* 1, 1934.

256. Taylor, Richard. "Knowing What One Knows," *Analysis* 16, 1955-56.

257. Urmson, J. O. "Two of the Senses of 'Probable'," *Analysis* 8, 1947-48.

258. Venn, John. *The Logic of Chance*. London, 1876. (2'nd edition).

259. Waismann, F. "Logische Analyse des Wahrscheinlichkeitsbegriffs," *Erkenntnis* 1, 1930-31.

260. Wald, Abraham. "Contributions to the Theory of Statistical Estimation and Testing Hypotheses," *Annals of Mathematical Statistics* 10, 1939.

261. —, *On the Principles of Statistical Inference*, Notre Dame, 1942.

262. —, *Statistical Decision Functions*, Wiley, New York, 1950.

263. —, "Die Widerspruchsfreiheit des Kollektivsbegriffs der Wahrscheinlich-keitsrechnung," *Ergebnisse eines mathematisches Kolloquiums* 8, 1937.

264. Whitehead, A. N. *Science and the Modern World*, New York, 1925.

265. Whiteley, C. H. "On the Justification of Induction," *Analysis* 7, 1939-40.

266. —, "More About Probability," *Analysis* 8, 1947-48.

267. Wilks, S. S. *Elementary Statistical Analysis*, Princeton University Press, Princeton, 1951.

268. —, "Shortest Average Confidence Intervals from Large Samples," *Annals of Mathematical Statistics* 9, 1938.

269. Will, F. L. "Is There a Problem of Induction?" *Journal of Philosophy* 39,. 1942.

270. —, "Will the Future Be Like the Past?" *Mind* 55, 1946.

271. —, "The Contrary-to-Fact Conditional," *Mind* 56, 1947.

272. —, "Generalization and Evidence," in *Philosophical Analysis*, ed. M. Black. Cornell University Press, Ithaca, 1950.

273. —, "The Justification of Theories," *Philosophical Review* 64, 1955.

274. Williams, Donald C. "The Realistic Interpretation of Scientific Sentences," *Erkenntnis* 7, 1937-38.

275. —, "On the Derivation of Probabilities from Frequencies," *Philosophy and Phenomenological Research* 5, 1945.

276. —, "The Challenging Situation in the Philosophy of Probability," *Philosophy and Phenomenological Research* 6, 1945-46.

277. —, "The Problem of Probability," *Philosophy and Phenomenological Research* 6, 1945-46.

278. —, *The Ground of Induction*, Harvard University Press, Cambridge (Mass.) 1947.

279. –, "Mr. Chatalian on Probability and Induction," *Philosophical Studies* 4, 1953.

280. Wilson, Neil L. "In Defense of Proper Names," *Philosophical Studies* 4, 1953.

281. Wright, G. H. von. "On Probability," *Mind* 49, 1940.

282. –, *The Logical Problem of Induction*, Helsinki 1941.

283. –, *Uber Wahrscheinlichkeit, eine Logische und Philosophische Untersuchung*, Helsinki, 1945.

284. –, *A Tratise on Induction and Probability*. Harcourt Brace and Co., New York, 1951.

285. –, "The Meaning of Probability," abstract of an invited address for the Association for Symbolic Logic, *Journal of Symbolic Logic* 20, 1955.

286. Xenakis, Jason. "Sentence and Statement: Professor Quine on Mr. Strawson," *Analysis* 16, 1955-56.

Anthologies containing reprints of papers mentioned above:

1. *Philosophical Analysis*, ed: Max Black. Cornell University Press, Ithaca, 1950.

2. *Readings in Philosophical Analysis*, eds: Herbert Feigl and Wilfrid Sellars. Appleton-Century-Crofts, New York, 1949.

3. *Readings in the Philosophy of Science*, eds: Herbert Feigl and May Brodbeck. Appleton-Century-Crofts, New York, 1953.

4. *Naturalism and the Human Spirit*, ed.: Krikorian, Columbia University Press, New York, 1944.

5. *Semantics and the Philosophy of Language*. ed: Leonard Linsky. The University of Illinois Press, Urbana, 1952.

6. *Philosophy and Analysis*, ed. Margaret McDonald. Oxford, 1954.

7. *Readings in the Philosophy of Science*, ed. Philip Wiener. Charles Scribner's Sons, New York, 1953.

ADDENDA

Brown, G. Spencer. *Probability and Scientific Inference*, Longmans, Green and Co., New York, 1957.

Campbell, Norman. *What is Science?* Dover Publications, New York, 1952.

Harrod, Roy. "New Argument for Induction: reply to Professor Popper," *British Journal for the Philosophy of Science* 10, 1960.

Koopman, B. O. "The Axioms and Algebra of Intuitive Probability," *Annals of Mathematics* 41, 1940.

–, "Intuitive Probabilities and Sequences," *Annals of Mathematics*, 42, 1941.

Kyburg, Henry E. "Probability and Rationality," *Philosophical Quarterly*, forthcoming.

–, "A Modest Proposal Concerning Simplicity," *Philosophical Review*, forthcoming.

Leblanc, Hughes. "On So-called Degrees of Confirmation," *British Journal for the Philosophy of Science* 10, 1960.

—, "Evidence logique et lege de confirmation," Revue Philosophique de Louvain 52, 1954.

Menger, Karl. "Random Variables and the General Theory of Variables," *Proceedings of the Third Berkley Symposium on Mathematical Statistics and Probability* 2, 1954.

Nagel, Ernest. *Sovereign Reason.* Glencoe, Illinois, 1954.

Popper, Karl. "Probabilistic Independence and Corroboration by Empirical Tests," *British Journal for the Philosophy of Science* 10, 1960.

—, *The Logic of Scientific Inference*, London, 1959.